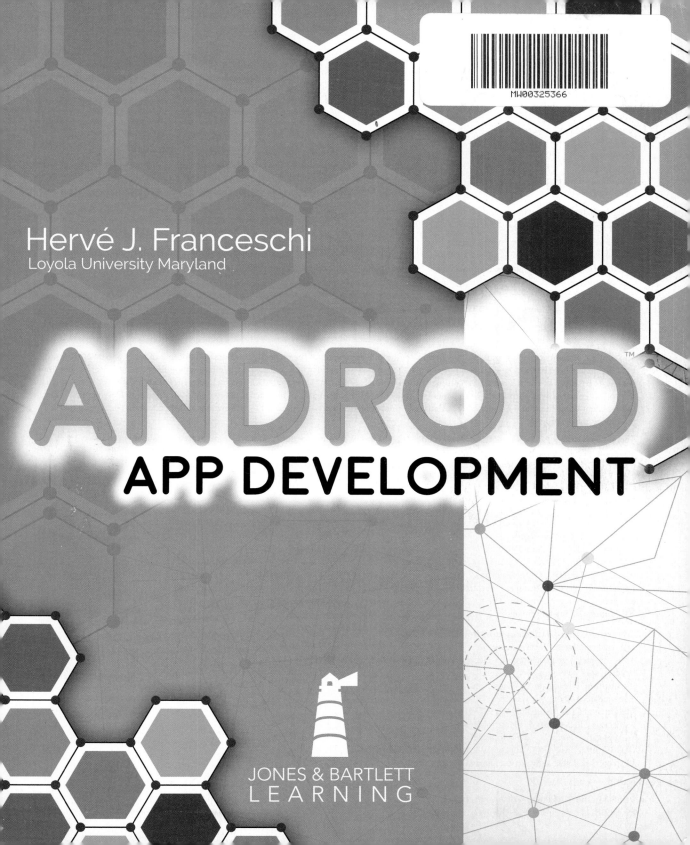

Hervé J. Franceschi
Loyola University Maryland

ANDROID™
APP DEVELOPMENT

JONES & BARTLETT
LEARNING

World Headquarters
Jones & Bartlett Learning
5 Wall Street
Burlington, MA 01803
978-443-5000
info@jblearning.com
www.jblearning.com

Jones & Bartlett Learning books and products are available through most bookstores and online booksellers. To contact Jones & Bartlett Learning directly, call 800-832-0034, fax 978-443-8000, or visit our website, www.jblearning.com.

09365-0

Production Credits

VP, Executive Publisher: David D. Cella
Executive Editor: Matt Kane
Acquisitions Editor: Laura Pagluica
Associate Editor: Taylor Ferracane
Associate Production Editor: Rebekah Linga
Director of Marketing: Andrea DeFronzo
Marketing Manager: Amy Langlais
VP, Manufacturing and Inventory Control: Therese Connell

Composition: S4Carlisle Publishing Services
Cover Design: Kristin E. Parker
Rights & Media Specialist: Merideth Tumasz
Media Development Editor: Shannon Sheehan
Cover Image: © Fon_nongkran/Shutterstock
Printing and Binding: LSC Communications
Cover Printing: LSC Communications

Library of Congress Cataloging-in-Publication Data
Names: Franceschi, Hervé, author.
Title: Android app development / Herve J. Franceschi, Loyola University
   Maryland.
Description: Burlington, Massachusetts : Jones & Bartlett Learning, [2017] |
   Includes bibliographical references and index.
Identifiers: LCCN 2016038890 | ISBN 9781284092127
Subjects: LCSH: Android (Electronic resource) | Mobile computing. |
   Application software—Development.
Classification: LCC QA76.76.A65 F73 2017 | DDC 005.3—dc23
LC record available at https://lccn.loc.gov/2016038890

6048

Printed in the United States of America
20 19 18 17 16   10 9 8 7 6 5 4 3 2 1

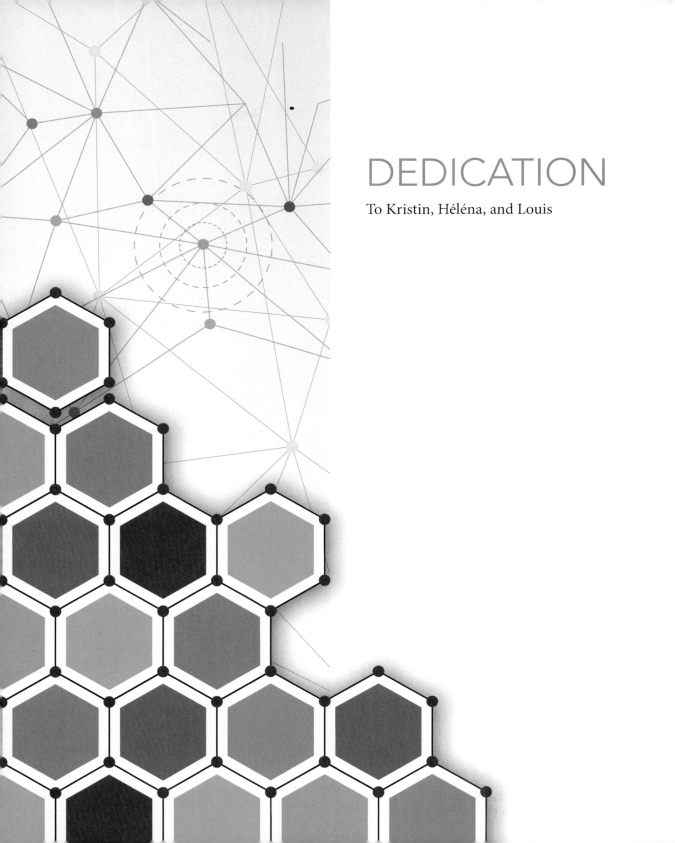

DEDICATION

To Kristin, Héléna, and Louis

TABLE OF CONTENTS

v

PREFACE

Purpose of This Text and Its Audience

Android App Development covers the essential topics of Android Development: XML resources, including styles, XML defined GUIs, programmatically defined GUI, event-driven programming, activity life cycle, how to manage several activities, transitions between activities, persistent data (including SQLite), how to manage orientation, fragments, how to make a device-independent app, and how to use an app within another app. It covers "fun" topics such as touches, swipes, graphics, sounds, and game programming. Finally, it also covers more specialized topics of interest: maps, voice recognition, how to make a content app including remote data retrieval and XML parsing, GPS, how to make a widget, in-app advertising, and encryption.

This course ideally follows a Java course. Although it is preferable that students have been exposed to event handling programming prior to taking an Android course, it is not a requirement. GUI programming and event handling are thoroughly explained.

Coverage and Approach

The approach in this book is to use an app throughout each chapter to illustrate the concepts presented. The app typically uses the Model View Controller architecture. It is constructed in a very progressive manner starting with version 0, then version 1, and so on. We progress through the app versions, adding concepts and topics as needed by the app. Thus, each app is manageable in the classroom. The instructor can choose to download the Model and explain it briefly rather than cover it in detail. The Model classes use straightforward Java code and do not need much explanation. We also try to use apps that are simple yet meaningful and that the students can easily understand and relate to. It is possible to only cover the early versions of an app if the instructor does not want to cover some of the chapter's topics. Furthermore, many chapters are independent of each other and do not have to be covered in the sequence in which they are presented in this book.

Pedagogy

Within each chapter, and therefore within each app, the instructor can pick what topics he or she chooses to cover and in what depth as well as at what pace. The Model, which typically uses basic Java classes and is Android independent, can be downloaded and briefly explained. That allows the instructor to concentrate on the View and the Controller, which include Android-specific topics. Screenshots, examples, and tables are included throughout each chapter to illustrate the concepts at hand and the current state of the chapter app. Software Engineering and Common Error boxes highlight software engineering tips and common errors throughout the chapters. Chapter summaries are provided at the end of each chapter followed by exercises, problems, and projects to test students' knowledge. Each chapter includes extensive multiple-choice, fill in the code, and write an app exercises.

> **SOFTWARE ENGINEERING:** When defining an `EditText`, choose the appropriate value for `android:inputType` in order to match the data we expect the user will input.

▶   Model: `TipCalculator` class
▶   View: activity_main.xml
▶   Controller: `MainActivity` class

> **COMMON ERROR:** We need to add an *activity* element in the Android Manifest.xml file whenever we add an activity to our app. Otherwise, the app will crash when we try to go to that activity.

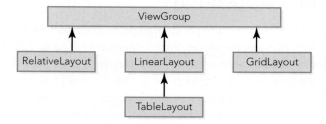

FIGURE 2.2 Selected layout manager classes

TABLE 2.6 The `android:textSize` and `android:hint` XML attributes of `TextView`

XML Attribute	Method	Description
android:textSize	void setTextSize(int unit, float size)	Sets the size of the text
android:hint	void setHint(int resource)	Sets the hint text to display

Chapter-by-Chapter Overview

The first nine chapters cover essential concepts of Android app development. The last seven chapters cover more specific topics.

The appendices include mini-chapters on concepts that are used in several chapters: retrieving the dimensions of a device, including the status and action bars, sizing the font of a TextView dynamically, performing a task in the background using AsyncTask (to retrieve data from a remote location), and using Google Play Services. This helps make most of the chapters independent so that the instructor can pick and choose which chapters to cover.

A lot of the fundamental concepts are covered in Chapters 1, 2, 3, and 4, so we recommend instructors cover those chapters early and in that order. Chapter 2 covers the concepts of XML resources, including strings, colors, and styles extensively, as well as event driven programming. These concepts are reused throughout the book. Chapter 3 is the first chapter in which we build the GUI programmatically. We also do so in Chapters 5, 7, and 13. Thus, it is better to cover Chapter 3 early. Chapter 4 is the first chapter that involves multiple activities. Chapters 5, 10, 12, and 13 also involve multiple activities. Thus, Chapter 4 should also be covered early. Some of the material in Chapter 7 (touches and gestures) is used in Chapter 8 (graphics, animation, and sound), so they should be covered in this order.

The following is a summary of the topics covered in each chapter:

Chapter 1: Basics of Android, First App: Hello World

We look at how to use the Android Studio development environment: how to use the emulator, how to run the app on a device, how to output to Logcat, using the debugger. We also look at the various resources associated with an app: the AndroidManifest.xml file, the various xml files to define string, color, dimension resources, and the xml file defining the GUI.

Chapter 2: Model View Controller, GUI Components, Events

We explain the Model View Controller architecture and make our first app, a tip calculator, using the MVC. We define a GUI using a RelativeLayout and TextViews, EditTexts and a Button. We explain how to separate the various styles used in an app from the contents of the app (similar to CSS in web design). We cover event handling: clicking on a button and typing on a soft keyboard.

Chapter 3: Coding the GUI Programmatically, Layout Managers

Continuing with the MVC architecture, we explain how to define a GUI and set up event handling programmatically for a tic-tac-toe app. We explain how to use inner classes, layout parameters, and alert dialogs.

Chapter 4: Multiple Activities, Passing Data between Activities, Transitions, Persistent Data

We cover how to include multiple activities within an app, and explain how to pass data between activities. We explore the life-cycle methods of an activity and how they can be used, particularly in the context of an app with multiple activities. We demonstrate how to set up an animated transition between one activity and another. We explore the RelativeLayout class in greater depth as well as the TableLayout class. Finally, we show how to deal with persistent data. We use a mortgage app as the vehicle for the concepts presented: the first screen displays mortgage data, including the monthly payment, and the second screen enables the user to edit the mortgage characteristics (amount, interest rate, and number of years).

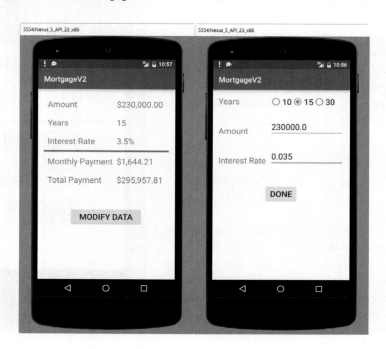

Chapter 5: Menus, SQLite

We show how to include a menu in an app and how to use SQLite to handle persistent data. We use a ScrollView when generating a GUI programmatically. The app is a candy store manager that enables the user to add, update, and delete candies, as well as ring the cash register for a customer using the Toast class.

Chapter 6: Managing the Device Orientation

In this chapter, we show how to detect a change in the device orientation and explore various ways of coding the GUI so that an app works in both vertical and horizontal orientations. In particular, we dynamically retrieve the dimensions of the device so that we can size and position the GUI components accordingly. There is no meaningful app in this chapter, we simply explore the various ways of managing the GUI with orientation changes.

Chapter 7: Touches and Swipes

We first show how to detect and handle a touch or a swipe event. More generally, we also show how to detect and handle a gesture, single tap, or double tap event. We use touch and gesture handling to build a puzzle game app: the user can solve a puzzle by touching and moving the puzzle pieces. The puzzle colors are generated randomly and feedback is given to the user when he or she solves the puzzle.

Chapter 8: Graphics, Animations, Sounds, and Gaming

We explore how to create a custom View, how to draw shapes and bitmaps, how to create a game by animating objects on the screen, handling events, and making sounds. We use the Timer and TimerTask classes to create a game loop and update the state of the game at a defined frequency. In this duck hunting app, a duck flies from the right of the screen in an animated fashion, using

four png frames. The user can control a cannon, a drawn shape, located at the bottom left of the screen by moving its barrel with touches. A double tap fires a bullet, a drawn shape, and we detect collision with the duck. If the duck is shot, a sound is played, we stop animating the duck, and it falls down vertically.

Chapter 9: Fragments

We cover various ways of using fragments within an activity, communication between two fragments, and how to make a fragment reusable. The app is a hangman game where the various fragments include the state of the game, the status of the game, the number of tries left, as well as an invisible fragment.

Chapter 10: Using Libraries and Their APIs: Speech Recognition and Maps

We use the Google maps activity template to display a map with annotations, and use speech recognition to change the map. We also explain how to use Google Play Services. In this app, the user can display a map centered on a city (London, Paris, Rome, or Washington, DC) by saying its name, and then move the map by saying north, south, west, or east.

Chapter 11: Using the GPS and Location Services

We explain how to use Google Play Services, and how to use a device's GPS within an app. The app manages the distance and time left to a destination, first enabling the user to update them, and eventually updating them both periodically and automatically.

Chapter 12: Using Another App within the App: Taking a Photo, Graying It, and Sending an Email

We explain how to use another app, such as a camera app, within an app, how to store files in external storage, and how to use an email app within an app. We also explore seek bars (sliders). The app opens a camera app and when the user takes a picture, enables the user to gray the picture using three seek bars. In the Model, we explain how to access each individual pixel of a Bitmap, both for reading and writing. After the user is done graying the image, the user can send an email to a friend and we automatically attach the grayed picture.

Chapter 13: XML and Content Apps

We parse local and remote XML documents using a SAX parser. We show how we can use the AsyncTask class to perform a task in the background of an app. We display results in a ListView and open a web browser inside the app. The app is a content app that retrieves data from a remote URL (http://blogs.jblearning.com/computer-science/feed/), parses its XML content into an ArrayList of items, and displays the items in a ListView. When the user clicks on one of the items, we open the browser at the URL corresponding to that item.

Chapter 14: Making an Android Widget

We cover the various steps to make a widget: we first make a very simple widget, then make it dynamic, then retrieve temperature data from a remoter website, and finally make the widget customizable by the user. We start with hard coded city and temperature, then give the widget a style, then add some dynamic data retrieving the date and time from the device, and enable the user to update the widget data by clicking on it. Next, we retrieve the temperature data from a remote website using the AsyncTask class. The data comes as a JSON string so we access the data we want within the JSON string (the temperature) and display it inside the widget. Finally, we make the widget customizable by enabling the user to set the city and state for which we retrieve the temperature data.

Chapter 15: In App Advertising

We place a Google ad in a simple app and explain the life-cycle methods of the AdView class. We also cover how to create a drawable resource and use it with a button. In this stopwatch app, we create three drawable resources (stop.xml, reset.xml, and start.xml) that we use as buttons for the app. We display a banner ad at the bottom of the screen and shows how we can retrieve a fake remote Google ad to test the app as well as how to use a live Google ad. There is no need to be a registered Google developer to ask for fake ads served by Google.

Chapter 16: Security and Encryption

We explain symmetric and asymmetric encryption, and how to use an encryption algorithm (AES) and an asymmetric encryption algorithm (RSA). There is no meaningful app in this chapter; the main objectives are to explain the various encryption schemes and algorithms, as well as how to use the classes and methods of the Java library that relate to encryption.

If students progress through all sixteen chapters, then they will have created the following apps:

Hello Android (Chapter 1)
Tip Calculator (Chapter 2)
TicTacToe (Chapter 3)
Mortgage Calculator (Chapter 4)
Candy Store Manager (Chapter 5)
Puzzle Game (Chapter 7)
Duck Hunting Game (Chapter 8)
Hangman Game (Chapter 9)

Map Display Using Speech Input (Chapter 10)
Travel App Using the GPS (Chapter 11)
Photo Graying (Chapter 12)
Content App (Chapter 13)
Temperature Widget (Chapter 14)
StopWatch with Advertising (Chapter 15)

Appendices

The appendices include the following:

▶ A micro-chapter on how to retrieve the height of the action bar and the status bar dynamically (including a micro-app for it): this is important if we intend to code the GUI programmatically and make the app device independent.

▶ A micro-chapter on how to size the font inside a TextView dynamically so that it fits perfectly on one line (including a micro-app for it): this is important if we display dynamic data whose length can vary significantly.

▶ How to use Google Play Services: this is important for apps involving maps, GPS, ads, and other services from Google.

▶ A micro-chapter on how to use the AsyncTask class (including a micro-app for it): this is important for apps that retrieve data from a remote location.

Instructor and Student Resources

Instructor and student resources are available for download at go.jblearning.com/FranceschiAndroid. These include:

▶ Access to the latest version of Android Studio
▶ Source code for all apps
▶ Answers to end of chapter multiple-choice and fill in the code questions
▶ Slides in PowerPoint format
▶ Test bank including sample midterm and final exams with mini-apps

Contacting the Author

If errors are found in this text, please contact the author at hjfranceschi@loyola.edu. Errata will be posted on the Jones & Bartlett catalog page at go.jblearning.com/FranceschiAndroid.

Acknowledgments

We would like to acknowledge the contributions of many partners, colleagues, and family members to this book.

First and foremost, we would like to thank our publisher, Jones & Bartlett Learning, especially Laura Pagluica, Acquisitions Editor, Taylor Ferracane, Associate Editor, Bharathi Sanjeev, Project Manager, and Rebekah Linga, Associate Production Editor.

Second, we extend our thanks to the reviewers:

Timothy E. Roden, PhD
Associate Professor of Computer Science
Lamar University, Texas

Jeremy Blum, DSc
Associate Professor of Computer Science
Pennsylvania State University, Harrisburg

Jamie Pinchot, DSc
Associate Professor of Computer and Information Systems
Robert Morris University

Allan M. Hart, PhD
Assistant Professor
Computer Information Science
Minnesota State University, Mankato

Dr. Marwan Shaban
Adjunct Professor
University of Central Florida

Georgia Brown, MS
Computer Science Department
Northern Illinois University

Roy Kravitz
Portland State University

Sonia M. Arteaga, PhD
Hartnell College

Dr. Shane Schartz
Assistant Professor of MIS, Informatics
Fort Hays State University

Finally, we recognize the support of my family, my wife Kristin, my daughter Héléna, and my son Louis, who provided support, feedback, and advice.

CHAPTER **ONE**

Basics of Android, First App: HelloAndroid

CHAPTER CONTENTS

Introduction

Today, it seems that almost everybody has a smartphone and is using apps. There are apps to check our email, check the weather, play games, calculate a mortgage payment, translate one language into another, learn algebra, or even apps for websites, social media, or news organizations such as Facebook, Twitter, or CNN. In this chapter, we learn how to develop our first app for Android devices.

1.1 Smartphones and Their Operating Systems

1.1.1 Smartphones

A smartphone is an intelligent cellular phone, or a cellular phone with a computer inside, as well as some extra hardware. Thus, programmers can write application software for them; such application software is called an app. A smartphone has the typical components of a regular computer: a CPU, memory, a storage device, an operating system, and other devices, such as a camera, an accelerometer, or a GPS.

The two most well-known operating systems are the Android operating system, from Google, and iOS, from Apple. Other popular operating systems for smartphones include BlackBerry, Windows, and Symbian. The annual number of smartphones sold worldwide is now over one billion. Furthermore, smartphones comprise an increasing percentage of the mobile phones sold.

1.1.2 Android Phones

There are over 100 different varieties of Android phones or tablets. They can have a different CPU, a different screen resolution, and a different amount of memory available. This makes it difficult for developers to test their apps on actual devices. The dimensions of the various components of the user interface of an app can be different depending on the Android phone or tablet. Furthermore, in complex games where speed is an issue, an app can run differently on an old and slow Android device as compared to a more recent one. This is something to keep in mind as we develop apps for the Android market.

1.1.3 Apps and Google Play

Android apps are distributed via Google Play (https://play.google.com), which used to be called the Android Market. Google Play is actually a store for digital content, much like the Apple's app store, not just apps. In order to distribute apps on Google Play, you need to become a registered developer, which costs $25.

There are now over one million apps in Google Play, and the vast majority of those apps are free. Top categories include entertainment (games), personalization, tools, books, and references. Most of the downloaded apps are free apps. One should also be aware that the Android operating system is open, so anyone can easily copy an app from one Android device to another. There is little protection for intellectual property.

1.2 Development Environment for Android Apps

The typical and recommended development environment for Android apps is comprised of the following:

▶ Java Development Kit (JDK)
▶ Android Studio
▶ Android Standard Development Kit (Android SDK)

It is not a requirement to use Android Studio to develop Android apps, we can run our code from the command line or use another integrated development environment, such as Eclipse. However, Android Studio is Google's official development environment and is likely to quickly become the industry standard; we use Android Studio in this book.

In order to set up a complete Android app development environment, we need to:

▶ Download and install the latest Java SDK (if we have not done it yet), which we can find at http://www.oracle.com/technetwork/java/javase/downloads/index.html.
▶ Download and install Android Studio, including the IDE, SDK tools, and the emulator system, which we can find at http://developer.android.com/sdk/index.html

1.3 Our First App: HelloAndroid

Let's create our first Android app.

1.3.1. Skeleton App

Open Android Studio. The first time we run Android Studio, the environment checks that it is up to date, asks us to download components if needed. Once that is done and we click on Finish (see **FIGURE 1.1**), we see the screen shown in **FIGURE 1.2**. Recent projects are listed on the left side; there will not be any the first time we use Android Studio. To start a new project, click on Start a new Android Studio project.

In the dialog box shown in **FIGURE 1.3**, we type in our project name (we choose HelloAndroid) and our domain (we chose jblearning.com; if we do not have a domain name, we can choose any name); the other two fields (package name and project location) are automatically filled. If we prefer a different project location, we can edit that field. Note that the package name is our domain name in reverse. It is typical for developers to name their package with their domain name in reverse; it insures that it is unique. When we are done, we click Next.

The next dialog box (**FIGURE 1.4**) is used to specify the minimum SDK for this project; depending on our app, this can be important. For example, if we incorporate advertising, this may require a higher SDK level than the default level; however, the more recent the SDK level we

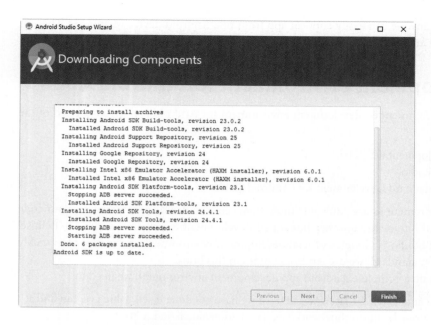

FIGURE 1.1 Downloading components

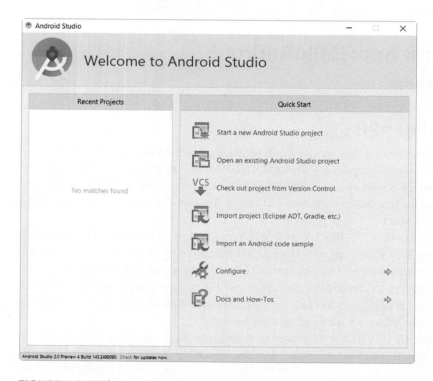

FIGURE 1.2 Welcome screen

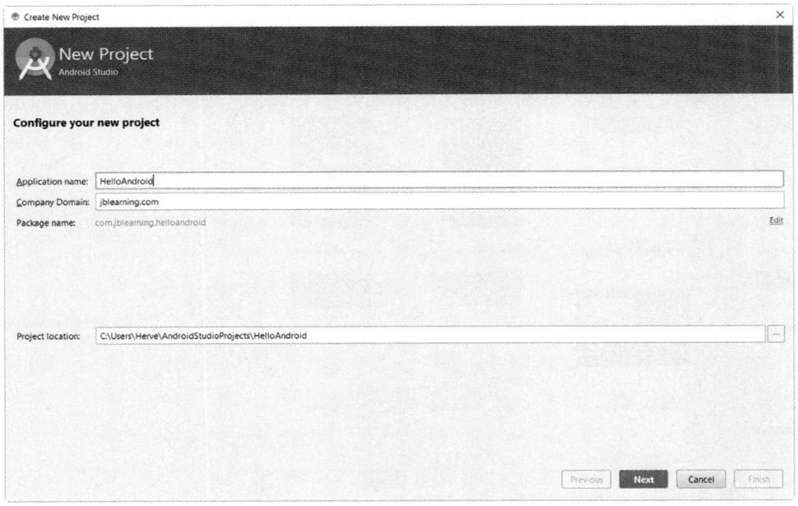

FIGURE 1.3 **Dialog box for new project**

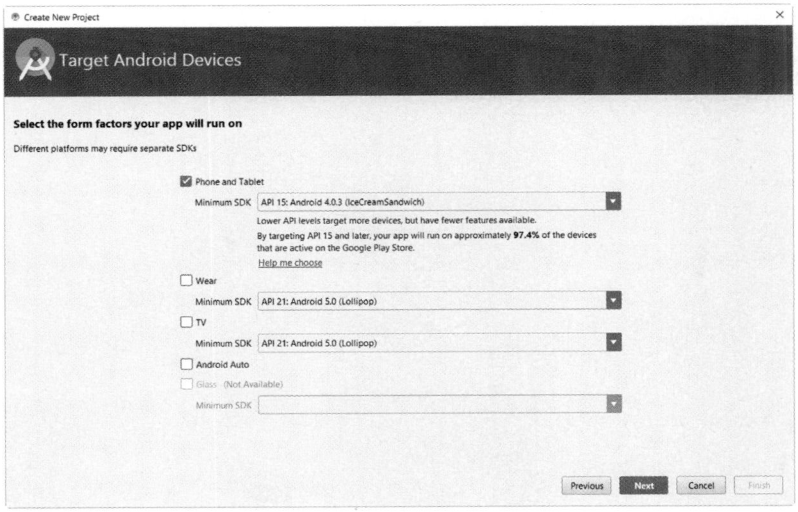

FIGURE 1.4 **Dialog box to specify the minimum SDK**

specify, the more we restrict the potential number of users for our app. For this app, we keep the default SDK level and click Next.

In the next dialog box (**FIGURE 1.5**), we can choose among several templates; a template creates skeleton code with some predefined user-interface functionality; often, it provides a user interface that is similar to what can be found in native apps. For this app, we choose the Empty Activity template—it creates a minimum skeleton code.

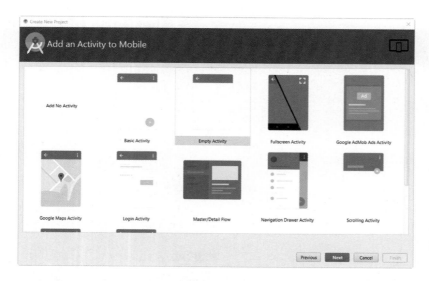

FIGURE 1.5 **Dialog box to choose the type of activity**

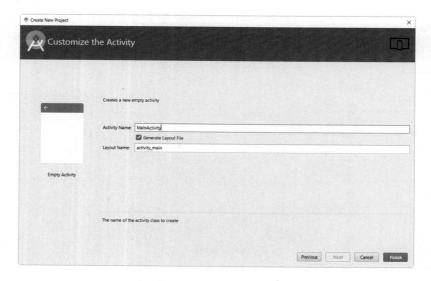

FIGURE 1.6 **File names dialog box**

In the next dialog box (**FIGURE 1.6**), we can specify various names for the first activity class and layout files. For this first app, we keep the default names, `MainActivity` for the class, and activity_main for the layout file. After we click on Finish, our project is created.

The project directory structure has been created along with many source files, which we can see on the left pane of the Android Studio development environment (shown in **FIGURE 1.7**).

FIGURE 1.7 **The app directory structure in the IDE**

The program generates a lot of directories and files automatically.

▶ The manifests directory contains the AndroidManifest.xml file, automatically generated and editable. Among other things, it specifies the resources that this app uses, such as activities, the file system, the Internet, the device's hardware resources... When a user downloads an app, this file tells the user about the resources that this app uses (e.g., if it writes to the file system of the device).

▶ The java directory contains the Java source files. We can add more Java source files as our app gets more complex.

▶ The res (`res` stands for "resources") directory contains resources such as utility files (to define strings, menus, layouts, colors, styles) and images, sounds, etc. Ids are automatically generated for these resources inside a file named R.java. R.java should not be modified.

▶ Inside the res directory, the drawable directory is meant to contain images and other drawable resources. It can contain jpegs, pngs, gifs, files to define gradients, etc. As needed, we can add resources to this directory.

▶ Inside the res directory, the mipmap directory contains the icon for the app. As needed, we can add resources to this directory.

▶ Inside the res directory, the layout directory contains XML files defining screen layouts. At this point, it contains the activity_main.xml file, an automatically generated layout file for our empty activity. We can edit this file to define the Graphical User Interface (GUI) for this app.

▶ Inside the res directory, the values directory contains XML files defining various resources such as colors (in the colors.xml file), dimensions (in the dimens.xml file), styles (in the styles.xml file), or strings (in the strings.xml file). We can edit these files to define more color, dimension, style, or string resources.

▶ The gradle scripts directory contains the scripts used to build the app.

In this chapter, we look at the following files in detail: AndroidManifest.xml, MainActivity.java, dimens.xml, strings.xml, styles.xml, colors.xml, and activity_main.xml. We also add an icon for the app.

1.3.2 GUI Preview

A nice feature of Android Studio is that it lets us preview a screen without running the app. A layout file needs to be selected for the preview to show. To select activity_main.xml, we double click on the file name. In the menu, if we select View, Tool Windows, Preview, a preview of the app shows on the right side of the environment, as shown in **FIGURE 1.8**. In this way, we can edit the GUI and preview it without running the app. We can preview a screen in both portrait and landscape orientations by choosing from a menu (**FIGURE 1.9**). **FIGURE 1.10** shows the preview in landscape orientation. We can also preview the app choosing a different theme by clicking on the AppTheme drop-down list (**FIGURE 1.11**) and choosing among many devices (**FIGURE 1.12**) by clicking on the device drop-down list.

1.3.3 XML Files: activity_main.xml, colors.xml, styles.xml, strings.xml, dimens.xml

The GUI for this app is defined in the activity_main.xml file. Note that we can also set the GUI by code.

To open activity_main.xml, we click on res, then click on layout, then double click on activity_main.xml. In order to see the actual XML code, we may need to click on the Text tab at the bottom of the panel.

Activity_main.xml, shown in **EXAMPLE 1.1**, is an **eXtensible Markup Language (XML)** file. The Android development environment uses XML extensively, in particular to define the user interface of the various screens of an app and also to define various resources such as strings, dimensions, menus, styles, shapes, or gradients.

We may already be familiar with **HyperText Markup Language (HTML)** and its syntax. HTML is the language that web browsers use, and has a fixed set of tags and attributes. XML uses essentially the same syntax as HTML, but we can create our own tags and attributes.

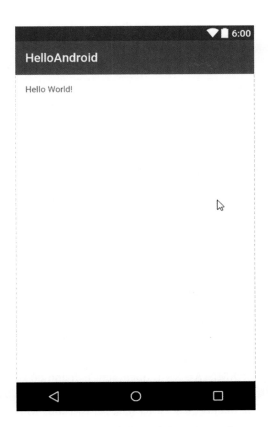

FIGURE 1.8 A preview of the app in the environment

FIGURE 1.9 Choosing the orientation for the preview

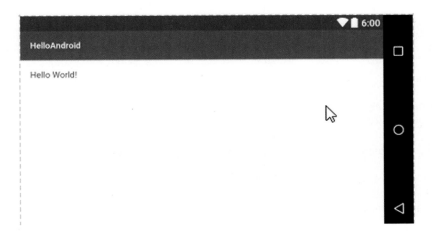

FIGURE 1.10 A preview of the app in landscape orientation

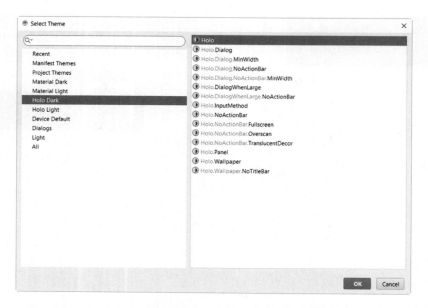

FIGURE 1.11 Choosing a theme for the preview (after selecting Holo Dark)

We can find the full XML documentation at http://www.w3.org/XML/.

We will next outline the main characteristics of XML. An XML document is made up of elements, and each element can have 0 or more attribute/value pairs. Elements can be nested. An element can have content or not. A non-empty element begins with a start tag and ends with an end tag. The text between the start tag and the end tag is called the element content.

Although the actual specification is a bit more complex, we will use the following simplified syntax to define a non-empty XML element:

```
<tagName attribute1="value1" attribute2="value2" ... >
Element Content
</tagName>
```

Here are two examples:

```
<price>46.00</price>
<app language="Java" version="7.0">Hello Android</app>
```

If an element has no content, then we can use an empty element tag with the following syntax:

```
<tagName attribute1="value1" attribute2="value2" ... />
```

Here are two examples:

```
<website name="twitter"/>
<app language="Java" version="7.0"/>
```

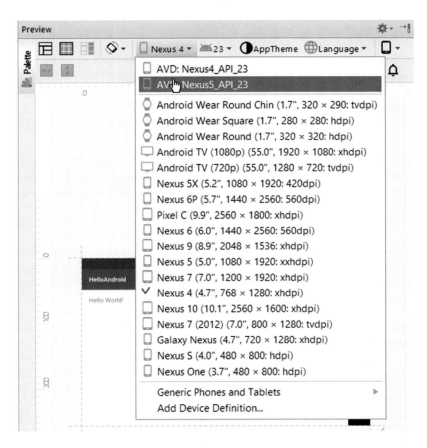

FIGURE 1.12 Choosing a device for the preview

There are rules for naming tags; we use only tag names that start with a letter or an underscore and are followed by 0 or more letters, underscores, or digits. The official specification for tag names is more complex than the earlier, and we can find it at http://www.w3.org/XML/Core/#Publications.

Comments use this syntax:

```
<!-- Write a comment here -->
```

The file activity_main.xml defines how the GUI should look like. The RelativeLayout element defines that the various graphical elements will be positioned and displayed in relation to each other or their parent graphical container.

In the activity_main.xml file the element RelativeLayout uses the first syntax and includes attributes android:layout_width and android:layout_height, which both have value match_parent (lines 5–6). This means that the RelativeLayout element will be as big as its parent element, which in this example is the screen. It also includes attributes android:paddingBottom, android:paddingLeft, android:paddingRight, and android:paddingTop (lines 7–10). The android:paddingBottom element has value @dimen/activity_vertical_margin (line 7): this means that there will be some padding on the left side of the screen equal to the value of the dimen element named activity_vertical_margin (in this case 16 px) in the dimens.xml file located in the values directory of the res directory.

Generally, if a constant named constant_name is defined in a resource file named resource_types.xml, we can access the value of that constant using the syntax @resource_type/constant_name.

Lines 13–16 define a TextView element that is nested inside the RelativeLayout element; a TextView element is an instance of the TextView class, which encapsulates a label. This TextView element is an empty element and as such has no content; it has three attribute/value pairs:

▸ The attributes android:layout_width and android:layout_height have value wrap_content (lines 14 and 15). That means that the TextView element's width and height are just as big as necessary to make the contents of the TextView element fit; the element "wraps" around its contents.

▸ The attribute android:text defines the String displayed inside the TextView; it has value Hello World!.

```
1   <?xml version="1.0" encoding="utf-8"?>
2   <RelativeLayout
3       xmlns:android="http://schemas.android.com/apk/res/android"
4       xmlns:tools="http://schemas.android.com/tools"
5       android:layout_width="match_parent"
6       android:layout_height="match_parent"
7       android:paddingBottom="@dimen/activity_vertical_margin"
8       android:paddingLeft="@dimen/activity_horizontal_margin"
9       android:paddingRight="@dimen/activity_horizontal_margin"
10      android:paddingTop="@dimen/activity_vertical_margin"
11      tools:context="com.jblearning.helloandroid.MainActivity">
12
13    <TextView
14        android:layout_width="wrap_content"
15        android:layout_height="wrap_content"
16        android:text="Hello World!"/>
17  </RelativeLayout>
```

EXAMPLE 1.1 The activity_main.xml file

The activity_horizonal_margin and the activity_vertical_margin values are defined within two dimen elements in the dimens.xml file (lines 3–4), shown in **EXAMPLE 1.2**. Their values are 16 px. The suffix dp stands for density pixels, which means that the value is device independent. If our app requires using a different value per screen size, we can define many values in the dimens.xml file, one per screen size.

Inside the dimens.xml file, the syntax for defining a `dimen` resource is:

```
     <dimen name="dimenName">valueOfDimension</dimen>

1    <resources>
2      <!-- Default screen margins, per the Android Design guidelines. -->
3      <dimen name="activity_horizontal_margin">16dp</dimen>
4      <dimen name="activity_vertical_margin">16dp</dimen>
5    </resources>
```

EXAMPLE 1.2 The dimens.xml file

Try to modify dimens.xml as in **EXAMPLE 1.3**. The environment updates its preview as shown in **FIGURE 1.13**.

```
1    <resources>
2      <!-- Default screen margins, per the Android Design guidelines. -->
3      <dimen name="activity_horizontal_margin">50dp</dimen>
4      <dimen name="activity_vertical_margin">100dp</dimen>
5    </resources>
```

EXAMPLE 1.3 The modified dimens.xml file

Similarly, the `String` whose value is `HelloAndroid` (see the blue title of the app in Figure 1.13) is defined at line 2 of the strings.xml file (**EXAMPLE 1.4**), located in the values directory of the res directory. We can create `String` constants in our Java files, but it is recommended to store `String` constants in the strings.xml file as much as possible. If we want to modify one or several `String` values later, it is easier to edit that file than to edit our Java code.

Inside the strings.xml file, the syntax for defining a `String` resource is:
```
<string name="stringName">valueOfString</string>
```

```
1    <resources>
2        <string name="app_name">HelloAndroid</string>
3    </resources>
```

EXAMPLE 1.4 The strings.xml file

Try to modify strings.xml as in **EXAMPLE 1.5**. The environment updates its preview as shown in **FIGURE 1.14**. The `String` app_name is used in the AndroidManifest.xml file, which is explained in paragraph 1.7.

FIGURE 1.13 A preview of the app in the environment after updating the dimens.xml file

FIGURE 1.14 A preview of the app in the environment after updating the strings.xml file

```
1    <resources>
2        <string name="app_name">My First App</string>
3    </resources>
```

EXAMPLE 1.5 The modified strings.xml file

The file styles.xml, located in the values directory of the res directory, defines the various styles used in the app. **EXAMPLE 1.6** shows its automatically generated contents.

Inside the styles.xml file, we can modify a style by adding an `item` element using this syntax:

```
<item name="styleAttribute">valueOfItem</item>
```

The name of the style attribute that specifies the text size inside a `TextView` is `android:-textSize`. In **EXAMPLE 11.7**, we change the default text size to 40 at line 6. The environment updates its preview as shown in **FIGURE 1.15**.

```
1    <resources>
2
3        <!-- Base application theme. -->
4        <style name="AppTheme" parent="Theme.AppCompat.Light.DarkActionBar">
5            <!-- Customize your theme here. -->
6            <item name="colorPrimary">@color/colorPrimary</item>
7            <item name="colorPrimaryDark">@color/colorPrimaryDark</item>
8            <item name="colorAccent">@color/colorAccent</item>
9        </style>
10
11   </resources>
```

EXAMPLE 1.6 The styles.xml file

```
1    <resources>
2
3        <!-- Base application theme. -->
4        <style name="AppTheme" parent="Theme.AppCompat.Light.DarkActionBar">
5            <!-- Customize your theme here. -->
6            <item name="android:textSize">40sp</item>
7            <item name="colorPrimary">@color/colorPrimary</item>
8            <item name="colorPrimaryDark">@color/colorPrimaryDark</item>
9            <item name="colorAccent">@color/colorAccent</item>
10       </style>
11
12   </resources>
```

EXAMPLE 1.7 The modified styles.xml file

Note that the style defined in styles.xml consists of three color constants using the syntax `@color/color_name`. These constants are defined in the colors.xml file, shown in **EXAMPLE 1.8**, and also located in the values directory of the res directory. Its contents are automatically generated. Inside the colors.xml file, the syntax for defining a `color` resource is:

```
<color name="colorName">valueOfColor</color>
```

```
1    <?xml version="1.0" encoding="utf-8"?>
2    <resources>
3        <color name="colorPrimary">#3F51B5</color>
4        <color name="colorPrimaryDark">#303F9F</color>
5        <color name="colorAccent">#FF4081</color>
6    </resources>
```

EXAMPLE 1.8 The colors.xml file

FIGURE 1.15 A preview of the app in the environment after updating the styles.xml file

FIGURE 1.16 A preview of the app in the environment after updating the colors.xml file

The color values are defined using the syntax #RRGGBB where R, G, and B are hexadecimal digits representing the amount of red, blue, and green, respectively.

If we modify the value of the color named colorPrimary to #FF0000 (full red), the preview is updated as shown in **FIGURE 1.16**.

1.3.4 The MainActivity Class

The entry point for our app is the MainActivity class, whose name is composed of the names Main and Activity. It is located in the com.jblearning.helloandroid package in the java directory (shown in **EXAMPLE 1.9**).

The source code for an Android app uses Java syntax. Line 1 is the package declaration. When this project was created, we told Android Studio to place the code in the package com.jblearning.helloandroid. Lines 3–4 import the classes used in this class. We need to import AppCompatActivity because MainActivity extends it (line 6) and thus inherits from it. AppCompatActivity inherits (indirectly) from the Activity class and includes an action bar (in red on Figure 1.16) above the activity screen, where the app title shows.

An activity is a component that provides and controls a screen with which users can interact. An app can consist of several activities, possibly passing data to each other. Activities are managed

```
 1    package com.jblearning.helloandroid;
 2
 3    import android.support.v7.app.AppCompatActivity;
 4    import android.os.Bundle;
 5
 6    public class MainActivity extends AppCompatActivity {
 7
 8      @Override
 9      protected void onCreate( Bundle savedInstanceState ) {
10        super.onCreate( savedInstanceState );
11        setContentView( R.layout.activity_main );
12      }
13    }
```

EXAMPLE 1.9 **The `MainActivity` class**

on a stack (a last-in, first-out data structure). To create an activity, we must subclass `Activity` or one of its subclasses as done in the skeleton code of `MainActivity`, which was automatically generated. Some methods of the `Activity` class are automatically called by the system when an activity starts, stops, resumes, or is destroyed.

The `onCreate` method (lines 8–12) is automatically called when the activity starts. We should override this method and if needed, create the components of the activity inside that method. At line 10, we call the `onCreate` method inherited from `Activity` via `AppCompatActivity`. At line 11, we define the layout of the app by calling the `setContentView` method, shown in **TABLE 1.1**. The layout is defined in the activity_main.xml file. The argument of the `setContentView` method is an integer that represents the id of a layout resource defining a screen layout. Ids of resources can be found in the R.java file inside the app/build/generated/source/r/debug/com/jblearning/helloandroid directory. The `R` class contains many inner classes: `anim`, `attr`, `bool`, `color`, `dimen`, `drawable`, `id`, `integer`, `layout`, `menu`, `string`, `style`, `styleable`. Each inner class is `public` and `static` and contains one or many `int` constants. Each `int` constant is accessible via the syntax:

```
R.className.constantName
```

The `activity_main` constant, the id for the activity_main.xml file, a layout resource, is defined in the `layout` class, inside the `R` class. Thus, it can be referenced using `R.layout.activity_main`.

TABLE 1.1 Selected `setContentView` methods of the `Activity` class

Method	Description
void setContentView(View view)	Sets the content of this Activity to view
void setContentView(int layoutResID)	Sets the content of this Activity using the resource with id layoutResID, which will be inflated

Calling `setContentView` with an integer argument that represents a layout XML file, in this case `R.layout.activity_main`, is called **inflating the XML**.

1.4 Running the App Inside the Emulator

Android Studio includes an emulator so that we can run and test an app inside the environment before testing it on a device. We first run the app in the emulator. In order for the emulator to work, we may need to do three things:

▶ If needed, enable the virtualization extension in the BIOS menu (if it is disabled; note that it may be enabled by default). When starting our computer, we need to interrupt the boot process, access the system's BIOS menu, and enable virtualization. If the computer does not support virtualization, it is unlikely that the emulator will work.

▶ If needed, download, install, and run the Intel Hardware Accelerated Execution Manager (HAXM). It may already be on our computer after we downloaded Android Studio. It is also possible that it needs to be updated. The file name should be intelhaxm-android.exe.

▶ Close and restart Android Studio.

Most, if not all, recent computers support virtualization.

The emulator runs inside an **Android Virtual Device (AVD)**. We can create AVDs with the

FIGURE 1.17 The AVD Manager icon

AVD Manager. To open the AVD Manager, choose Window, AVD Manager, or click on the AVD Manager icon, as shown in **FIGURE 1.17**. This opens the AVD Manager, as shown in **FIGURE 1.18**. To create a new AVD, we click on the + Create Virtual Device. . . button. That opens a new panel (**FIGURE 1.19**) that allows us to select among a list of premade AVDs. After selecting one from the list and clicking on Next, it is displayed in a new panel (**FIGURE 1.20**). We select the version we want and

FIGURE 1.18 Opening the AVD Manager for the first time

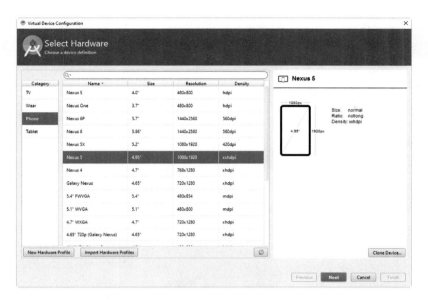

FIGURE 1.19 Selecting a new AVD

FIGURE 1.20 After selecting an AVD

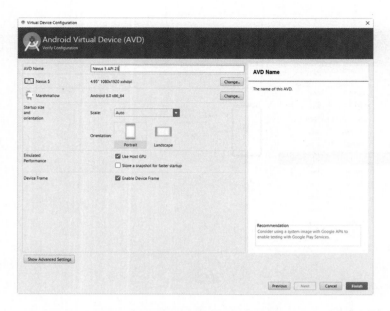

FIGURE 1.21 Characteristics of the selected AVD

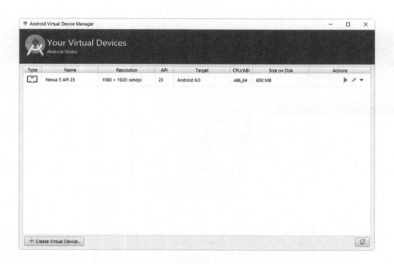

FIGURE 1.22 The AVD Manager showing the updated list of AVDs

click on next. The characteristics of the AVD are displayed, as shown in **FIGURE 1.21**. We can edit them if we want; in particular, we can edit the Scale attribute if we want to change the resolution of the AVD (and the size of the emulator as a result) when we run. After we click on Finish, the new AVD has been added, as shown in **FIGURE 1.22**.

In order to run the app, click on the Run icon in the icon bar, as shown in **FIGURE 1.23**.

FIGURE 1.23 Run configurations dialog box

A dialog box opens (**FIGURE 1.24**) and we choose the AVD we want to use by selecting one from the list; then, we click on OK. We can also access the AVD Manager by clicking on the Create New Emulator button. Note that if the emulator is already running or an actual device is connected to our computer, it will show in the panel under Connected Devices. After a couple of minutes, the app should be running in the emulator. In order to save time, we recommend that you leave the emulator open as long as Android Studio is open.

SOFTWARE ENGINEERING: Leave the emulator open for the length of your development session in order to save time.

Select Deployment Target   ×

No USB devices or emulators detected   Troubleshoot

Connected Devices
<none>

Available Emulators

Nexus 5 API 23

Create New Emulator

☐ Use same selection for future launches   OK   Cancel

FIGURE 1.24 Deployment target dialog box, after clicking on the Run icon

FIGURE 1.25 Emulator running the HelloAndroid app

FIGURE 1.26 The toolbar of the emulator, showing the Rotate tool

FIGURE 1.25 shows the app running in the emulator. By default, the emulator runs in vertical, also called **portrait**, orientation. It includes a toolbar on its right that enables us to control some of its features. In particular, we can rotate the emulator using the tool shown in **FIGURE 1.26**. We can also click on Ctrl+F11 to rotate the emulator to the horizontal, or **landscape**, orientation (see **FIGURE 1.27**; note that we did not include the toolbar in this screenshot). Ctrl+F12 brings the emulator back to the vertical orientation. We can move the emulator by clicking on the top, white part of its frame and dragging it. **TABLE 1.2** summarizes useful information about the emulator.

An interesting recent feature of Android Studio is **Instant Run**. With Instant Run, we can modify some selected components of an app, for example the strings.xml file, click on the Run icon, and the emulator automatically updates the app on the fly. Instant Run is enabled by default. If we want to disable it, we can choose File, Settings, and within the Build, Execution, Deployment section, select Instant Run, and then edit it, as shown in **FIGURE 1.28**. If we do not want to use Instant Run, we can uncheck it and check Restart activity on code changes.

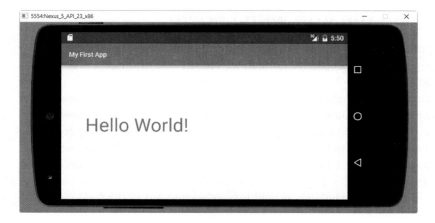

FIGURE 1.27 Emulator running the HelloAndroid app in horizontal orientation

TABLE 1.2 Useful information about the emulator	
Turn on virtualization in the BIOS (if necessary)	Enable the emulator to run
Install and run the HAXM executable (if necessary)	Enable the emulator to run
Ctrl+F11 and Ctrl+F12	Rotate the emulator
Toolbar	Control features of the emulator

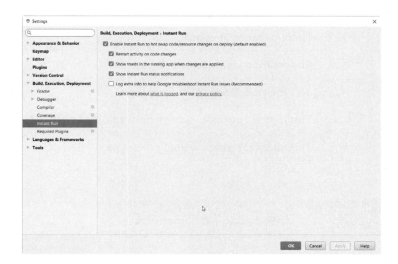

FIGURE 1.28 The Settings panel showing the Instant Run capability

1.5 Debugging the App with Logcat

Just like with a regular Java program, we can send output to the console, which can be very useful for debugging purposes. In order to do that, we can use one of the `static` methods of the `Log` class shown in TABLE 1.3. The `Log` class is part of the `android.util` package. This can be very useful at development time to provide us with feedback on various objects and variables as we test our app. Output from logging statements will show in the lower panel (click on the Android tab located at the bottom of the screen in order to open that panel) if we click on the **Logcat** tab, as shown in FIGURE 1.29. If the Logcat tab does not show, we should run the app in **Debug** mode first to force it to show. To run the app in Debug mode, click on the Debug button (the one with the bug icon, to the immediate right of the Run button) as shown in Figure 1.23. Logging statements should be commented out in the final version of the app.

The main difference in these methods is how verbose their output is. From the most to the least verbose, the order is: `v`, `d`, `i`, `w`, `e`.

There can be a lot of output inside Logcat. We can filter the output inside Logcat by using a filter so it only shows the output that we select from the app. To set up a filter, click on the drop-down list located on the top right corner inside the lower left panel; select Edit Filter Configuration (shown on the right side of FIGURE 1.30). Inside the dialog box shown on FIGURE 1.31, give the filter a tag. We choose `MainActivity`: in this way, it identifies that this output was generated

TABLE 1.3 Selected methods of the *Log* class	
Method	**Description**
static int d(String tag, String msg)	This method sends a debug message; tag identifies the source of the log message; it can be used to filter messages in Logcat.
static int e(String tag, String msg)	This method sends an error message.
static int i(String tag, String msg)	This method sends an info message.
static int v(String tag, String msg)	This method sends a verbose message.
static int w(String tag, String msg)	This method sends a warning message.

FIGURE 1.29 **The lower panel—the Logcat tab and the MainActivity filter are selected**

by some code inside the `MainActivity` class. When using the methods of the `Log` class to output data, we use `MainActivity` as the first argument (the tag) of those methods. In turn, when we run the app, if we select the filter named `MainActivity`, as shown in **FIGURE 1.32**, we only see the output that was tagged with `MainActivity`.

EXAMPLE 1.10 shows the updated `MainActivity` class, including a feedback output statement. The `Log` class is imported at line 5. We declare a constant named

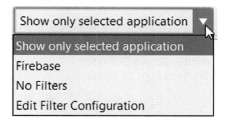

FIGURE 1.30 Opening the Logcat filter dialog box

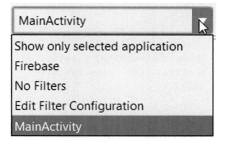

FIGURE 1.31 Setting up a Logcat filter

MA at line 8 to store the `String MainActivity`. The output statement at line 14 uses MA as its tag, and outputs the value of the resource `R.layout.activity_main`.

As we run the app, we see the result of our output statement in Figure 1.29. As the figure shows, the Logcat tab is selected (top left), and the `MainActivity` filter is selected (top right). We can verify that the id of the resource `R.layout.activity_main` (2130968601) matches the value found in the R.java file (hexadecimal number 0x7f040019).

FIGURE 1.32 Selecting the MainActivity filter

```
1   package com.jblearning.helloandroid;
2
3   import android.support.v7.app.AppCompatActivity;
4   import android.os.Bundle;
5   import android.util.Log;
6
7   public class MainActivity extends AppCompatActivity {
8     public static String MA = "MainActivity";
9
10    @Override
11    protected void onCreate( Bundle savedInstanceState ) {
12      super.onCreate( savedInstanceState );
13      setContentView( R.layout.activity_main );
14      Log.w( MA, "View resource: " + R.layout.activity_main );
15    }
16  }
```

EXAMPLE 1.10 **The modified** `MainActivity` **class, HelloAndroid, Version 1**

As always with programming, we could have compiler errors, runtime errors, and logic errors. By default, Android Studio compiles our code as we type. It flags compiler errors with a small red line and warnings with a small orange line on the right margin of our code; it also shows a red tilde where the error is. For example, if we forget to include the semicolon at the end of line 14, Android Studio will signal the error as shown in **FIGURE 1.33**. If we move the mouse over the red line on the right margin or the red tilde, we see one or more suggestions to help us correct the error. In this case, we see:

```
';' expected
```

```
public class MainActivity extends AppCompatActivity {
  public static String MA = "MainActivity";

  @Override
  protected void onCreate( Bundle savedInstanceState ) {
    super.onCreate( savedInstanceState );
    setContentView( R.layout.activity_main );
    Log.w( MA, "View resource: " + R.layout.activity_main )
  }                                                    ';' expected
}
```

FIGURE 1.33 **Compiler error flagged by Android Studio**

The Android Studio includes many features that improve the programmer's experience, saves time by automatically generating code and prevents errors. Here are a few of these features:

▶ When we type a double quote, it automatically closes it by adding another one; furthermore, if we close it ourselves, it automatically deletes the extra double quote.

▶ If we use a class that has not been imported yet, it will underline it and suggests to import it by typing Alt+Enter, saving us some time.

▶ If we type an object reference and then a dot, it suggests methods of the object's class that we can call, and updates and restricts the list as we type.

> **SOFTWARE ENGINEERING:** Use a filter to minimize the output inside Logcat.

1.6 Using the Debugger

In addition to Logcat, Android Studio includes traditional debugging tools, such as setting up breakpoints, checking the values of variables or expressions, stepping over code line by line, checking object memory allocation, taking screenshots and videos. In this section, we learn how to set up breakpoints and check the values of variables.

To set up a breakpoint, we click on the left of a statement—an orange filled circle appears. **FIGURE 1.34** shows that we have set up two breakpoints.

To run the app in debug mode, we click on the debug icon on the toolbar, shown in Figure 1.23. The app runs and stops at the first breakpoint. The debugger tab is selected in the panel at the bottom of the screen and we can see some debugging information and tools. Under Frames, we can see where in the code we are currently executing. Under Variables, we can check the values of the various variables, for example MA, which has value `MainActivity`. To resume the app, we click on the green Resume icon at the top left of the panel, as shown in **FIGURE 1.35**.

```java
    @Override
    protected void onCreate( Bundle savedInstanceState ) {
        super.onCreate( savedInstanceState );
        setContentView( R.layout.activity_main );
        Log.w( MA, "View resource: " + R.layout.activity_main );

        int count = 0;
        for( int i = 0; i < 3; i++ )
            count++;
    }
}
```

FIGURE 1.34 Breakpoints in the code

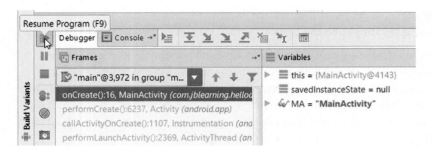

FIGURE 1.35 After stopping at the first breakpoint

FIGURE 1.36 Breakpoints in the code

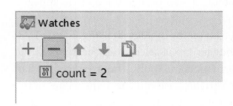

FIGURE 1.37 Managing a list of variables to watch

As we resume, stop at breakpoints, and resume the app a few times, the values of the various variables in our app are displayed under Variables. **FIGURE 1.36** shows that count and i both have a value of 2 at that point.

If there are too many variables showing up under Variables and we only want to look at a few of them, we can make a list of variables in the right bottom panel, under Watches. We click on the + sign to add a variable to the list and click on the – sign to take a variable off the list. **FIGURE 1.37** shows the value of count after we have added it to the list of watched variables.

1.7 Testing the App on an Actual Device

In order to test our app on an Android device, we need to:

▶ Download the driver for our Android device.
▶ Connect our Android device to our computer.

The driver for the Android device can be downloaded from the device manufacturer's website. For example, for Samsung's Android devices, the website is http://www.samsung.com/us/support/downloads#.

FIGURE 1.38 **The device's name and API level**

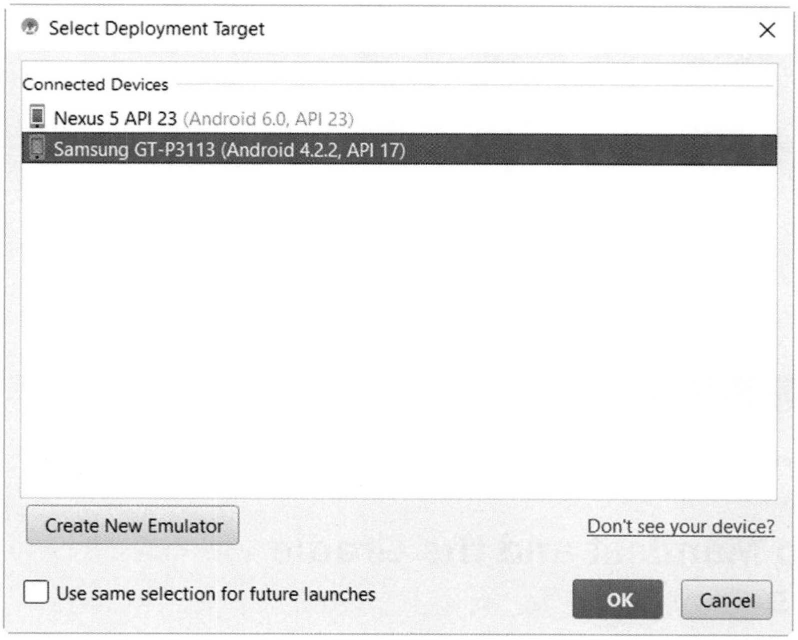

FIGURE 1.39 **Choose device dialog box**

Once we have done that, Android Studio will detect the connected device and display its name as well as its API level at the top left corner of the lower panel (assuming the lower panel is open, i.e., the Android tab is selected), as shown in **FIGURE 1.38**. We use a Samsung Galaxy Tab 2 7.0 tablet.

After we click on the Run or Debug button, a dialog box appears (**FIGURE 1.39**). The device appears in the list of devices or emulators we can run on. Select the device and click on OK. A few seconds later, the app runs (and is installed) on the device. Testing an app on an actual device is easier and faster than using the emulator. **FIGURE 1.40** shows the app running in the tablet. Note that we can still see the output in Logcat if we have output statements.

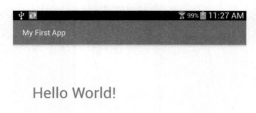

Hello World!

FIGURE 1.40 HelloAndroid app running inside the tablet

1.8 The App Manifest and the Gradle Build System

1.8.1 The AndroidManifest.xml File: App Icon and Device Orientation

The AndroidManifest.xml file, located in the manifests directory, specifies the resources that the app uses, such as activities, the file system, the Internet, and hardware resources. Before a user downloads an app on Google Play, the user is notified about these. **EXAMPLE 1.11** shows AndroidManifest.xml's automatically generated version. Among other things, it defines the icon (line 7) and the label or title for the app (line 8). The text inside the label is the app_name String defined in strings.xml.

We should supply a launcher icon for our app. This is the visual representation of our app on the Home screen or the apps screen. A launcher icon for a mobile device should be 48 × 48 dp. Various devices can have different screen densities, thus, we can supply several launcher icons,

```
1    <?xml version="1.0" encoding="utf-8"?>
2    <manifest package="com.jblearning.helloandroid"
3              xmlns:android="http://schemas.android.com/apk/res/android">
4
5      <application
6          android:allowBackup="true"
7          android:icon="@mipmap/ic_launcher"
8          android:label="@string/app_name"
9          android:supportsRtl="true"
10         android:theme="@style/AppTheme">
11        <activity android:name=".MainActivity">
12          <intent-filter>
13            <action android:name="android.intent.action.MAIN"/>
14
15            <category android:name="android.intent.category.LAUNCHER"/>
16          </intent-filter>
17        </activity>
18      </application>
19
20    </manifest>
```

EXAMPLE 1.11 The AndroidManifest.xml file

one for each density. When doing that, we should follow the 2/3/4/6/8 scaling ratios between the various densities from medium (2) to xxx-high (8). If we only supply one icon, Android Studio will use that icon and expand its density as necessary. TABLE 1.4 shows an example of possible dimensions using that rule. If we intend to publish, we should provide a 512×512 launcher icon for display in Google Play. We can find more information at https://www.google.com/design/spec/style/icons.html. FIGURE 1.41 shows the mipmap directory after we added a file named hi.png whose dimensions are 48×48.

To set the launch icon for the app to hi.png, we assign the String @mipmap/hi to the android:icon attribute of the application element in the AndroidManifest.xml file. The

TABLE 1.4 Launcher icon ratios and possible dimensions

Density	Medium	High	X-High	XX-High	XXX-High
Scaling ratio	2	3	4	6	8
Dots per inch	160 dpi	240 dpi	320 dpi	480 dpi	640 dpi
Dimensions	48×48 px	72×72 px	96×96 px	144×144 px	192×192 px

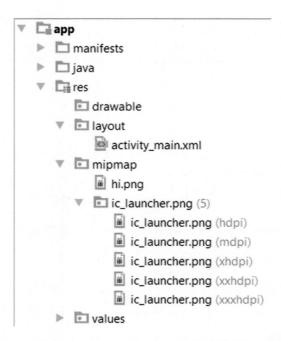

FIGURE 1.41 The hi.png file in the mipmap directory

`@mipmap/hi` expression defines the resource in the `mipmap` directory (of the `res` directory) whose name is `hi` (note that we do not include the extension). Line 7 of Example 1.11 becomes:

```
android:icon="@mipmap/hi"
```

One thing we have to worry about is that some users will use the app in vertical (portrait) orientation, and others will use the app in horizontal (landscape) orientation. The default behavior for an app is to rotate the screen as the user rotates the device, thus, our current app works in both orientations. **FIGURE 1.42** shows the app running inside the tablet in horizontal orientation. As an app gets more complex, this becomes an important issue. Later in the book, we discuss alternatives and strategies to manage orientations. Sometimes, we want the app to run in only one orientation, vertical for example, and therefore we do not want the app to rotate when the user rotates the device. Inside the `activity` element, we can add the `android:screenOrientation` attribute and specify either `portrait` or `landscape` as its value. For example, if we want our app to run in vertical orientation only, we add:

```
android:screenOrientation="portrait"
```

Note that we can control the behavior of the app on a per activity basis. In this app, there is only one activity, but there could be several. **EXAMPLE 1.12** shows the updated AndroidManifest.xml file. If we run the app on a device, the screen does not rotate as we rotate the device; it

```
1   <?xml version="1.0" encoding="utf-8"?>
2   <manifest package="com.jblearning.helloandroid"
3             xmlns:android="http://schemas.android.com/apk/res/android">
4
5     <application
6         android:allowBackup="true"
7         android:icon="@mipmap/hi"
8         android:label="@string/app_name"
9         android:supportsRtl="true"
10        android:theme="@style/AppTheme">
11      <activity android:name=".MainActivity"
12                android:screenOrientation="portrait">
13        <intent-filter>
14          <action android:name="android.intent.action.MAIN"/>
15
16          <category android:name="android.intent.category.LAUNCHER"/>
17        </intent-filter>
18      </activity>
19    </application>
20
21  </manifest>
```

EXAMPLE 1.12 The modified AndroidManifest.xml file

FIGURE 1.42 HelloAndroid app, running inside the tablet in horizontal orientation

FIGURE 1.43 **The emulator screen showing the app icon**

stays in portrait orientation. **FIGURE 1.43** shows the icon for the app in the emulator (among native apps).

1.8.2 The Gradle Build System

Android Application Package (APK), is the file format for distributing applications that run on the Android operating system. The file extension is .apk. To create an apk file, the project is compiled and its various parts are packaged into the apk file. At the time of this writing, the apk file can be found in the projectName/app/build/outputs/apk directory.

Apk files are built using the gradle build system, which is integrated in the Android Studio environment. When we start an app, the gradle build scripts are automatically created. They can be modified to build apps that require custom building, for example:

- Customize the build process.
- Create multiple apks for the app, each with different features, using the resources of the project. For example, different versions can be made for different audiences (paid versus free, consumer versus corporation).

Chapter Summary

- Android Studio is the official development environment for Android apps.
- In addition to the JDK, an Android SDK is available for development.
- Android Studio is free and available from Google.
- Android development uses XML files to define the Graphical User Interface (GUI), strings, styles, dimensions, etc.
- The res directory stores some of the app resources, such as activity_main.xml in the layout directory, and strings.xml, styles.xml, colors.xml, and dimens.xml in the values directory.
- The layout and GUI can be defined in XML files; the starting default file is activity_main.xml.
- `Strings` can be defined in the strings.xml file.
- Styles can be defined in the styles.xml file.
- Dimensions can be defined in the dimens.xml file.
- Colors can be defined in the colors.xml file.
- The R.java class is generated automatically and stores ids for various app resources.
- Android Studio includes a preview mode that can display the GUI for layout XML files.
- An activity is a component that provides a screen with which users can interact.
- An app can consist of several activities, possibly passing data to each other.
- Activities are managed on a stack (last-in, first-out data structure).
- To create an activity, we subclass the `Activity` class or an existing subclass of the `Activity` class.
- The `onCreate` method of the (entry point) `Activity` class is called automatically when the activity starts.
- We specify the View for an activity by calling the `setContentView` method.
- An app includes a manifest, the AndroidManifest.xml file, which defines the resources used by the app.
- The emulator enables us to simulate how an app would run on various devices.
- We can test an app in the emulator or on a device.
- The Instant Run feature enables us to modify various components of an app and run without restarting the app from scratch inside the emulator.
- When it is ready for installation, an app is packaged in a file with the .apk extension, known as the app's apk.
- Gradle is the build system for Android apps.

Exercises, Problems, and Projects

Multiple-Choice Exercises

1. AVD stands for
   - Android Validator
   - Android Virtual Device
   - Android Valid Device
   - Android Viral device

2. XML stands for
   - eXtended Mega Language
   - eXtended Multi Language
   - eXtensible Markup Language
   - eXtensible Mega Language

3. Mark the following XML snippets valid or invalid
   - `<a>hello</a>`
   - `</b>Hello<b>`
   - `<c digit="6"></c>`
   - `<d>He there</e>`
   - `<f letter='Z"/>`
   - `<1 digit="8">one</1>`
   - `<g digit1="1" digit2="2"></g>`
   - `<h><i name="Chris"></i></h>`
   - `<j><k name="Jane"></j>`
   - `<l><m name="Mary"></l></m>`

4. What is the name of the string that is defined by the following XML snippet inside strings.xml?

   ```
   <string name="abc">Hello</string>
   ```

   - `string`
   - `name`
   - `abc`
   - `Hello`

5. What is the value of the string that is defined by the following XML snippet inside strings.xml?

   ```
   <string name="abc">Hello</string>
   ```

   - `string`
   - `name`
   - `abc`
   - `Hello`

6. What will be the text displayed inside the TextView widget defined by the following XML snippet inside activity_main.xml?

   ```
   <TextView
       android:layout_width="match_parent"
       android:layout_height="wrap_content"
       android:text="@string/hi" />
   ```

   - `@string/hi`
   - `hi`
   - `the value of the String named hi as defined in strings.xml`
   - `android:text`

7. The AppCompatActivity class is found in the package
   - `android.app.Activity`
   - `android.app`
   - `android.Activity`
   - `android.support.v7.app`

8. The AppCompatActivity class is a subclass of the Activity class
   - `true`
   - `false`

Fill in the Code

9. Inside the XML snippet next activity_main.xml, add a line of XML so that the text displayed in the text field is the value of the string book (assume that the string book has been defined in strings.xml)

   ```
   <TextView
       android:layout_width="fill_parent"
       android:layout_height="wrap_content"

       />
   ```

10. Inside the onCreate method, fill in the code so that we set the layout and GUI defined in activity_main.xml

```
public void onCreate( Bundle savedInstanceState ){
        super.onCreate(savedInstanceState);
        // Your code goes here


}
```

Write an App

11. Write an app that displays "I like Android"

12. Write an app that only runs in horizontal orientation. It displays "This is fun!" on the top left corner of the screen with no margin either from the top or the left.

CHAPTER TWO

Model View Controller, GUI Components, Events

CHAPTER CONTENTS

Introduction

Good apps provide useful functionality and an easy to use interface. The user interface is made of various Graphical User Interface (GUI) components and typically waits for user interaction. Some of these GUI components enable user input, such as clicking on a button, entering data from the keyboard, selecting an item from a list, and spinning a wheel. . . Those user interactions are called **events**. When an event happens, the app processes the event and updates the screen; this is called **handling the event**. In this chapter, we learn about various GUI components, their associated events, and how to handle events on those components. We also learn how to style the look and feel of those components. Later, we will learn how to better arrange those components on the screen with layout managers.

2.1 Model-View-Controller Architecture

Previously, we created our first app, which had two parts:

▶ activity_main.xml, which defined the GUI: this is called the **View** part of the app.
▶ The `MainActivity` class, which displayed the GUI (more generally, the `Activity` class manages the GUI); this is called the **Controller** part of the app.

Our first app only displayed a label, so it did not have any functionality; the functionality of an app is called the **Model**.

It is good design practice to separate these three parts: the Model, the View, and the Controller. It makes the app much easier to design, code, maintain, and modify later on. We could also reuse parts of the app, for example the Model, to make another app.

In this chapter, we make a simple Tip Calculator app using the Model View Controller architecture; in order to do that, we code three important files:

▶ TipCalculator.java: the `TipCalculator` class encapsulates the functionality of a tip calculator; this class is the Model of the app,
▶ activity_main.xml: this file defines the View of the app, and
▶ MainActivity.java: this class is the Controller of the app.

What makes up the functionality of a tip calculator? We keep the Model to a minimum in order to focus more on the View and the Controller. Our minimum Model configuration includes the bill, the tip percentage, and two methods to compute the tip and the total bill. The View mirrors the Model and includes four GUI components to display the data specified in the Model.

The Controller is the middleman between the View and the Model. When the user inputs data in the View—for example, changes the tip percentage—the Controller asks the Model to perform some calculations, and then updates the View accordingly.

More generally, we can use the Model View Controller Store architecture. This is useful when we have persistent data; we can store and retrieve data in and from the Store.

The Model is typically straightforward Java code, and does not include any GUI-related code. It is generally a good place to start.

TABLE 2.1 API for the `TipCalculator` class

Constructor	
TipCalculator	TipCalculator(float newTip, float newBill) Constructs a TipCalculator object

Methods	
Return value	**Method name and argument list**
float	getTip( )
float	getBill( )
void	setTip(float)
void	setBill(float)
float	tipAmount( )
float	totalAmount( )

2.2 The Model

We start a new Android Studio project, we call it TipCalculatorV0, and we choose the Empty Activity template.

The Model encapsulates the Tip Calculator functionality. The Model should be platform independent. It should be coded so that it could be used to build not just this mobile app or another mobile app, but also a desktop application or even an Internet website.

For this app, the Model is simple and is only composed of one class that encapsulates a tip calculator, the `TipCalculator` class. It is a regular Java class. In fact, we can even code this class outside the Android development environment and test it before we bring it into our project. We choose to place our class in the com.jblearning.tipcalculatorv0 package (and directory) of our project, inside the Java directory. We select that directory, then select File → New → Java Class, write the name of the class, and click OK. The class skeleton appears. **TABLE 2.1** shows the API for the `TipCalculator` class.

EXAMPLE 2.1 shows the class code. In order to code the `TipCalculator` class and a Model in general, we do not need to know anything about Android programming. Furthermore, we can test the Model with a simple Java program that tests all the methods of the class; this is left as an exercise. We only have one class in this example, but in general, a Model can include many classes and can be placed in its own directory. The most useful methods for this app are the constructor (lines 7–10), and the `tipAmount` (lines 30–32) and `totalAmount` (lines 34–36) methods.

2.3 GUI Components

We now turn our attention to the View and the capabilities of the Android development environment for designing a GUI.

```
1   package com.jblearning.tipcalculatorv0;
2
3   public class TipCalculator {
4       private float tip;
5       private float bill;
6
7       public TipCalculator( float newTip, float newBill ) {
8           setTip( newTip );
9           setBill( newBill );
10      }
11
12      public float getTip( ) {
13          return tip;
14      }
15
16      public float getBill( ) {
17          return bill;
18      }
19
20      public void setTip( float newTip ) {
21          if( newTip > 0 )
22              tip = newTip;
23      }
24
25      public void setBill( float newBill ) {
26          if( newBill > 0 )
27              bill = newBill;
28      }
29
30      public float tipAmount( ) {
31          return bill * tip;
32      }
33
34      public float totalAmount( ) {
35          return bill + tipAmount( );
36      }
37  }
```

EXAMPLE 2.1 **The TipCalculator class**

In this chapter, we use the activity_main.xml file to create and define the GUI components that are displayed on the screen. We can also define and manipulate GUI components entirely by code, which we will do later in the book.

GUI Components are objects that have a graphical representation; they are also called **widgets**. The term widget also has another meaning for Android users—it refers to a mini-app that is displayed and is running on the Android's Home or Lock screen, typically showing the app's most relevant information. GUI components can:

- display information
- collect data from the user, and
- allow the user to interact with them and trigger a call to a method.

Android provides an extensive set of classes that encapsulate various GUI components. TABLE 2.2 lists some of them.

A lot of GUI components share some functionality, and inherit from each other. FIGURE 2.1 gives a summary of the inheritance hierarchy for some of them.

A `View` represents the basic building block for GUI components; the `View` class is in the `android.view` package. It occupies a rectangular area of the screen, is drawable, and can respond to events. `View` is the superclass for GUI components such as buttons, checkboxes, and lists. `ViewGroup` is the superclass for layout classes and is also in the `android.view` package; layouts are invisible containers that can contain other `Views` or other `ViewGroups`. Most other classes shown in Figure 2.1, such as `ImageView`, `TextView`, `Button`, `EditText`, `CompoundButton`, `AutoCompleteTextView`, `Checkbox`, `RadioButton`, `Switch`, and `ToggleButton` are in the `android.widget` package. `KeyboardView` is in the `android.inputmethodservice` package.

TABLE 2.2 Selected GUI components and their classes

GUI Component Type	Class	Description
View	View	A drawable rectangular area on the screen; can respond to events
Keyboard	KeyboardView	Renders a keyboard
Label	TextView	Displays text
Text field	EditText	Editable text field where user can enter data
Button	Button	Pressable and clickable push button
Radio button	RadioButton	Two-state button that can be checked by the user; when used in a group, checking a radio button automatically unchecks the other radio buttons in the group
Checkbox	CheckBox	Two-state button that can be checked or unchecked by the user
Two-state toggle button	ToggleButton	Two-state switch button that can select between two options
Two-state toggle button	Switch	Similar to a ToggleButton; user can also slide between the two states

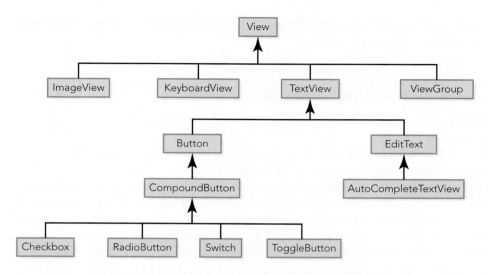

FIGURE 2.1 **Inheritance hierarchy for selected GUI components**

2.4 `RelativeLayout`, `TextView`, `EditText`, and `Button`: **Tip Calculator, Version 0**

In Version 0 of this app, we display some GUI components without any functionality. This version uses four GUI components: two `TextViews` that show labels for the bill and tip percentage, and two `EditTexts` where the user enters the bill and the tip percentage. In this version, we are not processing any user data, we are only concerned with placing the widgets on the screen; we do not even calculate or show the tip amount and the total amount.

In order to keep things simple, we only allow the app to work in vertical orientation, which we can specify in the AndroidManifest.xml file. We do that by assigning the value `portrait` to the `android:screenOrientation` attribute of the `activity` tag at line 13 in **EXAMPLE 2.2**.

We edit the activity_main.xml file to define the user interface. If the GUI is static and does not change as the user interacts with the app, activity_main.xml is a good way to define it. If the GUI is dynamic and changes as the app is running, then we can create and define the user interface by code. For example, if the app retrieves a list of links from a file and displays them, we do not know in advance how many links we will retrieve and that we will need to display. Typically, whatever we can do via XML attributes and values in the activity_main.xml file, we can also do programmatically.

Before editing the activity_main.xml file of our Tip Calculator app, let's look at the skeleton that is provided when we create a project. The `TextView` element has the following two attributes and values:

```
android:layout_width="match_parent"
android:layout_height="wrap_content"
```

```
1   <?xml version="1.0" encoding="utf-8"?>
2   <manifest package="com.jblearning.tipcalculatorv0"
3            xmlns:android="http://schemas.android.com/apk/res/android">
4
5     <application
6       android:allowBackup="true"
7       android:icon="@mipmap/ic_launcher"
8       android:label="@string/app_name"
9       android:supportsRtl="true"
10      android:theme="@style/AppTheme">
11      <activity
12        android:name=".MainActivity"
13        android:screenOrientation="portrait">
14        <intent-filter>
15          <action android:name="android.intent.action.MAIN"/>
16
17          <category android:name="android.intent.category.LAUNCHER"/>
18        </intent-filter>
19      </activity>
20    </application>
21
22  </manifest>
```

EXAMPLE 2.2 The AndroidManifest.xml file

Android: `layout_width` and android: `layout_height` are special attributes that can be specified with regular `View` attributes, but are instead parsed by the `View`'s parent. They belong to the `static` class `ViewGroup.LayoutParams`, which `Views` use to tell their parents how they want to be laid out. `ViewGroup.LayoutParams` is a `static` class nested inside the `ViewGroup` class.

The `ViewGroup.LayoutParams` class enables us to specify the width and height of a `View` relative to its parent. We can use its android: `layout_width` and android: `layout_height` XML attributes to specify the width and height of the `View`, not only with absolute values, but also relative to the `View`'s parent. The class provides two constants, `MATCH_PARENT` and `WRAP_CON-TENT`, to that effect, as seen in **TABLE 2.3**.

We can assign the android: `layout_width` and android: `layout_height` XML attributes a `match_parent` value or a `wrap_content` value. The `match_parent` value corresponds to the constant `MATCH_PARENT` (whose value is –1) of the `ViewGroup.LayoutParams` class, and means that the `View` should be as big as its parent, minus the padding. The `wrap_content` value, which corresponds to the constant `WRAP_CONTENT` (whose value is –2) of the `ViewGroup.LayoutParams` class, means that the `View` should just be dimensioned big enough to enclose its contents, plus the padding.

If we look at the `TextView` of the skeleton code provided in activity_main.xml, we see that we have dimensioned the width and the height of the `View` relative to the width and height of its contents.

TABLE 2.3 XML attributes and constants of `ViewGroup.LayoutParams`

Attribute Name	Description
android:layout_width	Sets the width of the View
android:layout_height	Sets the height of the View
Constant	**Value**
MATCH_PARENT	−1
WRAP_CONTENT	−2

We can also dimension the `View` with absolute coordinates. If we want to specify absolute dimensions, several units are available: px (pixels), dp (density-independent-pixels), sp (scaled pixels based on preferred font size), in (inches), mm (millimeters).

For example:

```
android:layout_width="200dp"
android:layout_height="50dp"
```

However, an app will eventually be run on many different devices that can have a variety of screen sizes. Thus, we recommend using relative positioning rather than absolute positioning. If we choose to use absolute dimensions, we recommend the dp units because they are independent of the screen density of the device that the app is installed on.

Furthermore, both `android:layout_width` and `android:layout_height` attributes are mandatory for each GUI element. Omitting one of them will result in a runtime exception; the app will stop and display the message:

```
Unfortunately, AppName has stopped
```

> **COMMON ERROR:** Not specifying the `android:layout_width` and `android:layout_height` attributes will result in a runtime exception.

As shown in Figure 2.1, EditText and `Button` are subclasses of `TextView`, itself a subclass of `View`; therefore, all these three classes inherit the attributes of `View`, in addition to having their own. **TABLE 2.4** shows some XML attributes of `View`, along with the corresponding methods and their descriptions. We can see the full list at http://www.developer.android.com/reference/android/view/View.html.

TABLE 2.4 Selected XML attributes and methods of `View`		
Attribute Name	**Related Method**	**Description**
android:id	setId(int)	Sets an id for the View; the View can then be retrieved by code using its id
android:minHeight	setMinimumHeight(int)	Defines the minimum height of the View
android:minWidth	setMinimumWidth(int)	Defines the minimum width of the View

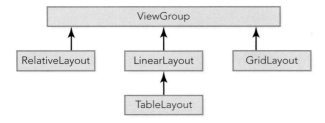

FIGURE 2.2 Selected layout manager classes

The Android Development Kit (ADK) provides layout manager classes to arrange the GUI components on the screen; they are subclasses of `ViewGroup`. **FIGURE 2.2** shows some of them.

The default layout manager used in activity_main.xml when an empty project is created is a `RelativeLayout`. It enables us to position components relative to other components. Typically, a layout manager class has a `public static` inner class, often named `LayoutParams`, containing XML attributes that enable us to position components. If the class name is `C`, then we refer to that inner class as `C.LayoutParams`. The `RelativeLayout` class has a `public static` inner class named `LayoutParams` (we refer to it using `RelativeLayout.LayoutParams`) that contains many XML attributes that enable us to arrange elements relative to each other, for example below a View, or to the right of another View. In order to reference another `View`, we can give that `View` an id and use that id to reference it. We can also position a `View` with respect to its parent `View`, in which case we do not need to reference the parent `View` with its id. We list some of these attributes in **TABLE 2.5**. The first eight attributes listed (`android:layout_alignLeft` to `android:layout_toRightOf`) expect their value to be the id of a `View`. The last four attributes listed expect their value to be `true` or `false`.

For a value to be the id of a `View`, that `View` must have been given an id.

The Android framework enables us to give an integer id to a `View` using the `android:id` XML attribute so we can reference it and also retrieve it by code using its id. The id must be a resource reference and is set using the `@+` syntax as follows:

```
android:id="@+id/idValue"
```

TABLE 2.5 Useful XML attributes of RelativeLayout.LayoutParams

XML attribute	Description
android:layout_alignLeft	View's left edge matches the value view's left edge
android:layout_alignRight	View's right edge matches the value view's right edge
android:layout_alignBottom	View's bottom edge matches the value view's bottom edge
android:layout_alignTop	View's top edge matches the value view's top edge
android:layout_above	View goes above the value view
android:layout_below	View goes below the value view
android:layout_toLeftOf	View goes left of the value view
android:layout_toRightOf	View goes right of the value view
android:layout_alignParentLeft	If true, view's left edge matches its parent's left edge
android:layout_alignParentRight	If true, view's right edge matches its parent's right edge
android:layout_alignParentBottom	If true, view's bottom edge matches its parent's bottom edge
android:layout_alignParentTop	If true, view's top edge matches its parent's top edge

EXAMPLE 2.3 shows the activity_main.xml file for Version 0. As compared to a skeleton app, we have added two EditText (lines 21–30 and 42–51), and another TextView element (lines 32–40). We use the two TextView elements as labels to describe the two EditTexts where we expect the user to enter some data. We want the TextView and the EditText for the bill to be displayed on the same horizontal line, and the TextView and the EditText for the tip percentage to be displayed on the line below. We do not want any of the four Views to take either

```
1   <?xml version="1.0" encoding="utf-8"?>
2   <RelativeLayout
3       xmlns:android="http://schemas.android.com/apk/res/android"
4       xmlns:tools="http://schemas.android.com/tools"
5       android:layout_width="match_parent"
6       android:layout_height="match_parent"
7       android:paddingBottom="@dimen/activity_vertical_margin"
8       android:paddingLeft="@dimen/activity_horizontal_margin"
```

EXAMPLE 2.3 **The activity_main.xml file, Tip Calculator app, Version 0 (*Continued*)**

```
 9          android:paddingRight="@dimen/activity_horizontal_margin"
10          android:paddingTop="@dimen/activity_vertical_margin"
11          tools:context="com.jblearning.tipcalculatorv0.MainActivity">
12
13    <TextView
14          android:id="@+id/label_bill"
15          android:layout_width="wrap_content"
16          android:layout_height="wrap_content"
17          android:minWidth="120dp"
18          android:textSize="28sp"
19          android:text="@string/label_bill"/>
20
21    <EditText
22          android:id="@+id/amount_bill"
23          android:layout_width="wrap_content"
24          android:layout_height="wrap_content"
25          android:layout_toRightOf="@+id/label_bill"
26          android:layout_alignBottom="@+id/label_bill"
27          android:layout_alignParentRight="true"
28          android:textSize="28sp"
29          android:hint="@string/amount_bill_hint"
30          android:inputType="numberDecimal" />
31
32    <TextView
33          android:id="@+id/label_tip_percent"
34          android:layout_width="wrap_content"
35          android:layout_height="wrap_content"
36          android:layout_below="@+id/label_bill"
37          android:layout_alignLeft="@+id/label_bill"
38          android:layout_alignRight="@+id/label_bill"
39          android:textSize="28sp"
40          android:text="@string/label_tip_percent"/>
41
42    <EditText
43          android:id="@+id/amount_tip_percent"
44          android:layout_width="wrap_content"
45          android:layout_height="wrap_content"
46          android:layout_toRightOf="@+id/label_tip_percent"
47          android:layout_alignBottom="@+id/label_tip_percent"
48          android:layout_alignRight="@id/amount_bill"
49          android:textSize="28sp"
50          android:hint="@string/amount_tip_percent_hint"
51          android:inputType="number" />
52
53    </RelativeLayout>
```

EXAMPLE 2.3 The activity_main.xml file, Tip Calculator app, Version 0

TABLE 2.6 The android:textSize and android:hint XML attributes of TextView

XML Attribute	Method	Description
android:textSize	void setTextSize(int unit, float size)	Sets the size of the text
android:hint	void setHint(int resource)	Sets the hint text to display

the whole width or height of the screen; thus, all the four `Views` use the `wrap_content` value for both the `android:layout_width` and `android:layout_height` attributes (lines 15–16, 23–24, 34–35, 44–45). We also specify that they use font size 28 (lines 18, 28, 39, 49).

We give all of them an id (lines 14, 22, 33, 43) so that we can refer to them when we position them relative to each other. We use the first `TextView`, storing the bill label, as the anchor element at the top left of the screen. At line 17, we give it a minimum width of 120 pixels; we choose that value so that the text of all the labels that we will position below the bill label will easily fit.

At line 25, we specify that the first `EditText`, where the user enters the bill, is to the right of the bill label. At line 26, we specify that its bottom edge is on the same horizontal line as the bottom edge of the bill label. At line 27, we specify that its right edge lines up with its parent's right edge, so that it extends to the right edge of the screen.

At line 36, we specify that the label for the tip percentage is below the bill label, whose id is `label_bill`. At lines 37 and 38, we specify that its left and right edges are lined up with the bill label.

At line 46, we specify that the first `EditText`, where the user enters the bill, is to the right of the bill label. At line 47, we specify that its bottom edge is on the same horizontal line as the bottom edge of the bill label. At line 48, we specify that its right edge lines up with the right edge of the `EditText` above it, whose id is `amount_bill`.

We assign hint values to both `EditTexts` at lines 29 and 50; both hint values are defined in the strings.xml file. **TABLE 2.6** shows the `android:textSize` and `android:hint` XML attributes of `TextView`, along with its corresponding method and description. Since `EditText` is a subclass of `TextView`, `EditText` inherits these two attributes. The default font size is small, so we set the font size of the `TextViews` and `EditTexts` to 28. By specifying `sp` units, we insure that the font size is screen-density independent. The size of the font has a direct impact on the size of the `TextViews` since they wrap around their contents. If we specify a large font size, then the components may not fit on the screen of small devices. In this app, do not worry about that issue. We will learn how to address that issue later in the book.

Both `EditText` elements contain one more attribute, `android:inputType` (lines 30 and 51), inherited from `TextView`; its value defines the type of data that is enabled for this field. **TABLE 2.7** lists some selected values. We want to enable the user to enter digits and the dot character only for the bill, so we choose `numberDecimal` for the first `EditText` element (line 30). When the app is running, we will not be able to enter anything different from a digit or the dot character (in fact,

TABLE 2.7	Selected possible values for the `android:inputType` XML attribute of `TextView`
Attribute Value	**Description**
text	Plain text
textPassword	Text is hidden; last character shows for a short time
number	Numeric values only
numberDecimal	Numeric values and one optional decimal point
phone	For entering a phone number
datetime	For entering a date and time
date	For entering a date
time	For entering a time

a maximum of one dot character). We want the user to enter digits only for the tip percentage, so choose `number` for the second `EditText` element (line 51). Try modifying line 30 or 51 using `textPassword` and run the app again. We would see that every character we enter is hidden and shows as a small plain circle.

SOFTWARE ENGINEERING: When defining an `EditText`, choose the appropriate value for `android:inputType` in order to match the data we expect the user will input.

SOFTWARE ENGINEERING: We should use ids that are unique.

COMMON ERROR: Define in the strings.xml file every `String` we use in the activity_main.xml file. Otherwise, we may have an error.

EXAMPLE 2.4 shows the strings.xml file.

```
1   <resources>
2       <string name="app_name">TipCalculatorV0</string>
3
4       <string name="label_bill">Bill</string>
5       <string name="label_tip_percent">Tip (%)</string>
6
7       <string name="amount_bill_hint">Enter bill</string>
8       <string name="amount_tip_percent_hint">Enter tip</string>
9   </resources>
```

EXAMPLE 2.4 **The strings.xml file, Tip Calculator app, Version 0**

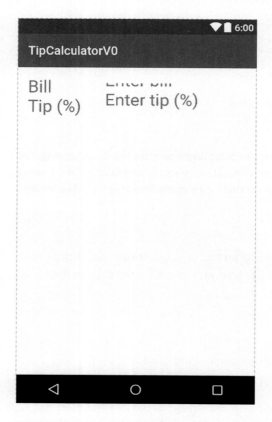

FIGURE 2.3 **Tip Calculator GUI, Version 0, shown in the Android Studio environment**

FIGURE 2.3 shows the current GUI in the Android Studio environment. We can see the two TextViews and EditTexts including the two hints: there is not enough space at the top of the screen to see Enter Bill properly. In Version 1, we fix that, add more GUI elements, and improve the look and feel.

2.5 GUI Components and More XML Attributes: Tip Calculator, Version 1

In Version 1, we complete the GUI, adding two labels and two `TextViews` to display the tip amount and the total amount, as well as one `Button`. In Version 2, we will update the tip and total amount when the user clicks on the `Button`. We also add colors, center the text in the `EditTexts`, and add margins around the various elements and padding inside them.

TABLE 2.8 shows more XML `View` attributes, along with the corresponding methods and their descriptions. There may not be a one-to-one mapping of each XML attribute to a method and vice versa. For example, a single method, such as `setPadding`, is used to set the values of several attributes (`paddingBottom`, `paddingLeft`, `paddingRight`, `paddingTop`). The padding attributes relate to extra spacing `inside` a GUI component, between the border of the component and its content. If we want to add extra space between GUI components (i.e., on the `outside`), we can use the margin attributes of the `ViewGroup.MarginLayoutParams` class, as shown in **TABLE 2.9**.

We can add some padding and margin to the first `TextView` of Example 2.3, as shown in the following code sequence:

```
<TextView
  android:id="@+id/label_bill"
  android:layout_width="wrap_content"
  android:layout_height="wrap_content"
  android:layout_marginTop="70dp"
  android:layout_marginLeft="50dp"
  android:padding="10dp"
```

TABLE 2.8 More selected XML attributes and methods of View

Attribute Name	Related Method	Description
android:background	setBackgroundColor(int)	Set the transparency and background color of the View
android:background	setBackgroundResource(int)	Set the drawable resource to be used as the background for the View
android:alpha	setAlpha(float)	Set the transparency value for the View
android:paddingBottom	setPadding(int, int, int, int)	Set the padding, in pixels, of the View's bottom edge
android:paddingLeft	setPadding(int, int, int, int)	Set the padding, in pixels, of the View's left edge
android:paddingRight	setPadding(int, int, int, int)	Set the padding, in pixels, of the View's right edge
android:paddingTop	setPadding(int, int, int, int)	Set the padding, in pixels, of the View's top edge

TABLE 2.9 Selected XML attributes and methods of ViewGroup.MarginLayoutParams		
Attribute Name	**Related Method**	**Description**
android:layout_marginBottom	setMargins(int, int, int, int)	Set extra space at the bottom of this View
android:layout_marginLeft	setMargins(int, int, int, int)	Set extra space at the left of this View
android:layout_marginRight	setMargins(int, int, int, int)	Set extra space at the right of this View
android:layout_marginTop	setMargins(int, int, int, int)	Set extra space at the top of this View

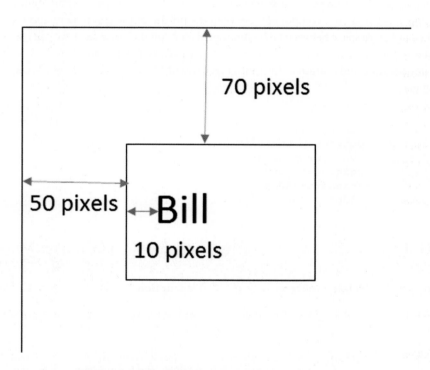

FIGURE 2.4 Margins around and padding inside a TextView

```
android:minWidth="120dp"
android:textSize="28sp"
android:text="@string/label_bill"/>
```

FIGURE 2.4 shows the resulting padding and margin. The top edge of the bill label is 70 pixels from the top edge of the screen (since there is no GUI component above the bill label). Its left edge is 50 pixels from the left edge of the screen (since there is no GUI component to the left of the bill label). There are 10 pixels of free space around the text Bill.

TABLE 2.10 Selected XML attributes of `TextView`		
XML Attribute	**Method**	**Description**
android:textColor	setTextColor(int)	Text color
android:textStyle	setTypeface(Typeface)	Style (bold, italic, regular) of the text
android:gravity	setGravity(int)	Text alignment within this TextView

We can also set more text attributes of a `TextView`, such as its color, style, or alignment. TABLE 2.10 shows the `android:textColor`, `android:textStyle`, and `android:gravity` XML attributes of `TextView`. The `android:gravity` attribute relates to the alignment of the text within the `TextView`; the default is left-aligned.

TABLE 2.11 shows the possible formats for the value of the `android:textColor` XML attribute of `TextView` (or any GUI component that inherits from `TextView`). The same applies to the `android:background` XML attribute of `View`. More generally, for an XML attribute of a `View`, it is common to have three strategies to set its value:

▶ Specify a value directly
▶ Reference a resource
▶ Reference a theme attribute

We will discuss themes later in this chapter. In this paragraph, we discuss the first two strategies.

TABLE 2.11 Possible formats for a color used with android:textColor or android:background		
Description	**Format**	**Explanation**
6 digits color value	"#rrggbb"	r, g, b are hex digits, representing the amount of red, green, and blue in the color
Transparency and 6 digits color value	"#aarrggbb"	a is a hex digit representing the transparency value (0 for transparent, f for opaque)
3 digits color value	"#rgb"	r, g, and b are duplicated
Transparency and 3 digits color value	"#argb"	a, r, g, and b are duplicated
Reference to a resource	"@[+][package:]type:name"	[ ] denote an optional field
Reference to a theme attribute	"?[package:][type:]name"	

To specify a yellow color (e.g., full red, full green, no blue) for the text, we can directly give a value to the `android:textColor` attribute in four different ways:

```
android:textColor="#FFFF00"
android:textColor="#FFFFFF00"
android:textColor="#FF0"
android:textColor="#FFF0"
```

If there are only three or four characters in the color string, then each character is duplicated to obtain an equivalent six- or eight-character color string. If there are six characters only, the first two characters specify the amount of red, the next two characters the amount of green, and the last two characters the amount of blue. If there are eight characters, the first two characters specify the opacity of the color, and the last six characters specify the various amounts of red, green, and blue as before. FF means fully opaque and 00 means fully transparent. If the opacity is not specified (if there are three or six characters), the default is fully opaque.

In `"FFFFFF00"`, the first two Fs indicate an opaque color; 00 would indicate a fully transparent color. In `"FFF0"`, the first F indicates an opaque color; 0 would indicate a fully transparent color.

Another way to specify a color is to use a resource of the form:

```
"@[+] [package:] type:name"
```

We have already learned that we can externalize string resources as we did in the strings.xml file. We can also externalize other resources such as: bool, color, dimension (using the tag name `dimen`), id, integer, integer array (using the tag name `integer-array`), and typed array (using the tag name `array`).

The brackets, [], in the syntax expression mean that the field is optional.

In order to use this syntax, we externalize some colors in a file, the resource, named colors.xml. The name of the file does not matter, but it is good practice to choose a file name that is meaningful; the file should have the .xml extension and must be located in the res/values/ directory of our project so that the Android framework can find it. Although not using the .xml extension will not prevent our app from running, we recommend that we use the .xml extension for these files.

If we place colors.xml in the wrong directory, for example in the res/layout/ directory, we will have compiler errors.

TABLE 2.12 shows the supported directories inside the `res` directory along with their descriptions.

To specify a color that is defined by the string named `lightGreen` in a newly created resource file named colors.xml, we write this code:

```
android:textColor="@color/lightGreen"
```

In the colors.xml file, we included the following code (line 8 of **EXAMPLE 2.5**) in order to define lightGreen:

```
<color name="lightGreen">#40F0</color>
```

TABLE 2.12 List of directories supported inside the res directory	
Directory	**Description of directory contents**
animator	XML files defining property animations
anim	XML files defining tween animations
color	XML files defining a state list of colors (that can be used to specify different colors for different states of a button, for example)
drawable	Bitmap files or XML files defining drawable resources (place drawable resources for the app here)
mipmap	Bitmap files or XML files defining drawable resources (place the icon for the app here)
layout	XML files defining a GUI layout
menu	XML files defining menus
raw	Files saved in their raw form
values	XML files defining strings, integers, colors, and other simple values
xml	XML files that can be read at runtime by calling Resources.getXML(resourceIdNumber)

```
1    <?xml version="1.0" encoding="utf-8"?>
2    <resources>
3      <color name="colorPrimary">#3F51B5</color>
4       <color name="colorPrimaryDark">#303F9F</color>
5       <color name="colorAccent">#FF4081</color>
6
7       <color name="lightGray">#DDDDDDDD</color>
8       <color name="lightGreen">#40F0</color>
9       <color name="darkGreen">#F0F0</color>
10      <color name="darkBlue">#F00F</color>
11   </resources>
```

EXAMPLE 2.5 The colors.xml file

Color is the resource type and lightGreen is its name. The name of the file, colors.xml, although that is the recommended name, is not important; we could choose any other name for it. We can even have several files defining colors. It is mandatory to use a resources element (line 2 of Example 2.5) as the parent element of color. If we use a different element instead, we will get an "invalid start tag" error message.

If we delete the `resources` start and end tags, we will get an error message that our XML document is not well formed. Any error in our XML documents will abort the build when we try to compile or run our app.

At compile time, each child of the `resources` element is converted into an application resource object at compile time; in colors.xml, `resources` has four children, all `color` elements. Each one can then be referenced in other files by its name, for example `lightGreen`.

COMMON ERROR: If we are creating an XML file for resources, we must use the `resources` element as their parent in our XML file. We also must place that file in one of the res/values/ directories of our project.

EXAMPLE 2.6 shows the updated activity_main.xml file. We have deleted lines 7 to 10 from Example 2.3 (specifying the padding around the app GUI) because we redefined the margins of the various GUI elements and the default padding is no longer needed.

```
1   <?xml version="1.0" encoding="utf-8"?>
2   <RelativeLayout
3       xmlns:android="http://schemas.android.com/apk/res/android"
4       xmlns:tools="http://schemas.android.com/tools"
5       android:layout_width="match_parent"
6       android:layout_height="match_parent"
7       tools:context="com.jblearning.tipcalculatorv1.MainActivity">
8
9   <TextView
10          android:id="@+id/label_bill"
11          android:layout_width="wrap_content"
12          android:layout_height="wrap_content"
13          android:layout_marginTop="20dp"
14          android:layout_marginLeft="20dp"
15          android:padding="10dp"
16          android:minWidth="120dp"
17          android:textSize="28sp"
18          android:background="@color/lightGray"
19          android:text="@string/label_bill"/>
20
21  <EditText
22          android:id="@+id/amount_bill"
23          android:layout_width="wrap_content"
24          android:layout_height="wrap_content"
25          android:padding="10dp"
```

EXAMPLE 2.6 The activity_main.xml file, Tip Calculator app, Version 1 (*Continued*)

```
26              android:layout_marginRight="20dp"
27              android:layout_toRightOf="@+id/label_bill"
28              android:layout_alignBottom="@+id/label_bill"
29              android:layout_alignParentRight="true"
30              android:textSize="28sp"
31              android:gravity="center"
32              android:textColor="@color/darkBlue"
33              android:hint="@string/amount_bill_hint"
34              android:inputType="numberDecimal" />
35
36  <TextView
37              android:id="@+id/label_tip_percent"
38              android:layout_width="wrap_content"
39              android:layout_height="wrap_content"
40              android:padding="10dp"
41              android:layout_marginTop="20dp"
42              android:layout_below="@+id/label_bill"
43              android:layout_alignLeft="@+id/label_bill"
44              android:layout_alignRight="@+id/label_bill"
45              android:textSize="28sp"
46              android:background="@color/lightGray"
47              android:text="@string/label_tip_percent"/>
48
49  <EditText
50              android:id="@+id/amount_tip_percent"
51              android:layout_width="wrap_content"
52              android:layout_height="wrap_content"
53              android:padding="10dp"
54              android:layout_toRightOf="@+id/label_tip_percent"
55              android:layout_alignBottom="@+id/label_tip_percent"
56              android:layout_alignRight="@id/amount_bill"
57              android:textSize="28sp"
58              android:gravity="center"
59              android:textColor="@color/darkBlue"
60              android:hint="@string/amount_tip_percent_hint"
61              android:inputType="number" />
62
63  <!-- red line -->
64  <View
65              android:id="@+id/red_line"
66              android:layout_below="@+id/label_tip_percent"
67              android:layout_marginTop="20dp"
68              android:layout_height="5dip"
69              android:layout_width="match_parent"
70              android:layout_alignLeft="@id/label_bill"
71              android:layout_alignRight="@id/amount_bill"
```

EXAMPLE 2.6 The activity_main.xml file, Tip Calculator app, Version 1 (*Continued*)

```
 72            android:background="#FF00" />
 73
 74    <TextView
 75            android:id="@+id/label_tip"
 76            android:layout_width="wrap_content"
 77            android:layout_height="wrap_content"
 78            android:layout_marginTop="20dp"
 79            android:padding="10dp"
 80            android:layout_below="@id/red_line"
 81            android:layout_alignLeft="@+id/label_bill"
 82        android:layout_alignRight="@+id/label_bill"
 83            android:textSize="28sp"
 84            android:background="@color/lightGray"
 85            android:text="@string/label_tip" />
 86
 87    <TextView
 88            android:id="@+id/amount_tip"
 89            android:layout_width="wrap_content"
 90            android:layout_height="wrap_content"
 91            android:padding="10dp"
 92            android:layout_toRightOf="@+id/label_tip"
 93            android:layout_alignBottom="@+id/label_tip"
 94            android:layout_alignRight="@id/amount_bill"
 95            android:background="@color/lightGreen"
 96            android:gravity="center"
 97            android:textSize="28sp" />
 98
 99    <TextView
100            android:id="@+id/label_total"
101            android:layout_width="wrap_content"
102            android:layout_height="wrap_content"
103            android:layout_marginTop="20dp"
104            android:padding="10dp"
105            android:layout_below="@id/label_tip"
106            android:layout_alignLeft="@+id/label_bill"
107            android:layout_alignRight="@+id/label_bill"
108            android:textSize="28sp"
109            android:background="@color/lightGray"
110            android:text="@string/label_total" />
111
112    <TextView
113            android:id="@+id/amount_total"
114            android:layout_width="wrap_content"
115            android:layout_height="wrap_content"
116            android:padding="10dp"
117            android:layout_toRightOf="@+id/label_total"
```

EXAMPLE 2.6 The activity_main.xml file, Tip Calculator app, Version 1 (*Continued*)

```
118              android:layout_alignBottom="@+id/label_total"
119              android:layout_alignRight="@id/amount_bill"
120              android:background="@color/lightGreen"
121              android:gravity="center"
122              android:textSize="28sp" />
123
123      <Button
125          android:layout_width="wrap_content"
126          android:layout_height="wrap_content"
127          android:layout_marginTop="20dp"
128          android:padding="10dp"
129          android:layout_centerHorizontal="true"
130          android:layout_below="@+id/amount_total"
131          android:textSize="28sp"
132          android:background="@color/darkGreen"
133          android:text="@string/button_calculate" />
134
135  </RelativeLayout>
```

EXAMPLE 2.6 **The activity_main.xml file, Tip Calculator app, Version 1**

We separate the input related elements, at the top, from the computed related elements, at the bottom, by a red line (lines 63–72). The red line is a View element (line 64) whose height is 5 pixels (line 68). We use the same positioning attributes that we use earlier in order to position the five new elements in relation to themselves and the existing four elements: android:layout_below, android:layout_alignLeft, android:layout_alignRight, and android:layout_toRightOf. We line up the four TextViews on the left of the screen and the red line by specifying that they all line up with the bill label (lines 43, 70, 81, 106). We specify a constant vertical spacing between elements of 20 pixels by using the android:layout_marginTop attribute (lines 41, 67, 78, 103, 127).

We add the same amount of padding, 10 pixels, to all the TextView, EditText, and Button elements (lines 15, 25, 40, 53, 79, 91, 104, 116, 128). At lines 13–15, we add margins and padding to the bill label, our anchor element.

We set the background of the four TextViews on the left to light gray at lines 18, 46, 84, 109. We set the background of the computed tip and total to light green at lines 95 and 120. We set the text color of the two EditText elements to dark blue at lines 32 and 59. We left the default left-alignment for the four TextViews on the left. We center-align the two EditTexts and two TextViews on the right (lines 31, 58, 96, 121). As **FIGURE 2.5** shows, Android Studio suggests the possible values for it as we type.

At line 129, we center the button horizontally. At this point, the button does not respond to a user click; we will implement that feature in Version 3.

EXAMPLE 2.7 shows the updated strings.xml file.

We can see the various component sizes, colors, font sizes, and font styles in **FIGURE 2.6**, which shows the GUI in the Android Studio environment.

```
<TextView
    android:id="@+id/amount_tip"
    android:layout_width="wrap_content"
    android:layout_height="wrap_content"
    android:padding="10dp"
    android:layout_toRightOf="@+id/label_tip"
    android:layout_alignBottom="@+id/label_tip"
    android:layout_alignRight="@id/amount_bill"
    android:background="@color/lightGreen"
    android:gravity="c
    android:textSize      center
                          center_horizontal
<TextView                 center_vertical
    android:id="@+id      clip_horizontal
    android:layout_w      clip_vertical
    android:layout_h      fill_vertical
    android:layout_m  Ctrl+Down and Ctrl+Up will move caret down and up in tl
    android:padding=
    android:layout_below="@id/label_tip"
```

FIGURE 2.5 **The Android Studio environment, showing suggested values for the**
`android:gravity` **attribute**

```
1   <resources>
2       <string name="app_name">TipCalculatorV1</string>
3
4       <string name="label_bill">Bill</string>
5       <string name="label_tip_percent">Tip (%)</string>
6       <string name="label_tip">Tip ($)</string>
7       <string name="label_total">Total</string>
8
9       <string name="amount_bill_hint">Enter bill</string>
10      <string name="amount_tip_percent_hint">Enter tip %</string>
11
12      <string name="button_calculate">CALCULATE</string>
13  </resources>
```

EXAMPLE 2.7 **The strings.xml file, Tip Calculator app, Version 1**

2.6 Styles and Themes: Tip Calculator, Version 2

In Version 1, many GUI components have the same attributes with the same values. For example, all the nine elements in the activity_main.xml file have a `wrap_content` value for both the `android:layout_width` and `android:layout_height` attributes. The Android Development

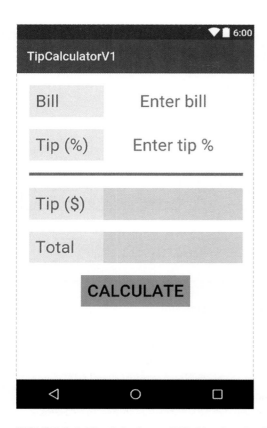

FIGURE 2.6 **Tip Calculator GUI, Version 1, shown in Android Studio**

Kit (ADK) allows us to externalize styles in resources that we can reuse in order to apply a common style to various elements.

The concept of styles is similar to the concept of CSS (Cascading Style Sheets) in HTML pages. A style is a collection of properties (XML attributes) that specify the look and feel of a View or a window. A style can specify such things as width, height, padding, background color, text color, text size. We can then use a style to specify values of XML attributes for one or several Views. Styles allow us to separate the look and feel of a View from its contents.

We can define styles in a file named styles.xml in one of the res/values directories. In it, we can define several styles, each with a list of XML attributes and values; each style has a name that we can use to reference it.

The syntax for defining a style is:

```
<style name="nameOfStyle" [parent="styleThisStyleInheritsFrom"]>
   <item name="attributeName">attributeValue</item>
   ...
</style>
```

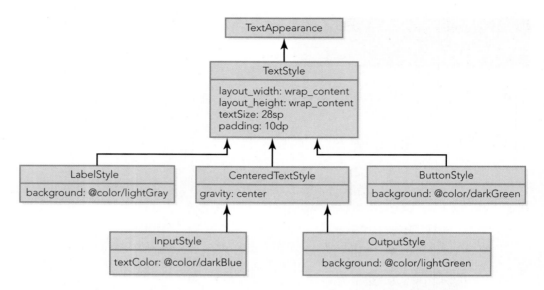

FIGURE 2.7 Inheritance hierarchy for styles defined in styles.xml

A style can inherit from another style. Inheritance is defined using the `parent` attribute, and is optional. The `parent` style can be a native Android style, or it can be a user-defined style.

By defining styles this way, we can build an inheritance hierarchy; not only several GUI elements can use the same style, but a style can reuse another style's attributes via inheritance. A style can also override the value of an attribute that it inherits. We define six styles as shown in **FIGURE 2.7**. We use `InputStyle` for the two `EditTexts`: it inherits from `CenteredTextStyle`, which itself inherits from `TextStyle`, which inherits from `TextAppearance`, an existing style from the Android Standard Development Kit (Android SDK). Thus, the text inside the `EditTexts` will be centered, have size 28, and be dark blue. Note that the default text color inherited from `Text Appearance` is black but is overridden. The two `EditTexts` will be sized based on their contents.

EXAMPLE 2.8 shows the styles.xml file. `TextStyle` is defined at lines 11–16; it inherits from the Android native style `TextAppearance` using the syntax `parent="@android:style/nameOfParentStyle"`. Note that the contents for each item element, for example `wrap_content` or `28sp`, are not inside double quotes.

> **COMMON ERROR:** Do not use double quotes when specifying a value for an XML attribute when defining a style.

At lines 18–20, `LabelStyle` inherits from our own `TextStyle` using the syntax `parent="nameOfParentStyle"`. Thus, it inherits the four attributes and their values defined in `TextStyle` at lines 12–15, `android:layout_width`, `android:layout_height`,

```
1   <resources>
2
3       <!-- Base application theme. -->
4       <style name="AppTheme" parent="Theme.AppCompat.Light.DarkActionBar">
5           <!-- Customize your theme here. -->
6           <item name="colorPrimary">@color/colorPrimary</item>
7           <item name="colorPrimaryDark">@color/colorPrimaryDark</item>
8           <item name="colorAccent">@color/colorAccent</item>
9       </style>
10
11      <style name="TextStyle" parent="@android:style/TextAppearance">
12          <item name="android:layout_width">wrap_content</item>
13          <item name="android:layout_height">wrap_content</item>
14          <item name="android:textSize">28sp</item>
15          <item name="android:padding">10dp</item>
16      </style>
17
18      <style name="LabelStyle" parent="TextStyle">
19          <item name="android:background">@color/lightGray</item>
20      </style>
21
22      <style name="CenteredTextStyle" parent="TextStyle">
23          <item name="android:gravity">center</item>
24      </style>
25
26      <style name="InputStyle" parent="CenteredTextStyle">
27          <item name="android:textColor">@color/darkBlue</item>
28      </style>
29
30      <style name="OutputStyle" parent="CenteredTextStyle">
31          <item name="android:background">@color/lightGreen</item>
32      </style>
33
34      <style name="ButtonStyle" parent="TextStyle">
35          <item name="android:background">@color/darkGreen</item>
36      </style>
37   </resources>
```

EXAMPLE 2.8 The styles.xml file

android:textSize, and android:padding. It specifies the light gray color defined in colors.xml for the android:background attribute at line 19. Thus, any element styled with LabelStyle will have a light gray background, 10 pixels of padding around its text, which will have size 28. The size of that element will be set based on the text inside it.

At lines 22–24, CenteredTextStyle also inherits from our own TextStyle, specifying that the text is centered. At lines 26–28, InputStyle inherits from CenteredTextStyle, specifying that the text color is the dark blue defined in colors.xml. At lines 30–32, OutputStyle also inherits from CenteredTextStyle, specifying that the background color is the light green defined in colors.xml. Finally, at lines 34–36, ButtonStyle inherits from TextStyle, specifying that the background color is the dark green defined in colors.xml.

Not only does an XML style file provide a centralized location to define styles, but it also makes our code better organized and easier to maintain and modify. Often, we will want to have the same styling themes for GUI components of the same type. If all our TextView components are styled red and we decide to change them to purple, we only have one line of code to change at a single location. We can also reuse styles in many apps. Furthermore, the expertise needed to create and edit a style file is different from the expertise needed to write Java code. If the app is complex and developed by a group of developers, it makes it easier to separate the work and distribute it among the team members based on their respective expertise.

> **SOFTWARE ENGINEERING:** It is good practice to externalize the various styles of your GUI components in a separate file.

In **EXAMPLE 2.9**, we style the GUI elements inside activity_main.xml with the styles defined in styles.xml. The result is an identical GUI to the one in Version 1. In order to style a GUI component, we use this syntax:

```
style="@style/nameOfStyle"
```

Writing android:style instead of style would result in a compiler error.

> **COMMON ERROR:** When using a style, do not write android: in front of the style attribute. It would result in a compiler error.

At lines 11, 29, 58, and 74, we style the four TextView elements on the left side of the screen with LabelStyle. At lines 19 and 38, we style the two EditText elements with InputStyle. At lines 67 and 83, we style the two output TextView elements with OutputStyle. The Button element is styled with ButtonStyle at line 89.

If we modify the styles.xml file, for example if we change the android:background attribute of LabelStyle from light gray to another color, we will see that change taking place as we run the app again.

A style is typically applied to one or several screens. Often, we will want the Views in a screen to have the same look and feel. Or we might want all the screens in the app to have the same look and feel. Using a style, we can give an activity, or give the whole app, a theme.

```
1   <?xml version="1.0" encoding="utf-8"?>
2   <RelativeLayout
3       xmlns:android="http://schemas.android.com/apk/res/android"
4       xmlns:tools="http://schemas.android.com/tools"
5       android:layout_width="match_parent"
6       android:layout_height="match_parent"
7       tools:context="com.jblearning.tipcalculatorv2.MainActivity">
8
9   <TextView
10          android:id="@+id/label_bill"
11          style="@style/LabelStyle"
12          android:layout_marginTop="20dp"
13          android:layout_marginLeft="20dp"
14          android:minWidth="120dp"
15          android:text="@string/label_bill"/>
16
17  <EditText
18          android:id="@+id/amount_bill"
19          style="@style/InputStyle"
20          android:layout_marginRight="20dp"
21          android:layout_toRightOf="@+id/label_bill"
22          android:layout_alignBottom="@+id/label_bill"
23          android:layout_alignParentRight="true"
24          android:hint="@string/amount_bill_hint"
25          android:inputType="numberDecimal" />
26
27  <TextView
28          android:id="@+id/label_tip_percent"
29          style="@style/LabelStyle"
30          android:layout_marginTop="20dp"
31          android:layout_below="@+id/label_bill"
32          android:layout_alignLeft="@+id/label_bill"
33          android:layout_alignRight="@+id/label_bill"
34          android:text="@string/label_tip_percent"/>
35
36  <EditText
37          android:id="@+id/amount_tip_percent"
38          style="@style/InputStyle"
39          android:layout_toRightOf="@+id/label_tip_percent"
40          android:layout_alignBottom="@+id/label_tip_percent"
41          android:layout_alignRight="@id/amount_bill"
42          android:hint="@string/amount_tip_percent_hint"
43          android:inputType="number" />
44
45  <!-- red line -->
46  <View
47          android:id="@+id/red_line"
```

EXAMPLE 2.9 **The activity_main.xml file, Tip Calculator app, Version 2 (*Continued*)**

```
48            android:layout_below="@+id/label_tip_percent"
49            android:layout_marginTop="20dp"
50            android:layout_height="5dip"
51            android:layout_width="match_parent"
52            android:layout_alignLeft="@id/label_bill"
53            android:layout_alignRight="@id/amount_bill"
54            android:background="#FF00" />
55
56    <TextView
57            android:id="@+id/label_tip"
58            style="@style/LabelStyle"
59            android:layout_marginTop="20dp"
60            android:layout_below="@id/red_line"
61            android:layout_alignLeft="@+id/label_bill"
62            android:layout_alignRight="@+id/label_bill"
63            android:text="@string/label_tip" />
64
65    <TextView
66            android:id="@+id/amount_tip"
67            style="@style/OutputStyle"
68            android:layout_toRightOf="@+id/label_tip"
69            android:layout_alignBottom="@+id/label_tip"
70            android:layout_alignRight="@id/amount_bill" />
71
72    <TextView
73            android:id="@+id/label_total"
74            style="@style/LabelStyle"
75            android:layout_marginTop="20dp"
76            android:layout_below="@id/label_tip"
77            android:layout_alignLeft="@+id/label_bill"
78            android:layout_alignRight="@+id/label_bill"
79            android:text="@string/label_total" />
80
81    <TextView
82            android:id="@+id/amount_total"
83            style="@style/OutputStyle"
84            android:layout_toRightOf="@+id/label_total"
85            android:layout_alignBottom="@+id/label_total"
86            android:layout_alignRight="@id/amount_bill" />
87
88    <Button
89            style="@style/ButtonStyle"
90            android:layout_marginTop="20dp"
91            android:layout_centerHorizontal="true"
92            android:layout_below="@+id/amount_total"
93            android:text="@string/button_calculate" />
94
95    </RelativeLayout>
```

EXAMPLE 2.9 **The activity_main.xml file, Tip Calculator app, Version 2**

To apply a style to the whole app, we add an `android:theme` attribute to the application element in the AndroidManifest.xml file using this syntax:

```
android:theme="@style/nameOfStyle"
```

The AndroidManifest.xml skeleton already includes the preceding syntax using the style `AppTheme`. `AppTheme` is already declared in the styles.xml skeleton, and we can edit `AppTheme` inside styles.xml. We can also use a style from styles.xml, and change line 10 of Example 2.2 as follows:

```
android:theme="@style/LabelStyle"
```

To apply a style to a given activity, we add an `android:theme` attribute to the activity element in the AndroidManifest.xml file as follows:

```
android:theme="@style/nameOfStyle"
```

For example, we could insert a line between lines 12 and 13 of Example 2.2 as follows:

```
android:theme="@style/OutputStyle"
```

There is only one activity in our current app, but in a more complex app, there could be many activities, and therefore there could be many activity elements in the AndroidManifest.xml file. Each one can be themed separately.

Now that we have a Model and a View, we can edit the Controller so that our app calculates and displays the tip and the total when the user enters a new amount for either the bill or the tip percentage rate and clicks on the Calculate button.

2.7 Events and Simple Event Handling: Coding the Controller, Tip Calculator, Version 3

Clicking on a button is called an **event**. Executing some code, for example updating the value of a text field, after the event happened is called **handling the event**. In GUI programming, there can be many types of events: clicking on a button, checking a checkbox, selecting an item from a list, pressing a key, tapping on the screen, swiping the screen, to name a few.

In the activity_main.xml file, we can assign to the `android:onClick` attribute of a `View` the name of method: that method will be called when the user clicks on a `View`. The syntax is:

```
android:onClick="methodName"
```

The method should be in the `Activity` class that is controlling the View, in this case `Main-Activity`. The `Button` class inherits from `View`, so we can use the `android:onClick` XML attribute within the `Button` element in our activity_main.xml file. If we want a method named `calculate` to execute when the user clicks on the `Button`, we write:

```
android:onClick="calculate"
```

```
87
88      <Button
89          style="@style/ButtonStyle"
90          android:layout_marginTop="20dp"
91          android:layout_centerHorizontal="true"
92          android:layout_below="@+id/amount_total"
93          android:text="@string/button_calculate"
94          android:onClick="calculate"/>
95
96   </RelativeLayout>
```

EXAMPLE 2.10 **The Button element of the activity_main.xml file**

EXAMPLE 2.10 shows the updated part of the activity_main.xml file.

We should code the method in the corresponding context, most likely an `Activity` class. If we do not code that method, the app will crash when the user clicks on the button. It must have the following header:

```
public void methodName(View v)
```

Inside the method, the `View` parameter v is a reference to the `View` that originated the event.

Thus, inside the `MainActivity` class, we need to code the `calculate` method, and it has the following header:

```
public void calculate(View v)
```

Inside that method, we need to access the `EditText` elements to retrieve the data input by the user and some of the `TextView` elements to update them accordingly.

If a `View` had been given an id, we can get a reference to that `View` using the `findViewById` method of the `Activity` class (inherited by the `AppCompatActivity` class), described in **TABLE 2.13**, with the following method call:

```
findViewById(R.id.idValue)
```

Now that the activity_main.xml file is defined, we can code the `MainActivity` class, shown in **EXAMPLE 2.11**, and its new method `calculate`.

The `calculate` method needs to retrieve the amount entered in the two `EditText` components, calculate the corresponding tip and total amounts, and update the two output `TextViews` accordingly.

At line 12, we declare a `TipCalculator` instance variable, `tipCalc`. With it, we can call any method of the `TipCalculator` class in order to perform various calculations. At lines 6–8, we import the `View`, `TextView`, and `EditText` classes. `View` is in the `android.view` package; `TextView` and `EditText` are in the `android.widget` package. We need to import them because we use them in the `calculate` method (lines 21–51). When `calculate` is called, the `View`

TABLE 2.13 Useful methods of the Activity and TextView classes	
Class	**Method**
Activity	View findViewById(int id) Finds and returns the View that is identified by the id attribute from the XML inflated in the onCreate method (for example, activity_main.xml)
TextView	CharSequence getText( ) Returns the text displayed in the TextView widget
TextView	void setText(CharSequence text) Sets the text to be displayed in the TextView widget

argument is a reference to the `View` that originated the event, in this case the button. We output it at line 23 for feedback purposes only. If we try to code the `calculate` method without the `View` parameter, our code will compile but when we run the app and click on the Calculate button, we will have a runtime exception.

At lines 24–27, we retrieve object references to our two `EditText` components using the method `findViewById` inherited from the `Activity` class, passing their ids, `R.id.amount_bill` and `R.id.amount_tip_percent`. Since the `findViewById` method returns a `View`, we typecast its return value to an `EditText`.

At lines 28–29, we retrieve the data input by the user in the two `EditText`s and assign the two values to the `billString` and `tipString` `String`s; we use the `getText` method (**TABLE 2.13**) of the `TextView` class, inherited by the `EditText` class. `GetText` returns a `CharSequence`, so we make an extra method call to the `CharSequence`'s `toString` method to convert each value retrieved from the `EditText` to a `String`.

The two values are `String`s; we use the `parseFloat` and `parseInt` static methods of the `Float` and `Integer` classes to convert them to a `float` and an `int` in order to process them. Although the exceptions thrown by the `parseFloat` and `parseInt` methods (lines 37 and 38) are unchecked, it is good practice to use `try` and `catch` blocks in order to prevent a runtime exception from being thrown in case the data retrieved is not a valid number. At lines 39–41, we update the Model: we set the bill and tip of `tipCalc` by calling `setBill` and `setTip`. At lines 42–44, we ask the Model to call `tipAmount` and `totalAmount` to compute the tip and total amounts. At lines 45–47, we use the

```
1   package com.jblearning.tipcalculatorv3;
2
3   import android.support.v7.app.AppCompatActivity;
4   import android.os.Bundle;
5   import android.util.Log;
6   import android.view.View;
```

EXAMPLE 2.11 The `MainActivity` class of the Tip Calculator app, Version 3 (*Continued*)

```
7   import android.widget.EditText;
8   import android.widget.TextView;
9   import java.text.NumberFormat;
10
11  public class MainActivity extends AppCompatActivity {
12      private TipCalculator tipCalc;
13      public NumberFormat money = NumberFormat.getCurrencyInstance( );
14
15      protected void onCreate( Bundle savedInstanceState ) {
16          super.onCreate( savedInstanceState );
17          tipCalc = new TipCalculator( 0.17f, 100.0f );
18          setContentView( R.layout.activity_main );
19      }
20
21      /** Called when the user clicks on the Calculate button */
22      public void calculate( View v ) {
23          Log.w("MainActivity", "v = " + v );
24          EditText billEditText =
25              ( EditText ) findViewById( R.id.amount_bill );
26          EditText tipEditText =
27              ( EditText ) findViewById( R.id.amount_tip_percent );
28          String billString = billEditText.getText( ).toString( );
29          String tipString = tipEditText.getText( ).toString( );
30
31          TextView tipTextView =
32              ( TextView ) findViewById( R.id.amount_tip );
33          TextView totalTextView =
34              ( TextView ) findViewById( R.id.amount_total );
35          try {
36              // convert billString and tipString to floats
37              float billAmount = Float.parseFloat( billString );
38              int tipPercent = Integer.parseInt( tipString );
39              // update the Model
40              tipCalc.setBill( billAmount );
41              tipCalc.setTip( .01f * tipPercent );
42              // ask Model to calculate tip and total amounts
43              float tip = tipCalc.tipAmount( );
44              float total = tipCalc.totalAmount( );
45              // update the View with formatted tip and total amounts
46              tipTextView.setText( money.format( tip ) );
47              totalTextView.setText( money.format( total ) );
48          } catch( NumberFormatException nfe ) {
49              // pop up an alert view here
50          }
51      }
52  }
```

EXAMPLE 2.11 The `MainActivity` class of the Tip Calculator app, Version 3

results to update the View: we place the formatted tip and total amounts in the `TextViews` using the `setText` method from Table 2.13. In this way, the Controller, the `MainActivity` class, gathers input from the View to update the Model, and retrieves updated data from the Model to update the View.

We should never get in the `catch` block (lines 48–50); indeed, the `numberDecimal` and `number` input types of the two `EditText` specified in activity_main.xml guarantee that the values of the bill and the tip percentage will be a valid floating point number and a valid integer. The `numberDec-imal` value for `android:inputType` only allows the user to enter digits and a maximum of one dot. The `number` value for `android:inputType` only allows the user to enter digits. However, it is good practice to trap potential errors and validate data even if we are reasonably sure that they will not happen. This practice is called **defensive programming**. Inside the `catch` block (line 49), we could pop up an alert view to inform the user to enter correct data.

COMMON ERROR: If we specify a method to be called using the `android:on-Click` attribute when the user clicks on a button, that method must be `public`, `void`, and take one and only parameter, a `View`; otherwise, we will have a run-time exception when the user clicks on the button when the app is running.

SOFTWARE ENGINEERING: Output statements are useful during development; they should be deleted or commented out in the final version of our app.

In Logcat, we should see some output similar to this:

```
v = android.support.v7.widget.AppCompatButton{fe17b58
VFED..C.....P.... 280,1063-799,1235}
```

This shows that the `View` argument is indeed a `Button` (the only one, clicked by the user; `AppCompatButton` is a class that extends Button and supports features of older versions); fe17b58 is a hexadecimal number representing its memory address.

FIGURE 2.8 shows our app running in the emulator after the user enters 154.50 in the bill `EditText` and 18 in the tip percentage `EditText` and clicks on the Calculate button. By default, when we have at least one `EditText` on the screen, the soft keyboard is open.

One may think that we do not really need a complete model, the `TipCalculator` class, for this very simple app. However, even for a simple app, it is good practice to use the Model-View-Controller architecture and therefore have a separate model. Over its lifetime, an app can have many versions and increase in complexity, each version requiring new features and functions that can easily be added to the model and used in the controller. For example, we may want to upgrade this app in the future and include the number of guests, and calculate the tip and total bill per guest. We could also format the tip amount and total bill with two decimal digits only. We might also be interested

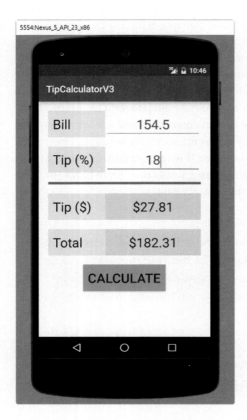

FIGURE 2.8 **Tip Calculator, Version 3, running in the emulator**

in building a different version of the app with the same functionality but a different GUI. We would just need to update the View and the Controller, but not the Model.

2.8 More Event Handling: Tip Calculator, Version 4

Our app now has some basic functionality, but we should update the tip and total amount any time the user changes the data (i.e., any time the user is typing on the keyboard) even if the user does not click on the Calculate button. In fact, we do not even need the Calculate button. In order to implement that, we have to edit the View (delete the `Button` element in the activity_main.xml file) and change the Controller (process any change in the text of the two `EditTexts`); there is no change needed in the Model. **EXAMPLE 2.12** shows the end of the updated activity_main.xml file. It no longer includes the `Button` element. Since we no longer use the `Button`, we can also delete

```
80
81        <TextView
82            android:id="@+id/amount_total"
83            style="@style/OutputStyle"
84            android:layout_toRightOf="@+id/label_total"
85            android:layout_alignBottom="@+id/label_total"
86            android:layout_alignRight="@id/amount_bill" />
87
88    </RelativeLayout>
```

EXAMPLE 2.12 The activity_main.xml file, Tip Calculator app, Version 4

the button_calculate String in strings.xml, the button style in styles.xml, and the dark green color element in colors.xml.

We have already learned that clicking on a Button is an event. Typing inside an EditText component, or more generally pressing a key, is also an event. The Android framework provides developers with tools that alert us whenever an event happens or something is changing or has changed inside a GUI component.

Generally, to capture and process an event, we need to do the following, in order:

1. Write an event handler (a class extending a listener interface).
2. Instantiate an object of that class.
3. Register that object on one or more GUI component.

A typical event handler implements a listener interface, which means that it needs to override all the abstract methods of that interface.

The static OnKeyListener interface, nested inside the View class, includes a method, onKey, that is called when a key event is dispatched to a View. However, key presses in software keyboards will generally not trigger a call to this method. We want our app to be as universal as possible and work equally well with mobile devices that have either a hardware keyboard or a software keyboard. For that reason, we do not use the OnKeyListener interface in this app.

The TextWatcher interface, from the android.text package, provides three methods that are called when the text inside a GUI component (a TextView or an object of a subclass of TextView, such as EditText) changes, assuming that a TextWatcher object is registered on the TextView. TABLE 2.14 shows these methods. As in any interface, these three methods are abstract.

In order to have a TextWatcher be notified of any change in the text inside a TextView, we need to do the following:

▶ Code a class (also called a **handler**) that implements the TextWatcher interface
▶ Declare and instantiate an object of that class
▶ Register that object on the TextView (in this app the two EditTexts)

TABLE 2.14 Methods of the TextWatcher interface

Method	When Is the Method Called?
void afterTextChanged (Editable e)	Somewhere within e, the text has changed
void beforeTextChanged (CharSequence cs, int start, int count, int after)	Within cs, the count characters beginning at start are about to be replaced with after characters
void onTextChanged (CharSequence cs, int start, int before, int count)	Within cs, the count characters beginning at start have just replaced before characters

In our handler class, we are only interested in the `afterTextChanged` method. We do not really care how many characters have changed and where within the text. We only care that something has changed within the text. So we will implement the other two methods, `beforeTextChanged` and `onTextChanged`, as "do nothing" methods. Because we need to access the two `EditText`s and the two `TextView`s, we choose to implement the handler class as a `private`, inner class of `MainActivity`. When coding a handler, we can also implement it as a separate `public` class if we choose to.

EXAMPLE 2.13 shows the complete code for the `MainActivity` class. We made one important change to the overall class design. We have added instance variables for the two `EditText`s (lines 14–15). This is not necessary but it is convenient to have direct references to GUI components if we need to access them at various places (when we register the handler and when we process the text changes). This is easier than to use the `findViewById` method every time we want to access them. They are instantiated at lines 23–24.

The handler class is coded at lines 57–69. The `afterTextChanged` method (lines 58–60) calls the `calculate` method (lines 31–55), which is very similar to the previous `calculate` method; note that we deleted its `View` parameter.

At line 26, we declare and instantiate a `TextChangeHandler` object, `tch`. At lines 27 and 28, we register `tch` with the two `EditText`s, `billEditText` and `tipEditText`. Thus, any time the user changes the bill or the tip percentage, `afterTextChanged` is automatically called; that triggers a call to `calculate`, which updates the Model, and then updates the View accordingly.

COMMON ERROR: Be sure that all the methods of the handler class are coded. If one or more `abstract` methods of the interface is not implemented, there will be a compiler error.

```
1   package com.jblearning.tipcalculatorv4;
2
3   import android.os.Bundle;
4   import android.support.v7.app.AppCompatActivity;
5   import android.text.Editable;
6   import android.text.TextWatcher;
7   import android.widget.EditText;
8   import android.widget.TextView;
9   import java.text.NumberFormat;
10
11  public class MainActivity extends AppCompatActivity {
12      private TipCalculator tipCalc;
13      public NumberFormat money = NumberFormat.getCurrencyInstance( );
14      private EditText billEditText;
15      private EditText tipEditText;
16
17      @Override
18      protected void onCreate( Bundle savedInstanceState ) {
19          super.onCreate( savedInstanceState );
20          tipCalc = new TipCalculator( 0.17f, 100.0f );
21          setContentView( R.layout.activity_main );
22
23          billEditText = ( EditText ) findViewById( R.id.amount_bill );
24          tipEditText = ( EditText ) findViewById( R.id.amount_tip_percent );
25
26          TextChangeHandler tch = new TextChangeHandler( );
27          billEditText.addTextChangedListener( tch );
28          tipEditText.addTextChangedListener( tch );
29      }
30
31      public void calculate( ) {
32          String billString = billEditText.getText( ).toString( );
33          String tipString = tipEditText.getText( ).toString( );
34
35          TextView tipTextView =
36              ( TextView ) findViewById( R.id.amount_tip );
37          TextView totalTextView =
38              (TextView) findViewById( R.id.amount_total );
39          try {
40              // convert billString and tipString to floats
41              float billAmount = Float.parseFloat( billString );
42              int tipPercent = Integer.parseInt( tipString );
43              // update the Model
44              tipCalc.setBill( billAmount );
45              tipCalc.setTip( .01f * tipPercent );
46              // ask Model to calculate tip and total amounts
```

EXAMPLE 2.13 The MainActivity class of the Tip Calculator app, Version 4 (*Continued*)

```
47                float tip = tipCalc.tipAmount( );
48                float total = tipCalc.totalAmount( );
49                // update the View with formatted tip and total amounts
50                tipTextView.setText( money.format( tip ) );
51                totalTextView.setText( money.format( total ) );
52            } catch( NumberFormatException nfe ) {
53                // pop up an alert view here
54            }
55        }
56
57        private class TextChangeHandler implements TextWatcher {
58            public void afterTextChanged( Editable e ) {
59                calculate( );
60            }
61
62            public void beforeTextChanged( CharSequence s, int start,
63            int count, int after ) {
64            }
65
66            public void onTextChanged( CharSequence s, int start,
67                int before, int after ) {
68            }
69        }
70    }
```

EXAMPLE 2.13 The MainActivity class of the Tip Calculator app, Version 4

As we run the app, the tip amount is updated after any key is pressed when either of the two EditText components is in focus (except when one of the EditTexts is empty; in that case, we execute inside the catch block and the components are not updated). **FIGURE 2.9** shows the app running after the user enters 125.59 for the bill value and starts entering the tip percentage. As soon as the user types 2, the tip and the total amounts are updated.

Instead of coding a separate class for the handler, then instantiate an object of that class and register that object on one or more GUI components, as we did in Example 2.13 (lines 57–69, line 26, and lines 27–28 respectively), some developers like to use anonymous objects instead and write code as follows:

```
tipEditText.addTextChangedListener( new TextWatcher( ) {
    // override afterTextChanged, beforeTextChanged
    // and onTextChanged here
} );
```

FIGURE 2.9 Tip Calculator, Version 4, running in Samsung Galaxy Tab 2 7.0

While that code looks more compact at first, we feel that it is less readable and less reusable, particularly if we need to have several handler objects or several GUI components that the handlers need to be registered on.

If we look at the overall code for this app, we can start seeing the benefits of the Model-View-Controller architecture and the resulting organization of the code as follows:

▶ Model: `TipCalculator` class
▶ View: activity_main.xml
▶ Controller: `MainActivity` class

As the apps that we develop get more complex, the benefits of the Model-View-Controller architecture will be more obvious.

Chapter Summary

- A sound design for an app involves using the Model-View-Controller architecture.
- The Model is a set of classes that encapsulate the functionality of the app.
- The View is the Graphical User Interface (GUI).
- The Controller is a middleman between the Model and the View: it takes some inputs from the View, updates the Model, asks the Model to perform some calculations, and updates the View accordingly.
- The Android framework provides a variety of components for building a GUI such as labels, buttons, text fields, checkboxes, radio buttons, and lists.
- We can use the activity_main.xml file to set up our GUI, including setting up some events.
- We can define styles and apply them to views.
- We can apply a style, as a theme, to the whole app or to an activity.
- A `RelativeLayout` enables us to position GUI components in relation to the position of other GUI components.
- We can assign an id to a `View` in order to retrieve it later using its id with the `findViewById` method from the `Activity` class. We can also refer to a component using its id in a layout XML file, which is useful if we use a `RelativeLayout`.
- Event-driven programming consists of using interactive components and event handlers to respond to events generated by user interaction with these components.
- If we want to handle the action of clicking on a `View`, we can assign the name of a method to the `android:onClick` attribute of that `View` in the XML layout file. We should then code that method as a `void` method accepting a `View` parameter in the corresponding `Activity` class.
- Generally, to respond to a user's interaction with a component, we need to write a handler class, instantiate an object of that class, and register that object on one or more components.
- Event handler classes implement a listener interface and need to override all their `abstract` method(s).
- Event handlers can be implemented as `private` inner classes; this enables the methods of that class to directly access the instance variables of its outer class. Event handlers can also be implemented with anonymous objects or as separate `public` classes.
- To listen to text changing inside a `TextView`, we can implement the `TextWatcher` interface from the `android.text` package.

Exercises, Problems, and Projects

Multiple-Choice Exercises

1. MVC stands for
   - Model View Code
   - Made View Controller
   - Model Visual Controller
   - Model View Controller

2. GUI components can be used to (check all that apply)
   - Display data to the user
   - Let the user interact with the app
   - Let the user input data

3. What is the name of the layout manager class that enables us to position GUI components relative to other GUI components?
   - LinearLayout
   - AbsoluteLayout
   - RelativeLayout
   - PositionLayout

4. In what package is the View class?
   - javax.swing
   - android.widget
   - java.util
   - android.view

5. What is the name of the attribute of style that lets you specify that a style inherits from another style?
   - superclass
   - inherits
   - parent
   - baseStyle

6. What is the name of the attribute of item (assuming an item element is nested inside a style element) that lets you specify the color of some text?
   - android:color
   - android:text
   - android:colorText
   - android:textColor

7. What is the name of the attribute of either the application or the activity tag that lets you specify a theme for the whole application or for the activity?
    - android:style
    - android:theme
    - android:@style
    - android:@theme

8. You have defined a color named myColor in the file colors.xml using the color XML element. Inside the activity_main.xml file, how do you specify that the background color of an EditText element will use the color myColor?
    - android:background="@color/myColor"
    - android:background="@myColor"
    - android:background="color/myColor"
    - android:backgroundColor="@color/myColor"

9. What is the name of the attribute of the Button element that lets you specify the method being called when the user clicks on the Button?
    - android:onPress
    - android:onButton
    - android:onClick
    - android:click

10. What class can we use to detect if there is a change within the text of a TextView?
    - TextChanger
    - TextWatcher
    - ViewWatcher
    - KeyListener

Fill in the Code

The following applies to questions 11 to 15

```
<TextView
    android:layout_width="wrap_content"
    android:layout_height="wrap_content"
/>
```

11. Add a line of XML so that the text displayed is the value of a string named book (defined in strings.xml).

12. Add a line of XML so that the background color of the TextView is red.

13. Add a line of XML so that the text displayed is centered inside the TextView element.

14. Add a line of XML so that the TextView is centered on a vertical axis within the View containing that TextView element.

15. Add a line of XML so that TextView uses a style named myStyle defined in styles.xml (using the XML element style).

16. Inside colors.xml, write the code to define a color named myColor that is green.

17. Inside styles.xml, define a style named myStyle so that paddingBottom is 10dp, and the background color is red.

18. Inside MainActivity.java, write the code to retrieve and assign to a TextView object reference a TextView element defined in activity_main.xml and whose id is look.

19. We have coded a class named MyWatcher extending the TextWatcher interface and declared an object of that class as follows:

    ```
    MyWatcher mw = new MyWatcher();
    ```

    Write one statement to register that object on an EditText object named myEditText.

Write an App

20. Modify this chapter's app. Allow the user to input the number of guests and calculate the tip and total per guest.

21. Write an app that performs an addition. It has three labels and one button. The first two labels are filled with two randomly generated integers between 1 and 10. When the user clicks on the button, the two integers are added and the result is displayed in the third label. The three labels should be styled using the same style. The button should have a red background and a blue text. All four components should be centered vertically. Include a Model.

22. Write an app that performs an addition. It has two text fields, one label and one button. The user can enter two integers in the text fields. When the user clicks on the button, the two integers are added and the result is displayed in the label. The two text fields should be styled using the same style. The label and the button should also be styled with the same style, but different from the other style. Each style should have a minimum of four attributes. All four components should be centered vertically. Include a Model.

23. Write an app that simulates a traffic light. It displays a label and a button. The label represents the current color of a traffic light and can be red, green, or yellow. When the user clicks on the button, the label cycles to the next color and simulates running the traffic light. You should look at the documentation of the View class to figure out how to change the color of a View programmatically. The two components should be centered vertically. Include a Model.

24. Write an app that lets the user create a color using the RGB color model. It displays three text fields and one label. We expect the user to enter integers between 0 and 255 included in the three text fields; if a value is negative, it should be converted to 0; if it is greater than 255, it should be converted to 255. The value of the text fields represents the amount of red, green, and blue of the background color in the label. When the user modifies the number in any text field, the background color of the label should be updated. You should look at the documentation of the View class to figure out how to change the color of a View programmatically. The three text fields should have the same style with a minimum of four attributes. All four components should be centered vertically. Include a Model.

25. Write an app that checks if two passwords match. It has two text fields, one label and one button. The user can enter two passwords in the text fields, which should be styled as such. When the user clicks on the button, the two passwords are compared for equality and either THANK YOU (if the passwords match) or PASSWORDS MUST MATCH (if the passwords do not match) is displayed in the label. The text fields and the label should have their own separate style, each with a minimum of four attributes. All four components should be centered vertically. Include a Model.

26. Write an app that evaluates if an email is valid. The app includes an edit text field, a label and a button. The user can enter his or her email in the edit text field. When the user clicks on the button, the app checks if the email entered contains the @ character. If it does, the label displays VALID, otherwise it displays INVALID. The text field and the label should have their own separate style, each with a minimum of four attributes. The text field and the label should be on the same horizontal axis; the button should be below them and centered. Include a Model.

27. Write an app that evaluates the strength of a password. It has a text field and a label; the user can enter his or her password. The label displays, as the user types, WEAK or STRONG. To keep things simple, we define a weak password as a string of eight characters or fewer; a strong password is defined as a string of nine characters or more. The text field and the label should have their own separate style, each with a minimum of four attributes. The two components should be centered vertically. Include a Model.

28. Write an app that asks the user to enter a password with a minimum strength level. It has a text field and a label. As the user enters his or her password, the label displays VALID or INVALID. For the purpose of this app, we define a valid password as a string of eight characters or more with at least one uppercase letter, one lowercase letter, and one digit. The text field and the label should have their own separate style, each with a minimum of four attributes. The two components should be centered vertically. The label displaying VALID or INVALID should be updated as the user types. Include a Model.

29. Write an app that keeps track of the calories for a meal. Present the user with a choice of several foods; assign a number of calories to each food choice. After the user enters the number of servings for each food, the total number of calories is updated. The text fields and the labels should have their own separate style, each with a minimum of four attributes. Include a Model.

30. Write an app that keeps track of the calories burned during a workout session. Present the user with a choice of workouts; assign a number of calories to each workout. After the user enters a number for each workout, the total number of calories burned is updated. The text fields and the labels should have their own separate style, each with a minimum of four attributes. Include a Model.

CHAPTER **THREE**

Coding the GUI Programmatically, Layout Managers

CHAPTER CONTENTS

Introduction

Sometimes the number of buttons (or other components) we want to display is dynamic—it could be different every time we run the app, such as in a content app. A content app is an app that gets its data from an external source, for example a website such as Facebook or Twitter, displays the data, and enables the user to interact with it. We do not know in advance how much data will be retrieved. It is also possible that an app lends itself well to a particular data structure, like a 3 × 3 two-dimensional array in a tic-tac-toe game. We can implement the GUI part of a tic-tac-toe game with nine buttons and we could define the nine buttons in the activity_main.xml file, but it is easier to manipulate a 3 × 3 two-dimensional array of buttons by code.

In this chapter, we build a Tic-Tac-Toe app, and create the GUI and handle the events programmatically. We leave the automatically generated activity_main.xml file as it is, and do everything by code.

3.1 Model View Controller Architecture

Although we define the View by code rather than in the activity_main.xml file, we still use the Model-View-Controller architecture. In order to define the View, we need to understand what will be in it. That depends on how the TicTacToe game is defined and played; that part is encapsulated in the Model. Thus, we define the Model first.

3.2 The Model

The Model is comprised of the TicTacToe class, which encapsulates the functionality of the TicTacToe game. Again, the Model is independent from any visual representation. In this app, it enables play and enforces the rules of the game. The API for this class is shown in TABLE 3.1.

EXAMPLE 3.1 shows the class code. The TicTacToe constructor (lines 8–11) calls reset-Game at line 10 after instantiating the two-dimensional array game as a 3 × 3 array. Having a separate resetGame method enables us to reuse the same object when playing back-to-back games. ResetGame (lines 80–85) clears the board by setting all the cells in game to 0; it also sets turn to 1 so that player 1 starts.

The method play (lines 13–26) first checks if the play is legal (lines 15–16). If it is not, it returns 0 (line 25). If it is, it updates game at line 17 and turn at lines 18–21. It then returns the value of currentTurn (line 22), which holds the old value of turn (line 14).

The method whoWon (lines 28–39) checks if a player has won the game and returns the player number if that is true; otherwise, it returns 0. We break down that logic using three protected methods: checkRows (lines 41–47), checkColumns (lines 49–55), and checkDiagonals (lines 57–65). There is no reason for a client of that class to access these methods so we declare them protected.

TABLE 3.1 API for the `TicTacToe` class

Instance Variables

private int[ ][ ] game	3 × 3 two-dimensional array representing the board
private int turn	1 = player 1's turn to play; 2 = player 2's turn to play

Constructor

TicTacToe( )	Constructs a TicTacToe object; clears the board and prepares to play by setting turn to 1

Public Methods

int play(int row, int column)	If the play is legal and the board cell is not taken, plays and returns the old value of turn
boolean canStillPlay( )	Returns true if there is still at least one cell not taken on the board; otherwise, returns false
int whoWon( )	Returns i if player i won, 0 if nobody has won yet
boolean gameOver( )	Returns true if the game is over, false otherwise
void resetGame( )	Clears the board and sets turn to 1

```
1    package com.jblearning.tictactoev0;
2
3    public class TicTacToe {
4        public static final int SIDE = 3;
5        private int turn;
6        private int [][] game;
7
8        public TicTacToe ( ) {
9            game = new int [SIDE][SIDE];
10           resetGame ( );
11       }
12
13       public int play ( int row, int col ) {
14           int currentTurn = turn;
15           if ( row >= 0 && col >= 0 && row < SIDE && col < SIDE
16                   && game [row][col] == 0 ) {
17               game [row][col] = turn;
18               if ( turn == 1 )
19                   turn = 2;
20               else
21                   turn = 1;
22               return currentTurn;
23           }
```

EXAMPLE 3.1 The `TicTacToe` class (*Continued*)

```
24              else
25                  return 0;
26          }
27
28      public int whoWon( ) {
29          int rows = checkRows( );
30          if ( rows > 0 )
31              return rows;
32          int columns = checkColumns( );
33          if( columns > 0 )
34              return columns;
35          int diagonals = checkDiagonals( );
36          if( diagonals > 0 )
37              return diagonals;
38          return 0;
39      }
40
41      protected int checkRows( ) {
42          for( int row = 0; row < SIDE; row++ )
43              if ( game[row][0] != 0 && game[row][0] == game[row][1]
44                      && game[row][1] == game[row][2] )
45                  return game[row][0];
46          return 0;
47      }
48
49      protected int checkColumns( ) {
50          for( int col = 0; col < SIDE; col++ )
51              if ( game[0][col] != 0 && game[0][col] == game[1][col]
52                      && game[1][col] == game[2][col] )
53                  return game[0][col];
54          return 0;
55      }
56
57      protected int checkDiagonals( ) {
58          if ( game[0][0] != 0 && game[0][0] == game[1][1]
59                  && game[1][1] == game[2][2] )
60              return game[0][0];
61          if ( game[0][2] != 0 && game[0][2] == game[1][1]
62                  && game[1][1] == game[2][0] )
63              return game[2][0];
64          return 0;
65      }
66
67      public boolean canNotPlay( ) {
68          boolean result = true;
69          for( int row = 0; row < SIDE; row++)
70              for( int col = 0; col < SIDE; col++ )
```

EXAMPLE 3.1 The TicTacToe class (*Continued*)

```
71                     if ( game[row][col] == 0 )
72                          result = false;
73             return result;
74         }
75
76         public boolean isGameOver( ) {
77             return canNotPlay( ) || ( whoWon( ) > 0 );
78         }
79
80         public void resetGame( ) {
81             for (int row = 0; row < SIDE; row++)
82                 for( int col = 0; col < SIDE; col++ )
83                     game[row][col] = 0;
84             turn = 1;
85         }
86    }
```

EXAMPLE 3.1 **The `TicTacToe` class**

The method `isGameOver` (lines 76–78) returns `true` if the game is over (i.e., somebody has won or no one can play); otherwise, it returns `false`.

3.3 Creating the GUI Programmatically, TicTacToe, Version 0

In Version 0 of our TicTacToe app, we use the empty activity template and only setup the GUI. We use a 3 × 3 two-dimensional array of `Buttons`, in order to mirror the 3 × 3 two-dimensional array game in our Model, the `TicTacToe` class. In order to keep things simple, we first place the View inside the `Activity` class, so the View and the Controller are in the same class. Later in the chapter, we separate the View from the Controller and place them in two different classes.

The Android framework provides classes, called layout classes, to help us organize window contents. We have already used the `RelativeLayout` class, which is the default layout that is automatically used in activity_main.xml when we create a project. These layout classes are subclasses of the `abstract` class `ViewGroup`, itself a subclass of `View`. A `ViewGroup` is a special `View` that can contain other `Views`, called its children.

TABLE 3.2 shows a few layout classes along with their descriptions. **FIGURE 3.1** shows the hierarchy of these classes.

In order to display the nine buttons in a 3 × 3 grid, we use a `GridLayout`.

As we know, there are many types of Android phones and tablets, and they all can have different screen dimensions. Thus, it is bad practice to hardcode widget dimensions and coordinates because a user interface could look good on some Android devices but poorly on others. In order to keep this example simple, we will assume that the user will only play in vertical orientation; thus, we assume that the width of the device is smaller than its height.

TABLE 3.2 `ViewGroup` and selected subclasses

Class	Description
ViewGroup	A View that contains other Views.
LinearLayout	A layout that arranges its children in a single direction (horizontally or vertically).
GridLayout	A layout that places its children in a rectangular grid.
FrameLayout	A layout designed to block out an area of the screen to display a single item.
RelativeLayout	A layout where the positions of the GUI components can be described in relation to each other or to their parent.
TableLayout	A layout that arranges its children in rows and columns.
TableRow	A layout that arranges its children horizontally. A TableRow should always be used as a child of a TableLayout.

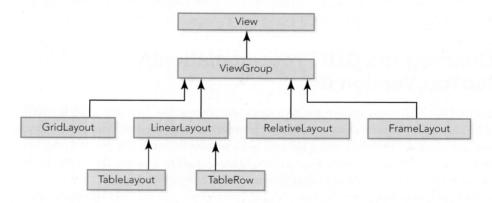

FIGURE 3.1 Inheritance hierarchy showing some layout classes

We can dynamically retrieve, by code, the width and height of the screen of the device that the app is currently running on. Using that information, we can then size the GUI components so that they fit within the device's screen no matter what the brand and model of the device are. In setting up the View, we perform the following steps:

▶ Retrieve the width of the screen
▶ Define and instantiate a `GridLayout` with three rows and three columns
▶ Instantiate the 3 × 3 array of `Buttons`
▶ Add the nine `Buttons` to the layout
▶ Set the `GridLayout` as the layout manager of the view managed by this activity

In **EXAMPLE 3.2**, the method `buildGuiByCode` (lines 19–42) implements the above.

```
1   package com.jblearning.tictactoev0;
2
3   import android.graphics.Point;
4   import android.os.Bundle;
5   import android.support.v7.app.AppCompatActivity;
6   import android.widget.Button;
7   import android.widget.GridLayout;
8
9   public class MainActivity extends AppCompatActivity {
10      private Button [][] buttons;
11
12      @Override
13      protected void onCreate( Bundle savedInstanceState ) {
14          super.onCreate( savedInstanceState );
15          // setContentView( R.layout.activity_main );
16          buildGuiByCode( );
17      }
18
19      public void buildGuiByCode( ) {
20          // Get width of the screen
21          Point size = new Point( );
22          getWindowManager( ).getDefaultDisplay( ).getSize( size );
23          int w = size.x / TicTacToe.SIDE;
24
25          // Create the layout manager as a GridLayout
26          GridLayout gridLayout = new GridLayout( this );
27          gridLayout.setColumnCount( TicTacToe.SIDE );
28          gridLayout.setRowCount( TicTacToe.SIDE );
29
30          // Create the buttons and add them to gridLayout
31          buttons = new Button[TicTacToe.SIDE][TicTacToe.SIDE];
32          for( int row = 0; row < TicTacToe.SIDE; row++ ) {
33              for( int col = 0; col < TicTacToe.SIDE; col++ ) {
34                  buttons[row][col] = new Button( this );
35                  gridLayout.addView( buttons[row][col], w, w );
36              }
37          }
38
39          // Set gridLayout as the View of this Activity
40          setContentView( gridLayout );
41      }
42  }
```

EXAMPLE 3.2 The MainActivity class, TicTacToe app Version 0

TABLE 3.3 Resources involved in retrieving the width of the screen		
Class or Interface	**Package**	**Method and fields**
Activity	android.app	WindowManager getWindowManager( )
WindowManager	android.view	Display getDefaultDisplay( )
Display	android.view	void getSize(Point)
Point	android.graphics	x and y public instance variables

At line 10, we declare the instance variable buttons, a two-dimensional array of Buttons. The Button class is imported at line 6.

At lines 20–23, we retrieve the width of the screen. At line 21, we declare a Point variable, size. The Point class, imported at line 3, has two public instance variables, x and y.

At line 22, we chain three method calls, successively calling getWindowManager, getDefaultDisplay, and getSize. GetWindowManager, from the Activity class, returns a WindowManager object that encapsulates the current window. With it, we call the method getDefaultDisplay of the WindowManager interface; it returns a Display object, which encapsulates the current display and can provide information about its size and its density. With it, we call the getSize method of the Display class; getSize is a void method but takes a Point object reference as a parameter. When that method executes, it modifies the Point parameter object and assigns to it the width and height of the display as its x and y instance variables. At line 23, we retrieve the width of the screen (size.x) and assign one third of it to the variable w. We later use the value of w to dimension the Buttons so that we can place three of them across the screen. TABLE 3.3 summarizes the resources involved in retrieving the size of the current device's screen.

At lines 25–28, we define and instantiate the GridLayout object gridLayout.

The GridLayout class belongs to the android.widget package; we import it at line 7. At line 26, we instantiate a GridLayout object, passing the argument this to the GridLayout constructor; as shown in TABLE 3.4, the GridLayout constructor takes a Context parameter. Context is an interface that encapsulates global information about the app environment. As shown in FIGURE 3.2, the Activity class inherits indirectly from the Context class, therefore, an Activity object "is a" Context object and this can be used as the Context object representing the app environment. At lines 27–28, we set the GridLayout's number of columns and rows to 3.

The Buttons are created and added to the layout at lines 30–37 by looping through the array buttons. We first instantiate buttons at line 31 as a 3 × 3 two-dimensional array of Buttons. The double loop at lines 32–37 instantiates each Button and adds it to gridLayout. The Button constructor called at line 34 takes a Context parameter representing the app environment. Again, we pass this, representing the current Context, as the argument. It is important to instantiate a

TABLE 3.4 `GridLayout` constructor and methods	
Constructor	
GridLayout(Context context)	Constructs a GridLayout within the app environment defined by context.
Public Methods	
setRowCount(int rows) setColumnCount(int cols) addView(View child, int w, int h)	Sets the number of rows in the grid to rows. Sets the number of columns in the grid to cols. Method inherited from ViewGroup; adds child to this ViewGroup using width w and height h.

GUI component before either calling a method with it or adding it to a `View`. Otherwise, we will have a `NullPointerException` at runtime and the app will stop. At line 35, we add the current button to the layout using the `addView` method and specify its width and height as equal to w. The `GridLayout` class inherits `addView` from `ViewGroup`.

Finally, at line 40, we set the contents of the view managed by this activity to `gridLayout` by calling the `setContentView` method from the `Activity` class. Remember that `GridLayout` inherits from `ViewGroup`, which inherits from `View`; therefore, `gridLayout` "is a" `View`.

The `buildGuiByCode` method is called at line 16, inside the `onCreate` method, which is called automatically when the app starts.

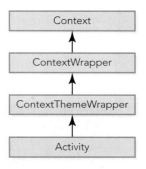

FIGURE 3.2 Inheritance hierarchy showing the `Context` and `Activity` classes

COMMON ERROR: We must instantiate a GUI component before using it. In particular, adding a GUI component that has not been instantiated to a `View` will result in a `NullPointerException`.

In order to keep things simple, we only allow the app to work in vertical orientation. Inside the AndroidManifest.xml file, we assign the value `portrait` to the `android:screenOrientation` attribute of the `activity` tag.

FIGURE 3.3 shows the app running inside the emulator.

At this point, we have coded two important components of our app: the Model (the `TicTacToe` class), and the View (the `buildGuiByCode` method of the `MainActivity` class). Next, we build the Controller.

5554:Nexus_5_API_23_x86

TicTacToeV0

FIGURE 3.3 TicTacToe app, Version 0, running inside the emulator

3.4 Event Handling: TicTacToe, Version 1

In Version 1, we add code to capture a click on any button, identify what button was clicked, and we place an X inside the button that was clicked. At that point, we are not concerned about playing the game or enforcing its rules. We will do that in Version 2.

In order to capture and process an event, we need to:

1. Write an event handler (a class extending a listener interface)
2. Instantiate an object of that class
3. Register that object listener on one or more GUI components

EXAMPLE 3.3 shows the updated `MainActivity` class, implementing the above.

The type of event that we want to capture determines the listener interface that we implement. `View.OnClickListener` is the listener interface that we should implement in order to capture and handle a click event on a `View`. Since it is defined inside the `View` class, importing the `View` class (line 7) automatically imports `View.OnClickListener`. **TABLE 3.5** lists the only abstract

TABLE 3.5 The `View.OnClickListener` interface	
public abstract void onClick(View v)	Called when a View has been clicked; the parameter v is a reference to that View.

method of that interface, `onClick`. Our event handler class, `ButtonHandler`, implements `OnClickListener` and overrides `onClick`. `ButtonHandler`, implemented as a `private` class, is coded at lines 53–61. At line 55, we add an output statement that gives feedback on the `View` parameter of the `onClick` method; we expect that it is a `Button`. At lines 56–59, we loop through the array `buttons` in order to identify the row and column values of the button that was clicked. We then call the `update` method, passing these row and column values at line 59.

The `update` method is coded at lines 48–51, but does not do much in this version. It outputs some feedback on the row and column of the button that was clicked (for debugging purposes), and writes an X inside it; this will change in Version 2.

We declare and instantiate a `ButtonHandler` object at line 34 and we register it on each element of `buttons` (line 39) as we loop through the array. Additionally, we set the text size of each button at line 38 so that it is relative to the size of each button, which we have sized relatively to the screen. In this way, we try to make our app as much device independent as possible. It is important to test an app on as many devices as possible and of various sizes to validate sizes and font sizes.

```
1    package com.jblearning.tictactoev1;
2
3    import android.graphics.Point;
4    import android.os.Bundle;
5    import android.support.v7.app.AppCompatActivity;
6    import android.util.Log;
7    import android.view.View;
8    import android.widget.Button;
9    import android.widget.GridLayout;
10
11   public class MainActivity extends AppCompatActivity {
12     private Button [][] buttons;
13
14     @Override
15     protected void onCreate( Bundle savedInstanceState ) {
16       super.onCreate( savedInstanceState );
17       // setContentView( R.layout.activity_main );
18       buildGuiByCode( );
19     }
20
```

EXAMPLE 3.3 The `MainActivity` class, TicTacToe app, Version 1 (*Continued*)

```
21    public void buildGuiByCode( ) {
22       // Get width of the screen
23       Point size = new Point( );
24       getWindowManager( ).getDefaultDisplay( ).getSize( size );
25       int w = size.x / TicTacToe.SIDE;
26
27       // Create the layout manager as a GridLayout
28       GridLayout gridLayout = new GridLayout( this );
29       gridLayout.setColumnCount( TicTacToe.SIDE );
30       gridLayout.setRowCount( TicTacToe.SIDE );
31
32       // Create the buttons and add them to gridLayout
33       buttons = new Button[TicTacToe.SIDE][TicTacToe.SIDE];
34       ButtonHandler bh = new ButtonHandler( );
35       for( int row = 0; row < TicTacToe.SIDE; row++ ) {
36         for( int col = 0; col < TicTacToe.SIDE; col++ ) {
37           buttons[row][col] = new Button( this );
38           buttons[row][col].setTextSize( ( int ) ( w * .2 ) );
39           buttons[row][col].setOnClickListener( bh );
40           gridLayout.addView( buttons[row][col], w, w );
41         }
42       }
43
44       // Set gridLayout as the View of this Activity
45       setContentView( gridLayout );
46    }
47
48    public void update( int row, int col ) {
49       Log.w( "MainActivity", "Inside update: " + row + ", " + col );
50       buttons[row][col].setText( "X" );
51    }
52
53    private class ButtonHandler implements View.OnClickListener {
54       public void onClick( View v ) {
55          Log.w( "MainActivity", "Inside onClick, v = " + v );
56          for( int row = 0; row < TicTacToe.SIDE; row ++ )
57            for( int column = 0; column < TicTacToe.SIDE; column++ )
58              if( v == buttons[row][column] )
59                update( row, column );
60       }
61    }
62 }
```

EXAMPLE 3.3 **The MainActivity class, TicTacToe app, Version 1**

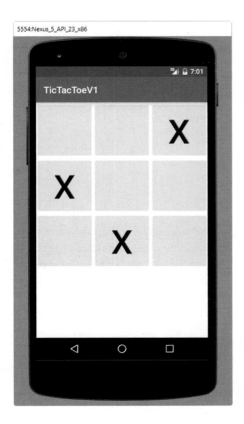

FIGURE 3.4 **TicTacToe app, Version 1, running inside the emulator**

COMMON ERROR: When overriding an `abstract` method of an interface, it is mandatory that the method header be the same, minus the keyword `abstract`, as the method header of the listener interface. Otherwise, the method will not override the `abstract` method of the interface, and that will generate a compiler error.

FIGURE 3.4 shows the app after the user clicked successively on three buttons. **FIGURE 3.5** shows a partial output of Logcat, resulting from the output statements at lines 55 and 49. It reveals that the user clicked on the button in the top right corner first, then on the left button in the middle row, and then on the middle button in the bottom row. Figure 3.5 also shows the three different memory addresses of the three `View` (`Buttons` in this case) arguments of `onClick`.

```
Inside onClick, v = android.widget.Button{dd7bc45 VFED..C.. ...P....
720,0-1080,360}
Inside update: 0, 2
Inside onClick, v = android.widget.Button{2965f9a VFED..C.. ...P....
0,360-360,720}
Inside update: 1, 0
Inside onClick, v = android.widget.Button{643d0cb VFED..C.. ...P....
360,720-720,1080}
Inside update: 2, 1
```

FIGURE 3.5 Partial output of Logcat

We now have a very simple Controller. It is made up of the `onCreate` and `update` methods, as well as the `ButtonHandler` private class of the `MainActivity` class. Note that in this app, the View and the Controller are in the same class. Later in the chapter, we put them in separate classes to make the code more reusable. The next step is to finish coding the Controller in order to enable game play.

3.5 Integrating the Model to Enable Game Play: TicTacToe, Version 2

We are assuming that two users will be playing on the same device against each other. Enabling game play does not just mean placing an X or an O on the grid of buttons at each turn. It also means enforcing the rules, such as not allowing someone to play twice at the same position on the grid, checking if one player won, indicating if the game is over. Our Model, the `TicTacToe` class, provides that functionality. In order to enable play, we add a `TicTacToe` object as an instance variable of our `Activity` class, and we call the methods of the `TicTacToe` class as and when needed. Play is happening inside the `update` method so we have to modify it. We also need to check if the game is over and, in that case, disable all the buttons.

EXAMPLE 3.4 shows the updated `MainActivity` class. At line 11, we declare a `TicTacToe` object, `tttGame`; we instantiate it at line 17.

Inside the `update` method (lines 48–56), we first call the `play` method of the `TicTacToe` class with `tttGame` at line 49. We know that it returns the player number (1 or 2) if the play is legal, 0 if the play is not legal. If the play is legal and the player is player 1, we write X inside the button (line 51). If the play is legal and the player is player 2, we write O inside the button (line 53). If the play is not legal, we do not do anything.

When the game is over, we want to disable all the buttons. At lines 58–62, the `enableButtons` method enables all the buttons if its parameter, `enabled`, is true. If it is `false`, it disables all the buttons. We can enable or disable a `Button` by calling the `setEnabled` method of the `Button` class using the argument `true` to enable the `Button`, `false` to disable it. We test if the game is over at line 54 and disable all the buttons if it is (line 55).

```
1    package com.jblearning.tictactoev2;
2
3    import android.graphics.Point;
4    import android.os.Bundle;
5    import android.support.v7.app.AppCompatActivity;
6    import android.view.View;
7    import android.widget.Button;
8    import android.widget.GridLayout;
9
10   public class MainActivity extends AppCompatActivity {
11     private TicTacToe tttGame;
12     private Button [][] buttons;
13
14     @Override
15     protected void onCreate( Bundle savedInstanceState ) {
16       super.onCreate( savedInstanceState );
17       tttGame = new TicTacToe( );
18       buildGuiByCode( );
19     }
20
21     public void buildGuiByCode( ) {
22       // Get width of the screen
23       Point size = new Point( );
24       getWindowManager( ).getDefaultDisplay( ).getSize( size );
25       int w = size.x / TicTacToe.SIDE;
26
27   // Create the layout manager as a GridLayout
28       GridLayout gridLayout = new GridLayout( this );
29       gridLayout.setColumnCount( TicTacToe.SIDE );
30       gridLayout.setRowCount( TicTacToe.SIDE );
31
32       // Create the buttons and add them to gridLayout
33       buttons = new Button[TicTacToe.SIDE][TicTacToe.SIDE];
34       ButtonHandler bh = new ButtonHandler( );
35       for( int row = 0; row < TicTacToe.SIDE; row++ ) {
36         for( int col = 0; col < TicTacToe.SIDE; col++ ) {
37             buttons[row][col] = new Button( this );
38             buttons[row][col].setTextSize( ( int ) ( w * .2 ) );
39             buttons[row][col].setOnClickListener( bh );
40             gridLayout.addView( buttons[row][col], w, w );
41         }
42       }
43
44       // Set gridLayout as the View of this Activity
45       setContentView( gridLayout );
46     }
```

EXAMPLE 3.4 The MainActivity class, TicTacToe app, Version 2 (*Continued*)

```
47
48    public void update( int row, int col ) {
49      int play = tttGame.play( row, col );
50      if( play == 1 )
51        buttons[row][col].setText( "X" );
52      else if( play == 2 )
53        buttons[row][col].setText( "O" );
54      if( tttGame.isGameOver( ) ) // game over, disable buttons
55        enableButtons( false );
56    }
57
58    public void enableButtons( boolean enabled ) {
59      for( int row = 0; row < TicTacToe.SIDE; row++ )
60        for( int col = 0; col < TicTacToe.SIDE; col++ )
61          buttons[row][col].setEnabled( enabled );
62    }
63
64    private class ButtonHandler implements View.OnClickListener {
65      public void onClick( View v ) {
66        for( int row = 0; row < TicTacToe.SIDE; row ++ )
67          for( int column = 0; column < TicTacToe.SIDE; column++ )
68            if( v == buttons[row][column] )
69              update( row, column );
70      }
71    }
72  }
```

EXAMPLE 3.4 **The MainActivity class, TicTacToe app, Version 2**

In Version 3, we will add a status label giving some feedback on the current state of the game. **FIGURE 3.6** shows the app running in the emulator. Player 1 just won and the buttons are disabled.

3.6 Inner Classes

A lot of the Android GUI classes are inner classes or inner interfaces. For example, OnClick-Listener is an inner interface of the View class. The layout manager classes have inner classes that are used to specify the position of a View child inside its parent layout. **TABLE 3.6** shows some of them. The dot notation used in the class name indicates that a class is an inner class of another class. For example, GridLayout.LayoutParams means that LayoutParams is an inner class of GridLayout.

The LayoutParams classes are all public, static inner classes.

EXAMPLE 3.5 shows a very simple example of how a public, static, inner class, B, can be defined inside another class, A. Class B is defined at lines 2–12. At line 2, the class header defines

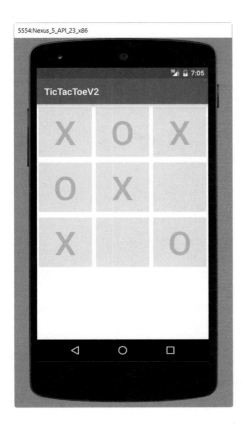

FIGURE 3.6 TicTacToe app, Version 2, running inside the emulator—player 1 just won

TABLE 3.6 Selected `LayoutParams` classes

Class	Description
ViewGroup.LayoutParams	Base class for the LayoutParams classes
GridLayout.LayoutParams	Layout info associated with a child of a GridLayout
LinearLayout.LayoutParams	Layout info associated with a child of a LinearLayout
TableLayout.LayoutParams	Layout info associated with a child of a TableLayout
RelativeLayout.LayoutParams	Layout info associated with a child of a RelativeLayout

```
1    public class A {
2      public static class B {
3        private int number;
4
5        public B( int newNumber ) {
6          number = newNumber;
7        }
8
9        public String toString( ) {
10         return "number: " + number;
11       }
12     }
13   }
```

EXAMPLE 3.5   **B is a `public`, `static`, inner class of class A**

B as `public` and `static`. It has a constructor (lines 5–7) and a `toString` method (lines 9–11). For convenience, we refer to the class `A.B` as opposed to class `B`, inner class of `A`.

EXAMPLE 3.6 shows a very simple example showing how we can use class `B` inside another class, `Test`. To reference an inner class, we use the following syntax:

```
OuterClassName.InnerClassName
```

At line 3, we use this syntax to declare and instantiate b, an object reference of type `A.B`.

```
1    public class Test {
2      public static void main( String [] args ) {
3        A.B b = new A.B( 20 );
4        System.out.println( b );
5      }
6    }
```

EXAMPLE 3.6   **Using B, a `public`, `static`, inner class of class A in another class**

The output of Example 3.6 is:

```
number: 20
```

If `B` was declared as a `private` class, we could only use `B` inside class `A` and not outside it. And if `B` was not declared `static`, we could not use the syntax `A.B`.

If `C`, an inner class of class `A`, is declared `public` but not `static`, we could declare and instantiate an object reference of class `C` as follows (using default constructors in this example):

```
A a = new A( );
A.C c = a.new C( );
```

3.7 Layout Parameters: TicTacToe, Version 3

We want to improve Version 2 by showing the current state of the game at the bottom of the screen, as shown in **FIGURE 3.9**.

The feedback message depends on the state of the game. It makes sense to let the TicTacToe class, our Model, define the message. **EXAMPLE 3.7** shows the result method (lines 87–94) of the TicTacToe class. It returns a String that reflects the state of the game.

```
86
87        public String result( ) {
88            if( whoWon( ) > 0 )
89                return "Player " + whoWon( ) + " won";
90            else if( canNotPlay( ) )
91                return "Tie Game";
92            else
93                return "PLAY !!";
94        }
95    }
```

EXAMPLE 3.7 The result method of the TicTacToe class

The GridLayout used in Version 2 suits the layout of TicTacToe or any View that requires a two-dimensional grid of GUI components very well. Sometimes we want to use a grid and we want to have the flexibility of combining several cells of the grid and place a single component there. The GridLayout class enables us to span widgets over several rows or columns, or both, in order to achieve a more customized look and feel.

In Version 3, we use a GridLayout with four rows and three columns. We place the buttons in the first three rows, and use the fourth row to place a TextView across the three columns to display the game status.

The ViewGroup.LayoutParams class enables us to specify how a View child is to be positioned inside its parent layout. GridLayout.LayoutParams inherits from the ViewGroup.LayoutParams class and we can use it to set the layout parameters of a GUI component before we add it to a GridLayout.

A GridLayout.LayoutParams object is defined by two components, rowSpec and columnSpec, both of type GridLayout.Spec. Spec is defined as a public static inner class of GridLayout. Thus, we refer to it using GridLayout.Spec. RowSpec defines a vertical span, starting at a row index and specifying a number of rows; columnSpec defines a horizontal span, starting at a column index and specifying a number of columns. Thus, by defining rowSpec, the vertical span, and columnSpec, the horizontal span, we define a rectangular area within the grid where we can place a View.

We can use the static spec methods of the GridLayout.Spec class to create and define a GridLayout.Spec object, which defines a span. Once we have defined two GridLayout.Spec

TABLE 3.7 Methods of the `GridLayout` and `GridLayout.LayoutParams` classes

Selected Methods of the GridLayout class

public static GridLayout.Spec spec(int start, int size)
   Returns a GridLayout.Spec object where start is the starting index and size is the size.
public static GridLayout.Spec spec(int start, int size, GridLayout.Alignment alignment)
   Returns a GridLayout.Spec object where start is the starting index and size is the size.
   Alignment is the alignment; common values include GridLayout.TOP,
   GridLayout,BOTTOM, GridLayout.LEFT, GridLayout.RIGHT, GridLayout.CENTER.

Constructor of the GridLayout.LayoutParams class

GridLayout.LayoutParams(Spec rowSpec, Spec columnSpec)
   Constructs a LayoutParams object with rowSpec and columnSpec.

objects, we can use them to define a `GridLayout.LayoutParams` object. **TABLE 3.7 shows** these methods.

FIGURE 3.7 shows a 4 × 6 grid of cells. The shaded area can be defined as follows:

The vertical span starts at index 1 and has size 2
The horizontal span starts at index 2 and has size 4

We could define a `GridLayout.LayoutParams` object for the shaded area as follows:

```
// vertical span
GridLayout.Spec rowSpec = GridLayout.spec( 1, 2 );
// horizontal span
GridLayout.Spec columnSpec = GridLayout.spec( 2, 4 );
GridLayout.LayoutParams lp
= new GridLayout.LayoutParams( rowSpec, columnSpec );
```

Note that we could use `Spec` instead of `GridLayout.Spec` if we include the following import statement:

```
import android.widget.GridLayout.Spec;
```

in addition to:

```
import android.widget.GridLayout;
```

FIGURE 3.8 shows a 4 × 3 grid of cells like the one in our app. The shaded area can be defined as follows:

The vertical span starts at index 3 and has size 1
The horizontal span starts at index 0 and has size 3

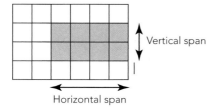

FIGURE 3.7 **An area of a 4 × 6 grid defined by a vertical span with start = 1 and size = 2, and a horizontal span with start = 2 and size = 4**

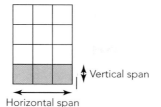

FIGURE 3.8 **An area of a 4 × 3 grid defined by a vertical span with start = 3 and size = 1, and a horizontal span with start = 0 and size = 3**

We define a `GridLayout.LayoutParams` object for the shaded area as follows:

```
GridLayout.Spec rowSpec = GridLayout.spec( 3, 1 );
GridLayout.Spec columnSpec = GridLayout.spec( 0, 3 );
GridLayout.LayoutParams lp
= new GridLayout.LayoutParams( rowSpec, columnSpec );
```

We use code similar to the one above in **EXAMPLE 3.8** at lines 48–53 to define the layout parameters of `status`. At line 54, we set them by calling `setLayoutParams`. At line 34, we set the number of rows of our `GridLayout` to four so that we can place `status` in the fourth row. At lines 57–58, we set the height and width of `status` so that it fills completely the area of the grid defined by its layout parameters. Note that it is possible to set the height and width of a component to be different from its layout parameters. We can then use the `spec` method with three parameters to set the alignment of the component with respect to its defined layout parameters. Table 3.7 shows some possible values for the third parameter of the `spec` method.

At lines 59–62, we center the text in `status`, set its background color to green, set its text font size, and set its text content based on the state of `tttGame`, respectively.

We add code to the `update` method at lines 77 and 79 to change the color and text of `status` when the game is over.

```
1    package com.jblearning.tictactoev3;
2
3    import android.graphics.Color;
4    import android.graphics.Point;
5    import android.os.Bundle;
6    import android.support.v7.app.AppCompatActivity;
7    import android.view.Gravity;
8    import android.view.View;
```

EXAMPLE 3.8 **The `MainActivity` class, TicTacToe app, Version 3 (*Continued*)**

```
 9    import android.widget.Button;
10    import android.widget.GridLayout;
11    import android.widget.TextView;
12
13    public class MainActivity extends AppCompatActivity {
14      private TicTacToe tttGame;
15      private Button [][] buttons;
16      private TextView status;
17
18      @Override
19      protected void onCreate( Bundle savedInstanceState ) {
20        super.onCreate( savedInstanceState );
21        tttGame = new TicTacToe( );
22        buildGuiByCode( );
23      }
24
25      public void buildGuiByCode( ) {
26        // Get width of the screen
27        Point size = new Point( );
28        getWindowManager( ).getDefaultDisplay( ).getSize( size );
29        int w = size.x / TicTacToe.SIDE;
30
31        // Create the layout manager as a GridLayout
32        GridLayout gridLayout = new GridLayout( this );
33        gridLayout.setColumnCount( TicTacToe.SIDE );
34        gridLayout.setRowCount( TicTacToe.SIDE + 1 );
35
36        // Create the buttons and add them to gridLayout
37        buttons = new Button[TicTacToe.SIDE][TicTacToe.SIDE];
38        ButtonHandler bh = new ButtonHandler( );
39        for( int row = 0; row < TicTacToe.SIDE; row++ ) {
40          for( int col = 0; col < TicTacToe.SIDE; col++ ) {
41            buttons[row][col] = new Button( this );
42            buttons[row][col].setTextSize( ( int ) ( w * .2 ) );
43            buttons[row][col].setOnClickListener( bh );
44            gridLayout.addView( buttons[row][col], w, w );
45          }
46        }
47
48        // set up layout parameters of 4th row of gridLayout
49        status = new TextView( this );
50        GridLayout.Spec rowSpec = GridLayout.spec( TicTacToe.SIDE, 1 );
51        GridLayout.Spec columnSpec = GridLayout.spec( 0, TicTacToe.SIDE );
52        GridLayout.LayoutParams lpStatus
53                = new GridLayout.LayoutParams( rowSpec, columnSpec );
54        status.setLayoutParams( lpStatus );
```

EXAMPLE 3.8 **The `MainActivity` class, TicTacToe app, Version 3 (*Continued*)**

```
55
56         // set up status' characteristics
57         status.setWidth( TicTacToe.SIDE * w );
58         status.setHeight( w );
59         status.setGravity( Gravity.CENTER );
60         status.setBackgroundColor( Color.GREEN );
61         status.setTextSize( ( int ) ( w * .15 ) );
62         status.setText( tttGame.result( ) );
63
64         gridLayout.addView( status );
65
66         // Set gridLayout as the View of this Activity
67         setContentView( gridLayout );
68     }
69
70     public void update( int row, int col ) {
71         int play = tttGame.play( row, col );
72         if( play == 1 )
73             buttons[row][col].setText( "X" );
74         else if( play == 2)
75             buttons[row][col].setText( "O" );
76         if( tttGame.isGameOver( ) ) {
77             status.setBackgroundColor( Color.RED );
78             enableButtons( false );
79             status.setText( tttGame.result( ) );
80         }
81     }
82
83     public void enableButtons( boolean enabled ) {
84         for( int row = 0; row < TicTacToe.SIDE; row++ )
85             for( int col = 0; col < TicTacToe.SIDE; col++ )
86                 buttons[row][col].setEnabled( enabled );
87     }
88
89     private class ButtonHandler implements View.OnClickListener {
90         public void onClick( View v ) {
91             for( int row = 0; row < TicTacToe.SIDE; row ++ )
92                 for( int column = 0; column < TicTacToe.SIDE; column++ )
93                     if( v == buttons[row][column] )
94                         update( row, column );
95         }
96     }
97 }
```

EXAMPLE 3.8 The **MainActivity class, TicTacToe app, Version 3**

FIGURE 3.9 **TicTacToe app, Version 3, running inside the emulator**

FIGURE 3.9 shows the app running inside the emulator, including the status of the game at the bottom of the screen.

3.8 Alert Dialogs: TicTacToe, Version 4

In Version 4, we enable the player to play another game after the current one is over. When the game is over, we want a dialog box asking the user if he or she wants to play again to pop up. If the answer is yes, he or she can play again. If the answer is no, we exit the activity (in this case the app since there is only one activity).

The `AlertDialog.Builder` class, part of the `android.app` package, provides the functionality of a pop-up dialog box. It offers several choices to the user and captures the user's answer. A dialog box of type `AlertDialog.Builder` can contain up to three buttons: negative, neutral, and positive buttons. In this app, we only use two of them: the positive and negative buttons. Typically, these two buttons correspond to yes or no answers from the user, although that is not required. **TABLE 3.8** shows the `AlertDialog.Builder` constructor and other methods of that class.

> **TABLE 3.8** Selected constructor and methods of the `AlertDialog.Builder` class
>
> **Constructor of the AlertDialog.Builder class**
>
> public AlertDialog.Builder(Context context)
>   Constructs an AlertDialog.Builder dialog box object for the context parameter.
>
> **Methods of the AlertDialog.Builder class**
>
> public AlertDialog.Builder setMessage(CharSequence message)
>   Sets the message to display to message; returns this AlertDialog.Builder object, which
>   allows chaining if desired.
> public AlertDialog.Builder setTitle(CharSequence title)
>   Sets the title of the alert box to title; returns this AlertDialog.Builder object, which
>   allows method call chaining if desired.
> public AlertDialog.Builder setPositiveButton(CharSequence text, DialogInterface.OnClickListener listener)
>   Sets listener to be invoked when the user clicks on the positive button; sets the text of
>   the positive button to text.
> public AlertDialog.Builder setNegativeButton(CharSequence text, DialogInterface.OnClickListener listener)
>   Sets listener to be invoked when the user clicks on the negative button; sets the text of
>   the negative button to text.
> public AlertDialog.Builder setNeutralButton(CharSequence text, DialogInterface.OnClickListener listener)
>   Sets listener to be invoked when the user clicks on the neutral button; sets the text of
>   the neutral button to text.
> public AlertDialog show( )
>   Creates, returns an AlertDialog box and shows it.

EXAMPLE 3.9 shows the updated `MainActivity` class. Inside the method `showNewGame-Dialog` (lines 98–106), we declare and instantiate `alert`, an `AlertDialog.Builder` object at line 99, passing `this`, the current `MainActivity` object. `MainActivity` inherits from `Activity`, which inherits from `Context`; thus, `this` "is a" `Context` object. In order to show the dialog box, we call the `show` method at line 105. If we do not call the `show` method, the dialog box does not show. However, showing a dialog box without buttons enabling interaction with the user results in a dialog box with a title and a message that cannot be closed. In this app, we want to ask the user if he or she wants to play another game, so we include only the positive and negative buttons.

The neutral, positive, or negative buttons can be included by calling the `setPositiveButton`, `setNegativeButton`, and `setNeutralButton` methods of `AlertDialog.Builder`. These three methods take two parameters. The first one is either a `CharSequence` or an `int` resource id representing the `String` to be displayed inside the button. The second one is an object of type `DialogInterface.OnClickListener`, an interface.

Thus, we need to implement the `DialogInterface.OnClickListener` interface in order to declare and instantiate an object of that type and pass it as the second argument of these three methods. We implement it as a `private` class in order to have access to the instance variables and methods of our `MainActivity` class, in particular the object `tttGame` and the methods to reset

```
1   package com.jblearning.tictactoev4;
2
3   import android.app.DialogInterface;
4   import android.graphics.Color;
5   import android.graphics.Point;
6   import android.os.Bundle;
7   import android.support.v7.app.AlertDialog;
8   import android.support.v7.app.AppCompatActivity;
9   import android.view.Gravity;
10  import android.view.View;
11  import android.widget.Button;
12  import android.widget.GridLayout;
13  import android.widget.TextView;
14
15  public class MainActivity extends AppCompatActivity {
16    private TicTacToe tttGame;
17    private Button [][] buttons;
18    private TextView status;
19
20    @Override
21    protected void onCreate( Bundle savedInstanceState ) {
22      super.onCreate( savedInstanceState );
23      tttGame = new TicTacToe( );
24      buildGuiByCode( );
25    }
26
27    public void buildGuiByCode( ) {
28      // Get width of the screen
29      Point size = new Point( );
30      getWindowManager( ).getDefaultDisplay( ).getSize( size );
31      int w = size.x / TicTacToe.SIDE;
32
33      // Create the layout manager as a GridLayout
34      GridLayout gridLayout = new GridLayout( this );
35      gridLayout.setColumnCount( TicTacToe.SIDE );
36      gridLayout.setRowCount( TicTacToe.SIDE + 1 );
37
38      // Create the buttons and add them to gridLayout
39      buttons = new Button[TicTacToe.SIDE][TicTacToe.SIDE];
40      ButtonHandler bh = new ButtonHandler( );
41      for( int row = 0; row < TicTacToe.SIDE; row++ ) {
42        for( int col = 0; col < TicTacToe.SIDE; col++ ) {
43          buttons[row][col] = new Button( this );
44          buttons[row][col].setTextSize( ( int ) ( w * .2 ) );
45          buttons[row][col].setOnClickListener( bh );
```

EXAMPLE 3.9 **The MainActivity class, TicTacToe app, Version 4 (*Continued*)**

```
46              gridLayout.addView( buttons[row][col], w, w );
47          }
48      }
49
50      // set up layout parameters of 4th row of gridLayout
51      status = new TextView( this );
52      GridLayout.Spec rowSpec = GridLayout.spec( TicTacToe.SIDE, 1 );
53      GridLayout.Spec columnSpec = GridLayout.spec( 0, TicTacToe.SIDE );
54      GridLayout.LayoutParams lpStatus
55              = new GridLayout.LayoutParams( rowSpec, columnSpec );
56      status.setLayoutParams( lpStatus );
57
58      // set up status' characteristics
59      status.setWidth( TicTacToe.SIDE * w );
60      status.setHeight( w );
61      status.setGravity( Gravity.CENTER );
62      status.setBackgroundColor( Color.GREEN );
63      status.setTextSize( ( int ) ( w * .15 ) );
64      status.setText( tttGame.result( ) );
65
66      gridLayout.addView( status );
67
68      // Set gridLayout as the View of this Activity
69      setContentView( gridLayout );
70   }
71
72   public void update( int row, int col ) {
73      int play = tttGame.play( row, col );
74      if( play == 1 )
75        buttons[row][col].setText( "X" );
76      else if( play == 2 )
77        buttons[row][col].setText( "O" );
78      if( tttGame.isGameOver( ) ) {
79        status.setBackgroundColor( Color.RED );
80        enableButtons( false );
81        status.setText( tttGame.result( ) );
82        showNewGameDialog( );   // offer to play again
83      }
84   }
85
86   public void enableButtons( boolean enabled ) {
87      for( int row = 0; row < TicTacToe.SIDE; row++ )
88        for( int col = 0; col < TicTacToe.SIDE; col++ )
89          buttons[row][col].setEnabled( enabled );
90   }
```

EXAMPLE 3.9 **The `MainActivity` class, TicTacToe app, Version 4 (*Continued*)**

```
91
92    public void resetButtons( ) {
93      for( int row = 0; row < TicTacToe.SIDE; row++ )
94        for( int col = 0; col < TicTacToe.SIDE; col++ )
95          buttons[row][col].setText( "" );
96    }
97
98    public void showNewGameDialog( ) {
99      AlertDialog.Builder alert = new AlertDialog.Builder( this );
100     alert.setTitle( "This is fun" );
101     alert.setMessage( "Play again?" );
102     PlayDialog playAgain = new PlayDialog( );
103     alert.setPositiveButton( "YES", playAgain );
104     alert.setNegativeButton( "NO", playAgain );
105     alert.show( );
106   }
107
108   private class ButtonHandler implements View.OnClickListener {
109     public void onClick( View v ) {
110       for( int row = 0; row < TicTacToe.SIDE; row ++ )
111         for( int column = 0; column < TicTacToe.SIDE; column++ )
112           if( v == buttons[row][column] )
113             update( row, column );
114     }
115   }
116
117   private class PlayDialog implements DialogInterface.OnClickListener {
118     public void onClick( DialogInterface dialog, int id ) {
119       if( id == -1 ) /* YES button */ {
120         tttGame.resetGame( );
121         enableButtons( true );
122         resetButtons( );
123         status.setBackgroundColor( Color.GREEN );
124         status.setText( tttGame.result( ) );
125       } else if( id == -2 ) // NO button
126         MainActivity.this.finish( );
127     }
128   }
129 }
```

EXAMPLE 3.9 The `MainActivity` class, **TicTacToe app, Version 4**

the `Buttons` and the `TextView` to their original state. The `private` class `PlayDialog` (lines 117–128) implements `DialogInterface.OnClickListener`.

The `DialogInterface.OnClickListener` interface contains one `abstract` method, `onClick`, which we override at lines 118–127. The `onClick` method's second parameter, `id`, of type `int`, contains information about what button was clicked by the user. If it is –1, the user clicked the positive button. If it is –2, the user clicked the negative button.

At line 119, we test if the value of `id` is –1. If it is, we reset the instance variables of `tttGame` to their starting values by calling `resetGame` with `tttGame` (line 120), we enable the buttons at line 121, clear them of any text at line 122, and update the background color and text in `status` at lines 123–124. The `enableButtons` and `resetButtons` methods, coded at lines 86–90 and 92–96, enable or disable the nine buttons and reset their text content to the empty `String`, respectively. If the value of `id` is –2, we exit the activity by calling the `finish` method at line 126. Note that the expression `this.finish()` would be incorrect, because this would refer to the current `PlayDialog` object since we are inside that class. Because we want to call the `finish` method with the current object of the `MainActivity` class, we use `MainActivity.this` to access it.

> **COMMON ERROR:** Inside a `private` class, the keyword `this` refers to the current object of the `private` class, not to the current object of the `public` class that contains the `private` class. In order to access the current object of class `A` from inside its inner class `B`, do not use `this` but use `A.this` instead.

FIGURE 3.10 shows the app at the end of the game with the status reflecting that player 1 won, and asking the user to play again.

3.9 Splitting the View and the Controller: TicTacToe, Version 5

In Version 5, we split the View and the Controller. In this way, we make the View reusable. The Controller is the middleman between the View and the Model, so we keep the View independent from the Model.

In the View, in addition to the code creating the View, we also provide methods to:

▶ Update the View.
▶ Get user input from the View.

This is similar to the Model class, which provides methods to retrieve its state and update it.

In the Controller, in addition to an instance variable from the Model, we add an instance variable from the View. With it, we can call the various methods of the View to update it and get user input from it.

The array of buttons and the `TextView` status are now inside the View. Updating the View means updating the buttons and the `TextView` status. To that end, we provide the following methods:

▶ A method to set the text of a particular button

FIGURE 3.10 TicTacToe app, Version 4, running inside the emulator, showing the alert dialog box at the end of a game

▶ A method to set the text of the TextView status
▶ A method to set the background color of the TextView status
▶ A method to reset the text of all the buttons to the empty String (we need it when we start a new game)
▶ A method to enable or disable all the buttons (we also need it when we start a new game)

User input for this View is clicking on one of the buttons. Typically, event handling is performed in the Controller. Thus, we provide a method to check if a particular button was clicked.

EXAMPLE 3.10 shows the ButtonGridAndTextView class, the View for Version 5 of this app. In Version 4, our View was a GridLayout, thus, the ButtonGridAndTextView class extends GridLayout (line 10), and therefore, it "is" a GridLayout. We have three instance variables (lines 11–13):

▶ buttons, a two-dimensional array of Buttons
▶ status, a TextView
▶ side, an int, the number of rows and columns in buttons

```
1    package com.jblearning.tictactoev5;
2
3    import android.content.Context;
4    import android.graphics.Color;
5    import android.view.Gravity;
6    import android.widget.Button;
7    import android.widget.GridLayout;
8    import android.widget.TextView;
9
10   public class ButtonGridAndTextView extends GridLayout {
11     private int side;
12     private Button [][] buttons;
13     private TextView status;
14
15     public ButtonGridAndTextView( Context context, int width,
16                     int newSide, View.OnClickListener listener ) {
17       super( context );
18       side = newSide;
19       // Set # of rows and columns of this GridLayout
20       setColumnCount( side );
21       setRowCount( side + 1 );
22
23       // Create the buttons and add them to this GridLayout
24       buttons = new Button[side][side];
25       for( int row = 0; row < side; row++ ) {
26         for( int col = 0; col < side; col++ ) {
27           buttons[row][col] = new Button( context );
28           buttons[row][col].setTextSize( ( int ) ( width * .2 ) );
29           buttons[row][col].setOnClickListener( listener );
30           addView( buttons[row][col], width, width );
31         }
32       }
33
34       // set up layout parameters of 4th row of gridLayout
35       status = new TextView( context );
36       GridLayout.Spec rowSpec = GridLayout.spec( side, 1 );
37       GridLayout.Spec columnSpec = GridLayout.spec( 0, side );
38       GridLayout.LayoutParams lpStatus
39               = new GridLayout.LayoutParams( rowSpec, columnSpec );
40       status.setLayoutParams( lpStatus );
41
42       // set up status' characteristics
43       status.setWidth( side * width );
44       status.setHeight( width );
45       status.setGravity( Gravity.CENTER );
46       status.setBackgroundColor( Color.GREEN );
```

EXAMPLE 3.10 The ButtonGridAndTextView class, TicTacToe app, Version 5 (*Continued*)

```
47        status.setTextSize( ( int ) ( width / .15 ) );
48
49        addView( status );
50    }
51
52    public void setStatusText( String text ) {
53        status.setText( text );
54    }
55
56    public void setStatusBackgroundColor( int color ) {
57        status.setBackgroundColor( color );
58    }
59
60    public void setButtonText( int row, int column, String text ) {
61        buttons[row][column].setText( text );
62    }
63
64    public boolean isButton( Button b, int row, int column ) {
65        return ( b == buttons[row][column] );
66    }
67
68    public void resetButtons( ) {
69        for( int row = 0; row < side; row++ )
70            for( int col = 0; col < side; col++ )
71                buttons[row][col].setText( "" );
72    }
73
74    public void enableButtons( boolean enabled ) {
75        for( int row = 0; row < side; row++ )
76            for( int col = 0; col < side; col++ )
77                buttons[row][col].setEnabled( enabled );
78    }
79 }
```

EXAMPLE 3.10 **The `ButtonGridAndTextView` class, TicTacToe app, Version 5**

Because we want to keep the View independent from the model, we do not use the SIDE constant of the TicTacToe class to determine the number of rows and columns in buttons. Instead, the side instance variable stores that value. The constructor includes a parameter, newSide, that is assigned to side (lines 15–16 and 18). When we create the View from the Controller, we have access to the Model, thus, we will pass the SIDE constant of the TicTac-Toe class so that it is assigned to side. The ButtonGridAndTextView constructor includes three more parameters: a Context, an int, and a View.OnClickListener. The Context parameter is needed to instantiate the widgets of the View (the Buttons and the TextView).

Since the `Activity` class inherits from `Context`, an `Activity` "is a" `Context`. Thus, when we create the `ButtonGridAndTextView` from the Controller, we can pass this for the `Context` parameter. We pass that `Context` parameter to the `Button` and `TextView` constructors at lines 27 and 35. The `int` parameter represents the width of the View. By having the width as a parameter, we let the `Activity` client determine the dimensions of the View. We assign the `newSide` parameter to `side` at line 18. Finally, the `View.OnClickListener` parameter enables us to set up event handling. We want to handle events in the Controller but the `Button`s are in the View, so event handling needs to be set up in the View. We do that at line 29. The constructor code can be made more robust by testing if `newSide` and `width` are positive. This is left as an exercise.

At lines 30 and 49, we add each `Button` and the `TextView` to this `ButtonGridAndTextView`.

The `setStatusText`, `setStatusBackgroundColor`, `setButtonText`, `resetButtons`, and `enableButtons` methods provide the ability to a client of the View (the Controller) to update the View. The `isButton` method (lines 64–66) enables a client of the View (the Controller) to compare a `Button` with a `Button` from the array `buttons` identified by its row and column. From the Controller, we will call that method to identify the row and the column of the `Button` that was clicked.

EXAMPLE **3.11** shows the updated `MainActivity` class. A `ButtonGridAndTextView` instance variable, `tttView`, is declared at line 14 and instantiated at line 24. Inside `onClick` (lines 40–58), we first identify which button was clicked at line 43, and call `setButtonText` to update the View at lines 46 and 48 depending on whose turn it is to play. If the game is over (line 49), we update the View accordingly by calling the `setStatusBackgroundColor` and `setStatusText` methods at lines 50 and 52. We also disable the buttons at line 51.

```
1    package com.jblearning.tictactoev5;
2
3    import android.app.DialogInterface;
4    import android.graphics.Color;
5    import android.graphics.Point;
6    import android.os.Bundle;
7    import android.support.v7.app.AlertDialog;
8    import android.support.v7.app.AppCompatActivity;
9    import android.view.View;
10   import android.widget.Button;
11
12   public class MainActivity extends AppCompatActivity {
13       private TicTacToe tttGame;
14       private ButtonGridAndTextView tttView;
15
16       @Override
17       protected void onCreate( Bundle savedInstanceState ) {
```

EXAMPLE **3.11** The `MainActivity` class, TicTacToe app, Version 5 (*Continued*)

```
18        super.onCreate( savedInstanceState );
19        tttGame = new TicTacToe( );
20        Point size = new Point( );
21        getWindowManager().getDefaultDisplay( ).getSize( size );
22        int w = size.x / TicTacToe.SIDE;
23        ButtonHandler bh = new ButtonHandler( );
24        tttView = new ButtonGridAndTextView( this, w, TicTacToe.SIDE, bh );
25        tttView.setStatusText( tttGame.result( ) );
26        setContentView( tttView );
27      }
28
29      public void showNewGameDialog( ) {
30        AlertDialog.Builder alert = new AlertDialog.Builder( this );
31        alert.setTitle( "This is fun" );
32        alert.setMessage( "Play again?" );
33        PlayDialog playAgain = new PlayDialog( );
34        alert.setPositiveButton( "YES", playAgain );
35        alert.setNegativeButton( "NO", playAgain );
36        alert.show( );
37      }
38
39      private class ButtonHandler implements View.OnClickListener {
40        public void onClick( View v ) {
41          for( int row = 0; row < TicTacToe.SIDE; row++ ) {
42            for( int column = 0; column < TicTacToe.SIDE; column++ ) {
43              if( tttView.isButton( ( Button ) v, row, column ) ) {
44                int play = tttGame.play( row, column );
45                if( play == 1 )
46                  tttView.setButtonText( row, column, "X" );
47                else if( play == 2 )
48                  tttView.setButtonText( row, column, "O" );
49                if( tttGame.isGameOver( ) ) {
50                  tttView.setStatusBackgroundColor( Color.RED );
51                  tttView.enableButtons( false );
52                  tttView.setStatusText( tttGame.result( ) );
53                  showNewGameDialog( );    // offer to play again
54                }
55              }
56            }
57          }
58        }
59      }
60
61      private class PlayDialog implements DialogInterface.OnClickListener {
62        public void onClick( DialogInterface dialog, int id ) {
63          if( id == -1 ) /* YES button */ {
```

EXAMPLE 3.11 **The MainActivity class, TicTacToe app, Version 5 (*Continued*)**

```
64              tttGame.resetGame( );
65              tttView.enableButtons( true );
66              tttView.resetButtons( );
67              tttView.setStatusBackgroundColor( Color.GREEN );
68              tttView.setStatusText( tttGame.result( ) );
69          } else if( id == -2 ) // NO button
70              MainActivity.this.finish( );
71          }
72      }
73  }
```

EXAMPLE 3.11 **The `MainActivity` class, TicTacToe app, Version 5**

By separating the View from the Controller, we make the View reusable.

Chapter Summary

- To create a GUI, we can either use XML or do it programmatically. For some apps, the number of widgets is dynamic and we have to do it programmatically. For some other apps, although we could do it using XML, it may be more convenient to do it programmatically.
- The Android framework provides layout managers to help us organize a `View`.
- Layout managers are subclasses of `ViewGroup`.
- The `addView` method adds a child `View` to a `ViewGroup`.
- Using the methods `getWindowManager` and `getDefaultDisplay`, we can retrieve the characteristics of the display of the current device, in particular its width and height.
- We can use the screen dimensions to properly size GUI components so that the look and feel is device-independent.
- We can implement the `View.OnClickListener` interface to handle a click event on a `View`, for example a `Button`. If we do, we need to implement its `onClick` method.
- We can specify layout parameters for a `View` so that it is properly positioned when the `View` is added to its `ViewGroup` parent.
- A `GridLayout` places its children in a rectangular grid.
- A `GridLayout` offers the flexibility to span components over several rows or columns.
- We can use the `AlertDialog.Builder` class and the `DialogInterface.OnClickListener` interface to build an alert box.
- We can call the `finish` method to close an activity.

Exercises, Problems, and Projects

Multiple-Choice Exercises

1. How do we import View.OnClickListener (if we want to use code like View.
   OnClickListener listener;)?
   - Importing the View class is sufficient
   - It is automatically imported
   - We must import View.OnClickListener;
   - We must import OnClickListener;

2. What is the name of the abstract method of View.OnClickListener?
   - listen
   - click
   - onClick
   - clickListen

3. What method of the ViewGroup class do we use to add a child View to a parent View?
   - addChild
   - addView
   - moreView
   - newView

4. We are coding inside the private class Y, which is coded inside the public class X. How do
   we access the current object of the Y class?
   - this
   - X.this
   - Y.this
   - this.X

5. We are coding inside the private class Y, which is coded inside the public class X. How do
   we access the current object of the X class?
   - this
   - X.this
   - Y.this
   - this.X

6. How do we retrieve the size of the screen (assuming that size is a Point object reference)?
   - getWindowManager( ).getSize( );
   - getDefaultDisplay( ).getSize( );
   - getWindowManager( ).getDefaultDisplay( ).getSize(size);
   - getWindowManager( ).getDefaultDisplay( ).getSize( );

7. What is the data type of this in the code GridLayout gridLayout = new GridLayout(this)?
   - GridLayout
   - Context
   - Grid
   - View

8. What method of the GridLayout class do we use to set the number of rows of the grid?
   - setRows
   - setRowCount
   - setCount
   - numberOfRows

9. What method of the Activity class do we use to set the view for an activity?
   - setLayout
   - setContentView
   - setView
   - view

10. Inside an Activity class, how do we instantiate a button?
    - Button b = new Activity( );
    - Button b = new Button( );
    - Button b = new Button(this);
    - Button b = new Button(Activity);

11. What class is used by views to tell their parents how they want to be laid out?
    - Layout
    - Params
    - ViewParams
    - LayoutParams

12. What method do we use to specify the alignment of the text within a TextView?
    - setAlignment
    - center
    - setGravity
    - align

Fill in the Code

13. Assign the width of the current screen to a variable name width.

    ```
    // Your code goes here
    ```

14. This code creates a GridLayout within the current context and sets its number of rows to four and its number of columns to two.

    ```
    // Your code goes here
    ```

15. This code creates a button within the current context.

    ```
    // Your code goes here
    ```

16. This code creates a 5 × 2 two-dimensional array of buttons within the current context.

    ```
    // Your code goes here
    ```

17. This code adds a Button object named b, specifying its width and height as 200 pixels each, to an already created GridLayout object named gl.

    ```
    // Your code goes here
    ```

18. This code defines a GridLayout.LayoutParams object for the shaded area below.

    ```
    // Your code goes here
    ```

19. This code defines a `GridLayout.LayoutParams` object for the shaded area below.

    ```
    // Your code goes here
    ```

20. This code sets up an alert view for the current activity. It sets its title to HELLO and its message to HAVE FUN

```
AlertDialog.Builder alert = new AlertDialog.Builder( this );
// Your code starts here
PlayDialog pd = new PlayDialog( );
alert.setPositiveButton( "YES", pd );
alert.setNegativeButton( "NO", pd );
// And continues here so that the alert view shows
```

21. This code checks if the button that was clicked is a button named b. If it is, it outputs to Logcat YES, otherwise, it outputs to Logcat NO.

```
private class ButtonHandler implements View.OnClickListener {
  public void onClick( View v ){
    // Your code goes here


  }
}
```

Write an App

22. Write an app that displays one label and one button. Every time the user clicks on the button, the label toggles between being visible and not being visible. Do not use XML.

23. Write an app that has three labels and one button. The three labels represent a traffic light. When the app starts, only the label with the red background shows. When the user clicks on the button, only the label with the yellow background shows. When the user clicks again on the button, only the label with the green background shows. When the user clicks again on the button, only the label with the red background shows . . . and the cycle continues. Do not use XML.

24. Write an app that displays one label and one button. The label represents the current color of a traffic light and can be red, yellow, or green. When the user clicks on the button, the label cycles to the next color and simulates running the traffic light. Do not use XML.

25. Write an app that displays one label and one button. Every time the user clicks on the button, the label moves down by 10 pixels. When the label reaches the bottom of the screen, it no longer moves when the user clicks on the button. Do not use XML.

26. Write an app that displays two labels and one button. The first label should display a randomly generated integer between 50 and 100. When the user clicks on the button, the

second label moves to a position whose y-coordinate is the integer displayed in the first label. Do not use XML.

27. Write an app that has one text field, one label, and one button. The user can enter his or her email in the text field. When the user clicks on the button, the app checks if the email entered contains the @ character and a dot somewhere after the @ character. If it does, the label displays VALID, otherwise it displays INVALID in the label. The text field and the label should have their own separate style, each with a minimum of four attributes. Include a Model. Do not use XML.

28. Write an app that has one text field and one label. The user can enter his or her password. The label displays, as the user types, WEAK or STRONG. For the purpose of this app, we define a weak password as having eight or fewer characters. A strong password is defined as having nine or more characters. Include a Model. Do not use XML.

29. Write an app that displays a chessboard on a grid with black and white pieces. You can represent each piece by a letter or two, for example, P for pawn, Q for queen, R for rook, K for knight, B for bishop, and KG for king. When the user clicks on a knight, color in green the cells where the knight can move. Include a Model. Do not use XML.

30. Write an app that displays four labels and a button. The first two labels represent two cards in a simplified blackjack game and are filled with two randomly generated integers with values between 1 and 11 inclusive. The total of the two is displayed inside the fourth label. When the user clicks on the button, if the current total shown inside the fourth label is 15 or less, the third label is filled with a randomly generated number between 1 and 11 inclusive and the total inside the fourth label is updated to equal the sum of the three numbers in labels one, two, and three. If the current total shown inside the fourth label is greater than 15, nothing happens. Include a Model. Do not use XML.

CHAPTER FOUR

Multiple Activities, Passing Data between Activities, Transitions, Persistent Data

CHAPTER CONTENTS

Introduction

Most apps involve the use of several screens. In this chapter, we learn how to code several activities, how to go from one to another and back, how to share data between activities, how to set up transitions between them, and how to save the state of an app and retrieve it whenever the user starts the app again (i.e., how to make the data persistent). We build a mortgage calculator app as a vehicle to learn all these concepts.

We explore two layout managers: a `TableLayout` for the first screen and a `Relative-Layout` for the second screen. In the second screen, we explore more GUI components: radio buttons, which are used to display mutually exclusive choices.

4.1 Model: The Mortgage Class

The Model for this app is the `Mortgage` class, which encapsulates a mortgage. A typical mortgage has three parameters: the mortgage amount, the interest rate, and the number of years for the mortgage. For simplicity, we assume that the interest rate parameter is the annual rate, and is compounded monthly; we also assume that the monthly payment is constant. TABLE 4.1 shows the flow of money. M is the mortgage amount that we receive at time 0 from the bank. P is the monthly payment that we pay every month to the bank, starting at month 1, and ending at month n*12, where n is the number of years.

If r is annual interest rate, then mR = r/12 is the monthly interest rate. The present value of all the monthly payments discounted using the monthly interest rate of mR is equal to M, the mortgage amount. Thus, we have the following equation between M and P, mR, and n.

$$M = P/(1 + mR) + P/(1 + mR)^2 + P/(1 + mR)^3 + \ldots + P/(1 + mR)^{n*12} = \sum_{i=1}^{n*12} P/(1 + mR)^i$$

Let's set a = 1/(1 + mR); thus, we have:

$$M = P(\sum_{i=1}^{n*12} a^i) = P(-1 + \sum_{i=0}^{n*12} a^i) = P(-1 + (1 - a^{n*12 + 1})/(1 - a))$$

Month	0	1	2	3	4	. . .	. . .	n*12 — 1	n*12
Mortgage	M								
Payment		P	P	P	P	. . .		P	P

TABLE 4.1 Monthly cash flow for a mortgage, M, of n years with monthly payment P

$$M = P((-1 + a + 1 - a^{n*12 + 1})/(1 - a)) = P(a - a^{n*12 + 1})/(1 - a)$$
$$M = P\,a(1 - a^{n*12})/(1 - a) = P(1 - a^{n*12})\,a/(1 - a)$$

$$1 - a = 1 - 1/(1 + mR) = mR(1 + mR)$$

Therefore, $a/(1 - a) = 1/mR$

Thus, $M = P(1 - a^{n*12})/mR$; our formula for the monthly payment is:

$$P = mR * M/(1 - a^{n*12}) \text{ where } a = 1/(1+mR).$$

EXAMPLE 4.1 shows the Mortgage class, including its three instance variables, amount, years, and rate (lines 9–11), constructor (lines 13–17), mutators (lines 19–32), and accessors (lines 34–36, 42–44, and 46–48). The monthlyPayment method is at lines 50–54. We have included a DecimalFormat constant MONEY (lines 6–7) so that we can format the mortgage amount, the monthly payment, and the total payment with a dollar sign and two digits after the decimal point. The methods getFormattedAmount (lines 38–40), formattedMonthlyPayment (lines 56-58), and formattedTotalPayment (lines 64–66) return string representations of amount, the monthly payment, and the total payment respectively. The DecimalFormat class, part of the java.text package is imported at line 3. We choose not to provide a formatting method for the interest rate because we want to show its exact value in the app.

```
1    package com.jblearning.mortgagev0;
2
3    import java.text.DecimalFormat;
4
5    public class Mortgage {
6      public final DecimalFormat MONEY
7                  = new DecimalFormat( "$#,##0.00" );
8
9      private float amount;
10     private int years;
11     private float rate;
12
13     public Mortgage( ) {
14        setAmount( 100000.0f );
15        setYears( 30 );
16        setRate( 0.035f );
17     }
18
19     public void setAmount( float newAmount ) {
20        if( newAmount >= 0 )
21           amount = newAmount;
22     }
23
```

EXAMPLE 4.1 The Mortgage class (Continued)

```java
24    public void setYears( int newYears ) {
25      if( newYears >= 0 )
26        years = newYears;
27    }
28
29    public void setRate( float newRate ) {
30      if( newRate >= 0 )
31        rate = newRate;
32    }
33
34    public float getAmount( ) {
35      return amount;
36    }
37
38    public String getFormattedAmount( ) {
39      return MONEY.format( amount );
40    }
41
42    public int getYears( ) {
43      return years;
44    }
45
46    public float getRate( ) {
47      return rate;
48    }
49
50    public float monthlyPayment( ) {
51      float mRate = rate / 12;  // monthly interest rate
52      double temp = Math.pow( 1/( 1 + mRate ), years * 12 );
53      return amount * mRate / ( float ) ( 1 - temp );
54    }
55
56    public String formattedMonthlyPayment( ) {
57      return MONEY.format( monthlyPayment( ) );
58    }
59
60    public float totalPayment( ) {
61      return monthlyPayment( ) * years * 12;
62    }
63
64    public String formattedTotalPayment( ) {
65      return MONEY.format( totalPayment( ) );
66    }
67  }
```

EXAMPLE 4.1 The `Mortgage` class

4.2 Using a `TableLayout` for the Front Screen GUI: Mortgage Calculator App, Version 0

We use the empty activity template for this app. The View part of the Model-View-Controller for this app consists of two screens. The first screen displays the characteristics of a mortgage: the amount, the number of years, the interest rate, the monthly payment, and the total payments over the course of the mortgage. The user does not interact with this screen, it is read-only. We want to display all this information as a table of six rows and two columns. For each of the first five rows, the first column is a label describing the data displayed in the second column. The last row is a button that will enable the user to go to another screen to update the data for the mortgage amount, number of years, and interest rate. **FIGURE 4.1** shows a preview of Version 0 of the app inside the environment.

We use a `TableLayout` to manage the first screen of the app. A `TableLayout` arranges its children in rows and columns. It typically contains `TableRow` elements, and each of those defines a row. The row with the most columns determines the number of columns for the layout. A cell

FIGURE 4.1 Preview of the Mortgage Calculator app, Version 0

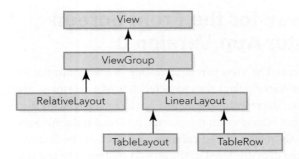

FIGURE 4.2 Inheritance hierarchy for `TableLayout` and `TableRow`

is defined as the rectangular area of a row spanning over one or more columns. We can also use a `View` or one of its subclasses instead of a `TableRow`, in which case the `View` will span the entire row. A `TableLayout` has very few XML attributes of its own, other than those inherited from its ancestor classes, such as `LinearLayout`, `ViewGroup`, and `View`. **FIGURE 4.2** shows the inheritance hierarchy.

We want to use a standard margin of 16 pixels for both our `TableLayout` and our `RelativeLayout`. Thus, we modify the dimens.xml file and create a `dimen` element named `activity_margin` with value `16dp` as shown in **EXAMPLE 4.2**.

```
1   <resources>
2       <dimen name="activity_margin">16dp</dimen>
3   </resources>
```

EXAMPLE 4.2 The dimens.xml file

EXAMPLE 4.3 shows the activity_main.xml file, using a `TableLayout` to define the GUI with six `TableRow` elements. At line 7, we specify a margin around the `TableLayout` of 16 pixels, using the `dimen` element `activity_margin` previously defined in dimens.xml. The top three rows are defined at lines 10–19, 21–30, and 32–41 and show the mortgage parameters. Each row contains two `TextView` elements; the first one is a descriptive label and the second one shows the corresponding data. For the first `TextView` element of each new `TableRow` element, we specify a padding of 10 dip (lines 15, 26, 37) to space out the GUI component in the new row from the element above and from the left edge of the screen. We assign text to all these `TextView` elements using `Strings` (at lines 14, 18, 25, 29, 36, 40) that are defined in the strings.xml file (**EXAMPLE 4.4**). We use default values $100000, 30 years, and 3.5% in strings.xml for the mortgage parameters; the corresponding monthly payment is $449.04 and the total payment over 30 years is $161654.66. Since we intend to later update by code the text inside the `TextView` elements in the second column, we give each of them an id (lines 17, 28, and 39) so that we can retrieve them using the `findViewById` method. The `findViewById` method returns a reference to the GUI component whose id is the argument of the method.

```
1   <?xml version="1.0" encoding="utf-8"?>
2   <TableLayout
3       xmlns:android="http://schemas.android.com/apk/res/android"
4       xmlns:tools="http://schemas.android.com/tools"
5       android:layout_width="match_parent"
6       android:layout_height="match_parent"
7       android:layout_margin="@dimen/activity_margin"
8       tools:context="com.jblearning.mortgagev0.MainActivity">
9
10      <TableRow
11          android:layout_width="wrap_content"
12          android:layout_height="wrap_content">
13          <TextView
14              android:text="@string/label_amount"
15              android:padding="10dip" />
16          <TextView
17              android:id="@+id/amount"
18              android:text="@string/amount" />
19      </TableRow>
20
21      <TableRow
22          android:layout_width="wrap_content"
23          android:layout_height="wrap_content">
24          <TextView
25              android:text="@string/label_years"
26              android:padding="10dip" />
27          <TextView
28              android:id="@+id/years"
29              android:text="@string/years" />
30      </TableRow>
31
32      <TableRow
33          android:layout_width="wrap_content"
34          android:layout_height="wrap_content">
35          <TextView
36              android:text="@string/label_rate"
37              android:padding="10dip" />
38          <TextView
39              android:id="@+id/rate"
40              android:text="@string/rate" />
41      </TableRow>
42
43      <!-- red line -->
44      <View
45          android:layout_height="5dip"
46          android:background="#FF0000" />
```

EXAMPLE 4.3 **The activity_main.xml file (*Continued*)**

```
47
48      <TableRow
49          android:layout_width="wrap_content"
50          android:layout_height="wrap_content">
51          <TextView
52              android:text="@string/label_monthly_payment"
53              android:padding="10dip" />
54          <TextView
55              android:id="@+id/payment"
56              android:text="@string/monthly_payment" />
57      </TableRow>
58
59      <TableRow
60          android:layout_width="wrap_content"
61          android:layout_height="wrap_content">
62          <TextView
63              android:text="@string/label_total_payment"
64              android:padding="10dip" />
65          <TextView
66              android:id="@+id/total"
67              android:text="@string/total_payment" />
68      </TableRow>
69
70      <TableRow
71          android:layout_width="wrap_content"
72          android:layout_height="wrap_content"
73          android:gravity="center"
74          android:paddingTop="50dip">
75          <Button
76              android:text="@string/modify_data"
77              android:onClick="modifyData" />
78      </TableRow>
79
80  </TableLayout>
```

EXAMPLE 4.3 The activity_main.xml file

At lines 43–46, we insert a `View` element that is 5 pixels high and red. This defines a thin red rectangle that spans the width of the screen, showing as a red line. This enables us to separate the top area of the screen displaying the mortgage parameters from the bottom area of the screen showing the calculated data (i.e., monthly payment and total payment). These are shown in the next two rows. The XML code for these two rows is similar to the code for the first three rows, using the same padding, some `String`s from strings.xml, and ids.

The last row shows a button. Since there is only one element in that row, we center the row at line 73 using the `android:gravity` attribute with value `center`. We specify 50 dip for the padding above the row (line 74) to better separate the button from the row above it. At line 77, we specify `modifyData` as the method that will be called when the user clicks on the button.

```
1   <resources>
2     <string name="app_name">MortgageV0</string>
3     <string name="label_amount">Amount</string>
4     <string name="amount">$100000.00</string>
5     <string name="label_years">Years</string>
6     <string name="years">30</string>
7     <string name="label_rate">Interest Rate</string>
8     <string name="rate">3.5%</string>
9     <string name="label_monthly_payment">Monthly Payment</string>
10    <string name="monthly_payment">$449.04</string>
11    <string name="label_total_payment">Total Payment</string>
12    <string name="total_payment">$161654.66</string>
13    <string name="modify_data">Modify Data</string>
14  </resources>
```

EXAMPLE 4.4 **The strings.xml file**

We want the font size for all elements to be larger than the default font size, thus, we specify a text size of 22sp at line 3 of the file styles.xml (**EXAMPLE 4.5**). This font size may work well for some Android devices and not as well for others, but we do not worry about this issue in this app—we cover that topic later in the book. The AppTheme style, at line 2, is the default style specified in the AndroidManifest.xml file as the theme for the app.

```
1   <resources>
2       <style name="AppTheme" parent="Theme.AppCompat.Light.DarkActionBar">
3           <item name="android:textSize">22sp</item>
4           <item name="colorPrimary">@color/colorPrimary</item>
5           <item name="colorPrimaryDark">@color/colorPrimaryDark</item>
6           <item name="colorAccent">@color/colorAccent</item>
7       </style>
8   </resources>
```

EXAMPLE 4.5 **The styles.xml file**

In order to keep this app simple, we only allow the app to run in vertical orientation. Thus, inside the AndroidManifest.xml file, we add an android:screenOrientation attribute to the activity element and set its value to portrait.

4.3 Using a `RelativeLayout` for the Second Screen GUI

The second component of the View part of the app is the second screen. It enables the user to change the three mortgage parameters: the amount, the number of years, and the interest rate. We use this opportunity to explore radio buttons, which we use to select the number of years for the mortgage.

When we first create a project, it automatically creates an `Activity` class and the XML file (whose default names are `MainActivity` and activity_main.xml) for its GUI. Since we are adding a second screen to the app, we add another XML file, activity_data.xml, to define its GUI, and another `Activity` class, `DataActivity`, to control it. Be sure to create the activity_data.xml file in the res/layout directory, and do not use uppercase letters in the file name. If we need to separate nouns in our file names, we use an underscore character.

> **COMMON ERROR:** We should not use upper case letters in our XML file names. Android Studio does not allow them. File names for resources must start with a lowercase letter and only contain lowercase letters, digits, and underscores.

For the GUI of this second screen, we use the `RelativeLayout` class, a subclass of `View-Group`, as shown in Figure 4.2. It enables us to position components relative to other components.

The `RelativeLayout` class has a `public static` inner class named `LayoutParams` (we refer to it using `RelativeLayout.LayoutParams`) that contains many XML attributes that specifically relate to arranging elements relative to each other. These attributes enable us to position a `View` relative to another `View` on the screen. In order to reference another `View`, we can give that `View` an id and use that id to reference it. We can also position a `View` with respect to its parent `View`, in which case we do not need to reference the parent `View` with its id. Some of these attributes are listed in **TABLE 4.2**. The first eight attributes listed (`android:layout_alignLeft`, to `android:layout_toRightOf`) expect their value to be the id of a `View`.

For example, at line 15 of **EXAMPLE 4.6**, we use the code:

```
android:layout_toRightOf="@+id/label_years"
```

in order to specify that the radio buttons group is positioned to the right of the `View` whose id is `label_years`. That `View`, a `TextView`, is defined at lines 8–12, and its id is specified at line 9.

At line 18, we use the code

```
android:layout_alignLeft="@+id/data_rate"
```

to further define the position of the radio buttons group. This specifies that it is left-aligned with the `View` whose id is `data_rate`. That `View`, an `EditText`, is defined at lines 67–76, and its id is defined at line 68.

Thus, when we use a `RelativeLayout`, we typically assign ids to a lot of `View` elements for the purpose of referring to them when we define the position of other `View` elements relative to them.

We can use the last four attributes listed in Table 4.2 to position a `View` relative to its parent `View`. The attributes `android:layout_alignParentLeft` and `android:layout_align-ParentRight` relate to vertical alignment, while `android:layout_alignParentBottom` and `android:layout_alignParentTop` relate to horizontal alignment.

TABLE 4.2 Useful XML attributes of RelativeLayout.LayoutParams

XML attribute	Description
android:layout_alignLeft	View's left edge matches the value of the view's left edge.
android:layout_alignRight	View's right edge matches the value of the view's right edge.
android:layout_alignBottom	View's bottom edge matches the value of the view's bottom edge.
android:layout_alignTop	View's top edge matches the value of the view's top edge.
android:layout_above	View goes above the value view.
android:layout_below	View goes below the value view.
android:layout_toLeftOf	View goes left of the value view.
android:layout_toRightOf	View goes right of the value view.
android:layout_alignParentLeft	If true, view's left edge matches its parent's left edge.
android:layout_alignParentRight	If true, view's right edge matches its parent's right edge.
android:layout_alignParentBottom	If true, view's bottom edge matches its parent's bottom edge.
android:layout_alignParentTop	If true, view's top edge matches its parent's top edge.

```
1    <?xml version="1.0" encoding="utf-8"?>
2    <RelativeLayout xmlns:android="http://schemas.android.com/apk/res/android"
3      android:layout_width="match_parent"
4      android:layout_height="match_parent"
5      android:orientation="vertical"
6      android:layout_margin="@dimen/activity_margin">
7
8      <TextView
9        android:id="@+id/label_years"
10       android:layout_width="wrap_content"
11       android:layout_height="wrap_content"
12       android:text="@string/label_years"/>
13
14     <RadioGroup
15       android:layout_toRightOf="@+id/label_years"
16       android:layout_width="match_parent"
17       android:layout_height="wrap_content"
```

EXAMPLE 4.6 The activity_data.xml file (*Continued*)

```
18          android:layout_alignLeft="@+id/data_rate"
19          android:orientation="horizontal">
20
21        <RadioButton
22          android:layout_width="wrap_content"
23          android:layout_height="wrap_content"
24          android:id="@+id/ten"
25          android:text="@string/ten" />
26        <RadioButton
27          android:layout_width="wrap_content"
28          android:layout_height="wrap_content"
29          android:id="@+id/fifteen"
30          android:text="@string/fifteen" />
31        <RadioButton
32          android:layout_width="wrap_content"
33          android:layout_height="wrap_content"
34          android:id="@+id/thirty"
35          android:checked="true"
36          android:text="@string/thirty" />
37
38      </RadioGroup>
39
40      <TextView
41        android:id="@+id/label_amount"
42        android:layout_width="wrap_content"
43        android:layout_height="wrap_content"
44        android:layout_below="@+id/label_years"
45        android:layout_marginTop="50dp"
46        android:text="@string/label_amount" />
47
48      <EditText
49        android:id="@+id/data_amount"
50        android:layout_width="wrap_content"
51        android:layout_height="wrap_content"
52        android:layout_alignBottom="@+id/label_amount"
53        android:layout_alignLeft="@+id/data_rate"
54        android:layout_alignParentRight="true"
55        android:layout_toRightOf="@+id/label_amount"
56        android:text="@string/amountDecimal"
57        android:inputType="numberDecimal" />
58
59      <TextView
60        android:id="@+id/label_rate"
61        android:layout_width="wrap_content"
62        android:layout_height="wrap_content"
63        android:layout_marginTop="50dp"
```

EXAMPLE 4.6 The activity_data.xml file (*Continued*)

```
64          android:layout_below="@+id/label_amount"
65          android:text="@string/label_rate" />
66
67      <EditText
68          android:id="@+id/data_rate"
69          android:layout_width="wrap_content"
70          android:layout_height="wrap_content"
71          android:layout_alignBottom="@+id/label_rate"
72          android:layout_alignParentRight="true"
73          android:layout_toRightOf="@+id/label_rate"
74          android:layout_marginLeft="10dp"
75          android:text="@string/rateDecimal"
76          android:inputType="numberDecimal" />
77
78      <Button
79          android:layout_width="wrap_content"
80          android:layout_height="wrap_content"
81          android:layout_centerHorizontal="true"
82          android:layout_below="@+id/data_rate"
83          android:layout_marginTop="50dp"
84          android:onClick="goBack"
85          android:text="@string/done" />
86
87  </RelativeLayout>
```

EXAMPLE 4.6 The activity_data.xml file

At line 54, we use the code

```
android:layout_alignParentRight="true"
```

to specify that the `EditText` should be right aligned with its parent, the `RelativeLayout`, which is a `View`, and in this case encompasses the whole screen; so that means that the `EditText`'s right edge should be vertically aligned with the right edge of the screen.

At line 81, we center the button element horizontally. At line 82, we specify that it should be positioned below the `View` whose id is `data_rate` and that it should be 50dp below it (line 83). We also specify that the method `goBack` will execute when the user clicks on the button (line 84).

We specify both `EditText`'s `android:inputType` attribute to be `numberDecimal` (lines 57 and 76). In this way, the user can only enter digits and a maximum of one . (dot) character.

EXAMPLE 4.7 shows the updated strings.xml, with some `String` variables added at lines 16–21. The strings are used in the activity_data.xml file at lines 25, 30, 36, 56, 75, and 85 (Example 4.6).

At this point, when we run the app, we can only see the first screen, because we have no way to go to the second screen, yet. However, we can temporarily modify the statement in MainActivity.java that sets the resource to be used for the first screen in MainActivity.java and show the second screen instead. We show that at lines 11–12 of **EXAMPLE 4.8**.

```
1    <?xml version="1.0" encoding="utf-8"?>
2      <resources>
3      <string name="app_name">MortgageV0</string>
4      <string name="label_amount">Amount</string>
5      <string name="amount">$100000.00</string>
6      <string name="label_years">Years</string>
7      <string name="years">30</string>
8      <string name="label_rate">Interest Rate</string>
9      <string name="rate">3.5%</string>
10     <string name="label_monthly_payment">Monthly Payment</string>
11     <string name="monthly_payment">$449.04</string>
12     <string name="label_total_payment">Total Payment</string>
13     <string name="total_payment">$161654.66</string>
14     <string name="modify_data">Modify Data</string>
15
16     <string name="ten">10</string>
17     <string name="fifteen">15</string>
18     <string name="thirty">30</string>
19     <string name="amountDecimal">100000.00</string>
20     <string name="rateDecimal">.035</string>
21     <string name="done">Done</string>
22   </resources>
```

EXAMPLE 4.7 **The updated strings.xml file**

```
7
8        @Override
9        protected void onCreate( Bundle savedInstanceState ) {
10         super.onCreate( savedInstanceState );
11         // setContentView( R.layout.activity_main );
12         setContentView( R.layout.activity_data );
13       }
14     }
```

EXAMPLE 4.8 **Edits in the `MainActivity` class, replacing activity_main with activity_data**

FIGURE 4.3 shows what the second screen looks like inside the environment.

4.4 Connecting Two Activities: Mortgage Calculator App, Version 1

We have now defined and coded the Model and the View part of the app, for which we have two XML files defining two Views. Next, we code the Controller part of the app. We want to be able to

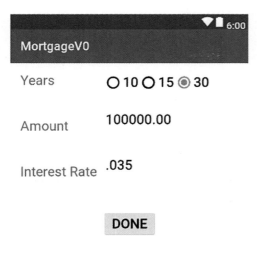

FIGURE 4.3 Preview of the second screen of our Mortgage Calculator app, Version 0

navigate back and forth between the two Views that we have created. For this, we need to complete the following steps:

▶ Add some code in the first Activity class so that we can go to the second View via some user interaction, in this case when the user clicks on the Modify Data button.

▶ Add a new class, DataActivity, which extends Activity, to manage the second View. Include the code so that we can dismiss that activity and go back to the first View when the user clicks on the Done button.

▶ Add another activity element (for the second activity) in the AndroidManifest.xml file.

The Intent and Activity classes provide the functionality to start a new activity and go back to a previous activity. The Intent class encapsulates the concept of an operation to be performed. It is typically used to launch a new activity, and can also be used to launch a service.

TABLE 4.3 shows one of the Intent constructors. It accepts two parameters: context, a Context parameter, and cls, a Class parameter. Cls represents the type of class that this Intent intends to execute. In this case, it is an argument whose type should be Class. Context represents the context of this application package. The Activity class is a subclass of Context,

TABLE 4.3 Constructor of the `Intent` class

`Intent` **Constructor**
Intent(Context context, Class <?> cls)   Constructs an `Intent` that is intended to execute a class modeled by type ? (probably some `Activity` class) that is in the same application package as `context`

TABLE 4.4 Methods of the `Activity` class

`Activity` **Class Methods**
public void startActivity(Intent intent)   Launches a new activity using `intent` as the `Intent` to start it.
public void finish( )   Closes this activity and pops it off the stack; the screen for the prior activity is shown.

thus, an `Activity` object "is a" `Context` object. Typically, if we are already executing an activity from the current application package, the current `Activity` object, represented by the keyword `this`, is therefore a `Context` object as well, and is used as the first argument of this constructor.

TABLE 4.4 shows the `startActivity` and `finish` methods of the `Activity` class. `StartActivity` is typically called by the current `Activity` object reference to execute its `Intent` argument.

EXAMPLE 4.9 shows the `MainActivity` class, including the `modifyData` method at lines 16–19, which tells the app to go to a `DataActivity`. In order to do that, we do two things:

▶ Create an `Intent` to go to a `DataActivity`
▶ Execute that `Intent` and start that `DataActivity`

The `Intent` class belongs to the `android.content` package. We import it at line 3. At line 17, we instantiate `myIntent`, passing `this` and `DataActivity.class` (whose type is `Class`) to the `Intent` constructor. At line 18, we call `startActivity` with `myIntent`, and thus start a new activity of type `DataActivity`.

To create a second activity, we create a new class, named `DataActivity`, which extends `AppCompatActivity`. **EXAMPLE 4.10** shows the `DataActivity` class. It has a similar `onCreate` method to the one in the `MainActivity` class, using the resource `activity_data` instead of `activity_main` at line 11. The method `goBack`, called when the user clicks on the Done button, is coded at lines 14–16. In this version, it just calls the `finish` method, which dismisses this activity, returning the app to the View associated with the main activity. At this point, the `DataActivity` class only enables the user to display its associated View and to go back to the first View by clicking on the Done button.

```
1    package com.jblearning.mortgagev1;
2
3    import android.content.Intent;
4    import android.os.Bundle;
5    import android.support.v7.app.AppCompatActivity;
6    import android.view.View;
7
8    public class MainActivity extends AppCompatActivity {
9
10     @Override
11     protected void onCreate( Bundle savedInstanceState ) {
12       super.onCreate( savedInstanceState );
13       setContentView( R.layout.activity_main );
14     }
15
16     public void modifyData( View v ) {
17       Intent myIntent = new Intent( this, DataActivity.class );
18       this.startActivity( myIntent );
19     }
20   }
```

EXAMPLE 4.9 **The `MainActivity` class of the Mortgage Calculator app, Version 1**

```
1    package com.jblearning.mortgagev1;
2
3    import android.os.Bundle;
4    import android.support.v7.app.AppCompatActivity;
5    import android.view.View;
6
7    public class DataActivity extends AppCompatActivity {
8
9      public void onCreate( Bundle savedInstanceState ) {
10       super.onCreate( savedInstanceState );
11       setContentView( R.layout.activity_data );
12     }
13
14     public void goBack( View v ) {
15       this.finish( );
16     }
17   }
```

EXAMPLE 4.10 **The `DataActivity` class of the Mortgage Calculator app, Version 1**

When we add an activity to an app, we need to add a corresponding activity element to the AndroidManifest.xml file. **EXAMPLE 4.11** shows the updated file. We specify the second activity element at lines 20–23.

```
1    <?xml version="1.0" encoding="utf-8"?>
2    <manifest xmlns:android="http://schemas.android.com/apk/res/android"
3      package="com.jblearning.mortgagev1">
4
5      <application
6        android:allowBackup="true"
7        android:icon="@mipmap/ic_launcher"
8        android:label="@string/app_name"
9        android:supportsRtl="true"
10       android:theme="@style/AppTheme">
11       <activity android:name=".MainActivity"
12         android:screenOrientation="portrait">
13         <intent-filter>
14           <action android:name="android.intent.action.MAIN" />
15
16           <category android:name="android.intent.category.LAUNCHER" />
17         </intent-filter>
18       </activity>
19
20       <activity
21         android:name=".DataActivity"
22         android:screenOrientation="portrait">
23       </activity>
24
25     </application>
26
27   </manifest>
```

EXAMPLE 4.11 **The AndroidManifest.xml file**

The `activity` tag has many possible attributes. An important one is `android:name`: it specifies the name of the corresponding `Activity` class. The syntax is:

```
android:name="ActivityClassName"
```

The value must be specified (there is no default value) and can be a fully qualified class name such as `com.jblearning.mortgagev1.MainActivity`. If the value starts with a. (dot) as at lines 11 and 21 (`.MainActivity` and `.DataActivity`), then the value is appended to the package name listed as the `package` attribute value of the `manifest` element (lines 2–3).

COMMON ERROR: We need to add an `activity` element in the AndroidManifest.xml file whenever we add an activity to our app. Otherwise, the app will crash when we try to go to that activity.

We can now run the app and go back and forth between the first and second Views (Figures 4.1 and 4.3). We can also edit the mortgage amount, interest rate, and number of years in the second screen. However, the values in the first View are unchanged at this point. This will change in Version 2.

4.5 The Life Cycle of an Activity

An activity goes through a life cycle, and methods are called automatically as an activity is started, paused, stopped, or closed. TABLE 4.5 lists these methods.

To illustrate which methods are called and when as the user runs the app, we include all the methods of Table 4.5 in our `MainActivity` and `DataActivity` classes. Each method calls its `super` method and outputs something to Logcat. **EXAMPLE 4.12** and **EXAMPLE 4.13** show the two classes. Note that if we do not call the `super` methods, the app will crash.

For convenience, we add a constant in each class (lines 10 and 9, respectively) that we use in each of the Log statements. These two constants have the same value, `MainActivity`, the name of the filter. We could have added a second filter for the `DataActivity` class, however, in this case, we want to check the order of execution of the activity life cycle methods from both activities. So it is convenient to click on only one filter and see all the outputs at once and in the correct sequence.

> **COMMON ERROR:** When overriding a method of the activity life cycle, if we do not call the corresponding `super` method, the app will crash.

TABLE 4.5 Life cycle methods of the `Activity` class

Method	Description
onCreate(Bundle)	Called when the activity is created; the Bundle argument stores the activity's previously frozen state, if there is one.
onStart()	Called after onCreate, when the activity becomes visible.
onResume()	Called after onStart, when the user starts interacting with the activity.
onPause()	Called when android starts or resumes another activity.
onStop()	Called when the activity becomes invisible to the user.
onRestart()	Called when the activity is about to restart.
onDestroy()	Called when the activity has ended or is being destroyed by the system because the system is running out of memory and needs to free some memory.

```
1    package com.jblearning.mortgagev1lifecycle;
2
3    import android.content.Intent;
4    import android.os.Bundle;
5    import android.support.v7.app.AppCompatActivity;
6    import android.util.Log;
7    import android.view.View;
8
9    public class MainActivity extends AppCompatActivity {
10     public static final String MA = "MainActivity";
11
12     protected void onCreate( Bundle savedInstanceState ) {
13       super.onCreate( savedInstanceState );
14       Log.w( MA, "Inside MainActivity:onCreate\n" );
15       setContentView( R.layout.activity_main );
16     }
17
18     public void modifyData( View v ) {
19       Intent myIntent = new Intent( this, DataActivity.class );
20       this.startActivity( myIntent );
21     }
22
23     protected void onStart( ) {
24       super.onStart( );
25       Log.w( MA, "Inside MainActivity:onStart\n" );
26     }
27
28     protected void onRestart( ) {
29       super.onRestart( );
30       Log.w( MA, "Inside MainActivity:onReStart\n" );
31     }
32
33     protected void onResume( ) {
34       super.onResume( );
35       Log.w( MA, "Inside MainActivity:onResume\n" );
36     }
37
38     protected void onPause( ) {
39       super.onPause( );
40       Log.w( MA, "Inside MainActivity:onPause\n" );
41     }
42
43     protected void onStop( ) {
44       super.onStop( );
45       Log.w( MA, "Inside MainActivity:onStop\n" );
46     }
```

EXAMPLE 4.12 **The `MainActivity` class with its life cycle methods (*Continued*)**

```
47
48     protected void onDestroy( ) {
49       super.onDestroy( );
50       Log.w( MA, "Inside MainActivity:onDestroy\n" );
51     }
52   }
```

EXAMPLE 4.12 The `MainActivity` class with its life cycle methods

```
1    package com.jblearning.mortgagev1lifecycle;
2
3    import android.os.Bundle;
4    import android.support.v7.app.AppCompatActivity;
5    import android.util.Log;
6    import android.view.View;
7
8    public class DataActivity extends AppCompatActivity {
9      public staticfinal String DA = "MainActivity";
10
11     public void onCreate( Bundle savedInstanceState ) {
12       super.onCreate( savedInstanceState );
13       Log.w( DA, "Inside DataActivity:onCreate\n" );
14       setContentView( R.layout.activity_data );
15     }
16
17     public void goBack( View v ) {
18       this.finish( );
19     }
20
21     protected void onStart( ) {
22       super.onStart( );
23       Log.w( DA, "Inside DataActivity:onStart\n" );
24     }
25
26     protected void onRestart( ) {
27       super.onRestart( );
28       Log.w( DA, "Inside DataActivity:onReStart\n" );
29     }
30
31     protected void onResume( ) {
32       super.onResume( );
33       Log.w( DA, "Inside DataActivity:onResume\n" );
34     }
35
```

EXAMPLE 4.13 The `DataActivity` class with its life cycle methods (*Continued*)

```
36      protected void onPause( ) {
37        super.onPause( );
38        Log.w( DA, "Inside DataActivity:onPause\n" );
39      }
40
41      protected void onStop( ) {
42        super.onStop( );
43        Log.w( DA, "Inside DataActivity:onStop\n" );
44      }
45
46      protected void onDestroy( ) {
47        super.onDestroy( );
48        Log.w( DA, "Inside DataActivity:onDestroy\n" );
49      }
50    }
```

EXAMPLE 4.13 **The `DataActivity` class with its life cycle methods**

An activity remains in memory until it is destroyed, at which time the `onDestroy` method is called. Activities are organized on a stack—whenever a new activity is started, it goes to the top of the stack. When an activity is destroyed, it is popped off the stack.

TABLE 4.6 shows the state of the output and the activity stack as the user starts the app and interacts with the app on the device.

When the app starts, the `onCreate`, `onStart`, and `onResume` methods of `MainActivity`, the starting activity, are called in that order. When the user touches the Modify Data button, the `onPause` method of `MainActivity` is called, then the `onCreate`, `onStart`, and `onResume` methods of the `DataActivity` class are called, and then the `onStop` method of `MainActivity` is called. The `onDestroy` method of the `MainActivity` class is not called, because the instance of `MainActivity` is still in memory and at the bottom of the activity stack. The instance of `Data-Activity` is now at the top of the stack. When the user touches the Done button, the `onPause` method of `DataActivity` is called, then the `onRestart`, `onStart`, and `onResume` methods of `MainActivity` are called, and then the `onStop` and `onDestroy` methods of `DataActivity` are called. The call to `onDestroy` shows that the `DataActivity` instance, previously at the top of the stack, is popped off the stack and is no longer in memory. The call to the `onRestart` method of `MainActivity` shows that the `MainActivity` instance, now at the top of the stack (the only one on the stack at this point), is restarted. Note that the `onCreate` method is not called because the `MainActivity` instance was created before and is still in memory.

At that point, if the user just waits and stops interacting with the app, the app goes to the background and is no longer visible; the `onPause` and `onStop` methods of `MainActivity`, the current activity, are called. Then, when the user touches the Power button and swipes the screen, the `onRestart`, `onStart`, and `onResume` methods of `MainActivity` are called as the current activity of the app comes to the foreground.

TABLE 4.6 Output and state of Activity stack as the user interacts with the app		
Action	**Output**	**Activity Stack**
User starts app	Inside MainActivity:onCreate Inside MainActivity:onStart Inside MainActivity:onResume	Main activity
User touches the Modify Data button	Inside MainActivity:onPause Inside DataActivity:onCreate Inside DataActivity:onStart Inside DataActivity:onResume Inside MainActivity:onStop	Data activity Main activity
User touches the Done button	Inside DataActivity:onPause Inside MainActivity:onRestart Inside MainActivity:onStart Inside MainActivity:onResume Inside DataActivity:onStop Inside DataActivity:onDestroy	Main activity
User waits a while, app goes to the background, is no longer visible	Inside MainActivity:onPause Inside MainActivity:onStop	Main activity
User touches the device's Power button, then swipes the screen	Inside MainActivity:onRestart Inside MainActivity:onStart Inside MainActivity:onResume	Main activity
User hits the device's Home Key button	MainActivity:onPause MainActivity:onStop	Main activity
User touches the app icon	Inside MainActivity:onRestart Inside MainActivity:onStart Inside MainActivity:onResume	Main activity
User touches the device's Back Key button	Inside MainActivity:onPause Inside MainActivity:onStop Inside MainActivity:onDestroy	

Then, if the user touches the Home button, `onPause` and `onStop` are called. When the user touches the app icon on the screen, the app restarts, thus, `onRestart`, `onStart`, and `onResume` are called again.

Finally, if the user touches the Back Key button, `onPause`, `onStop,` and `onDestroy` are called and we exit the current activity. The activity stack is now empty and we exit the app.

SOFTWARE ENGINEERING TIP: If the app is dealing with persistent data, it is a good idea to provide code to save the current data in the `onPause` method.

4.6 Sharing Data between Activities: Mortgage Calculator App, Version 2

In Version 2, we add functionality to the Controller in order to have a fully functional app. For this, we need to be able to pass the values input by the user in the second View to the activity managing the first View so that we can compute the monthly and total payments and display them. When we go back to the second View to edit the values again, we need to retrieve and show the most recent values, not the default values.

There are several ways that we can pass data from one activity to another, including:

▶ Pass data using the `putExtra` methods of the `Intent` class. Data must be either primitive data types or `Strings`.

▶ Declare a `public static` instance of a class of the Model (in this app, the `Mortgage` class) in one `Activity` class. That makes that instance globally accessible by any other `Activity` class.

▶ Rewrite the `Mortgage` class as a "singleton" class so that all the `Activity` classes can access and share the same object.

▶ Write data to a file and read it from that file.

▶ Write data to a SQLite database and read it from it.

In this app, we want to share a `Mortgage` object between the two screens, rather than sharing primitive data types or `Strings`. Thus, we will not use the `putExtra` methods of `Intent`. Later in the book, we show how to use the `putExtra` methods. Writing data to a file or a SQLite database is an overkill if we only want to pass data between two activities.

A singleton class is a class from which only one object can be instantiated. We can declare several object references of that class, but after instantiation, they will all point to the same object in memory. Thus, activities can share that same object, reading data from it and writing data to it. We could recode the `Mortgage` class so that it is a singleton class, but if we write other apps, we may want to be able to instantiate more than one `Mortgage` object. Thus, we decide not to implement the `Mortgage` class as a singleton.

We implement the second strategy, the most simple for this app. We declare a `public static` variable of type `Mortgage` in the `MainActivity` class and we access it from the `DataActivity` class. In `MainActivity`, we have the following declaration:

```
public static Mortgage mortgage;
```

We can access it inside the `DataActivity` class using the expression:

```
MainActivity.mortgage
```

In this way, the same `Mortgage` object can be referenced from both `Activity` classes. This is what we want for this app, only one `Mortgage` object rather than two identical `Mortgage` objects.

EXAMPLE 4.14 shows the updated `MainActivity` class. We declare the `Mortgage` variable `mortgage` as `public` and `static` at line 10. It is instantiated at line 14 inside the `onCreate` method.

The `onStart` method (lines 18–21) is called automatically when we start the app, when we come back from the data activity, or when we bring back the main activity to the foreground after

```
1   package com.jblearning.mortgagev2;
2
3   import android.content.Intent;
4   import android.os.Bundle;
5   import android.support.v7.app.AppCompatActivity;
6   import android.view.View;
7   import android.widget.TextView;
8
9   public class MainActivity extends AppCompatActivity {
10    public static Mortgage mortgage;
11
12    protected void onCreate( Bundle savedInstanceState ) {
13      super.onCreate( savedInstanceState );
14      mortgage = new Mortgage( );
15      setContentView( R.layout.activity_main );
16    }
17
18    public void onStart( ) {
19      super.onStart( );
20      updateView( );
21    }
22
23    public void updateView( ) {
24      TextView amountTV = ( TextView ) findViewById( R.id.amount );
25      amountTV.setText( mortgage.getFormattedAmount( ) );
26      TextView yearsTV = ( TextView ) findViewById( R.id.years );
27      yearsTV.setText( "" + mortgage.getYears( ) );
28      TextView rateTV = ( TextView ) findViewById( R.id.rate );
29      rateTV.setText( 100 * mortgage.getRate( ) + "%" );
30      TextView monthlyTV = ( TextView ) findViewById( R.id.payment );
31      monthlyTV.setText( mortgage.formattedMonthlyPayment( ) );
32      TextView totalTV = ( TextView ) findViewById( R.id.total );
33      totalTV.setText( mortgage.formattedTotalPayment( ) );
34    }
35
36    public void modifyData( View v ) {
37      Intent myIntent = new Intent( this, DataActivity.class );
38      this.startActivity( myIntent );
39    }
40  }
```

EXAMPLE 4.14 **The `MainActivity` class, Mortgage Calculator app, Version 2**

it went to the background. We want the data to be updated every time those events happen, so we call the updateView method at line 20. The updateView method, coded at lines 23–34, updates the five TextView elements with current mortgage data. We retrieve each TextView element using the findViewById method and typecast the returned View to a TextView. Then we call methods from the Mortgage class with the mortgage object in order to set the text of each TextView element with current mortgage data. For example, at line 31, we set the text inside the TextView displaying the monthly payment. We call the formattedMonthlyPayment method of the Mortgage class with the mortgage object in order to retrieve the monthly payment value. We then call the setText method with monthlyTV and pass that value.

EXAMPLE 4.15 shows the updated DataActivity class. It adds two functionalities:

▶ It updates the mortgage parameters displayed in the View controlled by this Activity.
▶ It updates the mortgage object of the MainActivity class when the user leaves this activity.

The updateView method (lines 16–30) updates the various elements of the View controlled by this Activity based on the values of the three instance variables of the static variable mortgage of the MainActivity class. It first gets a reference to the mortgage object of the MainActivity class at line 17. It then updates the states of the radio buttons at lines 18–24 based on the value of the years instance variable of mortgage. If that value is 10 (line 18), we turn on the 10 years radio button (line 20). If that value is 15 (line 21), we turn on the 15 years radio button (line 23).Otherwise, we do nothing, because the 30 years radio button's state is specified as on in the activity_data.xml file. Since the three radio buttons are defined in the activity_data file as part of a RadioGroup element, they are mutually exclusive—turning one on automatically turns the others off. We use the findViewById method to retrieve the radio buttons. The EditText element displaying the mortgage amount is updated at line 27, and the EditText element displaying the interest rate is updated at line 29.

```
1    package com.jblearning.mortgagev2;
2
3    import android.os.Bundle;
4    import android.support.v7.app.AppCompatActivity;
5    import android.view.View;
6    import android.widget.EditText;
7    import android.widget.RadioButton;
8
9    public class DataActivity extends AppCompatActivity {
10     public void onCreate( Bundle savedInstanceState ) {
11       super.onCreate( savedInstanceState );
12       setContentView( R.layout.activity_data );
13       updateView( );
14     }
15
```

EXAMPLE 4.15 **The DataActivity class of the Mortgage Calculator app, Version 2 (***Continued***)**

```
16     public void updateView( ) {
17       Mortgage mortgage = MainActivity.mortgage;
18       if( mortgage.getYears( ) == 10 ) {
19         RadioButton rb10 = ( RadioButton ) findViewById( R.id.ten );
20         rb10.setChecked( true );
21       } else if( mortgage.getYears( ) == 15 ) {
22         RadioButton rb15 = ( RadioButton ) findViewById( R.id.fifteen );
23         rb15.setChecked( true );
24       } // else do nothing (default is 30)
25
26       EditText amountET = ( EditText ) findViewById( R.id.data_amount );
27       amountET.setText( "" + mortgage.getAmount( ) );
28       EditText rateET = ( EditText ) findViewById( R.id.data_rate );
29       rateET.setText( "" + mortgage.getRate( ) );
30     }
31
32     public void updateMortgageObject( ) {
33       Mortgage mortgage = MainActivity.mortgage;
34       RadioButton rb10 = ( RadioButton ) findViewById( R.id.ten );
35       RadioButton rb15 = ( RadioButton ) findViewById( R.id.fifteen );
36       int years = 30;
37       if( rb10.isChecked( ) )
38         years = 10;
39       else if( rb15.isChecked( ) )
40         years = 15;
41       mortgage.setYears( years );
42       EditText amountET = ( EditText ) findViewById( R.id.data_amount );
43       String amountString = amountET.getText( ).toString( );
44       EditText rateET = ( EditText ) findViewById( R.id.data_rate );
45       String rateString = rateET.getText( ).toString( );
46       try {
47         float amount = Float.parseFloat( amountString );
48         mortgage.setAmount( amount );
49         float rate = Float.parseFloat( rateString );
50         mortgage.setRate( rate );
51       } catch( NumberFormatException nfe ) {
52         mortgage.setAmount( 100000.0f );
53         mortgage.setRate( .035f );
54       }
55     }
56
57     public void goBack( View v ) {
58       updateMortgageObject( );
59       this.finish( );
60     }
61   }
```

EXAMPLE 4.15 **The DataActivity class of the Mortgage Calculator app, Version 2**

The goBack method (lines 57–60), executes when the user clicks on the Done button. Before the user leaves this activity (line 59) and returns to the main activity, we want to update the state of the mortgage object based on the values the user inputs. We call the method updateMortgageObject at line 58. As in the updateView method, the first thing we do inside the updateMortgageObject method (lines 32–55) is get a reference to the mortgage object. Then, we update the values of its instance variables amount, years, and rate. At lines 34–41, we update years based on the current state of the three radio buttons. We call the method isChecked, inherited by RadioButton from CompoundButton, to check if a radio button is on or off. At line 42, we get a reference to the EditText element displaying the mortgage amount and retrieve its text value and assign it to the String variable amountString at line 43. We do the same for the interest rate value and assign the value retrieved to the String variable rateString at line 45. Because the amount and rate instance variable of the mortgage object are floats, we need to convert the two Strings to floats. In the activity_data.xml file, we specified numberDecimal for the android:inputType attribute associated with the two EditTexts; therefore, we are guaranteed to get Strings that look like floats. However, we still take the extra precaution of using try and catch blocks when converting the two Strings to floats at lines 46–54. We use default values for amount and rate in the catch block.

FIGURE 4.4 and FIGURE 4.5 show the two screens after the user has updated the mortgage parameters on the second screen.

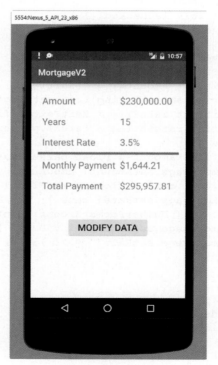

FIGURE 4.4 The Mortgage Calculator app running inside the emulator, Version 2 (second screen)

FIGURE 4.5 The Mortgage Calculator app running inside the emulator, Version 2 (first screen after coming back from the second screen)

4.7 Transitions between Activities: Mortgage Calculator App, Version 3

We want to improve Version 2 by adding animated transitions between the two screens.

A transition is typically an animation special effect when going from one screen to another: for example, we can fade out of the current screen into the new one, or fade in to present the new screen, or bring a screen with a sliding motion from left to right (or right to left). Two types of animations can be used: **tween animation** and **frame animation**. A tween animation is defined with its starting and ending points, and intermediary frames are automatically generated. A frame animation is defined by using a sequence of various images from the beginning to the end of the animation.

In Version 3, we make a tween animation that slides from left to right to go from the first to the second screen, and a combination of fade in and scaling transitions to come back from the second screen to the first one. Like a layout, a `String`, or a style, a transition can be defined as a resource defined in an XML file. It can also be defined programmatically.

> **COMMON ERROR:** The Android framework has rigid rules for naming resource directories and resource files. Transition resources must be placed in the anim directory of the res directory.

When looking for resources, the Android framework looks inside the res directory. We create a directory named anim in the res directory, and add two XML files, `slide_from_left.xml` and `fade_in_and_scale.xml` in it. **FIGURE 4.6** shows the directory structure. R represents the res directory, and we access these two resources using the expressions `R.anim.fade_in_and_scale` and `R.anim.slide_from_left`. The Android framework automatically creates `fade_in_and_scale` and `slide_from_left` as `public static int` constants in the anim class, itself a `public static` inner class of the R class.

The `abstract` class `Animation` is the root class for animation classes. It defines some XML attributes that we can use to define an animation using an XML file. It also defines some methods we can use to define the animation by code. It has five direct subclasses: `AnimationSet`, `AlphaAnimation`, `RotateAnimation`, `ScaleAnimation`, and `TranslateAnimation`. **TABLE 4.7** shows these five classes and their corresponding XML elements. An `AnimationSet` can be used to define a group of animations to be run concurrently. We can also run several animations sequentially by using several `AnimationSets` in sequence.

An XML animation file must have a single root element such as `<alpha>`, `<rotate>`, `<translate>`, `<scale>`, or `<set>`. We can use the element to nest other elements inside it and define several animations that run concurrently.

TABLE 4.8 shows some selected XML attributes and their meaning for the XML elements in Table 4.7. The `android:duration` and the `android:interpolator` attributes are common

FIGURE 4.6 **The directory structure showing the transition XML files**

TABLE 4.7 Selected animation XML elements and their corresponding classes

XML Element	Class	Description
set	AnimationSet	Defines a set of (concurrent) animations
alpha	AlphaAnimation	A fade in or fade out animation
rotate	RotateAnimation	A rotating animation around a fixed point
scale	ScaleAnimation	A scaling animation from a fixed point
translate	TranslateAnimation	A sliding (horizontal or vertical) animation

to all animations. The `android:interpolator` attribute specifies a resource that defines the smoothness of the animation, in particular its acceleration or deceleration. The default is linear speed, or no acceleration.

When assigning values to these attributes, we can use either absolute values or relative values. A relative value can be relative to the element itself using the syntax value%, for example, `30%`, or can be relative to its parent using the syntax value%p, for example, `50%p`.

TABLE 4.8 Selected XML attributes of the various `Animation` classes

XML Element	XML Attribute	Description
	android:duration	Amount of time in milliseconds the animation should run
	android:interpolator	An interpolator to apply to the animation
alpha	android:fromAlpha	Starting opacity value between 0.0 and 1.0
alpha	android:toAlpha	Ending opacity value between 0.0 and 1.0
rotate	android:fromDegrees	Starting angle of the rotation
rotate	android:toDegrees	Ending angle of the rotation
rotate	android:pivotX	X-coordinate of the fixed point of the rotation
rotate	android:pivotY	Y-coordinate of the fixed point of the rotation
scale	android:fromXScale	Starting X scaling value between 0.0 and 1.0
scale	android:toXScale	Ending X scaling value between 0.0 and 1.0
scale	android:fromYScale	Starting X scaling value of between 0.0 and 1.0
scale	android:toYScale	Ending Y scaling value between 0.0 and 1.0
scale	android:pivotX	X-coordinate of fixed point when scaling takes place
scale	android:pivotY	Y-coordinate of fixed point when scaling takes place
translate	android:fromXDelta	X-coordinate of the starting point of the translation
translate	android:toXDelta	X-coordinate of the ending point of the translation
translate	android:fromYDelta	Y-coordinate of the starting point of the translation
translate	android:toYDelta	Y-coordinate of the ending point of the translation

EXAMPLE 4.16 shows the sliding from the left side of the screen transition. For a horizontal sliding transition, we define the starting x-coordinate using the attribute `android:fromXDelta` and the ending x-coordinate using the attribute `android:toXDelta`, which should be set to 0. The `android:fromXDelta` value should be negative if the screen comes in left to right (and positive if the screen comes in right to left). The two values are defined at lines 5 and 6. The time of the transition is defined using the attribute `android:duration`; its value is in milliseconds. Line 7 defines a transition lasting 4 seconds.

```
1   <?xml version="1.0" encoding="utf-8"?>
2   <set xmlns:android="http://schemas.android.com/apk/res/android">
3
4     <translate
5       android:fromXDelta="-100%p"
6       android:toXDelta="0"
7       android:duration="4000" />
8
9   </set>
```

EXAMPLE 4.16 **The slide_from_left.xml file**

EXAMPLE **4.17** shows a fade in and scaling transitions that run concurrently. They are both defined inside a set element.

For the fade animation (lines 4–7), we use an alpha element and we define the starting opacity using the android:fromAlpha attribute and the ending opacity using the android:toAlpha attribute. For a full fade in, the starting opacity is 0 and the ending opacity is 1. They are defined at lines 5 and 6. Line 7 defines a transition lasting 3 seconds.

For the scaling animation (lines 9–16), we use a scale element and we define the starting and ending x and y scaling values using the android:fromXScale, android:toXScale, android:fromYScale, and android:toYScale attributes. Usually, we want to finish with scale 1. Thus, the values of android:toXScale and android:toYScale are both 1.0 (lines 11 and 13). For a full scaling animation, we specify 0.0 for android:fromXScale and android:fromYScale (lines 10 and 12). We define the pivot point to be the center of the scaling animation. The android:pivotX

```
1   <?xml version="1.0" encoding="utf-8"?>
2   <set xmlns:android="http://schemas.android.com/apk/res/android">
3
4     <alpha
5       android:fromAlpha="0.0"
6       android:toAlpha="1.0"
7       android:duration="3000" />
8
9     <scale
10      android:fromXScale="0.0"
11      android:toXScale="1.0"
12      android:fromYScale="0.0"
13      android:toYScale="1.0"
14      android:pivotX="50%"
15      android:pivotY="50%"
16      android:duration="3000" />
17
18  </set>
```

EXAMPLE 4.17 **The fade_in_and_scale.xml file**

Method	Description
void overridePendingTransition (int enterAnimResource, int exitAnimResource)	The enterAnimResource and exitAnimResource parameters, both resource ids, specify the animations to enter a new activity and exit the current activity, respectively. A value 0 specifies no animation.

TABLE 4.9 The `overridePendingTransition` method of the `Activity` class

and `android:pivotY` attributes specify the x- and y-coordinates of that pivot point. If we want to define the scaling animation as starting on the top left corner and expanding toward the bottom right corner, we set these two values to 0.0. If we want to define the scaling animation to start at the center of the screen and expanding outward, we use a relative value and set these two values to 50% (lines 14 and 15). Since we run both animations concurrently, we specify the same duration, 3 seconds (line 16), as we specified for the fade in animation.

The `overridePendingTransition` method, inherited from the `Activity` class, shown in **TABLE 4.9**, allows us to specify one or two transitions when switching from one activity to another. It should be called immediately after calling `startActivity` (to start a new activity) or `finish` (to go back to the previous activity).

In the `MainActivity` class, the method `modifyData` (**EXAMPLE 4.18**) includes the code to go to the second screen. We call `overridePendingTransition` at line 39 and specify the `slide_from_left` resource as the animation to use to transition to the second screen. The value `0` for the second argument specifies that no animation is used to transition from the first screen.

```
35
36     public void modifyData( View v ) {
37        Intent myIntent = new Intent( this, DataActivity.class );
38        this.startActivity( myIntent );
39        overridePendingTransition( R.anim.slide_from_left, 0 );
40     }
41  }
```

EXAMPLE 4.18 **The `modifyData` method in the `MainActivity` class**

In the `DataActivity` class, the method `goBack` (**EXAMPLE 4.19**) includes the code to go back to the first screen. We call `overridePendingTransition` at line 60 and specify the `fade_in_and_scale` resource to use to transition to the first screen and no transition from the current screen.

EXAMPLE 4.20 shows part of the R.java, which is automatically generated. Inside the project, it is located in the app/build/generated/source/r/debug/com/jblearning/mortgagev3 directory.

```
56
57     public void goBack( View v ) {
58       updateMortgageObject( );
59       this.finish( );
60       overridePendingTransition( R.anim.fade_in_and_scale, 0 );
61     }
62   }
```

EXAMPLE 4.19 **The** `goBack` **method in the** `DataActivity` **class**

```
package com.jblearning.mortgagev3;

public finalclass R {
    public static final class anim {
        ...
        public static final int fade_in_and_scale=0x7f05000a;
        public static final int slide_from_left=0x7f05000b;
    }
    ...
    public static final class id {
        ...
        public static final int data_amount=0x7f080045;
        public static final int data_rate=0x7f080040;
        ...
        public static final int years=0x7f080048;
    }
    ...
    public static final class layout {
        ...
        public static final int activity_data=0x7f030017;
        public static final int activity_main=0x7f030018;
    }
    public static final class string {
        ...
        public static final int total_payment=0x7f0a0020;
        public static final int years=0x7f0a0021;
    }
    ...
```

EXAMPLE 4.20 **Selected contents of the R.java file**

This file should not be modified. Among other things, it includes public static classes containing constants for the transitions, the ids, the layouts, the strings, etc.

If we run the app, we can see the sliding to the left transition going to the second screen, and the fade in and scaling transition coming back to the first screen (shown in **FIGURE 4.7**).

FIGURE 4.7 **The Mortgage Calculator app in the middle of the** `fade_in_and_scale`
transition, Version 3

4.8 Handling Persistent Data: Mortgage Calculator App, Version 4

In Version 4 of the app, we want to make the data chosen by the user persistent. When the user uses the app for the first time, we show the default values for the three mortgage parameters, the mortgage amount, the interest rate, and the number of years. But when the user uses the app again, we want to show the values that were used the last time the user used the app.

In order to implement that functionality, we write to a file on the device the mortgage parameters every time they are changed. When we start the app the first time, the file does not exist and we use the default parameters for the mortgage. When we run the app afterward, we read the mortgage parameters from the file. Although we could use the `openFileOutput` and `openFileInput` methods of the `ContextWrapper` class to open a file for writing and reading, it is easier to use the user preferences system in order to store and retrieve persistent data. Preferences for an app

TABLE 4.10 Selected methods of the `SharedPreferences.Editor` interface

Method	Description
SharedPreferences. Editor putInt(String key, int value)	Associates value with key in this `SharedPreferences.Editor`. These key/value pairs should be committed by calling either the commit or apply method. Returns this `SharedPreferences.Editor` so that method calls can be chained.
SharedPreferences. Editor putFloat(String key, float value)	Associates value with key in this `SharedPreferences.Editor`. These key/value pairs should be committed by calling either the commit or apply method. Returns this `SharedPreferences.Editor` so that method calls can be chained.
boolean commit()	Commits the preferences changes made by this `SharedPreferences.Editor` (using putDataType method calls) to the corresponding `SharedPreferences` object.

are organized as a set of key/value pairs, like a hashtable. In this app, since we have three values for a mortgage, we have three key/value pairs.

The `SharedPreferences` interface includes the functionality to write to and read from the user preferences. Its `static` inner interface, `Editor`, enables us to store user preferences. **TABLE 4.10** shows some of its methods. The `putDataType` methods have this general method header:

```
public SharedPreferences.Editor putDataType( String key, DataType
value )
```

It associates value with key in this `SharedPreferences.Editor`. The data type can be either a primitive data type or a `String`. In order to actually write to the user preferences, we need to call the `commit` or `apply` method. Assuming we have a `SharedPreferences.Editor` reference named `editor`, in order to associate the value 10 with the key rating, we write:

```
// editor is a SharedPreferences.Editor
editor.putInt( "rating", 10 );
```

To retrieve data previously written to the user preferences, we use the `getDataType` methods of the `SharedPreferences` interface. **TABLE 4.11** shows some of them. The `getDataType` methods have this general method header:

```
public DataType getDataType( String key, DataType defaultValue )
```

The return value is the value that was previously associated with key when user references were written to. If the key does not exist, `defaultValue` is returned. Assuming we have a `Shared-Preferences` reference named `pref`, in order to retrieve the value that was previously associated with the key `rating` and written to the preferences, we write:

```
// pref is a SharedPreferences
int storedRating = pref.getInt( "rating", 1 );
```

TABLE 4.11 Selected methods of the `SharedPreferences` interface

Method	Description
int getInt(String key, int defaultValue)	Returns the int value associated with key in this `SharedPreferences` object. Returns defaultValue if the key is not found.
float getFloat(String key, float defaultValue)	Returns the float value associated with key in this `SharedPreferences` object. Returns defaultValue if the key is not found.

TABLE 4.12 The `getDefaultSharedPreferences` method of the `PreferenceManager` class

Method	Description
static SharedPreferences getDefaultSharedPreferences(Context context)	Returns the `SharedPreferences` for context.

We can use the `getDefaultSharedPreferences` `static` method of the `PreferenceManager` class, shown in **TABLE 4.12**, in order to get a `SharedPreferences` reference. Since the `Activity` class inherits from `Context` and our `MainActivity` and `DataActivity` classes inherit from `Activity`, we can pass the keyword `this` as the argument of this method. Thus, inside an `Activity` class, in order to get a `SharedReferences` inside our two classes, we can write:

```
SharedPreferences pref =
    ReferenceManager.getDefaultSharedPreferences( this );
```

The View components of our app are still the same. Most of the changes take place in the Model. We modify the `Mortgage` class, so that it includes a method to write mortgage data to the user preferences system and a constructor to read data from it. In both the `MainActivity` and `DataActivity` classes, which make up the Controller parts of the app, we use these methods to either load or write the mortgage parameters from and to the user preferences system.

EXAMPLE 4.21 shows the updated parts of the `Mortgage` class. The `SharedPreferences` interface and the `PreferenceManager` class are imported at lines 5–6. Lines 11–13 define three `String` constants that hold the preferences key names for amount, years, and rate.

The method `setPreferences` is coded at lines 84–93. We include a `Context` parameter so we can pass it to the `getDefaultSharedPreferences` method. When we call the `setPreferences` method from the `DataActivity` class using the `Mortgage` object reference `mortgage`, we will pass `this`. The `Context` class is imported at line 4.

At lines 86–87, we call the `getDefaultSharedPreferences` in order to obtain a `SharedPreferences` reference. At line 88, we call the `edit` method and get a `SharedPreferences.Editor`

```
1   package com.jblearning.mortgagev4;
2
3   import java.text.DecimalFormat;
4   import android.content.Context;
5   import android.content.SharedPreferences;
6   import android.preference.PreferenceManager;
7
8   public class Mortgage {
9     public final DecimalFormat MONEY
10                 = new DecimalFormat( "$#,##0.00" );
11    private static final String PREFERENCE_AMOUNT = "amount";
12    private static final String PREFERENCE_YEARS = "years";
13    private static final String PREFERENCE_RATE = "rate";
14
15    private float amount;
16    private int years;
17    private float rate;
...
26    // Instantiate Mortgage from preferences
27    public Mortgage( Context context ) {
28      SharedPreferences pref =
29        PreferenceManager.getDefaultSharedPreferences( context );
30      setAmount( pref.getFloat( PREFERENCE_AMOUNT, 100000.0f ) );
31      setYears( pref.getInt( PREFERENCE_YEARS, 30 ) );
32      setRate ( pref.getFloat( PREFERENCE_RATE, 0.035f ) );
33    }
...
84    // Write mortgage data to preferences
85    public void setPreferences( Context context ) {
86      SharedPreferences pref =
87        PreferenceManager.getDefaultSharedPreferences( context );
88      SharedPreferences.Editor editor = pref.edit( );
89      editor.putFloat( PREFERENCE_AMOUNT, amount );
90      editor.putInt( PREFERENCE_YEARS, years );
91      editor.putFloat( PREFERENCE_RATE, rate );
92      editor.commit( );
93    }
94  }
```

EXAMPLE 4.21 The `Mortgage` class, Mortgage Calculator app, Version 4

reference. With it, we write our mortgage data at lines 89–91 using the three keys defined at lines 11–13. At line 92, we call `commit` to actually write to the preferences.

We add an overloaded constructor at lines 26–33. We read mortgage data from the preferences at lines 30–32 and call the mutators in order to assign the three values read to the `amount`, `years`, and `rate` instance variables. If a key is not found, we specify an appropriate default value.

> **COMMON ERROR:** Do not forget to call `commit` or `apply` after putting data into the user defaults using the various `putDataType` methods. If we do not, no data is written to them.

There is only one line of code to change in the `MainActivity` class: the statement that instantiates `mortgage`. Instead of using the default constructor, we use the overloaded constructor of the `Mortgage` class (line 14 of **EXAMPLE 4.22**). The argument `this` represents the current `MainActivity`, therefore an `Activity`, and therefore a `Context` object reference.

```
11
12    protected void onCreate( Bundle savedInstanceState ) {
13      super.onCreate( savedInstanceState );
14      mortgage = new Mortgage( this );
15      setContentView( R.layout.activity_main );
16    }
17
```

EXAMPLE 4.22 **The `onCreate` method in the `MainActivity` class, Mortgage Calculator app, Version 4**

There is also only one line of code to add to the `DataActivity` class: a statement that writes the data in `mortgage` to the user preferences for this app. We do this toward the end of the `updateMortgage-Object` method by calling the `setPreferences` method with `mortgage`, once again passing `this` as its argument (line 51 of **EXAMPLE 4.23**). The `updateMortgageObject` method is called right after the user has updated the mortgage parameters on the second screen and before going back to the first screen.

```
31
32    public void updateMortgageObject( ) {
...
46      try {
47        float amount = Float.parseFloat( amountString );
48        mortgage.setAmount( amount );
49        float rate = Float.parseFloat( rateString );
50        mortgage.setRate( rate );
51        mortgage.setPreferences( this );
52      } catch( NumberFormatException nfe ) {
53        mortgage.setAmount( 100000.0f );
54        mortgage.setRate( .035f );
55      }
56    }
57
```

EXAMPLE 4.23 **The `updateMortgageObject` method in the `DataActivity` class, Mortgage Calculator app, Version 4**

As we can see from the previous example, it is simple to implement persistent data for this app. Other than one line of code in each `Activity` class (the two Controllers for this app), we coded two methods, one writing to a file, and the other one reading from a file, in our Model, the `Mortgage` class. The two Views remain unchanged. Simple updates and improvements are one of the benefits of the Model-View-Controller architecture.

When an app writes to the user preferences, it writes to the device file system. Generally, when we release an app to Google Play that requires interaction with a device, we may need to include a `uses-permission` element in the AndroidManifest.xml file so that the app operates correctly. Furthermore, before somebody downloads the app, he or she is informed that the app writes to the device's file system. The syntax for such an element is:

```
<uses-permission android:name="permissionName" />
```

The `android:name` attribute is the name of the permission: its value relates to the fact that the app wants to use a function or service of the device, for example, its camera, its list of contacts, or its ability to read or send SMS messages. There are many values that can be assigned to this attribute, for example `android.permission.CAMERA`, `android.permission.READ_CON-TACTS`, `android.permission.FLASHLIGHT`, or in this app's case `android.permission.WRITE_EXTERNAL_STORAGE`.

For this app, since we are writing on the device file system, we need to include the following inside the `manifest` element in AndroidManifest.xml (note that this is not necessary when we run the app in the emulator):

```
<uses-permission android:name="android.permission.WRITE_EXTERNAL_
STORAGE" />
```

When we run the app the second time, the data that we entered on the second screen the first time we ran the app is now shown on the first screen. The app is pulling data from the preferences that were written into the first time we ran the app.

Chapter Summary

- The Android framework provides layouts to help us organize a View.
- Layouts are subclasses of `ViewGroup`.
- A `TableLayout` arranges its children in rows and columns.
- A `RelativeLayout` positions components relative to other components.
- We can call the `startActivity` method of the `Activity` class, passing an `Intent` argument, to start a new `Activity` for that `Intent`.
- Activities are managed on a stack—the most recently started `Activity` is on top of the stack.
- We can call the `finish` method to close an `Activity`. This pops it off the stack and the app returns to the previous `Activity`.

- An `Activity` goes through a life cycle, and methods are called automatically as an activity is started, paused, stopped, or closed.
- There are many ways to either pass data or share data between two activities, which include: using the `putExtra` methods of the `Intent` class, using a singleton class for the Model, or using a global variable representing the Model.
- One way for activities to share data is to declare a `public static` instance of a class of the Model in one `Activity` class. In this way, it is global and can be accessed by any other `Activity` class.
- A transition is an animation special effect going from one screen to another.
- The android framework provides classes for fading, scaling, translating, and rotating animations. Animations can be coded in XML files and placed in the anim directory, which should be placed in the res directory.
- The `SharedPreferences` interface provides the functionality to write and read preferences to the file system.
- The `getDefaultSharedPreferences static` method of the `PreferenceManager` class returns a `SharedPreferences` reference.
- If an app writes to the file system, we need to include a `uses-permission` element in the AndroidManifest.xml file.

Exercises, Problems, and Projects

Multiple-Choice Exercises

1. The TableLayout class can be used to organize various GUI components
   - As a table of rows and columns
   - As a table of multiple rows with only one column each
   - As a table of only one row and multiple columns
   - As a table of only one row and one column

2. The direct superclass of LinearLayout and RelativeLayout is
   - View
   - ViewGroup
   - Layout
   - Object

3. TableLayout and TableRow are direct subclasses of
   - LinearLayout
   - ViewGroup
   - RelativeLayout
   - View

4. The RelativeLayout class is a good choice to organize various GUI components
   - To give the components absolute x- and y-coordinates
   - So that we position components relative to other components
   - As a grid of multiple rows and columns
   - It is never a good choice

5. In what package is the Intent class?
   - java.intent
   - android.widget
   - android.activity
   - android.content

6. After you have created an Intent for a new activity, what method of the Activity class do you call with that Intent parameter in order to start a new activity?
   - startActivity
   - newActivity
   - startIntent
   - newIntent

7. What method of the Activity class is automatically called when an activity is about to restart?
   - onCreate
   - onDestroy
   - onRestart
   - onGo

8. What methods of the Activity class (and in what order) are automatically called when an activity is first created?
   - onCreate
   - onCreate, onStart, and onResume (in that order)
   - onCreate and onResume
   - onStart, onCreate, and onResume (in that order)

9. What method of the Activity class is automatically called when an activity becomes invisible to the user?
   - onResume
   - onStop
   - onPause
   - onInvisible

10. Two activities can share the same data
    - No, it is not possible
    - Yes, but it is only possible by writing to and reading from the same file
    - Yes, but it is only possible by writing to and reading from a SQLite database
    - Yes, for example by each accessing a public static instance variable from another class

11. In what package do we find the Animation class?
    - android.animation
    - android.view
    - android.view.animation
    - android.animation.view

12. What is not a subclass of the Animation class?
    - ScaleAnimation
    - RotateAnimation
    - AlphaAnimation
    - MoveAnimation

13. What class do we use to play several animations together?
    - AnimationSequence
    - SequenceAnimation
    - SeveralAnimation
    - AnimationSet

14. What static method of the class PreferenceManager do we use to get SharedPreferences?
    - getPreferences
    - sharedPreferences
    - getDefaultPreferences
    - getDefaultSharedPreferences

Fill in the Code

15. Inside a TableLayout element, this code adds a row that contains an EditText and a TextView whose ids are game and player.

```
<TableRow
    android:layout_width="wrap_content"
    android:layout_height="wrap_content" >
    <!--Your code goes here -->



</TableRow>
```

16. This code draws a blue line that is 2 pixels thick.

```
<!-- blue line; your code goes here -->
```

17. Inside a TableRow of a RelativeLayout element, this code adds an EditText whose id is age and is positioned to the right of a View whose id is name

```
<EditText
    android:layout_width="wrap_content"
    android:layout_height="wrap_content"
    <!-- Your code goes here -->


    android:inputType="numberDecimal" />
```

18. Inside the AndroidManifest.xml file, add an activity element of the type `MyActivity` class

```
<!-- Your code goes here -->
```

19. Inside an activity, when the user clicks on a button, the method goToSecondActivity executes. Write the code to start a new activity from the SecondActivity class.

```
public void goToSecondActivity( View v ) {
// Your code goes here



}
```

20. When the user comes back to this activity from another activity, we want the method modifyThisActivity to execute. Override the appropriate method and make the call to the modifyThisActivity method inside it.

```
public void modifyThisActivity( ) {
  // this method is already coded
}
// Your code goes here
```

21. This XML file defines a resource for a full scaling transition starting on the top left corner and expanding toward the bottom right corner and lasting 2 seconds.

```
<?xml version="1.0" encoding="utf-8"?>
<set xmlns:android="http://schemas.android.com/apk/res/android">
  <scale
```

```
      android:fromXScale="0.0"
      android:fromYScale="0.0"
      <!--Your code goes here -->


  </set>
```

22. This XML file defines a resource for a transition rotating 180 degrees clockwise around the top left corner, finishing in the normal position and lasting five seconds.

```
<?xml version="1.0" encoding="utf-8"?>
<set xmlns:android="http://schemas.android.com/apk/res/android">
  <rotate
  <!--Your code goes here -->


  </set>
```

23. This code writes the values 45 and "Hello" to user preferences using the keys number and hi.

```
SharedPreferences preferences = PreferenceManager.
getDefaultSharedPreferences( );
SharedPreferences.Editor editor = preferences.edit( );
// Your code goes here
```

24. This code reads the integer value associated with the key grade and the String value associated with the key course from the user preferences and assigns them to two variables. If the keys do not exist, the default values 80 and CS3 should be assigned to the two variables.

```
SharedPreferences preferences = PreferenceManager.
getDefaultSharedPreferences();
SharedPreferences.Editor editor = preferences.edit();
// Your code goes here
```

Write an app

25. Write an app using two activities: one activity plays TicTacToe, and the other activity asks the user to choose who plays first (X or O) and the colors for the Xs and Os. Include a Model. Include transitions between the two activities.

26. Write an app using two activities: one activity asks the user to give the answer to a simple math problem—addition, subtraction, or multiplication—the other activity asks the user

to choose the arithmetic operation. Include a Model. Include transitions between the two activities.

27. Write an app using two activities: one activity performs a unit conversion from Celsius to Fahrenheit or Fahrenheit to Celsius, and the other activity asks the user to choose which way to make that conversion. Include a Model. Include transitions between the two activities.

28. Write an app using two activities: one activity performs a unit conversion from miles to kilometers or kilometers to miles, and the other activity asks the user to choose which way to make that conversion. Include a Model. Include transitions between the two activities.

29. Write an app using two activities: one activity performs the translation from English to another language of the sentence `Hello World`, and the other activity asks the user to choose one of five languages for the translation. Include a Model. Include transitions between the two activities.

30. Write an app using two activities: one activity performs a unit conversion from pounds to kilograms or kilograms to pounds, and the other activity asks the user to choose which way to make that conversion. Include a Model. Include transitions between the two activities. Make the user choice persistent so that next time the user runs the app, his or her previous choice is the default.

31. Write an app using two activities: one activity performs a currency conversion from dollars to another currency, and the other activity asks the user to choose which currency to use among five currencies. Include a Model. Include transitions between the two activities. Make the user choice persistent so that next time the user runs the app, his or her previous choice is the default.

32. Write an app using two activities: one activity calculates the monthly payment for a car lease, and the other activity asks the user for the car lease parameters—duration in months, down payment, lease rate, and car value at the end of the lease. Include a Model. Include transitions between the two activities. Make the user choice persistent so that next time the user runs the app, his or her previous choices are the default values when the app starts.

33. Write an app using two activities: one activity encrypts with a fixed shift (using a Caesar cipher) a text that the user types in a text field, and the other activity asks the user to define the shift, an integer between 1 and 25 (if the shift value is 3, then the word `the` will be encrypted into `wkh`. If the word is `zoo`, the encrypted word is `crr`). Assume that only lowercase letters from a to z will be used. Include a Model. Include transitions between the two activities. Make the user choice persistent so that next time the user runs the app, his or her previous shift value is the default value when the app starts.

CHAPTER FIVE

Menus, SQLite

CHAPTER CONTENTS

Introduction

In order to manage persistent data, we can store the data in a file or in a database. In this chapter, we learn how to use SQLite, a light **relational database management system** (**RDBMS**) available on Android devices. An RDBMS is a software program that manages relational databases. Although SQLite uses flat files to store data and is therefore not optimized for speed as compared to a regular RDBMS, it enables us to organize our data as if we were using a regular RDBMS and to use SQL syntax. The typical SQL operations are insert, delete, update, and select. In this chapter, we also explore how to use menus: each menu item corresponds to an SQL (insert, delete, update, select) operation. To keep things simple, we only allow the device to run in vertical orientation.

> **SOFTWARE ENGINEERING:** If the app data is complex, consider using SQLite to store it. The data can be logically organized and we can use SQL syntax.

5.1 Menus and Menu Items: Candy Store App, Version 0

When we start an app using the Basic Activity template, Android Studio generates two layout XML files and one menu XML file: activity_main.xml, content_main.xml, and menu_main.xml. This is different from the Empty Activity template, which only generates the activity_main.xml file.

The activity_main.xml file, shown in **EXAMPLE 5.1**, uses a `CoordinatorLayout` to arrange the elements. A `CoordinatorLayout` is typically used as a top-level container for an app and as a container for specific interactions with one or more child Views.

It includes three elements:

▸ An `AppBarLayout` (lines 11–23), itself including a `ToolBar` (lines 16–21). This is the action bar and this is where the menu items go.
▸ The View defined by content_main.xml (line 25), a `RelativeLayout` with a `TextView` inside it.
▸ A `FloatingActionButton` (lines 27–33) positioned at the bottom right and whose icon is a standard email icon from the Android icon library. In this app, we do not want that functionality, so we delete lines 27–33.

Inside the `onCreate` method of the `MainActivity` class, there is existing code to handle user interaction with the floating action button, as shown in **EXAMPLE 5.2**. Since we do not use the floating action button for this app, we delete that code inside the `MainActivity` class.

```
1    <?xml version="1.0" encoding="utf-8"?>
2    <android.support.design.widget.CoordinatorLayout
3        xmlns:android="http://schemas.android.com/apk/res/android"
4        xmlns:app="http://schemas.android.com/apk/res-auto"
5        xmlns:tools="http://schemas.android.com/tools"
6        android:layout_width="match_parent"
7        android:layout_height="match_parent"
8        android:fitsSystemWindows="true"
9        tools:context="com.jblearning.candystorev0.MainActivity">
10
11       <android.support.design.widget.AppBarLayout
12           android:layout_width="match_parent"
13           android:layout_height="wrap_content"
14           android:theme="@style/AppTheme.AppBarOverlay">
15
16           <android.support.v7.widget.Toolbar
17               android:id="@+id/toolbar"
18               android:layout_width="match_parent"
19               android:layout_height="?attr/actionBarSize"
20               android:background="?attr/colorPrimary"
21               app:popupTheme="@style/AppTheme.PopupOverlay"/>
22
23       </android.support.design.widget.AppBarLayout>
24
25       <include layout="@layout/content_main"/>
26
27       <android.support.design.widget.FloatingActionButton
28           android:id="@+id/fab"
29           android:layout_width="wrap_content"
30           android:layout_height="wrap_content"
31           android:layout_gravity="bottom|end"
32           android:layout_margin="@dimen/fab_margin"
33           android:src="@android:drawable/ic_dialog_email"/>
34
35   </android.support.design.widget.CoordinatorLayout>
```

EXAMPLE 5.1 The automatically generated activity_main.xml file when using the Basic Activity template

```
21       FloatingActionButton fab =
22           ( FloatingActionButton ) findViewById( R.id.fab );
23       fab.setOnClickListener( new View.OnClickListener( ) {
24         @Override
25         public void onClick( View view ) {
26           Snackbar.make( view, "Replace with your own action",
27               Snackbar.LENGTH_LONG ).setAction( "Action", null ).show( );
28         }
29       });
```

EXAMPLE 5.2 Selected generated code inside MainActivity.java when using the Basic Activity template

EXAMPLE 5.3 shows the menu_main.xml file. It defines a menu with one item. Menu items are shown in the action bar, starting from the right. However, if we run the skeleton app, no menu item shows. This is because the only menu item has the value never for the attribute app:showAsAction (line 9).

```
1    <menu xmlns:android="http://schemas.android.com/apk/res/android"
2         xmlns:app="http://schemas.android.com/apk/res-auto"
3         xmlns:tools="http://schemas.android.com/tools"
4         tools:context="com.jblearning.candystorev0.MainActivity">
5      <item
6         android:id="@+id/action_settings"
7         android:orderInCategory="100"
8         android:title="@string/action_settings"
9         app:showAsAction="never"/>
10   </menu>
```

EXAMPLE 5.3 The menu_main.xml automatically generated file

The Menu interface, part of the android.view package, encapsulates a menu. A menu is made up of menu items: the MenuItem interface encapsulates a menu item. **TABLE 5.1** shows a few attributes and methods of MenuItem. There can be several methods corresponding to the same attribute. One setTitle method accepts a CharSequence parameter (similar to the String data type), whereas the other setTitle method accepts an int parameter representing a resource. Menu items can be given an id so that we can get a reference to them in the corresponding Activity class. **TABLE 5.2** shows some constants of MenuItem that are possible arguments of the setShow-AsAction and the corresponding values for the showAsAction XML attribute.

We update the menu_main.xml file, shown in **EXAMPLE 5.4**, and include three items with the titles add, delete, and update. The three Strings are defined in the strings.xml file, shown in **EXAMPLE 5.5**. We provide these three items so that the user can add a candy to the database, delete one, or edit one. The android:orderInCategory attribute enables us to order the items as they are placed on the menu (the highest value item will be on the far right). Without specifying a value

TABLE 5.1 Selected XML attributes and methods of MenuItem		
Attribute Name	**Related Method(s)**	**Description**
android:title	setTitle(int), setTitle(CharSequence)	Sets the title for the menu item
app:showAsAction	setShowAsAction(int)	Defines how this item displays within the action bar
android:icon	setIcon(int), setIcon(Drawable)	Sets the icon for the menu item

TABLE 5.2 Selected constants of `MenuItem` to be used as arguments of `setShowAsAction` and their corresponding value for the `showAsAction` attribute

Constant	Attribute Value	Description
SHOW_AS_ACTION_NEVER	never	Never show the item in the action bar
SHOW_AS_ACTION_ALWAYS	always	Always show the item in the action bar
SHOW_AS_ACTION_IF_ROOM	ifRoom	Show the item in the action bar if there is room

```
1    <menu xmlns:android="http://schemas.android.com/apk/res/android"
2          xmlns:app="http://schemas.android.com/apk/res-auto"
3          xmlns:tools="http://schemas.android.com/tools"
4          tools:context="com.jblearning.candystorev0.MainActivity">
5      <item android:id="@+id/action_add"
6            android:title="@string/add"
7            app:showAsAction="ifRoom"/>
8
9      <item android:id="@+id/action_delete"
10           android:title="@string/delete"
11           app:showAsAction="ifRoom"/>
12
13     <item android:id="@+id/action_update"
14           android:title="@string/update"
15           app:showAsAction="ifRoom"/>
16   </menu>
```

EXAMPLE 5.4 **The menu_main.xml file, Candy Store app, Version 0**

```
1    <resources>
2      <string name="app_name">CandyStoreV0</string>
3      <string name="action_settings">Settings</string>
4      <string name="add">ADD</string>
5      <string name="delete">DELETE</string>
6      <string name="update">UPDATE</string>
7    </resources>
```

EXAMPLE 5.5 **The strings.xml file, Candy Store app, Version 0**

for that attribute, the items will be placed left to right in the action bar. Since this is satisfactory, we delete the `android:orderInCategory` attribute for all three items.

If there are too many items to fit in the action bar, the ones on the far right will not be immediately visible, but they are still accessible via a sub menu.

EXAMPLE 5.6 shows the edited `MainActivity` class. As discussed earlier, we deleted the code related to the floating action button inside the `onCreate` method. At line 16 of `onCreate`, we get a reference to the `Toolbar` defined in activity_main.xml. We call the `setSupportActionBar` method (line 17), shown in **TABLE 5.3**, to set it as the action bar for this app.

The `onCreateOptionsMenu` method (lines 20–26) inflates menu_main.xml (line 24) in order to create a menu and places that menu in the toolbar. The `onOptionsItemSelected` method is called when the user selects a menu item. Its parameter is a `MenuItem` reference to the menu item selected. We retrieve its id at line 33 and use a `switch` statement to compare it to the ids of the various menu items defined in menu_main.xml and output what action is selected to Logcat. **TABLE 5.4** shows the menu-related classes and methods used for this.

If we select the menu_main.xml file, the menu items are visible in the preview pane, as shown in **FIGURE 5.1.** When we run the app inside the emulator or a device, the UPDATE menu item may or may not be visible depending on the available space. If there are items that are not shown, there is a . . . that will show instead and the non-visible items will become visible when the user clicks on . . . If we click on the various menu items, the corresponding output will show in Logcat.

```
1    package com.jblearning.candystorev0;
2
3    import android.os.Bundle;
4    import android.support.v7.app.AppCompatActivity;
5    import android.support.v7.widget.Toolbar;
6    import android.util.Log;
7    import android.view.Menu;
8    import android.view.MenuItem;
9
10   public class MainActivity extends AppCompatActivity {
11
12     @Override
13     protected void onCreate( Bundle savedInstanceState ) {
14       super.onCreate( savedInstanceState );
15       setContentView( R.layout.activity_main );
16       Toolbar toolbar = ( Toolbar ) findViewById( R.id.toolbar );
17       setSupportActionBar( toolbar );
18     }
19
20     @Override
21     public boolean onCreateOptionsMenu( Menu menu ) {
22       // Inflate the menu;
23       // this adds items to the action bar if it is present.
24       getMenuInflater( ).inflate( R.menu.menu_main, menu );
25       return true;
26     }
27
```

EXAMPLE 5.6 The `MainActivity` class, Candy Store app, Version 0 (*Continued*)

```
28    @Override
29    public boolean onOptionsItemSelected( MenuItem item ) {
30      // Handle action bar item clicks here. The action bar will
31      // automatically handle clicks on the Home/Up button, so long
32      // as you specify a parent activity in AndroidManifest.xml.
33      int id = item.getItemId( );
34      switch ( id ) {
35        case R.id.action_add:
36          Log.w( "MainActivity", "Add selected" );
37          return true;
38        case R.id.action_delete:
39          Log.w( "MainActivity", "Delete selected" );
40          return true;
41        case R.id.action_update:
42          Log.w( "MainActivity", "Update selected" );
43          return true;
44        default:
45          return super.onOptionsItemSelected( item );
46      }
47    }
48  }
```

EXAMPLE 5.6 **The `MainActivity` class, Candy Store app, Version 0**

TABLE 5.3 The `setSupportActionBar` of the `AppCompatActivity` class

Method	Description
void setSupportActionBar(Toolbar toolbar)	Sets toolbar to act as the action bar for this Activity; the toolbar's menu will be populated with the activity's options menu

TABLE 5.4 Selected menu-related methods

Class or Interface	Method	Description
Activity	boolean onCreateOptionsMenu(Menu menu)	Initializes the contents of this activity's menu. Must return true to display the menu.
Activity	boolean onOptionsItemSelected(MenuItem menuItem)	Called when a menu item is selected by the user.
Activity	MenuInflater getMenuInflater( )	Returns a MenuInflater.
MenuInflater	void inflate(int menuRes, Menu menu)	Inflates the menuRes resource and creates menu with it.
MenuItem	int getItemId( )	Returns the id of this menu item.

FIGURE 5.1 **The menu showing in the action bar, Candy Store app, Version 0**

5.2 Icon Items, Candy Store app, Version 1

In Version 1, we use icons instead of `Strings` for the menu items and we provide an activity with its layout for the add menu item. To include an icon for a menu item, we use the `android:icon` XML attribute shown in Table 5.1. We can use existing icons available in the Android library or create our own icons. Existing icons can be referenced using the following syntax and pattern:

```
@android:drawable/name_of_icon
```

For add, edit (update), and delete, the names of the icon resources are `ic_menu_add`, `ic_menu_edit`, and `ic_menu_delete`.

EXAMPLE 5.7 shows the updated menu_main.xml file, with the `android:icon` attributes added at lines 7, 12, and 17. Note that although the icons show in the action bar and the titles do not, we still specify titles for the three items (lines 6, 11, 16). Indeed, if the user long presses on an icon, the title shows. This can be very helpful for visually impaired users.

```
1    <menu xmlns:android="http://schemas.android.com/apk/res/android"
2          xmlns:app="http://schemas.android.com/apk/res-auto"
3          xmlns:tools="http://schemas.android.com/tools"
4          tools:context="com.jblearning.candystorev0.MainActivity">
5      <item android:id="@+id/action_add"
6            android:title="@string/add"
7            android:icon="@android:drawable/ic_menu_add"
8            app:showAsAction="ifRoom"/>
9
10     <item android:id="@+id/action_delete"
11           android:title="@string/delete"
12           android:icon="@android:drawable/ic_menu_delete"
13           app:showAsAction="ifRoom"/>
14
15     <item android:id="@+id/action_update"
16           android:title="@string/update"
17           android:icon="@android:drawable/ic_menu_edit"
18           app:showAsAction="ifRoom"/>
19   </menu>
```

EXAMPLE 5.7 The menu_main.xml file, Candy Store app, Version 1

FIGURE 5.2 shows a preview of the app in the Android Studio environment: the three icons appear on the right side of the action bar.

When the user clicks on the add icon, we want to enable the user to add a candy to the database. We keep things simple and our database only contains one table storing candies: a candy has an id, a name, and a price. Ids are expected to be integers starting at 0 and being automatically incremented by 1 as we add candies. Thus, our second screen, where the user can add a candy to the database, only includes two widgets for user input: one for the name and one for the price of the candy. EXAMPLE 5.8 shows the XML layout file for it, activity_insert.xml.

We use a RelativeLayout to organize the GUI. Each of the two EditTexts has a TextView element to its left to tell the user what to input. We specify that the user must enter a floating point number for the price (line 43). We also add two buttons, one to add the candy to the database (lines 45–53), and the second one to go back to the first activity (lines 55–62). The buttons, when clicked, trigger a call to the insert method (line 52), and the goBack method (line 61), respectively. The various elements are given ids so we can retrieve them (for the two editTexts) or position other elements relative to their position.

The additional String constants used in the activity_insert.xml file are defined in strings.xml, shown in EXAMPLE 5.9.

We create the InsertActivity class to control the second screen, defined in activity_insert.xml. Before coding it, we update the MainActivity class, so that when the user clicks on the Add icon, we start an InsertActivity. The updated MainActivity class is shown in EXAMPLE 5.10. The only change is at lines 33–34: when the user clicks on the ADD icon (line 31), we create an Intent for an InsertActivity at line 33 and start that activity at line 34.

FIGURE 5.2 The first screen of the Candy Store app, Version 1

```
1    <?xml version="1.0" encoding="utf-8"?>
2    <RelativeLayout xmlns:android="http://schemas.android.com/apk/res/android"
3      android:layout_width="match_parent"
4      android:layout_height="match_parent"
5      android:orientation="vertical"
6      android:paddingLeft="@dimen/activity_horizontal_margin"
7      android:paddingRight="@dimen/activity_horizontal_margin"
8      android:paddingTop="@dimen/activity_vertical_margin"
9      android:paddingBottom="@dimen/activity_vertical_margin">
10
11     <TextView
12       android:id="@+id/label_name"
13       android:layout_marginTop="50dp"
14       android:layout_width="wrap_content"
15       android:layout_height="wrap_content"
16       android:text="@string/label_name"/>
17
18     <EditText
19       android:id="@+id/input_name"
```

EXAMPLE 5.8 The activity_insert.xml file, Candy Store app, Version 1 (*Continued*)

```
20        android:layout_toRightOf="@+id/label_name"
21        android:layout_width="wrap_content"
22        android:layout_height="wrap_content"
23        android:layout_alignBottom="@+id/label_name"
24        android:layout_marginLeft="50dp"
25        android:orientation="horizontal" />
26
27     <TextView
28        android:id="@+id/label_price"
29        android:layout_width="wrap_content"
30        android:layout_height="wrap_content"
31        android:layout_below="@+id/label_name"
32        android:layout_marginTop="50dp"
33        android:text="@string/label_price" />
34
35     <EditText
36        android:id="@+id/input_price"
37        android:layout_width="wrap_content"
38        android:layout_height="wrap_content"
39        android:layout_alignBottom="@+id/label_price"
40        android:layout_alignLeft="@+id/input_name"
41        android:layout_alignParentRight="true"
42        android:layout_toRightOf="@+id/label_price"
43        android:inputType="numberDecimal" />
44
45     <Button
46        android:id="@+id/button_add"
47        android:layout_width="wrap_content"
48        android:layout_height="wrap_content"
49        android:layout_centerHorizontal="true"
50        android:layout_below="@+id/label_price"
51        android:layout_marginTop="50dp"
52        android:onClick="insert"
53        android:text="@string/button_add" />
54
55     <Button
56        android:layout_width="wrap_content"
57        android:layout_height="wrap_content"
58        android:layout_centerHorizontal="true"
59        android:layout_below="@+id/button_add"
60        android:layout_marginTop="50dp"
61        android:onClick="goBack"
62        android:text="@string/button_back" />
63
64  </RelativeLayout>
```

EXAMPLE 5.8 The activity_insert.xml file, Candy Store app, Version 1

```
1   <resources>
2     <string name="app_name">CandyStoreV1</string>
3     <string name="action_settings">Settings</string>
4     <string name="add">ADD</string>
5     <string name="delete">DELETE</string>
6     <string name="update">UPDATE</string>
7
8     <string name="label_name">Name</string>
9     <string name="label_price">Price</string>
10    <string name="button_add">ADD</string>
11    <string name="button_back">BACK</string>
12  </resources>
```

EXAMPLE 5.9 **The strings.xml file, Candy Store app, Version 1**

```
1   package com.jblearning.candystorev1;
2
3   import android.content.Intent;
4   import android.os.Bundle;
5   import android.support.v7.app.AppCompatActivity;
6   import android.support.v7.widget.Toolbar;
7   import android.util.Log;
8   import android.view.Menu;
9   import android.view.MenuItem;
10
11  public class MainActivity extends AppCompatActivity {
12
13    @Override
14    protected void onCreate( Bundle savedInstanceState ) {
15      super.onCreate( savedInstanceState );
16      setContentView( R.layout.activity_main );
17      Toolbar toolbar = ( Toolbar ) findViewById( R.id.toolbar );
18      setSupportActionBar( toolbar );
19    }
20
21    @Override
22    public boolean onCreateOptionsMenu( Menu menu ) {
23      getMenuInflater( ).inflate( R.menu.menu_main, menu );
24      return true;
25    }
26
27    @Override
28    public boolean onOptionsItemSelected(MenuItem item) {
29      int id = item.getItemId( );
```

EXAMPLE 5.10 **The `MainActivity` class, Candy Store app, Version 1 (*Continued*)**

```
30        switch ( id ) {
31          case R.id.action_add:
32            Log.w( "MainActivity", "Add selected" );
33            Intent insertIntent = new Intent( this, InsertActivity.class );
34            this.startActivity( insertIntent );
35            return true;
36          case R.id.action_delete:
37            Log.w( "MainActivity", "Delete selected" );
38            return true;
39          case R.id.action_update:
40            Log.w( "MainActivity", "Update selected" );
41            return true;
42          default:
43            return super.onOptionsItemSelected( item );
44        }
45      }
46    }
```

EXAMPLE 5.10 **The `MainActivity` class, Candy Store app, Version 1**

EXAMPLE 5.11 shows the `InsertActivity` class. We inflate the XML layout defined in the insert_activity.xml file (line 11), and we include the `insert` and `goBack` methods. The `goBack` method (lines 28–30) executes when the user clicks on the BACK button; it pops the current activity off the activity stack, returning the app to the previous activity (i.e., the first screen). Inside the `insert` method (lines 14–26), we retrieve the user input at lines 15–19, plan to insert a new candy in the database using user input (line 21), and clear the two `EditText`s (lines 23–25) in case the user wants to add another candy.

```
1    package com.jblearning.candystorev1;
2
3    import android.os.Bundle;
4    import android.support.v7.app.AppCompatActivity;
5    import android.view.View;
6    import android.widget.EditText;
7
8    public class InsertActivity extends AppCompatActivity  {
9      public void onCreate( Bundle savedInstanceState ) {
10       super.onCreate( savedInstanceState );
11       setContentView( R.layout.activity_insert );
12     }
13
```

EXAMPLE 5.11 **The `InsertActivity` class, Candy Store app, Version 1 (*Continued*)**

```
14    public void insert( View v ) {
15      // Retrieve name and price
16      EditText nameEditText = ( EditText) findViewById( R.id.input_name );
17      EditText priceEditText = ( EditText) findViewById( R.id.input_price );
18      String name = nameEditText.getText( ).toString( );
19      String priceString = priceEditText.getText( ).toString( );
20
21      // insert new candy in database
22
23      // clear data
24      nameEditText.setText( "" );
25      priceEditText.setText( "" );
26    }
27
28    public void goBack( View v ) {
29      this.finish( );
30    }
31  }
```

EXAMPLE 5.11 The `InsertActivity` **class, Candy Store app, Version 1**

Finally, we add an `activity` element in the AndroidManifest.xml file, as shown at lines 23–26 of **EXAMPLE 5.12**. We also allow both activities to run in vertical orientation only.

```
1   <?xml version="1.0" encoding="utf-8"?>
2   <manifest package="com.jblearning.candystorev1"
3             xmlns:android="http://schemas.android.com/apk/res/android">
4
5     <application
6         android:allowBackup="true"
7         android:icon="@mipmap/ic_launcher"
8         android:label="@string/app_name"
9         android:supportsRtl="true"
10        android:theme="@style/AppTheme">
11      <activity
12          android:name=".MainActivity"
13          android:label="@string/app_name"
14          android:theme="@style/AppTheme.NoActionBar"
15          android:screenOrientation="portrait">
16        <intent-filter>
17          <action android:name="android.intent.action.MAIN"/>
18
```

EXAMPLE 5.12 The AndroidManifest.xml file, Candy Store app, Version 1 (*Continued*)

```
19        <category android:name="android.intent.category.LAUNCHER"/>
20            </intent-filter>
21        </activity>
22
23        <activity
24            android:name=".InsertActivity"
25            android:screenOrientation="portrait">
26        </activity>
27
28        </application>
29
30    </manifest>
```

EXAMPLE 5.12 The AndroidManifest.xml file, Candy Store app, Version 1

Finally, in styles.xml, we specify that the text size in the various views is 24, as shown at line 5 of **EXAMPLE 5.13**.

```
1    <resources>
2
3      <!-- Base application theme. -->
4      <style name="AppTheme" parent="Theme.AppCompat.Light.DarkActionBar">
5        <item name="android:textSize">24sp</item>
6        <item name="colorPrimary">@color/colorPrimary</item>
7        <item name="colorPrimaryDark">@color/colorPrimaryDark</item>
8        <item name="colorAccent">@color/colorAccent</item>
9      </style>
10
11      <style name="AppTheme.NoActionBar">
12        <item name="windowActionBar">false</item>
13        <item name="windowNoTitle">true</item>
14      </style>
15
16      <style name="AppTheme.AppBarOverlay"
17            parent="ThemeOverlay.AppCompat.Dark.ActionBar"/>
18
19      <style name="AppTheme.PopupOverlay"
20            parent="ThemeOverlay.AppCompat.Light"/>
21
22    </resources>
```

EXAMPLE 5.13 The styles.xml file, Candy Store app, Version 1

FIGURE 5.3 The add a candy screen of the Candy Store app, Version 1

FIGURE 5.3 shows a preview of the insert screen of the app inside the Android Studio environment.

5.3 SQLite: Creating a Database, a Table, and Inserting Data: Candy Store App, Version 2

In Version 2, we create a database, create a table to store candies, and insert data in that table.

SQLite is available on Android devices; there is no setup required. It enables us to organize data as in a SQL relational database and execute SQL commands, although the data is stored in text files. The `android.database.sqlite` package contains classes and interfaces to manage databases, execute SQL queries, process their results, etc.

When creating a SQLite table, we are restricted to the following data types: `null`, `integer`, `real`, `text`, and `blob`. We use `real` for `floats` and `doubles`, and `text` for strings. SQLite includes support for date and time using the `integer`, `real`, or `text` data types.

TABLE 5.5 Selected Classes of the `android.database.sqlite` package	
Class	**Description**
SQLiteOpenHelper	Extend this abstract class to manage a database and its version. We must override the onCreate and onUpgrade methods.
SQLiteDatabase	Includes methods to execute SQL statements
Cursor	Encapsulates a table returned by a select SQL query.

TABLE 5.6 Sample SQL table for candies		
id	**Name**	**Price**
1	Chocolate cookie	1.49
2	Chocolate fudge	1.99
3	Walnut chocolate	2.99

TABLE 5.5 shows several useful classes of the `android.database.sqlite` package.

We include in the Model a class that mirrors the columns of a SQL table. We intend to store names and prices for candies as in **TABLE 5.6**, where `id` is an `int`, `name` is a `String`, and `price` is a `double`.

The `Candy` class, shown in **EXAMPLE 5.14**, mirrors the type of data we have in Table 5.6. It is a straightforward Java class with constructor, accessors, and mutators. We included a `toString` method, which is always very useful for debugging and feedback purposes.

```
1    package com.jblearning.candystorev2;
2
3    public class Candy {
4      private int id;
5      private String name;
6      private double price;
7
8      public Candy( int newId, String newName, double newPrice ) {
9        setId( newId );
10       setName( newName );
11       setPrice( newPrice );
12     }
13
```

EXAMPLE 5.14 The `Candy` class, Candy Store app, Version 2 (*Continued*)

```
14      public void setId( int newId ) {
15        id = newId;
16      }
17
18      public void setName( String newName ) {
19        name = newName;
20      }
21
22      public void setPrice( double newPrice ) {
23        if( newPrice >= 0.0 )
24          price = newPrice;
25      }
26
27      public int getId( ) {
28        return id;
29      }
30
31      public String getName( ) {
32        return name;
33      }
34
35      public double getPrice( ) {
36        return price;
37      }
38
39      public String toString( ) {
40        return id + " " + name + " " + price;
41      }
42    }
```

EXAMPLE 5.14 **The `Candy` class, Candy Store app, Version 2**

As part of the Model, we include a class containing methods to execute various basic SQL statements. When executing an insert, update, or delete statement, we can use the execSQL method of the SQLiteDatabase class, shown in TABLE 5.7. When executing a select statement, we can use the rawQuery method of the SQLiteDatabase class to execute it, and the methods of the Cursor class shown in TABLE 5.8 to process the results.

EXAMPLE 5.15 shows the DatabaseManager class, which extends SQLiteOpenHelper. The SQLiteOpenHelper class provides functionality to open, create, or upgrade a database. It is an abstract class and has two abstract methods, onCreate and onUpgrade, which we must override. It opens the database if it exists, creates it if it does not exist, and upgrades it as necessary (by calling onUpgrade automatically). The first time we call getWritableDatabase, onCreate will be called automatically. TABLE 5.9 shows these methods. In addition to that, we create a table named candy, and supply insert, delete, update, and select operations on that table. In order to keep it simple, we only include methods to insert a record, delete a record based on the value of

TABLE 5.7 Selected Methods of the `SQLiteDatabase` class

Method	Description
void execSQL(String sql)	Executes sql, a SQL query that does not return data. Can be used for create, insert, update, delete, but not for select queries.
Cursor rawQuery(String sql, String [ ] selectionArgs)	Executes sql and returns a Cursor; selectionArgs can be provided to match ?s in the where clause of the query.

TABLE 5.8 Selected Methods of the `Cursor` class

Method	Description
boolean moveToNext( )	Move this Cursor to the next row when processing results.
DataType getDataType(int column)	Returns the value for the current row at column index column. DataType can be a basic data type, String or Blob.

```
1   package com.jblearning.candystorev2;
2
3   import android.content.Context;
4   import android.database.Cursor;
5   import android.database.sqlite.SQLiteDatabase;
6   import android.database.sqlite.SQLiteOpenHelper;
7   import java.util.ArrayList;
8
9   public class DatabaseManager extends SQLiteOpenHelper {
10    private static final String DATABASE_NAME = "candyDB";
11    private static final int DATABASE_VERSION = 1;
12    private static final String TABLE_CANDY = "candy";
13    private static final String ID = "id";
14    private static final String NAME = "name";
15    private static final String PRICE = "price";
16
17    public DatabaseManager( Context context ) {
18      super( context, DATABASE_NAME, null, DATABASE_VERSION );
19    }
20
```

EXAMPLE 5.15 The `DatabaseManager` class, Candy Store app, Version 2 (*Continued*)

```
21    public void onCreate( SQLiteDatabase db ) {
22      // build sql create statement
23      String sqlCreate = "create table " + TABLE_CANDY + "( " + ID;
24      sqlCreate += " integer primary key autoincrement, " + NAME;
25      sqlCreate += " text, " + PRICE + " real )" ;
26
27      db.execSQL( sqlCreate );
28    }
29
30    public void onUpgrade( SQLiteDatabase db,
31                           int oldVersion, int newVersion ) {
32      // Drop old table if it exists
33      db.execSQL( "drop table if exists " + TABLE_CANDY );
34      // Re-create tables
35      onCreate( db );
36    }
37
38    public void insert( Candy candy ) {
39      SQLiteDatabase db = this.getWritableDatabase( );
40      String sqlInsert = "insert into " + TABLE_CANDY;
41      sqlInsert += " values( null, '" + candy.getName( );
42      sqlInsert += "', '" + candy.getPrice( ) + "' )";
43
44      db.execSQL( sqlInsert );
45      db.close( );
46    }
47
48    public void deleteById( int id ) {
49      SQLiteDatabase db = this.getWritableDatabase( );
50      String sqlDelete = "delete from " + TABLE_CANDY;
51      sqlDelete += " where " + ID + " = " + id;
52
53      db.execSQL( sqlDelete );
54      db.close( );
55    }
56
57    public void updateById( int id, String name, double price ) {
58      SQLiteDatabase db = this.getWritableDatabase();
59
60      String sqlUpdate = "update " + TABLE_CANDY;
61      sqlUpdate += " set " + NAME + " = '" + name + "', ";
62      sqlUpdate += PRICE + " = '" + price + "'";
63      sqlUpdate += " where " + ID + " = " + id;
64
65      db.execSQL( sqlUpdate );
66      db.close( );
```

EXAMPLE 5.15 The `DatabaseManager` class, Candy Store app, Version 2 (*Continued*)

```
67      }
68
69      public ArrayList<Candy> selectAll( ) {
70        String sqlQuery = "select * from " + TABLE_CANDY;
71
72        SQLiteDatabase db = this.getWritableDatabase( );
73        Cursor cursor = db.rawQuery( sqlQuery, null );
74
75        ArrayList<Candy> candies = new ArrayList<Candy>( );
76        while( cursor.moveToNext( ) ) {
77          Candy currentCandy
78              = new Candy( Integer.parseInt( cursor.getString( 0 ) ),
79                      cursor.getString( 1 ), cursor.getDouble( 2 ) );
80          candies.add( currentCandy );
81        }
82        db.close( );
83        return candies;
84      }
85
86      public Candy selectById( int id ) {
87        String sqlQuery = "select * from " + TABLE_CANDY;
88        sqlQuery += " where " + ID + " = " + id;
89
90        SQLiteDatabase db = this.getWritableDatabase( );
91        Cursor cursor = db.rawQuery( sqlQuery, null );
92
93        Candy candy = null;
94        if( cursor.moveToFirst( ) )
95          candy = new Candy( Integer.parseInt( cursor.getString( 0 ) ),
96                      cursor.getString( 1 ), cursor.getDouble( 2 ) );
97        return candy;
98      }
99    }
```

EXAMPLE 5.15 The `DatabaseManager` class, Candy Store app, Version 2

its id, update a record, select a record, and select all the rows in the candy table. We could add more methods, for example, deleting or selecting records based on the value of the candy name.

The constructor (lines 17–19) calls the super constructor shown in Table 5.9. The onCreate method (lines 21–28) is automatically called when the database is first created. Inside it, we should create the tables that we need. We define a String representing an SQL statement to create the candy table at lines 22–25 and actually create the table at line 27. Note that a database is specific to the app that uses it. If we have two different apps, we have two different databases.

The insert, deleteById, and updateById methods (lines 38–46, 48–55, 57– 67) share the same pattern: we get a SQLiteDatabase reference by calling the getWritableDatabase

TABLE 5.9 Selected Methods of the `SQLiteOpenHelper` class

Method	Description
SQLiteOpenHelper(Context context, String name, SQLiteDatabase.CursorFactory factory, int newVersion)	Constructor: creates a SQLiteOpenHelper object. Name is the name of the database. Factory can be used to create Cursor objects, use null for default.
abstract void onCreate(SQLiteDatabase db)	Called when the database is created for the first time. We must implement that method.
abstract void onUpgrade(SQLiteDatabase db, int oldVersion, int newVersion)	Called when the database needs to be upgraded. We must implement that method.
SQLiteDatabase getWritableDatabase( )	Creates and/or opens a database that we will use for reading and writing. Triggers a call to onCreate the first time it is called. Returns a SQLiteDatabase reference, which we can use to perform SQL operations.

of the `SQLiteOpenHelper` class, build an SQL query, execute it by calling the `execSQL` method, and close the database.

The `selectAll` and `selectById` methods (lines 69–84 and 86–98) get a `SQLiteDatabase` reference, build a select SQL query, execute it by calling the `rawQuery` method, process the results, close the database, and return an `ArrayList` of Candy objects (`selectAll` method) or one `Candy` object (`selectById` method). The `rawQuery` method returns a `Cursor` object reference. The `moveToNext` method (line 76) makes the `Cursor` object point to the next row of results and returns `false` if we have processed all the rows. Thus, we process all the rows returned by our query using a `while` loop (lines 76–81). Inside the body of the loop, we construct a `Candy` object for the current row (lines 77–79), and add it to the `ArrayList candies` at line 80. We return `candies` at line 83. For the `selectById` method, we expect either 0 or 1 row returned by the query since we are selecting based on the value of the table's primary key, `id`. Thus, we do not need to loop. We call the `moveToFirst` method at line 94 . If it returns `true`, one row is returned by the query. We build the corresponding `Candy` object at lines 95–96. We return it at line 97.

Note that during the debugging stage, we can use `try` and `catch` blocks when calling these methods because they throw an unchecked `SQLException` when the SQL `String` is invalid.

Now that our Model is ready, we can use it in the Controller, the `InsertActivity` class, in order to add a candy in our database, as shown in **EXAMPLE 5.16**. We declare an instance variable of type `DatabaseManager` at line 10 and instantiate it at line 14. We insert the data input by the user at lines 25–33. We create and instantiate a `Candy` object at line 28 and insert it in the candy table at line 29. We use `try` and `catch` blocks to convert the user input for `price` from a `String` to a `double`. Note that we do not care what `id` value we pass to the `Candy` constructor at line 28 because the `id` column of the `candy` table has type `auto_increment`; the `insert` method of `DatabaseManager` does not use the `id` value of the `Candy` object it inserts.

```
1   package com.jblearning.candystorev2;
2
3   import android.os.Bundle;
4   import android.support.v7.app.AppCompatActivity;
5   import android.view.View;
6   import android.widget.EditText;
7   import android.widget.Toast;
8
9   public class InsertActivity extends AppCompatActivity  {
10    private DatabaseManager dbManager;
11
12    public void onCreate( Bundle savedInstanceState ) {
13      super.onCreate( savedInstanceState );
14      dbManager = new DatabaseManager( this );
15      setContentView( R.layout.activity_insert );
16    }
17
18    public void insert( View v ) {
19      // Retrieve name and price
20      EditText nameEditText = ( EditText ) findViewById( R.id.input_name );
21      EditText priceEditText = ( EditText ) findViewById( R.id.input_price );
22      String name = nameEditText.getText( ).toString( );
23      String priceString = priceEditText.getText( ).toString( );
24
25      // insert new candy in database
26      try {
27        double price = Double.parseDouble( priceString );
28        Candy candy = new Candy( 0, name, price );
29        dbManager.insert( candy );
30        Toast.makeText( this, "Candy added", Toast.LENGTH_SHORT ).show( );
31      } catch( NumberFormatException nfe ) {
32        Toast.makeText( this, "Price error", Toast.LENGTH_LONG ).show( );
33      }
34
35      // clear data
36      nameEditText.setText( "" );
37      priceEditText.setText( "" );
38    }
39
40    public void goBack( View v ) {
41      this.finish( );
42    }
43  }
```

EXAMPLE 5.16 The InsertActivity class, Candy Store app, Version 2

TABLE 5.10 Selected Methods and Constants of the `Toast` class	
Method	**Description**
static Toast makeText(Context context, CharSequence text, int duration)	Creates a Toast within context with content text and a duration specified by duration.
void show( )	Shows this Toast.
Constant	**Value**
LENGTH_SHORT	0; use this constant for a Toast of approximately 3 seconds.
LENGTH_LONG	1; use this constant for a Toast of approximately 5 seconds.

We provide feedback to the user at lines 30 and 32, showing a `Toast`. A `Toast` is a temporary pop-up that can be used to provide visual feedback on an operation. It automatically disappears after a short time. The `Toast` class is in the `android.widget` package. **TABLE 5.10** shows methods and constants of the `Toast` class. To create a `Toast` inside an `Activity` class, we use the `makeText` static method, pass `this` (an `Activity` "is a" `Context`), a `String` (a `String` "is a" `CharSequence`), and one of the two constants of the `Toast` class to specify the duration of the `Toast`. We then can show the `Toast` by calling the `show` method. The following code sequence illustrates this. Lines 30 and 32 chain the two method calls.

```
Toast toast = Toast.makeText( this, "Hi", Toast.LENGTH_SHORT );
toast.show( );
```

COMMON ERROR: When creating a `Toast`, do not forget to call the `show` method. Otherwise, the `Toast` will not show.

Finally, we delete the `TextView` element in the content_main.xml file so that the first screen does not show "Hello World!".

When we run the app, enter some data and click on the ADD icon, the `Toast` message appears. If we want to check that a new row is added to the `candy` table, we can call the `selectAll` method of the `DatabaseManager` class and loop through the resulting `ArrayList` of `Candy` objects. We can write these statements at the end of the `insert` method and check the output in Logcat:

```
ArrayList<Candy> candies = dbManager.selectAll( );
for( Candy candy : candies )
  Log.w( "MainActivity", "candy = " + candy.toString( ) );
```

5.4 Deleting Data: Candy Store App, Version 3

In Version 3, we enable the user to delete a candy from the database. To implement this functionality, we need to do the following:

▶ Create a delete activity.

▶ Modify `MainActivity` so that when the user clicks on the DELETE icon, the user goes to the delete activity.

▶ Add an activity element in AndroidManifest.xml for the delete activity.

We create a new class named **DeleteActivity**. We update the `onOptionsItemSelected` method of the `MainActivity` class (see **EXAMPLE 5.17**) so that when the user clicks on the delete icon (line 36), we create an intent for a `DeleteActivity` (line 37), and then start that activity (line 38).

```
1    package com.jblearning.candystorev3;
...
11   public class MainActivity extends AppCompatActivity {
...
27     @Override
28     public boolean onOptionsItemSelected( MenuItem item ) {
29       int id = item.getItemId( );
30       switch ( id ) {
31         case R.id.action_add:
32           Log.w( "MainActivity", "Add selected" );
33           Intent insertIntent = new Intent( this, InsertActivity.class );
34           this.startActivity( insertIntent );
35           return true;
36         case R.id.action_delete:
37           Intent deleteIntent = new Intent( this, DeleteActivity.class );
38           this.startActivity( deleteIntent );
39           Log.w( "MainActivity", "Delete selected" );
40           return true;
41         case R.id.action_update:
42           Log.w( "MainActivity", "Update selected" );
43           return true;
44         default:
45           return super.onOptionsItemSelected( item );
46       }
47     }
48   }
```

EXAMPLE 5.17 The `MainActivity` class, Candy Store app, Version 3

EXAMPLE 5.18 shows the updated AndroidManifest.xml file. It includes an additional activity element for a `DeleteActivity` at lines 28–31.

```
 1    <?xml version="1.0" encoding="utf-8"?>
 2    <manifest package="com.jblearning.candystorev3"
 3             xmlns:android="http://schemas.android.com/apk/res/android">
...
 5      <application
...
11        <activity
12          android:name=".MainActivity"
...
21        </activity>
22
23        <activity
24            android:name=".InsertActivity"
25            android:screenOrientation="portrait">
26        </activity>
27
28        <activity
29            android:name=".DeleteActivity"
30            android:screenOrientation="portrait">
31        </activity>
32
33      </application>
34
35    </manifest>
```

EXAMPLE 5.18 **The AndroidManifest.xml file, Candy Store app, Version 3**

EXAMPLE 5.19 shows the DeleteActivity class. As **FIGURE 5.4** shows, we want to display a list of all the candies as radio buttons. Clicking on a radio button deletes the candy and refreshes the screen. When we delete an item from a database or a file, we usually ask the user to confirm via an alert box before we actually delete the item. In the interest of keeping this example simple, this is left as an exercise.

Because the number of records in the candy table varies over time, the number of radio buttons varies as well. Thus, we need to create the GUI programmatically. At line 21 of the onCreate method, we call the updateView method, which creates the GUI. We code updateView at lines 24–64: we retrieve all the records from the candy table and create one radio button per record. In order to do this, we call the selectAll method of the DatabaseManager class at line 26, using the instance variable dbManager (line 16) that we instantiate at line 20.

Because we do not know how many candies there are, it is possible that we will not have enough space on the screen to display all the necessary radio buttons. Thus, we place the RadioGroup that contains all the radio buttons inside a ScrollView (lines 28 and 50). In this way, we can scroll through the radio buttons if necessary.

```
1    package com.jblearning.candystorev3;
2
3    import android.os.Bundle;
4    import android.support.v7.app.AppCompatActivity;
5    import android.view.View;
6    import android.widget.Button;
7    import android.widget.RadioButton;
8    import android.widget.RadioGroup;
9    import android.widget.RelativeLayout;
10   import android.widget.ScrollView;
11   import android.widget.Toast;
12
13   import java.util.ArrayList;
14
15   public class DeleteActivity extends AppCompatActivity {
16     private DatabaseManager dbManager;
17
18     public void onCreate( Bundle savedInstanceState ) {
19       super.onCreate( savedInstanceState );
20       dbManager = new DatabaseManager( this );
21       updateView( );
22     }
23
24     // Build a View dynamically with all the candies
25     public void updateView( ) {
26       ArrayList<Candy> candies = dbManager.selectAll( );
27       RelativeLayout layout = new RelativeLayout( this );
28       ScrollView scrollView = new ScrollView( this );
29       RadioGroup group = new RadioGroup( this );
30       for ( Candy candy : candies ) {
31         RadioButton rb = new RadioButton( this );
32         rb.setId( candy.getId( ) );
33         rb.setText( candy.toString( ) );
34         group.addView( rb );
35       }
36       // set up event handling
37       RadioButtonHandler rbh = new RadioButtonHandler( );
38       group.setOnCheckedChangeListener(rbh);
39
40       // create a back button
41       Button backButton = new Button( this );
42       backButton.setText( R.string.button_back );
43
```

EXAMPLE 5.19 The `DeleteActivity` class, Candy Store app, Version 3 (*Continued*)

```
44        backButton.setOnClickListener( new View.OnClickListener( ) {
45          public void onClick(View v) {
46            DeleteActivity.this.finish();
47          }
48        });
49
50        scrollView.addView(group);
51        layout.addView( scrollView );
52
53        // add back button at bottom
54        RelativeLayout.LayoutParams params
55            = new RelativeLayout.LayoutParams(
56            RelativeLayout.LayoutParams.WRAP_CONTENT,
57            RelativeLayout.LayoutParams.WRAP_CONTENT );
58        params.addRule( RelativeLayout.ALIGN_PARENT_BOTTOM );
59        params.addRule( RelativeLayout.CENTER_HORIZONTAL );
60        params.setMargins( 0, 0, 0, 50 );
61        layout.addView( backButton, params );
62
63        setContentView( layout );
64      }
65
66      private class RadioButtonHandler
67        implements RadioGroup.OnCheckedChangeListener {
68        public void onCheckedChanged( RadioGroup group, int checkedId ) {
69          // delete candy from database
70          dbManager.deleteById( checkedId );
71          Toast.makeText( DeleteActivity.this, "Candy deleted",
72            Toast.LENGTH_SHORT ).show( );
73
74          // update screen
75          updateView( );
76        }
77      }
78    }
```

EXAMPLE 5.19 The `DeleteActivity` **class, Candy Store app, Version 3**

Although the user can use the device's back button to go back to the previous activity, we add a button to do that as a convenience (lines 40–42; we use a string named `button_back` from strings.xml). We set up event handling for the button at lines 44–48 using an anonymous object of type `View.OnClickListener`. When the user clicks on the button, the current activity is popped off the stack and we go back to the previous activity, the first screen. However, a `ScrollView` does not allow more than one `ViewGroup` inside it. Thus, we cannot add the button inside the `ScrollView`.

FIGURE 5.4 The Delete Screen of the Candy Store app, Version 3

We place the `ScrollView` inside a `RelativeLayout` (line 51) and place the button at the bottom of the `RelativeLayout` (lines 53–61).

We create the `RadioGroup` at line 29. At lines 30–35, we loop through the `ArrayList` of `Candy` objects: we create one `RadioButton` per `Candy` (line 31), set its text to the `String` representation of that `Candy` object (line 33), and add it to the `RadioGroup` at line 34. At line 32, set the `id` of the `RadioButton` to the `id` of the corresponding `Candy` object. In this way, when the user selects a radio button, we can access the correct `Candy` object.

At lines 36–38, we set up event handling for the group of radio buttons. TABLE 5.11 shows the `setOnCheckedChangeListener` method of the `RadioGroup` class that we use to handle the selection of a radio button within a group. The parameter of that method is a `RadioGroup`. `OnCheckedChangeListener`. `OnCheckedChangeListener` is a `public static` inner interface of `RadioGroup`. We code a `private` class that implements `RadioGroup.OnCheckedChangeListener` at lines 66–77. At lines 69–70, we delete the candy selected from the candy

TABLE 5.11 Selected Methods of the `RadioGroup` class	
Method	**Description**
void setOnCheckedChangeListener(RadioGroup. OnCheckedChangeListener listener)	Registers listener on this RadioGroup. When the selected radio button changes in this group, the onCheckedChange of method of the RadioGroup. OnCheckedChangeListener interface is called.

table. Because we assigned the `Candy id` to the corresponding `RadioButton`, we know that the `checkedId` parameter is not only the `id` of the `RadioButton` that is selected, but also the `id` of the correct `Candy` to delete. At lines 71–72, using a `Toast`, we provide some visual feedback that a candy was deleted. At lines 74–75, we call `updateView` to update the list of radio buttons, reflecting that the deleted candy is no longer in the database.

> **SOFTWARE ENGINEERING:** When building a GUI programmatically, consider placing the various components inside a `ScrollView`.

Figure 5.4 shows the delete screen of the app after the user selects the DELETE icon. All candies are displayed as radio buttons. Clicking on one deletes it and refreshes the screen. Note that the database in Version 3 is different from the database in Version 2. Thus, if we run Version 3 without inserting candies, the `candy` table is empty and no candy will show when we click on the DELETE icon.

5.5 Updating Data: Candy Store App, Version 4

In Version 4, we enable the user to update the name and price of a candy from the database. To implement this functionality, we need to do the following:

▶   Create an update activity.
▶   Modify `MainActivity` so that when the user clicks on the UPDATE icon, the user goes to the update activity.
▶   Add an activity element in AndroidManifest.xml for the update activity.

This is very similar to Version 3 in which we added the delete activity. We create a new class named **UpdateActivity**. We update the `onOptionsItemSelected` method of the `MainActivity` class (see lines 39–40 of **EXAMPLE 5.20**) and the AndroidManifest.xml file (see lines 33–36 of **EXAMPLE 5.21**) in the same way as we did for the delete activity.

```
 1   package com.jblearning.candystorev4;
...
10   public class MainActivity extends AppCompatActivity {
...
26     @Override
27     public boolean onOptionsItemSelected(MenuItem item) {
28       int id = item.getItemId( );
29       switch ( id ) {
30         case R.id.action_add:
31           Intent insertIntent = new Intent( this, InsertActivity.class );
32           this.startActivity( insertIntent );
33           return true;
34         case R.id.action_delete:
35           Intent deleteIntent = new Intent( this, DeleteActivity.class );
36           this.startActivity( deleteIntent );
37           return true;
38         case R.id.action_update:
39           Intent updateIntent = new Intent( this, UpdateActivity.class );
40           this.startActivity( updateIntent );
41           return true;
42         default:
43           return super.onOptionsItemSelected( item );
44       }
45     }
46   }
```

EXAMPLE 5.20 The `MainActivity` class, Candy Store app, Version 4

```
 1   <?xml version="1.0" encoding="utf-8"?>
 2   <manifest package="com.jblearning.candystorev4"
 3             xmlns:android="http://schemas.android.com/apk/res/android">
 4
 5     <application
...
28       <activity
29           android:name=".DeleteActivity"
30           android:screenOrientation="portrait">
31       </activity>
32
33       <activity
34           android:name=".UpdateActivity"
35           android:screenOrientation="portrait">
36       </activity>
37
38     </application>
39
40   </manifest>
```

EXAMPLE 5.21 The AndroidManifest.xml file, Candy Store app, Version 4

EXAMPLE 5.22 shows the `UpdateActivity` class. As **FIGURE 5.5** shows, we want to display a list of all the candies. For each candy, we display its id in a `TextView`, its name and its price in `EditTexts` so they can be edited, and a button to update the name and price of that candy in the database. As for the delete activity, clicking on a button updates the candy and refreshes the screen.

As in the delete activity, we need to create the GUI by code and will wrap a `ScrollView` in the list of candies. To keep this example simple, we do not provide a BACK button to go back to the previous activity. The user can go back using the device's BACK button. We organize the components in a grid with four columns: we place the id in the first column in a `TextView`, the name and the price in the second and third columns in `EditTexts`, and a button in the fourth column. As before, the `updateView` method creates the GUI, and is called by `onCreate` and after the user updates a candy.

The `ScrollView` and `GridLayout` are created at lines 32–36. We create arrays for the `TextViews`, `EditTexts`, and `Buttons` at lines 38–41.

```
1  package com.jblearning.candystorev4;
2
3  import android.graphics.Point;
4  import android.os.Bundle;
5  import android.support.v7.app.AppCompatActivity;
6  import android.text.InputType;
7  import android.view.Gravity;
8  import android.view.View;
9  import android.view.ViewGroup;
10 import android.widget.Button;
11 import android.widget.EditText;
12 import android.widget.GridLayout;
13 import android.widget.ScrollView;
14 import android.widget.TextView;
15 import android.widget.Toast;
16
17 import java.util.ArrayList;
18
19 public class UpdateActivity extends AppCompatActivity  {
20   DatabaseManager dbManager;
21
22   public void onCreate( Bundle savedInstanceState ) {
23     super.onCreate( savedInstanceState );
24     dbManager = new DatabaseManager( this );
25     updateView( );
26   }
```

EXAMPLE 5.22 The `UpdateActivity` class, Candy Store app, Version 4 (*Continued*)

```
27
28      // Build a View dynamically with all the candies
29      public void updateView( ) {
30        ArrayList<Candy> candies = dbManager.selectAll( );
31        if( candies.size( ) > 0 ) {
32          // create ScrollView and GridLayout
33          ScrollView scrollView = new ScrollView( this );
34          GridLayout grid = new GridLayout( this );
35          grid.setRowCount( candies.size( ) );
36          grid.setColumnCount( 4 );
37
38          // create arrays of components
39          TextView [] ids = new TextView[candies.size( )];
40          EditText [][] namesAndPrices = new EditText[candies.size( )][2];
41          Button [] buttons = new Button[candies.size( )];
42          ButtonHandler bh = new ButtonHandler( );
43
44          // retrieve width of screen
45          Point size = new Point( );
46          getWindowManager( ).getDefaultDisplay( ).getSize( size );
47          int width = size.x;
48
49          int i = 0;
50
51          for ( Candy candy : candies ) {
52            // create the TextView for the candy's id
53            ids[i] = new TextView( this );
54            ids[i].setGravity( Gravity.CENTER );
55            ids[i].setText( "" + candy.getId( ) );
56
57            // create the two EditTexts for the candy's name and price
58            namesAndPrices[i][0] = new EditText( this );
59            namesAndPrices[i][1] = new EditText( this );
60            namesAndPrices[i][0].setText( candy.getName( ) );
61            namesAndPrices[i][1].setText( "" + candy.getPrice( ) );
62            namesAndPrices[i][1]
63               .setInputType( InputType.TYPE_CLASS_NUMBER );
64            namesAndPrices[i][0].setId( 10 * candy.getId( ) );
65            namesAndPrices[i][1].setId( 10 * candy.getId( ) + 1 );
66
67            // create the button
68            buttons[i] = new Button( this );
69            buttons[i].setText( "Update" );
70            buttons[i].setId( candy.getId( ) );
71
```

EXAMPLE 5.22 **The** `UpdateActivity` **class, Candy Store app, Version 4 (*Continued*)**

```
72          // set up event handling
73          buttons[i].setOnClickListener( bh );
74
75          // add the elements to grid
76          grid.addView( ids[i], width / 10,
77                        ViewGroup.LayoutParams.WRAP_CONTENT );
78          grid.addView( namesAndPrices[i][0], ( int ) ( width * .4 ),
79                        ViewGroup.LayoutParams.WRAP_CONTENT );
80          grid.addView( namesAndPrices[i][1], ( int ) ( width * .15 ),
81                        ViewGroup.LayoutParams.WRAP_CONTENT );
82          grid.addView( buttons[i], ( int ) ( width * .35 ),
83                        ViewGroup.LayoutParams.WRAP_CONTENT );
84
85          i++;
86        }
87      scrollView.addView( grid );
88      setContentView( scrollView );
89    }
90  }
91
92  private class ButtonHandler implements View.OnClickListener {
93    public void onClick( View v ) {
94      // retrieve name and price of the candy
95      int candyId = v.getId( );
96      EditText nameET = ( EditText ) findViewById( 10 * candyId );
97      EditText priceET = ( EditText ) findViewById( 10 * candyId + 1 );
98      String name = nameET.getText( ).toString( );
99      String priceString = priceET.getText( ).toString( );
100
101      // update candy in database
102      try {
103        double price = Double.parseDouble( priceString );
104        dbManager.updateById( candyId, name, price );
105        Toast.makeText( UpdateActivity.this, "Candy updated",
106          Toast.LENGTH_SHORT ).show( );
107
108        // update screen
109        updateView( );
110      } catch( NumberFormatException nfe ) {
111        Toast.makeText( UpdateActivity.this,
112                        "Price error", Toast.LENGTH_LONG ).show( );
113      }
114    }
115  }
116 }
```

EXAMPLE 5.22 The `UpdateActivity` class, Candy Store app, Version 4

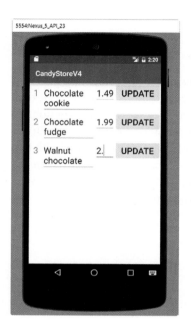

FIGURE 5.5 The update screen of the Candy Store app, Version 4

We distribute the width of the screen among the four components across it as follows:

▶ 10% for the id,
▶ 40% for the name,
▶ 15% for the price, and
▶ 35% for the button.

We assign each component a width as specified above when we add it to the GridLayout at lines 75–83. We retrieve the width of the screen at lines 44–47 and assign it to the variable width.

At lines 51–86, we loop through the ArrayList of Candy objects. We create the TextViews for the ids at lines 52–55. We create the EditTexts at lines 57–65. We give them a unique id at lines 64–65 so that we can later access them in order to retrieve the name and price input by the user. We create the Buttons at lines 67–70. We also give each Button a unique id (line 70), the id of the corresponding Candy object. The parameter of the onClick method of the View.OnClickListener interface is a View that is a reference to the View that was clicked. In this way, we can retrieve the id of the candy to update by retrieving the id of that View. At lines 72–73, we set up event handling.

We add the grid to the ScrollView at line 87 and assign the ScrollView as the content View of this activity at line 88.

Figure 5.5 shows the update screen. Clicking on an UPDATE button updates the corresponding candy and refreshes the screen. The user is updating the price of the walnut chocolate candy. Once again, if we run Version 4 without inserting candies first, the candy table is empty and no candy will show when we click on the UPDATE icon.

5.6 Running the Cash Register: Candy Store App, Version 5

In Version 5, we enable the user to run the app as a cash register using the first screen. We provide a grid of buttons, one button per candy. The store employee can use the buttons to compute the total amount of money due by a customer who buys candies. Each time the user clicks on a button, we add the price of the corresponding candy to the total for that customer and show the total in a Toast.

When the user clicks on a button, we need to access the price of the candy associated with that button. An easy way to solve that problem is to create a new class, CandyButton, which extends the Button class and has a Candy instance variable. It is shown in **EXAMPLE 5.23**. We include a getPrice method (lines 14–16) that returns the price of the Candy instance variable. In this way, a CandyButton "knows" the price of its associated Candy.

```
1   package com.jblearning.candystorev5;
2
3   import android.content.Context;
4   import android.widget.Button;
5
6   public class CandyButton extends Button {
7     private Candy candy;
8
9     public CandyButton( Context context, Candy newCandy ) {
10      super( context );
11      candy = newCandy;
12    }
13
14    public double getPrice( ) {
15      return candy.getPrice( );
16    }
17  }
```

EXAMPLE 5.23 The CandyButton **class, Candy Store app, Version 5**

The app needs to work for more than one customer. Thus, we need to have a way to reset the running total to 0 whenever we are done with the current customer and are ready for the next one. An easy way to do that is to provide an additional item in the menu and reset the total to 0 when the user clicks on that item. Thus, we add an item in the menu as shown in **EXAMPLE 5.24** at lines 5–8. We add a String named reset with value RESET in the strings.xml file (not shown). We also add our own icon, stored in the ic_reset.png file, which we place in the drawable directory. We access that icon at line 7 using the expression @drawable/ic_reset.

As we did in the delete and update activities, we need to place our buttons inside a ScrollView because we do not know how many there are each time we run the app . An easy way to do this is

```
1    <menu xmlns:android="http://schemas.android.com/apk/res/android"
2          xmlns:app="http://schemas.android.com/apk/res-auto"
3          xmlns:tools="http://schemas.android.com/tools"
4          tools:context="com.jblearning.candystorev5.MainActivity">
5       <item android:id="@+id/action_reset"
6             android:title="@string/reset"
7             android:icon="@drawable/ic_reset"
8             app:showAsAction="ifRoom"/>
9
10      <item android:id="@+id/action_add"
11            android:title="@string/add"
12            android:icon="@android:drawable/ic_menu_add"
13            app:showAsAction="ifRoom"/>
14
15      <item android:id="@+id/action_delete"
16            android:title="@string/delete"
17            android:icon="@android:drawable/ic_menu_delete"
18            app:showAsAction="ifRoom"/>
19
20      <item android:id="@+id/action_update"
21            android:title="@string/update"
22            android:icon="@android:drawable/ic_menu_edit"
23            app:showAsAction="ifRoom"/>
24   </menu>
```

EXAMPLE 5.24 **The menu_main.xml file, Candy Store app, Version 5**

to replace the RelativeLayout inside content_main.xml with a ScrollView element as shown in **EXAMPLE 5.25**. We give it an id (line 12) so that we can retrieve it inside the MainActivity class. We also eliminate the padding inside the ScrollView.

```
1    <?xml version="1.0" encoding="utf-8"?>
2    <ScrollView
3        xmlns:android="http://schemas.android.com/apk/res/android"
4        xmlns:app="http://schemas.android.com/apk/res-auto"
5        xmlns:tools="http://schemas.android.com/tools"
6        android:layout_width="match_parent"
7        android:layout_height="match_parent"
8
9        app:layout_behavior="@string/appbar_scrolling_view_behavior"
10       tools:context="com.jblearning.candystorev5.MainActivity"
11       tools:showIn="@layout/activity_main"
12       android:id="@+id/scrollView">
13
14   </ScrollView>
```

EXAMPLE 5.25 **The content_main.xml file, Candy Store app, Version 5**

EXAMPLE 5.26 shows the updated `MainActivity` class. It has four instance variables (lines 19–22): A `DatabaseManager`, `dbManager`, so that we can query the database to retrieve the candies; `total`, a `double`, to keep track of the running total for the current customer; `scrollView`, a reference to the `ScrollView` defined in content_main.xml; and `buttonWidth`, the width of each button. We instantiate `dbManager` at line 30, initialize `total` to `0.0` at line 31, instantiate `scrollView` at line 32, and calculate `buttonWidth` at lines 33–35. We want to size the buttons so that their width is half the width of the screen. Thus, we assign half the width of the screen to the variable `buttonWidth`. When the user has finished processing the current customer and clicks on the reset icon (line 104), we reset the running total to `0.0` (line 105) so that the app is ready to compute the total for the next customer.

```
1   package com.jblearning.candystorev5;
2
3   import android.content.Intent;
4   import android.graphics.Point;
5   import android.os.Bundle;
6   import android.support.v7.app.AppCompatActivity;
7   import android.support.v7.widget.Toolbar;
8   import android.view.Menu;
9   import android.view.MenuItem;
10  import android.view.View;
11  import android.widget.GridLayout;
12  import android.widget.ScrollView;
13  import android.widget.Toast;
14
15  import java.text.NumberFormat;
16  import java.util.ArrayList;
17
18  public class MainActivity extends AppCompatActivity {
19    private DatabaseManager dbManager;
20    private double total;
21    private ScrollView scrollView;
22    private int buttonWidth;
23
24    @Override
25    protected void onCreate( Bundle savedInstanceState ) {
26      super.onCreate( savedInstanceState );
27      setContentView( R.layout.activity_main );
28      Toolbar toolbar = ( Toolbar ) findViewById( R.id.toolbar );
29      setSupportActionBar( toolbar );
30      dbManager = new DatabaseManager( this );
31      total = 0.0;
32      scrollView = ( ScrollView ) findViewById( R.id.scrollView );
```

EXAMPLE 5.26 The `MainActivity` class, Candy Store app, Version 5 (*Continued*)

```
33        Point size = new Point( );
34        getWindowManager( ).getDefaultDisplay( ).getSize( size );
35        buttonWidth = size.x / 2;
36        updateView( );
37     }
38
39     protected void onResume( ) {
40        super.onResume( );
41        updateView( );
42     }
43
44     public void updateView( ) {
45        ArrayList<Candy> candies = dbManager.selectAll( );
46        if( candies.size( ) > 0 ) {
47           // remove subviews inside scrollView if necessary
48           scrollView.removeAllViewsInLayout( );
49
50           // set up the grid layout
51           GridLayout grid = new GridLayout( this );
52           grid.setRowCount( ( candies.size( ) + 1 ) / 2 );
53           grid.setColumnCount( 2 );
54
55           // create array of buttons, 2 per row
56           CandyButton [] buttons = new CandyButton[candies.size( )];
57           ButtonHandler bh = new ButtonHandler( );
58
59           // fill the grid
60           int i = 0;
61           for ( Candy candy : candies ) {
62             // create the button
63             buttons[i] = new CandyButton( this, candy );
64             buttons[i].setText( candy.getName( )
65                 + "\n" + candy.getPrice( ) );
66
67             // set up event handling
68             buttons[i].setOnClickListener( bh );
69
70             // add the button to grid
71             grid.addView( buttons[i], buttonWidth,
72                 GridLayout.LayoutParams.WRAP_CONTENT );
73             i++;
74           }
75           scrollView.addView( grid );
76        }
77     }
78
```

EXAMPLE 5.26 **The `MainActivity` class, Candy Store app, Version 5 (*Continued*)**

```
79      @Override
80      public boolean onCreateOptionsMenu( Menu menu ) {
81        getMenuInflater( ).inflate( R.menu.menu_main, menu );
82        return true;
83      }
84
85      @Override
86      public boolean onOptionsItemSelected(MenuItem item) {
87        int id = item.getItemId( );
88        switch ( id ) {
89          case R.id.action_add:
90            Intent insertIntent
91              = new Intent( this, InsertActivity.class );
92            this.startActivity( insertIntent );
93            return true;
94          case R.id.action_delete:
95            Intent deleteIntent
96              = new Intent( this, DeleteActivity.class );
97            this.startActivity( deleteIntent );
98            return true;
99          case R.id.action_update:
100           Intent updateIntent
101             = new Intent( this, UpdateActivity.class );
102           this.startActivity( updateIntent );
103           return true;
104         case R.id.action_reset:
105           total = 0.0;
106           return true;
107         default:
108           return super.onOptionsItemSelected( item );
109       }
110     }
111
112     private class ButtonHandler implements View.OnClickListener {
113       public void onClick( View v ) {
114         // retrieve price of the candy and add it to total
115         total += ( ( CandyButton ) v ).getPrice( );
116         String pay =
117           NumberFormat.getCurrencyInstance( ).format( total );
118         Toast.makeText( MainActivity.this, pay,
119             Toast.LENGTH_LONG ).show( );
120       }
121     }
122   }
```

EXAMPLE 5.26 **The** `MainActivity` **class, Candy Store app, Version 5**

The updateView method (lines 44–77) creates the GUI and sets up event handling. We call updateView inside onCreate (line 36) when the app starts and also inside onResume (line 41) when the user comes back from a secondary activity such as add, delete, or update. Indeed, the contents of the candy table may have changed when the user comes back from a secondary activity so it is necessary to update the first screen by calling updateView. The onResume method is automatically called when the user comes back to this activity.

The updateView method has similarities with the updateView method in the UpdateActivity class. It is possible that the user added, deleted, or updated one or more candies before coming back to this View. Thus, we first remove all the buttons inside scrollView at lines 47–48 before rebuilding scrollView. We create a grid of buttons dynamically, one button per candy. We include two buttons per row (line 53). We size the number of rows to guarantee to have enough room for all the buttons (line 52). As in the delete and update activities, we put the grid inside a ScrollView so that we have automatic scrolling if needed (line 75).

Inside each button, we put the name and the price of the candy, each on one line (lines 62–65). Long candy names may require two lines of their own. We could set the font size of each button dynamically to make each candy name fit on one line. This is beyond the scope of this chapter, but we explain it in Appendix A. We set up event handling at lines 67–68.

The onClick method of the ButtonHandler class (lines 113–120) is called when the user clicks on a button. We update total (line 115) and show a Toast whose value is formatted as currency (lines 116–119). The benefit of using the CandyButton class is illustrated at line 115, where we cast the View parameter v, which represents the button clicked, to a CandyButton and call getPrice to retrieve the price of the corresponding candy.

FIGURE 5.6 Running the cash register of the Candy Store app, Version 5

FIGURE 5.6 shows all the candies and a current running total of $4.48 after the user selected chocolate cookie and walnut chocolate. Note the three vertical dots showing on the right of the menu because there is not enough space for all the icons. Touching the three dots opens a submenu showing the missing items.

Chapter Summary

- We can place menu items in the action bar.
- A menu item can be either text or an icon.
- A menu can be defined in an XML file, such as the automatically generated menu_main.xml, using item elements inside a menu element.

- The onCreateOptionsMenu method of the Activity class is automatically called when the activity starts.
- Clicking on an item in a menu triggers a call to the onOptionsItemSelected method.
- We can retrieve which item was selected if we give each item an id.
- SQLite is available on every Android device.
- SQLite allows us to organize our data in a relational database manner and perform SQL queries.
- In order to perform database operations, we extend the SQLiteOpenHelper class.
- The getWritableDatabase method of the SQLiteOpenHelper creates or returns a SQLiteDatabase object for the current app.
- The SQLiteDatabase class includes methods to perform SQL queries.
- To perform insert, update, and delete queries, we use the execSQL method of SQLiteDatabase.
- To perform a select query, we use the rawQuery method of SQLiteDatabase.
- The rawQuery method returns a Cursor object, which allows us to loop through the results of the query.
- We can use the Toast class to provide temporary visual feedback to the user.
- Using SQLite typically involves building a GUI programmatically since we do not know in advance how many components will be in the GUI.
- Using SQLite also involves using a ScrollView in case the screen is not big enough to hold all the components.

 # Exercises, Problems, and Projects

Multiple-Choice Exercises

1. The menu whose code is automatically generated when using a Basic Activity template is placed in
   - The whole screen
   - The action bar
   - The bottom of the screen

2. It is possible to place icons in a menu
   - True
   - False

3. What is typically inside an XML file defining a menu?
   - A menu element and item elements inside it
   - An item element and menu elements inside it
   - Item elements only
   - Menu elements only

4. SQLite is available on Android devices
   - True, without any special installation
   - No
   - No, but it can be installed

5. What is the name of the class that we extend in order to manage database operations?
   - Sqlite
   - SQLite
   - SQLiteOpenHelper
   - DatabaseHelper

6. The onCreate method of the class in question 5
   - Is never called
   - Is called every time we instantiate an object of that class
   - Is called the first time (only) we instantiate an object of that class

7. The name of the method of the SQLiteDatabase class to execute insert, delete, or update SQL queries is
   - execSQL
   - sqlExec
   - queryExec
   - exec

8. The name of the method of the SQLiteDatabase class to execute a select SQL query is
   - execSQL
   - query
   - rawQuery
   - sqlExec

9. The return type of the method in question 8 is
   - SQL
   - Cursor
   - ResultSet
   - Result

Fill in the Code

10. Inside an item element of a menu, this line of code makes the item visible in the action bar if there is room for it.

```
<item
  ...

/>
```

11. Inside an item element of a menu, this line of code specifies that the title of the item is the value of the string test, defined in strings.xml.

```
<item
  ...

/>
```

12. Inside an item element of a menu, this line of code specifies that the icon of the item is the file named image.png, which is stored in the drawable directory.

```
<item
  ...

/>
```

13. Inside the AndroidManifest.xml file, add an activity element of the type SecondActivity class.

```
        </activity>
        <!-- Your code goes here -->


    </application>
```

14. When the user selects from the menu an item whose id is second, write the code to go to another activity of type SecondActivity. Otherwise, we do nothing.

```
public boolean onOptionsItemSelected( MenuItem item ) {
  // your code goes here

}
```

15. Write the class header of the MyDBManager class. Inside that class, we intend to create a database and perform SQL operations.

```
// Your code goes here
```

16. Inside a class that extends SQLiteOpenHelper, write the code for the constructor. The name of the database we want to create is FRIENDS, and its version is 3.

```
public DatabaseManager( Context context ) {
    // Your code goes here

}
```

17. Inside a class that extends SQLiteOpenHelper, write the code for the onCreate method. We want to create the table emails defined as follows: the key is email, a string; it has two other columns, first and last, both strings.

```
public void onCreate( SQLiteDatabase db ) {
    // your code goes here

}
```

18. Inside a class that extends SQLiteOpenHelper , write the code for the insert method below. We want to insert one record in the emails table from question 17 using the three parameter values of the insert method below.

```
public void insert( String email, String first, String last ) {
    // your code goes here

}
```

19. Inside a class that extends SQLiteOpenHelper, write the code for the delete method below. We want to delete the records in the emails table from question 17 with a last value equal to the value of the parameter of the method.

```
public void delete( String last ) {
    // your code goes here

}
```

20. Inside a class that extends SQLiteOpenHelper, write the code for the update method below. We want to update the records in the emails table from question 17 whose email value is email. We want to change the first and last names of that record to first and last.

```
public void update( String email, String first, String last) {
    // your code goes here
}
```

Write an app

21. Modify the app of this chapter. Add a BACK button to the update activity.

22. Write an app similar to the chapter's app to manage a group of friends: a friend is defined as having a first name, a last name, and an email address. The friends should be stored in a database: a friend can be added or deleted; his/her data can be modified.

23. Write an app similar to the chapter's app to manage a group of friends: a friend is defined as having a first name, a last name, and an email address. The friends should be stored in a database: a friend can be added, updated, or deleted; his/her data can be modified. On the first screen, you should display a list of all the friends.

24. Same as # 22 with the following feature: on the first screen, provide a search engine where the user enters an email; the app searches the database and returns the corresponding first and last names if the email exists.

25. Same as #24 with an autocomplete feature for the search engine text field: as the user types, a drop-down list suggests possible matching emails retrieved from the database. You should look at the AutoCompleteTextView to implement this feature.

26. Write an app that does error correction. Build a database with one table. That table has two columns: one stores misspelled words and the other stores their corresponding correct words (e.g., the is the correct word for teh). The contents of that table can be hard coded and should include at least five pairs of words. The app shows an EditText: as the user types, the app corrects misspelled words based on the contents of the table.

27. Same as # 26 with the following feature: the user can add pairs of misspelled and correct words in the table.

28. Same as # 26 with the following feature: the user can delete and update misspelled and correct word pairs.

29. Write a quiz app where the questions and the answers are stored in a table of a database. The contents of the table can be hard coded.

30. Same as # 29 with the following feature: the user can add pairs of questions and answers in the table.

31. Same as # 29 with the following feature: the user can delete and update question and answer pairs.

32. Write an app that maintains a TO DO list stored in a database. The user can add items to the list and delete them.

33. Same as # 32 with the following feature: the TO DO list is displayed on the first screen.

34. Same as # 32 with the following feature: along with each item on the TO DO list, we store a deadline in the database. The first screen should display all the items in the TO DO list, and the past due items should be colored in red.

CHAPTER **SIX**

Managing the Device Orientation

CHAPTER CONTENTS

Chapter opener image: © Fon_nongkran/Shutterstock

Introduction

When we run an app and we rotate the device that the app is running on, the Graphical User Interface (GUI) may or may not rotate. Some apps, in particular games, are best run in one orientation only, often horizontal. But sometimes, we want to build an app that works in both horizontal and vertical orientations in order to provide a better experience for the user and also to expand the reach of the app. Some users might prefer to run an app in horizontal position while others might prefer to run it in vertical position. The default behavior is that the app automatically rotates. If we want to prevent our app from rotating, we need to specify either `portrait` or `landscape` as the value for the `android:screen Orientation` attribute inside the `activity` element of the AndroidManifest.xml. For example, if we want the app to run in horizontal position only, we specify the following:

```
<activity
    android:screenOrientation="landscape"
```

In this chapter, we want the app to run in both orientations. We use the Empty Activity template so that our View has nothing in it when we start.

6.1 The `Configuration` Class

The `Configuration` class, from the `android.content.res` package, encapsulates a device's configuration information such as locale, input modes, screen size, or screen orientation. In this chapter, we focus on screen orientation. TABLE 6.1 shows some `public` fields and methods of that class. The orientation field can have two values as shown in TABLE 6.2: `ORIENTATION_LANDSCAPE`, a constant that has value 2, and `ORIENTATION_PORTRAIT`, another constant that has value 1.

TABLE 6.1 Selected `public` fields and methods of the `Configuration` class

Field or Method	Description
public int keyboard	Keyboard for the device.
public Locale locale	User preference for the locale.
public int orientation	An integer value representing the orientation of the screen.
public int screenHeightDp	Height of the screen, not including the status bar, in dp units (density independent pixels).
public int screenWidthDp	Width of the screen in dp units.
public boolean isLayoutSizeAtLeast(int size)	Checks if the device's screen is at least a given size.

TABLE 6.2 Constant values for the orientation field of the Configuration class

Constant	Value
ORIENTATION_LANDSCAPE	2
ORIENTATION_PORTRAIT	1

TABLE 6.3 Constant values of the Configuration class related to a device's screen size

Constant	Value
SCREENLAYOUT_SIZE_UNDEFINED	0
SCREENLAYOUT_SIZE_SMALL	1
SCREENLAYOUT_SIZE_NORMAL	2
SCREENLAYOUT_SIZE_LARGE	3
SCREENLAYOUT_SIZE_XLARGE	4

TABLE 6.4 The getResources and getConfiguration methods

Class	Method
Context	Resources getResources( )
Resources	Configuration getConfiguration( )

The Configuration class provides constants to use as an argument of the isLayoutSizeAtLeast method (listed in **TABLE 6.3**). The SCREENLAYOUT_SIZE_SMALL and SCREENLAYOUT_SIZE_NORMAL constants apply to smartphones, whereas SCREENLAYOUT_SIZE_LARGE and SCREENLAYOUT_SIZE_XLARGE apply to tablets.

Using these resources, we can detect information about the device that our app is running on when the app starts. In order to use these resources, we need a Configuration reference. Inside the Activity class, we can call the getResources method from the Context class (that Activity inherits from) to get a Resources reference for the application's package. Using that Resources reference, we can call the getConfiguration method of the Resources class to obtain a Configuration reference. **TABLE 6.4** lists these two methods.

Thus, inside an `Activity` class, we can use these two methods in order to obtain a `Configuration` object as follows:

```
Resources resources = getResources();
Configuration config = resources.getConfiguration();
```

We can also chain these two method calls as follows:

```
Configuration config = getResources().getConfiguration();
```

Using a modified HelloAndroid app, we demonstrate how we can retrieve device information in **EXAMPLE 6.1**. We retrieve the `Configuration config` reference for the current app environment at line 18. At lines 19–20, we output the height and width of the screen in density independent pixels (dp). To obtain the actual size, we need to multiply those values by the pixel density. Note that `screenHeightDp` stores the height of the screen excluding the status bar.

At lines 22–27, we retrieve the size of the screen in actual pixels and output its width and height. At lines 29–32, we retrieve and output the pixel density of the screen. Appendix A gives us a detailed explanation.

At lines 34–47, we test for the relative size of the screen and output it. Note that we test for the relative sizes in descending order. If we tested for "at least" a small screen first, it would always evaluate to `true`. We output the two constants `ORIENTATION_LANDSCAPE` and `ORIENTATION_PORTRAIT` of the `Configuration` class (2 and 1, respectively) at lines 49–52. At line 53, we output the `orientation` value of the device as an integer. At lines 54–59, we compare that value to the two previous constants and output the device's orientation.

```
1   package com.jblearning.orientationv0;
2
3   import android.content.res.Configuration;
4   import android.content.res.Resources;
5   import android.graphics.Point;
6   import android.os.Bundle;
7   import android.support.v7.app.AppCompatActivity;
8   import android.util.DisplayMetrics;
9   import android.util.Log;
10
11  public class MainActivity extends AppCompatActivity {
12      public final static String MA = "MainActivity";
13
14      protected void onCreate( Bundle savedInstanceState ) {
15        super.onCreate( savedInstanceState );
16        setContentView( R.layout.activity_main );
17
```

EXAMPLE 6.1 Obtaining information on the device running the app (Continued)

```
18          Configuration config = getResources( ).getConfiguration( );
19          Log.w( MA, "screen dp height: " + config.screenHeightDp );
20          Log.w( MA, "screen dp width: " + config.screenWidthDp );
21
22          Point size = new Point( );
23          getWindowManager( ).getDefaultDisplay( ).getSize( size );
24          int screenWidth = size.x;
25          int screenHeight = size.y;
26          Log.w( MA, "screen height in pixels = " + screenHeight );
27          Log.w( MA, "screen width in pixels = " + screenWidth );
28
29          Resources res = getResources( );
30          DisplayMetrics metrics = res.getDisplayMetrics( );
31          float pixelDensity = metrics.density;
32          Log.w( MA, "logical pixel density = " + pixelDensity );
33
34          if( config.isLayoutSizeAtLeast(
35             Configuration.SCREENLAYOUT_SIZE_XLARGE ) )
36            Log.w( MA, "Extra large size screen" );
37          else if( config.isLayoutSizeAtLeast(
38             Configuration.SCREENLAYOUT_SIZE_LARGE ) )
39            Log.w( MA, "Large size screen" );
40          else if( config.isLayoutSizeAtLeast(
41             Configuration.SCREENLAYOUT_SIZE_NORMAL ) )
42            Log.w( MA, "Normal size screen" );
43          else if( config.isLayoutSizeAtLeast(
44             Configuration.SCREENLAYOUT_SIZE_SMALL ) )
45            Log.w( MA, "Small size screen" );
46          else
47            Log.w( MA, "Unknown size screen" );
48
49          Log.w( MA, "Landscape constant: "
50               + Configuration.ORIENTATION_LANDSCAPE );
51          Log.w( MA, "Portrait constant: "
52               + Configuration.ORIENTATION_PORTRAIT );
53          Log.w( MA, "Orientation: " + config.orientation );
54          if( config.orientation == Configuration.ORIENTATION_LANDSCAPE )
55            Log.w( MA, "Horizontal position" );
56          else if( config.orientation == Configuration.ORIENTATION_PORTRAIT )
57            Log.w( MA, "Vertical position" );
58          else
59            Log.w( MA, "Undetermined position" );
60        }
61      }
```

EXAMPLE 6.1 Obtaining information on the device running the app

> **COMMON ERROR:** When testing the screen's size using the `isLayoutSize` `AtLeast`, we should test the sizes in descending order. Otherwise, if we start testing with argument SCREENLAYOUT_SIZE_SMALL, the method will always return `true`.

FIGURE 6.1 shows the various parts of a device's screen. In yellow is the device's status bar. It typically includes some icons for system and application notifications, including the clock. In red is the app's action bar, which typically includes the app name on the left and optional menu items on the right, although it can be different depending on the app. In blue is the app content View. This is where the contents of our app go. The visible display frame is made up of the app's action bar (in red) and the app content View (in blue).

FIGURE 6.2 shows the output of Example 6.1 in Logcat when running using the emulator for the Nexus 5 started in vertical position. The output confirms that the device is in vertical position, that the screen of the device is 568 dp × 360 dp in that position and is considered a normal size screen. The orientation value is 1, equal to the portrait constant. The height dimension (568 dp) includes the action bar height but does not include the status bar height. The logical pixel density is 3; 568 dp is equivalent to 1,704 pixels (568 × 3), 72 pixels less than the 1,776 pixels screen height. The 72 pixels are equivalent to 24 dp, the height of the status bar.

If we rotate the emulator (Ctrl+F11), we notice more output, which means that the `onCreate` method executes again. Furthermore, the screen dimensions are different in horizontal orientation: the height is 336 dp and the width is 598 dp. The action bar height, 56 dp in vertical position, is only 48 dp in horizontal orientation. Furthermore, the Back and Home buttons are at the bottom of the screen in vertical orientation, but are to the right of the screen in horizontal orientation.

If we leave the emulator in horizontal position and restart the app, the output shows that we detect that the device is in the horizontal position.

If we run the app in the Nexus 4 emulator, we can see that the logical pixel density for the Nexus 4 is only 2, and the height and width are 568 dp and 384 dp, respectively.

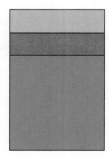

```
screen dp height: 568
screen dp width: 360
screen height in pixels = 1776
screen width in pixels = 1080
logical pixel density = 3.0
Normal size screen
Landscape constant: 2
Portrait constant: 1
Orientation: 1
Vertical position
```

FIGURE 6.1 View components of the screen

FIGURE 6.2 Logcat output of Example 6.1

COMMON ERROR: Do not confuse dimensions in physical pixels and dp unit. The ratio between the two is the logical pixel density.

6.2 Capturing a Device Rotation Event

The user could start an app in a given orientation but might rotate the device later. If we are building an app that works in both orientations, we need to code our app so that it will react properly to a change in device orientation. By default, the onCreate method of the Activity class is called when the user rotates the device. However, the onCreate method typically does more than just handling orientation changes. Thus, it could be a waste of CPU resources to let onCreate execute every time the user rotates the device.

The onConfigurationChanged method of the Activity class, shown in TABLE 6.5, is called automatically whenever the device's configuration changes (e.g., when the user rotates the device), provided that we specify it in the AndroidManifest.xml file. In turn, the onCreate method is only called when the user starts the app and no longer called when the user rotates the device. The newConfig parameter of the onConfigurationChanged method represents the latest configuration of the device.

Inside the activity element for which we want to be notified if the device configuration changes, we need to add the android:configChanges attribute and assign to it the appropriate value or values. We can assign several values, separated by the | character. TABLE 6.6 shows selected

TABLE 6.5 The onConfigurationChanged method of the Activity class

Method	Description
void onConfigurationChanged(Configuration newConfig)	Called when one of the configurations specified in the AndroidManifest.xml file has changed.

TABLE 6.6 Selected values for the android:configChanges attribute of the activity element

Attribute Value	Meaning
orientation	The user has rotated the device.
screenSize	The size of the screen has changed.
locale	The locale has changed (the user has selected a new language).
keyboard	The keyboard type has changed.
fontScale	The user has selected a new global font size.

values. If we want to be notified whenever the user rotates the device, we need to assign the value `orientation` to `android:configChanges`. However, starting with API level 13, we also need to add the value `screenSize`. Indeed, the system considers that the screen size changes when the user rotates the device. Thus, we need to specify the value `orientation | screenSize` for the `android:configChanges` attribute as follows (note that there is no space between `orientation` and |, and between | and `screenSize`):

```
<activity
    android:name=".MainActivity"
    android:configChanges="orientation|screenSize" >
```

Using another modified HelloAndroid app, we demonstrate how we execute inside the `onConfigurationChanged` method when the user rotates the device in **EXAMPLE 6.2**. We can use the `newConfig` parameter of that method (lines 16–28) to detect what orientation the device is in

```
1   package com.jblearning.orientationv1;
2
3   import android.content.res.Configuration;
4   import android.os.Bundle;
5   import android.support.v7.app.AppCompatActivity;
6   import android.util.Log;
7
8   public class MainActivity extends AppCompatActivity {
9     public final static String MA = "MainActivity";
10
11    protected void onCreate( Bundle savedInstanceState ) {
12      super.onCreate( savedInstanceState );
13      setContentView( R.layout.activity_main );
14    }
15
16    public void onConfigurationChanged( Configuration newConfig ) {
17      super.onConfigurationChanged( newConfig );
18      Log.w( MA, "Height: " + newConfig.screenHeightDp );
19      Log.w( MA, "Width: " + newConfig.screenWidthDp );
20
21      Log.w( MA, "Orientation: " + newConfig.orientation );
22      if( newConfig.orientation == Configuration.ORIENTATION_LANDSCAPE )
23        Log.w( MA, "Horizontal position" );
24      else if( newConfig.orientation == Configuration.ORIENTATION_PORTRAIT )
25        Log.w( MA, "Vertical position" );
26      else
27        Log.w( MA, "Undetermined position" );
28    }
29  }
```

EXAMPLE 6.2 Detecting configuration changes inside the `onConfigurationChanged` **method**

and code the appropriate changes for the app. In this simple app, we output screen size information at lines 18–19 and orientation information at lines 21–27.

If we run the app starting in vertical position, there is no output until we rotate the device (Ctrl+F11) to the horizontal position. When we do, the first four lines of **FIGURE 6.3** are output. When we rotate the device back (Ctrl+F12) to the vertical position, the next four lines of Figure 6.2 are output. We can see that the dimensions of the screen differ depending on the device's orientation.

```
Height: 336
Width: 598
Orientation: 2
Horizontal position
Height: 568
Width: 360
Orientation: 1
Vertical position
```

FIGURE 6.3 **Logcat output of Example 6.1**

We now have the tools to detect orientation and screen dimensions whenever the user rotates the device. There are many possible ways to display the correct layout to the user, including:

▶ Have one layout XML file per orientation and inflate it whenever the user rotates the device.

▶ Have the same layout XML file for both orientations and modify the characteristics of some of the GUI components whenever the user rotates the device.

▶ Manage layouts 100% by code and make the appropriate modifications whenever the user rotates the device.

6.3 Strategy 1: One Layout XML File per Orientation

We already have one layout XML file, activity_main.xml, shown in **EXAMPLE 6.3**. We use it for the vertical orientation: we add a background color (green) to the TextView element at line 17 and modify the text displayed, using the String named portrait at line 18. We add another layout XML file, activity_main_landscape.xml, shown in **EXAMPLE 6.4**, which we use for the horizontal orientation. This time, we set the background color of the TextView element to red at line 17 and the text is displayed using the String landscape at line 18. The portrait and landscape Strings are defined at lines 3 and 4 of the strings.xml file in **EXAMPLE 6.5**. We also edit the styles.xml file, shown in **EXAMPLE 6.6**, so that the size of the text is large enough (line 3).

Now that the resource files are set, we code the MainActivity class. If the device is in the vertical position, we use the activity_main.xml file for the layout. If the device is in the horizontal position, we use the activity_main_landscape.xml file for the layout. Not only do we need to do this inside the onConfigurationChanged method, but we must also do this inside the onCreate method so that the proper layout file is used when the app starts. Indeed, the device could either be in horizontal or vertical position when the app starts. Since the same code will be run two times, we code a new method, modifyLayout (lines 20–25 of **EXAMPLE 6.7**), which we call from onCreate (line 12) and onConfigurationChanged (line 17). The modifyLayout method tests what the orientation of the device is, and sets the layout for it, inflating the appropriate XML file.

```
1    <?xml version="1.0" encoding="utf-8"?>
2    <RelativeLayout xmlns:android="http://schemas.android.com/apk/res/android"
3                    xmlns:tools="http://schemas.android.com/tools"
4                    android:layout_width="match_parent"
5                    android:layout_height="match_parent"
6                    android:paddingLeft="@dimen/activity_horizontal_margin"
7                    android:paddingRight="@dimen/activity_horizontal_margin"
8                    android:paddingTop="@dimen/activity_vertical_margin"
9                    android:paddingBottom="@dimen/activity_vertical_margin"
10                   tools:context=".MainActivity">
11
12     <TextView
13       android:layout_width="wrap_content"
14       android:layout_height="wrap_content"
15       android:layout_centerHorizontal="true"
16       android:layout_centerVertical="true"
17       android:background="#FF00FF00"
18       android:text="@string/portrait" />
19
20   </RelativeLayout>
```

EXAMPLE 6.3 **The activity_main.xml file, for portrait orientation**

```
1    <?xml version="1.0" encoding="utf-8"?>
2    <RelativeLayout xmlns:android="http://schemas.android.com/apk/res/android"
3                    xmlns:tools="http://schemas.android.com/tools"
4                    android:layout_width="match_parent"
5                    android:layout_height="match_parent"
6                    android:paddingLeft="@dimen/activity_horizontal_margin"
7                    android:paddingRight="@dimen/activity_horizontal_margin"
8                    android:paddingTop="@dimen/activity_vertical_margin"
9                    android:paddingBottom="@dimen/activity_vertical_margin"
10                   tools:context="com.jblearning.orientationv2.MainActivity">
11
12     <TextView
13       android:layout_width="wrap_content"
14       android:layout_height="wrap_content"
15       android:layout_centerHorizontal="true"
16       android:layout_centerVertical="true"
17       android:background="#FFFF0000"
18       android:text="@string/landscape" />
19
20   </RelativeLayout>
```

EXAMPLE 6.4 **The activity_main_landscape.xml file, for landscape orientation**

```
1    <resources>
2      <string name="app_name">OrientationV2</string>
3      <string name="portrait">PORTRAIT VIEW</string>
4      <string name="landscape">LANDSCAPE VIEW</string>
5    </resources>
```

EXAMPLE 6.5 **The strings.xml file**

```
1    <resources>
2      <style name="AppTheme" parent="Theme.AppCompat.Light.DarkActionBar">
3        <item name="android:textSize">42sp</item>
4        <item name="colorPrimary">@color/colorPrimary</item>
5        <item name="colorPrimaryDark">@color/colorPrimaryDark</item>
6        <item name="colorAccent">@color/colorAccent</item>
7      </style>
8    </resources>
```

EXAMPLE 6.6 **The styles.xml file**

COMMON ERROR: If we are building an app working in both orientations, not only should we display the appropriate layout when the user rotates the device, but also when the app starts. Our code needs to account for the fact that we do not know the position of the device when the app starts.

```
1    package com.jblearning.orientationv2;
2
3    import android.content.res.Configuration;
4    import android.os.Bundle;
5    import android.support.v7.app.AppCompatActivity;
6
7    public class MainActivity extends AppCompatActivity {
8
9      protected void onCreate( Bundle savedInstanceState ) {
10        super.onCreate( savedInstanceState );
11        Configuration config = getResources( ).getConfiguration( );
12        modifyLayout( config );
13      }
14
```

EXAMPLE 6.7 **Managing orientation changes using two XML layout files (*Continued*)**

```
15     public void onConfigurationChanged( Configuration newConfig ) {
16       super.onConfigurationChanged( newConfig );
17       modifyLayout( newConfig );
18     }
19
20     public void modifyLayout( Configuration newConfig ) {
21       if( newConfig.orientation == Configuration.ORIENTATION_LANDSCAPE )
22         setContentView( R.layout.activity_main_landscape );
23       else if( newConfig.orientation == Configuration.ORIENTATION_PORTRAIT )
24         setContentView( R.layout.activity_main );
25     }
26   }
```

EXAMPLE 6.7 Managing orientation changes using two XML layout files

FIGURE 6.4 shows the app running inside the emulator when the device is in vertical position, and **FIGURE 6.5** shows the app after we rotate the device to the horizontal position. If we place output statements to Logcat inside onCreate and onConfigurationChanged, we see that onCreate is only called when the app starts and is no longer called afterward when we rotate the device. Instead, onConfigurationChanged is called. As discussed earlier, this is because we added

```
android:configChanges="orientation|screenSize"
```

inside the activity element in the AndroidManifest.xml file.

FIGURE 6.4 App running inside the emulator, starting in vertical position

FIGURE 6.5 App running inside the emulator, after rotating to horizontal position

6.4 Strategy 2: One Layout XML File for Both Orientations, Modify the Layout by Code

We now look at another strategy to control the layout depending on screen orientation. We use only one XML layout file but we modify the layout parameters of some of its components programmatically depending on the screen orientation. To better illustrate this, we modify the activity_main.xml, as shown in **EXAMPLE 6.8**. It displays three buttons (lines 10, 15, and 21) inside a LinearLayout (line 2). A LinearLayout organizes elements linearly, either horizontally or vertically depending on the value of its android:orientation attribute. In this app, we specify a vertical organization of its elements (line 6). If we keep the spacing constant between the buttons no matter the orientation of the screen, for example 50 pixels, it is possible that the app looks good in one orientation (vertical for example) but looks bad in the other orientation (horizontal). Instead, we can set the spacing between the buttons by code, depending on orientation. For this, we need to access the second and third buttons at run time, so we give them an id at lines 16 and 22. Lines 13, 19, and 25 specify the text of the three buttons using the view1, view2, and view3 Strings defined in the strings.xml file, shown in **EXAMPLE 6.9**. We use the same styles.xml file as the one in Example 6.6.

```
1   <?xml version="1.0" encoding="utf-8"?>
2   <LinearLayout xmlns:android="http://schemas.android.com/apk/res/android"
3                 xmlns:tools="http://schemas.android.com/tools"
4                 android:layout_width="match_parent"
5                 android:layout_height="match_parent"
6                 android:orientation="vertical"
7                 android:gravity="center"
8                 tools:context=" com.jblearning.orientationv3.MainActivity" >
9
10    <Button
11      android:layout_width="wrap_content"
12      android:layout_height="wrap_content"
13      android:text="@string/view1" />
14
15    <Button
16      android:id="@+id/button2"
17      android:layout_width="wrap_content"
18      android:layout_height="wrap_content"
19      android:text="@string/view2" />
20
21    <Button
22      android:id="@+id/button3"
23      android:layout_width="wrap_content"
24      android:layout_height="wrap_content"
25      android:text="@string/view3" />
26  </LinearLayout>
```

EXAMPLE 6.8 The activity_main.xml file

```
1    <resources>
2      <string name="app_name">OrientationV3</string>
3      <string name="view1">GO TO VIEW 1</string>
4      <string name="view2">GO TO VIEW 2</string>
5      <string name="view3">GO TO VIEW 3</string>
6      <string name="action_settings">Settings</string>
7    </resources>
```

EXAMPLE 6.9 **The strings.xml file**

In order to make the app look good in both positions, we need to set the spacing between the buttons by code in the `MainActivity` class. If the device is in the vertical position, we set the spacing to 50 pixels, and if the device is in the horizontal position, we set the spacing to 25 pixels.

EXAMPLE 6.10 shows the new `MainActivity` class. This time, we inflate the XML inside the `onCreate` method. Like before, both `onCreate` and `onConfigurationChanged` call `modifyLayout`, which sets the spacing parameters between the buttons.

The `modifyLayout` method (lines 25–41) retrieves the second and third buttons at lines 26 and 29, and then retrieves their associated margin layout parameters at lines 27–28 and 30–31.

```
1    package com.jblearning.orientationv3;
2
3    import android.content.res.Configuration;
4    import android.os.Bundle;
5    import android.support.v7.app.AppCompatActivity;
6    import android.view.ViewGroup;
7    import android.widget.Button;
8
9    public class MainActivity extends AppCompatActivity {
10     public final static int SPACING_VERTICAL = 50;
11     public final static int SPACING_HORIZONTAL = 25;
12
13     protected void onCreate( Bundle savedInstanceState ) {
14       super.onCreate( savedInstanceState );
15       setContentView( R.layout.activity_main );
16       Configuration config = getResources( ).getConfiguration( );
17       modifyLayout( config );
18     }
19
20     public void onConfigurationChanged( Configuration newConfig ) {
21       super.onConfigurationChanged( newConfig );
22       modifyLayout( newConfig );
23     }
24
```

EXAMPLE 6.10 **Managing orientation changes using two XML layout files (*Continued*)**

```
25      public void modifyLayout( Configuration newConfig ) {
26        Button b2 = ( Button ) findViewById( R.id.button2 );
27        ViewGroup.MarginLayoutParams params2
28          = ( ViewGroup.MarginLayoutParams ) b2.getLayoutParams( );
29        Button b3 = ( Button ) findViewById( R.id.button3 );
30        ViewGroup.MarginLayoutParams params3
31          = ( ViewGroup.MarginLayoutParams ) b3.getLayoutParams( );
32
33        if( newConfig.orientation == Configuration.ORIENTATION_LANDSCAPE ) {
34          params2.setMargins( 0, SPACING_HORIZONTAL, 0, 0 );
35          params3.setMargins( 0, SPACING_HORIZONTAL, 0, 0 );
36        } else if( newConfig.orientation
37                  == Configuration.ORIENTATION_PORTRAIT ) {
38          params2.setMargins( 0, SPACING_VERTICAL, 0, 0 );
39          params3.setMargins( 0, SPACING_VERTICAL, 0, 0 );
40        }
41      }
42    }
```

EXAMPLE 6.10 **Managing orientation changes using two XML layout files**

The Android framework includes layout parameter classes that we can use to set the
layout parameters of the GUI components contained in a layout. The root class for those is
`ViewGroup.LayoutParams`. It has many specialized subclasses relating to specialized
`ViewGroups`, including `TableLayout.LayoutParams`, `RelativeLayout.Layout-
Params`, `LinearLayout.LayoutParams`, or `ViewGroup.MarginLayoutParams`. The
`ViewGroup.MarginLayoutParams` class (`MarginLayoutParams` is a `public static` inner
class of `ViewGroup`) is used to set margins for GUI components.

TABLE 6.7 shows some XML attributes of `ViewGroup.MarginLayoutParams`, along with
the corresponding method. Although there are four attributes, we can set them by using a single
method, `setMargins`.

TABLE 6.7 Selected XML attributes of `ViewGroup.MarginLayoutParams`
and the `setMargins` method

Attribute Name	Related Method
android:layout_marginBottom	setMargins(int left, int top, int right, int bottom)
android: layout_marginTop	setMargins(int left, int top, int right, int bottom)
android: layout_marginLeft	setMargins(int left, int top, int right, int bottom)
android: layout_marginRight	setMargins(int left, int top, int right, int bottom)

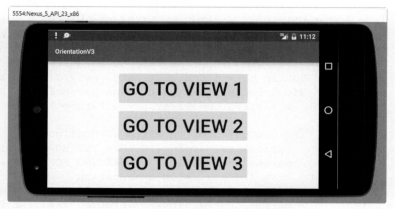

FIGURE 6.7 **App running in horizontal position using 25 pixels between buttons**

FIGURE 6.6 **App running in vertical position using 50 pixels between buttons**

We test for orientation at lines 33 and 36–37 and set the top margin of the layout parameters of the two buttons at lines 34–35 or 38–39 depending on orientation. We use the two constants SPACING_VERTICAL and SPACING_HORIZONTAL defined at lines 10–11. The MarginLayoutParams, params2 and params3 are object references, so when we modify them, we automatically modify the layout parameters of the two buttons associated with them.

As we did earlier, we add

```
android:configChanges="orientation|screenSize"
```

inside the activity element in the AndroidManifest.xml file.

FIGURES 6.6 and **6.7** show the app running inside the emulator when the device is in vertical position and horizontal position, respectively.

In this example, we hard coded the spacing between the buttons. As a result, the app may not look as good in some devices. In the next example, we set the spacing dynamically, relative to the dimensions of the device that the app is running on.

6.5 Strategy 3: Manage Layout and Orientation 100% by Code

In the previous example, we could have set up some dimen elements in the dimens.xml file to define several spacing values to go with different screen sizes. This strategy would work for most current devices, but may or may not work well for future devices. In order to have maximum flexibility and tailor the GUI to any screen size, we can control everything by code, without using any layout XML file. Instead of inflating a layout XML file, we call a method that sets up the layout programmatically. Additionally, we call another method that sets the layout parameters for the GUI components of the View. The basic principles of the previous example apply as far as managing orientations: each time the user rotates the device, `onConfigura-tionChanged` is called, and in turn it calls `modifyLayout`. This app is more complex, however, because we need to capture information related to the screen dimensions when the app starts in order to display the GUI components properly based on the starting orientation. Overall, we replace the layout XML file and the call to `setContentView` with a method setting up the GUI programmatically and a call to that method. Again, we use the same styles.xml file as the one in Example 6.6.

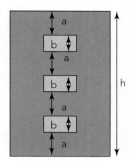

FIGURE 6.8 Three buttons with equal spacing

We need to display our buttons inside the app content View, the blue area of the screen in Figure 6.1. And we want our buttons to be equally distributed, whatever the orientation of the device, as shown in **FIGURE 6.8**.

If h is the height of the screen, a is the space between buttons, and b is the height of a button, we have (assuming we are using three buttons):

$$h = 4 * a + 3 * b$$

Therefore,

$$a = (h - 3 * b)/4$$

We can measure the dimensions of a View that has not been displayed yet by calling its `measure` method, and then its `getMeasuredHeight` method, shown in **TABLE 6.8**. If `button` is a `Button` reference, we can obtain its height as follows:

```
button.measure( LayoutParams.WRAP_CONTENT, LayoutParams.WRAP_CONTENT );
int buttonHeight = button.getMeasuredHeight();
```

In order to compute a, the space between the buttons, we need to calculate h, the height of the app's content view, first. We can retrieve the height of the action bar as shown next. Once we have it, we can easily compute the height of the app content View. Appendix A provides detailed explanations.

```
// set default value for action bar height
int actionBarHeight = ( int ) ( pixelDensity * 56 );
TypedValue tv = new TypedValue( );
if( getTheme( ).resolveAttribute( android.R.attr.actionBarSize, tv, true ))
    actionBarHeight = TypedValue.complexToDimensionPixelSize( tv.data,
                            getResources( ).getDisplayMetrics( ) );
```

TABLE 6.8 The `measure` and `getMeasuredHeight` methods of the `View` class

public void measure(int widthMeasureSpec, int heightMeasureSpec)	The two parameters are dimensional constraint information supplied by the parent of this View.
public int getMeasuredHeight( )	Returns the measured height of this View.

In Example 6.1, we learned how to retrieve the height of the screen minus the status bar. Thus, to compute the height of the content view, we do the following:

```
Retrieve the height of the screen minus the status bar: appScreenHeight
Retrieve the height of the action bar: actionBarHeight
Height of content view = appScreenHeight - actionBarHeight
```

EXAMPLE 6.11 shows a simple app whose View is defined by code and whose orientation changes are managed by code. As shown in Figure 6.8, the screen contains three buttons that are equally spaced vertically in both horizontal and vertical orientations. In addition to the three buttons, we also declare instance variables to store various dimensions: the height of the action bar, the height of the screen in both orientations, and the spacing between the buttons. We also declare

```
1  package com.jblearning.orientationv4;
2
3  import android.content.res.Configuration;
4  import android.content.res.Resources;
5  import android.os.Bundle;
6  import android.support.v7.app.AppCompatActivity;
7  import android.util.DisplayMetrics;
8  import android.util.Log;
9  import android.util.TypedValue;
10 import android.view.ViewGroup.MarginLayoutParams;
11 import android.view.ViewGroup.LayoutParams;
12 import android.widget.Button;
13 import android.widget.LinearLayout;
14
15 public class MainActivity extends AppCompatActivity {
16   public static String MA = "MainActivity";
17   public static int ACTION_BAR_HEIGHT = 56; // vertical, in dp units
18
19   private float pixelDensity;
20   private boolean verticalDimensionsSet;
21   public static int screenHeightInVP;
22   private int spacingInVP;
23
24   private boolean horizontalDimensionsSet;
25   public static int screenHeightInHP;
26   private int spacingInHP;
27
28   private Button b1, b2, b3;
29   private int actionBarHeight;
30
```

EXAMPLE 6.11 **Managing orientation by code only (*Continued*)**

```
31    protected void onCreate( Bundle savedInstanceState ) {
32      super.onCreate( savedInstanceState );
33      setUpGui( );
34      Resources res = getResources( );
35      DisplayMetrics metrics = res.getDisplayMetrics( );
36      pixelDensity = metrics.density;
37      Configuration config = getResources( ).getConfiguration( );
38      checkDimensions( config );
39      modifyLayout( config );
40    }
41
42    public void checkDimensions( Configuration config ) {
43      // retrieve ActionBar height
44      actionBarHeight = ( int ) ( pixelDensity * ACTION_BAR_HEIGHT );
45      TypedValue tv = new TypedValue( );
46      if( getTheme( ).resolveAttribute( android.R.attr.actionBarSize,
47                                        tv, true ) )
48        actionBarHeight = TypedValue.complexToDimensionPixelSize( tv.data,
49                                        getResources( ).getDisplayMetrics( ) );
50      Log.w( MA, "action bar height = " + actionBarHeight );
51
52      // measure button height
53      b1.measure( LayoutParams.WRAP_CONTENT, LayoutParams.WRAP_CONTENT );
54      int buttonHeight = b1.getMeasuredHeight( );
55
56      // set spacing between buttons depending on orientation
57      if( config.orientation == Configuration.ORIENTATION_LANDSCAPE ) {
58        screenHeightInHP = ( int ) ( config.screenHeightDp * pixelDensity );
59        spacingInHP =
60            ( screenHeightInHP - actionBarHeight - 3 * buttonHeight ) / 4;
61        horizontalDimensionsSet = true;
62      } else if ( config.orientation == Configuration.ORIENTATION_PORTRAIT ) {
63        screenHeightInVP = ( int ) ( config.screenHeightDp * pixelDensity );
64        spacingInVP =
65            ( screenHeightInVP - actionBarHeight - 3 * buttonHeight ) / 4;
66        verticalDimensionsSet = true;
67      }
68    }
69
70    public void setUpGui( ) {
71      LinearLayout linearLayout = new LinearLayout( this );
72      linearLayout.setOrientation( LinearLayout.VERTICAL );
73      linearLayout.setGravity( LinearLayout.VERTICAL );
74
75      b1 = new Button( this );
76      b2 = new Button( this );
```

EXAMPLE 6.11 Managing orientation by code only (*Continued*)

```
77      b3 = new Button( this );
78
79      b1.setText( "GO TO VIEW 1" );
80      b2.setText( "GO TO VIEW 2" );
81      b3.setText( "GO TO VIEW 3" );
82
83      LayoutParams params = new LayoutParams
84        ( LayoutParams.WRAP_CONTENT, LayoutParams.WRAP_CONTENT );
85      b1.setLayoutParams( params );
86      b2.setLayoutParams( params );
87      b3.setLayoutParams( params );
88
89      linearLayout.addView( b1 );
90      linearLayout.addView( b2 );
91      linearLayout.addView( b3 );
92
93      setContentView( linearLayout );
94    }
95
96    public void onConfigurationChanged( Configuration newConfig ) {
97      super.onConfigurationChanged( newConfig );
98      if( !verticalDimensionsSet || !horizontalDimensionsSet )
99        checkDimensions( newConfig );
100     modifyLayout( newConfig );
101   }
102
103   public void setLayoutMargins( int spacing ) {
104     MarginLayoutParams params1 =
105       ( MarginLayoutParams ) b1.getLayoutParams( );
106     MarginLayoutParams params2 =
107       ( MarginLayoutParams ) b2.getLayoutParams( );
108     MarginLayoutParams params3 =
109       ( MarginLayoutParams ) b3.getLayoutParams( );
110
111     params1.setMargins( 0, spacing, 0, 0 );
112     params2.setMargins( 0, spacing, 0, 0 );
113     params3.setMargins( 0, spacing, 0, 0 );
114   }
115
116   public void modifyLayout( Configuration config ) {
117     if( config.orientation == Configuration.ORIENTATION_LANDSCAPE )
118       setLayoutMargins( spacingInHP );
119     else if( config.orientation == Configuration.ORIENTATION_PORTRAIT )
120       setLayoutMargins( spacingInVP );
121   }
122 }
```

EXAMPLE 6.11 Managing orientation by code only

two `boolean` state variables, `verticalDimensionsSet` and `horizontalDimensionsSet` (lines 20 and 24), so that we only set all these variables once and not every time the device changes orientation. Some of these variables are declared as `public` and `static` so they can be easily accessed from other activities if necessary—most likely, if we have other activities in the app, we will need to access these values in other activities for the same reason that we need to access them in this activity, and we do not want to rewrite the same code to retrieve them.

The `onCreate` method (lines 31–40) calls `setUpGui` at line 33. The `setUpGui` method is coded at lines 70–94: it sets up the layout manager for the View, creates the buttons, and adds them to the View. In order to retrieve the action bar height, the screen dimensions, and to calculate the space between the buttons, we call a separate method, `checkDimensions`, at line 38. At line 39, we call `modifyLayout`, which displays the buttons properly depending on the orientation of the device. Since we do not know what orientation the device is in when the app starts, we assign the current configuration to the variable `config` at line 37 and pass `config` to `checkDimensions` and `modifyLayout`.

Inside `setUpGui`, we declare and instantiate `linearLayout`, a `LinearLayout`, at line 71 and set its orientation to vertical at line 72. This means that the buttons inside it are arranged vertically. We set its gravity to vertical at line 73. That means that the buttons inside it are centered vertically. We instantiate the three buttons at lines 75–77 and set their respective texts at lines 79–81. We instantiate a `LayoutParams` object at lines 83–84 and use it to set the layout parameters to `WRAP_CONTENT` for all three buttons at lines 85–87. We add the buttons to `linearLayout` at lines 89–91 and set the content view of this activity to `linearLayout` at line 93. The `setUpGui` method does not set the space between the buttons because that value depends on the device orientation. Thus, we want to set it when the `onConfigurationChanged` method is called and also when the app starts. We code a separate method, `setLayoutMargins`, to do that at lines 103–114. That method accepts one parameter, the space between two buttons. Depending on the position of the device, we pass a different value for that parameter when calling that method.

The `checkDimensions` method (lines 42–68) retrieves the action bar height and assigns values to the various dimension-related instance variables. We only want to do that twice: when the app starts, and after the user has rotated the device the first time. Thus, inside `onConfig`-`urationChanged`, we only call `checkDimensions` if either `verticalDimensionsSet` or `horizontalDimensionsSet` is `false` (line 98). The `checkDimensions` method retrieves the height of the action bar, and the height of the screen in both orientations. We assign them to the instance variables `actionBarHeight`, `screenHeightInHP`, and `screenHeightInVP`. We also retrieve the height of the buttons (lines 52–54) and calculate the values of `spacingInHP` and `spacingInVP` at lines 59–60 and 64–65. We output the value of the action bar height at line 50 for feedback purposes. **FIGURE 6.9** shows the output after we start the app in vertical orientation and rotate the device. The height of the action bar is 168 pixels (56 dp) and 144 pixels (48 dp) in vertical and horizontal orientations, respectively.

Earlier in the chapter, we showed that the height of the screen, not including the status bar, is 1,704 pixels (568 dp × 3) and 1,008 pixels (336 dp × 3) in vertical and horizontal orientations, respectively. Thus, the height of

```
action bar height = 168
action bar height = 144
```

FIGURE 6.9 Logcat output of Example 6.11

Status Bar: 72 pixels high
App Title Bar: 168 pixels high
App Content: 1,536 pixels high

Status Bar: 72 pixels high
App Title Bar: 144 pixels high
App Content: 864 pixels high

FIGURE 6.10 Heights in vertical orientations for the Nexus 5 emulator

FIGURE 6.11 Heights in horizontal orientations for the Nexus 5 emulator

the app content view for our emulator is 1,536 pixels (1,704 – 168) in vertical orientation, and 864 pixels (1,008 – 144) in horizontal orientation as shown in **FIGURES 6.10** and **6.11**.

The `modifyLayout` method, coded at lines 116–121, tests the orientation of the device (lines 117 and 119) and calls the `setLayoutMargins` method with the appropriate argument (lines 118 and 120), either `spacingInHP` or `spacingInVP`.

The `onConfigurationChanged` method is coded at lines 96–101. If the values of the various instance variables have not been set yet (line 98), we call `checkDimensions` (line 99). This will happen only once, the first time the user rotates the device. Currently, the action bar height is the same in both orientations. If this changes in the future, the code in this Example will need to be modified. At line 100, we call `modifyLayout` so that the buttons are displayed according to the device orientation.

The `setLayoutMargins` method is coded at lines 103–114. We first retrieve `MarginLayoutParams` references `params1`, `params2`, and `params3` to the three buttons at lines 104–109. We then call `setMargins` at lines 111–113, passing `spacing` as its second argument, in order to set the y-coordinate of the top of each button. Remember that the `params1`, `params2`, and `params3` are object references, so when we modify them, we modify the layout parameters of the three buttons.

Finally, remember that since we want the `onConfigurationChanged` method to be called when the user rotates the device, we need to add the `android:configChanges` attribute of the `activity` element in the androidManifest.xml file:

```
<activity
    android:name=".MainActivity"
  android:configChanges="orientation|screenSize" >
```

SOFTWARE ENGINEERING TIP: We can send some output to Logcat in the development stage of the app for feedback and debugging purposes. In the final version of the app, these output statements should be commented out.

> **COMMON ERROR:** Do not forget to add an `android:configChanges` attribute to the `activity` element in the AndroidManifest.xml file. Otherwise, the `onConfigurationChanged` method will not be called when the user rotates the device.

If we run the app and rotate the device, the vertical and horizontal Views look like the ones in Figures 6.6 and 6.7, with the buttons evenly spaced in both orientations.

At the time of this writing, the height of the status bar is 24 dp in both orientations. If necessary, it can be retrieved by code as follows (Appendix A provides detailed explanations):

```
// set default value for status bar height
int statusBarHeight = ( int ) ( pixelDensity * 24 );
// res is a Resources reference
int resourceId =
    res.getIdentifier( "status_bar_height", "dimen", "android" );
    // res.getIdentifier( "android:dimen/status_bar_height", "", "" );
if( resourceId != 0 ) // found resource for status bar height
  statusBarHeight = res.getDimensionPixelSize( resourceId );
```

Chapter Summary

- It is possible to build an app that runs in both orientations: we can have two separate layout XML files, combine one layout XML file with some code to handle both orientations, or manage both the layout and orientation programmatically.
- The `Configuration` class includes resources to access device information such as its keyboard, locale, orientation, screen dimensions, and many others. It also includes a method and constants to test if the current device is at least a certain size.
- The `getResources` and `getConfiguration` methods can be used to obtain a `Configuration` reference representing the current device configuration.
- The `onConfigurationChanged` is called automatically when the user rotates the device, provided that the `android:onChanges` attribute is defined inside the `activity` element of the AndroidManifest.xml file.
- In order to detect a change in orientation, the value of `android:onChanges` should be `orientation|screenSize`.
- The `LayoutParams` class and its subclasses can be used to set the various layout parameters of a GUI component.
- When an app is running, the screen is typically divided into three parts: the status bar at the top, the action bar (which may include other GUI components in addition to the app name), and the app's content view. Their respective heights can be retrieved programmatically.

- At the time of this writing, the height of the status bar is 24 dp and is the same in vertical and horizontal orientation.
- At the time of this writing, the height of the action bar is 56 dp and 48 dp in vertical and horizontal orientations, respectively.
- Appendix A provides detailed explanations on how to retrieve the heights of the status bar and action bar.

Exercises, Problems, and Projects

Multiple-Choice Exercises

1. In what package is the Configuration class?
   - android.config
   - android.configuration
   - android.content
   - android.content.res

2. In what class is the getConfiguration method?
   - Configuration
   - Resources
   - Activity
   - Context

3. The getResources method
   - Can be called from the Activity class because Activity inherits it from Context
   - Cannot be called from the Activity class
   - Is automatically called by the system
   - Is called by a Configuration reference

4. ORIENTATION_PORTRAIT and ORIENTATION_LANDSCAPE
   - Are constants of the Resources class
   - Are constants of the Activity class
   - Are constants of the Configuration class
   - Are constants of the View class

5. The name of the instance variable of the Configuration class that stores the value of the device orientation is
   - config
   - name

- position
- orientation

6. The screenHeightDp instance variable of the Configuration class stores (in dp units)
   - the height of the status bar
   - the height of the whole screen, including the status bar
   - the height of the whole screen, excluding the status bar
   - the height of the whole screen, excluding the status bar and the action bar

7. What method is automatically called when the user rotates the device, provided the AndroidManifest.xml file is correctly coded?
   - onConfigurationChanged
   - onRotate
   - onChange
   - onRotation

8. For the method in question 7 to be called automatically when the user rotates the device, what attribute needs to be set in the AndroidManifest.xml file?
   - android:changes
   - android:configChanges
   - android:rotate
   - android:onRotate

9. The height of the status bar
   - cannot be retrieved programmatically
   - can be retrieved programmatically
   - is currently equal to 20 pixels
   - is always different in vertical and horizontal orientations

10. Margins around a GUI component
    - Must be set in the layout xml file—they cannot be set by code
    - can be set using the setMargins method of the View class
    - can be set using the setMargins method of the MarginLayoutParams class
    - can be set using the setMargins method of the Activity class

Fill in the Code

11. Write the code to get a Configuration reference.

12. Write the code to retrieve the width of the screen in pixels.

13. Write the code to retrieve the width of the screen in dp.

14. Write the code to output to Logcat the current orientation of the device.

15. Write the code to test if a device has an extra large screen and output the result to Logcat.

16. Write the code to test if a device has a screen that is considered at least large but not extra large and output the result to Logcat.

17. Write the code to set the view to be inflated from portrait.xml if the device is in vertical position and from landscape.xml if the device is in horizontal position. Assume that you already have a Configuration reference.

18. Write the code to retrieve the height of the action bar in pixels.

19. Write the code to output to Logcat the width and height of a TextView named label.

    ```
    /* Assume that the TextView label has been instantiated and has
    been added to the View */
    // Your code goes here
    ```

20. Write the code to set the margins of a button to 30 pixels on the left and 50 pixels on the right.

    ```
    /* Assume that the Button myButton has been instantiated and has
    been added to the View */
    MarginLayoutParams params =
      ( MarginLayoutParams ) myButton.getLayoutParams( );
    // Your code goes here
    ```

Write an App

21. Write an app that works in both vertical and horizontal orientations using two layout XML files: the app asks the user to enter the result of an addition and checks the answer. Use randomly generated integers between 0 and 20 for the operands of the addition. Include a Model. The GUI should look nice in both orientations.

22. Write an app that works in both vertical and horizontal orientations. The app is a variety of the game of nim. Two players take turns removing identical objects from a set of objects. A player can remove one, two, or three objects at a time. The player who takes the last object loses. You can store the current number of objects in a TextView and get user input via an EditText. Include a Model. Generate randomly the starting number of objects, an integer between 10 and 20. The GUI should look nice in both orientations.

23. Write an app that works in both vertical and horizontal orientations using two layout XML files. The app is a simple calculator: the user can click on buttons showing digits from 1 to 9, click on buttons displaying +, -, and *, and the app shows the result. Include

a Model. The GUI should look nice in both orientations. Use one color theme for an orientation, and another color theme for the other orientation.

24. Write an app that works in both vertical and horizontal orientations using two layout XML files. The app is a tip calculator: the user can enter a restaurant bill, a number of guests, and a tip percentage, and the app shows the total tip, the total amount, the tip per guest, and the total per guest. Include a Model. The GUI should look nice in both orientations.

25. Write an app that works in both vertical and horizontal orientations. The app is a tic-tac-toe game. Include a Model. The GUI should look nice in both orientations. Use Xs and Os in one orientation, and As and Zs in the other orientation.

26. Write an app that works in both vertical and horizontal orientations. The app displays a chessboard in its starting position. Include a Model. The GUI should look nice in both orientations. Use black and white colors in one orientation, and two other colors in the other orientation. In vertical position, position the chessboard at the top of the screen, using the full width of the screen. In horizontal position, position the chessboard in the middle of the screen, using the full height of the screen. Use chars to represent the various pieces (K for King, Q for Queen, etc.).

CHAPTER **SEVEN**

Touches and Swipes

CHAPTER CONTENTS

Introduction

Many mobile games use screen touching, tapping, or swiping as a way to interact with the user. In most map apps, the user can zoom in and out of the map by doing some gesture such as pinching or spreading his or her fingers. All these things are events and follow the same rules as event handling in general:

▸ There is an event handling class, typically implementing an interface.
▸ We create an object of the class, a listener.
▸ We register that listener on one or more Graphical User Interface (GUI) components.

In this chapter, we learn how to detect and handle touches, swipes, and taps. We also build a simple puzzle app that lets the user move a piece of the puzzle by touching it and dragging it to another position in the puzzle. **FIGURE 7.1** shows the puzzle, which uses five `TextViews` whose order has been scrambled and need to be placed in the correct order.

FIGURE 7.1 **The Puzzle app, Version 2, running inside the emulator**

7.1 **Detecting a Touch Event**

Before working on the puzzle app, we build a simple practice app containing one `TextView`. When the user touches it, we move the `TextView` along as the user moves his or her finger. We use the Empty Activity template for this app. The `View.OnTouchListener` interface, a `public static` inner interface of the `View` class, provides a method, `onTouch`, that is called when the user interacts with the screen. A method that is called when something happens, for example an event, is called a **Callback** method. **TABLE 7.1** shows that method.

In order to handle a touch event using the `View.OnTouchListener` interface, we need to:

▶ Define a class that implements `View.OnTouchListener` and overrides the `onTouch` method.
▶ Create an object of that class.
▶ Register that object on one or more `Views`.

We can define that class as a private class of the current activity class:

```
// private class inside the MainActivity class
private class TouchHandler implements View.OnTouchListener {
  // the TouchHandler class needs to override onTouch
  public boolean onTouch( View v, MotionEvent event ) {
    // process the event here
  }
}
```

In order to register an object of type `View.OnTouchListener` on a `View`, we use the `setOnTouchListener` method of the `View` class, shown in **TABLE 7.2**.

```
// Inside MainActivity, if we want the View v to respond to touch events
TouchHandler th = new TouchHandler( );
v.setOnTouchListener( th );
```

An alternative to defining a new class implementing `View.OnTouchListener` is for the current `Activity` class to implement `View.OnTouchListener`. Then, `this` is a

TABLE 7.1 The `View.OnTouchListener` interface

Method	Description
boolean onTouch(View v, MotionEvent event)	Called when a touch event occurs. v is the View where the event occurred (assuming that this listener is registered on v). If this method returns true, the event is consumed. If it returns false, the event is propagated to the Views that are underneath v in the View stack.

TABLE 7.2 The `setOnTouchListener` method of the `View` class

Method	Description
void setOnTouchListener(View.OnTouchListener listener)	Registers listener on this View. When a touch event is sent to this View, the onTouch method of listener will be called.

`View.OnTouchListener` object and we can register it on one or more `Views`. If the `Activity` class is `MainActivity`, we would write:

```
// MainActivity implements View.OnTouchListener
public class MainActivity extends Activity implements
          View.OnTouchListener {

// if we want the View v to respond to touch events
v.setOnTouchListener( this );

// the MainActivity class needs to override onTouch
public boolean onTouch( View v, MotionEvent event ) {
  // process the event here

}
```

The first parameter of the `onTouch` method is a `View` where the event occurred, assuming that the listener is registered on that `View`. The second parameter is a `MotionEvent` reference. It contains information about the event. When the user touches the screen, moves his or her finger, and then lifts it up, there is actually a series of events that happen in sequence. The `onTouch` method is called many times, each time with a different value for the `event` parameter. This allows us to test that `event` parameter and process the event accordingly. The `MotionEvent` parameter `event` contains information about the current event within the sequence of events. It can even include information about how much time has passed during the whole sequence, how hard the touch on the screen was, etc. The method `getAction`, listed with other methods of the `MotionEvent` class in **TABLE 7.3**, returns an integer value that identifies the type of action that occurred. We can compare that value to one of the action constants of the `MotionEvent` class. Some of them are listed in **TABLE 7.4**. Thus, inside `onTouch`, we can call `getAction` with `event`, compare the result to a constant of the `MotionEvent` class that corresponds to an event we are interested in, and process the result accordingly. A good way to do that is with a `switch` statement as follows (replacing `SOME_ACTION` and `SOME_OTHER_ACTION` with actual constants like `ACTION_DOWN`, `ACTION_UP`, etc.):

```
public boolean onTouch( View v, MotionEvent event ) {
  int action = event.getAction( );
  switch( action ) {
```

TABLE 7.3 Selected methods of the `MotionEvent` class

Method	Description
float getRawX( )	Returns the x-coordinate of the touch within the screen.
float getRawY( )	Returns the y-coordinate of the touch within the screen.
float getX( )	Returns the x-coordinate of the touch within the View where it happened.
float getY( )	Returns the y-coordinate of the touch within the View where it happened.
int getAction( )	Returns the type of action that occurred within the touch event.

TABLE 7.4 Selected constants of the `MotionEvent` class that can be compared to the return value of the `getAction` method

Constant	Description
ACTION_DOWN	The user touched the screen.
ACTION_UP	The user stopped touching the screen.
ACTION_MOVE	The user is moving his or her finger on the screen.

```
    case MotionEvent.SOME_ACTION:
      // some action happened; process that information
      break;
    case MotionEvent.SOME_OTHER_ACTION:
      // some other action happened; process that information
      break;
      ...
    }
    ...
  }
```

We concentrate on the first touch (`ACTION_DOWN` constant), the dragging of the finger (`ACTION_MOVE` constant), and the lifting of the finger (`ACTION_UP` constant). In this first example, we simply output to Logcat some information about what action is being processed, for what event, and on what `View`. **EXAMPLE 7.1** shows the `MainActivity` class.

We declare that `MainActivity` implements the `View.OnTouchListener` interface at lines 9–10. Inside `onCreate`, we retrieve the content view for the activity at line 17 using the default id `content`, which identifies it by default. We output it at line 18, so that we can compare its value to the value of the `View` parameter of the `onTouch` method. At line 19, we register `this`, a

```
1    package com.jblearning.touchesv0;
2
3    import android.os.Bundle;
4    import android.support.v7.app.AppCompatActivity;
5    import android.util.Log;
6    import android.view.MotionEvent;
7    import android.view.View;
8
9    public class MainActivity extends AppCompatActivity
10                               implements View.OnTouchListener {
11     public static final String MA = "MainActivity";
12
13     protected void onCreate( Bundle savedInstanceState ) {
14       super.onCreate( savedInstanceState );
15       setContentView( R.layout.activity_main );
16       // set up touch event handling
17       View view = findViewById( android.R.id.content );
18       Log.w( MA, "view = " + view );
19       view.setOnTouchListener( this );
20     }
21
22     public boolean onTouch( View v, MotionEvent event ) {
23       int action = event.getAction( );
24       switch( action ) {
25         case MotionEvent.ACTION_DOWN:
26           Log.w( MA, "DOWN: v = " + v + "; event = " + event );
27           break;
28         case MotionEvent.ACTION_MOVE:
29           Log.w( MA, "MOVE: v = " + v + "; event = " + event );
30           break;
31         case MotionEvent.ACTION_UP:
32           Log.w( MA, "UP: v = " + v + "; event = " + event );
33           break;
34       }
35       return true;
36     }
37   }
```

EXAMPLE 7.1 **The `MainActivity` class, tracking touch events, Touches app, Version 0**

`View.OnTouchListener`, on that content `View`. In this way, whenever the user interacts with the screen via touches, the `onTouch` method executes and its `View` parameter is the content `View`.

Inside the `onTouch` method (at lines 22–36), we first retrieve the action performed at line 23. We compare its value to the `ACTION_DOWN`, `ACTION_MOVE`, and `ACTION_UP` constants of the `MotionEvent` class using a `switch` construct. For each case, we output to Logcat information about v, the `View` parameter, and event, the `MotionEvent` parameter.

```
view = android.support.v7.widget.ContentFrameLayout{e61a782 V.E........
....I. 0,0-0,0 #1020002 android:id/content}

DOWN: v = android.support.v7.widget.ContentFrameLayout{e61a782 V.E......
........ 0,168-1080,1704 #1020002 android:id/content}; event = MotionEvent {
action=ACTION_DOWN, actionButton=0, id[0]=0, x[0]=289.0, y[0]=370.0,
toolType[0]=TOOL_TYPE_FINGER, buttonState=0, metaState=0, flags=0x0,
edgeFlags=0x0, pointerCount=1, historySize=0, eventTime=94301,
downTime=94301, deviceId=0, source=0x1002}

MOVE: v = android.support.v7.widget.ContentFrameLayout{e61a782 V.E......
........ 0,168-1080,1704 #1020002 android:id/content}; event = MotionEvent {
action=ACTION_MOVE, actionButton=0, id[0]=0, x[0]=328.0, y[0]=459.0,
toolType[0]=TOOL_TYPE_FINGER, buttonState=0, metaState=0, flags=0x0,
edgeFlags=0x0, pointerCount=1, historySize=2, eventTime=94404,
downTime=94301, deviceId=0, source=0x1002}

MOVE: v = android.support.v7.widget.ContentFrameLayout{e61a782 V.E......
........ 0,168-1080,1704 #1020002 android:id/content}; event = MotionEvent {
action=ACTION_MOVE, actionButton=0, id[0]=0, x[0]=361.5, y[0]=483.5,
toolType[0]=TOOL_TYPE_FINGER, buttonState=0, metaState=0, flags=0x0,
edgeFlags=0x0, pointerCount=1, historySize=2, eventTime=94418,
downTime=94301, deviceId=0, source=0x1002}

...

MOVE: v = android.support.v7.widget.ContentFrameLayout{e61a782 V.E......
........ 0,168-1080,1704 #1020002 android:id/content}; event = MotionEvent {
action=ACTION_MOVE, actionButton=0, id[0]=0, x[0]=614.0, y[0]=798.85583,
toolType[0]=TOOL_TYPE_FINGER, buttonState=0, metaState=0, flags=0x0,
edgeFlags=0x0, pointerCount=1, historySize=2, eventTime=94594,
downTime=94301, deviceId=0, source=0x1002}

MOVE: v = android.support.v7.widget.ContentFrameLayout{e61a782 V.E......
........ 0,168-1080,1704 #1020002 android:id/content}; event = MotionEvent {
action=ACTION_MOVE, actionButton=0, id[0]=0, x[0]=614.0, y[0]=804.0,
toolType[0]=TOOL_TYPE_FINGER, buttonState=0, metaState=0, flags=0x0,
edgeFlags=0x0, pointerCount=1, historySize=0, eventTime=94601,
downTime=94301, deviceId=0, source=0x1002}

UP: v = android.support.v7.widget.ContentFrameLayout{e61a782 V.E......
........ 0,168-1080,1704 #1020002 android:id/content}; event = MotionEvent {
action=ACTION_UP, actionButton=0, id[0]=0, x[0]=614.0, y[0]=804.0,
toolType[0]=TOOL_TYPE_FINGER, buttonState=0, metaState=0, flags=0x0,
edgeFlags=0x0, pointerCount=1, historySize=0, eventTime=94615,
downTime=94301, deviceId=0, source=0x1002}
```

FIGURE 7.2 Logcat output from Example 7.1

FIGURE 7.2 shows the output in Logcat from Example 7.1 as the user makes a small swipe somewhere on the screen. We can observe several things:

▶ The method is called first with a DOWN action, then many times with a MOVE action, then once with an UP action.

▶ The `View` parameter `v` is always the same and it is the content view for the activity.

▶ The parameter event contains information such as the action, x- and y-coordinates, time, etc. We can see that each time the method is called on a `MOVE` action, the x- and y-coordinate values are different. Together, they form a discrete set of values that mirrors the swipe. Note that we do not get continuous, pixel by pixel information on the swipe.

7.2 Handling a Swipe Event: Moving a `TextView`

In the first example, we register the touch listener on the content `View`. In this second example, we add a `TextView` to the screen and we move it as the user touches it and moves his or her finger on the screen. This time, we register the listener on the `TextView`. This illustrates the difference between the `getX` and `getY` methods on one hand, and the `getRawX` and `getRawY` methods on the other hand, shown in Table 7.3. The `getX` and `getY` methods return the x- and y-coordinates relative to the `View` where the event happened, which is the `View v` passed to `onTouch` as the first parameter. The `getRawX` and `getRawY` return the x- and y-coordinates within the screen, including the screen decorations such as the status bar and the action bar. If we use the `getRawX` and `getRawY` methods and we want the x- and y-coordinates relative to the content `View`, we can use the following code inside `onTouch` to convert them:

```
int [] location = new int[2];
// view represents the content view for the activity
view.getLocationInWindow( location );
float relativeX = event.getRawX( ) - location[0];
float relativeY = event.getRawY( ) - location[1];
```

The `getLocationInWindow` method of the `View` class accepts an array of two `int`s as a parameter, and sets its two values to the x- and y-coordinates of the top left corner of the `View` calling that method within the window. We can then subtract their values from the values returned by `getRawX` and `getRawY` to obtain the relative x- and y-coordinates of the touch event within the content view of the activity.

By contrast, if the listener has been registered on a `TextView` and the first touch is at the top left corner of the `TextView`, then the `View v` parameter of the `onTouch` method is that `Text-View`, and the `getX` and `getY` method return 0 and 0 (or close to it) independently of where the `TextView` is located on the screen.

EXAMPLE 7.2 shows the `MainActivity` class. We build the GUI by code and include one `TextView` in it. We want to move that `TextView` based on user touches, so we need to use absolute coordinates. The `AbsoluteLayout` class, originally intended to work with absolute coordinates, is deprecated. We use the `RelativeLayout` class instead. A `RelativeLayout` allows us to position components either relative to each other or using absolute coordinates. Each component's dimension and position can be defined and controlled inside that `RelativeLayout` by associating it with it a `RelativeLayout.LayoutParams` object when we add it to the `RelativeLayout`. The `TextView` instance variable, `tv`, is declared at line 12, along with `params`, its `RelativeLayout.LayoutParams` parameters at line 13. By declaring them as instance variables, we can access them inside the `onTouch` method.

```
1    package com.jblearning.touchesv1;
2
3    import android.os.Bundle;
4    import android.support.v7.app.AppCompatActivity;
5    import android.view.MotionEvent;
6    import android.view.View;
7    import android.widget.RelativeLayout;
8    import android.widget.TextView;
9
10   public class MainActivity extends AppCompatActivity
11                              implements View.OnTouchListener {
12     private TextView tv;
13     private RelativeLayout.LayoutParams params;
14     private int startX;
15     private int startY;
16     private int startTouchX;
17     private int startTouchY;
18
19     protected void onCreate( Bundle savedInstanceState ) {
20       super.onCreate( savedInstanceState );
21       buildGuiByCode( );
22     }
23
24    public void buildGuiByCode( ) {
25       tv = new TextView( this );
26       tv.setBackgroundColor( 0xFFFF0000 );
27
28       RelativeLayout rl = new RelativeLayout( this );
29       params = new RelativeLayout.LayoutParams( 300, 200 );
30       params.leftMargin = 50;
31       params.topMargin = 150;
32
33       rl.addView( tv, params );
34       setContentView( rl );
35
36       tv.setOnTouchListener( this );
37     }
38
39     public boolean onTouch( View v, MotionEvent event ) {
40       int action = event.getAction( );
41       switch( action ) {
42         case MotionEvent.ACTION_DOWN:
43           startX = params.leftMargin;
44           startY = params.topMargin;
45           startTouchX = ( int ) event.getX( );
46           startTouchY = ( int ) event.getY( );
47           break;
```

EXAMPLE 7.2 The `MainActivity` class, moving a `TextView` with a swipe, Touches app, Version 1 (*Continued*)

```
48              case MotionEvent.ACTION_MOVE:
49                params.leftMargin = startX + ( int ) event.getX( ) - startTouchX;
50                params.topMargin = startY + ( int ) event.getY( ) - startTouchY;
51                tv.setLayoutParams( params );
52                break;
53            }
54          return true;
55        }
56  }
```

EXAMPLE 7.2 **The `MainActivity` class, moving a `TextView` with a swipe, Touches app, Version 1**

We build the GUI by code inside the `buildGuiByCode` method (lines 24–37), called at line 21. At line 25, we instantiate `tv` and we give it a red background at line 26. At line 28, we create a `RelativeLayout` and we set the content view with it at line 34. At lines 29–31, we define `params`, and use it to add `tv` to the relative layout at line 33. Inside the `onTouch` method, when we modify `params` and reset the layout parameters of `tv` with `params`, we automatically modify the position of `tv`. `RelativeLayout.LayoutParams` is a subclass of `ViewGroup.MarginLayoutParams` and inherits its margin-related fields, shown in **TABLE 7.5**.

We add more instance variables at lines 14–17 to keep track of the original position of the `TextView` and the location of the touch when the swipe starts. We use them inside the `onTouch` methods to recalculate the left corner position of the `TextView` as the user moves his or her finger on the screen. Inside the `onTouch` method (lines 39–55), we initialize these four variables when the user first touches the screen (lines 43–46), which is captured by the DOWN action (line 42). When the user moves his or her finger (MOVE action, line 48), we update the `leftMargin` and `topMargin` parameters of `params` at lines 49–50 and update the position of `tv` accordingly at line 51 by calling the `setLayoutParams` method, shown in **TABLE 7.6**, passing the updated value of `params`. There is nothing to do when the user lifts up his or her finger from the screen, so we do not account for the UP action in our code.

TABLE 7.5 The public fields of the `ViewGroup.MarginLayoutParams` class

Method	Description
int bottomMargin	The bottom margin in pixels of the child
int leftMargin	The left margin in pixels of the child
int rightMargin	The right margin in pixels of the child
int topMargin	The top margin in pixels of the child

TABLE 7.6 The `setLayoutParams` method of the `View` class	
Method	**Description**
void setLayoutParams(ViewGroup. LayoutParams params)	Sets the layout parameters associated with this View

Note that in this example, we register the listener on `tv` at line 36, and not on the content view. Thus, the calls to `onTouch` are triggered only when the touch starts inside `tv`, but no call to `onTouch` is triggered when the touch starts outside `tv`.

As we run this practice app, if we touch the red rectangle and move our finger, the red rectangle moves along.

7.3 The Model

Now that we understand how touch events work and how to move a `TextView`, we can start building our Puzzle app. As shown in Figure 7.1, it presents the user with several `TextViews` that need to be reordered. The first step is to design our Model, the `Puzzle` class, which includes the following:

▶   An array of `Strings`, `parts`, storing the puzzle in the correct order.
▶   A method returning an array of `Strings` storing the puzzle in a random incorrect order.
▶   A method checking if an array of `Strings` is in the correct order.
▶   A method returning the number of pieces in the puzzle (i.e., the number of elements in `parts`).

EXAMPLE 7.3 shows the `Puzzle` class. To keep things simple, we hard code the contents of the `parts` array in the default constructor (lines 10–17). We could envision a more complex model, with a constructor reading a puzzle data from a file or a database. In this case, we would not know the number of pieces in the puzzle before we read the data. For this reason, we provide an accessor for the number of pieces in the puzzle, `getNumberOfParts`, at lines 47–49. In this way, whenever the Controller needs to know how many pieces are in the puzzle, it can call that method, rather than use the constant `NUMBER_PARTS`, whose value is hard coded. We could also have many puzzles stored in a file or a database and read one at random. In this example, we can change the number of pieces of the puzzle inside the Model and the app would still work. For example, we can delete lines 15 and 16 and change the value of `NUMBER_PARTS` to 3, and the app would still work properly.

The `solved` method, at lines 19–29, returns `true` if its parameter array has the same content as `parts`, `false` otherwise. The `scramble` method, at lines 31–45, returns an array of `Strings` containing all the elements of the puzzle but in a different order. To do this, we first create a new array, `scrambled`, at line 32, and initialize it with the elements of `parts` at lines 33–34. At lines 36–43, we use a `while` loop to shuffle the elements of `scrambled` in place until the `scrambled` elements are in a different order as compared to the `parts` elements. To test for that, we use the `solved` method (line 36).

```
1   package com.jblearning.puzzlev0;
2
3   import java.util.Random;
4
5   public class Puzzle {
6     public static final int NUMBER_PARTS = 5;
7     String [] parts;
8     Random random = new Random( );
9
10    public Puzzle( ) {
11      parts = new String[NUMBER_PARTS];
12      parts[0] = "I LOVE";
13      parts[1] = "MOBILE";
14      parts[2] = "PROGRAMMING";
15      parts[3] = "USING";
16      parts[4] = "JAVA";
17    }
18
19    public boolean solved( String [] solution ) {
20      if( solution != null && solution.length == parts.length ) {
21        for( int i = 0; i < parts.length; i++ ) {
22          if( !solution[i].equals( parts[i] ) )
23            return false;
24        }
25        return true;
26      }
27      else
28        return false;
29    }
30
31    public String [] scramble( ) {
32      String [] scrambled = new String[parts.length];
33      for( int i = 0; i < scrambled.length; i++ )
34        scrambled[i] = parts[i];
35
36      while( solved( scrambled ) ) {
37        for( int i = 0; i < scrambled.length; i++ ) {
38          int n = random.nextInt( scrambled.length - i ) + i;
39          String temp = scrambled[i];
40          scrambled[i] = scrambled[n];
41          scrambled[n] = temp;
42        }
43      }
44      return scrambled;
45    }
46
47    public int getNumberOfParts( ) {
48      return parts.length;
49    }
50  }
```

EXAMPLE 7.3 The `Puzzle` class, Puzzle app, Version 0

The `for` loop at lines 37–42 shuffle the elements of `scrambled` in place going from left to right, starting at index 0. At each iteration of the loop, the elements between indexes 0 and i − 1 have already been shuffled. The current iteration of the loop swaps the element at index i with an element at a random index between i and `scrambled.length` − 1. At line 38, we generate a random index between i and `scrambled.length` − 1 included. Then, we swap the element at that index with the element at index i (lines 39–41).

7.4 The View: Setting Up the GUI, Puzzle App, Version 0

Now that we understand touch events and we have a Model, we can start building a functional puzzle app. In this section, we build the View part of the app. To keep things simple, we only allow the app to display in vertical orientation. in the AndroidManifest.xml file, we specify this as follows:

```
<activity
    android:screenOrientation="portrait"
```

Inside the styles.xml file, we set the font size for `TextViews` to be 32 as follows:

```
<item name="android:textSize">32sp</item>
```

Each piece of the puzzle is displayed in a `TextView`. Although the `Puzzle`'s default constructor specifies a puzzle with five pieces, we could easily envision having another constructor that lets the user specify the number of pieces, and then retrieves the `Strings` from a file or a database. Thus, we define our `View` by code rather than with an XML file so that it can accommodate a variable number of `TextViews`. Furthermore, we place the `View` in a separate class, different from the `MainActivity` class, which represents the Controller.

EXAMPLE 7.4 shows the `PuzzleView` class. Rather than extend `View` and manage the `View` with a `RelativeLayout` inside, we extend `RelativeLayout` instead. Since `RelativeLayout` inherits from `View`, it is a `View` and can be assigned to an `Activity` as its `View`. We use the `RelativeLayout` class to organize the `TextViews` because it can manage its children `Views` using absolute coordinates.

We code a constructor that takes four parameters as follows:

▶ `activity`, an `Activity` reference—we will instantiate a `PuzzleView` from an `Activity` class.
▶ `width`, an `int`, representing the width of the screen.
▶ `height`, an `int`, representing the height of the screen.
▶ `numberOfPieces`, an `int`, representing the number of pieces in the puzzle.

We build the entire GUI by code using the `buildGuiByCode` method, coded at lines 23–41, and called from the `PuzzleView` constructor at line 20, passing all the constructor's parameters to `buildGuiByCode`. Each component's dimension and position can be defined and controlled

```
1    package com.jblearning.puzzlev0;
2
3    import java.util.Random;
4    import android.app.Activity;
5    import android.view.Gravity;
6    import android.widget.RelativeLayout;
7    import android.widget.TextView;
8    import android.graphics.Color;
9
10   public class PuzzleView extends RelativeLayout {
11     private TextView [] tvs;
12     private RelativeLayout.LayoutParams [] params;
13     private int [] colors;
14
15     private int labelHeight;
16
17     public PuzzleView( Activity activity, int width, int height,
18                        int numberOfPieces ) {
19       super( activity );
20       buildGuiByCode( activity, width, height, numberOfPieces );
21     }
22
23     public void buildGuiByCode( Activity activity, int width, int height,
24                        int numberOfPieces ) {
25       tvs = new TextView[numberOfPieces];
26       colors = new int[tvs.length];
27       params = new RelativeLayout.LayoutParams[tvs.length];
28       Random random = new Random( );
29       labelHeight = height / numberOfPieces;
30       for( int i = 0; i < tvs.length; i++ ) {
31         tvs[i] = new TextView( activity );
32         tvs[i].setGravity( Gravity.CENTER );
33         colors[i] = Color.rgb( random.nextInt( 255 ),
34           random.nextInt( 255 ), random.nextInt( 255 ) );
35         tvs[i].setBackgroundColor( colors[i] );
36         params[i] = new RelativeLayout.LayoutParams( width, labelHeight );
37         params[i].leftMargin = 0;
38         params[i].topMargin = labelHeight * i;
39         addView( tvs[i], params[i] );
40       }
41     }
42
43     public void fillGui( String [] scrambledText ) {
44       for( int i = 0; i < tvs.length; i++ )
45         tvs[i].setText( scrambledText[i] );
46     }
47   }
```

EXAMPLE 7.4 **The** `PuzzleView` **class, Puzzle app, Version 0**

by associating with it a `RelativeLayout.LayoutParams` object when we add it to the `RelativeLayout`. We declare the following instance variables:

- ▶   `tvs`, an array of `TextViews` (line 11). There is one `TextView` for each puzzle piece.
- ▶   `params`, an array of `RelativeLayout.LayoutParams` (line 12).
- ▶   `colors`, an array of integer values representing colors (line 13). We generate them randomly in order to color the `TextViews`.
- ▶   `labelHeight`, the height of each `TextView` (line 15).

The three arrays above are parallel arrays. We use the `params` array to position and size the `TextViews` in `tvs`, and the `colors` array to color them. They are instantiated at lines 25–27. At lines 30–40, we loop through the elements in the array `tvs`. Each `TextView` is colored, positioned, and sized using the corresponding values in the three arrays above. At lines 33–34, we generate three random integers between `0` and `255` included and pass them to the `rgb static` method of the `Color` class in order to generate a random color for the current `TextView`. Note that we are using the `Color` class from the `android.graphics` package (imported at line 8), not the `Color` class from the traditional `java.awt` package.

We want all the `TextViews` to have the same height, which we store in `labelHeight`. At line 29, we assign `labelHeight` the `height` parameter (representing the height of the screen), divided by `numberOfPieces`. At line 36, we instantiate each element of `params` using `width` and `labelHeight`. At lines 37–38, we set the coordinates of the left upper corner of each element of `params`. At line 39, each `TextView` is added to this `PuzzleView` using the `addView` method of the `ViewGroup` class (the direct superclass of `RelativeLayout`) that accepts a `ViewGroup.LayoutParams` (a superclass of `RelativeLayout.LayoutParams`) object as its second parameter.

The `fillGui` method, coded at lines 43–46, provides code to fill the `TextViews` with an array of `Strings` representing the scrambled pieces of the puzzle.

EXAMPLE 7.5 shows the `MainActivity` class. It includes two instance variables: `puzzleView`, a `PuzzleView` reference representing the View (line 13), and `puzzle`, a `Puzzle` reference representing the Model (line 14).

The `onCreate` method (lines 16–49) instantiates `puzzle` at line 18 and `puzzleView` at lines 43–44. It sets the content View of this `Activity` to `puzzleView` at line 48. We retrieve the height and width of the screen at lines 20–23. While the width of the screen is also the width of the puzzle, the height of the screen includes the height of the status bar and the action bar, which should not be included in the puzzle. At the time of this writing, and according to Google's design guidelines, the height of the status bar is 24 dp and the height of the action bar is 56 dp. Thus, we declare two constants defining default values for the status bar and action bar heights at lines 11–12.

We start by assigning these default values multiplied by the pixel density to the `actionBarHeight` and `statusBarHeight` variables at lines 29 and 36 before attempting to retrieve them programmatically. We retrieve the pixel density of the current device at lines 25–27 by first retrieving a `Resources` reference, then retrieving a `DisplayMetrics` reference for the current device, and then accessing its `density` field. The `DisplayMetrics` class contains information about the display, including its size, its density, and font scaling. There is no guarantee that the height of the action bar will not change in the future. Thus, it is better to retrieve it programmatically. At lines 30–34, we attempt to retrieve the height of the action bar and assign it to `actionBarHeight` if

```
1    package com.jblearning.puzzlev0;
2
3    import android.content.res.Resources;
4    import android.graphics.Point;
5    import android.os.Bundle;
6    import android.support.v7.app.AppCompatActivity;
7    import android.util.DisplayMetrics;
8    import android.util.TypedValue;
9
10   public class MainActivity extends AppCompatActivity {
11     public static int STATUS_BAR_HEIGHT = 24; // in dp
12     public static int ACTION_BAR_HEIGHT = 56; // in dp
13     private PuzzleView puzzleView;
14     private Puzzle puzzle;
15
16     protected void onCreate( Bundle savedInstanceState ) {
17       super.onCreate( savedInstanceState );
18       puzzle = new Puzzle( );
19
20       Point size = new Point( );
21       getWindowManager( ).getDefaultDisplay( ).getSize( size );
22       int screenHeight = size.y;
23       int puzzleWidth = size.x;
24
25       Resources res = getResources( );
26       DisplayMetrics metrics = res.getDisplayMetrics( );
27       float pixelDensity = metrics.density;
28
29       int actionBarHeight = ( int ) ( pixelDensity * ACTION_BAR_HEIGHT );
30       TypedValue tv = new TypedValue( );
31       if( getTheme( ).resolveAttribute( android.R.attr.actionBarSize,
32                                         tv, true ) )
33         actionBarHeight = TypedValue.complexToDimensionPixelSize( tv.data,
34                         metrics );
35
36       int statusBarHeight = ( int ) ( pixelDensity * STATUS_BAR_HEIGHT );
37       int resourceId =
38           res.getIdentifier( "status_bar_height", "dimen", "android" );
39       if( resourceId != 0 ) // found resource for status bar height
40         statusBarHeight = res.getDimensionPixelSize( resourceId );
41
42       int puzzleHeight = screenHeight - statusBarHeight - actionBarHeight;
43       puzzleView = new PuzzleView( this, puzzleWidth, puzzleHeight,
44                                    puzzle.getNumberOfParts( ) );
45       String [] scrambled = puzzle.scramble( );
46       puzzleView.fillGui( scrambled );
47
48       setContentView( puzzleView );
49     }
50   }
```

EXAMPLE 7.5 The `MainActivity` class, Puzzle app, Version 0

we can. At lines 37–40, we attempt to retrieve the height of the status bar and assign it to status-BarHeight if we can. Appendix A provides a detailed explanation of this.

At line 42, we subtract the heights of the status bar and the action bar from the height of the screen in order to compute the height of the puzzle.

We call the scramble method of Puzzle at line 45 in order to generate a scrambled array of Strings for our puzzle, and then pass it to the fillGui method of PuzzleView at line 46. From a Model-View-Controller perspective, the Controller asks the Model to provide an array of scrambled Strings at line 45, and updates the View with it at line 46.

At this point, there is no event handling so the user cannot move any piece of the puzzle, but the app runs and shows the unsolved puzzle, as shown in Figure 7.1.

7.5 Moving the Pieces, Puzzle App, Version 1

We now start building the Controller part of the app, in order to give the app its functionality. In Version 1, we enable the user to move the various pieces of the puzzle (i.e., the TextViews). At this point, we do not care if the pieces are well positioned and whether the puzzle has been solved.

FIGURE 7.3 The red View is higher than the blue View in the stacking order. It partially hides the blue View.

Whenever the user is moving a piece of the puzzle, we bring that piece on top of the others so the user can see it at all times. Views are arranged in a stack using a **stacking order**. The first View added to a ViewGroup is at the bottom of the stack and the last View added is at the top of the stack. **FIGURE 7.3** illustrates the stacking order concept. The red View, which was added after the blue View, is higher in the stacking order and partially hides the blue View. **TABLE 7.7** shows the bringToFront method of the View class, which we can use to bring a View to the top of the stack so that it is not hidden by its sibling Views. To force a View named view to be at the top of the stack, we call the bringToFront method with it as in the following statement:

```
view.bringToFront( );
```

In order to implement the preceding functionality, the MainActivity class implements the View.OnTouchListener interface, and overrides the onTouch method. At this point, the pseudo-code of the onTouch method is:

```
If the action is DOWN
   Store the y position of the piece of the puzzle touched
   Store the y position of the touch
   Bring the piece of the puzzle at the top of the stacking order
If the action is MOVE
   Move the piece of the puzzle as the user moves his or her finger
```

TABLE 7.7 The bringToFront method of the View class

Method	Description
void bringToFront( )	Brings this View to the top of the stack so that it is on top of all its siblings.

All of the preceding involves managing the TextViews in the PuzzleView class. Thus, we provide methods in the PuzzleView class to perform these actions, and call these methods from the MainActivity class. **EXAMPLE 7.6** shows the MainActivity class. It implements View.OnTouchListener (lines 12–13) and overrides the onTouch method at lines 54–70. At line 50, inside the onCreate method, we call the enableListener method of the PuzzleView class with puzzleView. That method registers this listener, MainActivity, on all the TextViews.

Inside onTouch, we first call indexOfTextView to retrieve the index of the TextView that is the target of the touch event at line 55 and the type of action within the touch event at line 56. At this point, we only care about the DOWN and MOVE actions. We do not care about the UP action yet. If it is a DOWN action (line 58), the user is picking up a piece of the puzzle and is getting ready to move it. We call updateStartPositions with puzzleView (lines 59–60) in order to update the y position of the touched TextView and the y position of the touch (we need these two y values to calculate the new location of the TextView if the action is MOVE). We bring the touched TextView to the front at lines 61–62.

```
1    package com.jblearning.puzzlev1;
2
3    import android.content.res.Resources;
4    import android.graphics.Point;
5    import android.os.Bundle;
6    import android.support.v7.app.AppCompatActivity;
7    import android.util.DisplayMetrics;
8    import android.util.TypedValue;
9    import android.view.MotionEvent;
10   import android.view.View;
11
12   public class MainActivity extends AppCompatActivity
13                        implements View.OnTouchListener {
14     public static int STATUS_BAR_HEIGHT = 24; // in dp
15     public static int ACTION_BAR_HEIGHT = 56; // in dp
16     private PuzzleView puzzleView;
17     private Puzzle puzzle;
18
19     protected void onCreate( Bundle savedInstanceState ) {
20       super.onCreate( savedInstanceState );
21       puzzle = new Puzzle( );
22
23       Point size = new Point( );
24       getWindowManager( ).getDefaultDisplay( ).getSize( size );
25       int screenHeight = size.y;
26       int puzzleWidth = size.x;
```

EXAMPLE 7.6 The MainActivity class, Puzzle app, Version 1 (*Continued*)

```
27
28        Resources res = getResources( );
29        DisplayMetrics metrics = res.getDisplayMetrics( );
30        float pixelDensity = metrics.density;
31
32        TypedValue tv = new TypedValue( );
33        int actionBarHeight = ( int ) ( pixelDensity * ACTION_BAR_HEIGHT );
34        if( getTheme( ).resolveAttribute( android.R.attr.actionBarSize,
35                                   tv, true ) )
36          actionBarHeight = TypedValue.complexToDimensionPixelSize( tv.data,
37                          metrics );
38
39        int statusBarHeight = ( int ) ( pixelDensity * STATUS_BAR_HEIGHT );
40        int resourceId =
41           res.getIdentifier( "status_bar_height", "dimen", "android" );
42        if( resourceId != 0 ) // found resource for status bar height
43          statusBarHeight = res.getDimensionPixelSize( resourceId );
44
45        int puzzleHeight = screenHeight - statusBarHeight - actionBarHeight;
46        puzzleView = new PuzzleView( this, puzzleWidth, puzzleHeight,
47                               puzzle.getNumberOfParts( ) );
48        String [] scrambled = puzzle.scramble( );
49        puzzleView.fillGui( scrambled );
50        puzzleView.enableListener( this );
51        setContentView( puzzleView );
52      }
53
54      public boolean onTouch( View v, MotionEvent event ) {
55        int index = puzzleView.indexOfTextView( v );
56        int action = event.getAction( );
57        switch( action ) {
58          case MotionEvent.ACTION_DOWN:
59            // initialize data before move
60            puzzleView.updateStartPositions( index, ( int ) event.getY( ) );
61            // bring v to front
62            puzzleView.bringChildToFront( v );
63            break;
64          case MotionEvent.ACTION_MOVE:
65            // update y position of TextView being moved
66            puzzleView.moveTextViewVertically( index, ( int ) event.getY( ) );
67            break;
68        }
69        return true;
70      }
71  }
```

EXAMPLE 7.6 The `MainActivity` class, Puzzle app, Version 1

When the user moves his or her finger (move touch action, line 64), we call moveText-ViewVertically with puzzleView (lines 65–66) in order to move the touched TextView, following the user's finger along the vertical axis.

EXAMPLE 7.7 shows the updated PuzzleView class. It includes all the methods called by the PuzzleView instance variable in the MainActivity class: indexOfTextView, tvPosition, enableListener, updateStartPositions, and moveTextViewVertically.

The enableListener method (lines 73–76) expects a View.OnTouchListener parameter and registers it on all the TextViews. When we call it from MainActivity, we pass this, which "is a" View.OnTouchListener reference since MainActivity implements View.OnTouchListener.

```
1    package com.jblearning.puzzlev1;
2
3    import java.util.Random;
4    import android.app.Activity;
5    import android.view.Gravity;
6    import android.view.View;
7    import android.widget.RelativeLayout;
8    import android.widget.TextView;
9    import android.graphics.Color;
10
11   public class PuzzleView extends RelativeLayout {
12     private TextView [] tvs;
13     private RelativeLayout.LayoutParams [] params;
14     private int [] colors;
15
16     private int labelHeight;
17     private int startY; // start y coordinate of TextView being moved
18     private int startTouchY; // start y coordinate of current touch
19
20     public PuzzleView( Activity activity, int width, int height,
21                        int numberOfPieces ) {
22       super( activity );
23       buildGuiByCode( activity, width, height, numberOfPieces );
24     }
25
26     public void buildGuiByCode( Activity activity, int width, int height,
27                        int numberOfPieces ) {
28       tvs = new TextView[numberOfPieces];
29       colors = new int[tvs.length];
30       params = new RelativeLayout.LayoutParams[tvs.length];
31       Random random = new Random( );
```

EXAMPLE 7.7 The PuzzleView class, Puzzle app, Version 1 (*Continued*)

```
32        labelHeight = height / numberOfPieces;
33        for( int i = 0; i < tvs.length; i++ ) {
34          tvs[i] = new TextView( activity );
35          tvs[i].setGravity( Gravity.CENTER );
36          colors[i] = Color.rgb( random.nextInt( 255 ),
37            random.nextInt( 255 ),    random.nextInt( 255 ) );
38          tvs[i].setBackgroundColor( colors[i] );
39          params[i] = new RelativeLayout.LayoutParams( width, labelHeight );
40          params[i].leftMargin = 0;
41          params[i].topMargin = labelHeight * i;
42          addView( tvs[i], params[i] );
43        }
44      }
45
46      public void fillGui( String [] scrambledText ) {
47        for( int i = 0; i < tvs.length; i++ )
48          tvs[i].setText( scrambledText[i] );
49      }
50
51      // Returns the index of tv within the array tvs
52      public int indexOfTextView( View tv ) {
53        if( ! ( tv instanceof TextView ) )
54          return -1;
55        for( int i = 0; i < tvs.length; i++ ) {
56          if( tv == tvs[i] )
57            return i;
58        }
59        return -1;
60      }
61
62      public void updateStartPositions( int index, int y ) {
63        startY = params[index].topMargin;
64        startTouchY = y;
65      }
66
67      // moves the TextView at index index
68      public void moveTextViewVertically( int index, int y ) {
69        params[index].topMargin = startY + y - startTouchY;
70        tvs[index].setLayoutParams( params[index] );
71      }
72
73      public void enableListener( View.OnTouchListener listener ) {
74        for( int i = 0; i < tvs.length; i++ )
75          tvs[i].setOnTouchListener( listener );
76      }
77    }
```

EXAMPLE 7.7 **The `PuzzleView` class, Puzzle app, Version 1**

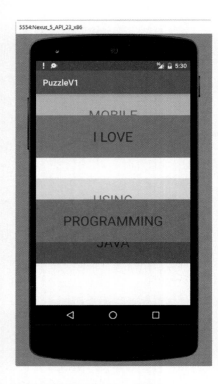

FIGURE 7.4 The Puzzle app, Version 1, after the user moved a few pieces

In order to help us manage the dragging of the TextViews, we add the following instance variables:

▸ An integer instance variable, startY (line 17), storing the y-coordinate of the top of the piece of the puzzle that we are moving.

▸ An integer instance variable, startTouchY (line 18), storing the y-coordinate of the initial touch.

The indexOfTextView method, coded at lines 51–60, returns the index of its View parameter, tv, within the array tvs. We expect tv to be a TextView, but we test for it at line 53. We loop through the elements of tvs and compare the element at index i to tv (line 56) and return i if they are equal (line 57). If tv is not a TextView or we do not find it, we return –1 (lines 54 and 59).

The updateStartPositions method, coded at lines 62–65, is called on a touch action DOWN. We update the values of the instance variables startY and startTouchY at lines 63–64; startY stores the original y-coordinate of the TextView for that piece, and startTouchY stores the y-coordinate of the touch within the TextView. We need both of them to update the y-coordinate of the TextView on a MOVE touch action.

The moveTextViewVertically method, coded at lines 67–71, updates the layout parameters of the TextView at index index, its first parameter, based on the value of y, its second parameter, which represents the y-coordinate of a touch. By changing the layout parameters of a TextView, it automatically moves it to a new location defined by these layout parameters.

FIGURE 7.4 shows the puzzle after the user has moved a few pieces.

7.6 Solving the Puzzle, Puzzle App, Version 2

We now continue to build the Controller part of the app, in order to give the app its functionality. When the user moves a piece of the puzzle, a TextView, and releases it, we swap its position with the piece of the puzzle that is under it. We consider that a piece of the puzzle is over another one if at least half of the piece of the puzzle is over the other one, as shown in **FIGURE 7.5**. The green piece is more than halfway over the blue piece. If the user releases it, the green piece will take the blue piece's place, and the blue piece will be placed where the green piece was when the touch event started. After each move, we check if the user has solved the puzzle. If the user has, we disable the touch events.

In addition to processing the DOWN and MOVE actions, we also need to process the UP action in order to swap the two pieces of the puzzle. Inside MainActivity, the pseudo-code of the onTouch method is now:

FIGURE 7.5 The green piece is closer to the blue piece than the red piece

```
If the action is DOWN
    Store the y position of the piece of the puzzle touched
```

Store the y position of the touch
Store the position of the "empty" puzzle slot
Bring the piece of the puzzle at the top of the stacking order
If the action is MOVE
Move the piece of the puzzle as the user moves his or her finger
If the action is UP
Swap the piece of the puzzle with the piece of the puzzle that is
under it
Check if the puzzle is solved; if it is, disable the listener

In order to implement the added functionality, we provide additional methods in the PuzzleView class, and call these methods from the MainActivity class. **EXAMPLE 7.8** shows the updated onTouch method of the MainActivity class.

```
11
12   public class MainActivity extends AppCompatActivity
13                            implements View.OnTouchListener {
...
54      public boolean onTouch( View v, MotionEvent event ) {
55         int index = puzzleView.indexOfTextView( v );
56         int action = event.getAction( );
57         switch( action ) {
58           case MotionEvent.ACTION_DOWN:
59             // initialize data before move
60             puzzleView.updateStartPositions( index, ( int ) event.getY( ) );
61             // bring v to front
62             puzzleView.bringChildToFront( v );
63             break;
64           case MotionEvent.ACTION_MOVE:
65             // update y position of TextView being moved
66             puzzleView.moveTextViewVertically( index, ( int ) event.getY( ) );
67             break;
68           case MotionEvent.ACTION_UP:
69             // move is complete: swap the 2 TextViews
70             int newPosition = puzzleView.tvPosition( index );
71             puzzleView.placeTextViewAtPosition( index, newPosition );
72             // if user just won, disable listener to stop the game
73             if( puzzle.solved( puzzleView.currentSolution( ) ) )
74               puzzleView.disableListener( );
75             break;
76         }
77         return true;
78      }
79   }
```

EXAMPLE 7.8 The updated onTouch **method of the** MainActivity **class, Puzzle app, Version 2**

When the user lifts up his or her finger (up touch action, line 68), we swap the touched TextView with the TextView currently underneath the touch: we first call tvPosition with puzzleView at line 70 in order to retrieve the new position index of the touched TextView, and then call placeTextViewAtPosition at line 71 with puzzleView in order to swap the two TextViews. Finally, we check if the user solved the puzzle at line 73. From a Model-View-Controller perspective, the Controller retrieves the state of the puzzle from the View, and asks the Model to check if this is the correct ordering of the puzzle. If it is, the Controller asks the View to disable touch event listening by calling disableListener at line 74 in order to disable touch listening. In this way, we prevent the user from moving the TextViews.

EXAMPLE 7.9 shows the updated PuzzleView class. It includes all the following additional methods called by the PuzzleView instance variable in the MainActivity class: tvPosition, placeTextViewAtPosition, disableListener, and currentSolution. We also update the buildGuiByCode, fillGui, and updateStartPositions methods as needed.

```
1  package com.jblearning.puzzlev2;
2
3  import java.util.Random;
4  import android.app.Activity;
5  import android.view.Gravity;
6  import android.view.View;
7  import android.widget.RelativeLayout;
8  import android.widget.TextView;
9  import android.graphics.Color;
10
11 public class PuzzleView extends RelativeLayout {
12    private TextView [] tvs;
13    private RelativeLayout.LayoutParams [] params;
14    private int [] colors;
15
16    private int labelHeight;
17    private int startY; // start y coordinate of TextView being moved
18    private int startTouchY; // start y coordinate of current touch
19    private int emptyPosition;
20    private int [ ] positions;
21
22    public PuzzleView( Activity activity, int width, int height,
23                       int numberOfPieces ) {
24      super( activity );
25      buildGuiByCode( activity, width, height, numberOfPieces );
26    }
27
```

EXAMPLE 7.9 The PuzzleView class, Puzzle app, Version 2 (*Continued*)

```
28    public void buildGuiByCode( Activity activity, int width, int height,
29                                int numberOfPieces ) {
30      positions = new int[numberOfPieces];
31      tvs = new TextView[numberOfPieces];
32      colors = new int[tvs.length];
33      params = new RelativeLayout.LayoutParams[tvs.length];
34      Random random = new Random( );
35      labelHeight = height / numberOfPieces;
36      for( int i = 0; i < tvs.length; i++ ) {
37        tvs[i] = new TextView( activity );
38        tvs[i].setGravity( Gravity.CENTER );
39        colors[i] = Color.rgb( random.nextInt( 255 ),
40          random.nextInt( 255 ),   random.nextInt( 255 ) );
41        tvs[i].setBackgroundColor( colors[i] );
42        params[i] = new RelativeLayout.LayoutParams( width, labelHeight );
43        params[i].leftMargin = 0;
44        params[i].topMargin = labelHeight * i;
45        addView( tvs[i], params[i] );
46      }
47    }
48
49    public void fillGui( String [] scrambledText ) {
50      for( int i = 0; i < tvs.length; i++ ) {
51        tvs[i].setText( scrambledText[i] );
52        positions[i] = i;
53      }
54    }
55
56    // Returns the index of tv within the array tvs
57    public int indexOfTextView( View tv ) {
58      if( ! ( tv instanceof TextView ) )
59        return -1;
60      for( int i = 0; i < tvs.length; i++ ) {
61        if( tv == tvs[i] )
62          return i;
63      }
64      return -1;
65    }
66
67    public void updateStartPositions( int index, int y ) {
68      startY = params[index].topMargin;
69      startTouchY = y;
70      emptyPosition = tvPosition( index );
71    }
72
73    // moves the TextView at index index
```

EXAMPLE 7.9 The `PuzzleView` class, Puzzle app, Version 2 (*Continued*)

```
74    public void moveTextViewVertically( int index, int y ) {
75      params[index].topMargin = startY + y - startTouchY;
76      tvs[index].setLayoutParams( params[index] );
77    }
78
79    public void enableListener( View.OnTouchListener listener ) {
80      for( int i = 0; i < tvs.length; i++ )
81        tvs[i].setOnTouchListener( listener );
82    }
83
84    public void disableListener( ) {
85      for( int i = 0; i < tvs.length; i++ )
86        tvs[i].setOnTouchListener( null );
87    }
88
89    // Returns position index within screen of TextView at index tvIndex
90    // Accuracy is half a TextView's height
91    public int tvPosition( int tvIndex ) {
92      return ( params[tvIndex].topMargin + labelHeight/2 ) / labelHeight;
93    }
94
95    // Swaps tvs[tvIndex] and tvs[positions[toPosition]]
96    public void placeTextViewAtPosition( int tvIndex, int toPosition ) {
97      // Move current TextView to position toPosition
98      params[tvIndex].topMargin = toPosition * labelHeight;
99      tvs[tvIndex].setLayoutParams( params[tvIndex] );
100
101     // Move TextView just replaced to empty spot
102     int index = positions[toPosition];
103     params[index].topMargin = emptyPosition * labelHeight;
104     tvs[index].setLayoutParams( params[index] );
105
106     // Reset positions values
107     positions[emptyPosition] = index;
108     positions[toPosition] = tvIndex;
109   }
110
111   // Returns the current user solution as an array of Strings
112   public String [ ] currentSolution( ) {
113     String [] current = new String[tvs.length];
114     for( int i = 0; i < current.length; i++ )
115       current[i] = tvs[positions[i]].getText( ).toString( );
116
117     return current;
118   }
119 }
```

EXAMPLE 7.9 The `PuzzleView` class, Puzzle app, Version 2

The disableListener method (lines 84–87) sets the listener of all the TextViews to null, effectively disabling touch listening.

In order to help us manage the swapping of the TextViews, we add the following instance variables:

▶ An integer instance variable, emptyPosition (line 19), storing the y position of the "empty position", where the TextView the user is currently moving was before the move.

▶ An integer-array instance variable, positions (line 20), storing the y positions of all the elements in tvs.

As the user picks up or releases a piece of the puzzle, we need to evaluate its position on the screen. **FIGURES 7.6** and **7.7** show a possible starting puzzle situation and a second puzzle situation after the user switched the two bottom pieces of the puzzle. Figure 7.7 shows the difference between the position of a TextView (listed in the right column) and its index (within the array tvs, listed in the left column): tvs[4] is at position 3 (one position above the bottom position on the screen), tvs[3] is at position 4 (bottom of the screen). Thus, the value of positions[3] is 4 (the index of the TextView that is at position 3), and the value of positions[4] is 3 (the index of the TextView that is at position 4). The other TextViews have not been moved yet.

The tvPosition method, coded at lines 89–93, returns the position (0, 1, 2, 3, or 4 in this example) of the array element of tvs at index tvIndex, the parameter of the method. The expression params[tvIndex].topMargin returns the y-coordinate of the top of the TextView. We add half the height of a TextView and then divide by the height of a TextView in order to compute its position within this PuzzleView.

Inside the updateStartPositions method, coded at lines 67–71, we update the value of emptyPosition at line 70. The emptyPosition instance variable stores the position within

Index of TextView	Text	Position
0	MOBILE	0
1	PROGRAMMING	1
2	USING	2
3	JAVA	3
4	I LOVE	4

FIGURE 7.6 A possible start of the puzzle

Index of TextView	Text	Position
0	MOBILE	0
1	PROGRAMMING	1
2	USING	2
4	I LOVE	3
3	JAVA	4

FIGURE 7.7 After switching I LOVE and JAVA

the `PuzzleView` of the `TextView` that was touched. We retrieve it by calling the `tvPosition` method, passing the array index of that `TextView` (line 70).

The `placeTextViewAtPosition` method is coded at lines 95–109. We call it when the user releases a piece of the puzzle. It swaps it with the piece underneath it. Its first parameter, `tvIndex`, is the index of the `TextView` that the user is releasing. Its second parameter, `toPosition`, is the position that `TextView` will be after the user releases it and ends the touch event. This method does three things:

▶ Place the `TextView` (TextView A) at index `tvIndex` to its new position, identified by `toPosition`. It is replacing a `TextView` at that position (TextView B).
▶ Place `TextView` B at the old position of `TextView` A, `emptyPosition`.
▶ Update the `positions` array.

FIGURE 7.8 shows the various states of the `TextView`s and those variables as the user picks up the I LOVE piece of the puzzle and moves it to where the PROGRAMMING piece of the puzzle is. At that stage, the user is moving the `TextView` at index 4 (the value of `tvIndex`) and position 3 (the value of `emptyPosition`) to the position 0 (the value of `toPosition`), where the `TextView` at index 1 (the value of `positions[toPosition]`) is.

The `tvs` and `params` arrays parallel each other. At line 98, we set the top margin of the `params` array element at index `tvIndex` to the y-coordinate where that `tvs` array element is moving to. At line 99, we force a re-layout of the `TextView` array element at `tvIndex` based on the value of its corresponding `params` array element, effectively placing the `TextView` in its new slot. At lines 101–104, we do the same for the `TextView` element that was at position `toPosition`. It is moving to the position `emptyPosition`. At lines 106–108, we update the `positions` array to reflect that the two `TextView`s have been moved.

The `positions` array is instantiated at line 30 inside the `buildGuiByCode` method and initialized at line 52 inside the `fillGui` method.

Index of TextView	Text	Position	toPosition	tvIndex	emptyPosition
1	PROGRAMMING	0	0		
0	MOBILE	1			
2	USING	2			
4	I LOVE	3		4	3
3	JAVA	4			

FIGURE 7.8 **Moving I LOVE to the PROGRAMMING position**

FIGURE 7.9 **The Puzzle app, Version 2, after the user solves the puzzle**

The currentSolution method, coded at lines 111–118, constructs and returns a String array that reflects the current positions of the TextViews in our puzzle. The value of positions[i] is the index of the TextView that is at position i within the screen as illustrated in Figures 7.6 and 7.7. We access the text inside the TextView at position i within the PuzzleView using the expression tvs[positions[i]].getText( ). Because the getText method returns a CharSequence, we call toString to convert the returned value to a String.

FIGURE 7.9 shows the solved puzzle.

7.7 Gesture and Tap Detection and Handling

Sometimes we need to detect a **confirmed** single tap, or a double tap. A single tap is confirmed when it is identified by the system as a single tap only (i.e., no tap following the first tap has been detected). Or we need to detect the speed of a swipe to assign to the velocity of an object on the screen. The `GestureDetector` class, along with its `static` inner interfaces, `GestureDetector.OnGestureListener` and `GestureDetector.OnDoubleTapListener`, provide the tools and functionality for gestures and taps.

▶ The `GestureDetector.OnGestureListener` interface notifies us of gestures via its six callback methods (listed in **TABLE 7.8**).

▶ The `GestureDetector.OnDoubleTapListener` interface notifies us of double taps or confirmed single taps via its three callback methods (listed in **TABLE 7.9**).

TABLE 7.10 shows some methods of the `GestureDetector` class, including a constructor, the `setOnDoubleTapListener`, and the `onTouchEvent` methods.

TABLE 7.8 Methods of the `GestureDetector.OnGestureListener` interface

Method	Description
boolean onDown(MotionEvent e)	Called on the DOWN action when a touch occurs.
boolean onFling(MotionEvent e1, MotionEvent e2, float velocityX, float velocityY)	Called when a swipe occurs. Velocity is measured in pixels per second in both directions.
void onLongPress(MotionEvent me)	Called when a long press occurs.
boolean onScroll(MotionEvent e1, MotionEvent e2, float distanceX, float distanceY)	Called when a scroll occurs. Distances are measured between this onScroll method call and the previous one.
void onShowPress(MotionEvent e)	Called when the user touches the screen and does not move or lift up his or her finger.
boolean onSingleTapUp(MotionEvent e)	Called on the UP action when a touch occurs.

TABLE 7.9 Methods of the `GestureDetector.OnDoubleTapListener` interface

Method	Description
boolean onDoubleTap(MotionEvent e)	Called on the DOWN action when a double tap occurs.
boolean onDoubleTapEvent(MotionEvent e)	Called on the DOWN, possibly MOVE, and UP actions when a double tap occurs.
boolean onSingleTapConfirmed(MotionEvent e)	Called on the DOWN action when a confirmed single tap occurs (i.e., the single tap is not the first tap of a double tap).

TABLE 7.10 Selected methods of the `GestureDetector` class

Method	Description
GestureDetector(Context context, GestureDetector.OnGestureListener gestureListener)	Creates a GestureDetector object for the context and using gestureListener as the listener called for gesture events. We must use this constructor from a User-Interface thread.
void setOnDoubleTapListener(GestureDetector. OnDoubleTapListener doubleTapListener)	Sets doubleTapListener as the listener called for double tap and related gestures.
boolean onTouchEvent(MotionEvent e)	Called when a touch event occurs; triggers a call to the appropriate callback methods of the GestureDetector.OnGestureListener interface.

In order to handle a touch event using the `GestureDetector` class and the `Gesture-Detector.OnDoubleTapListener` and `GestureDetector.OnGestureListener` interfaces, we need to:

▶ Declare a `GestureDetector` instance variable.
▶ Define a handler class that implements the `GestureDetector.OnGestureListener` and `GestureDetector.OnDoubleTapListener` interfaces and overrides their methods.
▶ Create a handler object of that class.
▶ Instantiate the `GestureDetector` instance variable and pass the handler object as the second argument of the constructor.
▶ Set the handler object as the listener handling the tap events (if necessary).
▶ Inside the `onTouchEvent` method of the `Activity` class, call the `onTouchEvent` method of the `GestureDetector` class with the `GestureDetector` instance variable. This triggers the dispatching of the touch event: depending on the touch event, the appropriate method of the handler class will be automatically called.

We can define the handler class as a `private` class of the current activity class. The following code sequences would implement the preceding:

```
// GestureDetector instance variable inside the activity class
private GestureDetector detector;

// Inside the onCreate method of the activity class
GestureAndTapHandler gth = new GestureAndTapHandler( );
detector = new GestureDetector( this, gth );
detector.setOnDoubleTapListener( gth );
```

```
// Inside the onTouchEvent method of the activity class
// event is the MotionEvent parameter of the onTouchEvent method
detector.onTouchEvent( event );

// Private class inside the activity class
private class GestureAndTapHandler implements
            GestureDetector.OnGestureListener,
            GestureDetector.OnDoubleTapListener {
  // The GestureAndTapHandler class needs to override all 9 methods
}
```

As before with the `View.OnTouchListener` interface, an alternative to defining a new class implementing `GestureDetector.OnGestureListener` and `GestureDetector.OnDoubleTapListener` is for the current activity class to implement them. Then, we would need to override the nine methods inside the `Activity` class and we would use `this` instead of `gth` in the preceding code.

The `onTouchEvent` method of the `GestureDetector` class acts as a dispatcher and calls the appropriate method or methods of the `GestureDetector.OnGestureListener` and `GestureDetector.OnDoubleTapListener` interfaces based on the nature of the event that just happened. For some apps, it is possible that all we need is to execute inside the `onTouchEvent` method. For other apps, we may be interested in capturing double taps and, therefore, we will want to place our code inside the `onDoubleTapEvent` method. Or we may be interested in capturing the speed of a swipe and therefore we will want to place our code inside the `onFling` method. Depending on what action we are interested in capturing and processing, we place our code in the corresponding method. Note that when we override `onTouchEvent`, we need to call the `onTouchEvent` method of the `GestureDetector` class because it performs the dispatching.

COMMON ERROR: If we do not call the `onTouchEvent` method of the `GestureDetector` class from inside the `onTouchEvent` method of the `Activity` class, the touch event will not be dispatched to the appropriate method(s) of the listener interfaces.

EXAMPLE 7.10 shows the `MainActivity` class of a practice app. It implements the `GestureDetector.OnGestureListener` and the `GestureDetector.OnDoubleTapListener` interfaces at lines 10–11. We declare a `GestureDetector` instance variable, `detector`, at line 13. We instantiate it at line 17, passing `this` as the first and second argument. As the first argument, `this` represents the application's context (an `Activity` object "is a" `Context` object). As the second argument, it represents a `GestureDetector.OnGestureListener` (`MainActivity` inherits from `GestureDetector.OnGestureListener` and, therefore, `this` "is a" `GestureDetector.OnGestureListener`). Thus, since `detector` calls its

```
1    package com.jblearning.touchesv2;
2
3    import android.os.Bundle;
4    import android.support.v7.app.AppCompatActivity;
5    import android.util.Log;
6    import android.view.MotionEvent;
7    import android.view.GestureDetector;
8
9    public class MainActivity extends AppCompatActivity
10          implements GestureDetector.OnGestureListener,
11                     GestureDetector.OnDoubleTapListener {
12     public static final String MA = "MainActivity";
13     private GestureDetector detector;
14
15     protected void onCreate( Bundle savedInstanceState ) {
16       super.onCreate( savedInstanceState );
17       detector = new GestureDetector( this, this );
18       detector.setOnDoubleTapListener( this );
19     }
20
21     public boolean onTouchEvent( MotionEvent event ) {
22       Log.w( MA, "Inside onTouchEvent" );
23       detector.onTouchEvent( event );
24       return true;
25     }
26
27     public boolean onFling( MotionEvent e1, MotionEvent e2,
28                   final float velocityX, final float velocityY )  {
29       Log.w( MA, "Inside onFling" );
30       return true;
31     }
32
33     public boolean onDown( MotionEvent e ) {
34       Log.w( MA, "Inside onDown" );
35       return true;
36     }
37
38     public void onLongPress( MotionEvent e ) {
39       Log.w( MA, "Inside onLongPress" );
40     }
41
42     public boolean onScroll( MotionEvent e1, MotionEvent e2,
43                        float distanceX, float distanceY ) {
44       Log.w( MA, "Inside onScroll" );
45       return true;
46     }
```

EXAMPLE 7.10 **The `MainActivity` class, Touches app, Version 2 (*Continued*)**

```
47
48   public void onShowPress( MotionEvent e ) {
49      Log.w( MA, "Inside onShowPress" );
50   }
51
52   public boolean onSingleTapUp( MotionEvent e ) {
53      Log.w( MA, "Inside onSingleTapUp" );
54      return true;
55   }
56
57   public boolean onDoubleTap( MotionEvent e ) {
58      Log.w( MA, "Inside onDoubleTap" );
59      return true;
60   }
61
62   public boolean onDoubleTapEvent( MotionEvent e ) {
63      Log.w( MA, "Inside onDoubleTapEvent" );
64      return true;
65   }
66
67   public boolean onSingleTapConfirmed( MotionEvent e ) {
68      Log.w( MA, "Inside onSingleTapConfirmed" );
69      return true;
70   }
71 }
```

EXAMPLE 7.10 **The `MainActivity` class, Touches app, Version 2**

onTouchEvent method at line 23, gestures events will trigger calls to some of the six callback methods implemented in the `MainActivity` class depending on the touch event. At line 18, we set this as the listener registered by detector as the listener for tap events. Thus, since detector calls its onTouchEvent method at line 23, tap events will trigger calls to some of the three callback methods inherited from GestureDetector.OnDoubleTapListener and implemented in the `MainActivity` class, depending on the touch event.

The onTouchEvent method is coded at lines 21–25. Detector calls its own onTouchEvent method at line 23, passing the `MotionEvent` event, setting up the dispatching discussed previously. All the nine overridden methods of the two listeners interface output a feedback statement to Logcat.

FIGURE 7.10 shows the output inside Logcat of Example 7.10 when the user taps on the screen

```
Inside onTouchEvent
Inside onDown
Inside onTouchEvent
Inside onSingleTapUp
Inside onSingleTapConfirmed
```

FIGURE 7.10 Possible Logcat output when the user taps on the screen once, Touches app, Version 2

```
Inside onTouchEvent
Inside onDown
Inside onTouchEvent
Inside onSingleTapUp
Inside onTouchEvent
Inside onDoubleTap
Inside onDoubleTapEvent
Inside onDown
Inside onTouchEvent
Inside onDoubleTapEvent
```

FIGURE 7.11 Possible Logcat output when the user double taps on the screen, Touches app, Version 2

```
Inside onTouchEvent
Inside onDown
Inside onTouchEvent
Inside onScroll
Inside onTouchEvent
Inside onScroll
Inside onTouchEvent
Inside onScroll
Inside onTouchEvent
Inside onFling
```

FIGURE 7.12 Possible Logcat output when the user swipes the screen, Touches app, Version 2

once on the emulator. It shows that the onTouchEvent method triggers calls to the onDown, onSingleTapUp, and onSingleTapConfirmed, successively. When onSingleTapUp is called, we do not know yet that this was a single tap event, because a double tap event would also trigger a call to onSingleTapUp. Thus, if we want to execute some code based on a single tap event only, we should place that code inside the onSingleTapConfirmed method.

FIGURE 7.11 shows the output inside Logcat of Example 7.10 when the user taps on the screen twice quickly (i.e., double taps on the emulator). It shows that the onTouchEvent method triggers calls to the onDown, onSingleTapUp, onDoubleTap, onDoubleTapEvent, and the onDown and onDoubleTapEvent again. It is possible that we get a slightly different output, possibly an additional call to onTouchEvent and onDoubleTapEvent. Note that the onSingleTapConfirmed method is not called. If we want to process taps, we can place our code inside the onSingleTapUp and onDoubleTap methods. If we want to process the double tap event, we can place our code inside the onDoubleTapEvent method. Note that it is called twice, once on a DOWN action and the second time on an UP action. It can even be called three times, if a (slight) MOVE action is detected in between the DOWN and UP actions.

A triple tap is interpreted as a double tap followed by a single tap. A quadruple tap is interpreted as a double tap followed by another double tap.

FIGURE 7.12 shows a possible output inside Logcat of Example 7.10 when the user swipes the screen. The onScroll method is called several times, at various points within the swipe. The onFling method is called once and last. It is possible that we get a slightly different output depending on the swipe or if we use the emulator and the computer mouse.

Once we have decided what method we want to execute in, we can use its parameter or parameters to retrieve values relative to the action that is taking place. For example, if we want to capture the point of origin and the velocity of a swipe, we can place our code inside the onFling method and retrieve these values as shown in **EXAMPLE 7.11**.

As we run the modified app and swipe the screen, the output looks like the one in **FIGURE 7.13**.

```
26
27   public boolean onFling( MotionEvent e1, MotionEvent e2,
28                  final float velocityX, final float velocityY ) {
29     long deltaTime = e2.getEventTime( ) - e1.getEventTime( );
30     Log.w( MA, "Inside onFling: deltaTime (in ms) = " + deltaTime );
31
32     Log.w( MA, "x1 = " + e1.getRawX( ) + "; y1 = " + e1.getRawY( ) );
33     Log.w( MA, "x2 = " + e2.getRawX( ) + "; y2 = " + e2.getRawY( ) );
34
35     Log.w( MA, "measured vX (in pixels/second) = " + velocityX );
36     Log.w( MA, "measured vY (in pixels/second) = " + velocityY );
37
38     return true;
39   }
40
```

EXAMPLE 7.11 Expanded `onFling` method within the `MainActivity` class, Touches app, Version 3

```
Inside onFling: deltaTime (in ms) = 82
x1 = 392.0; y1 = 1375.0
x2 = 775.0; y2 = 1061.0
measured vX (in pixels/second) = 1448.4669
measured vY (in pixels/second) = -573.99493
```

FIGURE 7.13 Logcat output when the user swipes the screen, Touches app, Version 3

7.8 Detecting a Double Tap, Puzzle App, Version 3

The `GestureDetector.SimpleOnGestureListener` is a convenient class that implements the `GestureDetector.OnGestureListener` and the `GestureDetector.OnDoubleTapListener` interfaces with do-nothing methods returning `false`. So if we are interested in only one or two methods of the nine methods in these two interfaces, it is easier to extend that class than to implement one or both interfaces. In our Puzzle app, Version 3, we want to process a double tap and change MOBILE to ANDROID when the user double taps on the `TextView` that shows MOBILE. We can ignore the other eight methods and only need to code inside the `onDoubleTapEvent` method.

SOFTWARE ENGINEERING: If we are only interested in implementing one or two methods of the `GestureDetector.OnGestureListener` and the `Gesture-Detector.OnDoubleTapListener` interfaces, we should consider extending `GestureDetector.SimpleOnGestureListener` instead of implementing both interfaces.

We update the `Puzzle` class, our Model, and add two methods to it: one that returns the word to be changed, and one that returns the replacement word. We keep this change as simple as possible in order to focus more on the Controller and View parts of the app. **EXAMPLE 7.12** shows these two methods.

```
50
51     public String wordToChange( ) {
52        return "MOBILE";
53     }
54
55     public String replacementWord( ) {
56        return "ANDROID";
57     }
58   }
```

EXAMPLE 7.12 The `wordToChange` and `replacementWord` methods of the `Puzzle` class, Puzzle app, Version 3

In order to use the `GestureDetector.SimpleOnGestureListener` class, we can do the following:

▶ Code a `private` class that extends `GestureDetector.SimpleOnGestureListener` and override inside that class the method(s) that we are interested in.

▶ Declare and instantiate an object of that class, a gesture handler.

▶ Declare a `GestureDetector` instance variable. When instantiating it, pass the gesture handler as the second argument of the constructor.

▶ If we are interested in processing tap events, call `setDoubleTapListener` with the gesture detector instance variable and pass the gesture handler.

▶ Override the `onTouchEvent` method of the `Activity` class inside the subclass of `Activity`. Inside it, call the `onTouchEvent` method of the `GestureDetector` class with the gesture detector instance variable. That sets up the dispatching of touch events to the appropriate method(s) of the gesture handler class.

Note that `MainActivity` already extends `AppCompatActivity` and, therefore, cannot extend `GestureDetector.SimpleOnGestureListener`. Thus, contrary to Example 7.10, in which `MainActivity` implements both listener interfaces, we need to code a separate class that extends `GestureDetector.SimpleOnGestureListener`.

EXAMPLE 7.13 shows the new parts of the `MainActivity` class. The `private` class `Double-TapHandler`, coded at lines 93–106, only overrides the `onDoubleTapEvent` method because we are only interested in processing a double tap event. In it, we retrieve the index of the `TextView` that the user double tapped on, check if its label is MOBILE, and change it to ANDROID if it is. We first retrieve the y-coordinate of the double tap within the `PuzzleView` at line 96. We then call the `indexOfTextView` method (which we add to the `PuzzleView` class) of `PuzzleView` to obtain the index of the `TextView` where the double tap happened (lines 99–100). Because we

```
  8
  9  import android.view.GestureDetector;
...
 14  public class MainActivity extends AppCompatActivity
 15                            implements View.OnTouchListener {
...
 19    private int statusBarHeight;
 20    private int actionBarHeight;
 21    private GestureDetector detector;
 22
 23    protected void onCreate( Bundle savedInstanceState ) {
...
 57      DoubleTapHandler dth = new DoubleTapHandler( );
 58      detector = new GestureDetector( this, dth );
 59      detector.setOnDoubleTapListener( dth );
 60    }
...
 88    public boolean onTouchEvent( MotionEvent event ) {
 89      detector.onTouchEvent( event );
 90      return true;
 91    }
 92
 93    private class DoubleTapHandler
 94      extends GestureDetector.SimpleOnGestureListener {
 95      public boolean onDoubleTapEvent( MotionEvent event ) {
 96        int touchY = ( int ) event.getRawY( );
 97        // y coordinate of the touch within puzzleView is
 98        // touchY - actionBarHeight - statusBarHeight
 99        int index = puzzleView.indexOfTextView( touchY
100                    - actionBarHeight - statusBarHeight );
101        if( puzzleView.getTextViewText( index )
102                    .equals( puzzle.wordToChange( ) ) )
103          puzzleView.setTextViewText( index, puzzle.replacementWord( ) );
104        return   true;
105      }
106    }
107  }
```

EXAMPLE 7.13 Additions to the `MainActivity` class, Puzzle app, Version 3

need to subtract the heights of the status bar and action bar from the y-coordinate of the double tap, we declare `statusBarHeight` and `actionBarHeight` as instance variables at lines 19–20. In this way, we do not have to compute their value twice.

At lines 101–102, we retrieve the text inside that `TextView` by calling the `getTextViewText` method (which we also add to the `PuzzleView` class) and test if it matches the word to change in the `Puzzle` class. If it does, we call the `setTextViewText` method (which we also add to the `PuzzleView` class) to change the text of the `TextView` to the new word retrieved from the `Puzzle` class. From the Model-View-Controller perspective, the Controller asks the View to retrieve the text of the `TextView` and compares it to the word to change retrieved from the Model. If they match, the Controller asks the Model for the replacement word and tells the view to place it inside the `TextView` at line 103.

At line 57, we declare and instantiate `dth`, a `DoubleTapHandler` object. The instance variable `detector`, a `GestureDetector`, is declared at line 21 and instantiated at line 58. The second argument passed to the constructor is `dth`. That means that the gesture-related methods of the `GestureDetector.OnGestureListener` interface, which `DoubleTapHandler` class inherits via the `GestureDetector.SimpleOnGestureListener` class, will be called when a gesture event happens. However, we are not interested in handling simple touches, swipes, or flings in this case. We are only interested in handling double taps. Thus, we call the `setOnDoubleTapListener` method at line 59 so that the three methods inherited from the `GestureDetector.OnDouble-TapListener` interface are called when a tap event occurs. The `GestureDetector` class, which belongs to the `android.view` package, is imported at line 9.

We override the `onTouchEvent` method at lines 88–91. At line 89, `detector` calls the `onTouch-Event` of the `GestureDetector` class, which sets up the dispatching of gestures and tap events to the methods of the class that `dth` belongs to, `DoubleTapHandler`. Thus, when the user double taps on the screen, we execute inside the `onDoubleTapEvent` of our `DoubleTapHandler` class.

EXAMPLE 7.14 shows the three methods added to the `PuzzleView` class. Inside the `indexOfTextView` method (lines 120–124), we divide the y-coordinate of the tap by the height of a `TextView` and assign it to `position` at line 122. The index of the `TextView` located at `position` is positions[position]. We return it at line 123.

Inside `getTextViewText` (lines 126–129), we call `toString` at line 128 because the `getText` method of `TextView` returns a `CharSequence`.

```
119
120     // returns index of TextView whose location includes y
121     public int indexOfTextView( int y ) {
122       int position = y / labelHeight;
123       return positions[position];
124     }
125
126     // returns text inside TextView whose index is tvIndex
127     public String getTextViewText( int tvIndex ) {
128       return tvs[tvIndex].getText( ).toString( );
129     }
130
131     // replace text inside TextView whose index is tvIndex with s
132     public void setTextViewText( int tvIndex, String s ) {
133       tvs[tvIndex].setText( s );
134     }
135   }
```

EXAMPLE 7.14 The three methods added to the `PuzzleView` class, Puzzle app, Version 3

If we run the app and double tap on MOBILE after we solve the puzzle, it changes to ANDROID. Note that if we double tap on either I LOVE, PROGRAMMING, USING, or JAVA, nothing happens. The onTouch method, which is part of the MainActivity class and is shown at lines 54–78 of Example 7.8, returns true. That means that we stop propagating the touch event. As we run the app, if we double tap on MOBILE before the puzzle is solved, nothing happens because the onDoubleTapEvent method does not execute. Once the puzzle is solved, we disable listening on the TextViews (at line 74 of Example 7.8). There is no longer a touch listener registered on the TextViews, so the touch event's target is now the content View for the activity, and the event is dispatched by the onTouchEvent method to the onDoubleTapEvent method.

If we change the onTouch method so that it returns false at line 77 of Example 7.8, then a double tap event on a TextView would propagate to the content View, which is the View underneath the View that is the target of the touch. In that case, the onDoubleTapEvent method would execute. If we double tap on MOBILE, it would change to ANDROID. More generally, if the onTouch method returns false, not only the touch event happens on the top View but also **propagates** to Views underneath that top View.

FIGURE 7.14 shows the state of the puzzle after the user solved it and double tapped on MOBILE.

FIGURE 7.14 The Puzzle app, Version 3, after the user solves the puzzle and double taps on MOBILE

7.9 Making the App Device Independent, Puzzle App, Version 4

When we publish an app, we do not know what device it will run on, in particular what the screen width and height dimensions will be. In Version 4, we use our `DynamicFontSizing` class in **EXAMPLE 7.15** so that the size of the font is optimal for the device on which the app runs. Given a `TextView`, the `setFontSizeToFitInView` static method (lines 11–32) sizes the text font inside the `TextView` so that it is maximal and the text fits on one line—it returns that maximal font size. Appendix B explains in detail the `DynamicSizing` class.

```
1   package com.jblearning.puzzlev4;
2
3   import android.util.TypedValue;
4   import android.view.View.MeasureSpec;
5   import android.widget.TextView;
6
7   public class DynamicSizing {
8     public static final int MAX_FONT_SIZE = 200;
9     public static final int MIN_FONT_SIZE = 1;
10
11    /*
12     * Sets the maximum font size of tv so that the text inside tv
13     *        fits on one line
14     * @param  tv    the TextView whose font size is to be changed
15     * @return the resulting font size
16     */
17    public static int setFontSizeToFitInView( TextView tv ) {
18      int fontSize = MAX_FONT_SIZE;
19      tv.setTextSize( TypedValue.COMPLEX_UNIT_SP, fontSize );
20      tv.measure( MeasureSpec.UNSPECIFIED, MeasureSpec.UNSPECIFIED );
21      int lines = tv.getLineCount( );
22      if( lines > 0 ) {
23        while( lines != 1 && fontSize >= MIN_FONT_SIZE + 2 ) {
24          fontSize--;
25          tv.setTextSize( TypedValue.COMPLEX_UNIT_SP, fontSize );
26          tv.measure( MeasureSpec.UNSPECIFIED, MeasureSpec.UNSPECIFIED );
27          lines = tv.getLineCount( );
28        }
29        tv.setTextSize( TypedValue.COMPLEX_UNIT_SP, --fontSize );
30      }
31      return fontSize;
32    }
33  }
```

EXAMPLE 7.15 The `DynamicFontSizing` class, Puzzle app, Version 4

```
49
50   public void fillGui( String [] scrambledText ) {
51     int minFontSize = DynamicSizing.MAX_FONT_SIZE;
52     for( int i = 0; i < tvs.length; i++ ) {
53       tvs[i].setText( scrambledText[i] );
54       positions[i] = i;
55
56       tvs[i].setWidth( params[i].width );
57       tvs[i].setPadding( 20, 5, 20, 5 );
58
59       // find font size dynamically
60       int fontSize = DynamicSizing.setFontSizeToFitInView( tvs[i] );
61       if( minFontSize > fontSize )
62         minFontSize = fontSize;
63     }
64
65     // set font size for TextViews
66     for( int i = 0; i < tvs.length; i++ )
67       tvs[i].setTextSize( TypedValue.COMPLEX_UNIT_SP, minFontSize );
68   }
69
```

EXAMPLE 7.16 **The updated** `fillGui` **method of the** `PuzzleView` **class, Puzzle app, Version 4**

EXAMPLE 7.16 shows the updated `fillGui` method, the only change in the `PuzzleView` class, in addition to importing the `TypedValue` class from the `android.util` package. We optimize the font size for the `TextViews` in the `fillGui` method because that is where their text is set.

We want to use the same font size for all the `TextViews`. However, the text inside each `TextView` is different. Thus, we compute the minimum font size returned by all the calls to `set-FontSizeToFitInView` for each `TextView`. After initializing `minFontSize` at line 51 with `MAX_FONT_SIZE`, we update it as necessary at lines 59–62. Once `minFontSize` is set, we loop again through all the `TextViews` and reset their font size with `minFontSize` at lines 65–67. After this method executes, all the `TextViews` have the same font size, and it is the maximal font size so that their text contents fit on one line.

Before we compute the font size for each `TextView`, we make sure that their width is equal to the width of the screen at line 56. We give some padding to each `TextView` at line 57 so that there is space around the text. The font size ends up being 46 when running on the Nexus 5 emulator.

FIGURE 7.15 shows the Puzzle app, Version 4, running inside the emulator. PROGRAMMING fills up almost the whole `TextView`.

FIGURE 7.15 The Puzzle app, Version 4, running inside the emulator

Chapter Summary

- We can use the `View.OnTouchListener` interface to capture and handle a touch event.
- To register a `View.OnTouchListener` on a GUI component, we can use the `setOnTouchListener` method of the `View` class.
- The `onTouch` callback method of the `View.OnTouchListener` interface is called when a touch event occurs.
- The `onTouch` method includes a `View` parameter that is a reference to the `View` on which the touch happened.
- The `onTouch` method includes a `MotionEvent` parameter that contains information about the current touch event, such as the x- and y-coordinates, the type of event, etc.
- If the `onTouch` method returns `true`, the touch event does not propagate to `Views` below the current `View` that might have an event handler for that touch event. If it returns `false`, it does.

- The getAction method of the MotionEvent class returns an integer value representing the type of action that just occurred within the touch event.
- The MotionEvent class includes some constants to identify a touch event action, such as ACTION_DOWN, ACTION_MOVE, or ACTION_UP.
- View components are displayed inside a ViewGroup using a stacking order. The View added first is at the bottom of the stack, whereas the View added last is at the top of the stack.
- We can use the bringToFront method to bring a View to the top of the stack in order to guarantee that that View is not hidden by other Views.
- We can use the GestureDetector class, along with its static inner interfaces, GestureDetector.OnGestureListener and GestureDetector.OnDoubleTapListener, to capture and handle gesture and tap events.
- Inside the onTouchEvent method of the activity class, a GestureDetector object is expected to call its onTouchEvent method to set up the dispatching of the touch event to the appropriate method of the handler class that implements the GestureDetector.OnGestureListener and/or GestureDetector.OnDoubleTapListener interfaces.
- The GestureDetector.SimpleOnGestureListener is a convenient class that implements the GestureDetector.OnGestureListener and the GestureDetector.OnDoubleTapListener interfaces with do-nothing methods.

Exercises, Problems, and Projects

Multiple-Choice Exercises

1. What method do we use to register a View.OnTouchListener on a component?
   - setOnTouchListener
   - addOnTouchListener
   - registerOnTouchListener
   - isOnTouchListener

2. What method of the MotionEvent class do we use to retrieve the type of action that just happened?
   - action
   - getAction
   - getEvent
   - getTouch

3. What method do we use to bring a View to the top of the stacking order?
   - bringToTop
   - gotToTop
   - bringToFront
   - bringChildToTop

4. What class can be used to capture gestures and tap events?
   - Gesture
   - GestureDetector
   - TapDetector
   - GestureAndTapDetector

5. OnGestureListener and OnDoubleTapListener are
   - Private static inner classes of GestureDetector
   - Private static inner interfaces of GestureDetector
   - Public static inner interfaces of GestureDetector
   - Classes independent of GestureDetector

6. In order to identify a touch event action, the MotionEvent class has
   - A special constructor
   - Private instance variables
   - Private methods
   - Constants that the action can be compared to

7. What method of the GestureDetector class acts as a dispatcher to the various methods of OnGestureListener and OnDoubleTapListener?
   - onTouch
   - onTouchEvent
   - onMotionTouchEvent
   - onEvent

8. How many methods do OnGestureListener and OnDoubleTapListener have, respectively?
   - six and six
   - three and three
   - three and six
   - six and three

9. When inheriting from OnGestureListener and OnDoubleTapListener, if we are only interested in one or two methods, an alternative is to
   - Implement the SimpleOnGestureListener interface
   - Extend the SimpleOnGestureListener class
   - Implement the SimpleOnGestureListener class
   - Extend the SimpleOnGestureListener interface

10. Which method is not a method of OnDoubleTapListener?
    - onSingleTapConfirmed
    - onDoubleTapConfirmed
    - onDoubleTap
    - onDoubleTapEvent

Fill in the Code

11. Write the class header of a class named MyActivity that inherits from Activity and View.OnTouchListener.

12. We are coding inside the onTouch method of View.OnTouchListener. If it is a DOWN action, assign the x-coordinate of the touch to the variable x1. If it is an UP action, assign the y-coordinate of the touch to the variable y2.

13. Write the code to place a View named view at the top of the stack it belongs to.

14. We have already coded a class named MyHandler that extends View.OnTouchListener. Write the code to use an object of that class so that we can listen to touch events occurring inside a View named myView.

15. Write the class header of a class named MyActivity that inherits from Activity, GestureDetector.OnGestureListener, and GestureDetector.OnDoubleTapListener.

16. Write a private class that inherits from GestureDetector.SimpleOnGestureListener. We only want to process single tap events. Every time there is a single tap, we color the background of a View named myView with a random color.

17. Write a private class that inherits from GestureDetector.SimpleOnGestureListener. We want to count the number of taps and accumulate them in an instance variable of an Activity class named total, which has already been initialized. Every time there is a tap, total goes up by 1.

The following applies to Questions 18 and 19:

The MyActivity class extends Activity and implements GestureDetector.OnGestureListener and GestureDetector.OnDoubleTapListener. We have declared an instance variable of type GestureDetector named d as follows:

```
private GestureDetector d;
```

18. We are coding inside the onCreate method of an Activity class. Write the code so that the current Activity will handle the gestures and tap events.

```
protected void onCreate( Bundle savedInstanceState ){
   super.onCreate( savedInstanceState );
   // Your code goes here

}
```

19. We are coding inside the onTouchEvent method of an Activity class. Write the code so that if there is a gesture event, it gets dispatched to the appropriate method of GestureDetector.OnGestureListener.

```
public boolean onTouchEvent( MotionEvent event ){
   // Your code goes here

}
```

Write an app

20. Modify Example 7.13 so that MainActivity does not implement View.OnTouchListener. Instead, the touch event handler is a private class.

21. Modify Example 7.10 so that MainActivity does not implement GestureDetector.OnGestureListener and GestureDetector.OnDoubleTapListener. Instead, they are private classes.

22. Modify Example 7.13 so that when the user double taps, we restart a new puzzle.

23. Write an app that shows in one or more TextViews the distances of a swipe along each axis whenever the user swipes the screen.

24. Write an app that has two TextViews. One of them has a red background—when the user taps inside it, it changes to blue, and when the user double taps inside it, it changes back to red, and so on. If the user taps or double taps outside the TextView, its color does not change. The other TextView displays the accumulated tap count.

25. Write an app that has one TextView that has a red background—when the user taps inside it, it becomes invisible, and when the user double taps anywhere on the screen, it becomes visible again.

26. Write an app that displays a chessboard using two colors—as the user taps, the colors change to the next pair of colors, and so on. We should include at least five pairs of colors that the app cycles through. Include a Model.

27. Write an app that has three activities—each activity has one TextView that displays some text that identifies the activity. For each activity, if the user swipes the screen from right to left, the app moves to the next activity (from activity 1 to activity 2, or from activity 2 to activity 3). If the user swipes the screen from left to right, the app moves back to the previous activity (from activity 3 to activity 2, or from activity 2 to activity 1).

28. Write an app that shows a TextView in the middle of the screen. The user can touch it and fling it toward an edge of the screen (the TextView should follow the fling). If the x or y velocity is above a certain threshold (that you determine), the TextView disappears at the end of the fling and reappears at some random location on the screen, and so on.

29. Write an app that implements the tile puzzle game: on a 3 × 3 grid, the digits 1 through 8 are randomly positioned inside TextViews on the grid. By touching a TextView, it moves to its adjacent empty square (if it is next to the empty square). When the digits are in order (1, 2, 3 on the first row, 4, 5, 6 on the second row, and 7, 8 on the last row), the game is over and touch events are disabled. Include a Model.

30. Write an app that implements the following algebra game: five TextViews display two random integers between 1 and 9, the + operator, the = operator, and the result of the addition. When the user double taps the + operator, the result shows. When the user double taps outside the + operator, two new random digits take the place of the existing ones. Include a Model.

31. Write an app that implements the following total accumulator using two TextViews. One contains a randomly generated digit between 1 and 9, the other displays the current total, whose initial value is 0. When the user touches the first TextView and brings it over the other TextView and releases it, the digit is added to the total, and the first TextView goes back to its original position and displays a new random digit between 1 and 9. Include a Model.

32. Write an app that simulates the dealing of the community cards in a game of poker (Texas hold 'em). The first three cards are dealt on a double tap. The last two cards should be dealt on a single tap, one at a time. A swipe hides the cards so that we are ready to start another round. Cards are represented by TextViews. Include a Model.

33. Write an app that simulates a modified game of blackjack. The first two cards are dealt on a double tap. Additional cards are dealt one by one on a single tap only (not a double tap). Cards are represented by TextViews. Another TextView shows the result. If the total is more than 17, taps should be disabled and the user wins. If the total goes beyond 21, the user loses. Include a Model.

CHAPTER EIGHT

Graphics, Animations, Sounds, and Gaming

CHAPTER CONTENTS

Introduction

The Android development framework provides us with a set of classes for drawing shapes and bitmaps, animating those shapes and bitmaps, and making sounds. In this chapter, we build a simple game where the user shoots from a cannon at a duck flying across the screen. We learn how to draw basic shapes such as a line, a circle, or a rectangle; drawing a bitmap from a file; playing a sound; and how to capture and respond to touch events. We also learn how to refresh the screen at a given frequency so we can animate objects on the screen.

8.1 Graphics

The `android.graphics` package contains classes to draw and paint. **TABLE 8.1** shows some of its selected classes.

Typically, we draw on a custom View (i.e., a user-defined subclass of the `View` class). Drawing takes place in the `onDraw` method, inherited from the `View` class. For this, we can use the following template:

```
public class CustomView extends View {
  ...
  public void onDraw( Canvas canvas ) {
    super.onDraw( canvas );
    // as needed, define style and color to draw with using a Paint object
    // call some drawing methods of the Canvas class with canvas
  }
  ...
```

TABLE 8.1 Selected classes of the `android.graphics` package

Class	Description
Bitmap	Encapsulates a bitmap.
BitmapFactory	Factory class to create Bitmap objects from various sources.
Camera	Generates 3D transformations that can be applied to a Canvas.
Canvas	Draws shapes and bitmaps.
Color	Defines constants and methods for defining colors represented by integers.
Paint	Defines style and color for drawing.
Picture	Records drawing calls.
Point	A point defined by two integer coordinates.
Rect	A rectangle defined by integer coordinates.

TABLE 8.2 Selected methods of the `Paint` class

Method	Description
void setARGB(int a, int r, int g, int b)	Sets the alpha, red, green, and blue color components of this Paint object to values a, r, g, and b (all between 0 and 255).
void setColor(int color)	Sets the color of this Paint object to color (including the alpha component).
void setStrokeWidth(float width)	Sets the stroke width of this Paint object to width.
void setTextSize(float textSize)	Sets the text size of this Paint object to textSize.
void setStyle(Paint.Style style)	Sets the style of this Paint object to style. Paint.Style is an enum whose possible values are STROKE, FILL, and FILL_AND_STROKE. The default is FILL.
void setAntiAlias(boolean flag)	Sets this Paint to use anti-alias when drawing shapes if flag is true, default is false.

To specify how we draw (i.e., define the drawing style and color), we use the `Paint` class. TABLE 8.2 shows some of its methods.

For example, to define a `Paint` object and set its color to red and its stroke width to 5 pixels, we can use the following code sequence:

```
Paint paint = new Paint( );
paint.setColor( 0xFFFF0000 );
paint.setStrokeWidth( 5.0f );
```

To draw, we use the `Canvas` class. It provides the tools to draw basic shapes and bitmaps previously generated, for example, from a file containing a picture, such as a jpeg. TABLE 8.3 shows some of its methods.

Assuming we already have declared, instantiated, and defined a `Paint` object named `paint`, here is how we can draw a circle inside the `onDraw` method of the `View` class so that it is centered at the point (50, 100) and has a radius of 25.

```
// canvas is the Canvas parameter of the onDraw method
canvas.drawCircle( 50, 100, 25, paint );
```

The default style for `Paint` is that shapes are filled when they are drawn. If we do not want shapes to be filled, we can set the style of the `Paint` object to STROKE (see Table 8.2) as in the following statement:

```
// paint is a Paint reference
paint.setStyle( Paint.Style.STROKE );
```

TABLE 8.3 Selected methods of the `Canvas` class

Method	Description
void drawLine(float startX, float startY, float endX, float endY, Paint paint)	Draws a line between the points (startX, startY) and (endX, endY) using the style and color defined in paint.
void drawLines (float [ ] points, Paint paint)	Draws lines defined in points using the style and color defined in paint. Each line is defined as four consecutive values in points.
void drawOval(RectF rect, Paint paint)	Draws an oval within the rectangle rect using the style and color defined in paint. RectF is similar to Rect, but uses floats instead of ints.
void drawCircle(float centerX, float centerY, float radius, Paint paint)	Draws a circle whose center is the point (centerX, centerY) and whose radius is radius using the style and color defined in paint.
void drawPicture(Picture picture, Rect dst)	Draws picture and stretches it to fit into the dst rectangle.
void drawBitmap(Bitmap bitmap, Rect src, Rect dst, Paint paint)	Draws the src rectangle from bitmap inside the dst rectangle using paint. If src is null, then the whole bitmap is drawn. The bitmap is drawn to the dimensions of dst.
void drawRect(Rect rect, Paint paint)	Draws the rectangle rect using the style and color defined in paint.
void drawText(String text, float x, float y, Paint paint)	Draws the String text starting at coordinates (x, y) using the style, including alignment, and color defined in paint.

We can also use the `Canvas` class to draw some graphics from a file. If we have a file named `duck.png`, we should place that file in the `drawable` directory of our project. Once a file is in the `drawable` directory, it is a resource that we can refer to using `R.drawable.nameOfFile`. In this case, we can refer to it using `R.drawable.duck`. Note that we do not include the file extension.

First, we instantiate a `Bitmap` object for that file. Then, we draw it with the `canvas` parameter of the `onDraw` method. In order to create a `Bitmap`, we can use one of the many `static` methods of the `BitmapFactory` class. **TABLE 8.4** lists some of them. Once we have a `Bitmap` reference, we can retrieve or set some of its characteristics with various methods of the `Bitmap` class. **TABLE 8.5** lists some of them.

Assuming we have a file named `duck.jpg` in the `drawable` directory of our project, we can use the following code to draw it inside our custom View inside a rectangle defined by the following code sequence:

```
// duck.png is in the drawable directory
Bitmap duck = BitmapFactory.decodeResource( getResources( ),
          R.drawable.duck );
```

TABLE 8.4 Selected methods of the `BitmapFactory` class

Method	Description
static Bitmap decodeResource(Resources res, int id)	Creates and returns a Bitmap from the resource whose id is id that is contained in the Resources object res.
static Bitmap decodeFile(String pathName)	Creates and returns a Bitmap from the file pathName.
static Bitmap decodeStream(InputStream is)	Reads is and creates and returns a Bitmap from it.

TABLE 8.5 Selected methods of the `Bitmap` class

Method	Description
int getWidth( )	Returns the width of this Bitmap.
int getHeight( )	Returns the height of this Bitmap.
int getPixel(int x, int y)	Returns the color, as an integer, at the (x, y) coordinate of this Bitmap; x and y must be greater than or equal to 0 and less than the width and the height of this Bitmap, respectively.
void setPixel(int x, int y, int color)	Sets to color the color of the pixel of this Bitmap located at the (x, y) coordinate. The same constraints as in the getPixel method apply.

```
Rect rect = new Rect( 20, 50, 20 + duck.getWidth( ),
            50 + duck.getHeight( ) );
// canvas is the Canvas parameter of the onDraw method
// paint is a Paint object
canvas.drawBitmap( duck, null, rect, paint );
```

Note that the last two parameters of the `Rect` constructor used previously are the right and bottom edges of the rectangle, not its width and height.

COMMON ERROR: When using the `Rect` constructor with four parameters, be aware that the last two parameters represent the right and bottom edges of the rectangle, not its width and height.

8.2 Making a Custom View, Drawing, Duck Hunting App, Version 0

We use the Empty Activity template for this app. In Version 0, we display the cannon on the lower left corner of the screen and a duck at the top right corner of the screen. As in many games, and to keep the example simple, we only allow the game to be played in horizontal position. Thus, we add the following inside the `activity` element of the AndroidManifest.xml file:

```
android:screenOrientation="landscape"
```

To bring a jpeg or png file into our project, we copy it and paste it in the `drawable` directory. The name of our file is `duck.png`.

In order to subclass the `View` class, we must provide a constructor that overrides a constructor of the `View` class and call the `super` constructor with its first statement. Otherwise, our code will not compile. Note that the `View` class does not supply a default constructor. TABLE 8.6 shows some constructors and methods of the `View` class.

TABLE 8.6 Selected constructors and methods of the `View` class

Constructor	Description
View(Context context)	Use this constructor when creating a View by code.
View(Context context, AttributeSet attrs)	Called when constructing a View by inflating an xml resource; attrs are attributes that are specified in the xml file.
View(Context context, AttributeSet attrs, int defStyle)	Called when constructing a View by inflating an xml resource; attrs are attributes that are specified in the xml file, and defStyle is the default style to be applied to the View created.
Method	**Description**
void onFinishInflate( )	Called after a View has finished inflating from its xml resource.
void onAttachedToWindow( )	Called when this View is attached to its window.
void onMeasure(int widthMeasuredSpec, int heightMeasuredSpec)	Called to measure this View and its contents in order to determine the width and height of this View.
void onSizeChanged(int width, int height, int oldWidth, int oldHeight)	Called when the size of this View is changed.
void onLayout(boolean changed, int left, int top, int right, int bottom)	Called when this View assigns positions and dimensions to its children. The parameters relate to this View relative to its parent.
void onDraw(Canvas canvas)	Called when the View draws its contents.

When a `View` is set as the content View of an activity, the following methods of the `View` class are automatically called, several times for some: `onAttachedToWindow`, `onMeasure`, `onSizeChanged`, `onLayout`, `onDraw`; `onFinishInflate` is only called if the View is inflated from an xml file. If we add all these methods to this example with an output statement to Logcat inside, the output in Logcat is as follows:

```
Inside GameView constructor
Inside onAttachedToWindow
Inside onMeasure
Inside onMeasure
Inside onSizeChanged
Inside onLayout
Inside onMeasure
Inside onLayout
Inside onDraw
```

EXAMPLE 8.1 shows the `GameView` class, which inherits from `View`. Later in this chapter, we expect the `onDraw` method to be called often as we redraw the screen at a high frequency in order to update the game. Thus, we want to avoid declaring variables inside `onDraw` so that our code is as efficient as possible. At lines 12–16, we declare various instance variables to store resources for the duck: a `Paint` object to define styles and colors for drawing, a `Bitmap` for the duck (`duck`), a rectangle in which we draw the duck within the View (`duckRect`), and the height of the screen.

The constructor is coded at lines 18–31. We expect to instantiate a `GameView` object from an `Activity` class. Thus, the constructor includes two integer parameters representing the width and height available within that activity. We assign the `height` parameter to the instance variable `height` at line 20 and initialize `duck` at line 21. We store height in an instance variable because we need to access it in the `onDraw` method. At lines 23–25, we set the coordinates of `duckRect` in relation to the width and height values passed by the activity to the constructor. We position the rectangle in the top right corner of the screen, set its width to 1/5 of `width`, and set its height so that we keep the same proportions of the original duck image. Thus, we assign width – width / 5 to its left edge coordinate and `width` to its right edge coordinate. We want to set the height of our duck to change by the same scaling factor as the width does. We can easily compute the scaling factor as follows:

```
new duck width = width / 5 = old duck width * scale
```

Thus,

```
scale = width/( 5 * old duck width )
```

We assign the preceding value to the `scale` variable at line 23. Be careful when performing floating point division: we want the rounding to an integer dimension to take place at the very end in order to minimize the loss of precision.

```
1    package com.jblearning.duckhuntingv0;
2
3    import android.content.Context;
4    import android.graphics.Bitmap;
5    import android.graphics.BitmapFactory;
6    import android.graphics.Canvas;
7    import android.graphics.Paint;
8    import android.graphics.Rect;
9    import android.view.View;
10
11   public class GameView extends View {
12     public static final int TARGET = R.drawable.duck;
13     private Paint paint;
14     private Bitmap duck;
15     private Rect duckRect;
16     private int height;
17
18     public GameView( Context context, int width, int height ) {
19       super( context );
20       this.height = height;
21       duck = BitmapFactory.decodeResource( getResources( ), TARGET );
22
23       float scale = ( ( float ) width / ( duck.getWidth( ) * 5 ) );
24       duckRect = new Rect( width - width / 5 , 0, width,
25           ( int ) ( duck.getHeight( ) * scale ) );
26
27       paint = new Paint( );
28       paint.setColor( 0xFF000000 );
29       paint.setAntiAlias( true );
30       paint.setStrokeWidth( 10.0f );
31     }
32
33     public void onDraw( Canvas canvas ) {
34       super.onDraw( canvas );
35       // draw Cannon
36       canvas.drawCircle( 0, height, height / 10, paint );
37
38       // draw cannon barrel using a 45 degrees angle
39       canvas.drawLine( 0, height, height / 5, height - height / 5, paint );
40
41       // draw duck
42       canvas.drawBitmap( duck,  null, duckRect, paint );
43     }
44   }
```

EXAMPLE 8.1 The GameView class, Duck Hunting app, Version 0

We initialize paint at line 27, set its color to black at line 28, the anti-alias option to true at line 29, and the stroke width of paint to 10 at line 30.

The onDraw method, at lines 33–43, is also called automatically, after onAttachedToWindow, onMeasure, onSizeChanged, and onLayout are called. After calling its super method at line 34, we successively draw the cannon base at lines 35–36, draw the cannon barrel at lines 38–39, and draw the duck at lines 41–42. We draw the cannon using the drawCircle method of the Canvas class. The first two parameters are the x- and y-coordinates of the center of the circle, the third parameter is the radius of the circle, and the fourth parameter is a Paint object defining the style and color of the circle. To draw a circle whose center is (0, height) and whose radius is 50, we use this statement:

```
canvas.drawCircle( 0, height, 50, paint );
```

The coordinate (0, height) denotes the bottom left corner of the View. The style attributes of paint are used to draw the circle. Because of the position of its center, only the top right quarter of the circle is visible.

We actually want to size the radius (50 above) relative to the size of the View. We use a 10% ratio for this. Thus, we draw the cannon base at line 36 using this statement:

```
canvas.drawCircle( 0, height, height / 10, paint );
```

Note that since we only draw a quarter of a circle, we could use the drawArc method instead. It has the following API:

```
public void drawArc( RectF oval, float startAngle, float sweepAngle,
                     boolean useCenter, Paint paint )
```

The RectF class encapsulates a rectangle using float coordinates. We can create a RectF using the following constructor:

```
public RectF( float left, float top, float right, float bottom )
```

The two angle parameters of drawArc are in degrees: startAngle specifies the starting angle: 0 specifies three o'clock. If sweepAngle is positive, the arc is drawn clockwise, otherwise it is drawn counterclockwise. If useCenter is true, we draw a wedge, going through the center of the oval (the center of the circle if the RectF argument is a square). Here is how we could draw the cannon base using drawArc:

```
RectF cannonRect = new RectF( - height / 10, height - height / 10,
                              height / 10, height + height / 10 );
canvas.drawArc( cannonRect, 0.0f, -90.0f, true, paint );
```

At line 39, we draw the cannon barrel using the drawLine method of the Canvas class. The first two parameters are the x- and y-coordinates of one end of the line, and the next two parameters are the x- and y-coordinates of the other end of the line. The fifth parameter is a `Paint` object defining the style and color of the line. If we want to draw a line whose end points are (`0`, `height`) and (`100`, `height` – `100`) so that it is at a 45-degree angle, we use this statement:

```
canvas.drawLine( 0, height, 100, height - 100, paint );
```

Again, we want to size the length of the cannon barrel relative to the size of the View. We use a 20% ratio for this (note that the 20% ratio is along the x- and y-axis whereas the cannon barrel is at a 45-degree angle and therefore longer. Part of the barrel is hidden by the cannon base). Thus, we draw the cannon barrel at line 39 using this statement:

```
canvas.drawLine( 0, height, height / 5, height - height / 5,
                 paint );
```

Later in the chapter, we will allow the user to change the angle of the cannon by touching the screen.

At line 42, we draw the duck using one of the `drawBitmap` methods of the `Canvas` class. The first parameter is a `Bitmap` reference, the second parameter defines the rectangle to draw within the bitmap, the third parameter defines the rectangle where to perform the drawing on the View, and the fourth parameter is a `Paint` object defining the style and color of the drawn bitmap. We draw the entire `Bitmap` `duck` within the rectangle `duckRect`, using this statement:

```
canvas.drawBitmap( duck, null, duckRect, paint );
```

The value `null` for the second argument means that we are drawing the entire bitmap. The duck is drawn within the rectangle represented by the third argument, `duckRect`, defined inside the `onLayout` method.

EXAMPLE 8.2 shows the `MainActivity` class. Because we want to have as big a screen as possible, we extend the `Activity` class, not the `AppCompatActivity` class. In this way, the screen does not include the action bar and is a little bigger. Instead of inflating an XML resource, it sets its content View to a `GameView`. At line 10, we declare a `GameView` instance variable, `gameView`. It is instantiated inside `onCreate` at line 26. We set the content View of the activity to `gameView` at line 27.

We retrieve the size of the screen at lines 24–25 in order to pass its width and height to the `GameView` constructor. However, the height of the screen includes the height of the status bar. Thus, we retrieve it at lines 16–22 and subtract it from the height of the screen at line 26 and pass the resulting value to the `GameView` constructor. Appendix A explains in greater detail how to retrieve the heights of the status and action bars.

FIGURE 8.1 shows the Duck Hunting Game app, Version 0, running inside the emulator. The circle we drew for the cannon is smooth without ragged edges, as a result of using the anti-alias feature.

```
1   package com.jblearning.duckhuntingv0;
2
3   import android.app.Activity;
4   import android.content.res.Resources;
5   import android.graphics.Point;
6   import android.os.Bundle;
7
8   public class MainActivity extends Activity {
9
10    private GameView gameView;
11
12    @Override
13    protected void onCreate( Bundle savedInstanceState ) {
14      super.onCreate( savedInstanceState );
15
16      // get status bar height
17      Resources res = getResources( );
18      int statusBarHeight = 0;
19      int statusBarId =
20        res.getIdentifier( "status_bar_height", "dimen", "android" );
21      if( statusBarId > 0 )
22        statusBarHeight = res.getDimensionPixelSize( statusBarId );
23
24      Point size = new Point( );
25      getWindowManager( ).getDefaultDisplay( ).getSize( size );
26      gameView = new GameView( this, size.x, size.y - statusBarHeight );
27      setContentView( gameView );
28    }
29  }
```

EXAMPLE 8.2 The `MainActivity` class, Duck Hunting app, Version 0

FIGURE 8.1 Duck Hunting Game app, Version 0, running inside the emulator

8.3 The Model

In a game, there can be many shapes and objects on the screen, moving, changing, and colliding. The functionality of a game can be quite complex and it is easier and cleaner to encapsulate it inside a Model. Our Model will reflect the state of the game and its rules. We have three objects in this game: the cannon, the bullet, and the duck. In order to keep things simple, the user can only shoot one bullet at a time from the cannon. If the bullet hits the duck or goes outside the screen, then the user can shoot again. Thus, there is either no or one bullet on the screen at all times. We can define the state of the game as follows:

- Overall game parameters: size (width and height), frequency of updates
- Cannon: position, angle
- Bullet: fired or not, size, position, velocity
- Duck: position, size, velocity, shot or flying

To keep things simple, the duck is expected to fly right to left, and the cannon is expected to be at the lower bottom of the screen. Those constraints are enforced in the Game class.

The values we use for drawing purposes inside the GameView class, such as the position of the duck and the cannon, as well as the dimensions of the game, should be retrieved from the Model.

We also need some functionality to capture what happens during the game:

- Start the game.
- Move the duck.
- Move the bullet.
- Test if the duck is outside the screen.
- Test if the bullet is outside the screen.
- Manage the state of the bullet (fired or not fired).
- Test if the duck was shot.

We encapsulate the Model in the Game class, shown in **EXAMPLE 8.3**. We choose to have a lot of instance variables (lines 8–29) instead of constants to store the game parameters, such as the duck or the bullet velocity. The advantage of having instance variables over constants is that their value can be modified as the user plays. If we want to implement various game levels with increasing difficulty, we can, for example, increase the speed of the duck or the bullet, or reduce the size of the bullet. Note that we have an instance variable for the cannon angle and another one for the bullet angle. When the bullet is fired, we want the user to be able to modify the angle of the cannon for the next shot without modifying the angle of the bullet that has been fired.

A lot of the accessor methods are needed because when we need to redraw the corresponding View, we need to access the data related to the various objects that we draw. The setCannon method (lines 90–102) sets not only the position of the cannon, but also the original position of the bullet inside the cannon.

From lines 137 to 199, we code the various methods that enable us to change the state of the game, move the duck, move the bullet, test if the duck or the bullet has gone outside the screen (outside the hunting rectangle in this Model), reload the bullet in its original position, change the

```
1   package com.jblearning.duckhuntingv1;
2
3   import android.graphics.Point;
4   import android.graphics.Rect;
5   import java.util.Random;
6
7   public class Game {
8     private Rect huntingRect;
9     private int deltaTime; // in milliseconds
10
11    private Rect duckRect;
12    private int duckWidth;
13    private int duckHeight;
14    private float duckSpeed;
15    private boolean duckShot;
16
17    private Point cannonCenter;
18    private int cannonRadius;
19    private int barrelLength;
20    private int barrelRadius;
21    private float cannonAngle;
22
23    private Point bulletCenter;
24    private int bulletRadius;
25    private boolean bulletFired;
26    private float bulletAngle;
27    private float bulletSpeed;
28
29    private Random random;
30
31    public Game( Rect newDuckRect, int newBulletRadius,
32                 float newDuckSpeed, float newBulletSpeed ) {
33      setDuckRect( newDuckRect );
34      setDuckSpeed( newDuckSpeed );
35      setBulletRadius( newBulletRadius );
36      setBulletSpeed( newBulletSpeed );
37      random = new Random( );
38      bulletFired = false;
39      duckShot = false;
40      cannonAngle = ( float ) Math.PI / 4; // starting cannon angle
41    }
42
43    public Rect getHuntingRect( ) {
44      return huntingRect;
45    }
46
```

EXAMPLE 8.3 **The** Game **class, Duck Hunting app, Version 1 (*Continued*)**

```
47    public void setHuntingRect( Rect newHuntingRect ) {
48     if( newHuntingRect != null )
49        huntingRect = newHuntingRect;
50    }
51
52    public void setDeltaTime( int newDeltaTime ) {
53      if( newDeltaTime > 0 )
54        deltaTime = newDeltaTime;
55    }
56
57    public Rect getDuckRect( ) {
58      return duckRect;
59    }
60
61    public void setDuckRect( Rect newDuckRect ) {
62      if( newDuckRect != null ) {
63        duckWidth = newDuckRect.right - newDuckRect.left;
64        duckHeight = newDuckRect.bottom - newDuckRect.top;
65        duckRect = newDuckRect;
66      }
67    }
68
69    public void setDuckSpeed( float newDuckSpeed ) {
70      if( newDuckSpeed > 0 )
71        duckSpeed = newDuckSpeed;
72    }
73
74    public Point getCannonCenter( ) {
75      return cannonCenter;
76    }
77
78    public int getCannonRadius( ) {
79      return cannonRadius;
80    }
81
82    public int getBarrelLength( ) {
83      return barrelLength;
84    }
85
86    public int getBarrelRadius( ) {
87      return barrelRadius;
88    }
89
90    public void setCannon( Point newCannonCenter, int newCannonRadius,
91                        int newBarrelLength, int newBarrelRadius ) {
92      if( newCannonCenter != null && newCannonRadius > 0
93                          && newBarrelLength > 0 ) {
```

EXAMPLE 8.3 The `Game` class, Duck Hunting app, Version 1 (*Continued*)

```
 94            cannonCenter = newCannonCenter;
 95            cannonRadius = newCannonRadius;
 96            barrelLength = newBarrelLength;
 97            barrelRadius = newBarrelRadius;
 98            bulletCenter = new Point(
 99              ( int ) ( cannonCenter.x + cannonRadius * Math.cos( cannonAngle ) ),
100              ( int ) ( cannonCenter.y - cannonRadius * Math.sin( cannonAngle ) ) );
101          }
102        }
103
104        public Point getBulletCenter( ) {
105          return bulletCenter;
106        }
107
108        public int getBulletRadius( ) {
109          return bulletRadius;
110        }
111
112        public void setBulletRadius( int newBulletRadius ) {
113          if( newBulletRadius > 0 )
114            bulletRadius = newBulletRadius;
115        }
116
117        public void setBulletSpeed( float newBulletSpeed ) {
118          if( newBulletSpeed > 0 )
119            bulletSpeed = newBulletSpeed;
120        }
121
122        public float getCannonAngle( ) {
123          return cannonAngle;
124        }
125
126        public void setCannonAngle( float newCannonAngle ) {
127          if( newCannonAngle >= 0 && newCannonAngle <= Math.PI / 2 )
128            cannonAngle = newCannonAngle;
129          else if( newCannonAngle < 0 )
130            cannonAngle = 0;
131          else
132            cannonAngle = ( float ) Math.PI / 2;
133          if( !isBulletFired( ) )
134            loadBullet( );
135        }
136
137        public boolean isBulletFired( ) {
138          return bulletFired;
139        }
```

EXAMPLE 8.3 **The Game class, Duck Hunting app, Version 1 (*Continued*)**

```
140
141    public void fireBullet( ) {
142      bulletFired = true;
143      bulletAngle = cannonAngle;
144    }
145
146    public boolean isDuckShot( ) {
147      return duckShot;
148    }
149
150    public void setDuckShot( boolean newDuckShot ) {
151      duckShot = newDuckShot;
152    }
153
154    public void startDuckFromRightTopHalf( ) {
155      duckRect.left = huntingRect.right;
156      duckRect.right = duckRect.left + duckWidth;
157      duckRect.top = random.nextInt( huntingRect.bottom / 2 );
158      duckRect.bottom = duckRect.top + duckHeight;
159    }
160
161    public void moveDuck( ) {
162      if( !duckShot ) { // move left
163        duckRect.left -= duckSpeed * deltaTime;
164        duckRect.right -= duckSpeed * deltaTime;
165      } else { // move down
166        duckRect.top += 5 * duckSpeed * deltaTime;
167        duckRect.bottom += 5 * duckSpeed * deltaTime;
168      }
169    }
170
171    public boolean duckOffScreen( ) {
172      return duckRect.right < 0 || duckRect.bottom < 0
173          || duckRect.top > huntingRect.bottom
174          || duckRect.left > huntingRect.right;
175    }
176
177    public void moveBullet( ) {
178      bulletCenter.x += bulletSpeed * Math.cos( bulletAngle ) * deltaTime;
179      bulletCenter.y -= bulletSpeed * Math.sin( bulletAngle ) * deltaTime;
180    }
181
182    public boolean bulletOffScreen( ) {
183      return bulletCenter.x - bulletRadius > huntingRect.right
184          || bulletCenter.y + bulletRadius < 0;
185    }
```

EXAMPLE 8.3 The Game **class, Duck Hunting app, Version 1 (*Continued*)**

```
186
187    public void loadBullet( ) {
188      bulletFired = false;
189      bulletCenter.x = ( int ) ( cannonCenter.x
190        + cannonRadius * Math.cos( cannonAngle ) );
191      bulletCenter.y = ( int ) ( cannonCenter.y
192        - cannonRadius * Math.sin( cannonAngle ) );
193    }
194
195    public boolean duckHit( ) {
196      return duckRect.intersects(
197        bulletCenter.x - bulletRadius, bulletCenter.y - bulletRadius,
198        bulletCenter.x + bulletRadius, bulletCenter.y + bulletRadius );
199    }
200  }
```

EXAMPLE 8.3 **The Game class, Duck Hunting app, Version 1**

TABLE 8.7 Selected intersects method of the Rect class

Method	Description
boolean intersects(int left, int top, int right, int bottom)	Returns true if this Rect intersects the rectangle defined by the four parameters, false if it does not. This Rect is not modified.

angle at which the bullet is fired, and test if the bullet hits the duck. The instance variable duckShot represents whether the duck has been shot. The method duckHit tests if the bullet hit the duck. If the duck is not shot, the moveDuck method (lines 161–169) moves the duck from right to left. If the duck is shot, it moves it down at five times its flying speed.

In order to test if the bullet hit the duck (method duckHit at lines 195–199), we compare the rectangle around the duck to the rectangle around the bullet and test if they intersect. We use one of the intersects methods of the Rect class, shown in TABLE 8.7. It returns true if the rectangle defined by its four parameters intersects with the Rect reference calling the method, false if it does not.

8.4 Animating an Object: Flying the Duck, Duck Hunting App, Version 1

Now we can use the Model to make the duck fly across the screen from right to left. In order to do that, we need to redraw the View at a certain frequency. The human eye thinks that things move in continuous motion when the frame rate is at 20–30 frames per second or more. The higher the frame rate, the more things will look like they move in continuous motion. However, the higher

TABLE 8.8 Selected methods of the `Timer` class

Method	Description
void schedule(TimerTask task, long delay, long period)	Schedules task to run after delay milliseconds and every period milliseconds afterward.
void cancel( )	Cancels the scheduled tasks of this Timer.

TABLE 8.9 Selected methods of the `TimerTask` class

Method	Description
void run( )	Called automatically with the specified frequency; override this method and execute the task here.
boolean cancel( )	Cancels this TimerTask.

the frame rate, the more demand there is on the CPU. If we ask the CPU to do too much in too short a period of time, movement will start to be jerky and the quality of our app will deteriorate. Furthermore, the CPU speed varies from device to device, which complicates things further. For complex games with a lot of objects moving and interacting with each other, it is recommended to use **OpenGL** (Open Graphics Library) so that drawings are rendered faster. OpenGL defines an API so that developers can interact directly with the graphics processor. Often, game developers use a game engine, which uses OpenGL, in order to develop a game. High performance game programming is beyond the scope of this book. We keep our game simple so that the CPU can handle it.

The `Timer` class, from the `java.util` package, provides several `schedule` and `scheduleAtFixedRate` methods to set up a given task, of type `TimerTask`, to be performed either once or at a specified frequency, starting after a specified delay. We can also cancel tasks that are currently scheduled by a `Timer`. **TABLE 8.8** shows a `schedule` method and the `cancel` method.

The first parameter of the various `schedule` and `scheduleAtFixedRate` methods is a `TimerTask` object. The `TimerTask` class `implements` the `Runnable` interface and is also from the `java.util` package. It is `abstract` and meant to be overridden in order to define a custom task to be performed. When we subclass `TimerTask`, we should provide a constructor and override the `run` method. The `run` method is automatically called at the specified frequency and executes the task. **TABLE 8.9** shows the `run` and `cancel` methods.

We define a `GameTimerTask` class that `extends` the `TimerTask` class. Inside the `run` method, we update the state of the game using the Model. Before exiting the `run` method, we force the View to be redrawn so that what the user sees on the screen reflects the state of the game at that time. For this, we need a reference to both the game and the View inside the `GameTimerTask`. There are several methods that can be used to redraw a View. **TABLE 8.10** lists some of them.

TABLE 8.10 Methods of the `View` class that force a call to `onDraw`

Method	Description
void invalidate( )	Refreshes this whole View by calling onDraw. This method must be called from a user-interface thread.
void postInvalidate( )	Refreshes this whole View by calling onDraw. This method can be called from outside a user-interface thread.
void invalidate(int top, int left, int right, int bottom)	Refreshes the rectangle within this View defined by the four parameters by calling onDraw. This method must be called from a user-interface thread.
void postInvalidate(int top, int left, int right, int bottom)	Refreshes the rectangle within this View defined by the four parameters by calling onDraw. This method can be called from outside a user-interface thread.

The methods with four parameters enable us to redraw the rectangle of the View defined by these four parameters. If we know that only part of the View changes, this can save valuable CPU time. The `postInvalidate` method of the View class automatically calls `onDraw` and can be called from a non-user interface thread, which is the case when we execute inside the `run` method of the `GameTimerTask`. Thus, at the end of the `run` method, we call `postInvalidate` in order to redraw the View.

The overall logic is as follows:

```
// Inside the MainActivity class
Timer timer = new Timer( );
// Start the task now, run it 10 times per second (every 100 milliseconds)
timer.schedule( new GameTimerTask( this ), 0, 100 );

// Inside the run method of the GameTimerTask class
// 1 - Update the state of the game with a Game reference to our game
// 2 - Assuming that gameView is a reference to our View,
// call postInvalidate to force a call to onDraw
gameView.postInvalidate( );

// Inside the onDraw method of GameView
// Draw the cannon, bullet, and duck based on the state of game
```

To summarize:

▶ The `run` method of the `GameTimerTask` class asks the Model to update the state of the game, and then asks the game View to redraw itself.

▶ The `onDraw` method of the `GameView` class updates the View based on the state of the game.

```
1    package com.jblearning.duckhuntingv1;
2
3    import java.util.TimerTask;
4
5    public class GameTimerTask extends TimerTask {
6      private Game game;
7      private GameView gameView;
8
9      public GameTimerTask( GameView view ) {
10       gameView = view;
11       game = view.getGame( );
12       game.startDuckFromRightTopHalf( );
13     }
14
15     public void run( ) {
16       game.moveDuck( );
17       if( game.duckOffScreen( ) )
18         game.startDuckFromRightTopHalf( );
19       gameView.postInvalidate( );
20     }
21   }
```

EXAMPLE 8.4 **The `GameTimerTask` class, Duck Hunting app, Version 1**

EXAMPLE 8.4 shows the `GameTimerTask` class. We import `TimerTask` at line 3 and the class `extends` it at line 5. We declare two instance variables (lines 6–7), `game`, a `Game` reference to our game, and `gameView`, a `GameView` reference to our View. We use `game` to start the game at line 12 and update the state of the game at lines 16–18 inside the `run` method. We use `gameView` to call `postInvalidate` at line 19, in order to trigger a call to the `onDraw` method of `GameView`.

We provide a constructor that accepts a `GameView` parameter, `view`, at lines 9–13; `view` is assigned to `gameView` at line 10. We call the `getGame` accessor (we need to add the `getGame` method to the `GameView` class) at line 11 in order to assign a reference to our game to `game`. We expect a `GameTimerTask` object to be instantiated from inside the `GameView` class, passing `this` to the constructor.

EXAMPLE 8.5 shows the `GameView` class. Instead of displaying a simple duck, we animate the duck when it is flying using three `Bitmaps` that we create from three transparent png files. We place the three files `anim_duck0.png`, `anim_duck1.png`, and `anim_duck2.png` in the `drawable` directory of our project. We intend to use these three files to create a four frames animation (0-1-2-1) and store these drawable resources in the array `TARGETS` (lines 14–15). There are four elements in the array in this example, but we could easily add more frames to improve the duck animation. Instead of one `Bitmap`, we now have an array of `Bitmaps`, `ducks`, declared at line 17. The instance variable `duckFrame` (line 18) stores the current index within the array `ducks`. We use it to access the correct `Bitmap` to draw inside the `onDraw` method. We declare a `Game` instance variable, `game`, at line 20. Usually, we include a reference to the Model inside the

```
1    package com.jblearning.duckhuntingv1;
2
3    import android.content.Context;
4    import android.graphics.Bitmap;
5    import android.graphics.BitmapFactory;
6    import android.graphics.Canvas;
7    import android.graphics.Paint;
8    import android.graphics.Point;
9    import android.graphics.Rect;
10   import android.view.View;
11
12   public class GameView extends View {
13     public static int DELTA_TIME = 100;
14     private int [ ] TARGETS = { R.drawable.anim_duck0, R.drawable.anim_duck1,
15                                 R.drawable.anim_duck2, R.drawable.anim_duck1 };
16     private Paint paint;
17     private Bitmap [ ] ducks;
18     private int duckFrame;
19
20     private Game game;
21
22     public GameView( Context context, int width, int height ) {
23       super( context );
24       ducks = new Bitmap[TARGETS.length];
25       for( int i = 0; i < ducks.length; i++ )
26         ducks[i] =
27             BitmapFactory.decodeResource( getResources( ), TARGETS[i] );
28       float scale = ( ( float ) width / ( ducks[0].getWidth( ) * 5 ) );
29       Rect duckRect = new Rect( 0, 0, width / 5,
30           ( int ) ( ducks[0].getHeight( ) * scale ) );
31       game = new Game( duckRect, 5, .03f, .2f );
32       game.setDuckSpeed( width * .00003f );
33       game.setBulletSpeed( width * .0003f );
34       game.setDeltaTime( DELTA_TIME );
35
36       game.setHuntingRect( new Rect( 0, 0, width, height ) );
37       game.setCannon( new Point( 0, height ), width / 30,
38         width / 15, width / 50);
39
40       paint = new Paint( );
41       paint.setColor( 0xFF000000 );
42       paint.setAntiAlias( true );
43       paint.setStrokeWidth( game.getBarrelRadius( ) );
44     }
45
```

EXAMPLE 8.5 The `GameView` class, Duck Hunting app, Version 1 (*Continued*)

```
46    public void onDraw( Canvas canvas ) {
47      super.onDraw( canvas );
48      // draw cannon
49      canvas.drawCircle( game.getCannonCenter( ).x, game.getCannonCenter( ).y,
50          game.getCannonRadius( ), paint );
51
52      // draw cannon barrel
53      canvas.drawLine(
54          game.getCannonCenter( ).x, game.getCannonCenter( ).y,
55          game.getCannonCenter( ).x + game.getBarrelLength( )
56              * ( float ) Math.cos( game.getCannonAngle( ) ),
57          game.getCannonCenter( ).y - game.getBarrelLength( )
58              * ( float ) Math.sin( game.getCannonAngle( ) ),
59          paint );
60
61      // draw animated duck
62      duckFrame = ( duckFrame + 1 ) % ducks.length;
63      canvas.drawBitmap( ducks[duckFrame], null, game.getDuckRect( ), paint );
64    }
65
66    public Game getGame( ) {
67      return game;
68    }
69  }
```

EXAMPLE 8.5 **The `GameView` class, Duck Hunting app, Version 1**

Controller (i.e., the `MainActivity` class). In this case, we set several parameters of what we draw inside the `onDraw` method (cannon base and barrel, duck, bullet) based on values from the Model. Thus, it is convenient to have a `Game` reference inside `GameView` so that we can access the values of the various instance variables of `Game` inside the `onDraw` method.

The array `ducks` parallels the array `TARGETS` and is instantiated at line 24 and filled with `Bitmaps` generated from the elements in `TARGETS` at lines 25–27.

We assume that all the png files have the same width and height and use the first one to construct a `Rect` at lines 29–30, after computing the scaling factor at line 28. We pass that `Rect` to the `Game` constructor at line 31 when we instantiate `game`. We also want to set the duck and bullet speeds dynamically. Indeed, the duck and the bullet should move faster if the screen has higher resolution. If the screen is 1,000 pixels wide, then the duck speed is .03 pixel per second and the bullet speed is 10 times faster, .3 pixel per second. After setting the game's hunting rectangle at line 36, we call `setCannon` at lines 37–38 in order to set the dimensions of the cannon: we position the cannon at the left bottom corner of the hunting rectangle and size it relative to the size of the View in order to be as device-independent as possible.

We want our screen to be refreshed at about 10 times per second for this game. Thus, we define the constant `DELTA_TIME` at line 13 and assign to it the value `100`. We pass that value to `game` at line 34 and set the dimension of the cannon barrel at line 43.

The onDraw method is coded at lines 46–64. We draw the cannon at lines 48–50, retrieving its center coordinates and radius from game. We draw the cannon barrel at lines 52–59, also retrieving its coordinates, dimensions, and angle from game. Before drawing the Bitmap for the duck at line 63, we update the value of duckFrame at line 62, so that we access the next Bitmap in the array ducks.

We provide an accessor for game at lines 66–68. We call inside the GameTimerTask of Example 8.6.

EXAMPLE 8.6 shows the edits in the MainActivity class. We instantiate a Timer object at line 30, and schedule a GameTimerTask to run 10 times per second, starting immediately, at lines 31–32.

```
 6
 7    import java.util.Timer;
 8
 9    public class MainActivity extends Activity {
...
27        gameView = new GameView( this, size.x, size.y - statusBarHeight );
28        setContentView( gameView );
29
30        Timer gameTimer = new Timer( );
31        gameTimer.schedule( new GameTimerTask( gameView ),
32                            0, GameView.DELTA_TIME );
33    }
34  }
```

EXAMPLE 8.6 Edits in the MainActivity class, Duck Hunting app, Version 1

FIGURE 8.2 shows the Duck Hunting Game app, Version 1, running inside the emulator, with the duck flying in the middle of the screen. Note that the emulator has significantly less power than an actual device, and it is possible that it would not be able to draw the ducks at the specified frame rate.

FIGURE 8.2 Duck Hunting Game app, Version 1, running inside the emulator

8.5 Handling Touch Events: Moving the Cannon and Shooting, Duck Hunting App, Version 2

In Version 2, we allow the user to move the cannon barrel using a single tap or swiping the screen. Wherever the user touches the screen, we point the cannon barrel toward that point. We also enable shooting by double tapping anywhere on the screen. However, we do not want a double tap to change the angle of the cannon barrel. In order to implement that, we need to capture the touch event and handle it as either a confirmed single tap or a swipe, moving the cannon barrel, or as a double tap, shooting. If it is a confirmed single tap or a swipe, we retrieve the x- and y-coordinates of the touch, and set the value of the cannon angle in game. The redrawing of the cannon barrel should happen automatically since we take into account the value of the cannon barrel angle when we draw it inside the onDraw method. If it is a double tap, we call the fireBullet method with game.

The easiest way to implement this is to use a GestureDetector inside the GameView class, create a private class that extends the GestureDetector.SimpleOnGestureListener class, and override the following methods: onSingleTapConfirmed, onScroll, and onDoubleTapEvent.

Generally, events should be handled inside the Controller. Thus, we add all the event-related code to the MainActivity class. **EXAMPLE 8.7** shows the new parts of the MainActivity class. At lines 7 and 8, we import the GestureDetector and MotionEvent classes. A GestureDetector instance variable, detector, is declared at line 14. Because we need to access and update the Model (changing the cannon angle, fire the bullet, etc.) based on user interaction, it is convenient to have a Game instance variable (game at line 15). The game instance variable references the same Game object as the game instance variable of the GameView class (line 38).

We code the private class, TouchHandler, extending GestureDetector.Simple OnGestureListener at lines 49–74. Whether we execute inside the onSingleTapConfirmed or onScroll methods, we want to execute the same code, so we create a separate method, update-Cannon, and call it, passing the MouseEvent parameter. Inside updateCannon, coded at lines 68–73, we calculate the x- and y-coordinates of the touch relative to the center of the cannon at lines 69–70, and use the atan2 method of the Math class to calculate the angle at line 71. We then call the setCannonAngle method with game and pass that calculated angle at line 72. To retrieve the touch coordinates, we use the getX and getY methods because they give us the x- and y-coordinates relative to the View, as opposed to the getRawX and getRawY methods that give us the absolute x- and y-coordinates.

Inside the onCreate method, we instantiate detector at line 40, passing th, a TouchHandler declared and instantiated at line 39, as its second argument. Then, we call the setOnDoubleTapListener method at line 41, passing th. Thus, gestures and touches trigger execution of the methods inside the TouchHandler class, assuming that event dispatching has been set up inside onTouchEvent. Inside the onTouchEvent method (lines 44–47), we call the onTouchEvent method of the GestureDetector class with detector so that the various touch events are dispatched to the appropriate methods among the nine methods of the TouchHandler class (three overridden inside the class and six do-nothing methods inherited from GestureDetector.SimpleOnGestureListener).

```
1    package com.jblearning.duckhuntingv2;
2
3    import android.app.Activity;
4    import android.content.res.Resources;
5    import android.graphics.Point;
6    import android.os.Bundle;
7    import android.view.GestureDetector;
8    import android.view.MotionEvent;
9    import java.util.Timer;
10
11   public class MainActivity extends Activity {
12
13     private GameView gameView;
14     private GestureDetector detector;
15     private Game game;
16
17     @Override
18     protected void onCreate( Bundle savedInstanceState ) {
19       super.onCreate( savedInstanceState );
20
21       // get status bar height
22       Resources res = getResources( );
23       int statusBarHeight = 0;
24       int statusBarId =
25           res.getIdentifier( "status_bar_height", "dimen", "android" );
26       if ( statusBarId > 0 )
27         statusBarHeight = res.getDimensionPixelSize( statusBarId );
28
29       Point size = new Point( );
30       getWindowManager( ).getDefaultDisplay( ).getSize( size );
31       gameView = new GameView( this, size.x, size.y - statusBarHeight );
32       setContentView( gameView );
33
34       Timer gameTimer = new Timer( );
35       gameTimer.schedule( new GameTimerTask( gameView ),
36                           0, GameView.DELTA_TIME );
37
38       game = gameView.getGame( );
39       TouchHandler th = new TouchHandler( );
40       detector = new GestureDetector( this, th );
41       detector.setOnDoubleTapListener( th );
42     }
43
44     public boolean onTouchEvent( MotionEvent event ) {
45       detector.onTouchEvent( event );
46       return true;
```

EXAMPLE 8.7 The `MainActivity` class, Duck Hunting app, Version 2 (*Continued*)

```
47        }
48
49        private class TouchHandler
50                  extends GestureDetector.SimpleOnGestureListener {
51          public boolean onDoubleTapEvent( MotionEvent event ) {
52            if( !game.isBulletFired( ) )
53              game.fireBullet( );
54            return true;
55          }
56
57          public boolean onSingleTapConfirmed( MotionEvent event ) {
58            updateCannon( event );
59            return true;
60          }
61
62          public boolean onScroll( MotionEvent event1, MotionEvent event2,
63                                    float d1, float d2 ) {
64            updateCannon( event2 );
65            return true;
66          }
67
68          public void updateCannon( MotionEvent event )  {
69            float x = event.getX( ) - game.getCannonCenter( ).x;
70            float y = game.getCannonCenter( ).y - event.getY( );
71            float angle = ( float ) Math.atan2( y, x );
72            game.setCannonAngle( angle );
73          }
74        }
75      }
```

EXAMPLE 8.7 The `MainActivity` class, **Duck Hunting app, Version 2**

The only change in the `GameView` class is to draw the bullet. This is done inside the `onDraw` method. **EXAMPLE 8.8** shows the updated `onDraw` method. If the bullet is not off the screen (line 62), we draw it at lines 63–64 using its position and radius stored in the instance variable game. As the game is played, the position of the bullet is updated every 100 ms. This takes place inside the `run` method of the `GameTimerTask` class.

EXAMPLE 8.9 shows the updated `GameTimerTask` class. The only changes are at lines 17–20 of the `run` method. If the bullet is off the screen (line 17), we load it inside the cannon (line 18). If it is on the screen, we test if it has been fired (line 19). If it has, we update its position by calling `moveBullet` with game at line 20. After the call to `postInvalidate` at line 23, it is redrawn by the `onDraw` method of the `GameView` class at its new position on the screen. If the bullet is on the screen but has not been fired, that means that it is inside the cannon and there is nothing to update in this case.

```
45
46    public void onDraw( Canvas canvas ) {
47      super.onDraw( canvas );
48      // draw cannon
49      canvas.drawCircle( game.getCannonCenter( ).x, game.getCannonCenter( ).y,
50          game.getCannonRadius( ), paint );
51
52      // draw cannon barrel
53      canvas.drawLine(
54          game.getCannonCenter( ).x, game.getCannonCenter( ).y,
55          game.getCannonCenter( ).x + game.getBarrelLength( )
56              * ( float ) Math.cos(game.getCannonAngle( ) ),
57          game.getCannonCenter( ).y - game.getBarrelLength( )
58              * ( float ) Math.sin( game.getCannonAngle( ) ),
59          paint );
60
61      // draw bullet
62      if( ! game.bulletOffScreen( ) )
63        canvas.drawCircle( game.getBulletCenter( ).x,
64            game.getBulletCenter( ).y, game.getBulletRadius( ), paint );
65
66      // draw animated duck
67      duckFrame = ( duckFrame + 1 ) % ducks.length;
68      canvas.drawBitmap( ducks[duckFrame], null, game.getDuckRect( ), paint );
69    }
70
71    public Game getGame( ) {
72      return game;
73    }
74  }
75
```

EXAMPLE 8.8 The `onDraw` Method of the `GameView` class, Duck Hunting app Version 2

```
1    package com.jblearning.duckhuntingv2;
2
3    import java.util.TimerTask;
4
5    public class GameTimerTask extends TimerTask {
6      private Game game;
7      private GameView gameView;
8
9      public GameTimerTask( GameView view ) {
10       gameView = view;
```

EXAMPLE 8.9 The `GameTimerTask` class, Duck Hunting app, Version 2 (*Continued*)

```
11        game = view.getGame( );
12        game.startDuckFromRightTopHalf( );
13      }
14
15    public void run( ) {
16      game.moveDuck( );
17      if( game.bulletOffScreen( ) )
18        game.loadBullet( );
19      else if( game.isBulletFired( ) )
20        game.moveBullet( );
21      if( game.duckOffScreen( ) )
22        game.startDuckFromRightTopHalf( );
23      gameView.postInvalidate( );
24    }
25  }
```

EXAMPLE 8.9 The `GameTimerTask` class, Duck Hunting app, Version 2

FIGURE 8.3 Duck Hunting app, Version 2, running inside the emulator

FIGURE 8.3 shows the Duck Hunting Game app, Version 2, running inside the emulator, after the user moved the cannon barrel and shot a bullet.

8.6 Playing a Sound: Shooting, Collision Detection, Duck Hunting App, Version 3

In Version 2, when the bullet hits the duck, nothing happens. In Version 3, when the duck is hit, we play a small sound and we let the duck fall down to the ground (in fact, we let the duck go through the ground). We also make a sound when we fire a bullet.

TABLE 8.11 Selected methods of the `SoundPool` class

Method	Description
int load(Context context, int resId, int priority)	Loads a sound from context identified by resId as its resource id. The priority parameter is not used at the time of this writing. Use 1 as a default value. Returns the sound id.
int play(int soundId, float leftVolume, float rightVolume, int priority, int loop, float rate)	Plays the sound whose sound id is soundId. If loop is 0, the sound plays once, and if loop is –1, the sound plays in a loop. Rate is the playback rate, ranging from 0.5 to 2.0, and 1.0 is the normal playback rate.
void pause(int soundId)	Pauses the sound whose sound id is soundId.
void resume(int soundId)	Resumes playing the sound whose sound id is soundId.

The `SoundPool` class, part of the `android.media` package, enables us to manage and play sounds. We can use its methods to:

▶ Preload a sound so that there is no delay when we play it once or in a loop.
▶ Adjust the sound volume and playback rate.
▶ Play, pause, resume a sound.
▶ Play several sounds simultaneously.

TABLE 8.11 lists some selected methods of the `SoundPool` class.

The `SoundPool` class contains a `public static` inner class, `Builder`, which we can use to create a `SoundPool` object. Because that class was introduced in API level 21, we need to make sure that the minimum SDK version specified in the module gradle file is 21, as shown in **EXAMPLE 8.10**. We first instantiate a `SoundPool.Builder` object using the default constructor

```
1    apply plugin: 'com.android.application'
2
3    android {
4        compileSdkVersion 23
5        buildToolsVersion "23.0.2"
6
7        defaultConfig {
8            applicationId "com.jblearning.duckhuntingv3"
9            minSdkVersion 21
10           targetSdkVersion 23
11           versionCode 1
12           versionName "1.0"
13       }
14
```

EXAMPLE 8.10 **Parts of the build.gradle (Module:app) file with a minimum SDK of 21**

TABLE 8.12 Default constructor and the `build` method of the `SoundPool.Builder` class

Default Constructor	Description
SoundPool.Builder( )	Constructs a SoundPool.Builder object that can play a maximum number of one stream at this point.
Method	**Description**
SoundPool build( )	Returns a SoundPool object reference.
SoundPool.Builder setMaxStreams (int maxStreams)	Sets the number of max streams that can be played at the same time. Returns this SoundPool.Builder.

of `SoundPool.Builder`, then call the `build` method, which returns a `SoundPool` reference. **TABLE 8.12** shows the `SoundPool.Builder` default constructor and the `build` method.

The following sequence shows how to create a `SoundPool` object.

```
SoundPool.Builder poolBuilder = new SoundPool.Builder( );
SoundPool pool = poolBuilder.build( );
```

After creating a `SoundPool`, the next step is to load a sound. Like we inflate a layout XML file using its id, we can load a sound using its resource id. When placing a sound resource in the `res` directory, it is common to create a directory named `raw` and place the sound file in it. In Version 3, we play a sound when a bullet is fired and play another sound when the duck is hit. Thus, we create the `raw` directory, and add (using copy and paste) the cannon_fire.wav and duck_hit.wav sound files in it. **FIGURE 8.4** shows the directory structure after having placed the cannon_fire.wav and duck_hit.wav files in the just created `raw` directory.

Inside an `Activity` class, we can load cannon_fire.wav using one of the load methods of `SoundPool` using this statement:

```
// Load the first sound, located inside the raw folder,
// using a Resource id
// this, this Activity, "is a" Context
int fireSoundId = pool.load( this, R.raw.cannon_fire, 1 );
```

Note that we do not include the extension of the file name when specifying a resource in the `raw` directory. That means that we should not have two sound files with the same name and different extensions in that directory.

Let's assume that a sound named `cannon_fire.wav` has been loaded and the `load` method returned an integer id that we stored in the `int` variable `fireSoundId`. We can play the sound once (we specify 0 as the next to last argument of `play`) as follows:

```
// Play cannon_fire.wav at regular speed once
pool.play( fireSoundId, 1.0f, 1.0f, 1, 0, 1.0f );
```

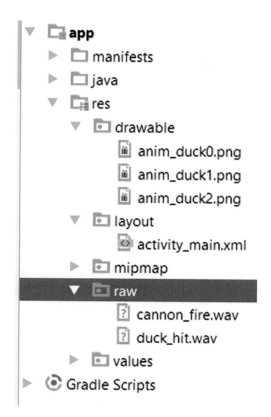

FIGURE 8.4 The cannon_fire.wav and duck_hit.wav files in the raw directory

If we have a sound named `background.wav` that has been loaded and its sound id is `backgroundSoundId`, we can play that sound and loop forever (we specify `-1` as the next to last argument of `play`) as follows:

```
// Play the sound at regular speed and loop forever
pool.play( backgroundSoundId, 1.0f, 1.0f, 1, -1, 1.0f );
```

We need to play sounds whenever we fire a bullet or the duck is hit. The code to fire a bullet is in the `MainActivity` class. The code to check if the duck has been hit is in the `GameTimerTask` class. Thus, inside the `MainActivity` class, we provide a method to play the hit sound that we can call from the `GameTimerTask` class.

EXAMPLE 8.11 shows the updated `MainActivity` class. At line 6, we import the `SoundPool` class. At lines 18–20, we declare three instance variables: `pool`, a `SoundPool` reference, and `fireSoundId` and `hitSoundId`, two `int`s storing the sound ids of the two sounds we play when a bullet is fired and when the duck is hit.

```
1    package com.jblearning.duckhuntingv3;
2
3    import android.app.Activity;
4    import android.content.res.Resources;
5    import android.graphics.Point;
6    import android.media.SoundPool;
7    import android.os.Bundle;
8    import android.view.GestureDetector;
9    import android.view.MotionEvent;
10   import java.util.Timer;
11
12   public class MainActivity extends Activity {
13
14     private GameView gameView;
15     private GestureDetector detector;
16     private Game game;
17
18     private SoundPool pool;
19     private int fireSoundId;
20     private int hitSoundId;
21
22     @Override
23     protected void onCreate( Bundle savedInstanceState ) {
24       super.onCreate( savedInstanceState );
25
26       // get status bar height
27       Resources res = getResources( );
28       int statusBarHeight = 0;
29       int statusBarId =
30         res.getIdentifier( "status_bar_height", "dimen", "android" );
31       if( statusBarId > 0 )
32         statusBarHeight = res.getDimensionPixelSize( statusBarId );
33
34       Point size = new Point( );
35       getWindowManager( ).getDefaultDisplay( ).getSize( size );
36       gameView = new GameView( this, size.x, size.y - statusBarHeight );
37       setContentView( gameView );
38
39       Timer gameTimer = new Timer( );
40       gameTimer.schedule( new GameTimerTask( gameView ),
41             0, GameView.DELTA_TIME );
42
43       game = gameView.getGame( );
44       TouchHandler th = new TouchHandler( );
45       detector = new GestureDetector( this, th );
46       detector.setOnDoubleTapListener( th );
```

EXAMPLE 8.11 **The** `MainActivity` **class, Duck Hunting app, Version 3 (*Continued*)**

```
47
48      SoundPool.Builder poolBuilder = new SoundPool.Builder( );
49      poolBuilder.setMaxStreams( 2 );
50      pool = poolBuilder.build( );
51      fireSoundId = pool.load( this, R.raw.cannon_fire, 1 );
52      hitSoundId = pool.load( this, R.raw.duck_hit, 1 );
53    }
54
55    public boolean onTouchEvent( MotionEvent event ) {
56      detector.onTouchEvent( event );
57      return true;
58    }
59
60    public void playHitSound( ) {
61      pool.play( hitSoundId, 1.0f, 1.0f, 1, 0, 1.0f );
62    }
63
64    private class TouchHandler
65            extends GestureDetector.SimpleOnGestureListener {
66      public boolean onDoubleTapEvent( MotionEvent event ) {
67        if ( !game.isBulletFired( ) ) {
68          game.fireBullet( );
69          pool.play( fireSoundId, 1.0f, 1.0f, 1, 0, 1.0f );
70        }
71        return true;
72      }
73
74      public boolean onSingleTapConfirmed( MotionEvent event ) {
75        updateCannon( event );
76        return true;
77      }
78
78     public boolean onScroll( MotionEvent event1, MotionEvent event2,
80                              float d1, float d2 ) {
81        updateCannon( event2 );
82        return true;
83      }
84
85      public void updateCannon( MotionEvent event )  {
86        float x = event.getX( ) - game.getCannonCenter( ).x;
87        float y = game.getCannonCenter( ).y - event.getY( );
88        float angle = ( float ) Math.atan2( y, x );
89        game.setCannonAngle( angle );
90      }
91    }
92  }
```

EXAMPLE 8.11 The `MainActivity` class, Duck Hunting app, Version 3

At lines 48–50, we instantiate the instance variable `pool` and we enable it to play two sounds simultaneously, although we do not need that feature: both sounds are very short and since we can only shoot one bullet at a time, the fire sound and the hit sound will always be played at different times.

We load the two sounds at lines 51–52, passing to the `load` method a sound resource id. `R.raw.cannon_fire` and `R.raw.duck_hit` identify the cannon_fire.wav and duck_hit.wav files in the `raw` directory of the `res` directory.

When the user double taps, we execute inside the `onDoubleTapEvent` method (lines 66–72) of the `TouchHandler` class. We play the `bullet_fire.wav` sound (line 69) whenever we fire a bullet.

At lines 60–62, we code the `playHitSound` method. Inside it, we play the `duck_hit.wav` sound once. That method is not used in this class, but we call it from the `GameTimerTask` class when the duck is hit.

EXAMPLE 8.12 shows the changes in the `run` method of the `GameTimerTask` class, the only changes in that class. We update the state of the game when the duck is shot and when the duck goes off the screen. We also play the hit sound when the duck is shot. If the duck is off the screen (line 21), not only do we want to start flying it again (line 23) but we also want to make sure that its status is that it is not shot (line 22). Indeed, it is possible that it has gone off the screen vertically after it has been shot (in which case its status was that it was shot).

If the duck is on the screen, we test if it has been hit (line 24). If it has not, there is nothing to do. If it has, we set its status to shot (line 25). That, in turn, impacts the way we move the duck inside the `Game` class (vertically from top to bottom and not horizontally from right to left). We also reload the bullet (line 27) and play the hit sound to indicate that the duck has been shot. We do that at line 26 by calling the `playHitSound` method of the `MainActivity` class. In order to

```
15     public void run( ) {
16       game.moveDuck( );
17       if( game.bulletOffScreen( ) )
18         game.loadBullet( );
19       else if( game.isBulletFired( ) )
20         game.moveBullet( );
21       if( game.duckOffScreen( ) ) {
22         game.setDuckShot( false );
23         game.startDuckFromRightTopHalf( );
24       } else if( game.duckHit( ) ) {
25         game.setDuckShot( true );
26         ( ( MainActivity ) gameView.getContext( ) ).playHitSound( );
27         game.loadBullet( );
28       }
29       gameView.postInvalidate( );
30     }
```

EXAMPLE 8.12 **The `run` method of the `GameTimerTask` class, Duck Hunting app, Version 3**

```
46      public void onDraw( Canvas canvas ) {
47         super.onDraw( canvas );
48         // draw cannon
49         canvas.drawCircle( game.getCannonCenter( ).x, game.getCannonCenter( ).y,
50            game.getCannonRadius( ), paint );
51
52         // draw cannon barrel
53         canvas.drawLine(
54            game.getCannonCenter( ).x, game.getCannonCenter( ).y,
55            game.getCannonCenter( ).x + game.getBarrelLength( )
56               * ( float ) Math.cos( game.getCannonAngle( ) ),
57            game.getCannonCenter( ).y - game.getBarrelLength( )
58               * ( float ) Math.sin( game.getCannonAngle( ) ),
59            paint );
60
61         // draw bullet
62         if( ! game.bulletOffScreen( ) )
63            canvas.drawCircle( game.getBulletCenter( ).x,
64               game.getBulletCenter( ).y, game.getBulletRadius( ), paint );
65
66         // draw animated duck
67         duckFrame = ( duckFrame + 1 ) % ducks.length;
68         if( game.isDuckShot( ) )
69            canvas.drawBitmap( ducks[0], null,
70               game.getDuckRect( ), paint );
71         else
72            canvas.drawBitmap( ducks[duckFrame], null,
73               game.getDuckRect( ), paint );
74      }
```

EXAMPLE 8.13 The updated `onDraw` method of the `GameView` class, Duck Hunting app, Version 3

get a `MainActivity` reference, we call the `getContext` method with `gameView`, and cast the returned `Context` to `MainActivity`.

We only need to make one change inside the `GameView` class: display the duck properly after it has been shot. If the duck is shot, we stop animating the duck and only show one frame, the last one (the first one in this example; we could modify this example using more than four frames to animate the duck so it makes sense to show the first one). Thus, the only change in the `GameView` class is the drawing of the duck, which takes place inside the `onDraw` method, shown in **EXAMPLE 8.13**.

We test if the duck is shot at line 68. If it is, we draw the `Bitmap` that corresponds to the first animation frame at lines 69–70. If the duck is not shot, we keep flying it, drawing the current `Bitmap` within the array `ducks` based on the value of `duckFrame` at lines 72–73.

FIGURE 8.5 shows the Duck Hunting Game app, Version 3, running inside the emulator, after the user shot the duck.

FIGURE 8.5 Duck Hunting Game app, Version 3, running inside the emulator, after the user shot the duck

SOFTWARE ENGINEERING: When testing our app, we want to test all possible situations that can happen. If a situation does not happen often, we can hard code some of our code during the testing phase so that it does and we can test it. For example, if we want to test what happens when we hit the duck twice, we can hard code the starting position of the duck at the top of the screen so that it is easier to shoot it twice. After we finish testing, we should delete the hard coded statements.

Chapter Summary

- The `android.graphics` package includes many classes like `Paint`, `Canvas`, `Bitmap`, `BitmapFactory` that we can use to draw.
- When we extend the `View` class, we must override a constructor of the `View` class and call the `super` constructor.
- To draw on a `View`, we can override the `onDraw` method of the `View` class.
- The `onDraw` method has one parameter of type `Canvas`. We can use it to draw shapes and bitmaps on the `View`.
- We can convert a file to a `Bitmap` using the `decodeResource` method of the `BitmapFactory` class.
- The various drawing methods of the `Canvas` class accept a `Paint` parameter. We define drawing attributes, such as color and style, by specifying the corresponding attributes of that `Paint` parameter.

- We can force a call to onDraw by calling postInvalidate with a View reference.
- We can use the Timer class to schedule a task to be performed at a specified frequency.
- To define that task, we extend the TimerTask class and override its run method.
- The SoundPool class can be used to manage and play sounds.
- A sound can be loaded from a resource, such as a .wav sound file.
- The SoundPool class includes methods to play, pause, and resume playing a sound.
- The play method of the SoundPool class accepts parameters to control how the sound is played (including volume and playback rate) in a loop or one or several times.

 # Exercises, Problems, and Projects

Multiple-Choice Exercises

1. What class is used to specify what (shapes, bitmaps, etc.) we are going to draw?
   - View
   - Paint
   - Canvas
   - Draw

2. What class is used to define how (style, color, etc.) we are going to draw?
   - View
   - Paint
   - Canvas
   - Draw

3. If we want to draw inside a View, what method do we override?
   - draw
   - paint
   - onDraw
   - onPaint

4. What method of the View class can we call to force a redrawing of the View?
   - reDraw
   - rePaint
   - post
   - postInvalidate

5. What class has static methods that we can use to create Bitmap objects?
   - Bitmap
   - BitmapFactory
   - MakeBitmap
   - CreateBitmap

6. What class can we use to schedule a task to be run at a specified frequency?
   - System
   - Timer
   - Task
   - Schedule

7. What class should we extend to define a task that is going to be run at a specified frequency?
   - Task
   - TimerTask
   - TaskTimer
   - Scheduler

8. What method of the class in question 7 should be overridden to perform the task that is scheduled to run at a specified frequency?
   - start
   - task
   - run
   - thread

9. How many sounds can a SoundPool object play at the same time?
   - 0
   - 1 only
   - 0, 1, or many

10. When we call the play method of the SoundPool class, what identifies the sound to be played?
    - The sound name
    - The SoundPool object
    - The sound id
    - The resource id of the sound

Fill in the Code

11. A Paint object named paint has been declared and instantiated. Modify it so that its color is yellow and its stroke thickness is 20.

12. Inside onDraw, draw a full red circle centered at (100, 200) and with radius 50.

13. Inside onDraw, draw an outlined green square (not green inside) centered in the middle of the current View and with side 50.

14. Inside onDraw, draw HELLO ANDROID in blue starting at (50, 200).

15. Inside onDraw, draw a bitmap somewhere on the screen from an image file named my_image.png located in the drawable directory.

16. Inside some class, you have an instance variable called myView that is a reference to a View. Write the code to force that View to be redrawn.

17. We have written a class named MyTask that extends TimerTask, including its run method. Schedule an instance of that class to run 50 times per second, starting in one second.

18. Inside the raw directory of the res directory, there is a sound file named my_sound.wav. Write the code to play it once.

```
SoundPool.Builder sb = new SoundPool.Builder( );
SoundPool pool = sb.build( );
// Your code goes here
```

Write an app

19. Modify the duck hunting app in the chapter so that there are two ducks, instead of one.

20. Modify the duck hunting app in the chapter so that we do not have to wait until the bullet is off the screen or the duck is hit in order to shoot another bullet.

21. Modify the duck hunting app in the chapter to include a nice background (water, sun, grass, etc.) made up of at least one picture and three shape drawings.

22. Modify the duck hunting app in the chapter so that we shoot with a shotgun instead of a cannon. A shotgun shoots a spray of bullets, for example, three. You can assume that these bullets are located within a circle and move at the same speed. At least one of these bullets has to hit the duck for the duck to be shot.

23. Write an app that shows a pool ball (you can use any number from 1 to 15). Use only shapes, do not use bitmaps.

24. Write an app that is a flashlight as follows: the color can go from one color (color A) to another (color B) in continuous motion. If the screen is colored with color A, when the user swipes the screen from left to right, the screen goes from color A to color B in continuous motion. When the user swipes the screen from right to left, the screen goes from color B to color A in continuous motion.

25. Write an app with two activities: the first activity presents the user with a few things to draw with some style or color options, and the second activity draws them.

26. Write an app with two activities: the first activity displays three buttons showing web names (for example Yahoo!, Google, or Facebook). When the user clicks on one, the second activity shows a drawing of its logo.

27. Write a drawing app where the user can draw lines between two points by swiping the screen between these two points. Offer the user a few options for the drawing: pick among several colors, pick a thickness for the line being drawn.

28. Write a drawing app where the user can draw by moving his or her finger on the screen (Hint: a curve can be made of several lines). Offer the user a few options for the drawing: pick among several colors, pick a thickness for what is being drawn.

29. Write an app that displays a chess piece of your choice on the screen. The user can pick it up and move it to another position on the screen by touching it, moving his or her finger, and releasing it.

30. Write an app about the following game: Some enemy comes down vertically from the top of the screen. The player is represented by a shape, a bitmap, or even a label, at the bottom of the screen. The user can move the player by touching it and moving his or her finger. Our objective is to avoid the enemy that is coming down. When the enemy goes off the screen, another one comes down from a random location at the top of the screen. The game is over when the enemy touches the player. Include a Model.

31. Same as problem 30 but we add a sound when an enemy starts at the top of the screen and another sound when the enemy hits the player.

32. Same as problem 30 but several enemies can come down at the same time—instead of one enemy, there is an array of enemies.

33. Write an app simulating the game of pong. The user can move a paddle at the bottom of the screen and a ball moves on the screen. The ball bounces off the side and top edges of the screen when it hits one of them. If the ball goes past the paddle, the game is over. Include a Model.

34. Write a jukebox-like app, where the user can make a selection from at least five sounds and play it. Offer some options for the selected sound: one time only or in a loop, different playback rates. Include a Model.

CHAPTER NINE

Fragments

CHAPTER CONTENTS

Introduction

In order to support larger screen devices like tablets, Google introduced **fragments** with API level 11. A fragment is a portion of an activity and can help manage a portion of the screen. We can think of a fragment as a mini-activity within an activity. **FIGURE 9.1** shows a screen for Version 4 of this chapter's app divided into three parts whose backgrounds are blue, red, and green. We can organize that screen so that each part is a fragment. Fragments are reusable. They can be reused within the same app or in a different app. Thus it is desirable to use them.

In this chapter, we demonstrate how to use and manage fragments. We build an app to play the hangman game. We use the Model-View-Controller architecture but we keep the Model as simple as possible so that we can focus on how fragments work. Furthermore, we also discuss how to nest layouts so that each fragment is managed by a separate layout manager.

9.1 The Model

The Model is the `Hangman` class, shown in **EXAMPLE 9.1**. It encapsulates a game where the user has to guess all the letters in a word but has only so many tries to do it. We keep our Model to the very minimum, and limit the number of possible words to just a few.

We provide a default value for the number of allowed guesses at line 6 and an array of hard coded words at line 7. At line 8, the instance variable `word` stores the word to guess. The `guessesAllowed` and `guessesLeft` instance variables keep track of the number of guesses allowed and the number of guesses that the user still has. Finally, the `indexesGuessed` array keeps track of the indexes of

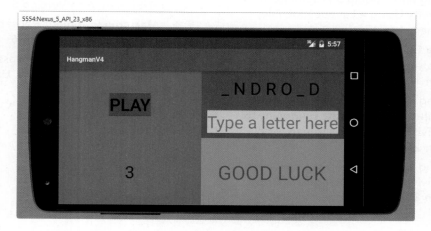

FIGURE 9.1 The Hangman app, Version 4, running in the horizontal position

```
1    package com.jblearning.hangmanv1;
2
3    import java.util.Random;
4
5    public class Hangman {
6      public static int DEFAULT_GUESSES = 6;
7      private String [ ] words = { "ANDROID", "JAVA", "APP", "MOBILE" };
8      private String word;
9      private boolean [ ] indexesGuessed;
10     private int guessesAllowed;
11     private int guessesLeft;
12
13     public Hangman( int guesses ) {
14       if( guesses > 0 )
15         guessesAllowed = guesses;
16       else
17         guessesAllowed = DEFAULT_GUESSES;
18       guessesLeft = guessesAllowed;
19       Random random = new Random( );
20       int index = random.nextInt( words.length );
21       word = words[index];
22       indexesGuessed = new boolean[word.length( )];
23     }
24
25     public int getGuessesAllowed( ) {
26       return guessesAllowed;
27     }
28
29     public int getGuessesLeft( ) {
30       return guessesLeft;
31     }
32
33     public void guess( char c ) {
34       boolean goodGuess = false;
35       for( int i = 0; i < word.length( ); i++ ) {
36         if( !indexesGuessed[i] && c == word.charAt( i ) ) {
37           indexesGuessed[i] = true;
38           goodGuess = true;
39         }
40       }
41       if( !goodGuess )
42         guessesLeft--;
43     }
44
45     public String currentIncompleteWord( ) {
46       String guess = "";
```

EXAMPLE 9.1 **The Hangman class (*Continued*)**

```
47       for( int i = 0; i < word.length( ); i++ )
48         if( indexesGuessed[i] )
49           guess += word.charAt( i ) + " ";
50         else
51           guess += "_ ";
52       return guess;
53     }
54
55   public int gameOver( ) {
56     boolean won = true;
57     for( int i = 0; i < indexesGuessed.length; i++ )
58       if( indexesGuessed[i] ==  false ) {
59         won = false;
60         break;
61       }
62
63     if( won ) // won
64       return 1;
65     else if( guessesLeft == 0 ) // lost
66       return -1;
67     else // game not over
68       return 0;
69     }
70   }
```

EXAMPLE 9.1 **The Hangman class**

the letters in the String word that the user has guessed correctly so far. A value of true means a correct guess at that index.

The Hangman constructor, coded at lines 13–23, sets the value of the number of guesses allowed (lines 14–17). It then randomly selects a word within the array words (lines 19–21), and instantiates the indexesGuessed array. We could envision a much more complex Model where another constructor could pull a list of possible words from a file, a database, or even a remote website, and then selects one at random.

We provide methods to play the game (lines 33–43), retrieve the state of completion of the word (lines 45–53), and check if the game is over (lines 55–69). We also provide accessors for guessesAllowed and guessesLeft (lines 25–27 and 29–31).

Figure 9.1 shows an actual game. At the bottom of the left pane, are the number of guesses that the user still has. Inside the upper right pane, are the letters that the user has correctly guessed so far, and we provide an EditText to input the next letter. At the bottom of the right pane, is the status or final result of the game.

9.2 Fragments

Since fragments have been available since API level 11, we need to specify API level 11 or higher when we create the app (at the time of this writing, the default is API level 15).

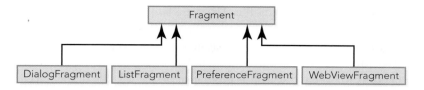

FIGURE 9.2 **Inheritance hierarchy for `Fragment` and selected subclasses**

A fragment must always be embedded inside an activity and although a fragment has its own life-cycle methods, they depend directly on the fragment's parent activity's life-cycle methods. For example, if the activity is stopped or destroyed, then the fragment is automatically stopped or destroyed. An activity can have several fragments inside it, and as long as the activity is running, these fragments can have their own life cycles independently of each other. A fragment is reusable and can be used in several activities. A fragment can define its own layout. It may also be invisible and perform tasks in the background.

In order to code our own user-defined fragments, we extend the `Fragment` class, a direct subclass of `Object`.

The `Fragment` class has several subclasses that encapsulate specialized fragments. **FIGURE 9.2** shows some of them. A `DialogFragment` displays a dialog window, which is displayed on top of its activity's view. A `ListFragment` displays a list of items and provides event handling when the user selects one of these items. A `PreferenceFragment` shows a hierarchy of preferences as a list. A `WebViewFragment` displays a web page.

These subclasses of the `Fragment` class encapsulate specialized fragment functionalities. For example, the `ListFragment` class is very useful when we want to display a list of items that the user can interact with in some part of the screen. Clicking on an item may trigger some changes inside another fragment on another part of the screen.

In this chapter, in order to better understand how fragments work, we build our own subclasses of `Fragment`. We explore the following topics:

▶   How to create and add a fragment for an activity using XML only.
▶   How to create and add a fragment for an activity using XML and code.
▶   How to create and add a fragment for an activity using code only.
▶   How a fragment and its activity communicate.
▶   How to create and add an invisible fragment.
▶   How to make a fragment reusable.

9.3 Defining and Adding a Fragment to an Activity Using a Layout XML File, Hangman, App Version 0

In Version 0 of the app, we show how we define and add a fragment; we do not use the Model yet and we keep the app as simple as possible. We choose the Empty Activity template when we create the app.

EXAMPLE 9.2 shows the activity_main.xml file. There are two elements inside the top LinearLayout element: a fragment element, defined at lines 9–15, and a LinearLayout element, defined at lines 17–37. At line 11, we specify that this fragment is an instance of the GameControlFragment class, which we code later in this section. The top LinearLayout element's orientation is horizontal(line 6), so the fragment is positioned on the left side of the screen,

```xml
1    <?xml version="1.0" encoding="utf-8"?>
2    <LinearLayout xmlns:android="http://schemas.android.com/apk/res/android"
3      xmlns:tools="http://schemas.android.com/tools"
4      android:layout_width="match_parent"
5      android:layout_height="match_parent"
6      android:orientation="horizontal"
7      tools:context=".MainActivity" >
8
9      <fragment
10       android:id="@+id/gameControl"
11       android:name="com.jblearning.hangmanv0.GameControlFragment"
12       android:layout_height="match_parent"
13       android:layout_weight="1"
14       android:layout_width="0dp"
15       tools:layout="@layout/fragment_game_control"/>
16
17     <LinearLayout
18       android:orientation="vertical"
19       android:layout_height="match_parent"
20       android:layout_weight="1"
21       android:layout_width="0dp" >
22
23       <LinearLayout
24         android:orientation="vertical"
25         android:layout_width="match_parent"
26         android:background="#F00F"
27         android:layout_weight="1"
28         android:layout_height="0dp" />
29
30       <LinearLayout
31         android:orientation="vertical"
32         android:layout_width="match_parent"
33         android:background="#F0F0"
34         android:layout_weight="1"
35         android:layout_height="0dp" />
36
37     </LinearLayout>
38
39   </LinearLayout>
```

EXAMPLE 9.2 The activity_main.xml file, Hangman app, Version 0

FIGURE 9.3 Width distribution with weights of 1 and 1

FIGURE 9.4 Width distribution with weights of 1 and 3

and the `LinearLayout` on the right side of the screen. They both have the same `android:layout_weight` value of 1 (lines 13 and 20), so they both occupy 50% (= $1/(1 + 1)$) of the screen, as shown in Figure 9.1 (the fragment is in red, the `LinearLayout` in blue and green) and illustrated in **FIGURE 9.3**. The `android:layout_weight` XML attribute of the `LinearLayout.LayoutParams` class enables us to specify how much space each `View` should occupy within its parent `LinearLayout`. We specify the value of `0dp` for the `android:layout_width` attribute for both the `fragment` and `LinearLayout` elements at lines 14 and 21. This is typical when the `android_layout:weight` attribute is used. The `0dp` value means that we want to let the system decide how much space is allocated to the various elements based on the values for the `layout_weight` attributes.

If we change the `android:layout_weight` values to 1 and 3, we get screen proportions of 25% ($1/(1 + 3)$) and 75% ($3/(1 + 3)$), as shown in **FIGURE 9.4**.

Inside the `LinearLayout` element, we define two `LinearLayout` elements at lines 23–28 and 30–35. Because that `LinearLayout` element has its orientation `vertical` (line 18), the two `LinearLayout` elements will be at the top and bottom of it (showing in blue and green in Figure 9.1). They have the same `android:layout_weight` value of 1 (lines 27 and 34), so they both occupy 50% of the right side of the screen (the heights of the blue and green parts are the same on Figure 9.1). To better visualize their position, we color them in blue (line 26) and green (line 33), respectively. Later in this chapter, we will place a fragment in each of them. We must give an id to the `fragment` element (line 10). If we do not, the app will crash at runtime.

EXAMPLE 9.3 shows the fragment_game_control.xml file (which we place in the layout directory). We use this layout XML file for the left pane of the screen, reserved by the `fragment` element in Example 9.2. It is managed by a `LinearLayout` (and its background is red (line 5)).

```
1    <?xml version="1.0" encoding="utf-8"?>
2    <LinearLayout xmlns:android="http://schemas.android.com/apk/res/android"
3      android:layout_width="match_parent"
4      android:layout_height="match_parent"
5      android:background="#FF00" >
6
7    </LinearLayout>
```

EXAMPLE 9.3 The fragment_game_control.xml file, Hangman app, Version 0

SOFTWARE ENGINEERING TIP: By giving a different color to each `ViewGroup` in a layout, it is easier to visualize the impact of the code on the layout when testing the app. We can change colors later, in the final version of the app.

Like an activity, a fragment has several life-cycle methods, as shown in **TABLE 9.1**. The methods identified with "a" in the table are automatically called when a fragment is created or

TABLE 9.1 Life-cycle methods of the `Fragment` class

Step	Method	Called
1a	void onAttach(Context context)	When the fragment is attached to its context.
2a	void onCreate(Bundle savedInstanceState)	When the fragment is created.
3a	View onCreateView(LayoutInflater inflater, ViewGroup container, Bundle savedInstanceState)	After onCreate; creates and returns the View associated with this fragment.
4a	void onViewCreated(View view, Bundle savedInstanceState)	After onCreateView, but before any saved state has been restored to the View.
5a	void onActivityCreated(Bundle savedInstanceState)	When the fragment's activity has finished executing its own onCreate method.
6a	void onViewStateRestored(Bundle savedInstanceState)	When the saved state of the fragment's View hierarchy has been restored (requires API level 17).
7a	void onStart( )	When the fragment becomes visible to the user.
8a	void onResume( )	When the fragment is visible to the user, who can start interacting with the fragment.
4b	void onPause( )	When the activity is being paused or another fragment is modifying it.
3b	void onStop( )	When the fragment is no longer visible to the user.
2b	void onDestroyView( )	After onStop; the View created by onCreateView has been detached from this fragment.
1b	void onDestroy( )	When the fragment is no longer in use.
0b	void onDetach( )	Just before the fragment is detached from its activity.

TABLE 9.2 Selected `inflate` methods of the `LayoutInflater` class	
View inflate(int resource, ViewGroup root, boolean attachToRoot)	Resource is an id for an XML resource that is being inflated. Root is an optional View to be the parent of the inflated layout if attachToRoot is true. If attachToRoot is false, root is only used to set the correct layout parameters for the root view in the XML resource.

restarted. The methods identified with "b" are automatically called when a fragment becomes inactive or is closed. Note that all these methods are `public`, contrary to the life-cycle methods in the `Activity` class, which are `protected`. When we want to inflate a fragment from a layout XML file, we must override the onCreateView method to do so. The onCreateView method provides a `LayoutInflater` parameter that enables us to inflate an XML file using its `inflate` method, shown in TABLE 9.2. Its `ViewGroup` parameter represents the `ViewGroup` inside which the fragment is to be placed. The `Bundle` parameter contains data from the previous instance of the fragment. That data can be read when a fragment is resumed.

EXAMPLE 9.4 shows the `GameControlFragment` class. At this point, we also keep it to a minimum: it only inflates the fragment_game_control.xml file at lines 16–17, inside the onCreate-View method (lines 13–18). The first argument we pass to the `inflate` method is the resource id for the fragment, `fragment_game_control`. The second argument is the container that the fragment goes into, the `ViewGroup` passed by the onCreateView method, `container`.

```
1    package com.jblearning.hangmanv0;
2
3    import android.app.Fragment;
4    import android.os.Bundle;
5    import android.view.LayoutInflater;
6    import android.view.View;
7    import android.view.ViewGroup;
8
9    public class GameControlFragment extends Fragment {
10     public GameControlFragment( ) {
11     }
12
13     @Override
14     public View onCreateView( LayoutInflater inflater,
15             ViewGroup container, Bundle savedInstanceState ) {
16       return inflater.inflate( R.layout.fragment_game_control,
17                         container, false );
18     }
19   }
```

EXAMPLE 9.4 The `GameControlFragment` class, Hangman app, Version 0

FIGURE 9.5 The Hangman app, Version 0, previewed in landscape orientation

The third argument is `false` because in this case, the inflated XML file is already inserted into `container`. Specifying `true` would create a redundant `ViewGroup` hierarchy.

When an activity state is restored, any fragment belonging to the activity is re-instantiated and its default constructor is called automatically. Thus, any fragment class must have a default constructor (lines 10–11).

FIGURE 9.5 shows a preview of the app, Version 0, in landscape orientation.

We can check what methods of the `Activity` and `Fragment` classes are automatically called and in what order by adding Log statements inside the various life-cycle methods of both the `MainActivity` and the `GameControlFragment` classes. If we add them to both classes, we would see the output shown in **FIGURE 9.6** as the user starts the app and interacts with the app and the device. It typically shows two things:

▶ When the activity is created or restarted, a method of the `Activity` class executes first and a similar method of the `Fragment` class executes afterward.

▶ When the activity becomes inactive or is closed, a method of the `Fragment` class executes first and a similar method of the `Activity` class executes afterward.

9.4 Adding GUI Components, Styles, Strings, and Colors, Hangman, App Version 1

In Version 1 of the app, we populate the left area of the screen (the fragment) with the two GUI components, and we start using the Model.

EXAMPLE 9.5 shows the updated activity_main.xml file. We give ids to the `LinearLayout` elements (at lines 24 and 32) at the top right and bottom right of the screen so that we can access them later to place fragments in them. We change from hard coded colors to colors defined in the colors.xml file (lines 27 and 35), as shown in **EXAMPLE 9.6**.

Action	Output
User starts app.	Inside MainActivity:onCreate Inside GameControlFragment:constructor Inside GameControlFragment:onAttach Inside GameControlFragment:onCreate Inside GameControlFragment:onCreateView Inside GameControlFragment:onViewCreated Inside GameControlFragment:onActivityCreated Inside GameControlFragment:onViewStateRestored Inside MainActivity:onStart Inside GameControlFragment:onStart Inside MainActivity:onResume Inside GameControlFragment:onResume
User waits a while, app goes to the background, is no longer visible.	Inside GameControlFragment:onPause Inside MainActivity:onPause Inside GameControlFragment:onStop Inside MainActivity:onStop
User touches the device's Power button, then swipes the screen.	Inside MainActivity:onRestart Inside MainActivity:onStart Inside GameControlFragment:onStart Inside MainActivity:onResume Inside GameControlFragment:onResume
User hits the device's Home Key button.	Inside GameControlFragment:onPause Inside MainActivity:onPause Inside GameControlFragment:onStop Inside MainActivity:onStop
User touches the app icon.	Inside MainActivity:onRestart Inside MainActivity:onStart Inside GameControlFragment:onStart Inside MainActivity:onResume Inside GameControlFragment:onResume
User touches the device's Back Key button.	Inside GameControlFragment:onPause Inside MainActivity:onPause Inside GameControlFragment:onStop Inside MainActivity:onStop Inside GameControlFragment:onDestroyView Inside GameControlFragment:onDestroy Inside GameControlFragment:onDetach Inside MainActivity:onDestroy

FIGURE 9.6 Output as the user interacts with the HangmanV0LifeCycle app, including life-cycle methods of the `Activity` and `Fragment` classes

```
1   <?xml version="1.0" encoding="utf-8"?>
2   <LinearLayout xmlns:android="http://schemas.android.com/apk/res/android"
3     xmlns:tools="http://schemas.android.com/tools"
4     android:layout_width="match_parent"
5     android:layout_height="match_parent"
6     android:orientation="horizontal"
7     tools:context="com.jblearning.hangmanv1.MainActivity" >
8
9     <fragment
10      android:id="@+id/gameControl"
11      android:name="com.jblearning.hangmanv1.GameControlFragment"
12      android:layout_height="match_parent"
13      android:layout_weight="1"
14      android:layout_width="0dp"
15      tools:layout="@layout/fragment_game_control"/>
16
17    <LinearLayout
18      android:orientation="vertical"
19      android:layout_height="match_parent"
20      android:layout_weight="1"
21      android:layout_width="0dp" >
22
23      <LinearLayout
24        android:id="@+id/game_state"
25        android:orientation="vertical"
26        android:layout_width="match_parent"
27        android:background="@color/game_state_background"
28        android:layout_weight="1"
29        android:layout_height="0dp" />
30
31      <LinearLayout
32        android:id="@+id/game_result"
33        android:orientation="vertical"
34        android:layout_width="match_parent"
35        android:background="@color/game_result_background"
36        android:layout_weight="1"
37        android:layout_height="0dp" />
38
39    </LinearLayout>
40
41  </LinearLayout>
```

EXAMPLE 9.5 **The activity_main.xml file, Hangman app, Version 1**

```
1    <?xml version="1.0" encoding="utf-8"?>
2    <resources>
3      <color name="colorPrimary">#3F51B5</color>
4      <color name="colorPrimaryDark">#303F9F</color>
5      <color name="colorAccent">#FF4081</color>
6
7      <color name="buttonColor">#F555</color>
8      <color name="game_control_background">#FF00</color>
9      <color name="game_state_background">#F00F</color>
10     <color name="game_result_background">#F0F0</color>
11     <color name="inputColor">#FFF0</color>
12   </resources>
```

EXAMPLE 9.6 **The colors.xml file, Hangman app, Version 1**

EXAMPLE 9.7 shows the updated fragment_game_control.xml file. We place two Linear-
Layouts (lines 9–14, 16–20) in it: they each contain a basic GUI component (a button and a label).
By placing one component per layout manager and giving each layout manager the same android:
layout_weight value of 1 via the wrapCenterWeight1 style at lines 9 and 16, we space out the
components evenly. The wrapCenterWeight1 style, which also sets android:layout_width

```
1    <?xml version="1.0" encoding="utf-8"?>
2    <LinearLayout xmlns:android="http://schemas.android.com/apk/res/android"
3      android:layout_width="match_parent"
4      android:layout_height="match_parent"
5      android:orientation="vertical"
6      android:background="@color/game_control_background"
7      android:gravity="center" >
8
9      <LinearLayout style="@style/wrapCenterWeight1" >
10       <Button
11         android:text="@string/play"
12         style="@style/buttonStyle"
13         android:onClick="play" />
14     </LinearLayout>
15
16     <LinearLayout style="@style/wrapCenterWeight1" >
17       <TextView
18         android:id="@+id/status"
19         style="@style/textStyle" />
20     </LinearLayout>
21
22   </LinearLayout>
```

EXAMPLE 9.7 **The fragment_game_control.xml file, Hangman app, Version 1**

and `android:layout_height` to `wrap_content` and `android:gravity` to `center`, is defined in the styles.xml file (lines 11–16), shown in **EXAMPLE 9.9**. The use of styles simplifies the coding of our layout XML files.

We give a background color defined in colors.xml to the outer `LinearLayout` (line 6). The button is styled at line 12 using the `buttonStyle` style, defined in Example 9.9 at lines 31–33. `ButtonStyle` inherits from `textStyle`, defined at lines 18–23 in Example 9.9.

The `TextView` element (lines 17–19) is styled with the `textStyle` style at line 19. The `TextView` element stores how many guesses the user has left. We retrieve that value from the Model. The button, whose text says PLAY (line 11—the value of the `play` `String` in the strings.xml file—line 3 of **EXAMPLE 9.8**), triggers execution of the `play` method when the user clicks on it (line 13).

```
1   <resources>
2     <string name="app_name">HangmanV1</string>
3     <string name="play">PLAY</string>
4   </resources>
```

EXAMPLE 9.8 **The strings.xml file, Hangman app, Version 1**

```
1    <resources>
2
3      <!-- Base application theme. -->
4      <style name="AppTheme" parent="Theme.AppCompat.Light.DarkActionBar">
5        <item name="android:textSize">42sp</item>
6        <item name="colorPrimary">@color/colorPrimary</item>
7        <item name="colorPrimaryDark">@color/colorPrimaryDark</item>
8        <item name="colorAccent">@color/colorAccent</item>
9      </style>
10
11     <style name="wrapCenterWeight1">
12       <item name="android:layout_height">wrap_content</item>
13       <item name="android:layout_width">wrap_content</item>
14       <item name="android:gravity">center</item>
15       <item name="android:layout_weight">1</item>
16     </style>
17
18     <style name="textStyle" parent="@android:style/TextAppearance">
19       <item name="android:layout_width">wrap_content</item>
20       <item name="android:layout_height">wrap_content</item>
21       <item name="android:textSize">36sp</item>
22       <item name="android:gravity">center</item>
23     </style>
24
```

EXAMPLE 9.9 **The styles.xml file, Hangman app, Version 1 (*Continued*)**

```
25      <style name="editTextStyle" parent="textStyle">
26        <item name="android:inputType">textCapCharacters</item>
27        <item name="android:background">@color/inputColor</item>
28        <item name="android:hint">Type a letter here</item>
29      </style>
30
31      <style name="buttonStyle" parent="textStyle">
32        <item name="android:background">@color/buttonColor</item>
33      </style>
34
35   </resources>
```

EXAMPLE 9.9 **The styles.xml file, Hangman app, Version 1**

We keep the `MainActivity` class, shown in **EXAMPLE 9.10**, to a minimum. It includes a `Hangman` instance variable representing the Model at line 10. Since the `onCreate` method can be called several times during the life cycle of this activity, we only instantiate it (line 16) if it has not been instantiated before (i.e., if it is `null`). We call the `getGuessesLeft` method of the Hangman

```
1    package com.jblearning.hangmanv1;
2
3    import android.os.Bundle;
4    import android.support.v7.app.AppCompatActivity;
5    import android.view.View;
6    import android.widget.TextView;
7
8    public class MainActivity extends AppCompatActivity {
9
10     private Hangman game;
11
12     @Override
13     protected void onCreate( Bundle savedInstanceState ) {
14       super.onCreate( savedInstanceState );
15       if ( game == null )
16         game = new Hangman( Hangman.DEFAULT_GUESSES );
17       setContentView( R.layout.activity_main );
18       TextView status = ( TextView ) findViewById( R.id.status );
19       status.setText( "" + game.getGuessesLeft( ) );
20     }
21
22     public void play( View view ) {
23     }
24   }
```

EXAMPLE 9.10 **The `MainActivity` class, Hangman app, Version 1**

FIGURE 9.7 The Hangman app, Version 1, running in horizontal orientation

class with it at line 19 in order to set the text inside the `TextView` of the fragment. We retrieve that `TextView` at line 18 using the `findViewById` method. The class also includes the `play` method (lines 22–23), which is implemented as a do-nothing method at this point (if we do not implement it, if we run and click on the button, the app will stop working).

FIGURE 9.7 shows the app, Version 1, running in horizontal orientation.

9.5 Defining a Fragment Using a Layout XML File and Adding the Fragment to an Activity by Code, Hangman, App Version 2

In Version 2, we display the fragment on the top right pane (with the blue background) of the screen showing the state of completion of the word, and an `EditText` for the user to enter a letter. We code the fragment in an XML file, fragment_game_state.xml, and create the fragment by code.

Furthermore, in order to better focus on fragments and keep things simple, we run the app in horizontal orientation only by adding this line to the AndroidManifest.xml file inside the `activity` element:

```
android:screenOrientation="landscape"
```

EXAMPLE 9.11 shows the fragment_game_state.xml file. It includes a `TextView`, which shows the state of completion of the word and an `EditText`, where the user can enter a letter. We give ids to these two elements at lines 11 and 17 so that we can later retrieve them using the `findViewById` method. They are styled with `textStyle` and `editTextStyle`, which are both defined in the styles.xml file shown in Example 9.9. Like in Example 9.7 for the left pane fragment, we wrap each element around a `LinearLayout` element styled with the `wrapCenterWeight1` style, so that the elements are centered and spaced evenly.

```
1    <?xml version="1.0" encoding="utf-8"?>
2    <LinearLayout xmlns:android="http://schemas.android.com/apk/res/android"
3      xmlns:tools="http://schemas.android.com/tools"
4      android:layout_width="match_parent"
5      android:layout_height="match_parent"
6      android:orientation="vertical"
7      android:gravity="center" >
8
9      <LinearLayout style="@style/wrapCenterWeight1" >
10        <TextView
11          android:id="@+id/state_of_game"
12          style="@style/textStyle" />
13      </LinearLayout>
14
15      <LinearLayout style="@style/wrapCenterWeight1" >
16        <EditText
17          android:id="@+id/letter"
18          style="@style/editTextStyle"
19          android:imeOptions="actionDone"/>
20      </LinearLayout>
21
22    </LinearLayout>
```

EXAMPLE 9.11 The fragment_game_state.xml file, Hangman app, Version 2

We want to close the soft keyboard when the user touches the Done key. In order to do that, we set the value of the android:imeOptions attribute, inherited from TextView, to actionDone at line 19. **IME** stands for **Input Method Editor**, and it enables the user to enter text. It is not restricted to a keyboard—the user can also enter text by voice. The attribute android:imeOptions enables us to specify the options that we want to enable.

We need to show the game state fragment when the app starts. We first need to create the fragment and add it to the activity, then set the text inside the TextView element of the fragment. For that, we can call the currentIncompleteWord method of our Model. To incorporate a fragment into an activity, we need to implement the following steps:

▶   Get a reference to the fragment manager for this Activity.
▶   Create a fragment transaction.
▶   Create a fragment.
▶   Have the fragment transaction add the fragment to a container (a ViewGroup).
▶   Commit the fragment transaction.

The FragmentManager abstract class provides the functionality to interact with fragments within an activity. A reference to the FragmentManager for the current Activity can be obtained by calling the getFragmentManager method, shown in TABLE 9.3, with the Activity reference. TABLE 9.4 lists some methods of the FragmentManager class.

TABLE 9.3 The getFragmentManager method of the `Activity` class

Method	Description
FragmentManager getFragmentManager( )	Returns the FragmentManager for this Activity.

TABLE 9.4 Selected methods of the `FragmentManager` class

Method	Description
FragmentTransaction beginTransaction( )	Starts a series of operations for this fragment manager. Returns a FragmentTransaction.
Fragment findFragmentById(int id)	Returns a Fragment identified by its id.
Fragment findFragmentByTag(String tag)	Returns a Fragment identified by its tag.

Thus, we can obtain a `FragmentManager` reference for the current `Activity` using:

```
FragmentManager fragmentManager = getFragmentManager();
```

To obtain a `FragmentTransaction` for the preceding `FragmentManager`, we write:

```
FragmentTransaction transaction = fragmentManager.beginTransaction( );
```

The `FragmentTransaction` class provides methods (see **TABLE 9.5**) to perform fragment operations, such as adding a fragment to an activity, removing it, replacing it, hiding it, showing it, etc. These methods return the `FragmentTransaction` that calls them, so that we can chain method calls. There are other methods, for example, to define animations or transitions when a fragment transaction is being performed. It is an `abstract` class so we cannot instantiate a `FragmentTransaction` object with a constructor. We can use the `beginTransaction` method of the `FragmentManager` class to instantiate a `FragmentTransaction` object.

After having obtained a `FragmentTransaction` named `transaction` for an `Activity`, we can add a `GameStateFragment` whose id is `game_state` to that `Activity` using the following code:

```
GameStateFragment fragment = new GameStateFragment( );
transaction.add( R.id.game_state, fragment );
transaction.commit( );
```

When performing a **fragment transaction**, for example, adding or removing a fragment to or from an activity, we can add it to the **back stack** of the activity by calling the `addToBackStack` method before calling the `commit` method. The back stack keeps track of the history of these

TABLE 9.5 Selected methods of the `FragmentTransaction` class

Method	Description
FragmentTransaction add(int containerViewId, Fragment fragment, String tag)	Adds a fragment to an activity. ContainerViewId is the resource id of the container that the fragment will be placed in; fragment is the fragment to be added. Tag is an optional tag name for the fragment. The added fragment can later be retrieved by the fragment manager using the findFragmentByTag method. Returns the FragmentTransaction reference calling this method; thus, method calls can be chained.
FragmentTransaction add(int containerViewId, Fragment fragment)	Calls the method above with a null tag parameter.
FragmentTransaction add(Fragment fragment, String tag)	Calls the method above with a resource id parameter equal to 0.
FragmentTransaction hide(Fragment fragment)	Hides fragment (i.e., hides its View).
FragmentTransaction show(Fragment fragment)	Shows fragment (i.e., shows its View if it had been hidden before—the default is that the fragment is shown).
FragmentTransaction remove(Fragment fragment)	Remove fragment from its activity.
FragmentTransaction replace(int containerViewId, Fragment fragment, String tag)	Similar to the first add method, but instead replaces an existing fragment inside the container whose id is containerViewId.
FragmentTransaction replace(int containerViewId, Fragment fragment)	Calls the method above with a null tag parameter.
int commit( )	Schedules that fragment transaction to be committed.
FragmentTransaction addToBackStack(String name)	Adds this transaction to the back stack of the activity; name is optional and stores the name of that back stack state.

fragment transactions within an activity so that the user can revert to a prior fragment by pressing the Back button of the device.

EXAMPLE 9.12 shows the updated `MainActivity` class. When the app starts, the `onCreate` method executes, and we create the fragment and attach it to the activity. At line 23, we get a reference to the fragment manager for this activity by calling the `getFragmentManager` method from the `Activity` class. We only want to create a new `GameStateFragment` and add

```
1    package com.jblearning.hangmanv2;
2
3    import android.app.FragmentManager;
4    import android.app.FragmentTransaction;
5    import android.os.Bundle;
6    import android.support.v7.app.AppCompatActivity;
7    import android.view.View;
8    import android.widget.TextView;
9
10   public class MainActivity extends AppCompatActivity {
11
12     private Hangman game;
13
14     @Override
15     protected void onCreate( Bundle savedInstanceState ) {
16       super.onCreate( savedInstanceState );
17       if ( game == null )
18         game = new Hangman( Hangman.DEFAULT_GUESSES );
19       setContentView( R.layout.activity_main );
20       TextView status = ( TextView ) findViewById( R.id.status );
21       status.setText( "" + game.getGuessesLeft( ) );
22
23       FragmentManager fragmentManager = getFragmentManager( );
24       if( fragmentManager.findFragmentById( R.id.game_state ) == null ) {
25         FragmentTransaction transaction = fragmentManager.beginTransaction( );
26         GameStateFragment fragment = new GameStateFragment( );
27         transaction.add( R.id.game_state, fragment );
28         transaction.commit( );
29       }
30     }
31
32     public Hangman getGame( ) {
33       return game;
34     }
35
36     public void play( View view ) {
37     }
38   }
```

EXAMPLE 9.12 The `MainActivity` class, Hangman app, Version 2

it to the activity if it has not been created yet. Using the `findFragmentById` method at line 24, we check if there is already a fragment with the id `game_state` within this activity. If there is, we do nothing. If there is not, we create one and add it to the activity at lines 25–28.

At line 25, using the `FragmentManager` reference, we get a `FragmentTransaction` reference, `transaction`. At line 26, we define and instantiate a `GameStateFragment` reference,

TABLE 9.6 The `getActivity` and `getView` methods of the `Fragment` class	
Method	**Description**
Activity getActivity( )	Returns the activity that this fragment belongs to.
View getView( )	Returns the root View for this fragment.

fragment. At line 27, we add `fragment` to this `Activity`, placing it inside the `ViewGroup` (a `LinearLayout` in this case) whose resource id is `game_state`. Finally, we commit the fragment transaction at line 28. At this point, we still need to place the text of the puzzle inside the `TextView` of the puzzle fragment that we just added to the activity. In order to do that, we first need to access the `View` of the fragment and use the `findViewById` method, passing the id of the `TextView` as its argument. However, at this point the `View` of the fragment is `null`, so attempting to use it would result in a `NullPointerException`, crashing the app. Thus, we do this inside the `GameStateFragment` class. Thus, in the `GameStateFragment` class, we need to access the value of the current incomplete word of the hangman game. To that end, we provide the `getGame` method (lines 32–34) in the `MainActivity` class. From the `GameStateFragment` class, we can access the activity by calling the `getActivity` method (see TABLE 9.6), inherited from the `Fragment` class. With a `MainActivity` reference, we can access the game by calling `getGame`, and then access the incomplete word as follows:

```
MainActivity fragmentActivity = ( MainActivity ) getActivity( );
String currentWord = fragmentActivity.getGame( ).currentIncompleteWord( );
```

> **COMMON ERROR:** Accessing a `View` inside a fragment too early could result in a `NullPointerException`. Be sure to access that `View` inside a life-cycle method of `Fragment` that guarantees that that `View` has been instantiated.

EXAMPLE 9.13 shows the `GameStateFragment` class. Since it inherits from `Fragment`, we provide a mandatory default constructor at lines 12–13. We inflate the fragment_game_state.xml file at lines 18–19 inside the `onCreateView` method. When the fragment transaction is committed at line 28 of Example 9.12, the constructor, the `onAttach`, `onCreate`, `onCreateView`, `onActivityCreated`, and `onStart` methods of the `Fragment` life cycle are called in that order. When the `onStart` method (lines 22–30) executes, the fragment's `View` and the `TextView` inside it have been instantiated. Thus, we can set the text inside the `TextView` at that point.

We get a reference to the fragment's `View` at line 24 using the `getView` method (shown in Table 9.6), inherited from the `Fragment` class. With it, we can call the `findViewById` method to access any `View` inside it that has been given an id. At lines 25–26, we call it and assign the

```
1    package com.jblearning.hangmanv2;
2
3    import android.app.Fragment;
4    import android.os.Bundle;
5    import android.view.LayoutInflater;
6    import android.view.View;
7    import android.view.ViewGroup;
8    import android.widget.TextView;
9
10   public class GameStateFragment extends Fragment {
11
12     public GameStateFragment( ) {
13     }
14
15     @Override
16     public View onCreateView( LayoutInflater inflater,
17                 ViewGroup container, Bundle savedInstanceState ) {
18       return inflater.inflate( R.layout.fragment_game_state,
19                                 container, false );
20     }
21
22     public void onStart( ) {
23       super.onStart( );
24       View fragmentView = getView( );
25       TextView gameStateTV
26         = ( TextView ) fragmentView.findViewById( R.id.state_of_game );
27       MainActivity fragmentActivity = ( MainActivity ) getActivity( );
28       gameStateTV.setText( fragmentActivity.getGame( )
29                 .currentIncompleteWord( ) );
30     }
31   }
```

EXAMPLE 9.13 **The `GameStateFragment` class, Hangman app, Version 2**

`TextView` whose id is `state_of_game` to `gameStateTV`. We get a reference to the parent `Activity` of this fragment at line 27, casting it to a `MainActivity`. We chain method calls to `getGame` and `currentIncompleteWord` in order to retrieve the game's incomplete word and assign the resulting value to the text of `gameStateTV` at lines 28–29.

COMMON ERROR: If we intend to call a method of we `Activity` class with the `Activity` of a fragment, it is important to cast the return object of the `get Activity` method to that type of `Activity`.

FIGURE 9.8 The Hangman app, Version 2, running in horizontal position, after the user enters a letter and hits the Done (or Check) button on the soft keyboard

FIGURE 9.8 shows the app running in the emulator after the user enters the letter U and hits the Done button on the soft keyboard.

9.6 Defining and Adding a Fragment to an Activity by Code, Hangman, App Version 3

In Version 3, we display the fragment on the bottom right pane (with the green background) of the screen showing a message about the result of the game in a TextView. This time, we do not use an XML file to define the fragment, we define and create it entirely by code.

Defining the fragment's Graphical User Interface (GUI) is similar to defining a View by code instead of using an XML file. We do this in the GameResultFragment class. Creating the fragment is identical to creating a game state fragment. It takes place in the MainActivity class.

EXAMPLE 9.14 shows the updated MainActivity class. It is very similar to its previous version shown in Example 9.12. We add a GameResultFragment in the LinearLayout whose id is game_result (lines 31–36).

In the GameResultFragment class, we define the fragment by code. This fragment only has a TextView in it. Furthermore, we need to access that TextView to set its text when the game ends. Rather than giving the TextView an id when we create it, we declare it as an instance variable so that we have a direct reference to it inside the GameResultFragment class (line 12 of EXAMPLE 9.15). The onCreateView method, at lines 14–20, calls the setUpFragmentGui method at line 17 in order to create the GUI for this fragment. It returns the View returned by its super method at lines 18–19. The setUpFragmentGui method is coded at lines 22–28. Since it is possible that onCreateView is called several times during the life cycle of the fragment, we can in turn expect setUpFragmentGui to be called several times too. Thus, we want to instantiate

```
1   package com.jblearning.hangmanv3;
2
3   import android.app.FragmentManager;
4   import android.app.FragmentTransaction;
5   import android.os.Bundle;
6   import android.support.v7.app.AppCompatActivity;
7   import android.view.View;
8   import android.widget.TextView;
9
10  public class MainActivity extends AppCompatActivity {
11
12    private Hangman game;
13
14    @Override
15    protected void onCreate( Bundle savedInstanceState ) {
16      super.onCreate( savedInstanceState );
17      if ( game == null )
18        game = new Hangman( Hangman.DEFAULT_GUESSES );
19      setContentView( R.layout.activity_main );
20      TextView status = ( TextView ) findViewById( R.id.status );
21      status.setText( "" + game.getGuessesLeft() );
22
23      FragmentManager fragmentManager = getFragmentManager( );
24      if( fragmentManager.findFragmentById( R.id.game_state ) == null ) {
25        FragmentTransaction transaction = fragmentManager.beginTransaction( );
26        GameStateFragment fragment = new GameStateFragment( );
27        transaction.add( R.id.game_state, fragment );
28        transaction.commit( );
29      }
30
31      if( fragmentManager.findFragmentById( R.id.game_result ) == null ) {
32        FragmentTransaction transaction = fragmentManager.beginTransaction( );
33        GameResultFragment fragment = new GameResultFragment( );
34        transaction.add( R.id.game_result, fragment );
35        transaction.commit( );
36      }
37    }
38
39    public Hangman getGame( ) {
40      return game;
41    }
42
43    public void play( View view ) {
44    }
45  }
```

EXAMPLE 9.14 **The MainActivity class, Hangman app, Version 3**

```
1    package com.jblearning.hangmanv3;
2
3    import android.app.Fragment;
4    import android.os.Bundle;
5    import android.view.Gravity;
6    import android.view.LayoutInflater;
7    import android.view.View;
8    import android.view.ViewGroup;
9    import android.widget.TextView;
10
11   public class GameResultFragment extends Fragment {
12     private TextView gameResultTV;
13
14     @Override
15     public View onCreateView( LayoutInflater inflater,
16              ViewGroup container, Bundle savedInstanceState ) {
17       setUpFragmentGui( container );
18       return super.onCreateView( inflater, container,
19                          savedInstanceState ) ;
20     }
21
22     public void setUpFragmentGui( ViewGroup container ) {
23       if( gameResultTV == null ) {
24         gameResultTV = new TextView( getActivity( ) );
25         gameResultTV.setGravity( Gravity.CENTER );
26         container.addView( gameResultTV );
27       }
28     }
29
30     public void onStart( ) {
31       super.onStart( );
32       gameResultTV.setText( "GOOD LUCK" );
33     }
34   }
```

EXAMPLE 9.15 The `GameResultFragment` class, Hangman app, Version 3

gameResultTV (line 24) and add it to the ViewGroup that is the root View of the fragment (line 26) only once, when it is null (line 23). We center the text inside gameResultTV at line 25.

In the onStart method (lines 30–33), which is automatically called after onCreateView and onActivityCreated, we hard code the text inside gameResultTV to "GOOD LUCK" (line 32).

We need to center the TextView of GameResultFragment within its parent LinearLayout. Inside the activity_main.xml file, we add the following attribute-value pair to the last Linear-Layout element (the one whose id is game_result and is located in the right bottom pane):

```
android:gravity="center"
```

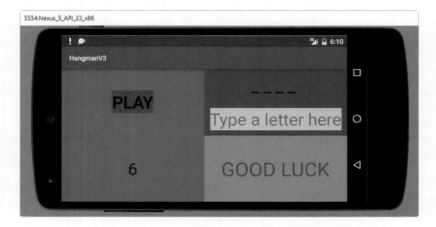

FIGURE 9.9 **The Hangman app, Version 3, running in horizontal position**

FIGURE 9.9 shows the app running in the emulator. All three fragments are now present:

▶ The left pane (game control) fragment in red is defined and created using XML.
▶ The top right pane (game status) fragment in blue is defined in XML and created by code.
▶ The bottom right pane (game result) fragment in green is defined and created by code.

9.7 Communication between Fragments and Their Activity: Enabling Play, Hangman, App Version 4

We have now created an activity with three fragments inside, defined and created in different ways. In Version 4, we complete the app by processing the user's letter and enabling the user to play the game. We also illustrate how fragments can communicate with their activity when processing an event.

The user enters a letter in the game state fragment, then clicks on the PLAY button on the left pane, which triggers execution of the `play` method inside the `MainActivity` class. To enable play, we do the following:

▶ Capture the letter entered by the user.
▶ Call the `guess` method of `Hangman`.
▶ Update the number of guesses left in the `TextView` inside the left pane.
▶ Update the incomplete word in the `TextView` inside the top right pane.
▶ Clear the `EditText`.
▶ If the game is over, update the message in the `TextView` inside the bottom right pane and clear the hint in the `EditText`.

EXAMPLE 9.16 shows the `play` method. We retrieve the `EditText` using its id at line 46 and assign it to the variable `input`. At line 47, we get an `Editable` reference for `input`. If it is not `null` and contains at least one character (line 48), we process the first character as the user's play. Otherwise, we do nothing.

```
 6
 7    import android.text.Editable;
 8
 9    import android.widget.EditText;
...
45      public void play( View view ) {
46         EditText input = ( EditText ) findViewById( R.id.letter );
47         Editable userText = input.getText( );
48         if( userText != null && userText.length( ) > 0 ) {
49           // update number of guesses left
50           char letter = userText.charAt( 0 );
51           game.guess( letter );
52           TextView status = ( TextView ) findViewById( R.id.status );
53           status.setText( "" + game.getGuessesLeft( ) );
54
55           // update incomplete word
56           FragmentManager fragmentManager = getFragmentManager( );
57           GameStateFragment gsFragment = ( GameStateFragment )
58             fragmentManager.findFragmentById( R.id.game_state );
59           View gsFragmentView = gsFragment.getView( );
60           TextView gameStateTV = ( TextView )
61             gsFragmentView.findViewById( R.id.state_of_game );
62           gameStateTV.setText( game.currentIncompleteWord( ) );
63
64           // clear EditText
65           input.setText( "" );
66
67           int result = game.gameOver( );
68           if( result != 0 ) /* game is over */ {
69             GameResultFragment grFragment = ( GameResultFragment )
70               fragmentManager.findFragmentById( R.id.game_result );
71
72             // update TextView in result fragment
73             if( result == 1 )
74               grFragment.setResult( "YOU WON" );
75             else if( result == -1 )
76               grFragment.setResult( "YOU LOST" );
77
78             // delete hint in EditText
79             input.setHint( "" );
80           }
81         }
82      }
82    }
```

EXAMPLE 9.16 The `play` method of the `MainActivity` class, Hangman app, Version 4

At lines 49–53, we play and update the number of guesses left. Since we gave the `TextView` that displays the number of guesses left an id (`status`) in the fragment_game_control.xml file, we retrieve it using the `findViewById` method at line 52. We call `getGuessesLeft` with `game` at line 53 to retrieve the number of guesses left and display it inside the `TextView`.

At lines 55–62, we update the state of the incomplete word. We first get a reference to the `GameStateFragment` at lines 56–58, then get a reference to the fragment's `View` at line 59. With it, we call `findViewById` at lines 60–61 in order to get a reference to the `TextView` whose id is `state_of_game`. We call the `currentIncompleteWord` of Hangman to set the text of that `TextView` at line 62. At lines 64–65, we clear the `EditText`.

We then check if the game is over at line 67. If it is not, we do nothing. If it is (line 68), we clear the hint in the `EditText` (lines 78–79), and we tell the user the result of the game. In order to do this, we need to access the `TextView` inside the `GameResultFragment`; however, that `TextView` does not have an id. Thus, in order to access it, we get a reference to the `GameResultFragment` that contains it (lines 69–70) with the `FragmentManager` and call `setResult`, a new method of the `GameResultFragment` class, with it (lines 72–76).

EXAMPLE 9.17 shows the `setResult` method of the `GameResultFragment` class. The rest of the class is unchanged. It sets the text of the `gameResultTV` instance variable.

```
34
35     public void setResult( String result ) {
36        gameResultTV.setText( result );
37     }
38  }
```

EXAMPLE 9.17 The `setResult` Method of the `GameResultFragment` class, Hangman app, Version 4

Figure 9.1, at the beginning of the chapter, shows the app running at some point in the game. **FIGURE 9.10** shows the app running after the user won. The `TextView` that was previously showing either a hint or a letter is no longer visible because its contents are empty and its `android:layout_width` and `android:layout_height` attributes are set to `wrap_content`.

FIGURE 9.10 The Hangman app, Version 4, running in horizontal position, after the user won

9.8 Using an Invisible Fragment, Hangman, App Version 5

We can also use a fragment that can perform some work in the background of the app, without any visual representation. For this, we use the add method of the FragmentTransaction class that does not have a View id parameter. If we want to be able to retrieve the fragment later, we should provide a tag name. Such a fragment could perform some work in the background of the app while the user is allowed to interact with the app. It could, for example, retrieve some data from a file, a database, a remote URL, or possibly use the device's GPS to retrieve some live location data.

To demonstrate how to use such a fragment, we keep our example to a minimum. Our fragment is hard coded and includes the warning method. We will give a warning to the user when he or she has only one guess left and display the String returned by the warning method. That information normally comes from the Model, but in the interest of keeping things as simple as possible, we hard code it in this class. EXAMPLE 9.18 shows the BackgroundFragment class.

```
1   package com.jblearning.hangmanv5;
2
3   import android.app.Fragment;
4
5   public class BackgroundFragment extends Fragment {
6
7       public BackgroundFragment( ) {
8       }
9
10      public String warning( ) {
11          return "ONLY 1 LEFT!";
12      }
13  }
```

EXAMPLE 9.18 The BackgroundFragment class, Hangman app, Version 5

Because this fragment is not visible, the onCreateView method is not called. Thus, we did not code it. At lines 10–12, we code the warning method, which we call from the MainActivity class.

EXAMPLE 9.19 shows parts of the updated MainActivity class. We create an invisible BackgroundFragment in the onCreate method at lines 40–45, without waiting for the user to interact with the app. This strategy can be used in apps where we need to bring data from an outside source. At line 43, we use the add method of the FragmentTransaction class with a Fragment and a String parameter. The String represents a tag name for the fragment, and later we can retrieve that fragment via its tag name, background, using the findFragmentByTag method of the FragmentManager class. We use the fragment in the play method (lines 52–99). If the user has only one guess left (line 75), we display a warning inside the TextView of the GameResultFragment. We retrieve the BackgroundFragment based on its tag at lines 76–77

```
  1  package com.jblearning.hangmanv5;
...
 12  public class MainActivity extends AppCompatActivity {
...
 16    @Override
 17    protected void onCreate( Bundle savedInstanceState ) {
...
 39
 40      if( fragmentManager.findFragmentByTag( "background" ) == null ) {
 41        FragmentTransaction transaction = fragmentManager.beginTransaction( );
 42        BackgroundFragment fragment = new BackgroundFragment( );
 43        transaction.add( fragment, "background" ); // tag is background
 44        transaction.commit( );
 45       }
 46     }
 47
 48    public Hangman getGame( ) {
 49      return game;
 50    }
 51
 52    public void play( View view ) {
 53      EditText input = ( EditText ) findViewById( R.id.letter );
 54      Editable userText = input.getText( );
 55      if( userText != null && userText.length( ) > 0 ) {
...
 73
 74        // check if there is only one guess left
 75        if( game.getGuessesLeft( ) == 1 ) {
 76          BackgroundFragment background = ( BackgroundFragment )
 77          fragmentManager.findFragmentByTag( "background" );
 78          GameResultFragment grFragment = ( GameResultFragment )
 79          fragmentManager.findFragmentById( R.id.game_result );
 80          // retrieve warning and display it
 81          grFragment.setResult( background.warning( ) );
 82        }
...
 98      }
 99    }
100  }
```

EXAMPLE 9.19 **The `MainActivity` class, Hangman app, Version 5**

and the `GameResultFragment` based on its id at lines 78–79. We then call `setResult` with the `GameResultFragment`, passing the warning retrieved by calling the `warning` method with the `BackgroundFragment` (line 81).

FIGURE 9.11 shows the app running in the emulator. The user only has one guess left.

FIGURE 9.11 The Hangman app, Version 5, running in horizontal position—the user only has one guess left

9.9 Making a Fragment Reusable, Hangman, App Version 6

Version 5 of the app works, but the GameStateFragment class is not really reusable. For example, at line 27 of Example 9.13, the use of the MainActivity reference and the call to getGame at line 28 inside the GameStateFragment class assume that the MainActivity class exists and includes the method getGame.

EXAMPLE 9.20 shows a better implementation, making the GameStateFragment class more reusable. Inside the fragment class, we use an inner interface, which we name Callbacks (lines 15–17), and transfer all the method calls using a MainActivity reference inside the fragment

```
1    package com.jblearning.hangmanv6;
2
3    import android.app.Fragment;
4    import android.content.Context;
5    import android.os.Bundle;
6    import android.view.LayoutInflater;
7    import android.view.View;
8    import android.view.ViewGroup;
9    import android.widget.TextView;
10
11   public class GameStateFragment extends Fragment {
12
13      private Callbacks mCallbacks = sDummyCallbacks;
14
```

EXAMPLE 9.20 The reusable GameStateFragment class, Hangman app, Version 6 (Continued)

```
15    public interface Callbacks {
16      public WordGame getGame( );
17    }
18
19    private static Callbacks sDummyCallbacks = new Callbacks( ) {
20      public WordGame getGame( ) {
21        return null;
22      }
23    };
24
25    public GameStateFragment( ) {
26    }
27
28    @Override
29    public View onCreateView( LayoutInflater inflater,
30                ViewGroup container, Bundle savedInstanceState ) {
31      return inflater.inflate( R.layout.fragment_game_state,
32                              container, false );
33    }
34
35    public void onStart( ) {
36      super.onStart( );
37      View fragmentView = getView( );
38      TextView gameStateTV
39        = ( TextView ) fragmentView.findViewById( R.id.state_of_game );
40      gameStateTV.setText( getGameFromActivity( )
41                .currentIncompleteWord( ) );
42    }
43
44    public void onAttach( Context context ) {
45      super.onAttach( context );
46      if ( !( context instanceof Callbacks ) ) {
47        throw new IllegalStateException(
48          "Context must implement fragment's callbacks." );
49      }
50      mCallbacks = ( Callbacks ) context;
51    }
52
53    public void onDetach( ) {
54      super.onDetach( );
55      mCallbacks = sDummyCallbacks;
56    }
57
58    public WordGame getGameFromActivity( ) {
59      return mCallbacks.getGame( );
60    }
61  }
```

EXAMPLE 9.20 **The reusable** `GameStateFragment` **class, Hangman app, Version 6**

class to the MainActivity class via that interface. Inside the fragment class, whenever we call a MainActivity method, we add a method to the Callbacks interface and call that method from the fragment class. The MainActivity class implements the interface and thus must override that method. In this way, we effectively transfer the MainActivity method calls from the fragment class to the MainActivity class.

Another reusability issue is that the method getGame returns a Hangman reference. Thus, since getGame is in the Callbacks interface, which is inside the GameStateFragment class, our GameStateFragment class is only reusable with the Hangman class. To solve that problem, we create an interface, which we name WordGame, and make getGame return a WordGame reference instead. The WordGame interface only has one method, currentIncompleteWord. This is needed because we call that method inside the GameStateFragment class with the WordGame reference returned by getGame. Thus, the GameStateFragment class is now reusable with any activity that implements the Callbacks interface and with any class that implements the WordGame interface, which are both very simple and generic. In this app, we modify Hangman so that it implements WordGame.

Here is how that method transfer mechanism is implemented in the GameStateFragment class.

Before: Inside GameStateFragment (old implementation), from Example 9.13:

```
27  MainActivity fragmentActivity = ( MainActivity ) getActivity( );
28  gameStateTV.setText( fragmentActivity.getGame( )
29              .currentIncompleteWord( ) );
```

After: Inside GameStateFragment (new implementation), from Example 9.20:

```
12
13  private Callbacks mCallbacks = sDummyCallbacks;
14
15  public interface Callbacks {
16    public WordGame getGame( );
17  }
...
40  gameStateTV.setText( getGameFromActivity( )
41              .currentIncompleteWord( ) );
...
58  public WordGame getGameFromActivity( ) {
59    return mCallbacks.getGame( );
60  }
```

The call to getGameFromActivity at line 40 triggers a call by the mCallbacks instance variable, declared and initialized at line 13, to the getGame method of the Callbacks interface (declared at line 16), which will execute inside a class implementing the Callbacks interface and, therefore, implementing getGame.

At lines 19–23, we declare and instantiate sDummyCallbacks, an object of an anonymous class implementing the Callbacks interface. That anonymous class overrides the getGame method, returning `null`, at lines 20–22; `sDummyCallbacks` is assigned to the instance variable `mCallbacks` of type `Callbacks` at line 13.

The `mCallbacks` instance variable is meant to be a reference to the activity that this fragment belongs to. The `onAttach` method, inherited from the `Fragment` class, is overridden at lines 44–51. This method is called when this fragment is attached to an activity. Furthermore, when that method is called, we expect its parameter, `context`, to be an instance of a superclass of `Context` (most likely a superclass of `Activity`) that implements the `Callbacks` interface. If it is not (line 46), we throw an `IllegalStateException` at lines 47–48. If it is, the `context` parameter is typecast to `Callbacks` and is assigned to `mCallbacks` at line 50.

In this new implementation, there is no mention of the `MainActivity` class, and there is no mention of a method from the `MainActivity` class named `getGame`. The only requirement is that the `MainActivity` class, or any activity class that we use with the `GameStateFragment` class, implements the `Callbacks` interface. This, in turn, forces `MainActivity`, or any class that implements the `Callbacks` interface, to override the `getGame` method. Note that in this example, there is only one method in the `Callbacks` interface, but more generally, there could be several.

The `onDetach` method, inherited from the `Fragment` class, is overridden at lines 53–56. That method is called when this fragment is detached from its activity. It reassigns the default `Callbacks` object `sDummyCallbacks` to `mCallbacks` at line 55.

EXAMPLE 9.21 shows the class header of the updated `MainActivity` class, which now implements the `Callbacks` inner interface of `GameStateFragment`. There is no other change as compared to Example 9.19: the `getGame` method was already implemented before and is still the same, but it now overrides the `getGame` method of the `Callbacks` interface.

```
11
12    public class MainActivity extends AppCompatActivity
13          implements GameStateFragment.Callbacks {
14
```

EXAMPLE 9.21 The class header of the `MainActivity` class, Hangman app, Version 6

EXAMPLE 9.22 shows the `WordGame` interface, which declares the `currentIncompleteWord` method (line 4).

```
1    package com.jblearning.hangmanv6;
2
3    public interface WordGame {
4      public abstract String currentIncompleteWord( );
5    }
```

EXAMPLE 9.22 The `WordGame` interface, Hangman app, Version 6

EXAMPLE 9.23 shows the class header of the updated `Hangman` class, which now implements the `WordGame` interface. There is no other change as compared to Example 9.1: the `currentIncompleteWord` method was already implemented before and is still the same, but it now overrides the `currentIncompleteWord` method of the `WordGame` interface.

```
4
5     public class Hangman implements WordGame {
6
```

EXAMPLE 9.23 The class header of the `Hangman` class, Hangman app, Version 6

Note that we implemented `Callbacks` as an inner interface of `GameStateFragment` and `WordGame` as a separate interface. Either can be implemented as an inner interface or as a separate interface.

9.10 Improving the GUI: Processing the Keyboard Input Directly, Hangman, App Version 7

Version 6 works but it is annoying to have to click on the PLAY button every time. In Version 7, we enable play as soon as the user closes the keyboard. We can either eliminate or convert the PLAY button to a "Play Another Game" button, which you can do in the exercises.

The `EditText` is located inside the game state fragment, so event handling for Version 7 takes place in that fragment. `OnEditorActionListener`, a `public static` inner interface of the `TextView` class, provides the functionality to handle a key event inside an `EditText`. **TABLE 9.7** lists its only method, `onEditorAction`.

As always, in order to set up event handling, we do the following:

1. Write an event handler (a class extending a listener interface).
2. Instantiate an object of that class.
3. Register that object listener on one or more GUI components.

EXAMPLE 9.24 shows the updated `GameStateFragment` class. At lines 79–94, we define the `private` class `OnEditorHandler`, which implements the `TextView.OnEditorActionListener` interface. It overrides its only method, `onEditorAction`, at lines 80–93. It does the following:

TABLE 9.7 The `onEditorAction` method of the `TextView.OnEditorActionListener` interface

Method	Description
boolean onEditorAction(TextView view, int keyCode, KeyEvent event)	view is the TextView that was clicked; keyCode is an integer identifying the key that was pressed; event is the Key event.

```
1    package com.jblearning.hangmanv7;
2
3    import android.app.Fragment;
4    import android.content.Context;
5    import android.os.Bundle;
6    import android.view.KeyEvent;
7    import android.view.LayoutInflater;
8    import android.view.View;
9    import android.view.ViewGroup;
10   import android.view.inputmethod.InputMethodManager;
11   import android.widget.EditText;
12   import android.widget.TextView;
13
14   public class GameStateFragment extends Fragment {
15
16     private Callbacks mCallbacks = sDummyCallbacks;
17
18     public interface Callbacks {
19       public WordGame getGame( );
20       public void play( );
21     }
22
23     private static Callbacks sDummyCallbacks = new Callbacks( ) {
24       public WordGame getGame( ) {
25         return null;
26       }
27
28       public void play( ) {
29       }
30     };
31
32     public GameStateFragment( ) {
33     }
34
35     @Override
36     public View onCreateView( LayoutInflater inflater,
37                  ViewGroup container, Bundle savedInstanceState ) {
38       return inflater.inflate( R.layout.fragment_game_state,
39         container, false );
40     }
41
42     public void onStart( ) {
43       super.onStart( );
44       View fragmentView = getView( );
45       TextView gameStateTV
46         = ( TextView ) fragmentView.findViewById( R.id.state_of_game );
47       gameStateTV.setText( getGameFromActivity( )
48         .currentIncompleteWord( ) );
```

EXAMPLE 9.24 The `GameStateFragment` class, Hangman app, Version 7 (*Continued*)

```
49
50        // set up event handling for the keyboard
51        EditText answerET
52           = ( EditText ) fragmentView.findViewById( R.id.letter );
53        OnEditorHandler editorHandler = new OnEditorHandler( );
54        answerET.setOnEditorActionListener( editorHandler );
55     }
56
57     public void onAttach( Context context ) {
58        super.onAttach( context );
59        if ( !( context instanceof Callbacks ) ) {
60           throw new IllegalStateException(
61              "Context must implement fragment's callbacks." );
62        }
63        mCallbacks = ( Callbacks ) context;
64     }
65
66     public void onDetach( ) {
67        super.onDetach( );
68        mCallbacks = sDummyCallbacks;
69     }
70
71     public void play( ) {
72        mCallbacks.play( );
73     }
74
75     public WordGame getGameFromActivity( ) {
76        return mCallbacks.getGame( );
77     }
78
79     private class OnEditorHandler implements TextView.OnEditorActionListener {
80        public boolean onEditorAction( TextView v,
81                                       int keyCode, KeyEvent event ) {
82        // hide the keyboard
83        InputMethodManager inputManager = ( InputMethodManager )
84           getActivity( ).getSystemService( Context.INPUT_METHOD_SERVICE );
85        inputManager.hideSoftInputFromWindow(
86           getActivity( ).getCurrentFocus( ).getWindowToken( ),
87           InputMethodManager.HIDE_NOT_ALWAYS );
88
89        // play
90        play( );
91
92        return true;
93        }
94     }
95  }
```

EXAMPLE 9.24 The `GameStateFragment` class, Hangman app, Version 7

▶ Hides the keyboard (lines 82–87).

▶ Plays (lines 89–90).

Since we already have a `play` method in the `MainActivity` class, we can reuse its code. The existing `play` method accepts a `View` parameter, expected to be a `Button`, which the method does not actually use. We could call it and pass `null`, but it is not good practice to pass `null` to a method from another class, since in theory (and in general), it could use that parameter to call methods. Thus, we create an additional `play` method in the `MainActivity` class (see **EXAMPLE 9.25**) that accepts no parameter and does exactly the same thing as the existing `play` method (which we can leave as a do-nothing method—if we choose to delete it, we also need to delete the `android:` `onClick` attribute in the fragment_game_control.xml file). We use the same strategy as in Version 6 to transfer the call to the `play` method of `MainActivity` via a `play` method of the `Callbacks` interface (declared at line 20), which we call with the fragment's `play` method (lines 71–73). Thus, the call to the fragment's `play` method at line 90 triggers a call to the Callbacks' `play` method. In this way, we keep our fragment class reusable (with a class implementing the Callbacks interface).

In order to close a keyboard by code, we can use an `InputMethodManager` reference. The `InputMethodManager` class manages the interaction between an application and its current input method. That class does not have a constructor but we can obtain an `InputMethodManager` reference by calling the `getSystemService` of the `Context` class using an `Activity` reference (which is a `Context` reference since `Activity` inherits from `Context`).

The `getSystemService` method has the following API:

```
Object getSystemService( String nameOfService )
```

Its `String` parameter represents a service, and **TABLE 9.8** lists some of the possible values. Depending on the service specified, it returns a manager object reference for that service. For example, if we specify `LOCATION_SERVICE`, it returns a `LocationManager` reference that we can use to gather location data from the device's GPS system. If we specify `WIFI_SERVICE`, it returns a `WifiManager` reference that we can use to access data regarding the device's Wi-Fi connectivity. Because that method returns a generic `Object`, we need to typecast the returned object reference to what we expect. We want to obtain an `InputMethodManager` reference, so we pass the argument `Context.INPUT_METHOD_SERVICE` and cast the resulting object reference to an `InputMethodManager` as follows (and as in lines 83–84):

```
InputMethodManager inputManager = ( InputMethodManager )
getActivity( ).getSystemService( Context.INPUT_METHOD_SERVICE );
```

To close the keyboard, we use one of the `hideSoftInputFromWindow` methods of the `InputMethodManager` class, shown in **TABLE 9.9**. The first parameter has type `IBinder`, an interface that encapsulates a **remotable** object. A remotable object is an object that can be accessed outside its context via a proxy. We want to pass to `hideSoftInputFromWindow` an `IBinder` reference that represents the window that the current `View` (in this case the `EditText`) is attached to. We

TABLE 9.8 Selected `string` constants and their values, as well as the corresponding return type of the `getSystemService` method of the `Context` class when using one of those constants as the method's parameter

String Constant	String Value	getSystemService Return Type
POWER_SERVICE	power	PowerManager
LOCATION_SERVICE	location	LocationManager
WIFI_SERVICE	wifi	WifiManager
DOWNLOAD_SERVICE	download	DownloadManager
INPUT_METHOD_SERVICE	input_method	InputMethodManager

TABLE 9.9 Selected `hideSoftInputFromWindow` method of the `InputMethodManager` class

Method	Description
boolean hideSoftInputFromWindow(IBinder token, int flags)	token is the token of the Window making the request as returned by the getWindowToken method of the View class; flags specifies additional condition for hiding the soft input.

call the `getCurrentFocus` method of the `Activity` class with the current `Activity` object. It returns the `View` that has the focus in the current window. Using that `View`, we call the `get WindowToken` of the `View` class. It returns a unique token that identifies the window that this `View` is attached to. At line 86, we chain these two method calls using the expression:

```
getActivity( ).getCurrentFocus( ).getWindowToken( )
```

TABLE 9.10 shows the two constants of the `InputMethodManager` class that can be used as values for the second parameter of the `hideSoftInputFromWindow` method. Since the user explicitly opens the keyboard when trying to enter some input, we should not use the HIDE_ IMPLICIT_ONLY constant in this case. We use HIDE_NOT_ALWAYS, so the second argument of we method call at line 87 is:

```
InputMethodManager.HIDE_NOT_ALWAYS
```

When we run the app, play happens as soon as the keyboard closes. We no longer need to click on the PLAY button.

TABLE 9.10 Selected `int` constants of the `InputMethodManager` class to be used as the second parameter of `hideSoftInputFromWindow`

Constant	Value	Meaning
HIDE_IMPLICIT_ONLY	1	The soft input window should only be hidden if it was not explicitly open by the user.
HIDE_NOT_ALWAYS	2	The soft input window should normally be hidden unless it was originally forced open by code.

```
52
53    public void play( ) {
...     /* same code as earlier play( View view ) method */
100   }
101
102   public void play( View view ) {
103   }
104 }
```

EXAMPLE 9.25 Changes in the `MainActivity` class, Hangman app, Version 7

Chapter Summary

- Fragments were introduced in API level 11 to provide better support for large screen devices such as tablets.
- A fragment is a portion of an activity, and can help manage a portion of the screen. We can think of a fragment as a mini-activity within an activity.
- There can be several fragments within one activity.
- A fragment can have a user interface or simply perform some work in the background of an activity.
- A fragment has its own life-cycle methods but depends on its activity running.
- An activity can use the `getFragmentManager` method to access its fragment manager. With it, it can access and manage its fragments.
- A fragment can access its activity using the `getActivity` method.
- A fragment can be defined, created, and added to an activity using XML only, code only, or a mix of both.
- When creating and adding a fragment to an activity, we use the `FragmentTransaction` class. When adding a fragment, we can identify it with an id, a tag, or both.
- A fragment manager can find fragments either by id or by tag.
- A fragment can be reused in several activities.
- A fragment class should be coded so that it is reusable and not tied to a particular activity class. We can do this by using an inner interface inside the fragment class.

Exercises, Problems, and Projects

Multiple-Choice Exercises

1. Fragments were introduced with API level
   - 2
   - 8
   - 11
   - 13

2. The direct superclass of Fragment is
   - Content
   - Activity
   - Object
   - FragmentActivity

3. How many fragments can there be in one activity?
   - 0
   - 1 only
   - 0 or more

4. What method of the following is not a life-cycle method of a fragment?
   - onStart
   - onCreate
   - onRestart
   - onStop

5. What method can be used by a fragment to access its activity?
   - activity
   - getActivity
   - getFragment
   - findActivity

6. What class can be used by an activity to access its fragments?
   - FragmentTransaction
   - Activity
   - FragmentManager
   - Manager

7. What method of the FragmentTransaction class is used to add a fragment to an activity?
   - add
   - addFragment
   - insert
   - insertFragment

8. An activity can retrieve one of its fragment via its
   - tag only
   - id only
   - tag or id
   - it cannot

9. We can make a fragment class reusable by transferring all the method calls by its activity inside the fragment class to the activity class via
   - an inner class
   - an interface
   - it is not possible

Fill in the Code

10. Inside an activity class, retrieve the fragment manager.

11. Inside an activity class, add a fragment of type MyFragment and place it inside a ViewGroup element whose id is my_id.

    ```
    // fm is a FragmentManager reference
    FragmentTransaction transaction = fm.beginTransaction( );
    // Your code goes here
    ```

12. Inside an activity class, add a fragment of type MyFragment and place it inside a ViewGroup element whose id is my_id. Give it the tag my_tag.

    ```
    // fm is a FragmentManager reference
    FragmentTransaction transaction = fm.beginTransaction( );
    // Your code goes here
    ```

13. Inside an activity class, add a fragment of type MyFragment that does not have a user interface. Give it the tag my_tag.

    ```
    // fm is a FragmentManager reference
    FragmentTransaction transaction = fm.beginTransaction( );
    // Your code goes here
    ```

14. Inside a fragment class, write the code so that the fragment is inflated from the my_fragment.xml file.

```
public View onCreateView( LayoutInflater inflater, ViewGroup
      container, Bundle savedInstanceState ) {
  // Your code goes here

}
```

15. Inside a fragment class, write the code to retrieve the activity that this fragment belongs to. Assume that the activity type is MyActivity.

```
// Your code goes here
```

16. The following fragment class is not reusable. Change it so that it is.

```
package com.you.myapp;
import android.app.Fragment;
public class MyFragment extends Fragment {
  public MyFragment( ) {
  }
  public void onStart( ) {
    super.onStart( );
    MyActivity activity = ( MyActivity ) getActivity( );
    activity.update( );
  }
}
// Your code goes here
```

Write an App

17. Write a mini app containing one activity using two fragments as shown below:

18. Write a mini app containing one activity using three fragments as shown below:

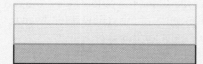

19. Write a mini app containing one activity using four fragments as shown below:

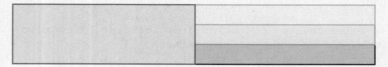

20. Write an app containing one activity using two fragments (one left and one right) as follows:
The left fragment contains a button and the right fragment contains a label that simulates a traffic light, red when we start. When the user clicks on the button, the label changes to green. When the user clicks on the button again, the label changes to yellow. When the user clicks on the button again, the label changes to red, and so on. Even though the functionality is simple, you should include a Model for this app.

21. Write an app containing one activity using several fragments (one at the top and one or more below) as follows:
The top fragment should occupy one fourth of the screen and contain three radio buttons, showing 1, 2, and 3. When the user selects one of them, the bottom of the screen displays the corresponding number of fragments (use a different color for each), and they all should occupy the same amount of space. For example, if the user clicks on the radio button that says 2, then two fragments of equal height are displayed at the bottom of the screen.

22. Write an app containing one activity using two fragments (one on top and one at the bottom) as follows:
The app simulates a flashlight. The top fragment comprises 20% of the screen and contains an on and off switch. You can use the Switch class for this. The bottom fragment comprises 80% of the screen and is black. When the user turns the switch on, the bottom fragment turns yellow. When the user turns the switch off, the bottom fragment reverts back to black. Even though the functionality is simple, you should include a Model for this app.

23. Write an app containing one activity using two fragments (one on top and one at the bottom) as follows:
The app simulates a dimmer. The top fragment comprises 20% of the screen and contains a slider. You can use the SeekBar class for this. The bottom fragment comprises 80% of the screen and is yellow. When the user moves the slider, the yellow fades. You can assume that the dimmer slider controls the transparency of the yellow color. Even though the functionality is simple, you should include a Model for this app.

24. Write an app containing one activity using two fragments (one on the left and one on the right) as follows:
The app simulates a traffic light. The left fragment contains a button and the right fragment contains three labels, the top one is red when we start and the others are transparent. When the user clicks on the button, the top label becomes transparent and the bottom label changes to green. When the user clicks on the button again, the bottom label becomes transparent and the middle label changes to yellow. When the user clicks on the button again, the middle label becomes transparent and the top label changes to red, and so on. Even though the functionality is simple, you should include a Model for this app.

25. Write an app containing one activity using two fragments (one at the top and one below) as follows:
The top fragment should occupy one fourth of the screen and contains a button, the bottom fragment three fourths of the screen. When the user clicks on the button, a tic-tac-toe game shows up inside the bottom fragment. Play should be enabled. You should include a Model for the tic-tac-toe game.

26. Write an app containing one activity using two fragments (one at the top occupying 75% of the space and one below occupying 25% of the space) as follows:
The app generates a random number between 1 and 5 and the user needs to guess it. The bottom fragment shows an EditText asking the user to enter a number. The top fragment shows some feedback to the user (for example, "You won" or "You lost"). Even though the functionality is simple, you should include a Model for this app.

27. Write the same app as in exercise 26 but add a third fragment, this one invisible: it provides the functionality of generating a random number.

28. Write an app that improves this chapter's app. On the left pane, add another fragment that contains a button so that the user can play another game by clicking on it.

29. Write the same app as in exercise 28 but add a file that stores a large number (1,000 or more) of potential words. The Hangman constructor should pick one at random from the file. Add an invisible fragment to instantiate a Hangman object and start the game with the word selected.

CHAPTER TEN

Using Libraries and Their APIs: Speech Recognition and Maps

CHAPTER CONTENTS

Introduction

The Android framework provides some powerful libraries for app developers. In this chapter, we learn how to use some of these libraries. We explore libraries for speech recognition and maps. We build a simple app including two activities. The first activity asks the user to say a location and compares it to a list of locations. If there is a match, the second activity displays a map with annotations for that location.

10.1 Voice Recognition

In order to test an app that involves speech recognition, we need an actual device—the emulator cannot recognize speech. Furthermore, some devices may not have speech recognition capabilities, so we should test for that. When the user says a word, the speech recognizer returns a list of possible matches for that word. We can then process that list. Our code can restrict what is returned in that list, for example, we can specify the maximum number of returned items, their confidence level, etc. **FIGURE 10.1** shows our app Version 0, using the standard user interface for speech recognition running inside the emulator.

FIGURE 10.1 Show A Map app, Version 0, running inside the tablet, expecting the user to speak

TABLE 10.1 Selected constants of the `RecognizerIntent` class

Constant	Description
ACTION_WEB_SEARCH	Use with an activity that searches the web with the spoken words.
ACTION_RECOGNIZE_SPEECH	Use with an activity that asks the user to speak.
EXTRA_MAX_RESULTS	Key to specify the maximum number of results to return.
EXTRA_PROMPT	Key to add text next to the microphone.
EXTRA_LANGUAGE_MODEL	Key to specify the language model.
LANGUAGE_MODEL_FREE_FORM	Value that specifies regular speech.
LANGUAGE_MODEL_WEB_SEARCH	Value that specifies that spoken words are used as web search terms.
EXTRA_RESULTS	Key to retrieve an ArrayList of results.
EXTRA_CONFIDENCE_SCORES	Key to retrieve a confidence scores array for results.

The `RecognizerIntent` class includes constants to support speech recognition when starting an intent. **TABLE 10.1** lists some of these constants. Most of them are `String`s.

To create a speech recognition intent, we use the `ACTION_RECOGNIZE_SPEECH` constant as the argument of the `Intent` constructor, as in the following statement:

```
Intent intent = new Intent( RecognizerIntent.ACTION_RECOGNIZE_SPEECH );
```

To create a web search intent that uses speech input, we use the `ACTION_WEB_SEARCH` constant of the `RecognizerIntent` class as the argument of the `Intent` constructor, as in the following statement:

```
Intent searchIntent = new Intent( RecognizerIntent.ACTION_WEB_SEARCH );
```

Once we have created the intent, we can refine it by placing data in it using the `putExtra` method, using constants of the `RecognizerIntent` class as keys for these values. For example, if we want to display a prompt, we use the key `EXTRA_PROMPT` and provide a `String` value for it as in the following statement:

```
intent.putExtra( RecognizerIntent.EXTRA_PROMPT, "What city?" );
```

We can use the `EXTRA_LANGUAGE_MODEL` constant as a key, specifying the value of the `LANGUAGE_MODEL_FREE_FORM` constant to tell the system to interpret the words said as regular speech or specifying the value of the `LANGUAGE_MODEL_WEB_SEARCH` constant to interpret the words said as a string of search words for the web.

TABLE 10.2 Useful classes and methods to assess if a device recognizes speech

Class	Method	Description
Context	PackageManager getPackageManager( )	Returns a PackageManager instance.
PackageManager	List queryIntentActivities(Intent intent, int flags)	Returns a list of ResolveInfo objects, representing activities that can be supported with intent. The flags parameter can be specified to restrict the results returned.
ResolveInfo		Contains information describing how well an intent is matched against an intent filter.

Not all devices support speech recognition. When building an app that uses speech recognition, it is a good idea to check if the Android device supports it.

We can use the `PackageManager` class, from the `android.content.pm` package, to retrieve information related to application packages installed on a device, in this case related to speech recognition. The `getPackageManager` method, from the `Context` class, which `Activity` inherits from, returns a `PackageManager` instance. Inside an activity, we can use it as follows:

```
PackageManager manager = getPackageManager( );
```

Using a `PackageManager` reference, we can call the `queryIntentActivities` method, shown in **TABLE 10.2** along with the `getPackageManager` method and the `ResolveInfo` class, to test if a type of intent is supported by the current device. We specify the type of intent as the first argument to that method, and it returns a list of `ResolveInfo` objects, one object per activity supported by the device that matches the intent. If that list is not empty, the type of intent is supported. If that list is empty, it is not.

We can use the `ACTION_RECOGNIZE_SPEECH` constant of the `RecognizerIntent`, to build an `Intent` object and pass that `Intent` as the first argument of the `queryIntentActivities` method. We pass 0 as the second argument, which does not place any restriction on what the method returns. Thus, we can use the following pattern to test if the current device supports speech recognition:

```
Intent intent = new Intent( RecognizerIntent. ACTION_RECOGNIZE_SPEECH );
List<ResolveInfo> list = manager.queryIntentActivities( intent, 0 );
if( list.size( ) > 0 ) { // speech recognition is supported
  // ask the user to say something and process it
} else {
  // provide an alternative way for user input
}
```

10.2 **Voice Recognition Part A, App Version 0**

In Version 0 of our app, we will only have one activity: we ask the user to say a word and we provide a list of possible matches for that word in Logcat. Once again, we choose the Empty Activity template. This will change in Version 1 when we add a map to our app. **EXAMPLE 10.1** shows the `MainActivity` class. It is divided into three methods:

- ▶ In the `onCreate` method (lines 17–32), we set the content View and check if speech recognition is supported. If it is, we call the listen method. If it is not, we display a message to that effect.
- ▶ In the `listen` method (lines 34–42), we set up the speech recognition activity.
- ▶ In the `onActivityResult` method (lines 44–63), we process the list of words understood by the device after the user speaks.

At line 22, we get a `PackageManager` reference. With it, we call `queryIntentActivities` at lines 23–24, passing an `Intent` reference of type `RecognizerIntent.ACTION_RECOGNIZE_SPEECH`, and assign the resulting list to `listOfMatches`. We test if `listOfMatches` contains more than one element at line 25, which means that speech recognition is supported by the current device, and call `listen` at line 26 if it does. If it does not, we show a temporary message at lines 28–30. We use the `Toast` class, shown in **TABLE 10.3**, a convenient class to show a quick message on the screen for a small period of time that still lets the user interact with the current activity.

```
1    package com.jblearning.showamapv0;
2
3    import android.content.Intent;
4    import android.content.pm.PackageManager;
5    import android.content.pm.ResolveInfo;
6    import android.os.Bundle;
7    import android.speech.RecognizerIntent;
8    import android.support.v7.app.AppCompatActivity;
9    import android.util.Log;
10   import android.widget.Toast;
11   import java.util.ArrayList;
12   import java.util.List;
13
14   public class MainActivity extends AppCompatActivity {
15     private static final int CITY_REQUEST = 1;
16
17     protected void onCreate( Bundle savedInstanceState ) {
18       super.onCreate( savedInstanceState );
19       setContentView( R.layout.activity_main );
20
```

EXAMPLE 10.1 The `MainActivity` class, capturing a word from the user, Version 0 (*Continued*)

```
21        // Test if device supports speech recognition
22        PackageManager manager = getPackageManager( );
23        List<ResolveInfo> listOfMatches = manager.queryIntentActivities(
24          new Intent( RecognizerIntent.ACTION_RECOGNIZE_SPEECH ), 0 );
25        if( listOfMatches.size( ) > 0 )
26          listen( );
27        else { // speech recognition not supported
28          Toast.makeText( this,
29            "Sorry - Your device does not support speech recognition",
30            Toast.LENGTH_LONG ).show( );
31        }
32      }
33
34      private void listen( ) {
35        Intent listenIntent =
36          new Intent( RecognizerIntent.ACTION_RECOGNIZE_SPEECH );
37        listenIntent.putExtra( RecognizerIntent.EXTRA_PROMPT, "What city?" );
38        listenIntent.putExtra( RecognizerIntent.EXTRA_LANGUAGE_MODEL,
39          RecognizerIntent.LANGUAGE_MODEL_FREE_FORM );
40        listenIntent.putExtra( RecognizerIntent.EXTRA_MAX_RESULTS, 5 );
41        startActivityForResult( listenIntent, CITY_REQUEST );
42      }
43
44      protected void onActivityResult( int requestCode,
45                                       int resultCode, Intent data ) {
46        super.onActivityResult( requestCode, resultCode, data );
47        if( requestCode == CITY_REQUEST && resultCode == RESULT_OK ) {
48          // retrieve list of possible words
49          ArrayList<String> returnedWords =
50            data.getStringArrayListExtra( RecognizerIntent.EXTRA_RESULTS );
51          // retrieve array of scores for returnedWords
52          float [ ] scores = data.getFloatArrayExtra(
53            RecognizerIntent.EXTRA_CONFIDENCE_SCORES );
54
55          // display results
56          int i = 0;
57          for( String word : returnedWords ) {
58            if( scores != null && i < scores.length )
59              Log.w( "MainActivity", word + ": " + scores[i] );
60            i++;
61          }
62        }
63      }
64    }
```

EXAMPLE 10.1 The `MainActivity` class, capturing a word from the user, Version 0

TABLE 10.3 Constants and selected methods of the `Toast` class

Constant	Description
LENGTH_LONG	Use this constant for a Toast lasting 3.5 seconds.
LENGTH_SHORT	Use this constant for a Toast lasting 2 seconds.
Method	**Description**
static Toast makeText(Context context, CharSequence message, int duration)	Static method to create a Toast in context, displaying message for duration seconds.
void show( )	Shows this Toast.

TABLE 10.4 The `putExtra` and `get...Extra` methods of the `Intent` class

Method	Description
Intent putExtra(String key, DataType value)	Stores value in this Intent, mapping it to key.
Intent putExtra(String key, DataType [ ] values)	Stores the array values in this Intent, mapping it to key.
DataType getDateTypeExtra(String key, DataType defaultValue)	Retrieves the value that was mapped to key. If there is not any, defaultValue is returned. DataType is either a primitive data type or a String.
DataType [ ] getDateTypeArrayExtra(String key)	Retrieves the array that was mapped to key.

Inside the `listen` method, at lines 35–36, we create and instantiate `listenIntent`, a speech recognition intent. Before starting an activity for it at line 41, we specify a few attributes for it at lines 37–40 by calling the `putExtra` methods of the `Intent` class, shown in **TABLE 10.4**. At line 37, we assign the value `What city?` to the `EXTRA_PROMPT` key so that it shows on the screen next to the microphone. At lines 38–39, we specify that the expected speech is regular human speech by setting the value of the key `EXTRA_LANGUAGE_MODEL` to `LANGUAGE_MODEL_FREE_FORM`. At line 40, we set the maximum number of words in the returned list to 5. We start the activity for `listenIntent` at line 41, and we associate it with the request code 1, the value defined by the constant `CITY_REQUEST` (line 15). When it finishes, the `onActivityResult` method is automatically called and the value of its first parameter should be the value of that request code, 1.

After the `listen` method executes, the user is presented with a user interface showing a microphone and the extra prompt, in this example `What city?`, and has a few seconds to say something. After that, the code executes inside the `onActivityResult` method, inherited from the `Activity` class. We call the `super onActivityResult` method at line 46, although it is a do-nothing method at the time of this writing, but that could change in the future. At line 47, we test if this method call corresponds to our earlier activity request and if the request was successful: we do this by checking the value of the request code, stored in the `requestCode` parameter, and the value of the result code, stored in the `resultCode` parameter. If they are equal to 1 (the value of `CITY_REQUEST`) and `RESULT_OK`, then we know that that method call is for the correct activity and that it was successful. `RESULT_OK` is a constant of the `Activity` class whose value is -1. It can be used to test if the result code of an activity is successful. The third parameter of the method is an `Intent` reference. With it, we can retrieve the results of the speech recognition process. We retrieve the list of possible words understood by the speech recognizer at lines 48–50 and assign it to the `ArrayList returnedWords`. We call the `getStringArrayListExtra` method with `data`, the `Intent` parameter of the method, and use the `EXTRA_RESULTS` key, shown in Table 10.1, in order to retrieve its corresponding value, an `ArrayList` of `Strings`. We retrieve the array of corresponding confidence scores assessed by the speech recognizer at lines 51–53 and assign it to the array `scores`.

In this version, we output the elements of `returnedWords` along with their scores to Logcat at lines 55–61.

We do not need the Hello world! label. Thus, we edit the activity_main.xml file and remove the `TextView` element.

We should not expect the speech recognition capability of the device to be perfect. Sometimes the speech recognizer understands correctly, sometimes it does not. And sometimes we can say the same word, slightly differently or with a different accent, and it can be understood differently. **FIGURE 10.2** shows a possible Logcat output when running the app and saying `Washington`, while **FIGURE 10.3** shows a possible Logcat output when running the app and saying `Paris`.

So when we process the user's speech, it is important to take these possibilities into account. There are many ways to do it. One way to do that is to provide feedback to the user by writing the word or words on the screen, or even having the device repeat the word or words to make sure the device understood the word correctly. However, this process can take extra time and be annoying to the user. We can also process all the elements of the list returned and compare them to our own list of words that we expect, and process the first matching word. We do that in Version 1. Another strategy is to try to process the elements of that list one at a time until we are successful processing one.

```
Paris: 0.48488528
parents: 0.0
paradise: 0.0
parent: 0.0
parrot: 0.0
```

```
Washington: 0.98762906
```

FIGURE 10.2 Possible Logcat output from Example 10.1 when the user says Washington

FIGURE 10.3 Possible Logcat output from Example 10.1 when the user says Paris

Note that if we failed to speak within a few seconds, the user interface showing the microphone goes away and it is then too late to speak. If we want to give more control to the user, we can include a button in the user interface, which when clicked, triggers a call to the listen method and brings up the microphone again.

10.3 Using the Google Maps Activity Template, App Version 1

The `com.google.android.gms.maps` and `com.google.android.gms.maps.model` packages include classes to display a map and place annotations on it. Depending on which version of Android Studio we use, we may need to update Google Play services and Google APIs using the SDK manager. Appendix C shows these steps.

The Google Maps Activity template already includes the skeleton code to display a map. Furthermore, it makes the necessary Google Play services libraries available to the project in the build. gradle (Module: app) file, as shown in Appendix C. When creating the project, instead of choosing the Empty Activity template as we usually do, we choose the Google Maps Activity template (see **FIGURE 10.4**). As **FIGURE 10.5** shows, the default names for the `Activity` class, the layout XML file, and the app title are MapsActivity, activity_main.xml, and Map, respectively.

In addition to the usual files, the google_maps_api.xml file is also automatically generated, and is located in the values directory. **EXAMPLE 10.2** shows it.

FIGURE 10.4 Choosing the Google Maps Activity template

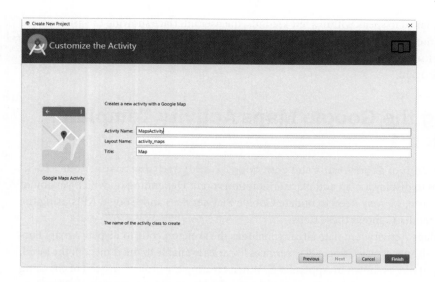

FIGURE 10.5 The names of the main files created by the template

```
1   <resources>
2       <!--
3       TODO: Before you run your application, you need a Google Maps API key.
4
5       To get one, follow this link, follow the directions and press "Create"
    at the end:
6
7       https://console.developers.google.com/flows/
    enableapi?apiid=maps_android_backend&keyType=CLIENT_SIDE_
    ANDROID&r=39:5D:BF:75:02:BE:44:45:3D:DE:9B:DA:AC:D5:9C:1B:D7:A7:27:07%3Bcom.
    jblearning.showamapv1
8
9       You can also add your credentials to an existing key, using this line:
10      39:5D:BF:75:02:BE:44:45:3D:DE:9B:DA:AC:D5:9C:1B:D7:A7:27:07;com.
    jblearning.showamapv1
11
12      Alternatively, follow the directions here:
13      https://developers.google.com/maps/documentation/android/start#get-key
14
15      Once you have your key (it starts with "AIza"), replace the
    "google_maps_key"
16      string in this file.
17      -->
18      <string name="google_maps_key" templateMergeStrategy="preserve"
    translatable="false">YOUR_KEY_HERE</string>
19  </resources>
```

EXAMPLE 10.2 The google_maps_api.xml file, Show A Map app, Version 1

```
18    <string name="google_maps_key" templateMergeStrategy="preserve"
19          translatable="false">AIza█████████████████W-Q4</string>
```

FIGURE 10.6 Lines 18–19 of the google_maps_api.xml file, with the key partially hidden

At line 18, we replace YOUR_KEY_HERE with an actual key obtained from Google based on the instructions in Appendix C. After editing, the author's lines 18–19 look like the one shown in **FIGURE 10.6**.

The layout file automatically generated by the template is called activity_maps.xml, as shown in **EXAMPLE 10.3**. It is typical to place a map inside a fragment (line 1). The type of fragment used here is a `SupportMapFragment` (line 2), a subclass of the `Fragment` class and the simplest way to include a map in an app. It occupies its whole parent View (lines 6–7) and has an id (line 1). Thus, we can retrieve it programmatically and change the characteristics of the map, for example, move the center of the map, or add annotations to it.

```
1    <fragment android:id="@+id/map"
2              android:name="com.google.android.gms.maps.SupportMapFragment"
3              xmlns:android="http://schemas.android.com/apk/res/android"
4              xmlns:map="http://schemas.android.com/apk/res-auto"
5              xmlns:tools="http://schemas.android.com/tools"
6              android:layout_width="match_parent"
7              android:layout_height="match_parent"
8              tools:context="com.jblearning.showamapv1.MapsActivity"/>
```

EXAMPLE 10.3 The activity_maps.xml file, Show A Map app, Version 1

The AndroidManifest.xml file already includes two additional elements, `uses-permission` and `meta-data`, to retrieve maps from Google Play services, as shown in **EXAMPLE 10.4**. The main additions as compared to the typical skeleton AndroidManifest.xml file are as follows:

▶ The activity element is of type `MapsActivity`.
▶ There is a `uses-permission` element specifying that the app can access the current device location.
▶ There is a `meta-data` element that specifies key information.

To request a permission in the AndroidManifest.xml file, we use the following syntax:

```
<uses-permission android:name="permission_name"/>
```

TABLE 10.5 lists some `String` constants of the `Manifest.permission` class that we can use as values in lieu of `permission_name`.

```
1    <?xml version="1.0" encoding="utf-8"?>
2    <manifest package="com.jblearning.showamapv1"
3              xmlns:android="http://schemas.android.com/apk/res/android">
4      <!--
5        The ACCESS_COARSE/FINE_LOCATION permissions are not required to use
6        Google Maps Android API v2, but you must specify either coarse or
7        fine location permissions for the 'MyLocation' functionality.
8      -->
9      <uses-permission
10       android:name="android.permission.ACCESS_FINE_LOCATION"/>
11
12     <application
13       android:allowBackup="true"
14       android:icon="@mipmap/ic_launcher"
15       android:label="@string/app_name"
16       android:supportsRtl="true"
17       android:theme="@style/AppTheme">
18
19       <!--
20         The API key for Google Maps-based APIs is defined as a string
21         resource (See the file "res/values/google_maps_api.xml").
22         Note that the API key is linked to the encryption key used to
23         sign the APK.
24         You need a different API key for each encryption key, including
25         the release key that is used to sign the APK for publishing.
26         You can define the keys for the debug and release targets in
27         src/debug/ and src/release/.
28       -->
29       <meta-data
30         android:name="com.google.android.geo.API_KEY"
31         android:value="@string/google_maps_key"/>
32
33       <activity
34         android:name=".MapsActivity"
35         android:label="@string/title_activity_maps">
36         <intent-filter>
37           <action android:name="android.intent.action.MAIN"/>
38
39           <category android:name="android.intent.category.LAUNCHER"/>
40         </intent-filter>
41       </activity>
42     </application>
43
44   </manifest>
```

EXAMPLE 10.4 The AndroidManifest.xml file, Show A Map app, Version 1

TABLE 10.5 Selected constants from the `Manifest.permission` class

Constant	Description
INTERNET	Allows an app to access the Internet.
ACCESS_NETWORK_STATE	Allows an app to access the information about a network.
WRITE_EXTERNAL_STORAGE	Allows an app to write to an external storage.
ACCESS_COARSE_LOCATION	Allows an app to access an approximate location for the device derived from cell towers and Wi-Fi.
ACCESS_FINE_LOCATION	Allows an app to access a precise location for the device derived from GPS, cell towers, and Wi-Fi.
RECORD_AUDIO	Allows an app to record audio.

Each app must declare what permissions are required by the app. When a user installs an app, the user is told about all the permissions that the app requires and has the opportunity to cancel the install at that time if he or she does not feel comfortable granting these permissions.

At lines 9–10, the automatically generated code includes a `uses-permission` element so that the app can use the device location using the GPS. At lines 29–31, the code includes a `meta-data` element to specify the value of the key for android maps. At lines 33–35, the code defines an `activity` element for our `MapsActivity` activity. At lines 36–40, we specify that it is the first activity to be launched when the app starts.

The `com.google.android.gms.maps` package provides us with classes to show maps and modify them. **TABLE 10.6** shows some of its selected classes. The `LatLng` class is part of the `com.google.android.gms.maps.model` package.

TABLE 10.6 Selected classes from the `com.google.android.gms.maps` and the `com.google.android.gms.maps.model` packages

Class	Description
SupportMapFragment	A container that contains a map.
GoogleMap	The main class for managing maps.
CameraUpdateFactory	Contains static methods to create CameraUpdate objects.
CameraUpdate	Encapsulates a camera move, such as a position change or zoom level change or both.
LatLng	Encapsulates a location on Earth using its latitude and longitude.

TABLE 10.7 The `getMapSync` method of the `SupportMapFragment` class and the `mapReady` method of the `OnMapReadyCallback` interface

Class or Interface	Method	Description
SupportMapFragment	void getMapAsync(OnMapReadyCallback callback)	Sets up callback so that its mapReady method will be called when the map is ready.
OnMapReadyCallback	void onMapReady(GoogleMap map)	This method is called when the map is instantiated and ready. This method needs to be implemented.

The `GoogleMap` class is the central class for modifying the characteristics of a map and handling map events. Our starting point is a `SupportMapFragment` object, which we can either retrieve through its id from a layout, or can construct programmatically. In order to modify the map that is contained in that `SupportMapFragment`, we need a `GoogleMap` reference to it. We can get the parameter by calling the `getMapAsync` method of the `SupportMapFragment` class, shown in **TABLE 10.7**.

The `OnMapReadyCallback` interface contains only one method, `onMapReady`, also shown in Table 10.7. The `onMapReady` method accepts one parameter, a `GoogleMap`. When the method is called, its `GoogleMap` parameter is instantiated and guaranteed not to be `null`.

The following code sequence will get a `GoogleMap` reference from a `SupportMapFragment` named `fragment` inside a class implementing the `OnMapReadyCallback` interface.

```
// Assuming fragment is a reference to a SupportMapFragment
GoogleMap map;
// assuming that this "is a" OnMapReadyCallback
fragment.getMapAsync( this );
public void onMapReady( GoogleMap googleMap ) {
  map = googleMap;
}
```

In order to modify a map, for example, its center point and its zoom level, we use the `animateCamera` and `moveCamera` methods of the `GoogleMap` class, which all take a `CameraUpdate` parameter. The `CameraUpdate` class encapsulates a **camera** move. A camera shows us the map we are looking at: if we move the camera, the map moves. We can also add annotations to a map using `addMarker`, `addCircle`, and other methods from the `GoogleMap` class. **TABLE 10.8** shows some of these methods.

In order to create a `CameraUpdate`, we use `static` methods of the `CameraUpdateFactory` class. **TABLE 10.9** shows some of these methods. A `CameraUpdate` object contains position and zoom level values. Zoom levels vary from 2.0 to 21.0. Zoom level 21.0 is the closest to the earth and shows the greatest level of details.

TABLE 10.8 Selected methods of the `GoogleMap` class

Method	Description
void animateCamera(CameraUpdate update)	Animates the camera position (and modifies the map) from the current position to update.
void animateCamera(CameraUpdate update, int ms, GoogleMap. CancelableCallback callback)	Animates the camera position (and modifies the map) from the current position to update, in ms (milliseconds). The onCancel method of callback is called if the task is cancelled. If the task is completed, then the onFinish method of the callback is called.
void moveCamera(CameraUpdate update)	Moves, without animation, the camera position (and modifies the map) from the current position to update.
void setMapType(int type)	Sets the type of map to be displayed: the constants MAP_TYPE_NORMAL, MAP_TYPE_SATELLITE, MAP_TYPE_TERRAIN, MAP_TYPE_NONE, and MAP_TYPE_HYBRID of the GoogleMap class can be used for type.
Marker addMarker(MarkerOptions options)	Adds a marker to this Map and returns it; options defines the marker.
Circle addCircle(CircleOptions options)	Adds a circle to this Map and returns it; options defines the circle.
Polygon addPolygon(PolygonOptions options)	Adds a polygon to this Map and returns it; options defines the polygon.
void setOnMapClickListener(GoogleMap. OnMapClickListener listener)	Sets a callback method that is automatically called when the user taps on the map; listener must be an instance of a class implementing the GoogleMap.OnMapClickListener interface and overriding its onMapClick(LatLng) method.

Often, we want to change the position of the center of the map. If we know the latitude and longitude coordinates of that point, we can use the `LatLng` class to create one using this constructor:

```
LatLng( double latitude, double longitude )
```

Thus, if we have a reference to a `MapFragment` named `fragment`, we can change the position of its map using the `moveCamera` method of the `GoogleMap` class as follows:

```
// someLatitute and someLongitude represent some location on Earth
GoogleMap map = fragment.getMap( );
LatLng newCenter = new LatLng( someLatitude, someLongitude );
CameraUpdate update1 = CameraUpdateFactory.newLatLng( newCenter );
map.moveCamera( update1 );
```

TABLE 10.9 Selected methods of the `CameraUpdateFactory` class

Method	Description
CameraUpdate newLatLng(LatLng location)	Returns a CameraUpdate that moves a map to location.
CameraUpdate newLatLngZoom(LatLng location, float zoom)	Returns a CameraUpdate that moves a map to location with zoom as the zoom level.
CameraUpdate zoomIn( )	Returns a CameraUpdate that zooms in.
CameraUpdate zoomOut( )	Returns a CameraUpdate that zooms out.
CameraUpdate zoomTo(float level)	Returns a CameraUpdate that zooms to the zoom level level.

We can then zoom in, using the `zoomIn` method of the `GoogleMap` class as follows:

```
CameraUpdate update2 = CameraUpdateFactory.zoomIn( );
map.animateCamera( update2 );
```

If we want to directly zoom to level 10, we can use the `zoomTo` method of the `GoogleMap` class as follows:

```
CameraUpdate update3 = CameraUpdateFactory.zoomTo( 10.0f );
map.animateCamera( update3 );
```

EXAMPLE 10.5 shows the `MapsActivity` class. It inherits from `FragmentActivity` (line 13) and `OnMapReadyCallback` (line 14). The map-related classes are imported at lines 6–11. This class inflates the activity_maps.xml layout file and then places a marker at Sydney, Australia.

A `GoogleMap` instance variable `mMap`, is declared at line 16. The `onCreate` method (lines 19–27) inflates the XML layout file at line 21, retrieves the map fragment at lines 24–25, and calls the `getMapSync` method with it at line 26.

The `onMapReady` method (lines 29–48) is automatically called when the map is ready. We assign its `GoogleMap` parameter to our `mMap` instance variable at line 41. At line 44, we create a `LatLng` reference with latitude and longitude values for Sydney, Australia. At lines 45–46, we add a marker to the map whose title is "Marker in Sydney" at that location using chained method calls and an anonymous `MarkerOptions` object. **TABLE 10.10** shows the constructor and various methods of the `MarkerOptions` class. This is equivalent to the following code sequence:

```
MarkerOptions options = new MarkerOptions( );
options.position( sydney );
options.title( "Marker in Sydney" );
mMap.addMarker( options );
```

```
1    package com.jblearning.showamapv1;
2
3    import android.os.Bundle;
4    import android.support.v4.app.FragmentActivity;
5
6    import com.google.android.gms.maps.CameraUpdateFactory;
7    import com.google.android.gms.maps.GoogleMap;
8    import com.google.android.gms.maps.OnMapReadyCallback;
9    import com.google.android.gms.maps.SupportMapFragment;
10   import com.google.android.gms.maps.model.LatLng;
11   import com.google.android.gms.maps.model.MarkerOptions;
12
13   public class MapsActivity extends FragmentActivity
14                             implements OnMapReadyCallback {
15
16     private GoogleMap mMap;
17
18     @Override
19     protected void onCreate( Bundle savedInstanceState ) {
20       super.onCreate( savedInstanceState );
21       setContentView( R.layout.activity_maps );
22       // Obtain the SupportMapFragment and get notified
23       // when the map is ready to be used.
24       SupportMapFragment mapFragment = ( SupportMapFragment )
25         getSupportFragmentManager( ).findFragmentById( R.id.map );
26       mapFragment.getMapAsync( this );
27     }
28
29     /**
30      * Manipulates the map once available.
31      * This callback is triggered when the map is ready to be used.
32      * This is where we can add markers or lines, add listeners or move the
33      * camera. In this case, we just add a marker near Sydney, Australia.
34      * If Google Play services is not installed on the device, the user
35      * will be prompted to install it inside the SupportMapFragment. This
36      * method will only be triggered once the user has installed Google Play
37      * services and returned to the app.
38      */
39     @Override
40     public void onMapReady( GoogleMap googleMap ) {
41       mMap = googleMap;
42
43       // Add a marker in Sydney and move the camera
44       LatLng sydney = new LatLng( -34, 151 );
45       mMap.addMarker( new MarkerOptions( ).position( sydney )
46                                          .title( "Marker in Sydney" ) );
47       mMap.moveCamera( CameraUpdateFactory.newLatLng( sydney ) );
48     }
49   }
```

EXAMPLE 10.5 The MapsActivity class, Show A Map app, Version 1

TABLE 10.10 Selected methods of the `MarkerOptions` class

Constructor	Description
MarkerOptions( )	Constructs a MarkerOptions object.
Method	**Description**
MarkerOptions position(LatLng latLng)	Sets the (latitude, longitude) position for this MarkerOptions.
MarkerOptions title(String title)	Sets the title for this MarkerOptions.
MarkerOptions snippet(String snippet)	Sets the snippet for this MarkerOptions.
MarkerOptions icon(BitmapDescriptor icon)	Sets the icon for this MarkerOptions.

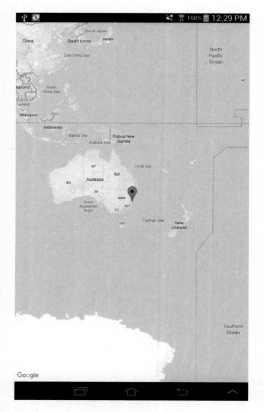

FIGURE 10.7 Show A Map app, Version 1, running inside the tablet

When the user touches the marker, the title is revealed in a callout. Finally, at line 47, we move the camera to the location on the map defined by the `LatLng` reference `sydney`, so that a map centered on Sydney, Australia, shows.

FIGURE 10.7 shows the app running inside the tablet. It is possible to run inside the emulator, but we may have to update Google Play services in order to do it.

10.4 Adding Annotations to the Map, App Version 2

In Version 2, we center the map on the White House in Washington, DC, set up the zoom level, add a marker, and draw a circle around the center of the map. The only part of the project impacted is the `onMapReady` method of the `MapsActivity` class. In order to do that, we use the `addMarker` and `addCircle` methods shown in Table 10.8. These two methods are similar: the `addMarker` takes a `MarkerOptions` parameter, and `addCircle` takes a `CircleOptions` parameter. **TABLE 10.11** shows selected methods of the `CircleOptions` class.

For both, we first use the default constructor to instantiate an object, and then call the appropriate methods to define the marker or the circle. We must specify a position, otherwise there

TABLE 10.11 Selected methods of the `CircleOptions` class	
Constructor	**Description**
CircleOptions( )	Constructs a CircleOptions object.
Method	**Description**
CircleOptions center(LatLng latLng)	Sets the (latitude, longitude) position of the center for this CircleOptions.
CircleOptions radius(double meters)	Sets the radius, in meters, for this CircleOptions.
CircleOptions strokeColor(int color)	Sets the stroke color for this CircleOptions.
CircleOptions strokeWidth(float width)	Sets the stroke width, in pixels, for this CircleOptions.

will be an exception at run time and the app will stop. All the methods shown in both tables return a reference to the object calling the method, so method calls can be chained.

> **COMMON ERROR:** Not specifying the position of a marker or a circle when adding it to a map results in a `NullPointerException` at run time and stops the app.

To add a circle to a `GoogleMap` named `mMap`, we can use the following code sequence:

```
LatLng whiteHouse = new LatLng( 38.8977, -77.0366 );
CircleOptions options = new CircleOptions( );
options.center( whiteHouse );
options.radius( 500 );
options.strokeWidth( 10.0f );
options.strokeColor( 0xFFFF0000 );
mMap.addCircle( options );
```

Because all the `CircleOptions` methods used previously return the `CircleOptions` reference that calls them, we can chain all these statements into one as follows:

```
map.addCircle( new CircleOptions( ).center( new LatLng( 38.8977,
-77.0366 ) ).radius( 500 ).strokeWidth( 10.0f ).strokeColor(
0xFFFF0000 ) );
```

The first format has the advantage of clarity. The second format is more compact. Many examples found on the web use the second format.

```
1   package com.jblearning.showamapv2;
2
3   import android.support.v4.app.FragmentActivity;
4   import android.os.Bundle;
5
6   import com.google.android.gms.maps.CameraUpdate;
7   import com.google.android.gms.maps.CameraUpdateFactory;
8   import com.google.android.gms.maps.GoogleMap;
9   import com.google.android.gms.maps.OnMapReadyCallback;
10  import com.google.android.gms.maps.SupportMapFragment;
11  import com.google.android.gms.maps.model.CircleOptions;
12  import com.google.android.gms.maps.model.LatLng;
13  import com.google.android.gms.maps.model.MarkerOptions;
14
15  public class MapsActivity extends FragmentActivity
16                            implements OnMapReadyCallback {
17
18    private GoogleMap mMap;
19
20    @Override
21    protected void onCreate( Bundle savedInstanceState ) {
22      super.onCreate( savedInstanceState );
23      setContentView( R.layout.activity_maps );
24      // Obtain the SupportMapFragment and get notified
25      // when the map is ready to be used.
26      SupportMapFragment mapFragment = ( SupportMapFragment )
27        getSupportFragmentManager( ).findFragmentById( R.id.map );
28      mapFragment.getMapAsync( this );
29    }
30
31    @Override
32    public void onMapReady( GoogleMap googleMap ) {
33      mMap = googleMap;
34
35      LatLng whiteHouse = new LatLng( 38.8977, -77.0366 );
36      CameraUpdate update
37          = CameraUpdateFactory.newLatLngZoom( whiteHouse, 15.5f );
38      mMap.moveCamera( update );
39
40      MarkerOptions options = new MarkerOptions( );
41      options.position( whiteHouse );
42      options.title( "Hello" );
43      options.snippet( "How is the food?" );
44      mMap.addMarker( options );
45
46      CircleOptions circleOptions = new CircleOptions( )
47          .center( whiteHouse ).radius( 500 )
48          .strokeWidth( 10.0f ).strokeColor( 0xFFFF0000 );
49      mMap.addCircle( circleOptions );
50    }
51  }
```

EXAMPLE 10.6 The `MapsActivity` class, Show A Map app, Version 2

FIGURE 10.8 The map of the White House with annotations, Show A Map app, Version 2

EXAMPLE 10.6 shows the updated `MapsActivity` class. At lines 40–44, we place a marker on the map specifying its location, title, and snippet. We instantiate the `MarkerOptions options` at line 40, sets its attributes at lines 41–43, and adds it to the map at line 44.

At lines 46–49, we place a circle on the map specifying its location, its radius, its stroke width, and its color. We instantiate a `CircleOptions` object and chain calls to the `center`, `radius`, `strokeWidth`, and `strokeColor` methods at lines 46–48. The center of the circle is at the White House location, its radius is `500` meters, its stroke is `10` pixels, and its color is red. We add it to the map at line 49. Although we prefer the first coding style (the one we use for the marker), there are many developers who use the second coding style, chaining method calls in one statement. Thus, we should be familiar with both.

FIGURE 10.8 shows the app running inside the tablet, after the user touches the marker. The title and snippet only show if the user touches the marker.

10.5 The Model

In Version 3, we place a speech recognition activity in front of the map activity: we expect the user to say one of a few predefined cities: Washington, Paris, New York, Rome, and London.

We analyze the words understood by the device and compare them to these five cities. If we have a match, we display a map of the matching city. We also place markers on the map with a description of a well-known attraction for each city. We still use the Google Maps Activity template. We need to modify the AndroidManifest.xml file to add an activity for the speech recognition activity as the starting activity for the app and therefore specify that the map activity is not the starting activity.

We keep our Model simple: we store (city, attraction) pairs in a **hash table**. A hash table is a data structure that maps keys to values. For example, we can map the integers 1 to 12 to the months of the year (January, February, March, etc.) and store them in a hash table. We can also store US states in a hash table: the keys are MD, CA, NJ, etc., and the values are Maryland, California, New Jersey, etc. In this app, cities (the keys) are New York, Washington, London, Rome, and Paris. The attractions (the values) are the Statue of Liberty, the White House, Buckingham Palace, the Colosseum, and the Eiffel Tower. We want to match a word said by the user to a city in our Model. In case we do not have a match, we use Washington as the default city.

EXAMPLE 10.7 shows the `Cities` class, which encapsulates our Model. At lines 11–13, we declare three constants to store the `String Washington`, its latitude and its longitude. At line 8, we declare a constant, `CITY_KEY`, to store the `String city`. When we go from the first to the second activity, we use that constant as the key for the name of the city understood by the speech recognizer in the intent that we use to start the activity. At line 9, we declare the constant `MIN_CONFIDENCE` and give it the value `0.5`. It defines a threshold of confidence level that any word understood by the speech recognizer needs to have for us to process it as a valid city. At line 14, we declare the constant `MESSAGE`. We use it when we add a marker to the map.

We declare our only instance variable, `places`, a `Hashtable`, at line 16. `Hashtable` is a generic type whose actual data types are specified at the time of declaration. The first `String` data type in `<String, String>` is the data type of the keys. The second `String` is the data type of the values. We code a constructor that accepts a `Hashtable` as a parameter and assign it to `places` at lines 18–20. At lines 43–45, the `getAttraction` method returns the attraction mapped to a given city in `places`. If there is no such city in `places`, it returns `null`.

At lines 22–41, the `firstMatchWithMinConfidence` method takes an `ArrayList` of `Strings` and an array of `floats` as parameters. The `ArrayList` represents a list of words provided by the speech recognizer. The array of `floats` stores the confidence levels for these words. We use a double loop to process the parameters: the outer loop loops through all the words (line 29), and the inner loop (line 34) checks if one of them matches a key in the hash table `places`. We expect the confidence levels to be ordered in descending order. Thus, if the current one falls below `MIN_CONFIDENCE` (line 30), the remaining ones will be as well, so we exit the outer loop and return the value of `DEFAULT_CITY` at line 40.

Inside the inner loop, we test if the current word matches a city listed as a key in the hash table `places` at line 36. If it does, we return it at line 37.

If we finish processing the outer loop and no match is found with an acceptable confidence level, we return the value of `DEFAULT_CITY` at line 40. Note that we process the parameter `words` in the outer loop (line 29) and the keys of `places` in the inner loop (line 34) and not the other way around because we expect `words` to be ordered by decreasing confidence levels.

```java
1    package com.jblearning.showamapv3;
2
3    import java.util.ArrayList;
4    import java.util.Enumeration;
5    import java.util.Hashtable;
6
7    public class Cities {
8      public static final String CITY_KEY = "city";
9      public static final float MIN_CONFIDENCE = 0.5f;
10
11     public static final String DEFAULT_CITY = "Washington";
12     public static final double DEFAULT_LATITUDE = 38.8977;
13     public static final double DEFAULT_LONGITUDE = -77.0366;
14     public static final String MESSAGE = "Thanks for visiting";
15
16     private Hashtable<String, String> places;
17
18     public Cities( Hashtable<String, String> newPlaces ) {
19       places = newPlaces;
20     }
21
22     public String firstMatchWithMinConfidence( ArrayList<String> words,
23                                               float [ ] confidLevels ) {
24       if( words == null || confidLevels == null )
25         return DEFAULT_CITY;
26
27       int numberOfWords = words.size( );
28       Enumeration<String> cities;
29       for( int i = 0; i < numberOfWords && i < confidLevels.length; i++ ) {
30         if( confidLevels[i] < MIN_CONFIDENCE )
31           break;
32         String word = words.get( i );
33         cities = places.keys( );
34         while( cities.hasMoreElements( ) ) {
35           String city = cities.nextElement( );
36           if( word.equalsIgnoreCase( city ) )
37             return word;
38         }
39       }
40       return DEFAULT_CITY;
41     }
42
43     public String getAttraction( String city ) {
44       return ( String ) places.get( city ); // null if city not found
45     }
46   }
```

EXAMPLE 10.7 The `Cities` class, Show A Map app, Version 2

10.6 Displaying a Map Based on Speech Input, App Version 3

In the first activity, we ask the user to say the name of a city and we use the Cities class to convert the list of words returned by the speech recognizer into a city name that we feel confident the user said. If there is no match, we use the default city stored in the DEFAULT_CITY constant of the Cities class. Then, we store that information in the intent that we create before launching the map activity. Inside the MapsActivity class, we can then access that intent, retrieve the city name and display the correct map.

We need to do the following:

▶ Create an activity that asks the user to speak.
▶ Add an XML layout file for that activity.
▶ After the user speaks, go to the map activity.
▶ Based on what the user says, display the correct map.
▶ Edit the AndroidManifest.xml.

We still use the Google Maps Activity template to automatically generate code, in particular the gradle file, the AndroidManifest.xml file and the MapsActivity class. As we add a MainActivity class that we intend to be the first activity, we modify the AndroidManifest.xml file so that MainActivity is the first activity and MapsActivity is the second activity.

We start with the MainActivity class of Version 0 and its activity_main.xml layout file, in which we delete the TextView element and the padding attributes.

EXAMPLE 10.8 shows the updated MainActivity class. After retrieving the city said by the user, we start a second activity to show a map centered on that city. In order to analyze the city said by the user, we use the Cities class. We declare cities, a Cities instance variable at line 16; it represents our Model. For convenience, because we need to access it from the MapsActivity class, we declare it as public and static. We instantiate it at lines 22–28 inside the onCreate method using a list of five cities. At lines 63–65 of the onActivityResult method, we call the firstMatchWithMinConfidence method with cities in order to retrieve the name of the city said by the user, and we assign it to the String variable firstMatch. At lines 68–69, we place firstMatch in an intent to start a MapsActivity using the putExtra method (shown in **TABLE 10.12**), mapping it to the key city. We start the activity at lines 70–71.

In the MapsActivity class, we need to do the following:

▶ Access the original intent for this activity and retrieve the name of the city stored in the intent.
▶ Convert that city name to latitude and longitude coordinates.
▶ Set the center of the map to that point.

To retrieve the name of city stored in the original intent, we use the getStringExtra method shown in Table 10.12.

We need to convert a city name to a point on Earth (latitude, longitude) in order to display a map centered on that point. More generally, the process of converting an address to a pair of latitude

```
1    package com.jblearning.showamapv3;
2
3    import android.content.Intent;
4    import android.content.pm.PackageManager;
5    import android.content.pm.ResolveInfo;
6    import android.os.Bundle;
7    import android.speech.RecognizerIntent;
8    import android.support.v7.app.AppCompatActivity;
9    import android.widget.Toast;
10   import java.util.ArrayList;
11   import java.util.Hashtable;
12   import java.util.List;
13
14   public class MainActivity extends AppCompatActivity {
15     private static final int CITY_REQUEST = 1;
16     public static Cities cities;
17
18     protected void onCreate( Bundle savedInstanceState ) {
19       super.onCreate( savedInstanceState );
20       setContentView( R.layout.activity_main );
21
22       Hashtable<String, String> places = new Hashtable<String, String>( );
23       places.put( "Washington", "White House" );
24       places.put( "New York", "Statue of Liberty" );
25       places.put( "Paris", "Eiffel Tower" );
26       places.put( "London", "Buckingham Palace" );
27       places.put( "Rome",   "Colosseum" );
28       cities = new Cities( places );
29
30       // Test if device supports speech recognition
31       PackageManager manager = getPackageManager( );
32       List<ResolveInfo> listOfMatches = manager.queryIntentActivities(
33          new Intent( RecognizerIntent.ACTION_RECOGNIZE_SPEECH ), 0 );
34       if( listOfMatches.size( ) > 0 )
35         listen( );
36       else { // speech recognition not supported
37         Toast.makeText( this,
38            "Sorry - Your device does not support speech recognition",
39            Toast.LENGTH_LONG ).show( );
40       }
41     }
42
43     private void listen( ) {
44       Intent listenIntent =
45          new Intent( RecognizerIntent.ACTION_RECOGNIZE_SPEECH );
46       listenIntent.putExtra( RecognizerIntent.EXTRA_PROMPT, "What city?" );
```

EXAMPLE 10.8 The `MainActivity` class, Show A Map app, Version 3 (*Continued*)

```
47        listenIntent.putExtra( RecognizerIntent.EXTRA_LANGUAGE_MODEL,
48            RecognizerIntent.LANGUAGE_MODEL_FREE_FORM );
49        listenIntent.putExtra( RecognizerIntent.EXTRA_MAX_RESULTS, 5 );
50        startActivityForResult( listenIntent, CITY_REQUEST );
51    }
52
53    protected void onActivityResult( int requestCode,
54                                     int resultCode, Intent data ) {
55      super.onActivityResult( requestCode, resultCode, data );
56      if( requestCode == CITY_REQUEST && resultCode == RESULT_OK ) {
57        // retrieve list of possible words
58        ArrayList<String> returnedWords =
59            data.getStringArrayListExtra( RecognizerIntent.EXTRA_RESULTS );
60        // retrieve array of scores for returnedWords
61        float [ ] scores = data.getFloatArrayExtra(
62            RecognizerIntent.EXTRA_CONFIDENCE_SCORES );
63        // retrieve first good match
64        String firstMatch =
65            cities.firstMatchWithMinConfidence( returnedWords, scores );
66        // Create Intent for map
67        Intent mapIntent = new Intent( this, MapsActivity.class );
68        // put firstMatch in mapIntent
69        mapIntent.putExtra( Cities.CITY_KEY, firstMatch );
70        // start map activity
71        startActivity( mapIntent );
72      }
73    }
74 }
```

EXAMPLE 10.8 The `MainActivity` class, Show A Map app, Version 3

TABLE 10.12 The `putExtra` and `getStringExtra` methods of the `Intent` class

Method	Description
Intent putExtra(String key, String value)	Puts value in this Intent, associating it with key; returns this Intent.
String getStringExtra(String key)	Retrieves and returns the value that was placed in this Intent using key.

and longitude coordinates is known as **geocoding**. The inverse, going from a pair of latitude and longitude coordinates to an address is known as **reverse geocoding**, as shown in TABLE 10.13. The Geocoder class provides methods for both geocoding and reverse geocoding. TABLE 10.14 lists two of its methods, getFromLocationName, a geocoding method, and getFromLocation,

TABLE 10.13 Geocoding versus reverse geocoding

Geocoding	Reverse Geocoding
Address → (latitude, longitude)	(latitude, longitude) → street address
Example: 1600 Pennsylvania Avenue, Washington, DC 20500 → (38.8977, –77.0366)	Example: (38.8977, –77.0366) → 1600 Pennsylvania Avenue, Washington, DC 20500

TABLE 10.14 Selected methods of the `Geocoder` class

Constructor	Description
Geocoder(Context context)	Constructs a Geocoder object.
Method	**Description**
List <Address> getFromLocationName(String address, int maxResults)	Returns a list of Address objects given an address. The list has maxResults elements at the most, ordered in descending order of matching. Throws an IllegalArgumentException if address is null, and throws an IOException if the network is not available or if there is any other IO problem.
List <Address> getFromLocation(double latitude, double longitude, int maxResults)	Returns a list of Address objects given a point on Earth defined by its latitude and longitude. The list has maxResults elements at the most, ordered in descending order of matching. Throws an IllegalArgumentException if latitude or longitude is out of range, and throws an IOException if the network is not available or if there is any other IO problem.

TABLE 10.15 Selected methods of the `Address` class

Method	Description
double getLatitude( )	Returns the latitude of this Address, if it is known at that time.
double getLongitude( )	Returns the longitude of this Address, if it is known at that time.

a reverse geocoding method. They both returned a `List` of `Address` objects, ordered by matching confidence level, in descending order. For this app, we keep it simple and process the first element in that list. The `Address` class, part of the `android.location` package, stores an address, including street address, city, state, zip code, country, etc., as well as latitude and longitude. **TABLE 10.15** shows its `getLatitude` and `getLongitude` methods.

EXAMPLE 10.9 shows the `MapsActivity` class, updated from Version 2. We declare `city`, a `String` instance variable storing the city name, at line 25. At lines 32–36, we retrieve the city

```
1   package com.jblearning.showamapv3;
2
3   import android.content.Intent;
4   import android.location.Address;
5   import android.location.Geocoder;
6   import android.os.Bundle;
7   import android.support.v4.app.FragmentActivity;
8
9   import com.google.android.gms.maps.CameraUpdate;
10  import com.google.android.gms.maps.CameraUpdateFactory;
11  import com.google.android.gms.maps.GoogleMap;
12  import com.google.android.gms.maps.OnMapReadyCallback;
13  import com.google.android.gms.maps.SupportMapFragment;
14  import com.google.android.gms.maps.model.CircleOptions;
15  import com.google.android.gms.maps.model.LatLng;
16  import com.google.android.gms.maps.model.MarkerOptions;
17
18  import java.io.IOException;
19  import java.util.List;
20
21  public class MapsActivity extends FragmentActivity
22                          implements OnMapReadyCallback {
23
24    private GoogleMap mMap;
25    private String city;
26
27    @Override
28    protected void onCreate( Bundle savedInstanceState ) {
29      super.onCreate( savedInstanceState );
30      setContentView( R.layout.activity_maps );
31
32      // retrieve city name from original intent
33      Intent originalIntent = getIntent( );
34      city = originalIntent.getStringExtra( Cities.CITY_KEY );
35      if( city == null )
36        city = Cities.DEFAULT_CITY;
37
38      // Obtain the SupportMapFragment and get notified
39      // when the map is ready to be used.
40      SupportMapFragment mapFragment = ( SupportMapFragment )
41        getSupportFragmentManager( ).findFragmentById( R.id.map );
42      mapFragment.getMapAsync( this );
43    }
44
```

EXAMPLE 10.9 The `MapsActivity` class, Show A Map app, Version 3 (*Continued*)

```
45      @Override
46      public void onMapReady( GoogleMap googleMap ) {
47        mMap = googleMap;
48
49        // default latitude and longitude for city before geocoding city
50        double latitude = Cities.DEFAULT_LATITUDE;
51        double longitude = Cities.DEFAULT_LONGITUDE;
52
53        // retrieve attraction for city
54        Cities cities = MainActivity.cities;
55        String attraction = cities.getAttraction( city );
56
57        // retrieve latitude and longitude of city/attraction
58        Geocoder coder = new Geocoder( this );
59        try {
60          // geocode city
61          String address = attraction + ", " + city;
62          List<Address> addresses = coder.getFromLocationName( address, 5 );
63          if( addresses != null ) {
64            latitude = addresses.get( 0 ).getLatitude( );
65            longitude = addresses.get( 0 ).getLongitude( );
66          } else // geocoding failed; use default values
67            city = Cities.DEFAULT_CITY;
68        } catch( IOException ioe ) {
69          // geocoding failed; use default city, latitude and longitude
70          city = Cities.DEFAULT_CITY;
71        }
72
73        // update the map
74        LatLng cityLocation = new LatLng( latitude, longitude );
75
76        CameraUpdate update
77            = CameraUpdateFactory.newLatLngZoom( cityLocation, 15.5f );
78        mMap.moveCamera( update );
79
80        MarkerOptions options = new MarkerOptions( );
81        options.position( cityLocation );
82        options.title( attraction );
83        options.snippet( Cities.MESSAGE );
84        mMap.addMarker( options );
85
86        CircleOptions circleOptions = new CircleOptions( )
87            .center( cityLocation ).radius( 500 )
88            .strokeWidth( 10.0f ).strokeColor( 0xFFFF0000 );
89        mMap.addCircle( circleOptions );
90      }
91    }
```

EXAMPLE 10.9 The `MapsActivity` class, Show A Map app, Version 3

name that was stored in the intent that was used to start this map activity. We get a reference to the intent at line 33, call `getStringExtra` and retrieve the city name and assign it to `city` at line 34. If `city` is `null` (line 35), we assign to it the default city defined in the `Cities` class at line 36.

Inside the `onMapReady` method, we geocode the address defined by the city chosen by the user and its attraction to its latitude and longitude coordinates. Then, we set up the map based on these coordinates, including a circle and a marker as in Version 2.

At lines 49–51, we declare `latitude` and `longitude`, two `double` variables that we use to store the latitude and longitude coordinates of `city`. We initialize them with the default values stored in the `DEFAULT_LATITUDE` and `DEFAULT_LONGITUDE` constants of the `Cities` class. At lines 53–55, we retrieve the attraction for city and assign it to the `String attraction`.

We declare and instantiate `coder`, a `Geocoder` object, at line 58. The `getFromLocation-Name` method throws an `IOException`, a checked exception, if an I/O problem occurred, such as a network-related problem, for example. Thus, we need to use `try` (lines 59–67) and `catch` (lines 68–71) blocks when calling this method. We define the address to geocode as the concatenation of the attraction and the city at line 61. We call `getFromLocationName` method at line 62, passing `address` and 5 to specify that we only want 5 or fewer results, and assign the return value to `addresses`. We test if `addresses` is `null` at line 63 before assigning the latitude and longitude data of the first element in it to `latitude` and `longitude` at lines 64 and 65. If we execute inside the `catch` block, that means that we failed to get latitude and longitude data for `city`, so we reset `city` to the default value.

Afterward, we update the center of the map to the point with coordinates (`latitude`, `longitude`) and set the zoom level at lines 73–78. We add the marker at lines 80–84 and add the circle at lines 86–89.

We need to update the AndroidManifest.xml file so that the app starts with the voice recognition activity and includes the map activity. **EXAMPLE 10.10** shows the updated

```
1   <?xml version="1.0" encoding="utf-8"?>
2   <manifest package="com.jblearning.showamapv3"
3            xmlns:android="http://schemas.android.com/apk/res/android">
4   <!--
5     The ACCESS_COARSE/FINE_LOCATION permissions are not required to use
6     Google Maps Android API v2, but you must specify either coarse or
7     fine location permissions for the 'MyLocation' functionality.
8   -->
9   <uses-permission
10       android:name="android.permission.ACCESS_FINE_LOCATION"/>
11
12  <application
13       android:allowBackup="true"
14       android:icon="@mipmap/ic_launcher"
```

EXAMPLE 10.10 The AndroidManifest.xml file, Show A Map app, Version 3 (*Continued*)

```
15            android:label="@string/app_name"
16            android:supportsRtl="true"
17            android:theme="@style/AppTheme">
18
19        <!--
20            The API key for Google Maps-based APIs is defined as a string
21            resource (See the file "res/values/google_maps_api.xml").
22            Note that the API key is linked to the encryption key used to
23            sign the APK.
24            You need a different API key for each encryption key, including
25            the release key that is used to sign the APK for publishing.
26            You can define the keys for the debug and release targets in
27            src/debug/ and src/release/.
28        -->
29        <meta-data
30            android:name="com.google.android.geo.API_KEY"
31            android:value="@string/google_maps_key"/>
32
33        <activity
34            android:name=".MainActivity"
35            android:label="@string/title_activity_maps">
36        <intent-filter>
37            <action android:name="android.intent.action.MAIN"/>
38
39            <category android:name="android.intent.category.LAUNCHER"/>
40        </intent-filter>
41      </activity>
42
43      <activity
44          android:name=".MapsActivity" >
45      </activity>
46    </application>
47
48  </manifest>
```

EXAMPLE 10.10 **The AndroidManifest.xml file, Show A Map app, Version 3**

AndroidManifest.xml file. At line 34, we specify `MainActivity` as the launcher activity. At lines 43–45, we add a `MapsActivity activity` element.

Finally, **EXAMPLE 10.11** shows the activity_main.xml file, a skeleton `RelativeLayout` for the first activity.

FIGURE 10.9 shows the second screen of our app Version 3, running inside the tablet. It shows a map of Paris, France, after the user said `Paris`. Note that the center of the map is the Eiffel Tower, because we add the attraction name to the city name so that the center of the map is at the attraction location.

```
1    <?xml version="1.0" encoding="utf-8"?>
2    <RelativeLayout xmlns:android="http://schemas.android.com/apk/res/android"
3      xmlns:tools="http://schemas.android.com/tools"
4      android:layout_width="match_parent"
5      android:layout_height="match_parent"
6      tools:context=".MainActivity">
7
8    </RelativeLayout>
```

EXAMPLE 10.11 The activity_main.xml file, Show A Map app, Version 3

FIGURE 10.9 The Show A Map app, Version 3, running inside the tablet

10.7 Controlling Speech Input, App Version 4

Note that if we run the app and we do not say anything, the microphone goes away and we are stuck on the first activity, which is now a blank screen. Furthermore, if we go to the second screen and come back to the first screen, we also have a blank screen. One way to fix this issue is to start the map activity no matter what. If the user does not say a word, the microphone goes away but onActivityResult still executes. We can place the code to start the map activity outside the if block of the onActivityResult method of Example 10.8. The map shown is a default map.

Another way to fix this issue is to add a button that when clicked, triggers a call to listen and brings back the microphone. This gives the user a chance to be in control, although there is the extra step of clicking on a button. We implement that feature in Version 4. We edit activity_main.xml to add a button to the first screen and we add a method to the MainActivity class to process that click.

EXAMPLE 10.12 shows the edited activity_main.xml file. At lines 8–14, we define a button that shows at the top of the screen. We give it the id speak at line 13 and specify the startSpeaking method to execute when the user clicks on the button at line 14.

```
1    <?xml version="1.0" encoding="utf-8"?>
2    <RelativeLayout xmlns:android="http://schemas.android.com/apk/res/android"
3      xmlns:tools="http://schemas.android.com/tools"
4      android:layout_width="match_parent"
5      android:layout_height="match_parent"
6      tools:context=".MainActivity">
7
8      <Button
9          android:layout_width="wrap_content"
10         android:layout_height="wrap_content"
11         android:layout_centerHorizontal="true"
12         android:text="@string/click_to_speak"
13         android:id="@+id/speak"
14         android:onClick="startSpeaking" />
15
16   </RelativeLayout>
```

EXAMPLE 10.12 **The activity_main.xml file, including a button, Show A Map app Version 4**

EXAMPLE 10.13 shows the edited strings.xml file. The click_to_speak string is defined at line 4.

```
1    <resources>
2      <string name="app_name">ShowAMapV4</string>
3      <string name="title_activity_maps">Map</string>
4      <string name="click_to_speak">Click to start speaking</string>
5    </resources>
```

EXAMPLE 10.13 **The strings.xml file, Show A Map app, Version 4**

EXAMPLE 10.14 shows the edited `MainActivity` class. It includes the instance variable `speak`, a `Button`, at line 20. It is assigned the button defined in activity_main.xml at line 25. If speech recognition is not supported, we disable the button at line 42. The `startSpeaking` method is defined at lines 49–51. It calls `listen` at line 50. Note that if we wanted to set up the button to

```
1   package com.jblearning.showamapv4;
2
3   import android.content.Intent;
4   import android.content.pm.PackageManager;
5   import android.content.pm.ResolveInfo;
6   import android.os.Bundle;
7   import android.speech.RecognizerIntent;
8   import android.support.v7.app.AppCompatActivity;
9   import android.view.View;
10  import android.widget.Button;
11  import android.widget.Toast;
12
13  import java.util.ArrayList;
14  import java.util.Hashtable;
15  import java.util.List;
16
17  public class MainActivity extends AppCompatActivity {
18    private static final int CITY_REQUEST = 1;
19    public static Cities cities;
20    private Button speak;
21
22    protected void onCreate( Bundle savedInstanceState ) {
23      super.onCreate( savedInstanceState );
24      setContentView( R.layout.activity_main );
25      speak = ( Button ) findViewById( R.id.speak );
26
27      Hashtable<String, String> places = new Hashtable<String, String>( );
28      places.put( "Washington", "White House" );
29      places.put( "New York", "Statue of Liberty" );
30      places.put( "Paris", "Eiffel Tower" );
31      places.put( "London", "Buckingham Palace" );
32      places.put( "Rome",   "Colosseum" );
33      cities = new Cities( places );
34
35      // Test if device supports speech recognition
36      PackageManager manager = getPackageManager( );
37      List<ResolveInfo> listOfMatches = manager.queryIntentActivities(
38          new Intent( RecognizerIntent.ACTION_RECOGNIZE_SPEECH ), 0 );
39      if( listOfMatches.size( ) > 0 )
40        listen( );
```

EXAMPLE 10.14 The `MainActivity` Class, Show A Map app, Version 4 (*Continued*)

```
41        else { // speech recognition not supported
42          speak.setEnabled( false );
43          Toast.makeText( this,
44              "Sorry - Your device does not support speech recognition",
45              Toast.LENGTH_LONG ).show( );
46        }
47      }
48
49    public void startSpeaking( View v ) {
50        listen( );
51    }
52
53    private void listen( ) {
54        speak.setEnabled( false );
55        Intent listenIntent =
56            new Intent( RecognizerIntent.ACTION_RECOGNIZE_SPEECH );
57        listenIntent.putExtra( RecognizerIntent.EXTRA_PROMPT, "What city?" );
58        listenIntent.putExtra( RecognizerIntent.EXTRA_LANGUAGE_MODEL,
59            RecognizerIntent.LANGUAGE_MODEL_FREE_FORM );
60        listenIntent.putExtra( RecognizerIntent.EXTRA_MAX_RESULTS, 5 );
61        startActivityForResult( listenIntent, CITY_REQUEST );
62    }
63
64    protected void onActivityResult( int requestCode,
65                                     int resultCode, Intent data ) {
66        super.onActivityResult( requestCode, resultCode, data );
67        if( requestCode == CITY_REQUEST && resultCode == RESULT_OK ) {
68          // retrieve list of possible words
69          ArrayList<String> returnedWords =
70              data.getStringArrayListExtra( RecognizerIntent.EXTRA_RESULTS );
71          // retrieve array of scores for returnedWords
72          float [ ] scores = data.getFloatArrayExtra(
73              RecognizerIntent.EXTRA_CONFIDENCE_SCORES );
74          // retrieve first good match
75          String firstMatch =
76              cities.firstMatchWithMinConfidence( returnedWords, scores );
77          // Create Intent for map
78          Intent mapIntent = new Intent( this, MapsActivity.class );
79          // put firstMatch in mapIntent
80          mapIntent.putExtra( Cities.CITY_KEY, firstMatch );
81          // start map activity
82          startActivity( mapIntent );
83        }
84        speak.setEnabled( true );
85      }
86  }
```

EXAMPLE 10.14 The `MainActivity` Class, Show A Map app, Version 4

call `listen` directly, we would need to add a `View` parameter to `listen`. When `listen` executes, we disable the button at line 54, and re-enable it at line 84 when `onActivityResult` finishes executing, so that it is enabled if we stay on this screen or when we come back to this screen from the map activity after hitting the back button.

If we run the app again, whenever the first screen goes blank, we can click on the button and bring back the microphone.

10.8 Voice Recognition Part B, Moving the Map with Voice Once, App Version 5

We have learned how to use speech recognition with an intent. Some users may like to interact with an app by voice, but they may find the user interface that comes with it annoying. In particular, if we allow the users to repeatedly provide input by voice, it may be desirable to do it without showing the microphone.

The `SpeechRecognizer` class, along with the `RecognitionListener` interface, both part of the `android.speech` package, allow us to listen to and process user speech without using a GUI. However, we still have the bleeping sound that alerts the user that the app expects him or her to say something. In Version 5 of the app, we enable the user to move the map based on speech input: if the user says `North`, `South`, `West`, or `East`, we move the center of the map North, South, West, or East, respectively. There is no change in `MainActivity` and activity_main.xml.

To implement this, we do the following:

▸   Edit the AndroidManifest.xml file so that we ask for audio recording permission.
▸   Add the functionality to compare a word (said by the user) to a list of possible directions.
▸   Capture speech input and process it inside the `MapsActivity` class.

In order to add a permission to record audio, we edit the AndroidManifest.xml file as shown at lines 12–13 of **EXAMPLE 10.15**.

```
 9
10      <uses-permission android:name="android.permission.ACCESS_FINE_LOCATION"/>
11
12      <!-- added for 2nd activity, SpeechRecognizer -->
13      <uses-permission android:name="android.permission.RECORD_AUDIO"/>
14
15      <application
```

EXAMPLE 10.15 The AndroidManifest.xml file, Show A Map app, Version 5

For convenience, we code the `Directions` class, which includes the `Directions` enum. We use it to compare user input to the various constants in `Directions`. Although we could use `String` constants, using an `enum` gives us better self-documentation for our code. **EXAMPLE 10.16** shows the `Directions` class.

```
1    package com.jblearning.showamapv5;
2
3    public enum Directions { NORTH, SOUTH, WEST, EAST }
```

EXAMPLE 10.16 **The `Directions` class, Show A Map app, Version 5**

As before when capturing speech input, we get a list of possible matching words along with a parallel array of confidence scores. In this version of the app, we compare that list to the constants in the enum `Directions` in order to assess if the user says a word that defines a valid direction. In order to do that, we code another class, `MatchingUtility`, shown in **EXAMPLE 10.17**. It includes a constant, `MIN_CONFIDENCE`, that defines the minimum acceptable score for a matching word, and a method, `firstMatchWithMinConfidence`, that tests if a list of words includes a `String` matching one of the constants defined in the enum `Directions`. It returns that `String` if it does. The `firstMatchWithMinConfidence` method is very similar to the method of the `Cities` class shown previously in Example 10.7, except that we compare a list of words to an enum list rather than a list of keys in a hash table. The main difference in the code is how we loop through

```
1    package com.jblearning.showamapv5;
2
3    import java.util.ArrayList;
4
5    public class MatchingUtility {
6      public static final float MIN_CONFIDENCE = 0.25f;
7
8      public static String firstMatchWithMinConfidence
9                  ( ArrayList<String> words, float [ ] confidLevels ) {
10        if( words == null || confidLevels == null )
11          return null;
12
13        int numberOfWords = words.size( );
14        for( int i = 0; i < numberOfWords && i < confidLevels.length; i++ ) {
15          if( confidLevels[i] < MIN_CONFIDENCE )
16            break;
17          String word = words.get( i );
18          for( Directions dir : Directions.values( ) ) {
19            if( word.equalsIgnoreCase( dir.toString( ) ) )
20              return word;
21          }
22        }
23        return null;
24      }
25    }
```

EXAMPLE 10.17 **The `MatchingUtility` class, Show A Map app, Version 5**

TABLE 10.16 Methods of the `RecognitionListener` interface

Method	Called when
void onReadyForSpeech(Bundle bundle)	The speech recognizer is ready for the user to start speaking.
void onBeginningOfSpeech( )	The user started to speak.
void onEndOfSpeech( )	The user stopped speaking.
void onPartialResults(Bundle bundle)	Partial results are ready. This method may be called 0, 1, or more times.
void onResults(Bundle bundle)	Results are ready.
void onBufferReceived(byte [ ] buffer)	More sound has just been received. This method may not be called.
void onEvent(int eventType, Bundle bundle)	This method is not currently used.
void onRmsChanged(float rmsdB)	The sound level of the incoming sound has changed. This method is called very often.
void onError(int error)	A recognition or network error has occurred.

the enum `Directions` at line 18. In general, to loop through an enum named `EnumName`, we use the following `for` loop header:

```
for( EnumName current: EnumName.values( ) ) {
  // process current here
}
```

In order to capture voice input without a user interface, we implement the `Recognition-Listener` interface. It has nine methods that all need to be overridden, as listed in **TABLE 10.16**.

When using the `RecognitionListener` interface to handle a speech event, we need to perform the following steps:

▶ Code a speech handler class that implements the `RecognitionListener` interface and override all of its methods.
▶ Declare and instantiate an object of that speech handler class.
▶ Declare and instantiate a `SpeechRecognizer` object.
▶ Register the speech handler object on the `SpeechRecognizer` object.
▶ Tell the `SpeechRecognizer` object to start listening.

TABLE 10.17 Selected methods of the `Bundle` class	
Method	**Description**
ArrayList getStringArrayList(String key)	Returns the ArrayList of Strings associated with key, or null if there is none.
float [] getFloatArray(String key)	Returns the float array associated with key, or null if there is none.

When testing on the tablet, the order of the calls of the various methods of the `RecognitionListener` interface, not including the calls to the `onRmsChanged` method, is as follows:

`onReadyForSpeech, onBeginningOfSpeech, onEndOfSpeech, onResults`

We process user input inside the `onResults` method. Its `Bundle` parameter enables us to access the list of possible matching words and their corresponding confidence scores. **TABLE 10.17** lists the two methods of the `Bundle` class that we use to retrieve the list of possible matching words and their associated confidences scores. We use the following pattern:

```
public void onResults( Bundle results ) {
  ArrayList<String> words =
    results.getStringArrayList( SpeechRecognizer.RESULTS_RECOGNITION );
  float [ ] scores =
    results.getFloatArray( SpeechRecognizer.CONFIDENCE_SCORES );
  // process words and scores
```

EXAMPLE 10.18 shows the edits in the `MapsActivity` class. At line 27, we declare `DELTA`, a constant that we use to change the latitude or longitude of the center of the map based on user input. At line 31, we declare a `SpeechRecognizer` instance variable, `recognizer`.

At lines 118–168, we code the `private SpeechListener` class, which `implements RecognitionListener`. In this version of the app, we only care about processing the results, so we

```
1 package com.jblearning.showamapv5;
2
3 import android.content.Intent;
4 import android.location.Address;
5 import android.location.Geocoder;
6 import android.os.Bundle;
7 import android.speech.RecognitionListener;
8 import android.speech.RecognizerIntent;
```

EXAMPLE 10.18 The `MapsActivity` class, Show A Map app, Version 5 (*Continued*)

```
 9  import android.speech.SpeechRecognizer;
10  import android.support.v4.app.FragmentActivity;
...
21  import java.io.IOException;
22  import java.util.ArrayList;
23  import java.util.List;
24
25  public class MapsActivity extends FragmentActivity
26                            implements OnMapReadyCallback {
27    public static final double DELTA = 0.01;
28
29    private GoogleMap mMap;
30    private String city;
31    private SpeechRecognizer recognizer;
...
51    @Override
52    public void onReadyForSpeech( Bundle params ){
...
97      // start listening to speech
98      listen( );
99    }
100
101   public void updateMap( LatLng location, float zoomLevel ) {
102     CameraUpdate center = CameraUpdateFactory.newLatLng( location );
103     CameraUpdate zoom = CameraUpdateFactory.zoomTo( zoomLevel );
104     mMap.moveCamera( center );
105     mMap.animateCamera( zoom );
106   }
107
108   public void listen( ) {
109     if( recognizer != null )
110       recognizer.destroy( );
111     recognizer = SpeechRecognizer.createSpeechRecognizer( this );
112     SpeechListener listener = new SpeechListener( );
113     recognizer.setRecognitionListener( listener );
114     recognizer.startListening( new Intent(
115         RecognizerIntent.ACTION_RECOGNIZE_SPEECH ) );
116   }
117
118   private class SpeechListener implements RecognitionListener {
119     public void onBeginningOfSpeech( ){
120     }
121
122     public void onEndOfSpeech( ) {
123     }
124
```

EXAMPLE 10.18 The MapsActivity class, Show A Map app, Version 5 (*Continued*)

```
125       public void onReadyForSpeech( Bundle params ){
126       }
127
128       public void onError( int error ) {
129       }
130
131       public void onResults( Bundle results ) {
132         ArrayList<String> words =
133           results.getStringArrayList( SpeechRecognizer.RESULTS_RECOGNITION );
134         float [ ] scores =
135           results.getFloatArray( SpeechRecognizer.CONFIDENCE_SCORES );
136
137         String match =
138           MatchingUtility.firstMatchWithMinConfidence( words, scores );
139         LatLng pos = mMap.getCameraPosition( ).target;
140         float zoomLevel = mMap.getCameraPosition( ).zoom;
141
142         if( match != null ) {
143           if( match.equalsIgnoreCase( Directions.NORTH.toString( ) ) )
144             pos = new LatLng( pos.latitude + DELTA, pos.longitude );
145           else if( match.equalsIgnoreCase( Directions.SOUTH.toString( ) ) )
146             pos = new LatLng( pos.latitude - DELTA, pos.longitude );
147           else if( match.equalsIgnoreCase( Directions.WEST.toString( ) ) )
148             pos = new LatLng( pos.latitude, pos.longitude - DELTA );
149           else if( match.equalsIgnoreCase( Directions.EAST.toString( ) ) )
150             pos = new LatLng( pos.latitude , pos.longitude + DELTA );
151
152           updateMap( pos, zoomLevel );
153         }
154         listen( );
155       }
156
157       public void onPartialResults( Bundle partialResults ) {
158       }
159
160       public void onBufferReceived( byte [ ] buffer ) {
161       }
162
163       public void onEvent( int eventType, Bundle params ) {
164       }
165
166       public void onRmsChanged( float rmsdB ) {
167       }
168     }
169   }
```

EXAMPLE 10.18 The `MapsActivity` class, Show A Map app, Version 5

override all the methods as do-nothing methods except `onResults`, which is the method processing the speech results. We retrieve the list of possible matching words and assign it to the `ArrayList` `words` at lines 132–133. We retrieve the array of corresponding confidence scores and assign it to the array `scores` at lines 134–135. At lines 137–138, we call the `firstMatchWithMinConfidence` method of the `MatchingUtility` class to retrieve the first element of `words` that would match the `String` equivalent value of one of the constants of the enum `Directions`. We assign it to the `String match`. Note that `match` could be `null` at this point.

Based on the value of `match`, we update the center of the map and refresh it. At line 139, we retrieve the current center of the map and assign it to the `LatLng` variable `pos`. At line 140, we retrieve the current zoom level of the map and assign it to the `float` variable `zoomLevel`. We do not intend to change the zoom level by code in this app, but the second parameter of our `update-Map` method represents the zoom level. If `match` is not `null` (line 142), we update the `pos` variable at lines 143–150, depending on the value of `match`. If `match` matches the enum constant `NORTH` (line 143), we increase the latitude component of `pos` by `DELTA` at line 144, and so on. Note that in order to modify the latitude or longitude of the object that `pos` refers to, we re-instantiate an object every time. This is because the `latitude` and `longitude` instance variables of the `LatLng` class, although `public`, are `final`. Thus, the following code does not compile:

```
pos.latitude = pos.latitude + DELTA;
```

Once `pos` is updated, we call `updateMap` at line 152 to redraw the map. We call `listen` at line 154 to enable the user to enter more voice input; `listen` is originally called at lines 97–98, after the map is displayed.

The `listen` method, coded at lines 108–116, sets up speech recognition. It uses various methods of the `SpeechRecognizer` class listed in **TABLE 10.18**. It initializes `recognizer` at line 111, instantiates a `SpeechListener` object at line 112, and registers it on `recognizer` at line 113. At lines 114–115, we call the `startListening` method with `recognizer`, passing to it an anonymous intent of the speech recognition type.

TABLE 10.18 Selected methods of the `SpeechRecognizer` class

Method	Description
static SpeechRecognizer createSpeechRecognizer(Context context)	Static method that creates a SpeechRecognizer object and returns a reference to it.
void setRecognitionListener(RecognitionListener listener)	Sets listener as the listener that will receive all the callback method calls.
void startListening(Intent intent)	Starts listening to speech.
void stopListening( )	Stops listening to speech.
void destroy( )	Destroys this SpeechRecognizer object.

FIGURE 10.10 **The Show A Map app, Version 5, running inside the tablet, after the user says** `North`

FIGURE 10.10 shows the app running in the tablet after the user says `Paris` and then `North`. Note that again, if we do not speak within a few seconds, the `onError` method is called with a speech timeout error, and speech is no longer processed. If we want to prevent that situation from happening, we can add some logic to detect that situation and restart a new speech recognizer if it occurs. We do that in Version 6.

10.9 Voice Recognition Part C, Moving the Map with Voice Continuously, App Version 6

In Version 6 of the app, we want to keep listening to the user and keep updating the map whenever the user tells us to, even if the user does not talk for a period of time. If that happens, the `onError` method is called and the speech recognizer stops listening so we need to restart it. Thus, we call the `listen` method (line 129 of **EXAMPLE 10.19**) inside the `onError` method in order to do that. In this way, we can keep talking to update the map.

```
...
127
128    public void onError( int error ) {
129      listen( );
130    }
131
```

EXAMPLE 10.19 **The onError method of the MapsActivity class, Show A Map app, Version 6**

Chapter Summary

- The RecognizerIntent class includes constants to support speech recognition that can be used to create an intent.
- To create a speech recognition intent, we use the ACTION_RECOGNIZE_SPEECH constant as the argument of the Intent constructor.
- We can use the PackageManager class, from the android.content.pm package, to retrieve information related to application packages installed on a device.
- The getPackageManager method, from the Context class, returns a PackageManager instance.
- We can use the getStringArrayListExtra method from the Intent class to retrieve a list of possible words that the speech recognizer may have understood.
- We can use the getFloatArrayExtra method from the Intent class to retrieve an array of confidence scores for the list of possible words that the speech recognizer may have understood.
- Map classes are not part of the standard Android Development Kit. If Android Studio is not up to date, they may need to be downloaded and imported. Furthermore, we need a key from Google to be able to use maps.
- Because maps, which are made of map tiles, are downloaded from Google, we need to specify a location access permission in the AndroidManifest,xml file.
- A map is typically displayed inside a fragment.
- The com.google.android.gms.maps package includes many useful map-related classes, such as GoogleMap, CameraUpdate, CameraUpdateFactory, LatLng, CircleOptions, MarkerOptions, etc.
- The LatLng class encapsulates a point on the Earth, defined by its latitude and its longitude.
- The SpeechRecognizer class, along with the RecognitionListener interface, both part of the android.speech package, allow us to listen to and process user speech without using a GUI.

Exercises, Problems, and Projects

Multiple-Choice Exercises

1. What constant do we use to create an intent for speech recognition?
   - ACTION _SPEECH
   - RECOGNIZE_SPEECH
   - ACTION_RECOGNIZE_SPEECH
   - ACTION_RECOGNITION_SPEECH

2. What class includes constants for speech recognition?
   - Activity
   - RecognizerIntent
   - Intent
   - Recognizer

3. What constant of the class in question 2 do we pass to the getStringArrayListExtra method of the Intent class in order to retrieve the possible words recognized from our speech?
   - RESULTS
   - EXTRA_RESULTS
   - RECOGNIZED_WORDS
   - WORDS

4. What constant of the class in question 2 do we pass to the getFloatArrayExtra method of the Intent class in order to retrieve the confidence scores for the words in question 3?
   - SCORES
   - EXTRA_CONFIDENCE_SCORES
   - CONFIDENCE_SCORES
   - CONFIDENCE_WORDS

5. What class can we use to find out if speech recognition is supported by the current device?
   - Manager
   - PackageManager
   - SpeechRecognition
   - Intent

6. Inside the AndroidManifest.xml file, what element do we use to express that this app needs some permission, like go on the Internet, for example?
   - need-permission
   - uses-permission
   - has-permission
   - permission-needed

7. What class can we use to retrieve the latitude and longitude of a point based on the address of that point?
   - Geocoder
   - Address
   - GetLatitudeLongitude
   - LatitudeLongitude

8. In which class are the moveCamera and animateCamera methods?
   - Camera
   - CameraFactory
   - CameraUpdate
   - GoogleMap

9. What class encapsulates a point on Earth defined by its latitude and longitude?
   - Point
   - EarthPoint
   - LatitudeLongitude
   - LatLng

10. What tools can we use to listen to speech without any user interface?
    - The SpeechRecognizer class and the RecognitionListener interface
    - The SpeechRecognizer interface and the RecognitionListener class
    - The SpeechRecognizer class and the RecognitionListener class
    - The SpeechRecognizer interface and the RecognitionListener interface

Fill in the Code

11. Write one statement to create an intent to recognize speech.

12. Assuming that you have created an Intent reference named myIntent to recognize speech, write one statement to start an activity for it.

13. You are executing inside the onActivityResult method, write the code to retrieve how many possible matching words there are for the speech captured.

```
protected void onActivityResult ( int requestCode, int resultCode,
                                   Intent data ) {
    // your code goes here


}
```

14. You are executing inside the onActivityResult method, write the code to count how many possible matching words have a confidence level of at least 25%.

```
protected void onActivityResult ( int requestCode, int resultCode,
                                   Intent data ) {
    // your code goes here



}
```

15. Inside the AndroidManifest.xml file, write one line so that this app is asking permission to access location.

16. A map is displayed on the screen and we have a GoogleMap reference to it named myMap. Write the code to set its zoom level to 7.

17. A map is displayed on the screen and we have a GoogleMap reference to it named myMap. Write the code to move the map so that it is centered on the point with latitude 75.6 and longitude –34.9.

18. A map is displayed on the screen and we have a GoogleMap reference to it named myMap. Write the code to move the map so that it is centered on the point at 1600 Amphitheatre Parkway, Mountain View, CA 94043.

19. A map is displayed on the screen and we have a GoogleMap reference to it named myMap. Write the code to display a blue circle of radius 100 meters and centered at the center of the map.

20. A map is displayed on the screen and we have a GoogleMap reference to it named myMap. Write the code to display an annotation located at the center of the map. If the user clicks on it, it says WELCOME.

21. A map is displayed on the screen and we have a GoogleMap reference to it named myMap. Make the map move so that the latitude of its center increases by 0.2 and the longitude of its center increases by 0.3.

22. You are overriding the onResults method of the RecognitionListener interface. If one of the matching words is NEW YORK, output USA to Logcat.

```
public void onResults( Bundle results ) {
  // your code goes here


}
```

23. You are overriding the onResults method of the RecognitionListener interface. If there is at least one matching word with at least a 25% confidence level, output YES lo Logcat.

```
public void onResults( Bundle results ) {
  // your code goes here


}
```

Write an App

24. Write an app that displays the city where you live with zoom level 14 and add two circles and an annotation to highlight things of interest.

25. Write an app that displays the city where you live and highlight, using something different from a circle or a pin (for example, use a polygon), something of interest (a monument, a stadium, etc.).

26. Write an app that asks the user to enter an address in several TextViews. When the user clicks on a button, the app displays a map centered on that address.

27. Write an app that asks the user to enter an address in several TextViews. When the user clicks on a button, the app displays a map centered on that address. When the user says a number, the map zooms in or out at that level. If the number is not a valid level, the map does not change.

28. Write an app that is a game that works as follows: The app generates a random number between 1 and 10 and the user tries to guess it using voice input. The user has three tries to guess it and the app gives some feedback for each guess. If the user wins or loses (after three tries), do not allow the user to speak again.

29. Write an app that draws circles at some random location on the screen in a color of your choice. The radius of the circle should be captured from speech input.

30. Write an app that displays a 3 × 3 tic-tac-toe grid. If the user says X, place an X at a random location on the grid. If the user says O, place an O at a random location on the grid.

31. Write an app that animates something (a shape or an image) based on speech input. If the user says left, right, up, or down, move that object to the left, right, up, or down by 10 pixels.

32. Write an app that is a mini-translator from English to another language. Include at least 10 words that are recognized by the translator. When the user says a word in English, the app shows the translated word.

33. Write an app that simulates the hangman game. The user is trying to guess a word one letter at a time by saying that letter. The user will lose after using seven incorrect letters (for the head, body, two arms, two legs, and one foot).

34. Write an app that is a math game. The app generates a simple addition equation using two digits between 1 and 9. The user has to submit the answer by voice, and the app checks if the answer is correct.

35. Write an app that is a math game. First, we ask the user (via speech) what type of operation should be used for the game: addition or multiplication. Then the app generates a simple equation using two digits between 1 and 9. The user has to submit the answer by voice, and the app checks if the answer is correct.

36. Write an app that displays a chessboard. When the app starts, all the squares are black and white with alternating colors. When the user says C8 (or another square), that square is colored in red.

37. Write an app that enables a user to play the game of tic-tac-toe by voice. Include a Model.

CHAPTER ELEVEN

Using the GPS and Location Services

CHAPTER CONTENTS

Introduction

Many apps today use the location services of the Android device. One such app is Uber, which people use to find a car to go somewhere for a fee. The app uses the device's **Global Positioning System (GPS)** to locate where we are and find registered car drivers who are nearby. It uses satellites to provide location and time information.

11.1 Accessing Google Play Services, GPS App, Version 0

In this app, we intend to retrieve the location of the device, ask the user for a destination, and calculate the distance and time to destination. In order for the app to retrieve the location of the device using its GPS, it needs to access Google Play services. We use an Empty Activity template for this app. In Version 0 of this app, we show how we can check if a device can access Google Play services. We need to do the following:

▸ Edit the build.gradle file in order to include Google Play services in the compilation process.

▸ Edit the `MainActivity` class in order to access Google Play services.

EXAMPLE 11.1 shows the build.gradle (Module: app) file. We edit it in order to make the Google Play services libraries available to the app (note that there are two build.gradle files). The only addition is at line 26: we include the appropriate version of the Google Play services libraries. At the time of this writing, it is 9.4.0.

```
21
22   dependencies {
23       compile fileTree( dir: 'libs', include: ['*.jar'])
24       testCompile 'junit:junit:4.12'
25       compile 'com.android.support:appcompat-v7:23.4.0'
26       compile 'com.google.android.gms:play-services:9.4.0'
27   }
```

EXAMPLE 11.1 The build.gradle (Module: app) file

After editing the build.gradle file, we should click on the Sync Project with Gradle Files icon on the tool bar, as shown on **FIGURE 11.1**.

Inside the `MainActivity` class, we do the following:

▸ Try to access Google Play services from the device.

▸ If we cannot and the issue can be resolved, we try to resolve it. Otherwise, we exit the app.

▸ Retrieve the current location and display it.

FIGURE 11.1 The Sync Project with Gradle Files icon

TABLE 11.1 Selected methods of the `GoogleApiClient.Builder` class	
Method	**Description**
GoogleApiClient.Builder(Context context)	Constructs a GoogleApiClient object.
GoogleApiClient.Builder addConnectionCallbacks(GoogleApiClient. ConnectionCallbacks listener)	Registers listener to receive connection events. Returns this GoogleApiClient.Builder reference so method calls can be chained.
GoogleApiClient.Builder addOnConnectionFailedListener(GoogleApiClient.ConnectionFailedListener listener)	Registers listener to receive failed connection events. Returns this GoogleApiClient.Builder reference so method calls can be chained.
GoogleApiClient.Builder addApi(API<? extends Api.ApiOptions. NotRequiredOptions> api)	Specifies api as an API requested by this app. We should use the API constant of LocationServices. Returns this GoogleApiClient.Builder reference so method calls can be chained.
GoogleApiClient build( )	Builds and returns a GoogleApiClient object for communicating with the Google APIs.

The `GoogleApiClient` abstract class, from the `com.google.android.gms.common.api` package, is the main entry point for Google Play services. It includes the functionality to establish a connection to Google Play services and manage it. Since it is `abstract`, we cannot instantiate an object of that class using the `new` operator. It includes a `static` inner class, `Builder`, which includes methods to specify attributes of a `GoogleApiClient` and a `build` method to create one. TABLE 11.1 lists some of these methods. These methods, except the `build` method, return the `GoogleApiClient.Builder` reference that calls them, so that method calls can be chained. The `build` method returns a `GoogleApiClient` reference.

The `GoogleApiClient` class includes the `ConnectionCallbacks` and `OnConnectionFailedListener` `static` inner interfaces. `ConnectionCallbacks` provides callback methods that are automatically called when we connect or are disconnected from the Google service. `OnConnectionFailedListener` provides a callback method that is automatically called if the connection attempt failed. TABLE 11.2 lists them. The `int` parameter of the

TABLE 11.2 The `ConnectionCallbacks` and `OnConnectionFailedListener` interfaces and their methods

Interface	Method	Description
ConnectionCallbacks	void onConnected(Bundle connectionHint)	Automatically called after successful completion of a connection request made by calling the connect method with a GoogleApiClient reference.
ConnectionCallbacks	void onConnectionSuspended(int cause)	Automatically called when the connection is lost. The GoogleApiClient object will automatically attempt to restore the connection.
OnConnectionFailedListener	void onConnectionFailed(ConnectionResult result)	Automatically called when there is an error connecting to the service.

onConnectionSuspended method can be tested against the CAUSE_SERVICE_DISCONNECTED and CAUSE_NETWORK_LOST constants of the ConnectionCallbacks interface in order to determine the cause of the disconnection.

Thus, assuming we are inside an Activity class that implements the ConnectionCallbacks and OnConnectionFailedListener interfaces, we can instantiate a GoogleApiClient object using the following sequence:

```
// Assuming that we are inside an Activity class and that it
// implements ConnectionCallbacks and OnConnectionFailedListener
GoogleApiClient.Builder builder = new GoogleApiClient.Builder( this );
builder.addConnectionCallbacks( this );
builder.addOnConnectionFailedListener( this );
builder.addApi( LocationServices.API );
GoogleApiClient gac = builder.build( );
```

Since we are inside an Activity class, we can use this as the argument of the GoogleApiClient.Builder constructor. Since the Activity class implements both interfaces, we can also use this as the argument of addConnectionCallbacks and addOnConnectionFailed Listener. We use the API constant of the LocationServices class, shown in **TABLE 11.3**, as the argument of the addApi method. Alternatively, since these three methods return the GoogleApiClient.Builder reference that calls them, we can chain method calls as follows:

```
GoogleApiClient gac = new GoogleApiClient.Builder( this )
                .addConnectionCallbacks( this )
                .addOnConnectionFailedListener( this )
                .addApi( LocationServices.API ).build( );
```

TABLE 11.3 Selected fields of the `LocationServices` class

Constant	Description
API	A constant that should be used to pass to the addApi method of the GoogleApi.Builder class during the process of building a GoogleApiClient.
FusedLocationAPI	Static constant of type FusedLocationProviderAPI, an interface that includes methods to retrieve the location of a device and manage location updates.

TABLE 11.4 Selected methods of the `GoogleApiClient` class

Methods	Description
void connect( )	Establishes a connection with Google Play services. If successful, the onConnected method of ConnectionCallbacks is called. If unsuccessful, onConnectionFailed is called.
void disconnect( )	Closes the connection with Google Play services.

Once we have a `GoogleApiClient` reference, and assuming its name is `gac`, we can attempt to establish a connection by calling the `connect` method of `GoogleApiClient`, shown in TABLE 11.4, as in the code that follows:

```
// Assuming that gac is a GoogleApiClient reference
gac.connect( );
```

If the connection is successful, the `onConnected` method of the `ConnectionCallbacks` interface is automatically called. Inside that method, we can retrieve the location of the device.

If the device fails to connect to Google Play services, the `onConnectionFailed` callback method is called. We want to check if that issue can be resolved (for example, Google Play services may need to be updated on the device). We can do that by calling the `hasResolution` method with the `ConnectionResult` parameter of `onConnectionFailed`. If that method returns `false`, the issue cannot be resolved and we can exit the app. If that method returns `true`, the issue can be resolved and we want to try to resolve it. We can do so by calling the `startResolutionForResult` method of `ConnectionResult`. TABLE 11.5 shows both methods. This requires user interaction. After it is over, the `onActivityResult` method of the `Activity` class will be called. Inside that method, we can check if the issue was resolved. If it was, we can try to connect again to Google Play services.

TABLE 11.5 Selected methods of the `ConnectionResult` class

Method	Description
boolean hasResolution( )	Returns true if there is a resolution that can be started to attempt to solve the connection issue.
void startResolutionForResult(Activity activity, int requestCode)	Starts an intent to attempt to resolve a connection issue. This requires user interaction.

We can implement this with the following pseudo-code:

```
// inside onConnectionFailed method
if( there is a possible resolution to the issue )
  call startResolutionForResult to try to resolve it
else
  exit the app
// inside onActivityResult
if( the problem was resolved )
  try to connect again
```

EXAMPLE 11.2 shows the `MainActivity` class. It implements the `ConnectionCallbacks` and `OnConnectionFailedListener` interfaces (lines 14–15). We declare a `GoogleApiClient` instance variable at line 18. We instantiate it at lines 25–28. The `onStart` method is automatically

```
1    package com.jblearning.gpsv0;
2
3    import android.content.Intent;
4    import android.content.IntentSender;
5    import android.os.Bundle;
6    import android.support.v7.app.AppCompatActivity;
7    import android.util.Log;
8    import android.widget.Toast;
9    import com.google.android.gms.common.ConnectionResult;
10   import com.google.android.gms.common.api.GoogleApiClient;
11   import com.google.android.gms.location.LocationServices;
12
13   public class MainActivity extends AppCompatActivity
14          implements GoogleApiClient.ConnectionCallbacks,
15                     GoogleApiClient.OnConnectionFailedListener {
16     public static final String MA = "MainActivity";
17     private final static int REQUEST_CODE = 100;
18     private GoogleApiClient gac;
19
20     @Override
```

EXAMPLE 11.2 The `MainActivity` class, GPS app, Version 0 (*Continued*)

```
21        protected void onCreate( Bundle savedInstanceState ) {
22          super.onCreate( savedInstanceState );
23          setContentView( R.layout.activity_main );
24
25          gac = new GoogleApiClient.Builder( this )
26                  .addConnectionCallbacks( this )
27                  .addOnConnectionFailedListener( this )
28                  .addApi( LocationServices.API ).build( );
29        }
30
31        public void onConnected( Bundle hint ) {
32          Log.w( MA, "connected" );
33          // make a request here
34        }
35
36        public void onConnectionSuspended( int cause ) {
37          Log.w( MA, "connection suspended" );
38          // Our GoogleApiClient will automatically try to restore the connection
39        }
40
41        public void onConnectionFailed( ConnectionResult result ) {
42          // test result here
43          Log.w( MA, "connection failed" );
44          if( result.hasResolution( ) ) { // a resolution can be started
45            try {
46              result.startResolutionForResult( this, REQUEST_CODE );
47            } catch( IntentSender.SendIntentException sie ) {
48              // Intent has been cancelled or cannot execute, exit app
49              Toast.makeText( this, "Google Play services problem, exiting",
50                      Toast.LENGTH_LONG ).show( );
51              finish( );
52            }
53          }
54        }
55
56        public void onActivityResult( int requestCode,
57                                      int resultCode, Intent data ) {
58          if( requestCode == REQUEST_CODE && resultCode == RESULT_OK ) {
59            // problem solved, try to connect again
60            gac.connect( );
61          }
62        }
63
64        protected void onStart( ) {
65          super.onStart( );
66          if( gac != null )
67            gac.connect( );
68        }
69    }
```

EXAMPLE 11.2 **The MainActivity class, GPS app, Version 0**

called after onCreate executes. If gac is not null (line 66), we try to establish the connection at line 67. If successful, this triggers a call to the onConnected method (lines 31–34). In this version, we simply output some feedback to Logcat. If the connection attempt fails, we execute inside onConnectionFailed (lines 41–54). At line 44, we test if there is a possible resolution to that problem. If there is, we try to start an activity to solve it at line 46. If we cannot, we exit the app after showing a Toast (lines 48–51). If we were successful in starting an activity to try to solve the connection problem, and after interaction with the user, the app will resume execution inside the onActivityResult method (lines 56–62). If the resolution was successful (line 58), we try to connect to Google Play services again at line 60.

When running the GPS app, Version 0, the output inside Logcat shows that we are connected.

11.2 Using the GPS to Retrieve Our Location, GPS App, Version 1

In Version 1, we retrieve the location of the device and display it in a TextView. Since the app accesses the GPS, it will not work in the emulator, although we could hard code latitude and longitude data using the emulator. To use our current location, we need to run it on a device. Because the app uses location services from Google, we need to specify that in the AndroidManifest.xml file. Thus, we need to do the following:

▶ In the AndroidManifest.xml file, specify that we use location services and add meta data about the Google Play services version this app uses.

▶ Inside the MainActivity class, capture our current location and display it.

EXAMPLE 11.3 shows the AndroidManifest.xml file. At lines 5–6, we specify that this app accesses the approximate location of the device. The ACCESS_COARSE_LOCATION and ACCESS_FINE_LOCATION String constants of the Manifest.permission class can be used to specify an approximate or a precise location, respectively. At lines 15–17, we specify the version of Google Play services that this app uses. To make it simple, we only allow the app to work in vertical orientation (line 20).

Inside the MainActivity class, we do the following:

▶ Establish a connection with Google Play services.
▶ Retrieve the location.
▶ Display the location.

The Location class, part of the android.location package, encapsulates a geographical location on Earth. A location is typically identified by its latitude and longitude. TABLE 11.6 lists a few methods of the Location class. Note that the Location class uses the metric system and distances, when calculated by methods, are returned in meters.

The lastLocation method of the FusedLocationProviderApi interface returns the current location of the device as a Location reference. It accepts a GoogleApiClient parameter, as shown in TABLE 11.7. We use this method to retrieve the device's location. Thus, in order to call that

```
1    <?xml version="1.0" encoding="utf-8"?>
2    <manifest xmlns:android="http://schemas.android.com/apk/res/android"
3      package="com.jblearning.gpsv1">
4
5      <uses-permission android:name
6        ="android.permission.ACCESS_COARSE_LOCATION" />
7
8      <application
9        android:allowBackup="true"
10       android:icon="@mipmap/ic_launcher"
11       android:label="@string/app_name"
12       android:supportsRtl="true"
13       android:theme="@style/AppTheme">
14
15       <meta-data
16         android:name="com.google.android.gms.version"
17         android:value="@integer/google_play_services_version" />
18
19       <activity android:name=".MainActivity"
20         android:screenOrientation="portrait">
21         <intent-filter>
22           <action android:name="android.intent.action.MAIN" />
23
24           <category android:name="android.intent.category.LAUNCHER" />
25         </intent-filter>
26       </activity>
27     </application>
28
29   </manifest>
```

EXAMPLE 11.3 **The AndroidManifest.xml file**

TABLE 11.6 Selected methods of the `Location` class

Method	Description
double getLatitude( )	Returns the latitude of this Location.
double getLongitude( )	Returns the longitude of this Location.
float getAccuracy( )	Returns the accuracy of this Location, in meters.
float distanceTo(Location destination)	Returns the distance between this Location and destination, in meters.

TABLE 11.7 The `getLastLocation` method of the `FusedLocationProviderApi` interface

Method	Description
Location getLastLocation(GoogleApiClient gac)	Returns the most recent location, null if no location is available.

method, we need a `FusedLocationProviderApi` reference to call it, and a `GoogleApiClient` reference to pass as its only argument. As shown in Table 11.3, the `LocationServices` class, part of the `com.google.android.gms.location` package, includes a `FusedLocationProviderApi` constant named `FusedLocationApi`. Thus, assuming we have a `GoogleApiClient` reference named `gac`, we can retrieve the current location using the following sequence:

```
// Assuming that gac is a GoogleApiClient reference
FusedLocationProviderApi flpa = LocationServices.FusedLocationApi;
Location location = flpa.getLastLocation( gac );
```

Once we have a `Location` reference for the current location, we can retrieve the latitude and longitude of that location by calling the `getLatitude` and `getLongitude` methods as follows:

```
double latitude = location.getLatitude( );
double longitude = location.getLongitude( );
```

EXAMPLE 11.4 shows the `MainActivity` class. We declare two additional instance variables at lines 23–24: `location`, a `Location` to store the current location; and `locationTV`, a

```
1    package com.jblearning.gpsv1;
2
3    import android.content.Intent;
4    import android.content.IntentSender;
5    import android.location.Location;
6    import android.os.Bundle;
7    import android.support.v7.app.AppCompatActivity;
8    import android.util.Log;
9    import android.widget.TextView;
10   import android.widget.Toast;
11   import com.google.android.gms.common.ConnectionResult;
12   import com.google.android.gms.common.api.GoogleApiClient;
13   import com.google.android.gms.location.FusedLocationProviderApi;
14   import com.google.android.gms.location.LocationServices;
```

EXAMPLE 11.4 The `MainActivity` class, GPS app, Version 1 (*Continued*)

```
15
16   public class MainActivity extends AppCompatActivity
17           implements GoogleApiClient.ConnectionCallbacks,
18                      GoogleApiClient.OnConnectionFailedListener {
19     public static final String MA = "MainActivity";
20     private final static int REQUEST_CODE = 100;
21
22     private GoogleApiClient gac;
23     private Location location;
24     private TextView locationTV;
25
26     @Override
27     protected void onCreate( Bundle savedInstanceState ) {
28       super.onCreate( savedInstanceState );
29       setContentView( R.layout.activity_main );
30       locationTV = ( TextView ) findViewById( R.id.location_tv );
31
32       gac = new GoogleApiClient.Builder( this )
33               .addConnectionCallbacks( this )
34               .addOnConnectionFailedListener( this )
35               .addApi( LocationServices.API ).build( );
36     }
37
38     public void displayLocation( ) {
39       FusedLocationProviderApi flpa = LocationServices.FusedLocationApi;
40       location = flpa.getLastLocation( gac );
41       if( location != null ) {
42         double latitude = location.getLatitude( );
43         double longitude = location.getLongitude( );
44         locationTV.setText( latitude + ", " + longitude );
45         Log.w( MA, "latitude = " + latitude + "; longitude = " + longitude );
46       } else
47         locationTV.setText( "Error locating the device" );
48     }
49
50     public void onConnected( Bundle hint ) {
51       Log.w( MA, "connected" );
52       displayLocation( );
53     }
54
55     public void onConnectionSuspended( int cause ) {
56       Log.w( MA, "connection suspended" );
57       // Our GoogleApiClient will automatically try to restore the connection
58     }
59
```

EXAMPLE 11.4 **The** `MainActivity` **class, GPS app, Version 1 (*Continued*)**

```
60    public void onConnectionFailed( ConnectionResult result ) {
61      // test result here
62      Log.w( MA, "connection failed" );
63      if( result.hasResolution( ) ) { // a resolution can be started
64        try {
65          result.startResolutionForResult( this, REQUEST_CODE );
66        } catch( IntentSender.SendIntentException sie ) {
67          // Intent has been cancelled or cannot execute, exit app
68          Toast.makeText( this, "Google Play services problem, exiting",
69                    Toast.LENGTH_LONG ).show( );
70          finish( );
71        }
72      }
73    }
74
75    public void onActivityResult( int requestCode,
76                                  int resultCode, Intent data ) {
77      if( requestCode == REQUEST_CODE && resultCode == RESULT_OK ) {
78        // problem solved, try to connect again
79        gac.connect( );
80      }
81    }
82
83      protected void onStart( ) {
84      super.onStart( );
85      if( gac != null )
86        gac.connect( );
87    }
88  }
```

EXAMPLE 11.4 **The MainActivity class, GPS app, Version 1**

TextView to display the location. Inside onCreate, we instantiate the TextView at line 30. This assumes that there is a TextView whose id is location_tv inside activity_main.xml. Inside the onConnected method, we call the displayLocation method at line 52. The displayLocation method (lines 38–48) retrieves the current device location at lines 39–40. If the location is not null (line 41), we retrieve its latitude and longitude, display them inside the TextView (line 44), and output them to Logcat (line 45).

    EXAMPLE 11.5 shows the activity_main.xml file. The id of the TextView is assigned at line 13. **EXAMPLE 11.6** shows the styles.xml file, which specifies a font size of 22 at line 5.

    FIGURE 11.2 shows the output of the app inside Logcat, showing the latitude and longitude data. Note that we must run this app on a connected device (which has GPS), not the emulator.

```
1    <?xml version="1.0" encoding="utf-8"?>
2    <RelativeLayout xmlns:android="http://schemas.android.com/apk/res/android"
3        xmlns:tools="http://schemas.android.com/tools"
4        android:layout_width="match_parent"
5        android:layout_height="match_parent"
6        android:paddingBottom="@dimen/activity_vertical_margin"
7        android:paddingLeft="@dimen/activity_horizontal_margin"
8        android:paddingRight="@dimen/activity_horizontal_margin"
9        android:paddingTop="@dimen/activity_vertical_margin"
10       tools:context="com.jblearning.gpsv1.MainActivity">
11
12       <TextView
13           android:id="@+id/location_tv"
14           android:layout_width="wrap_content"
15           android:layout_height="wrap_content" />
16   </RelativeLayout>
```

EXAMPLE 11.5 The activity_main.xml file, GPS app, Version 1

```
1    <resources>
2
3        <!-- Base application theme. -->
4        <style name="AppTheme" parent="Theme.AppCompat.Light.DarkActionBar">
5            <item name="android:textSize">22sp</item>
6            <item name="colorPrimary">@color/colorPrimary</item>
7            <item name="colorPrimaryDark">@color/colorPrimaryDark</item>
8            <item name="colorAccent">@color/colorAccent</item>
9        </style>
10
11   </resources>
```

EXAMPLE 11.6 The styles.xml file, GPS app, Version 1

```
connected
latitude = 39.567567567567565; longitude = -76.71181039801893
```

FIGURE 11.2 The Logcat output of the GPS app Version 1

11.3 Model for Distance and Time to Destination

In Version 2, we ask the user to input an address for his or her destination, and we provide a button to display the distance and time left to that destination. Before building the GUI and the controller for it, we add the TravelManager class, the Model for the app, shown in **EXAMPLE 11.7**.

```
1    package com.jblearning.gpsv2;
2
3    import android.location.Location;
4
5    public class TravelManager {
6      public static float DEFAULT_SPEED = 55.0f; // mph
7      public static int METERS_PER_MILE = 1600;
8
9      private Location destination;
10
11     public void setDestination( Location newDestination ) {
12       destination = newDestination;
13     }
14
15     // returns distance from current to destination in meters
16     public float distanceToDestination( Location current ) {
17       if( current!= null && destination != null )
18         return current.distanceTo( destination );
19       else
20         return -1.0f;
21     }
22
23     // returns distance from current to destination in miles
24     public String milesToDestination( Location current ) {
25       int distance =
26         ( int ) ( distanceToDestination( current ) / METERS_PER_MILE );
27       if( distance > 1 )
28         return distance + " miles";
29       else
30         return "0 mile";
31     }
32
33     // returns time from current to destination in hours and minutes
34     public String timeToDestination( Location current ) {
35       // # of meters from current location to destination
36       float metersToGo = distanceToDestination( current );
37       // hours from current location to destination at default speed
38       float timeToGo = metersToGo / ( DEFAULT_SPEED * METERS_PER_MILE );
39
40       String result = "";
41       int hours = ( int ) timeToGo;
42       if( hours == 1 )
43         result += "1 hour ";
44       else if( hours > 1 )
45         result += hours + " hours ";
46       int minutes = ( int ) ( ( timeToGo - hours ) * 60 );
```

EXAMPLE 11.7 **The `TravelManager` class, GPS app, Version 2 (Continued)**

```
47          if ( minutes == 1 )
48              result += "1 minute ";
49          else if ( minutes > 1 )
50              result += minutes + " minutes";
51          if ( hours <= 0 && minutes <= 0 )
52              result = "less than a minute left";
53          return result;
54      }
55  }
```

EXAMPLE 11.7 **The `TravelManager` class, GPS app, Version 2**

It includes a `Location` instance variable to store a destination (line 9) and methods to calculate the distance and time left from the current location to the destination location. In order to keep this app simple, we assume that the user travels at 55 miles per hour (line 6).

In the `distanceToDestination` method (lines 15–21), we call the `distanceTo` method of the `Location` class shown in Table 11.6 in order to calculate the distance between its `Location` parameter and `destination`. If one of them is `null`, it returns –1. Otherwise, we return the distance between them. The `milesToDestination` method (lines 23–31) converts and returns that distance to a `String` representing the number of miles.

The `timeToDestination` method (lines 33–54) calculates and returns the time that it takes to go from its `Location` parameter and destination, assuming a speed of 55 miles per hour. At lines 35–36, we compute the distance to the destination from its `Location` parameter in meters. At 37–38, we compute the time in hours, as a `float`, that it takes to drive that distance at a speed of 55 miles per hour. We then convert that value to the `String result`, which represents the number of hours and the number of minutes at lines 40–52. Note that if the time is either 0 or negative (line 51), we assign `less than a minute left` to `result` at line 52.

11.4 Distance and Time to Destination, GPS App, Version 2

We include the following elements in the GUI, all centered and lined up vertically:

▶ One EditText for the user to enter the destination address.
▶ Two TextViews to display the distance and time to destination.
▶ One `Button`: when the user clicks on it, we update the distance and time to destination in the two `TextViews`.

EXAMPLE 11.8 shows the updated activity_main.xml file. We give all the elements an id (lines 13, 18, 23, 28) so we can position them and retrieve them as needed in the `MainActivity` class. We want to specify the WRAP_CONTENT value for both the width and height of all the elements. We also want to have 20 pixels between them and center them horizontally. Thus, we define

```
1   <?xml version="1.0" encoding="utf-8"?>
2   <RelativeLayout xmlns:android="http://schemas.android.com/apk/res/android"
3       xmlns:tools="http://schemas.android.com/tools"
4       android:layout_width="match_parent"
5       android:layout_height="match_parent"
6       android:paddingBottom="@dimen/activity_vertical_margin"
7       android:paddingLeft="@dimen/activity_horizontal_margin"
8       android:paddingRight="@dimen/activity_horizontal_margin"
9       android:paddingTop="@dimen/activity_vertical_margin"
10      tools:context="com.jblearning.gpsv2.MainActivity">
11
12      <EditText
13          android:id="@+id/destination_et"
14          android:hint="@string/enter_destination"
15          style="@style/WrappedAndCentered" />
16
17      <TextView
18          android:id="@+id/distance_tv"
19          android:layout_below="@id/destination_et"
20          style="@style/WrappedAndCentered" />
21
22      <TextView
23          android:id="@+id/time_left_tv"
24          android:layout_below="@id/distance_tv"
25          style="@style/WrappedAndCentered" />
26
27      <Button
28          android:id="@+id/miles_time_button"
29          android:layout_below="@id/time_left_tv"
30          android:text="@string/button_text"
31          android:onClick="updateTrip"
32          style="@style/WrappedAndCentered" />
33  </RelativeLayout>
```

EXAMPLE 11.8 The activity_main.xml file, GPS app, Version 2

the `WrappedAndCentered` style in styles.xml (lines 11–16 of **EXAMPLE 11.9**) and use it for all the four elements (lines 15, 20, 25, 32). We specify a hint, `Enter destination`, defined in the strings.xml file (line 3 of **EXAMPLE 11.10**) for the `EditText` at line 14. At line 30, we define the text inside the button as the `String Update`, defined at line 4 of Example 11.10. At line 31, we specify that the `updateTrip` method is called when the user clicks on the `Button`.

Inside the `MainActivity` class, we need to make the following edits:

▶ Add the appropriate import statements.
▶ Add a `TravelManager` instance variable so that we can access the functionality of the Model.

```
1    <resources>
2
3        <!-- Base application theme. -->
4        <style name="AppTheme" parent="Theme.AppCompat.Light.DarkActionBar">
5            <item name="android:textSize">22sp</item>
6            <item name="colorPrimary">@color/colorPrimary</item>
7            <item name="colorPrimaryDark">@color/colorPrimaryDark</item>
8            <item name="colorAccent">@color/colorAccent</item>
9        </style>
10
11       <style name="WrappedAndCentered" parent="AppTheme">
12           <item name="android:layout_width">wrap_content</item>
13           <item name="android:layout_height">wrap_content</item>
14           <item name="android:layout_centerHorizontal">true</item>
15           <item name="android:layout_marginTop">20dp</item>
16       </style>
17
18   </resources>
```

EXAMPLE 11.9 **The styles.xml file, GPS app, Version 2**

```
1    <resources>
2        <string name="app_name">GpsV2</string>
3        <string name="enter_destination">Enter destination</string>
4        <string name="button_text">Update</string>
5    </resources>
```

EXAMPLE 11.10 **The strings.xml file, GPS app, Version 2**

▷ Add instance variables for the EditText and the two TextViews of the GUI and a String to store the destination address.

▷ Delete the displayLocation method: we are no longer interested in displaying our location.

▷ Add the updateTrip method.

▷ Delete the body of the onConnected method: we want to wait for the user to input a destination address before we do anything.

EXAMPLE 11.11 shows the updated MainActivity class. We declare the additional five instance variables at lines 29–33. The TravelManager and the three GUI components are instantiated inside onCreate at lines 39–42. Inside the updateTrip method (lines 50–79), we retrieve user input, update the Model if necessary, call methods of the Model to calculate the distance and time left to the destination, and update the View accordingly.

```
 1  package com.jblearning.gpsv2;
 2
 3  import android.content.Intent;
 4  import android.content.IntentSender;
 5  import android.location.Address;
 6  import android.location.Geocoder;
 7  import android.location.Location;
 8  import android.os.Bundle;
 9  import android.support.v7.app.AppCompatActivity;
10  import android.view.View;
11  import android.widget.EditText;
12  import android.widget.TextView;
13  import android.widget.Toast;
14
15  import com.google.android.gms.common.ConnectionResult;
16  import com.google.android.gms.common.api.GoogleApiClient;
17  import com.google.android.gms.location.FusedLocationProviderApi;
18  import com.google.android.gms.location.LocationServices;
19
20  import java.io.IOException;
21  import java.util.List;
22
23  public class MainActivity extends AppCompatActivity
24          implements GoogleApiClient.ConnectionCallbacks,
25                     GoogleApiClient.OnConnectionFailedListener {
26    private final static int REQUEST_CODE = 100;
27
28    private GoogleApiClient gac;
29    private TravelManager manager;
30    private EditText addressET;
31    private TextView distanceTV;
32    private TextView timeLeftTV;
33    private String destinationAddress = "";
34
35    @Override
36    protected void onCreate( Bundle savedInstanceState ) {
37      super.onCreate( savedInstanceState );
38      setContentView( R.layout.activity_main );
39      manager = new TravelManager( );
40      addressET = ( EditText ) findViewById( R.id.destination_et );
41      distanceTV = ( TextView ) findViewById( R.id.distance_tv );
42      timeLeftTV = ( TextView ) findViewById( R.id.time_left_tv );
43
44      gac = new GoogleApiClient.Builder( this )
45              .addConnectionCallbacks( this )
46              .addOnConnectionFailedListener( this )
```

EXAMPLE 11.11 The `MainActivity` class, GPS app, Version 2 (*Continued*)

```
47                  .addApi( LocationServices.API ).build( );
48      }
49
50    public void updateTrip( View v ) {
51      String address = addressET.getText( ).toString( );
52      boolean goodGeoCoding = true;
53      if( ! address.equals( destinationAddress ) ) {
54        destinationAddress = address;
55        Geocoder coder = new Geocoder( this );
56        try {
57          // geocode destination
58          List<Address> addresses
59                  = coder.getFromLocationName( destinationAddress, 5 );
60          if( addresses != null ) {
61            double latitude = addresses.get( 0 ).getLatitude( );
62            double longitude = addresses.get( 0 ).getLongitude( );
63            Location destinationLocation = new Location( "destination" );
64            destinationLocation.setLatitude( latitude );
65            destinationLocation.setLongitude( longitude );
66            manager.setDestination( destinationLocation );
67          }
68        } catch ( IOException ioe ) {
69          goodGeoCoding = false;
70        }
71      }
72
73      FusedLocationProviderApi flpa = LocationServices.FusedLocationApi;
74      Location current = flpa.getLastLocation( gac );
75      if( current != null && goodGeoCoding ) {
76        distanceTV.setText( manager.milesToDestination( current ) );
77        timeLeftTV.setText( manager.timeToDestination( current ) );
78      }
79    }
80
81    public void onConnected( Bundle hint ) {
82    }
83
84    public void onConnectionSuspended( int cause ) {
85    }
86
87    public void onConnectionFailed( ConnectionResult result ) {
88      if( result.hasResolution( ) ) { // a resolution can be started
89        try {
90          result.startResolutionForResult( this, REQUEST_CODE );
91        } catch( IntentSender.SendIntentException sie ) {
92          // Intent has been cancelled or cannot execute, exit app
```

EXAMPLE 11.11 **The** `MainActivity` **class, GPS app, Version 2 (***Continued***)**

```
 93              Toast.makeText( this, "Google Play services problem, exiting",
 94                    Toast.LENGTH_LONG ).show( );
 95            finish( );
 96          }
 97        }
 98      }
 99
100    public void onActivityResult( int requestCode,
101                              int resultCode, Intent data ) {
102      if( requestCode == REQUEST_CODE && resultCode == RESULT_OK ) {
103        // problem solved, try to connect again
104        gac.connect( );
105      }
106    }
107
108    protected void onStart( ) {
109      super.onStart( );
110      if( gac != null )
111        gac.connect( );
112    }
113  }
```

EXAMPLE 11.11 **The `MainActivity` class, GPS app, Version 2**

We first retrieve the destination address entered by the user at line 51. If the destination address is different from the current destination address (line 53), we update the current destination address (line 54). We then try to geocode it into a `Location` object (lines 57–59). Geocoding is the process of converting a street address into a (latitude, longitude) coordinate. **TABLE 11.8** shows a constructor and a `getFromLocationName` method of the `Geocoder` class. If the geocoding is successful (line 60), we assign the `Location` to the `destination` instance variable of the `TravelManager` (line 66). We keep track of whether the geocoding is successful or not with the state variable `goodGeocoding`. We initialize it to `true` at line 52, and switch it to `false` if we end up in the `catch` block at line 69. We retrieve the current location at lines 73–74. If we are successful retrieving the current location and if the geocoding was successful (line 75), we update

TABLE 11.8 Selected methods of the `Geocoder` class

Methods	Description
Geocoder(Context context)	Constructs a Geocoder.
List getFromLocationName(String locationName, int maxResults)	Returns a list of Address objects that match locationName. Throws an IllegalArgumentException and an IOException.

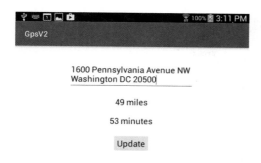

FIGURE 11.3 The GPS app, Version 2, running inside the tablet

the two `TextViews` displaying the distance and time left to the destination at lines 76–77. The `manager` instance variable calls the `milesToDestination` and `timeToDestination` methods, passing the current location.

FIGURE 11.3 shows the app running inside the tablet after the user enters the address of the White House and clicks on update.

11.5 Updating Distance and Time to Destination, GPS App, Version 3

In Version 3, we want to update the distance and time left to destination automatically, without having to click on the `Update` button. We keep the Update button in case the user wants an instant update. Thus, the user interface is identical to the one in Version 2.

The `LocationListener` interface, part of the `com.google.android.gms.location` package, provides a callback method, `onLocationChanged`, that is automatically called based on

TABLE 11.9 The `onLocationChanged` method of the `LocationListener` class

Method	Description
void onLocationChanged(Location location)	Callback method called automatically as defined by a LocationRequest; location represents the most recent location.

TABLE 11.10 Selected methods of the `FusedLocationProviderApi` interface

Method	Description
PendingResult requestLocationUpdates(GoogleApiClient gap, LocationRequest request, LocationListener listener)	Requests listener to listen to location updates based on request.
PendingResult removeLocationUpdates(GoogleApiClient gap, LocationListener listener)	Discontinues location updates for listener.

various specified parameters, such as frequency and distance travelled, as shown in TABLE 11.9. This is very similar to event handling; we need to do the following:

▶ Create a private class that implements `LocationListener` (and override `onLocationChanged`).
▶ Declare and instantiate an object of that class.
▶ Register that object on a fused location provider (a `FusedLocationProviderApi` reference).

Alternatively, we can do the following:

▶ Have our `Activity` class implement `LocationListener` (and override `onLocationChanged`).
▶ Register `this` on a fused location provider (a `FusedLocationProviderApi` reference).

We choose to implement the second strategy. TABLE 11.10 shows one of the `requestLocationUpdates` methods of the `FusedLocationProviderApi` interface. It requests that its `LocationListener` parameter provides location updates, via the `onLocationChanged` method, as defined by its `LocationRequest` parameter. Thus, assuming that we are inside an `Activity` class that implements the `LocationListener` interface, and that a `LocationRequest` named `request` has been defined, we can request location updates using the following code sequence:

```
// we are inside an Activity class that implements LocationListener
// thus, this "is a" LocationListener
// gac is a GoogleApiClient reference
// request is a LocationRequest reference
FusedLocationProviderApi flpa = LocationServices.FusedLocationApi;
flpa.requestLocationUpdates( gac, request, this );
```

TABLE 11.11 Selected methods of the `LocationRequest` class	
Method	**Description**
LocationRequest setInterval(long ms)	Sets the interval for location updates in milliseconds. Returns this LocationRequest so method calls can be chained.
LocationRequest setPriority(int priority)	Sets priority of this request. The LocationRequest class includes constants (see Table 11.12) that can be used as the argument. Returns this LocationRequest so method calls can be chained.
LocationRequest setSmallestDisplacement(float meters)	Sets the minimum distance between consecutive updates. Returns this LocationRequest so method calls can be chained.

At that point, we will receive updates and the `onLocationChanged` method will be called at the frequency specified by the `LocationRequest`. Its `Location` parameter stores the most recent location, as follows.

```
public void onLocationChanged( Location location ) {
  // location is the most recent location
}
```

The `LocationRequest` class provides the functionality to define a request for location updates by specifying the frequency of updates, their accuracy, etc.

TABLE 11.11 shows the two most important methods of the `LocationRequest` class. We use the `setInterval` method to specify the desired frequency, in milliseconds, of location updates. A location update consumes power, and frequent updates can drain the device's battery. We use the `setPriority` method to specify a desired accuracy level, which in turn is a hint at what source to use, GPS or Wi-Fi and cell tower. However, other factors, such as the current location and availability or such sources, as well as the device itself, can impact the accuracy of the location returned. All the set methods of the `LocationRequest` class return the `LocationRequest` reference that calls them, so that we can chain method calls. If we do not want updates—if we have not moved by a minimum distance—we can use the `setSmallestDisplacement` method and specify such minimum distance between two consecutive updates. For example, in a travel app, the user does not need distance updates if he or she is stuck in traffic and is not moving.

The following code sequence shows how to define a `LocationRequest`:

```
LocationRequest request = new LocationRequest( );
request.setInterval( 30000); // 30 seconds interval
request.setPriority( LocationRequest.PRIORITY_HIGH_ACCURACY );
request.setSmallestDisplacement(100); // 100 meters minimum
```

TABLE 11.12 shows the constants of the `LocationRequest` class that we can use as the argument of the `setPriority` method. The higher the accuracy requested, the higher the battery

TABLE 11.12 Priority constants of the `LocationRequest` class

Constant	Value	Description
PRIORITY_HIGH_ACCURACY	100	The highest available accuracy.
PRIORITY_BALANCED_POWER_ACCURACY	102	The default value—block level accuracy, around 100 meters.
PRIORITY_LOW_POWER	104	City level accuracy, around 10 kilometers.
PRIORITY_NO_POWER	105	The worst accuracy, requesting no power consumption.

usage. Without specifically setting the priority by calling `setPriority`, the default priority, defined by `PRIORITY_BALANCED_POWER_ACCURACY`, is used. If we build a golf app that measures the distance to the pin, we want accuracy to the nearest yard or meter, so we specify the highest possible accuracy. For this travel app, the default accuracy is adequate.

EXAMPLE 11.12 shows the changes in the `MainActivity` class. We only want to set up location updates if we are successfully connected. Thus, we do that inside the `onConnected` method (lines 98–108). We create and define a `LocationRequest` at lines 100–103. We added the calls to `setPriority` and `setSmallestDisplacement` in order to illustrate them, but commented them out. Indeed, if we test the app without moving, we do not want to set a minimum distance for location updates. It is actually possible that we get disconnected in the middle of the `onConnected` method, in which case the app will crash when we try to set up location updates. Thus, we test that we are connected (line 104) before we set up location updates (line 105). If we lost the connection, we try to establish another connection (line 107).

Inside the `onLocationChanged` method (lines 54–59), we call `updateTrip` at line 58 in order to update the two `TextViews` showing the distance and time left to the destination. For feedback, we output to Logcat information about the accuracy and the timeline of the automatic calls to `onLocationChanged`. TABLE 11.13 shows the `getAccuracy` and `getElapsedRealtimeNanos` methods. The `getElapsedRealtimeNanos` method requires API level 17. Thus, we update the build.gradle file accordingly.

If the app is running and goes in the background, we want to stop requesting location updates. When that happens, the `onPause` method (lines 92–96) is called automatically. We disable location updates at line 95 by calling the `removeLocationUpdates` method (shown in Table 11.10). When the app comes back to the foreground, `onStart` is called, reconnects to Google Play services if necessary, and we request location updates again when `onConnected` executes.

FIGURE 11.4 shows the Logcat output of the app when running on the author's tablet. The output shows that the accuracy of the location returned by the GPS can vary from measurement to measurement. In this instance, it varies from 30 meters to 64.5 meters. One nanosecond is equal to 10^{-9} second. The interval frequency of the measurements is always very close to the 30 seconds

```
  9
 10   import android.util.Log;
...
 19   import com.google.android.gms.location.LocationListener;
 20   import com.google.android.gms.location.LocationRequest;
...
 26   public class MainActivity extends AppCompatActivity
 27            implements GoogleApiClient.ConnectionCallbacks,
 28                     GoogleApiClient.OnConnectionFailedListener,
 29                     LocationListener {
...
 54     public void onLocationChanged( Location location ) {
 55       float accuracy = location.getAccuracy( );
 56       long nanos = location.getElapsedRealtimeNanos( );
 57       Log.w( "MainActivity", "accuracy " + accuracy + ", nanos = " + nanos );
 58       updateTrip( null );
 59     }
...
 92     protected void onPause( ) {
 93       super.onPause( );
 94       FusedLocationProviderApi flpa = LocationServices.FusedLocationApi;
 95       flpa.removeLocationUpdates( gac, this );
 96     }
 97
 98     public void onConnected( Bundle connectionHint ) {
 99       FusedLocationProviderApi flpa = LocationServices.FusedLocationApi;
100       LocationRequest request = new LocationRequest( );
101       request.setInterval( 30000 );
102       // request.setPriority( LocationRequest.PRIORITY_HIGH_ACCURACY );
103       // request.setSmallestDisplacement( 100 );
104       if( gac.isConnected( ) ) // in case connection was just lost !!
105         flpa.requestLocationUpdates( gac, request, this );
106       else
107         gac.connect( );
108     }
...
139   }
```

EXAMPLE 11.12 **The `MainActivity` class, GPS app, Version 3**

TABLE 11.13 Selected methods of the `Location` class

Method	Description
float getAccuracy( )	Returns the accuracy for this Location in meters.
long getElapsedRealtimeNanos( )	Returns the time since the last boot in nanoseconds.

```
accuracy 36.0, nanos = 43096038000000
accuracy 40.5, nanos = 43126109000000
accuracy 31.5, nanos = 43156156000000
accuracy 31.5, nanos = 43186190000000
accuracy 31.5, nanos = 43216241000000
accuracy 34.5, nanos = 43246275000000
accuracy 37.5, nanos = 43276291000000
```

FIGURE 11.4 Logcat output of the GPS app, Version 3, when running inside the tablet

specified. It varies between 30.016 seconds (time elapsed between the last and next to last measurements) and 30.034 seconds (time elapsed between the third and fourth measurements). When the app starts, the two `TextViews` show `0 mile` and `seconds left`. If we enter an address and wait, the distance and time to that location is automatically updated after fewer than 30 seconds without clicking on the `Update` button, illustrating that the `onLocationChanged` method has been called.

Accuracy can be device and location dependent too. Further testing on the author's tablet from his home shows an accuracy varying from 12 meters to 36 meters when setting the priority using `PRIORITY_HIGH_ACCURACY` (by un-commenting line 102 in Example 11.12).

Chapter Summary

- The `GoogleApiClient` class is the entry point to Google Play services.
- If Google Play services are not available, it is possible that they can be made available via user interaction.
- The `Builder` static inner class of `GoogleApiClient` enables us to build a `GoogleApiClient`.
- We can obtain the current location of the device by calling the `lastLocation` method of the `FusedLocationProviderApi` interface.
- The `LocationServices` has a `FusedLocationProviderApi` static constant field named `FusedLocationApi`.
- The `getLatitude` and `getLongitude` methods of the `Location` class return the latitude and longitude of a location.
- The `distanceTo` method of the `Location` class returns the distance, in meters, between the `Location` reference calling it and a parameter `Location` reference.
- If the app accesses Google Play services to retrieve the device's location, we should add a uses-permission element in the AndroidManifest.xml file and specify `ACCESS_COARSE_LOCATION` or `ACCESS_FINE_LOCATION`, two constants of the `Manifest.permission` class.
- The `Geocoder` class provides methods to convert an address into a `Location` object (i.e., latitude and longitude) and vice versa.

- We can get location updates at a regular interval by implementing the `LocationListener` interface. `LocationListener` contains one callback method, `onLocationChanged`. It takes a `Location` parameter that represents the current location of the device.
- We use the `requestLocationUpdates` method to register a `LocationListener` on a `FusedLocationProviderApi`, defining various parameters of the updates using a `LocationRequest` parameter. Such registration triggers automatic calls to the `onLocationChanged` method of `LocationListener`.
- The most important attributes of a `LocationRequest` are the frequency of the updates and the priority, which translates into the accuracy of the locations retrieved.

 # Exercises, Problems, and Projects

Multiple-Choice Exercises

1. How can we obtain a GoogleApiClient reference?
   - Use a constructor of GoogleApiClient
   - Use the getInstance method of GoogleApiClient
   - Create a GoogleApiClient.Builder and call the build method
   - We cannot

2. What is the name of the FusedLocationProviderApi constant of LocationServices?
   - Api
   - FusedLocationApi
   - FusedApi
   - Fused

3. The Location class encapsulates a location on Earth. What method can we use to retrieve its latitude?
   - latitude
   - getLat
   - getLatitude
   - locationLatitude

4. The distanceTo method of the Location class returns a distance in
   - yards
   - meters
   - miles
   - kilometers

5. What class contains methods to convert an address to a Location and vice versa?
   - Geocoder
   - LocationCoder
   - Mapping
   - Geography

6. If we want to get location updates at regular intervals, what interface should we implement?
   - Listener
   - UpdateListener
   - GeoListener
   - LocationListener

7. What is the meaning of the Location parameter of the onLocationChanged method of the interface of question 6?
   - It stores a random location
   - It stores the most recent location
   - It stores the next location
   - It is null

8. We call the requestLocationUpdates of the FusedLocationProviderApi interface to request regular location updates. Two of its parameters are a GoogleApiClient and a LocationListener. What is the type of the third one?
   - double
   - Request
   - Time
   - LocationRequest

Fill in the Code

9. Declare and instantiate a GoogleApiClient that listens to connection success and failures.

10. The Location reference myLocation stores a location. Output to Logcat its accuracy.

11. The String address stores an address. Output its latitude and longitude to Logcat. Use the first Address geocoded for this.

12. The MyActivity class wants to get location updates. Write its class header.

13. Code the onLocationChanged method so that we display the latitude and longitude of the current location in a TextView name MyTV.

14. Build a LocationRequest that can be used to trigger updates every 100 seconds with the highest possible accuracy.

15. We are coding inside an Activity class that implements LocationListener. We have already instantiated a FusedLocationProviderApi named providerApi, a GoogleClientApi named clientApi, and a LocationRequest named request. Write one statement so that we get location updates as defined by request inside this Activity class.

Write an App

16. Expand the app in the chapter by calculating the time left using the speed between the last two location updates rather than 55 miles per hour.

17. Expand the app in the chapter by calculating the time left using the average speed between the last five location updates rather than 55 miles per hour. If there have not been five location updates yet, use 55 miles per hour.

18. Write an app that identifies the closest location from where the user is among five locations. The five locations can be hard coded inside the Model of the app.

19. Write an app that identifies how far the user is from five locations. The five locations can be hard coded inside the Model of the app. As the user moves, the five distances should be updated at regular intervals. The app should let the user decide the frequency of the updates and the accuracy of the locations (priority).

20. Write an app that enables the user to select a friend in a list, retrieve his or her address, and calculate how far that friend is. The list should be stored either in a file or can be hard coded. Include a Model.

21. Same as 20 but the list is not hard coded, is persistent and is expandable. The user can add to the list.

22. Same as 21 but the user can also delete and update a friend's data from the list.

23. Write a 1-hole golf app. The app allows the user to enter the location of the middle of the green by simply clicking on a button. That data should be stored on the device. The app allows the user to compute the distance from where the user is to the middle of the green location (previously stored).

24. Same as 23 but the app is an 18-hole golf app, not a 1-hole golf app.

25. Write an app that stores a list of locations and descriptions on the device. The user can enter a description for a location (where the user is) and can click on a button to retrieve the current location and write to the device's storage the description and the location. The app also allows the user to retrieve the list of descriptions and locations and display them.

26. Write an app that sends an email and includes the latitude and longitude of the user's location in the body of the email.

27. Same as 26 but convert the current location to an address and include the current address in the body of the email.

28. Write an app that helps the user retrieve the parking location of his or her car. When the user parks his or her car, the user clicks on a button to store the car's location. If the user wants to know where his or her car is, the app displays a map with two circles showing both the car and the user location.

CHAPTER **TWELVE**

Using Another App within the App: Taking a Photo, Graying It, and Sending an Email

CHAPTER CONTENTS

Introduction

An app can start another app and process its results. It is more and more common for apps to communicate with and use other apps on a device. For example, we might want to access the phone directory of an app, or look for photos or videos. Photo apps are very popular among smartphone users. They include features to turn a color picture into a black-and-white picture, add a frame around a picture, post a picture on some social media website, etc. In this chapter, we learn how we can use another app: in particular, we learn how to use the camera and email apps inside another app. We build an app that uses the camera app (or at least one of them) of a device, takes a picture, processes that picture, and uses an email app to send it to a friend. The Android Studio environment does not include a camera so we need an actual device, phone or tablet, to test the apps in this chapter.

12.1 Accessing the Camera App and Taking a Picture, Photo App, Version 0

If we want to take a picture within an app, we have two options:

▶ Access the camera app and process its results.
▶ Use the Camera API and access the camera itself.

In this chapter, we use a camera app. In Version 0 of the app, we do three things:

▶ Enable the user to take a picture using a camera app.
▶ Capture the picture taken.
▶ Display the picture.

We can use the `PackageManager` class to gather information about application packages installed on the device: we can use a `PackageManager` reference to check if the device has a camera, a front-facing camera, a microphone, a GPS, a compass, a gyroscope, supports Bluetooth, supports Wi-Fi, etc.

We can test if the device has a given feature by calling the `hasSystemFeature` method of the `PackageManager` class, passing the constant of the `PackageManager` class that corresponds to that feature, and that methods returns `true` if the feature described by the constant is present on the device, `false` if it is not. The `hasSystemFeature` method has the following API:

```
public boolean hasSystemFeature( String feature )
```

We typically use a `String` constant of the `PackageManager` class in place of the feature argument. **TABLE 12.1** shows some of these `String` constants.

TABLE 12.1 Selected constants of the `PackageManager` class	
Constant	**Description**
FEATURE_BLUETOOTH	Use to check if device supports Bluetooth.
FEATURE_CAMERA	Use to check if device has a camera.
FEATURE_CAMERA_FRONT	Use to check if device has a front camera.
FEATURE_LOCATION_GPS	Use to check if device has a GPS.
FEATURE_MICROPHONE	Use to check if device has a microphone.
FEATURE_SENSOR_COMPASS	Use to check if device has a compass.
FEATURE_SENSOR_GYROSCOPE	Use to check if device has a gyroscope.
FEATURE_WIFI	Use to check if device supports Wi-Fi.

We use the `getPackageManager` method of the `Context` class, inherited by the `Activity` class, to get a `PackageManager` reference. Assuming that we are inside an `Activity` class, the following pseudo-code sequence illustrates the preceding:

```
// inside Activity class
PackageManager manager = getPackageManager( );
if( manager.hasSystemFeature( PackageManager.DESIRED_FEATURE_CONSTANT ) )
   // Desired feature is present; use it
else
   // Notify the user that this app will not work
```

In order to run the camera app, or more exactly "a" camera app, we first check that the device has a camera app. Table 12.1 shows two constants that we can use for that purpose. We can test if the device has a camera app by calling the `getSystemFeature` method of the `PackageMan`-`ager` class, passing the `FEATURE_CAMERA` constant of the `PackageManager` class, as shown by the code sequence that follows:

```
// inside Activity class
PackageManager manager = getPackageManager( );
if( manager.hasSystemFeature( PackageManager.FEATURE_CAMERA ) )
   // Camera app is present; use it
else
   // Notify the user that this app will not work
```

TABLE 12.2 The `startActivityForResult` and `onActivityResult` methods of the Activity class

Method	Description
void startActivityForResult(Intent intent, int requestCode)	Start an Activity for intent. If requestCode is >= 0, it will be returned as the first parameter of the onActivityResult method.
void onActivityResult(int requestCode, int resultCode, Intent data)	requestCode is the request code supplied to startActivityForResult. Data is the Intent returned to the caller by the activity.

Once we know that the device has a feature we want to use, we can launch an activity to use that feature. In this case, we are interested in capturing the photo picture and in displaying it on the screen. Generally, if we want to start an activity and we are interested in accessing the results of that activity, we can use the `startActivityForResult` and the `onActivityResult` methods of the `Activity` class, both shown in **TABLE 12.2**. The `onActivityResult` executes after the activity defined by the `Intent` parameter of `startActivityForResult` finishes executing.

In order to create an `Intent` to use a feature of the device, we can use the following `Intent` constructor:

```
public Intent( String action )
```

The `String action` describes the device feature we want to use. Once we have created the `Intent`, we can start an activity for it by calling the `startActivityForResult` method of the `Activity` class. The code sequence that follows illustrates how we can start another app within an app:

```
// create the Intent
Intent otherAppIntent = new Intent( otherAppAppropriateArgument );
// actionCode is some integer
startActivityForResult( otherAppIntent, actionCode );
```

To create an `Intent` to use a camera app, we pass the `ACTION_IMAGE_CAPTURE` constant of the `MediaStore` class to the `Intent` constructor. The following code sequence starts a camera app activity:

```
// inside Activity class
Intent takePictureIntent = new Intent
  ( MediaStore.ACTION_IMAGE_CAPTURE );
// actionCode is some integer
startActivityForResult( takePictureIntent, actionCode );
```

Once the activity has executed, we execute inside the `onActivityResult` method of the `Activity` class. Its `Intent` parameter contains the results of the `Activity` that just executed,

TABLE 12.3 The `getExtras` and get methods of the `Intent` and `BaseBundle` classes

Class	Method	Description
Intent	Bundle getExtras( )	Returns a Bundle object, which encapsulates a map (key/value pairs) of what was placed in this Intent.
BaseBundle	Object get(String key)	Returns the Object that was mapped to key.

in this case a `Bitmap` object that stores the picture that the user just took. The code that follows shows how we can access the picture taken as a `Bitmap` inside the `onActivityResult` method. As indicated in the first comment, we should check that the value of `requestCode` is identical to the request code passed to the `startActivityForResult` method, and that the `resultCode` value reflects that the activity executed normally.

We retrieve the `Bundle` object of the `Intent` using the `getExtras` method shown in **TABLE 12.3**. That `Bundle` object stores a map of key/value pairs that are stored in the `Intent`. With that `Bundle` object, we call the `get` method, inherited from the `BaseBundle` class by `Bundle` and also shown in Table 12.3, passing the key `data` in order to retrieve the `Bitmap`. Since the `get` method returns an `Object` and we expect a `Bitmap`, we need to typecast the returned value to a `Bitmap`.

```
protected void onActivityResult( int requestCode,
                                 int resultCode, Intent data ) {
    // Check that the request code is correct and the result code is good
    Bundle extras = data.getExtras( );
    Bitmap bitmap = ( Bitmap ) extras.get( "data" );
    // process bitmap here
}
```

The `ImageView` class, part of the `android.widget` package, can be used to display a picture and scale it. **TABLE 12.4** shows some of its methods.

TABLE 12.4 Selected methods of the `ImageView` class

Method	Description
ImageView(Context context)	Constructs an ImageView object.
void setImageBitmap(Bitmap bitmap)	Sets bitmap as the content of this ImageView.
void setImageDrawable(Drawable drawable)	Sets drawable as the content of this ImageView.
void setImageResource(int resource)	Sets resource as the content of this ImageView.
void setScaleType(ImageView.ScaleType scaleType)	Sets scaleType as the scaling mode of this ImageView.

In this app, we are getting the image dynamically, as the app is running, when the user takes a picture with the camera app. When the picture is taken, we retrieve the extras and then the corresponding `Bitmap` object using the `get` method of the `BaseBundle` class. Thus, we use the `setImageBitmap` method in this app to fill an `ImageView` with a picture that we take with the camera app. If we already have a `Bitmap` reference named `bitmap`, we can place it inside an `ImageView` named `imageView` using the following statement:

```
imageView.setImageBitmap( bitmap );
```

We want to notify potential users that this app uses the camera. Thus, we define a `uses-feature` element inside the `manifest` element of the `AndroidManifest.xml` file as follows:

```
<uses-feature android:name="android.hardware.camera2" />
```

To keep things simple, we only allow this app to run in vertical orientation, so we add this code inside the `activity` element:

```
android:screenOrientation="portrait"
```

EXAMPLE 12.1 shows the activity_main.xml file. We use a `LinearLayout` with a vertical orientation (line 10) because we intend to add elements at the bottom of the View in the other versions of the app. At lines 13–17, we add an `ImageView` element to store the picture. We give

```
1   <?xml version="1.0" encoding="utf-8"?>
2   <LinearLayout xmlns:android="http://schemas.android.com/apk/res/android"
3     xmlns:tools="http://schemas.android.com/tools"
4     android:layout_width="match_parent"
5     android:layout_height="match_parent"
6     android:paddingLeft="@dimen/activity_horizontal_margin"
7     android:paddingRight="@dimen/activity_horizontal_margin"
8     android:paddingTop="@dimen/activity_vertical_margin"
9     android:paddingBottom="@dimen/activity_vertical_margin"
10    android:orientation="vertical"
11    tools:context="com.jblearning.photograyingv0.MainActivity">
12
13    <ImageView
14      android:layout_width="match_parent"
15      android:layout_height="match_parent"
16      android:scaleType="fitCenter"
17      android:id="@+id/picture" />
18
19  </LinearLayout>
```

EXAMPLE 12.1 The activity_main.xml file, Photo app, Version 0

TABLE 12.5 Selected `enum` values and corresponding XML attribute values of the `ImageView.ScaleType` enum

Enum Value	XML Attribute Value	Description
CENTER	center	Centers the image inside the ImageView without doing any scaling.
CENTER_INSIDE	centerInside	Scales down the image as necessary so that it fits inside the ImageView and is centered, keeping the image's aspect ratio.
FIT_CENTER	fitCenter	Scales down or up the image as necessary so that it fits exactly (at least along one axis) inside the ImageView and is centered, keeping the image's aspect ratio.

it the id `picture` at line 17 so we can retrieve it from the `MainActivity` class using the `findViewById` method.

The `android:scaleType` XML attribute enables us to specify how we want a picture to be scaled and positioned inside an `ImageView`. The `ScaleType` enum, part of the `ImageView` class, contains values that we can use to scale and position a picture inside an `ImageView`. **TABLE 12.5** lists some of its possible values. At line 16, we use the value `fitCenter` to scale the picture perfectly so that it fits and position it in the middle of the `ImageView`. At lines 6–9, we provide some padding as defined in the dimens.xml file.

EXAMPLE 12.2 shows the `MainActivity` class. At lines 14–15, we declare two instance variables, `bitmap` and `imageView`, a `Bitmap` and an `ImageView`. We need to access them both whenever we want to change the picture so it is convenient to have direct references to them. Inside

```
1   package com.jblearning.photograyingv0;
2
3   import android.content.Intent;
4   import android.content.pm.PackageManager;
5   import android.graphics.Bitmap;
6   import android.os.Bundle;
7   import android.provider.MediaStore;
8   import android.support.v7.app.AppCompatActivity;
9   import android.widget.ImageView;
10  import android.widget.Toast;
11
12  public class MainActivity extends AppCompatActivity {
13    private static final int PHOTO_REQUEST = 1;
14    private Bitmap bitmap;
15    private ImageView imageView;
```

EXAMPLE 12.2 The `MainActivity` Class, Photo app, Version 0 (*Continued*)

```
16
17    protected void onCreate( Bundle savedInstanceState ) {
18      super.onCreate( savedInstanceState );
19      setContentView( R.layout.activity_main );
20      imageView = ( ImageView ) findViewById( R.id.picture );
21
22      PackageManager manager = this.getPackageManager( );
23      if( manager.hasSystemFeature( PackageManager.FEATURE_CAMERA ) ) {
24        Intent takePictureIntent
25          = new Intent( MediaStore.ACTION_IMAGE_CAPTURE );
26        startActivityForResult( takePictureIntent, PHOTO_REQUEST );
27      } else {
28        Toast.makeText( this,
29          "Sorry - Your device does not have a camera",
30          Toast.LENGTH_LONG ).show( );
31      }
32    }
33
34    protected void onActivityResult( int requestCode,
35                                     int resultCode, Intent data ) {
36      super.onActivityResult( requestCode, resultCode, data );
37      if( requestCode == PHOTO_REQUEST && resultCode == RESULT_OK ) {
38        Bundle extras = data.getExtras( );
39        bitmap = ( Bitmap ) extras.get( "data" );
40        imageView.setImageBitmap( bitmap );
41      }
42    }
43  }
```

EXAMPLE 12.2 **The `MainActivity` Class, Photo app, Version 0**

the onCreate method (lines 17–32), we initialize imageView at line 20. We get a PackageManager reference at line 22 and test if a camera app is present at line 23. If it is, we create an Intent to use a camera app at lines 24–25 and start an activity for it at line 26, passing the value stored in the PHOTO_REQUEST constant. If no camera app is present (line 27), we give a quick feedback to the user via a Toast at lines 28–30.

When the user runs the app and takes a picture, we execute inside the onActivityResult method, coded at lines 34–42. We retrieve the Bundle from the Intent parameter data at line 38. Since the Intent was created to take a picture with a camera app, we expect that the Bundle associated with that intent contains a Bitmap storing that picture. The get method of the Bundle class, when passed the String data, returns that Bitmap. We retrieve it at line 39. At line 40, we set the image inside imageView to that Bitmap.

When we run the app, the camera app starts. **FIGURE 12.1** shows our app after the user takes a picture. **FIGURE 12.2** shows our app after the user clicks on the Save button. The picture shows up on the screen.

FIGURE 12.1 The Photo app, Version 0, after taking the picture

FIGURE 12.2 The Photo app, Version 0, after clicking on Save

12.2 The Model: Graying the Picture, Photo App, Version 1

In Version 1 of our app, we gray the picture with a hard coded formula. Our Model for this app is the `BitmapGrayer` class. It encapsulates a `Bitmap` and a graying scheme that we can apply to that `Bitmap`.

In the RGB color system, there are 256 shades of gray; a gray color has the same amount of red, green, and blue. Thus, its RGB representation looks like (x, x, x) where x is an integer between 0 and 255. (0, 0, 0) is black and (255, 255, 255) is white.

TABLE 12.6 lists some `static` methods of the `Color` class of the `android.graphics` package. We should not confuse that class with the `Color` class of the `java.awt` package.

Generally, if we start from a color picture and we want to transform it into a black-and-white picture, we need to convert the color of every pixel in the picture to a gray color. There are several formulas that we can use to gray a picture, and we use the following strategy:

TABLE 12.6 Selected methods of the `Color` class of the `android.graphics` package

Method	Description
static int argb(int alpha, int red, int green, int blue)	Returns a color integer value defined by the alpha, red, green, and blue parameters.
static int alpha(int color)	Returns the alpha component of color as an integer between 0 and 255.
static int red(int color)	Returns the red component of color as an integer between 0 and 255.
static int green(int color)	Returns the green component of color as an integer between 0 and 255.
static int blue(int color)	Returns the blue component of color as an integer between 0 and 255.

▶   Keep the alpha component of every pixel the same.
▶   Use the red, green, and blue components of the pixel in order to generate a gray shade for it.
▶   Use the same transformation formula to generate the gray shade for every pixel.

For example, if red, green, and blue are the amount of red, green, and blue for a pixel, we could apply the following weighted average formula so that the new color for that pixel is (x, x, x):

```
x = red * redCoeff + green * greenCoeff + blue * blueCoeff
```

where

```
redCoeff, greenCoeff, and blueCoeff are between 0 and 1
```

and

```
redCoeff + greenCoeff + blueCoeff <= 1
```

This guarantees that x is between 0 and 255, that the color of each pixel is a shade of gray, and that the color transformation process is consistent for all the pixels in the picture.

Thus, if `color` is a `Color` reference representing the color of a pixel and we want to generate a gray color for that pixel using weights 0.5, 0.3, and 0.2 for red, green, and blue, respectively, we can use the following statement to generate that gray color:

```
int shade = ( int ) ( 0.5 * Color.red( color ) + 0.3 * Color.green( color )
                 + 0.2 * Color.blue( color ) );
```

A picture can be stored in a `Bitmap`. **TABLE 12.7** shows some methods of the `Bitmap` class. They enable us to loop through all the pixels of a `Bitmap` object, access the color of each pixel, and change it. In this app, we start with an image, get the corresponding `Bitmap`, change the colors to gray shades, and then put the `Bitmap` back into the image, which becomes black-and-white.

TABLE 12.7 Selected methods of the `Bitmap` class

Method	Description
int getWidth( )	Returns the width of this Bitmap.
int getHeight( )	Returns the height of this Bitmap.
int getPixel(int x, int y)	Returns the integer representation of the color of the pixel at coordinate(x, y) in this Bitmap.
void setPixel(int x, int y, int color)	Sets the color of the pixel at coordinate(x, y) in this Bitmap to color.
Bitmap.Config getConfig( )	Returns the configuration of this Bitmap. The Bitmap.Config class encapsulates how pixels are stored in a Bitmap.
static Bitmap createBitmap(int w, int h, Bitmap.Config config)	Returns a mutable Bitmap of width w, height h, and using config to create the Bitmap.

In order to access each pixel of a `Bitmap` named `bitmap`, we use the following double loop:

```
for( int i = 0; i < bimap.getWidth( ); i++ ) {
  for( int j = 0; j < bitmap.getHeight( ); j++ ) {
    int color = bitmap.getPixel( i, j );
    // process color here
  }
}
```

EXAMPLE 12.3 shows the `BitmapGrayer` class. It has four instance variables (lines 7–10): `originalBitmap`, a Bitmap, and `redCoeff`, `greenCoeff`, `blueCoeff`, three `float`s with values between 0 and 1. They represent the amounts of red, green, and blue that we take into account in order to generate a gray shade for each pixel of `originalBitmap`.

The three mutators, coded at lines 32–39, 41–48, and 50–57, enforce the following constraints:

▶ `redCoeff, greenCoeff, and blueCoeff are between 0 and 1`
▶ `redCoeff + greenCoeff + blueCoeff <= 1`

The `setRedCoeff` mutator, at lines 32–39, only updates `redCoeff` if the `newRedCoeff` parameter is between `0.0` and `1.0` (line 33). If the value of `newRedCoeff` is such that the sum of `greenCoeff`, `blueCoeff`, and `newRedCoeff` is 1 or less (line 34), it assigns `newRedCoeff` to `redCoeff` (line 35). If not, it sets the value of `redCoeff` so that the sum of `greenCoeff`, `blueCoeff`, and `redCoeff` is equal to 1 (line 37). The two other mutators follow the same logic.

The `grayScale` method, coded at lines 59–75, returns a `Bitmap` with the following characteristics:

▶ It has the same width and height as `originalBitmap`.
▶ Each of its pixels is gray.

```
1    package com.jblearning.photograyingv1;
2
3    import android.graphics.Bitmap;
4    import android.graphics.Color;
5
6    public class BitmapGrayer {
7      private Bitmap originalBitmap;
8      private float redCoeff;
9      private float greenCoeff;
10     private float blueCoeff;
11
12     public BitmapGrayer( Bitmap bitmap, float newRedCoeff,
13                          float newGreenCoeff, float newBlueCoeff ) {
14       originalBitmap = bitmap;
15       setRedCoeff( newRedCoeff );
16       setGreenCoeff( newRedCoeff );
17       setBlueCoeff( newRedCoeff );
18     }
19
20     public float getRedCoeff( ) {
21       return redCoeff;
22     }
23
24     public float getGreenCoeff( ) {
25       return greenCoeff;
26     }
27
28     public float getBlueCoeff( ) {
29       return blueCoeff;
30     }
31
32     public void setRedCoeff( float newRedCoeff ) {
33       if( newRedCoeff >= 0 && newRedCoeff <= 1 ) {
34         if( greenCoeff + blueCoeff + newRedCoeff <= 1 )
35           redCoeff = newRedCoeff;
36         else
37           redCoeff = 1 - greenCoeff - blueCoeff;
38       }
39     }
40
41     public void setGreenCoeff( float newGreenCoeff ) {
42       if( newGreenCoeff >= 0 && newGreenCoeff <= 1 ) {
43         if( redCoeff + blueCoeff + newGreenCoeff <= 1 )
44           greenCoeff = newGreenCoeff;
45         else
46           greenCoeff = 1 - redCoeff - blueCoeff;
47       }
48     }
```

EXAMPLE 12.3 The BitmapGrayer class, Photo app, Version 1 (*Continued*)

```
49
50     public void setBlueCoeff( float newBlueCoeff ) {
51       if( newBlueCoeff >= 0 && newBlueCoeff <= 1 ) {
52         if( redCoeff + greenCoeff + newBlueCoeff <= 1 )
53           blueCoeff = newBlueCoeff;
54         else
55           blueCoeff = 1 - redCoeff - greenCoeff;
56       }
57     }
58
59     public Bitmap grayScale( ) {
60       int width = originalBitmap.getWidth( );
61       int height = originalBitmap.getHeight( );
62       Bitmap.Config config = originalBitmap.getConfig( );
63       Bitmap bitmap = Bitmap.createBitmap( width, height, config );
64       for( int i = 0; i < width; i++ ) {
65         for( int j = 0; j < height; j++ ) {
66           int color = originalBitmap.getPixel( i, j );
67           int shade = ( int ) ( redCoeff * Color.red( color )+
68                                 greenCoeff * Color.green( color )+
69                                 blueCoeff * Color.blue( color ) ) ;
70           color = Color.argb( Color.alpha( color ), shade, shade, shade );
71           bitmap.setPixel( i, j, color );
72         }
73       }
74       return bitmap;
75     }
76   }
```

EXAMPLE 12.3 **The `BitmapGrayer` class, Photo app, Version 1**

▷ If red, green, and blue are the amount of red, green, and blue of a given pixel in
originalBitmap, the color of the pixel in the returned Bitmap at the same x- and
y-coordinates is gray and the value of the gray shade is red * redCoeff + green * greenCoeff
+ blue * blueCoeff.

We retrieve the width and height of originalBitmap at lines 60–61. We retrieve the configuration of originalBitmap at line 62 calling the getConfig method (see Table 12.7). We call
createBitmap (see Table 12.7) to create a mutable copy of originalBitmap, bitmap, at line
63, using the same width, height, and configuration as originalBitmap.

At lines 64–73, we use a double loop to define the color of each pixel in bitmap. We retrieve
the color of the current pixel in originalBitmap at line 66. We calculate the shade of gray for
the corresponding pixel in bitmap at lines 67–69, create a color with it at line 70, and assign that
color to that pixel at line 71. We return bitmap at line 74.

EXAMPLE 12.4 shows the MainActivity class, Version 1. The only change from Version 0 is
that we gray the picture that is inside imageView. We declare a BitmapGrayer instance variable,

```
 1   package com.jblearning.photograyingv1;
 2
 3   import android.content.Intent;
 4   import android.content.pm.PackageManager;
 5   import android.graphics.Bitmap;
 6   import android.os.Bundle;
 7   import android.provider.MediaStore;
 8   import android.support.v7.app.AppCompatActivity;
 9   import android.widget.ImageView;
10   import android.widget.Toast;
11
12   public class MainActivity extends AppCompatActivity {
13     private static final int PHOTO_REQUEST = 1;
14     private BitmapGrayer grayer;
15     private Bitmap bitmap;
16     private ImageView imageView;
17
18     protected void onCreate( Bundle savedInstanceState ) {
19       super.onCreate( savedInstanceState );
20       setContentView( R.layout.activity_main );
21       imageView = ( ImageView ) findViewById( R.id.picture );
22
23       PackageManager manager = this.getPackageManager( );
24       if( manager.hasSystemFeature( PackageManager.FEATURE_CAMERA ) ) {
25         Intent takePictureIntent
26           = new Intent( MediaStore.ACTION_IMAGE_CAPTURE );
27         startActivityForResult( takePictureIntent, PHOTO_REQUEST );
28       } else {
29         Toast.makeText( this,
30           "Sorry - Your device does not have a camera",
31           Toast.LENGTH_LONG ).show( );
32       }
33     }
34
35     protected void onActivityResult( int requestCode,
36                                      int resultCode, Intent data ) {
37       super.onActivityResult( requestCode, resultCode, data );
38       if( requestCode == PHOTO_REQUEST && resultCode == RESULT_OK ) {
39         Bundle extras = data.getExtras( );
40         bitmap = ( Bitmap ) extras.get( "data" );
41         grayer = new BitmapGrayer( bitmap, .34f, .33f, .33f );
42         bitmap = grayer.grayScale( );
43         imageView.setImageBitmap( bitmap );
44       }
45     }
46   }
```

EXAMPLE 12.4 The `MainActivity` class, Photo app, Version 1

FIGURE 12.3 The Photo app, Version 1, after clicking on save, showing a grayed picture

`grayer`, at line 14. Inside `onActivityResult`, we instantiate `grayer` at line 41 with `bitmap` and three default values for the red, green, and blue coefficients for the graying transformation process. Note that it would be too early to instantiate `grayer` inside the `onCreate` method because we need the picture to be taken so that we have a `Bitmap` object for that picture. At line 42, we call the `grayScale` method with `grayer` and assign the resulting `Bitmap` to `bitmap`.

   FIGURE 12.3 shows our app running inside the tablet after the user clicks on the Save button. The picture is now black-and-white.

12.3 Defining Shades of Gray Using `SeekBars`, Photo App, Version 2

In Version 1, the formula to generate the shade of gray for each pixel in the Bitmap is hard coded with coefficients 0.34, 0.33, and 0.33. In Version 2, we allow the user to specify the coefficients in the formula. We include three seek bars, also often called sliders, in the user interface. They allow

FIGURE 12.4 Inheritance hierarchy of `SeekBar`

the user to define the red, green, and blue coefficients that are used to calculate the shade of gray for each pixel.

The `SeekBar` class, part of the `android.widget` package, encapsulates a seek bar. **FIGURE 12.4** shows its inheritance hierarchy.

Visually, a seek bar includes a progress bar and a thumb. Its default representation includes a line (for the progress bar) and a circle (for the thumb). We can define a seek bar in a layout XML file using the element `SeekBar`. **TABLE 12.8** shows some of the XML attributes that we can use to define a seek bar using XML, along with their corresponding methods if we want to control a seek bar by code. We can set the current value of the seek bar, called progress, by using the `android:progress` attribute or by code using the `setProgress` method. Its minimum value is 0, and we can define its maximum value using the `android:max` attribute or the `setMax` method.

The progress bar and the thumb are light blue by default. We can customize a seek bar by replacing the progress bar or the thumb by a `drawable` resource, for example an image from a file or a shape. We can do that inside an XML layout file or programmatically. In this app, since each seek bar represents the coefficient of a particular color, we customize the thumb of each of

TABLE 12.8 Selected XML attributes and methods of `ProgressBar` and `AbsSeekBar`

Class	XML Attribute	Corresponding Method
ProgressBar	android:progressDrawable	void setProgressDrawable (Drawable drawable)
ProgressBar	android:progress	void setProgress (int progress)
ProgressBar	android:max	void setMax (int max)
AbsSeekBar	android:thumb	void setThumb (Drawable drawable)

the three seek bars to reflect the three colors that they represent: red, green, and blue. We define three `drawable` resources, one per color, and use them in the activity_main.xml file.

Inside the `drawable` directory, we create three files: `red_thumb.xml`, `green_thumb.xml`, and `blue_thumb.xml`.

EXAMPLE 12.5 shows the `red_thumb.xml` file. It defines a `shape` that we use for the thumb of the red seek bar. It defines an oval (line 4) of equal width and height (lines 5–7), that is, a circle. At lines 8–9, we define the color inside the circle, a full red. At lines 10–12, we define the thickness (line 11), and the color of the outline of the circle (line 12), also red but not completely opaque.

```
1    <?xml version="1.0" encoding="utf-8"?>
2    <shape
3        xmlns:android="http://schemas.android.com/apk/res/android"
4        android:shape="oval" >
5        <size
6            android:width="30dp"
7            android:height="30dp" />
8        <solid
9            android:color="#FF00" />
10       <stroke
11           android:width="20dp"
12           android:color="#AF00" />
13   </shape>
```

EXAMPLE 12.5 The `red_thumb.xml` file, Photo app, Version 2

The `green_thumb.xml` and `blue_thumb.xml` files are similar, using colors `#F0F0` and `#F00F`, respectively, with the same opacity values as in the `red_thumb.xml`.file

To access a `drawable` resource named `abc.xml`, we use the value `@drawable/abc` in an XML layout context, or the expression `R.drawable.abc` if we access the resource programmatically.

We need to add three `SeekBar` elements to our XML layout file. Other than their id and their thumb, these `SeekBar` elements are identical, so we use a style to define some of their attributes. We edit the styles.xml file and add a style element for the `SeekBar` elements. **EXAMPLE 12.6** shows the `styles.xml` file. The `seekBarStyle`, defined at lines 11–18, is used in activity_main.xml to style the seek bars. It defines all the attributes that the seek bars have in common.

At line 12, we allocate the same amount of horizontal space to all the elements using `seekBar-Style` and we center them vertically at line 15. We initialize any seek bar using `seekBarStyle` with a `progress` value of `0` at line 16 and give it a `max` value of `100` at line 17.

EXAMPLE 12.7 shows the activity_main.xml file. It organizes the screen into two parts: an `ImageView` (lines 13–18) at the top that occupies four fifths of the screen (line 14), and a `LinearLayout` (lines 20–39) at the bottom that contains one fifth of the screen (line 22), organizes its components horizontally (line 21), and contains three seek bars (lines 26–29, 30–33, 34–37).

We give each seek bar an id (lines 27, 31, 35) so we can retrieve it using the `findViewById` method. At lines 28, 32, and 36, we customize the three seek bars by setting their thumb to the

```
1    <resources>
2
3      <!-- Base application theme. -->
4      <style name="AppTheme" parent="Theme.AppCompat.Light.DarkActionBar">
5        <!-- Customize your theme here. -->
6            <item name="colorPrimary">@color/colorPrimary</item>
7            <item name="colorPrimaryDark">@color/colorPrimaryDark</item>
8            <item name="colorAccent">@color/colorAccent</item>
9      </style>
10
11     <style name="seekBarStyle">
12       <item name="android:layout_weight">1</item>
13       <item name="android:layout_width">wrap_content</item>
14       <item name="android:layout_height">wrap_content</item>
15       <item name="android:layout_gravity">center_vertical</item>
16       <item name="android:progress">0</item>
17       <item name="android:max">100</item>
18     </style>
19
20   </resources>
```

EXAMPLE 12.6 The `styles.xml` file, Photo app, Version 2

```
1    <?xml version="1.0" encoding="utf-8"?>
2    <LinearLayout xmlns:android="http://schemas.android.com/apk/res/android"
3      xmlns:tools="http://schemas.android.com/tools"
4      android:layout_width="match_parent"
5      android:layout_height="match_parent"
6      android:paddingLeft="@dimen/activity_horizontal_margin"
7      android:paddingRight="@dimen/activity_horizontal_margin"
8      android:paddingTop="@dimen/activity_vertical_margin"
9      android:paddingBottom="@dimen/activity_vertical_margin"
10     android:orientation="vertical"
11     tools:context="com.jblearning.photograyingv2.MainActivity">
12
13     <ImageView
14       android:layout_weight="4"
15       android:layout_width="match_parent"
16       android:layout_height="0dp"
17       android:scaleType="fitCenter"
18       android:id="@+id/picture" />
19
```

EXAMPLE 12.7 The **activity_main.xml** file, Photo app, Version 2 (*Continued*)

```
20       <LinearLayout
21         android:orientation="horizontal"
22         android:layout_weight="1"
23         android:layout_width="match_parent"
24         android:layout_height="0dp" >
25
26         <SeekBar
27           android:id="@+id/red_bar"
28           android:thumb="@drawable/red_thumb"
29           style="@style/seekBarStyle" />
30         <SeekBar
31           android:id="@+id/green_bar"
32           android:thumb="@drawable/green_thumb"
33           style="@style/seekBarStyle" />
34         <SeekBar
35           android:id="@+id/blue_bar"
36           android:thumb="@drawable/blue_thumb"
37           style="@style/seekBarStyle" />
38
39       </LinearLayout>
40
41     </LinearLayout>
```

EXAMPLE 12.7 **The activity_main.xml file, Photo app, Version 2**

shapes defined in red_thumb.xml, green_thumb.xml, and blue_thumb.xml. We style them with seekBarStyle at lines 29, 33, and 37.

We expect the user to interact with the seek bars and we need to process that event. In order to do that, we need to implement the OnSeekBarChangeListener interface, a public static inner interface of the SeekBar class. It has the three methods, shown in **TABLE 12.9**. In this app, we only care about the value of each slider as the user interacts with it. Thus we override the onStartTrackingTouch and onStopTrackingTouch methods as do-nothing

TABLE 12.9 Methods of the SeekBar.OnSeekBarChangeListener interface

Method	Description
void onStartTrackingTouch(SeekBar seekBar)	Called when the user starts touching the slider.
void onStopTrackingTouch(SeekBar seekBar)	Called when the user stops touching the slider.
void onProgressChanged(SeekBar seekBar, int progress, boolean fromUser)	Called continuously as the user moves the slider.

methods and place our event handling code inside the `onProgressChanged` method. Its first parameter, `seekBar`, is a reference to the `SeekBar` that the user is interacting with, and enables us to determine if the user is changing the red, green, or blue coefficients of our graying formula. Its second parameter, `progress`, stores the progress value of `seekBar`: we use it to set the coefficient of the corresponding color. Its third parameter `fromUser`, is `true` if the method was called due to user interaction, or `false` if it was called programmatically. We want the thumb position of each slider to reflect the actual value of its corresponding coefficient. Because of the constraint on our three coefficients of the graying formula, we do not want to allow the user to manipulate the sliders freely. The sum of the three coefficients must be `1` or less at all times. For example, we do not want the red and green sliders to show a value of `75%` each, because that would mean that the sum of the red, green, and blue coefficients would be at least `1.5`, a constraint violation. Thus, we need to reset the thumb position of each slider by code and that in turn triggers a call to the `onProgressChanged` method, which in this case, we do not want to process.

In order to set up event handling for a `SeekBar`, we do the following:

▸ Code a `private` handler class that implements the `SeekBar.OnSeekBarChangeListener` interface.
▸ Declare and instantiate a handler object of that class.
▸ Register that handler on a `SeekBar` component.

EXAMPLE 12.8 shows the `MainActivity` class, Version 2. At lines 57–82, we code the `GrayChangeHandler` class, which implements the `SeekBar.OnSeekBarChangeListener` interface. Three `SeekBar` references, `redBar`, `greenBar`, and `blueBar`, are defined as instance variables at line 18. Inside the `onCreate` method, at lines 25–27, we assign the three `SeekBars` defined in the activity_main.xml layout file to these three instance variables. At line 29, we declare and instantiate a `GrayChangeHandler` object. We register it on `redBar`, `greenBar`, and `blueBar`, at lines 30–32 as their listener.

Inside the `onActivityResult` method (lines 46–55), we instantiate `grayer` with default values 0, 0, 0 at line 52. In Version 1, we grayed the picture with a hard coded formula. In Version 2, we leave the picture as is, with its colors, and wait for the user to interact with the three sliders in order to gray the picture.

The `onProgressChanged` method is coded at lines 59–75. We test if the call to that method was triggered by user interaction at line 61. If it was not (i.e., `fromUser` is `false`), we do nothing. If it was (i.e., `fromUser` is `true`), we test which slider triggered the event. If it was the red slider (line 62), we call `setRedCoeff` with the value of progress scaled back to between `0` and `1` at line 63. It is possible that the new `redCoeff` value is such that the sum of the three coefficients is `1` or less. In this case, we want to prevent the thumb of the seek bar to go past the corresponding value of `redCoeff` (i.e., `100` times the value of `redCoeff`). Either way, we position the thumb based on the value of `redCoeff` by calling the `setProgress` method at line 64. We do the same if the seek bar is the green or blue seek bar at lines 65–67 and 68–70, respectively. Finally, we retrieve the `Bitmap` generated by the new coefficients at line 72 and reset the picture to that `Bitmap` at line 73.

```
1    package com.jblearning.photograyingv2;
2
3    import android.content.Intent;
4    import android.content.pm.PackageManager;
5    import android.graphics.Bitmap;
6    import android.os.Bundle;
7    import android.provider.MediaStore;
8    import android.support.v7.app.AppCompatActivity;
9    import android.widget.ImageView;
10   import android.widget.SeekBar;
11   import android.widget.Toast;
12
13   public class MainActivity extends AppCompatActivity {
14     private static final int PHOTO_REQUEST = 1;
15     private BitmapGrayer grayer;
16     private Bitmap bitmap;
17     private ImageView imageView;
18     private SeekBar redBar, greenBar, blueBar;
19
20     protected void onCreate( Bundle savedInstanceState ) {
21       super.onCreate( savedInstanceState );
22       setContentView( R.layout.activity_main );
23       imageView = ( ImageView ) findViewById( R.id.picture );
24
25       redBar = ( SeekBar ) findViewById( R.id.red_bar );
26       greenBar = ( SeekBar ) findViewById( R.id.green_bar );
27       blueBar = ( SeekBar ) findViewById( R.id.blue_bar );
28
29       GrayChangeHandler gch = new GrayChangeHandler( );
30       redBar.setOnSeekBarChangeListener( gch );
31       greenBar.setOnSeekBarChangeListener( gch );
32       blueBar.setOnSeekBarChangeListener( gch );
33
34       PackageManager manager = this.getPackageManager( );
35       if( manager.hasSystemFeature( PackageManager.FEATURE_CAMERA ) ) {
36         Intent takePictureIntent
37           = new Intent( MediaStore.ACTION_IMAGE_CAPTURE );
38         startActivityForResult( takePictureIntent, PHOTO_REQUEST );
39       } else {
40         Toast.makeText( this,
41           "Sorry - Your device does not have a camera",
42           Toast.LENGTH_LONG ).show( );
43       }
44     }
45
```

EXAMPLE 12.8 The `MainActivity` class, Photo app, Version 2 (*Continued*)

```
46    protected void onActivityResult( int requestCode,
47                                   int resultCode, Intent data )  {
48      super.onActivityResult( requestCode, resultCode, data );
49      if( requestCode == PHOTO_REQUEST && resultCode == RESULT_OK ) {
50        Bundle extras = data.getExtras( );
51        bitmap = ( Bitmap ) extras.get( "data" );
52        grayer = new BitmapGrayer( bitmap, 0.0f, 0.0f, 0.0f );
53        imageView.setImageBitmap( bitmap );
54      }
55    }
56
57    private class GrayChangeHandler
58           implements SeekBar.OnSeekBarChangeListener {
59      public void onProgressChanged( SeekBar seekBar,
60                                   int progress, boolean fromUser ) {
61        if( fromUser ) {
62          if( seekBar == redBar ) {
63            grayer.setRedCoeff( progress / 100.0f );
64            redBar.setProgress( ( int ) ( 100 * grayer.getRedCoeff( ) ) );
65          } else if( seekBar == greenBar ) {
66            grayer.setGreenCoeff( progress / 100.0f );
67            greenBar.setProgress( ( int ) ( 100 * grayer.getGreenCoeff( ) ) );
68          } else if( seekBar == blueBar ) {
69            grayer.setBlueCoeff( progress / 100.0f );
70            blueBar.setProgress( ( int ) ( 100 * grayer.getBlueCoeff( ) ) );
71          }
72          bitmap = grayer.grayScale( );
73          imageView.setImageBitmap( bitmap );
74        }
75      }
76
77      public void onStartTrackingTouch( SeekBar seekBar ) {
78      }
79
80      public void onStopTrackingTouch( SeekBar seekBar ) {
81      }
82    }
83  }
```

EXAMPLE 12.8 **The** `MainActivity` **class, Photo app, Version 2**

FIGURE 12.5 shows our app running after the user clicks on the Save button and the user interacts with the seek bars.

FIGURE 12.5 The Photo app, Version 2, after clicking on Save and user interaction

12.4 Improving the User Interface, Photo App, Version 3

Version 2 provides the user with the ability to customize the formula used to gray the picture, but the seek bars do not give a precise feedback regarding the value of each color coefficient. In Version 3, we add three TextViews below the three SeekBar components to display the color coefficients.

It would be annoying for the user to display numbers with a large number of digits after the decimal point. We limit the number of digits after the decimal point to two. In order to implement this, we build a utility class, MathRounding, with a static method, keepTwoDigits, that takes a float parameter and returns the same float with only the first two digits after the decimal point.

EXAMPLE 12.9 shows the MathRounding class. The keepTwoDigits method, coded at lines 4–7, multiplies the parameter f by 100 and casts the result to an int at line 5. It then casts that int to a float, divides it by 100, and returns the result at line 6. We cast the int to a float in order to perform floating-point division.

We could use this method inside the BitmapGrayer class or inside the MainActivity class. Because we think this feature relates to how we display things rather than the functionality of the

```
1   package com.jblearning.photograyingv3;
2
3   public class MathRounding {
4     public static float keepTwoDigits( float f ) {
5       int n = ( int ) ( 100 * f );
6       return ( ( float ) n ) / 100;
7     }
8   }
```

EXAMPLE 12.9 The `MathRounding` class, Photo app, Version 3

app, we use that method inside the Controller for the app, the `MainActivity` class, rather than the Model, the `BitmapGrayer` class. Thus, the `BitmapGrayer` class does not change.

We need to add three `TextView` elements to our XML layout file. Other than their id, these `TextView` elements are identical, so we use a style for them. We edit the styles.xml file and add a `style` element for the `TextView`. EXAMPLE 12.10 shows the `styles.xml` file.

```
1    <resources>
2
3        <!-- Base application theme. -->
4        <style name="AppTheme" parent="Theme.AppCompat.Light.DarkActionBar">
5            <!-- Customize your theme here. -->
6            <item name="colorPrimary">@color/colorPrimary</item>
7            <item name="colorPrimaryDark">@color/colorPrimaryDark</item>
8            <item name="colorAccent">@color/colorAccent</item>
9        </style>
10
11       <style name="seekBarStyle">
12           <item name="android:layout_weight">1</item>
13           <item name="android:layout_width">wrap_content</item>
14           <item name="android:layout_height">wrap_content</item>
15           <item name="android:layout_gravity">center_vertical</item>
16           <item name="android:progress">0</item>
17           <item name="android:max">100</item>
18       </style>
19
20       <style name="textStyle" parent="@android:style/TextAppearance">
21           <item name="android:layout_weight">1</item>
22           <item name="android:layout_width">0dp</item>
23           <item name="android:layout_height">match_parent</item>
24           <item name="android:gravity">center</item>
25           <item name="android:textStyle">bold</item>
26           <item name="android:textSize">30sp</item>
27           <item name="android:text">0.0</item>
28       </style>
29
30   </resources>
```

EXAMPLE 12.10 The `styles.xml` file, Photo app, Version 3

The `textStyle` style, at lines 20–28, defines the style we use for the three `TextView` elements. We specify a font size of 30 at line 26, which should work well for most devices, and specify that the text should be centered at line 24, make it bold at line 25, and initialize it to 0.0 at line 27.

EXAMPLE 12.11 shows the activity_main.xml file. The screen is still organized with a vertical `LinearLayout`. It now has three parts: the `ImageView` (lines 13–18) that occupies eight tenths of the screen (line 14), a `LinearLayout` (lines 20–39) that occupies one tenth of the screen (line 22), and another `LinearLayout` (lines 41–57) that also occupies one-tenth of the screen (line 43). The three `SeekBar` elements, defined at lines 26–37, now only take one-tenth of the screen.

```
1    <?xml version="1.0" encoding="utf-8"?>
2    <LinearLayout xmlns:android="http://schemas.android.com/apk/res/android"
3      xmlns:tools="http://schemas.android.com/tools"
4      android:layout_width="match_parent"
5      android:layout_height="match_parent"
6      android:paddingLeft="@dimen/activity_horizontal_margin"
7      android:paddingRight="@dimen/activity_horizontal_margin"
8      android:paddingTop="@dimen/activity_vertical_margin"
9      android:paddingBottom="@dimen/activity_vertical_margin"
10     android:orientation="vertical"
11     tools:context="com.jblearning.photograyingv3.MainActivity">
12
13     <ImageView
14       android:layout_weight="8"
15       android:layout_width="match_parent"
16       android:layout_height="0dp"
17       android:scaleType="fitCenter"
18       android:id="@+id/picture" />
19
20     <LinearLayout
21       android:orientation="horizontal"
22       android:layout_weight="1"
23       android:layout_width="match_parent"
24       android:layout_height="0dp" >
25
26       <SeekBar
27         android:id="@+id/red_bar"
28         android:thumb="@drawable/red_thumb"
29         style="@style/seekBarStyle" />
30       <SeekBar
31         android:id="@+id/green_bar"
32         android:thumb="@drawable/green_thumb"
```

EXAMPLE 12.11 **The activity_main.xml file, Photo app, Version 3 (*Continued*)**

```
33          style="@style/seekBarStyle" />
34      <SeekBar
35          android:id="@+id/blue_bar"
36          android:thumb="@drawable/blue_thumb"
37          style="@style/seekBarStyle" />
38
39      </LinearLayout>
40
41      <LinearLayout
42          android:orientation="horizontal"
43          android:layout_weight="1"
44          android:layout_width="match_parent"
45          android:layout_height="0dp" >
46
47      <TextView
48          android:id="@+id/red_tv"
49          style="@style/textStyle" />
50      <TextView
51          android:id="@+id/green_tv"
52          style="@style/textStyle" />
53      <TextView
54          android:id="@+id/blue_tv"
55          style="@style/textStyle" />
56
57      </LinearLayout>
58
59  </LinearLayout>
```

EXAMPLE 12.11 **The activity_main.xml file, Photo app, Version 3**

The three `TextView` elements are defined at lines 47–55. We give each of them an id at lines 48, 51, and 54 so that we can access them using the `findViewById` method in the `MainActivity` class. They are styled with `textStyle` at lines 49, 52, and 55.

EXAMPLE 12.12 shows the changes in the `MainActivity` class, Version 3. The `TextView` class is imported at line 11 and we declare three `TextView` instance variables `redText`, `greenText`, and `blueText` at line 20. They are initialized inside the `onCreate` method at lines 31–33.

Whenever the user interacts with one of the seek bars, we need to update the corresponding `TextView`. We do that at lines 71–72, 76–77, and 81–82, after we update `grayer` based on the `progress` value of the seek bar that the user is interacting with.

FIGURE 12.6 shows our app running after the user clicks on the Save button and then interacts with the seek bars.

```
10
11    import android.widget.TextView;
...
14    public class MainActivity extends AppCompatActivity {
. . .
20      private TextView redTV, greenTV, blueTV;
21
22      protected void onCreate( Bundle savedInstanceState ) {
...
31        redTV = ( TextView ) findViewById( R.id.red_tv );
32        greenTV = ( TextView ) findViewById( R.id.green_tv );
33        blueTV = ( TextView ) findViewById( R.id.blue_tv );
...
50      }
...
63      private class GrayChangeHandler
64              implements SeekBar.OnSeekBarChangeListener {
65        public void onProgressChanged( SeekBar seekBar,
66                                      int progress, boolean fromUser ) {
67          if( fromUser ) {
68            if( seekBar == redBar ) {
69              grayer.setRedCoeff( progress / 100.0f );
70              redBar.setProgress( ( int ) ( 100 * grayer.getRedCoeff( ) ) );
71              redTV.setText( ""
72                + MathRounding.keepTwoDigits( grayer.getRedCoeff( ) ) );
73            } else if( seekBar == greenBar ) {
74              grayer.setGreenCoeff( progress / 100.0f );
75              greenBar.setProgress( ( int ) ( 100 * grayer.getGreenCoeff( ) ) );
76              greenTV.setText( ""
77                + MathRounding.keepTwoDigits( grayer.getGreenCoeff( ) ) );
78            } else if( seekBar == blueBar ) {
79              grayer.setBlueCoeff( progress / 100.0f );
80              blueBar.setProgress( ( int ) ( 100 * grayer.getBlueCoeff( ) ) );
81              blueTV.setText( ""
82                + MathRounding.keepTwoDigits( grayer.getBlueCoeff( ) ) );
83            }
84            bitmap = grayer.grayScale( );
85            imageView.setImageBitmap( bitmap );
86          }
87        }
88
89        public void onStartTrackingTouch( SeekBar seekBar ) {
90        }
91
92        public void onStopTrackingTouch( SeekBar seekBar ) {
93        }
94      }
95    }
```

EXAMPLE 12.12 The MainActivity class, Photo app, Version 3

FIGURE 12.6 The Photo app, Version 3, after clicking on Save and user interaction

12.5 Storing the Picture, Photo App, Version 4

In Versions 0, 1, 2, and 3, our app uses a camera app to take a picture. By default, any picture taken with the camera is stored in the Gallery. However, the grayed picture is not stored in Versions 0, 1, 2, and 3. In Version 4, our app stores the grayed picture on the device. In general, we can store persistent data in either **internal storage** or **external storage**. In the early days of Android, internal storage referred to nonvolatile memory and external storage referred to a removable storage medium. In recent Android devices, storage space is divided into two areas: internal storage and external storage. We can save persistent data in files either in internal or external storage.

Internal storage is always available and files saved in some internal storage directory are, by default, only accessible by the app that wrote them. When the user uninstalls an app, the files related to the app located in internal storage are automatically deleted. Depending on the device, external storage is typically available, although that is not guaranteed, and files located in external storage are accessible by any app. When the user uninstalls an app, the files related to the app located in external storage are automatically deleted only if they are located in a directory returned by the

TABLE 12.10 Internal storage, external storage, and methods of the `Context` class

	Internal Storage	External Storage
Default File Access	Accessible by app.	World readable.
When to Use	If we want to restrict file access.	If we are not concerned about restricting file access.
Obtain a Directory	getFilesDir( ) or getCacheDir( )	getExternalFilesDir(String type)
Permission in Manifest	None needed.	Needed; WRITE_EXTERNAL_STORAGE
When user uninstalls the app	App-related files are deleted.	App-related files are deleted only if they are located in a directory obtained using getExternalFilesDir.

`getExternalFilesDir` method of the `Context` class. **TABLE 12.10** summarizes some of the differences between internal and external storage, including methods of the `Context` class.

In Version 4, we save our grayed picture in external storage. In order to implement this feature, we do the following:

▶ We add a button in the activity_main.xml layout file.
▶ We edit the `MainActivity` class so that we save the picture when the user clicks on the button.
▶ We create a utility class, `StorageUtility`, which includes a method to write a `Bitmap` to an external storage file.

EXAMPLE 12.13 shows the activity_main.xml file, Version 4. At lines 59–72, we add a button to the user interface. At line 70, we specify that the `savePicture` method is called when the user clicks on that button. We slightly change the percentage of the screen taken by the picture. At line 14, we set the `android:layout_weight` attribute value of the `ImageView` element to 7 so that it takes 70% of the screen. The `SeekBar` elements still take 10% (line 22), the `TextView` elements still take 10% (line 43), and the button takes 10% of the screen (line 61).

EXAMPLE 12.14 shows the `StorageUtility` class. It includes only one `static` method, `writeToExternalStorage`, at lines 13–62: that method writes a `Bitmap` to a file in external storage and returns a reference to that file. If a problem happens during that process, it `throws` an `IOException`. We return a `File` reference rather than `true` or `false` because we need to access that file in Version 5, when we send the picture to a friend via email, adding that file as an attachment. In addition to a `Bitmap` parameter, this method also takes an `Activity` parameter, which we use to access a directory for external storage.

The `Environment` class is a utility class that provides access to environment variables. Its `getExternalStorageState` static method returns a `String` representing the state of the external storage on a device. The API of `getExternalStorageState` is:

```
public static String getExternalStorageState( )
```

```
1   <?xml version="1.0" encoding="utf-8"?>
2   <LinearLayout xmlns:android="http://schemas.android.com/apk/res/android"
3     xmlns:tools="http://schemas.android.com/tools"
4     android:layout_width="match_parent"
5     android:layout_height="match_parent"
6     android:paddingLeft="@dimen/activity_horizontal_margin"
7     android:paddingRight="@dimen/activity_horizontal_margin"
8     android:paddingTop="@dimen/activity_vertical_margin"
9     android:paddingBottom="@dimen/activity_vertical_margin"
10    android:orientation="vertical"
11    tools:context="com.jblearning.photograyingv4.MainActivity">
12
13    <ImageView
14      android:layout_weight="7"
15      android:layout_width="match_parent"
16      android:layout_height="0dp"
17      android:scaleType="fitCenter"
18      android:id="@+id/picture" />
19
20    <LinearLayout
21      android:orientation="horizontal"
22      android:layout_weight="1"
23      android:layout_width="match_parent"
24      android:layout_height="0dp" >
25
26      <SeekBar
27        android:id="@+id/red_bar"
28        android:thumb="@drawable/red_thumb"
29        style="@style/seekBarStyle" />
30      <SeekBar
31        android:id="@+id/green_bar"
32        android:thumb="@drawable/green_thumb"
33        style="@style/seekBarStyle" />
34      <SeekBar
35        android:id="@+id/blue_bar"
36        android:thumb="@drawable/blue_thumb"
37        style="@style/seekBarStyle" />
38
39    </LinearLayout>
40
41    <LinearLayout
42        android:orientation="horizontal"
43        android:layout_weight="1"
44        android:layout_width="match_parent"
45        android:layout_height="0dp" >
46
```

EXAMPLE 12.13 The activity_main.xml file, Photo app, Version 4 (*Continued*)

```
47          <TextView
48              android:id="@+id/red_tv"
49              style="@style/textStyle" />
50          <TextView
51              android:id="@+id/green_tv"
52              style="@style/textStyle" />
53          <TextView
54              android:id="@+id/blue_tv"
55              style="@style/textStyle" />
56
57      </LinearLayout>
58
59      <LinearLayout
60          android:orientation="horizontal"
61          android:layout_weight="1"
62          android:layout_width="match_parent"
63          android:layout_height="0dp"
64          android:gravity="center" >
65
66        <Button
67            android:layout_width="wrap_content"
68            android:layout_height="wrap_content"
69            android:text="SAVE PICTURE"
70            android:onClick="savePicture" />
71
72      </LinearLayout>
73
74  </LinearLayout>
```

EXAMPLE 12.13 The activity_main.xml file, Photo app, Version 4

```
1   package com.jblearning.photograyingv4;
2
3   import android.app.Activity;
4   import android.graphics.Bitmap;
5   import android.os.Environment;
6   import android.os.SystemClock;
7   import java.io.File;
8   import java.io.FileOutputStream;
9   import java.io.IOException;
10  import java.util.Date;
11
12  public class StorageUtility {
13      /*
14       * This method write its bitmap parameter to external storage
15       *        in the Pictures directory
```

EXAMPLE 12.14 The StorageUtility class (Continued)

```
16        * @param activity, an Activity
17        * @param bitmap, a Bitmap reference
18        * @return returns the File it wrote bitmap to
19        */
20       public static File writeToExternalStorage
21         ( Activity activity, Bitmap bitmap ) throws IOException {
22         // get state of external storage
23         String storageState = Environment.getExternalStorageState( );
24
25         File file = null;
26         if( storageState.equals( Environment.MEDIA_MOUNTED ) ) {
27           // get external storage directory
28           File dir
29             = activity.getExternalFilesDir( Environment.DIRECTORY_PICTURES );
30           // generate a unique file name
31           Date dateToday = new Date( );
32           long ms = SystemClock.elapsedRealtime( );
33           String filename = "/" + dateToday + "_" + ms + ".png";
34
35           // create a file to write to
36           file = new File( dir + filename );
37           long freeSpace = dir.getFreeSpace( ); // in bytes
38           int bytesNeeded = bitmap.getByteCount( ); // in bytes
39           if( bytesNeeded * 1.5 < freeSpace ) {
40           // there is space for the bitmap
41             try {
42               FileOutputStream fos = new FileOutputStream( file );
43               // write to file
44               boolean result
45                 = bitmap.compress( Bitmap.CompressFormat.PNG , 100,  fos );
46               fos.close( );
47               if( result )
48                 return file;
49               else
50                throw new IOException( "Problem compressing the Bitmap"
51                                        + " to the output stream" );
52             } catch( Exception e ) {
53              throw new IOException( "Problem opening the file for writing" );
54             }
55           }
56           else
57             throw new IOException( "Not enough space in external storage"
58                                    + " to write Bitmap" );
59         }
60         else
61           throw new IOException( "No external storage found" );
62       }
63     }
```

EXAMPLE 12.14 The StorageUtility class

TABLE 12.11 Selected constants of the `Environment` class

Constant	Description
MEDIA_MOUNTED	Value returned by the getExternalStorageState method if external storage is present with read and write access.
DIRECTORY_PICTURES	Name of directory is Pictures.
DIRECTORY_DOWNLOADS	Name of directory is Download.
DIRECTORY_MUSIC	Name of directory is Music.
DIRECTORY_MOVIES	Name of directory is Movies.

If that `String` is equal to the value of the `MEDIA_MOUNTED` constant of the `Environment` class (shown in **TABLE 12.11**), that means that there is external storage on the device and it has read and write access. We can test if there is external storage with the following code sequence:

```
String storageState = Environment.getExternalStorageState( );
if( storageState.equals( Environment.MEDIA_MOUNTED ) ) {
  // there is external storage
```

We get the storage state at lines 22–23 and test if external storage is available on the device at line 26. If it is not, we `throw` an `IOException` at line 61. If it is, we obtain the path of a directory for the external storage at lines 27–29 by calling the `getExternalFilesDir` method of the `Context` class, inherited by the `MainActivity` class via the `Activity` class. **TABLE 12.12** shows the `getExternalFilesDir` method. On the author's tablet, the directory path returned if the argument is `null` is:

```
/storage/emulated/0/Android/data/com.jblearning.photograyingv4/files
```

If the argument is `MyGrayedPictures`, the directory path returned is:

```
/storage/emulated/0/Android/data/com.jblearning.photograyingv4/
files/MyGrayedPictures
```

TABLE 12.12 The `getExternalFilesDir` method of the `Context` class

Method	Description
File getExternalFilesDir(String type)	Returns the absolute path of an external storage directory where the app can place its files. This is app dependent. If type is not null, a subdirectory named with the value of type is created.

The `Environment` class includes some constants we can use for standard names for directories. Table 12.11 lists some of them. Note that we are not required to use a directory named `Music` to store music files, but it is good practice to do so. At line 29, we use the `DIRECTORY_PICTURES` constant, whose value is `Pictures`.

> **SOFTWARE ENGINEERING:** Use the appropriate constants provided by the `Environment` class to name subdirectories within the app external storage directory to store your files.

Because the `writeToExternalStorage` method can be called many times, we want to create a new file every time it is called and not overwrite an existing file. We also do not want to ask the user for a file name, because that can be annoying for the user. Thus, we generate the file name dynamically. Since we do not want to overwrite an existing file, we choose a file naming mechanism that guarantees that we generate a unique file name every time. One way to do this is to use today's date and the system clock. The `elapsedRealtime static` method of the `SystemClock` class, shown in **TABLE 12.13**, returns the number of milliseconds since the last boot. We combine it with today's date in order to generate the file name. It is virtually impossible for the user to modify one seek bar and click on the SAVE PICTURE button within the same millisecond as the previous click. Thus, our naming strategy guarantees a unique file name every time we generate one. We generate that unique file name at lines 30–33. At lines 35–36, we create a file using that file name and located in the external storage directory.

We retrieve the amount of free space in the directory where that file will be at line 37 and the number of bytes needed to write the bitmap into that file at line 38, using the `getByteCount` method of the `Bitmap` class, shown in **TABLE 12.14**. We test if we have enough space in the directory for the number of bytes we need (times `1.5`, to be safe) at line 39. If we do not, we `throw` an `IOException` at lines 57–58. If we do, we attempt to open that file for writing at line 42 and try to write `bitmap` to it at lines 43–45. If for some reason we are unsuccessful, we execute inside the `catch` block and we `throw` an `IOException` at line 53. Because the `FileOutputStream` constructor can throw several exceptions, we catch a generic `Exception` at line 52 to keep things simple.

In order to write the `Bitmap bitmap` to our file, we use the `compress` method of the `Bitmap` class, shown in Table 12.14. The first argument of the `compress` method is the file compression format. The `Bitmap.CompressFormat` enum contains constants that we can use to specify such a format, as listed in **TABLE 12.15**. The second argument of the `compress` method is the quality

TABLE 12.13 The `elapsedRealtime` method of the `SystemClock` class

Method	Description
static long elapsedRealtime( )	Returns the time since the last boot in milliseconds, including sleep time.

TABLE 12.14 The `getByteCount` and `compress` methods of the `Bitmap` class

Method	Description
public final int getByteCount( )	Returns the minimum number of bytes needed to store this Bitmap.
public boolean compress(Bitmap.Compress.Format format, int quality, OutputStream stream)	Writes a compressed version of this Bitmap to stream, using the format format and a compression quality specified by quality—quality is between 0 (smallest size) and 100 (highest quality). Some formats like PNG, which is lossless, ignore the value of quality.

TABLE 12.15 The constants of the `Bitmap.CompressFormat` enum

Constant	Description
JPEG	JPEG format
PNG	PNG format
WEBP	WebP format

of the compression. Some compression algorithms, such as the one for the PNG format, are lossless, and ignore the value of that parameter. The third argument of the `compress` method is the output stream. If we want to write to a file, we can use a `FileOutputStream` reference, since `FileOutputStream` is a subclass of `OutputStream`. At line 45, we specify the `PNG` format and a compression quality level of `100` (although it does not matter here).

After closing the file at line 46, we test if the `compress` method returned `true` at line 47 (i.e., the `Bitmap` was correctly written to the file). If it does, we return `file` at line 48, otherwise, we throw an `IOException` at lines 50–51.

EXAMPLE 12.15 shows the `MainActivity` class, Version 4. The `savePicture` method (lines 65–74) is called when the user clicks on the SAVE PICTURE button. At line 68, we call the `writeToExternalStorage` method, passing `this` and `bitmap`. We do not use the `File` reference returned so we do not capture it. The user can change the graying parameters many times and save many grayed pictures. Since we name our file using a unique name, we can save as many pictures as we want.

Since the app writes to external storage, it.is mandatory to notify potential users and to include a `uses-permission` element inside the `manifest` element of the `AndroidManifest.xml` file as follows:

```
<uses-permission android:name="android.permission.WRITE_EXTERNAL_
STORAGE" />
```

```
 8
 9  import android.view.View;
...
14  import java.io.IOException;
15
16  public class MainActivity extends AppCompatActivity {
...
65    public void savePicture( View view ) {
66      // Save the picture and give the user some feedback
67      try {
68        StorageUtility.writeToExternalStorage( this, bitmap );
69        Toast.makeText( this, "Your picture has been saved",
70                Toast.LENGTH_LONG ).show( );
71      } catch( IOException ioe ) {
72        Toast.makeText( this, ioe.getMessage( ), Toast.LENGTH_LONG ).show( );
73      }
74    }
...
108  }
```

EXAMPLE 12.15 **The `MainActivity` class, Photo app, Version 4**

COMMON ERROR: If the app writes to the external storage, failure to include a `uses-permission` element for it in the AndroidManifest.xml file will result in no storage space being available to write to a file.

FIGURE 12.7 shows our app running after the user interacts with the seek bars. The SAVE PICTURE button enables the user to save the grayed picture.

When we run the app and save a picture, the app gives a `Toast` feedback. We can also open the directory where the pictures stored by the app are located in the device's external storage and look for our files. **FIGURE 12.8** shows a screenshot of the tablet after we navigate to the `data` directory, after successively clicking on the `My Files` native app, then `storage`, `emulated`, `0`, `Android`, and `data` on the left pane. Next, we click on the `com.jblearning.photograyingv4` directory (at the top on the right) then `files`, and `Pictures`. Our pictures are now visible.

If we change lines 28–29 in Example 12.14 to

```
File dir = activity.getExternalFilesDir("MyPix");
```

and we run the app again, then navigate to the `MyPix` directory next to the `Pictures` directory, `MyPix` contains the new grayed pictures generated by the app.

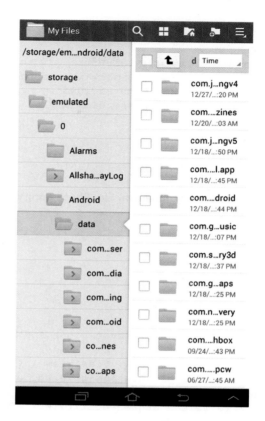

FIGURE 12.7 **The Photo app, Version 4, after clicking on Save and user interaction**

FIGURE 12.8 **Screenshot of the tablet as we navigate to find our stored grayed pictures**

12.6 Using the Email App: Sending the Grayed Picture to a Friend, Photo App, Version 5

Now that we know how to save the picture to a file, we can use that file as an attachment to an email. In Version 5, we replace the SAVE PICTURE text inside the button with SEND PICTURE, and we enable the user to share the picture or send it to a friend as an attachment to an email.

We modify the code for the button in the activity_main.xml file as shown in **EXAMPLE 12.16**.

EXAMPLE 12.17 shows the sendEmail method (lines 67–87) and the new import statements (lines 6 and 15) of the MainActivity class. The sendEmail method replaces the savePicture method of Example 12.16, Photo app, Version 4.

At line 70, we write bitmap to external storage, returning the File reference file. At line 71, we call the fromFile method of the Uri class, shown in **TABLE 12.16**, and create uri, a Uri

```
65
66        <Button
67          android:layout_width="wrap_content"
68          android:layout_height="wrap_content"
69          android:text="SEND PICTURE"
70          android:onClick="sendEmail" />
71
72      </LinearLayout>
73
74    </LinearLayout>
```

EXAMPLE 12.16 **The activity_main.xml file, Photo app, Version 5**

```
  5
  6  import android.net.Uri;
...
 15  import java.io.File;
...
 18  public class MainActivity extends AppCompatActivity {
...
 67    public void sendEmail( View view ) {
 68      // Send the picture and give the user some feedback
 69      try {
 70        File file = StorageUtility.writeToExternalStorage( this, bitmap );
 71        Uri uri = Uri.fromFile( file );
 72        Intent emailIntent = new Intent( Intent.ACTION_SEND );
 73        emailIntent.setType( "text/plain" );
 74        // String [] recipients = { "abc@xyz.com" };
 75        // emailIntent.putExtra( Intent.EXTRA_EMAIL, recipients );
 76        emailIntent.putExtra( Intent.EXTRA_SUBJECT,
 77              "Photo sent from my Android" );
 78        // emailIntent.putExtra( Intent.EXTRA_TEXT, "Hello from XYZ" );
 79        emailIntent.putExtra( Intent.EXTRA_STREAM, uri );
 80
 81        startActivity( Intent.createChooser( emailIntent,
 82              "Share your picture" ) );
 83      } catch( IOException ioe ) {
 84        Toast.makeText( this, ioe.getMessage( )
 85              + "; could not send it", Toast.LENGTH_LONG ).show( );
 86      }
 87    }
...
121  }
```

EXAMPLE 12.17 **The `MainActivity` class, Photo app, Version 5**

TABLE 12.16 The `fromFile` static method of the `Uri` class

Method	Description
static Uri fromFile(File file)	Creates and returns a Uri from file; encodes characters except /.

reference for `file`. We need a `Uri` reference in order to attach a file to an email. The `Uri` class, from the `android.net` package, not to be confused with the `URI` class from the `java.net` package, encapsulates a Uniform Resource Identifier (URI).

At lines 72–79, we create and define an `Intent` to send some data, using constants of the `Intent` class shown in **TABLE 12.17**. At line 72, we use the `ACTION_SEND` constant to create an `Intent` to send data. We set the Multipurpose Internet Mail Extensions (MIME) data type of the `Intent` at line 73 using the `setType` method shown in **TABLE 12.18**. We define a subject line at lines 76–77, mapping

TABLE 12.17 Selected constants of the `Intent` class

Constant	Description
ACTION_SEND	Used for an Intent to send some data to somebody.
EXTRA_EMAIL	Used to specify a list of email addresses.
EXTRA_STREAM	Used with ACTION_SEND to specify a URI holding a stream of data associated with an Intent.
EXTRA_SUBJECT	Used to specify a subject line in a message.
EXTRA_TEXT	Used with ACTION_SEND to define the text to be sent.

TABLE 12.18 The `setType` and `createChooser` methods of the `Intent` class

Method	Description
Intent setType(String type)	Sets the MIME data type of this Intent; returns this Intent so that method calls can be chained.
Intent putExtra(String name, dataType value)	Adds data to this Intent. Name is the key for the data, value is the data. There are many putExtra methods with various data types. It returns this Intent so that method calls can be chained.
static Intent createChooser(Intent target, CharSequence title)	Creates an action chooser Intent so that the user can choose among several activities to perform via a user interface. Title is the title of the user interface.

it to the value of EXTRA_SUBJECT. We add uri as an extra to the Intent at line 79, mapping it to the value of EXTRA_STREAM: that means that the file represented by file becomes the attachment when we send the data. We add and comment out lines 74–75 and 78. They show how we can add a list of recipients and email body text, using the EXTRA_EMAIL and EXTRA_TEXT constants. For this app, it is better to let the user fill in the blanks when the email app opens.

At lines 81–82, we call the createChooser method of the Intent class, shown in Table 12.18, and call startActivity, passing the returned Intent reference. The createChooser method returns an Intent reference such that when we start an activity with it, the user is presented with a choice of apps that match the Intent. Since we use the SEND_ACTION constant to create the original Intent, apps that send data, such as email, gmail, and other apps, will be presented to the user.

FIGURE 12.9 shows our app running after the user interacted with the seek bars. The SEND PICTURE button enables the user to save and send the grayed picture.

FIGURE 12.10 shows our app running after the user clicks on the SEND PICTURE button. All the available apps matching the intent to send data show.

FIGURE 12.9 The Photo app, Version 5, after the user interacted with the seek bars

FIGURE 12.10 The Photo app, Version 5, after the user clicks on SEND PICTURE

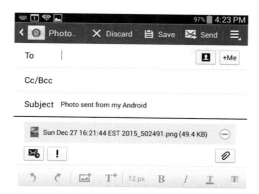

FIGURE 12.11 **The Photo app, Version 5, after selecting the email app**

FIGURE 12.11 shows our app running after the user selects email. We are now inside the email app, and we can edit it as we would edit any email.

Chapter Summary

- An app can use another app.
- In order to use a feature or another app, we include a `uses-feature` element in the AndroidManifest.xml file.
- The `hasSystemFeature` method of the `PackageManager` class enables us to check if a feature or an app is installed on an Android device.
- We can use the `ACTION_IMAGE_CAPTURE` constant of the `Intent` class to open a camera app.
- We can use the `ImageView` class as a container to display a picture.
- The `Bitmap` class encapsulates an image stored based on a format like PNG or JPEG.

- If a picture is stored in a `Bitmap`, we can access the color of every pixel of the picture.
- The `SeekBar` class, from the `android.widget` package, encapsulates a slider.
- We can capture and process `SeekBar` events by implementing the `SeekBar.OnSeekBarChangeListener` interface.
- To store persistent data, an Android device always has internal storage and typically, but not always, has external storage.
- The `Context` class provides methods that we can use to retrieve a directory path for external storage.
- In order to write to external storage, it is mandatory to include a `uses-permission` element in the AndroidManifest.xml file.
- We can use the `compress` method of the `Bitmap` class to write a `Bitmap` to a file.
- The `fromFile` method of the `Uri` class converts a `File` to a `Uri`.
- We can use the `ACTION_SEND` constant from the `Intent` class to create an `Intent` to send an email using an existing email app.
- We can use the `createChooser static` method of the `Intent` class to display several possible apps matching a given `Intent`.

 # Exercises, Problems, and Projects

Multiple-Choice Exercises

1. What method of the PackageManager class can we use to check if an app is installed on an Android device?
   - isInstalled
   - isAppInstalled
   - hasSystemFeature
   - hasFeature

2. What constant of the MediaStore class can we use to create an Intent to use a camera app?
   - ACTION_CAMERA
   - IMAGE_CAPTURE
   - ACTION_ CAPTURE
   - ACTION_IMAGE_CAPTURE

3. What class can we use as a container for a picture?
   - PictureView
   - ImageView
   - BitmapView
   - CameraView

4. What method of the class in question 3 is used to place a Bitmap object inside the container?
   - setBitmap
   - setImage
   - setImageBitmap
   - putBitmap

5. What key do we use to retrieve the Bitmap stored within the extras Bundle of a camera app Intent?
   - camera
   - picture
   - data
   - bitmap

6. What method of the Bitmap class do we use to retrieve the color of a pixel?
   - getPixel
   - getColor
   - getPixelColor
   - getPoint

7. What method of the Bitmap class do we use to modify the color of a pixel?
   - setPixel
   - setColor
   - setPixelColor
   - setPoint

8. How many parameters does the method in question 7 take?
   - 0
   - 1
   - 2
   - 3

9. What is the name of the class that encapsulates a slider?
   - Slider
   - Bar
   - SeekBar
   - SliderView

10. What are the types of storage on an Android device?
    - Internal and external
    - Internal only
    - External only
    - There is no storage on an Android device

11. What method of the Context class returns the absolute path of an external storage directory?
    - getExternalPath
    - getInternalPath
    - getExternalFiles
    - getExternalFilesDir

12. What method of the Bitmap class can we use to write a Bitmap to a file?
    - writeToFile
    - compress
    - write
    - format

13. What static method of the Uri class do we use to create a Uri from a file?
    - fromFile
    - a constructor
    - createFromFile
    - createUriFromFile

14. What constant of the Intent class do we use to create an Intent for sending data?
    - ACTION_SEND
    - DATA_SEND
    - EMAIL_SEND
    - SEND

Fill in the Code

15. Write a code sequence to output to Logcat that a camera app is available or not on a device.

16. Write the code to place a Bitmap named myBitmap inside an ImageView named myImageView.

17. Write the code to change all the pixels in a Bitmap named myBitmap to red.

18. Write the code to change all the pixels in a Bitmap named myBitmap to gray. The gray scale is defined with the following coefficients for red, green, and blue respectively: 0.5, 0.2, 0.3.

19. Write the code to output to Logcat EXTERNAL STORAGE or NO EXTERNAL STORAGE depending on whether there is external storage available on the current device.

20. Write the code to output to Logcat the number of bytes in a Bitmap named myBitmap.

21. Write the code to write a Bitmap named myBitmap to a file using the JPEG format, and a compression quality level of 50.

```
// assume that file is a File object reference
// previously and properly defined
try {
   FileOutputStream fos = new FileOutputStream( file );
   // your code goes here

}
catch( Exception e ) {
}
```

22. Write the code to create an Intent to send an email to mike@yahoo.com with the subject line HELLO and the message SEE PICTURE ATTACHED. Attach to the message a file that is stored in a File object named myFile.

Write an App

23. Write an app that enables the user to take a picture, display it, and has a button to eliminate the red color component in all the pixels of the picture. Include a Model.

24. Write an app that enables the user to take a picture, display it, and has three radio buttons to eliminate either the red, green, or blue color component in all the pixels of the picture. Include a Model.

25. Write an app that enables the user to take a picture, display it, and has a button to enable the user to change the picture to a mirror image of itself (the left and right sides of the picture are switched). If the user clicks on the button two times, the app shows the original picture again. Include a Model.

26. Write an app that enables the user to take a picture, display it, and has a button to enable the user to display a frame (of your choice) inside the picture. You can define a frame with a color and a number of pixels for its thickness. Include a Model.

27. Same as 26, but add a button to send an email with the framed picture. Include a Model.

28. Write an app that enables the user to take a picture, display it, and has a button to enable the user to display a frame around the picture of several possible colors (you can have at least three radio buttons for these colors). Include a Model.

29. Write an app that enables the user to take two pictures, and display them in the same ImageView container like an animated GIF: picture 1 shows for a second, then picture 2 shows for a second, then picture 1 shows for a second, and so on.

30. Same as 29, but add a button to send the two pictures via email.

31. Write an app that enables the user to take a picture, display it, and add some text of your choice on the picture. You can use the Canvas and Paint classes, in particular the Canvas constructor that takes a Bitmap as a parameter.

32. Same as 31, but add a bubble (you can hard code the drawing of the bubble). The text goes inside the bubble.

33. Write an app that enables the user to take a picture, display it, and add a vignette effect. A vignette effect is a reduction of the image's saturation at the periphery of the image. Include a Model.

CHAPTER **THIRTEEN**

XML and Content Apps

CHAPTER CONTENTS

Introduction

Smartphones and tablets include a browser so users can surf the Internet. However, a regular web page displayed on a small screen can be overwhelming. **Content apps** are apps that display selected content from a website so that the amount of information is manageable and the user experience is optimal. Such content apps exist for many sites, particularly social media websites and news sites. Often, websites offer frequently updated, consistently formatted information available to the outside world in general and app developers in particular. One such formatted information is called a **Really Simple Syndication (RSS) feed**. A typical RSS feed, not only is formatted in XML, but also often uses generic elements such as `item`, `title`, `link`, `description`, or `pubDate`. In order to build a content app for a particular site, we need to understand the formatting of that website's RSS feed, and we need to be able to parse the XML file that is exposed by that website so that we can display its contents.

13.1 Parsing XML, DOM, and SAX Parsers, Web Content App, Version 0

An XML document is typically accompanied by a **Document Type Declaration (DTD)** document: it contains the rules that an XML document should adhere to. For example, it can specify that an `rss` element can contain 0 or more `item` elements. It could specify that an `item` element must contain exactly one `title` element and one `link` element. It could also specify that a `title` element must contain plain text. In this chapter, we focus on the XML only, and we do not take into account the DTD. We assume that any XML document that we parse is properly formed and complies with the rules of its DTD.

There are two types of parsers to parse an XML document:

- **DOM** parsers
- **SAX** parsers

A **Document Object Model (DOM)** parser converts an XML file into a tree. Once the XML has been converted into a tree, we can navigate the tree to modify elements, add elements, delete elements, or search for elements or values. This is similar to what a browser does with an HTML document: it builds a tree, and once that tree data structure is in memory, it can be accessed, searched, or modified using JavaScript.

Using a DOM parser is a good option if we use an XML document as a replacement for a database and we are interested in accessing and modifying that database. That is often not the case for content apps. Content apps typically convert the XML document into a list and allow the user to interact with the list. Often, that list contains links to URLs.

In order to convert an XML document into a list, we use a **Simple API for XML (SAX)** parser. A SAX parser builds a list as it reads the XML document. The elements of that list are objects. It is generally thought that a SAX parser is faster than a DOM parser.

For example, let's assume that we want to parse the XML document shown in **EXAMPLE 13.1**.

```
<?xml version="1.0" encoding="utf-8" ?>
<rss>
  <item>
    <title>Facebook</title>
    <link>http://www.facebook.com</link>
  </item>
  <item>
    <title>Twitter</title>
    <link>http://www.twitter.com</link>
  </item>
  <item>
    <title>Google</title>
    <link>http://www.google.com</link>
  </item>
</rss>
```

EXAMPLE 13.1 A simple XML document

A DOM parser would convert that XML document to a tree similar to the tree shown in **FIGURE 13.1**. There are actually a few more branches in the tree than Figure 13.1 shows because empty strings between elements are also branches of the tree.

Instead of looking at that XML document as a tree, we can also look at it as a list of three items. In this document, each item has a title and a link. We can code an `Item` class with two `String` instance variables, `title` and `link`. A SAX parser would convert that XML document to a list of items containing three elements as shown in **FIGURE 13.2**.

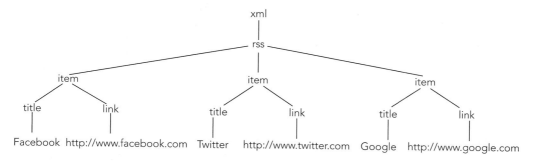

FIGURE 13.1 A tree for the XML document in Example 13.1

```
{ { title: Facebook; link: http://www.facebook.com }, { title:
Twitter; link: http://www.twitter.com }, { title: Google; link:
http://www.google.com } }
```

FIGURE 13.2 A list of items for the XML document in Example 13.1

TABLE 13.1 The `EntityResolver`, `DTDHandler`, `ContentHandler`, and `ErrorHandler` interfaces		
Interface	**Receives Notifications For**	**Method Names**
EntityResolver	Entity-related events	resolveEntity
DTDHandler	DTD-related events	notationDcl, unparsedEntityDcl
ContentHandler	Logic-related events	startDocument, endDocument, startElement, endElement, characters, and other methods
ErrorHandler	Errors and warnings	error, fatalError, warning

In Version 0 of our app, we concentrate on the process of XML parsing using a SAX parser. We use an existing SAX parser to parse the XML document in Example 13.1 and output feedback on the various steps of the parsing process to Logcat. In order to do this, we build two classes:

▸ The `SAXHandler` class processes the various elements of the XML document, such as start tags, end tags, and text between tags, as they are encountered by the SAX parser.
▸ The `MainActivity` class.

We will create a raw directory within the res directory and place a file named test.xml containing the XML document in Example 13.1 in it. Later in the chapter, we read an XML document dynamically from a URL. At this point, we do not create an `Item` class yet. We do that in Version 1.

The `DefaultHandler` class is the base class for SAX level 2 event handlers. The `Default-Handler` class implements four interfaces: `EntityResolver`, `DTDHandler`, `ContentHandler`, and `ErrorHandler`. It implements all the methods that it inherits from these four interfaces as do-nothing methods. **TABLE 13.1** shows these four interfaces and their methods.

When parsing an XML file using a SAX parser, there are many events that can happen: for example, whenever the parser encounters a start tag, an end tag, or text, it is an event. The `DefaultHandler` class includes a number of methods that are automatically called when parsing a document and an event occurs. **TABLE 13.2** shows some of these methods. For example, when the parser encounters a start tag, the `startElement` method is called. When the parser encounters an end tag, the `endElement` method is called. When the parser encounters text, the `characters` method is called. These methods are implemented as do-nothing methods. In order to handle these events, we need to subclass the `DefaultHandler` class and override the methods that we are interested in.

An XML document can contain **entity references**. An entity reference uses the special syntax `&nameOfTheEntity;`. For example, `&quot;` is an entity reference that represents a double quote ("), `&lt;` represents the less than sign (<), and `&amp;` represents the ampersand character (&). These are some of several predefined entity references. We can also add user-defined entity references

TABLE 13.2 Selected methods of the `DefaultHandler` class

Method	Description
void startElement(String uri, String localName, String startElement, Attributes attributes)	Called when a start tag is encountered by the parser; uri is the namespace uri and localName its local name; startElement is the name of the start tag; attributes contains a list of (name, value) pairs that are found inside the startElement tag.
void endElement(String uri, String localName, String endElement)	Called when an end tag is encountered by the parser.
void characters(char [ ] ch, int start, int length)	Called when character data is encountered by the parser; ch stores the characters, start is the starting index, and length is the number of characters to read from ch.

TABLE 13.3 Selected `parse` methods of the `SAXParser` class

Method	Description
void parse(InputStream is, DefaultHandler dh)	Parses the content of the XML input stream is and uses dh to handle events.
void parse(File f, DefaultHandler dh)	Parses the content of the XML file f and uses dh to handle events.
void parse(String uri, DefaultHandler dh)	Parses the content of the XML file located at uri and uses dh to handle events.

in the DTD. To keep things simple, we assume that the XML documents we parse in this chapter do not contain entity references.

To parse an XML document, we call one of the `parse` methods of the `SAXParser` class. **TABLE 13.3** lists some of them. They specify a `DefaultHandler` parameter that is used to handle the events encountered during parsing. When we override the `DefaultHandler` class, we need to override its methods so that we build our list of items inside these methods. **EXAMPLE 13.2** shows our `SAXHandler` class, Version 0. We override the `startElement`, `endElement`, and `characters` methods, which all throw a `SAXException`. Inside them, we output the values of some of their parameters. The SAX related classes are in the `org.xml.sax` and `org.xml.sax.helpers` packages. These classes are imported at lines 3–5.

As shown in Table 13.1, the `DefaultHandler` class includes other methods, such as `error` or `fatalError` that are called when an error in the XML document is encountered. In order to keep things simple, we assume that there is no error of any kind in the XML and the DTD documents, so we do not deal with XML errors.

```
1   package com.jblearning.webcontentv0;
2
3   import org.xml.sax.Attributes;
4   import org.xml.sax.SAXException;
5   import org.xml.sax.helpers.DefaultHandler;
6   import android.util.Log;
7
8   public class SAXHandler extends DefaultHandler {
9     public SAXHandler( ) {
10    }
11
12    public void startElement( String uri, String localName,
13                               String startElement, Attributes attributes )
14                               throws SAXException {
15      Log.w( "MainActivity", "Inside startElement, startElement = "
16             + startElement );
17    }
18
19    public void endElement( String uri, String localName,
20                             String endElement ) throws SAXException {
21      Log.w( "MainActivity", "Inside endElement, endElement = "
22             + endElement );
23    }
24
25    public void characters( char ch [], int start,
26                            int length ) throws SAXException {
27      String text = new String( ch, start, length );
28      Log.w( "MainActivity", "Inside characters, text = " + text );
29    }
30  }
```

EXAMPLE 13.2 **The** `SAXHandler` **class, Version 0**

TABLE 13.4 Selected methods of the `SAXParserFactory` class

Method	Description
SAXParserFactory newInstance( )	Static method that creates and returns a SAXParserFactory.
SAXParser newSAXParser( )	Creates and returns a SAXParser.

The `SAXParser` class is `abstract` so we cannot instantiate an object from it. The `SAXParser`-`Factory` class, also `abstract`, provides methods to create a `SAXParser` object. **TABLE 13.4** lists two of its methods. The `static` `newInstance` method creates a `SAXParserFactory` object

TABLE 13.5 The openRawResource method of the Resources class

Method	Description
InputStream openRawResource(int id)	Opens and returns an InputStream to read the data of the resource whose id is id.

and returns a reference to it, and the newSAXParser method creates a SAXParser object and returns a reference to it.

To create a SAXParser object, we can use the following sequence:

```
SAXParserFactory factory = SAXParserFactory.newInstance( );
SAXParser saxParser = factory.newSAXParser( );
```

In Version 0, we store a hard coded XML document in a file located in the raw directory of the res directory. Thus, if the name of our file is test.xml, we can access it using the resource R.raw.test. We can convert that resource to an input stream and use the first parse method listed in Table 13.3.

The getResources method of the Context class, inherited by the Activity class, returns a Resources reference to our application package. With that Resources reference, we can call the openRawResource method, listed in **TABLE 13.5**, in order to open and get a reference to an InputStream so that we can read the data in that resource.

We can chain method calls to getResources and openRawResource to open an input stream to read data from the file test.xml as follows:

```
InputStream is = getResources( ).openRawResource( R.raw.test );
```

In order to parse an InputStream named is containing an XML document with a SAX-Parser named saxParser that uses a DefaultHandler reference named handler to handle the events, we call the parse method as follows:

```
saxParser.parse( is, handler );
```

EXAMPLE 13.3 shows the MainActivity class. The SAXParser and SAXParserFactory classes, both part of the javax.xml.parsers package, are imported at lines 7–8. Many exceptions can be thrown by the various methods that we use:

newSAXParser throws a ParserConfigurationException and a SAXException.
openRawResource throws a Resources.NotFoundException.
parse throws an IllegalArgumentException, an IOException, and a SAXException.

Some of these exceptions are checked and some others are unchecked. To keep things simple, we use one try block at lines 14–20 and catch a generic Exception at line 20. Inside the try block, we create a SAXParser at lines 15–16 and declare and instantiate a SAXHandler

```
1    package com.jblearning.webcontentv0;
2
3    import android.os.Bundle;
4    import android.support.v7.app.AppCompatActivity;
5    import android.util.Log;
6    import java.io.InputStream;
7    import javax.xml.parsers.SAXParser;
8    import javax.xml.parsers.SAXParserFactory;
9
10   public class MainActivity extends AppCompatActivity {
11     protected void onCreate( Bundle savedInstanceState ) {
12       super.onCreate( savedInstanceState );
13       setContentView( R.layout.activity_main );
14       try {
15         SAXParserFactory factory = SAXParserFactory.newInstance( );
16         SAXParser saxParser = factory.newSAXParser( );
17         SAXHandler handler = new SAXHandler( );
18         InputStream is = getResources( ).openRawResource( R.raw.test );
19         saxParser.parse( is, handler );
20       } catch ( Exception e ) {
21         Log.w( "MainActivity", "e = " + e.toString( ) );
22       }
23     }
24   }
```

EXAMPLE 13.3 **The `MainActivity` class, Version 0**

named `handler` at line 17. We open an input stream to read the data in the test.xml file located in the raw directory of the res directory at line 18, and start parsing that input stream with `handler` at line 19. The parsing triggers a number of calls to the various methods inherited from `DefaultHandler` by `SAXHandler`, in particular the three methods that we overrode in Example 13.2.

FIGURE 13.3 shows the output inside Logcat when we run the app. We observe the following:

▶ Whenever a start tag is encountered, we execute inside the `startElement` method, and the value of the `startElement` parameter is the name of the tag.

▶ Whenever an end tag is encountered, we execute inside the `endElement` method, and the value of the `endElement` parameter is the name of the tag.

▶ Between the start and end tags of the same element, we execute inside the `characters` method and the array `ch` stores the characters between the start and end tags (also called the element contents).

▶ Between the end tag of an element and the start tag of another element, we execute inside the `characters` method and the text only contains white space characters.

```
    Inside startElement, startElement = rss
    Inside characters, text =
    Inside characters, text =
    Inside startElement, startElement = item
    Inside characters, text =
    Inside characters, text =
    Inside startElement, startElement = title
    Inside characters, text = Facebook
    Inside endElement, endElement = title
    Inside characters, text =
    Inside characters, text =
    Inside startElement, startElement = link
    Inside characters, text = http://www.facebook.com
    Inside endElement, endElement = link
    Inside characters, text =
    Inside characters, text =
    Inside endElement, endElement = item
    Inside characters, text =
    Inside characters, text =
    Inside startElement, startElement = item
    Inside characters, text =
    Inside characters, text =
    Inside startElement, startElement = title
    Inside characters, text = Twitter
    Inside endElement, endElement = title
    Inside characters, text =
    Inside characters, text =
    Inside startElement, startElement = link
    Inside characters, text = http://www.twitter.com
    Inside endElement, endElement = link
    Inside characters, text =
    Inside characters, text =
    Inside endElement, endElement = item
    Inside characters, text =
    Inside characters, text =
    Inside startElement, startElement = item
    Inside characters, text =
    Inside characters, text =
    Inside startElement, startElement = title
    Inside characters, text = Google
    Inside endElement, endElement = title
    Inside characters, text =
    Inside characters, text =
    Inside startElement, startElement = link
    Inside characters, text = http://www.google.com
    Inside endElement, endElement = link
    Inside characters, text =
    Inside characters, text =
    Inside endElement, endElement = item
    Inside characters, text =
    Inside endElement, endElement = rss
```

FIGURE 13.3 Logcat output of the Web Content app, Version 0

13.2 Parsing XML into a List, Web Content App, Version 1

In Version 1, we parse the test.xml file and convert it to a list. We code the Item class as part of our Model. The Item class encapsulates an item in the XML document: it has two String instance variables, title and link. In the SAXHandler class, we build an ArrayList of Item objects that reflect what we find in the XML document.

EXAMPLE 13.4 shows the Item class. It includes an overloaded constructor at lines 7–10, mutators at lines 12–13, and accessors at lines 14–15. We add a toString method at line 16, mostly to check the correctness of the parsing.

```java
1   package com.jblearning.webcontentv1;
2
3   public class Item {
4     private String title;
5     private String link;
6
7     public Item( String newTitle, String newLink ) {
8       setTitle( newTitle );
9       setLink( newLink );
10    }
11
12    public void setTitle( String newTitle ) { title = newTitle; }
13    public void setLink( String newLink ) { link = newLink; }
14    public String getTitle( ) { return title; }
15    public String getLink( ) { return link; }
16    public String toString( ) { return title + "; " + link; }
17  }
```

EXAMPLE 13.4 The Item class, Web Content app, Version 1

In the SAXHandler class, Version 1, shown in EXAMPLE 13.5, we build an ArrayList of Item objects. When the startElement method is called, if the tag is item, we need to instantiate a new Item object. If the tag is title or link, the text that we will read inside the characters method is the value for the title or link instance variable of the current Item object. When the endElement method is called, if the tag is item, we are done processing the current Item object and we need to add it to the list.

We need to be careful that inside the characters method, we process the correct data. There are white spaces that are typically present between tags, for example between an end tag and a start tag, in an XML document. We must be careful not to process them. The character data that we want to process is found between a start tag and the corresponding end tag. Thus, we use a state

```
1    package com.jblearning.webcontentv1;
2
3    import java.util.ArrayList;
4    import org.xml.sax.Attributes;
5    import org.xml.sax.SAXException;
6    import org.xml.sax.helpers.DefaultHandler;
7
8    public class SAXHandler extends DefaultHandler {
9      private boolean validText;
10     private String element = "";
11     private Item currentItem;
12     private ArrayList<Item> items;
13
14     public SAXHandler( ) {
15       validText = false;
16       items = new ArrayList<Item>( );
17     }
18
19     public ArrayList<Item> getItems( ) { return items; }
20
21     public void startElement( String uri, String localName,
22                               String startElement, Attributes attributes )
23                               throws SAXException {
24       validText = true;
25       element = startElement;
26       if( startElement.equals( "item" ) ) // start current item
27         currentItem = new Item( "", "" );
28     }
29
30     public void endElement( String uri, String localName,
31                             String endElement ) throws SAXException {
32       validText = false;
33       if( endElement.equals( "item" ) ) // add current item to items
34         items.add( currentItem );
35     }
36
37     public void characters( char ch [ ], int start,
38                             int length ) throws SAXException {
39       if( currentItem != null && element.equals( "title" ) && validText )
40         currentItem.setTitle( new String( ch, start, length ) );
41       else if( currentItem != null && element.equals( "link" ) && validText )
42         currentItem.setLink( new String( ch, start, length ) );
43     }
44   }
```

EXAMPLE 13.5 The SAXHandler class, Web Content app, Version 1

variable, `validText`, to assess if the character data that we process inside `characters` is the data that we want to process or not. When we encounter a start tag, we set `validText` to `true`. When we encounter an end tag, we set `validText` to `false`. We only process the character data in the `characters` method if `validText` is `true`.

We declare four instance variables at lines 9–12:

▸ `validText`, a `boolean` state variable. If its value is `true`, we process character data inside the `characters` method, otherwise we do not.

▸ `element`, a `String`, stores the current element (`xml`, `rss`, `item`, `title`, or `link` in this example).

▸ `currentItem`, an `Item`, stores the current `Item` object.

▸ `items`, an `ArrayList`, stores the list of `Item` objects that we build.

The constructor, at lines 14–17, initializes `validText` to `false` at line 15 and instantiates `items` at line 16. We code an accessor to `items` at line 19 so we can access it from an outside class.

In the `startElement` method (lines 21–28), we set `validText` to `true` at line 24 and assign `startElement`, the text inside the start tag, to `element` at line 25. If the start tag is equal to `item` (line 26), we instantiate a new `Item` object and assign its reference to `currentItem` at line 27.

COMMON ERROR: It is important to instantiate a new `Item` object every time we encounter a start tag whose value is `item`. Otherwise, we will keep over-writing the same `Item` object, and all the objects in our list will end up being identical.

If there is an end tag following the start tag, the `characters` method is called next. If `currentItem` is not `null` and `validText` is `true` and the value of `element` is either `title` or `link` (lines 39 and 41), we are in the middle of building the current `Item` object. If `element` is equal to `title` or `link`, we set the value of the `title` or `link` instance variable of the current `Item` object to the characters read (lines 40 and 42).

After the `startElement` and `characters` methods are called, the `endElement` method (lines 30–35) is called. We assign `false` to `validText` at line 32. In this way, any text found after an end tag and before a start tag is not processed by the `characters` method. If the value of `element` is `item` (line 33), we are done processing the current `Item` object, and we add it to `items` at line 34.

EXAMPLE 13.6 shows the `MainActivity` class, Version 1. At line 22, we retrieve the list of items that we parsed and assign it to the `ArrayList items`. At lines 23–24, we loop through it and output it to Logcat in order to check the correctness of the parsing.

FIGURE 13.4 shows the output inside Logcat when we run the app, Version 1. We can check that the `ArrayList items` contains the three `Item` objects that are listed in the test.xml file.

```
1    package com.jblearning.webcontentv1;
2
3    import android.os.Bundle;
4    import android.support.v7.app.AppCompatActivity;
5    import android.util.Log;
6    import java.io.InputStream;
7    import java.util.ArrayList;
8    import javax.xml.parsers.SAXParser;
9    import javax.xml.parsers.SAXParserFactory;
10
11   public class MainActivity extends AppCompatActivity  {
12     protected void onCreate( Bundle savedInstanceState ) {
13       super.onCreate( savedInstanceState );
14       setContentView( R.layout.activity_main );
15       try {
16         SAXParserFactory factory = SAXParserFactory.newInstance( );
17         SAXParser saxParser = factory.newSAXParser( );
18         SAXHandler handler = new SAXHandler( );
19         InputStream is = getResources( ).openRawResource( R.raw.test );
20         saxParser.parse( is, handler );
21
22         ArrayList<Item> items = handler.getItems( );
23         for( Item item : items )
24           Log.w( "MainActivity", item.toString( ) );
25       } catch ( Exception e ) {
26         Log.w( "MainActivity", "e = " + e.toString( ) );
27       }
28     }
29   }
```

EXAMPLE 13.6 **The `MainActivity` class, Web Content app, Version 1**

```
Facebook; http://www.facebook.com
Twitter; http://www.twitter.com
Google; http://www.google.com
```

FIGURE 13.4 **Logcat output of the Web Content app, Version 1**

13.3 Parsing a Remote XML Document, Web Content App, Version 2

In Version 2, we parse an XML document from a remote website. Instead of reading data from the test.xml file, we pull data from the rss feed for the computer science blog of Jones & Bartlett Learning. The URL is http://www.blogs.jblearning.com/computer-science/feed/. We access the

Internet, open that URL, and read the data at that URL. Starting with Version 3.0, Android does not allow an app to open a URL in its main thread. A **thread** is a sequence of code that executes inside an existing process. The existing process is often called the **main thread**. For an Android app, it is also called the **user-interface thread**. There can be several threads executing inside the same process. Threads can share resources, such as memory.

When we start the app, our code executes in the main thread, so we need to open that URL in a different thread. Furthermore, we need the XML parsing in the secondary thread to finish before trying to fill the list with data in the main thread because we use the data read in the secondary thread for the list. The `AsyncTask` class, from the `android.os` package, allows us to perform a background operation and then access the main thread to communicate its results. It is designed to execute short tasks, lasting a few seconds or less, and should not be used to start a thread that runs for a long time. `AsyncTask` is `abstract` so we must subclass it and instantiate an object of the subclass in order to use it. Appendix D explains the `AsyncTask` in detail, and it also includes a very simple app using `AsyncTask`.

We create the `ParseTask` class, a subclass of the `AsyncTask` class, in order to parse an rss feed from a remote server. We perform the following steps:

▶ We create `ParseTask`, a subclass of `AsyncTask`.
▶ We override the `doInBackground` method so that it parses the XML document we are interested in.
▶ Inside `ParseTask`, we include an instance variable that is a reference to the activity that starts the task. This enables us to call methods of the activity class from `ParseTask`.
▶ We override the `onPostExecute` method and call methods of the activity class to update the activity with the results of the task that we just completed.
▶ Inside the activity, we create and instantiate an object of `ParseTask`.
▶ We pass a reference to this activity to the `ParseTask` object.
▶ We call the `execute` method of `AsyncTask`, passing a URL, to start executing the task.

The `AsyncTask` class uses three generic types that we must specify when extending it. The class header of a subclass is as follows:

```
AccessModifier ClassName extends AsyncTask<Params, Progress, Result>
```

where `Params`, `Progress`, and `Result` are placeholders for actual class names and have the following meanings:

▶ `Params` is the data type of the array that is passed to the `execute` method of `AsyncTask` when we call it.
▶ `Progress` is the data type used for progress units as the task executes in the background. If we choose to report progress, that data type is often `Integer` or `Long`.
▶ `Result` is the data type of the value returned upon execution of the task.

In this app, we want to be able to pass an array of `Strings` (representing URLs) as the argument of the `execute` method, we do not care about reporting progress, and the task returns an `ArrayList` of `Item` objects. Thus, we use the following class header:

```
public ParseTask extends AsyncTask<String, Void, ArrayList<Item>>
```

TABLE 13.6 Selected methods of the `AsyncTask` class	
Method	**Description**
AsyncTask execute(Params. . . params)	params represent an array of values of type Params, a generic type.
Result doInBackground(Params. . . params)	params is the argument passed to execute when we call it.
void onPostExecute(Result result)	Automatically called after doInBackground finishes. Result is the value returned by doInBackground.

In order to launch a task using the `AsyncTask` class, we do the following:

▶ Create a subclass of `AsyncTask`.
▶ Declare and instantiate an object of that subclass.
▶ With that object, call the `execute` method to start the task.

After we call the `execute` method with a `ParseTask` reference, the `doInBackground` method executes and its argument is the same as the one we passed to `execute`. Its return value becomes the argument of `onPostExecute`, which is called automatically after `doInBackground` finishes. TABLE 13.6 shows these three methods. The `execute` and `doInBackground` method headers show that they both accept a variable number of arguments.

When we call the `execute` method, the following methods of the `AsyncTask` class execute in this order: `onPreExecute`, `doInBackground`, and `onPostExecute`.

Before the task executes, if we want to perform some initialization, we can place that code inside the `onPreExecute` method. We place the code for the task we want to execute in the `doInBackground` method. That method is `abstract` and must be overridden. The argument that is automatically passed to the `doInBackground` method is the same argument that we passed to the `execute` method when we called it. Inside `doInBackground`, as the task is executing, if we want to report progress to the main thread, we can call the `publishProgress` method. That in turn triggers a call to the `onProgressUpdate` method, which we can override: for example, we can update a progress bar in the user-interface thread. When the `doInBackground` method finishes executing, the `onPostExecute` method is called. We can override it to update the user interface with the results of the task that just completed. The argument that is automatically passed to the `onPostExecute` method is the value that is returned by the `doInBackground` method.

To summarize the flow of data, the argument that we pass to `execute` is passed to `doInBackground` and the returned value of `doInBackground` is passed as the argument of `onPostExecute`.

In our `ParseTask` class, the Params data type is `String` and the Result data type is `ArrayList`. Thus, the `doInBackground` method has the following method header:

```
protected ArrayList<Item> doInBackground( String... urls )
```

```
1    package com.jblearning.webcontentv2;
2
3    import android.os.AsyncTask;
4    import android.util.Log;
5    import java.util.ArrayList;
6    import javax.xml.parsers.SAXParser;
7    import javax.xml.parsers.SAXParserFactory;
8
9    public class ParseTask extends AsyncTask<String, Void, ArrayList<Item>> {
10     private MainActivity activity;
11
12     public ParseTask( MainActivity fromActivity ) {
13       activity = fromActivity;
14     }
15
16     protected ArrayList<Item> doInBackground( String... urls ) {
17       try {
18         SAXParserFactory factory = SAXParserFactory.newInstance( );
19         SAXParser saxParser = factory.newSAXParser( );
20         SAXHandler handler = new SAXHandler( );
21         saxParser.parse( urls[0], handler );
22         return handler.getItems( );
23       } catch( Exception e ) {
24         Log.w( "MainActivity", e.toString( ) );
25         return null;
26       }
27     }
28
29     protected void onPostExecute ( ArrayList<Item> returnedItems ) {
30       activity.displayList( returnedItems );
31     }
32   }
```

EXAMPLE 13.7 The `ParseTask` class, Web Content app, Version 2

EXAMPLE 13.7 shows the ParseTask class. In the class header (line 9), we specify String as the Params data type, Void as the Progress data type since we do not report progress in this app, and ArrayList as the Result data type.

At line 10, we declare the activity instance variable, a reference to MainActivity. The constructor (lines 12–4), accepts a MainActivity parameter and assigns it to activity. When we call that constructor from the MainActivity class, we pass this as the argument.

We override the doInBackground method at lines 16–27. The method header specifies that it returns an ArrayList of Item objects (the Result data type) and that it accepts Strings as parameters (the Params data type).

The code to parse the XML is essentially the same as in Example 13.6 except that we use a parse method whose first parameter is a String representing a URL at line 21, as opposed to an InputStream before. We expect that only one argument is passed to that method so we only process the first argument, which we access using the expression urls [0]. We do not expect that urls will be null at that point but even if it is, we catch that exception at line 23. At line 22, we return the ArrayList of Item objects generated when we parse the XML document.

We override the onPostExecute method at lines 29–31. When it is called automatically after the doInBackground method finishes execution, the value of its parameter returnedItems is the ArrayList of Item objects returned by doInBackground. We call the displayList method of the MainActivity class with the activity instance variable, passing returnedItems at line 30. Inside the MainActivity class, we need to code the displayList method.

Since our app accesses the Internet, we need to add the appropriate permission code inside the manifest element of the AndroidManifest.xml file as follows:

```
<uses-permission android:name="android.permission.INTERNET"/>
<uses-permission android:name="android.permission.ACCESS_NETWORK_STATE"/>
```

EXAMPLE 13.8 shows the MainActivity class. We declare a String constant named URL at lines 9–10 to store the URL of the RSS feed. At line 15, we declare and instantiate a ParseTask

```
1    package com.jblearning.webcontentv2;
2
3    import android.os.Bundle;
4    import android.support.v7.app.AppCompatActivity;
5    import android.util.Log;
6    import java.util.ArrayList;
7
8    public class MainActivity extends AppCompatActivity {
9      private final String URL
10             = "http://blogs.jblearning.com/computer-science/feed/";
11
12     protected void onCreate( Bundle savedInstanceState ) {
13       super.onCreate( savedInstanceState );
14       setContentView( R.layout.activity_main );
15       ParseTask task = new ParseTask( this );
16       task.execute( URL );
17     }
18
19     public void displayList( ArrayList<Item> items ) {
20       if( items != null ) {
21         for( Item item : items )
22           Log.w( "MainActivity", item.toString( ) );
23       }
24     }
25   }
```

EXAMPLE 13.8 The MainActivity class, Web Content app, Version 2

```
The Essentials of Computer Organization and Architecture Wins Third
Texty Award; http://blogs.jblearning.com/computer-science/2015/02/27/the-
essentials-of-computer-organization-and-architecture-wins-third-texty-award/

Computer Science Careers Among 2015 Best Jobs; http://blogs.jblearning.com/
computer-science/2015/02/17/computer-science-careers-among-2015-best-jobs/

Now Available: Computer Science Illuminated, Sixth Edition Includes Navigate
2 Advantage Access; -navigate-2-advantage-access/

. . .
```

FIGURE 13.5 Logcat output of the Web Content app, Version 2

object and call the execute method at line 16, passing URL. Since the execute method accepts a variable number of arguments, we can pass 0, 1, or more arguments. Alternatively, we could have passed an array of Strings containing only one element, URL, as follows:

```
task.execute( new String[ ] { URL } );
```

At lines 19–24, we code the displayList method. At this point, it outputs the contents of its parameter items to Logcat. Items could be null so we test for it at line 20 before the for loop.

Note that the sequencing of our code is important when we use an AsyncTask. After the call to execute at line 16, execution would continue inside the onCreate method if there were statements after line 16. In that case, there would be interleaved execution between those statements and the statements executing inside the ParseTask class. If we attempted to retrieve the ArrayList of Item objects right after line 16 inside the onCreate method, it would very likely be null. The correct way to process the result of a task is to do it inside the onPostExecute method.

FIGURE 13.5 shows a partial output inside Logcat when we run the app, Version 2. Note that this is a live blog, therefore contents may change daily and may not match the output in the figure.

13.4 Displaying the Results in a ListView, Web Content App, Version 3

In Versions 0, 1, and 2, we do not have any user interface. In Version 3, we display a list of all the titles retrieved from the XML document on the screen.

In order to keep this example simple, we only allow our app to run in vertical position. Thus, we add the following to the AndroidManifest.xml file inside the activity element:

```
android:screenOrientation="portrait"
```

To display the titles as a list on the screen, we use a ListView element in the activity_main.xml file. A ListView contains an arbitrary number of Strings. We do not have to specify how many elements when we define the ListView. Thus, we can build an ArrayList of Item objects dynamically and place the corresponding list of titles inside the ListView programmatically.

EXAMPLE 13.9 shows the activity_main.xml file, Version 3. We replace the TextView that displays Hello World! in the skeleton file with a ListView element at lines 12–16. We give it an id at line 12 so that we can access it by code using the findViewById method and populate it with data. We use the android:divider and the android:dividerHeight attributes at lines 15–16 to add a red, 2 pixels thick dividing line between the items displayed.

```
1    <?xml version="1.0" encoding="utf-8"?>
2    <RelativeLayout xmlns:android="http://schemas.android.com/apk/res/android"
3        xmlns:tools="http://schemas.android.com/tools"
4        android:layout_width="match_parent"
5        android:layout_height="match_parent"
6        android:paddingBottom="@dimen/activity_vertical_margin"
7        android:paddingLeft="@dimen/activity_horizontal_margin"
8        android:paddingRight="@dimen/activity_horizontal_margin"
9        android:paddingTop="@dimen/activity_vertical_margin"
10       tools:context="com.jblearning.webcontentv3.MainActivity">
11
12       <ListView android:id="@+id/list_view"
13           android:layout_width="match_parent"
14           android:layout_height="match_parent"
15           android:divider="#FF00"
16           android:dividerHeight="2dp" />
17
18   </RelativeLayout>
```

EXAMPLE 13.9 The activity_main.xml file, Web Content app, Version 3

EXAMPLE 13.10 shows the ParseTask class, Version 3. At lines 24–25, we replace the output statement to Logcat at line 24 of Example 13.7 with a Toast statement. Along with the statement importing Toast at line 4, these are the only changes.

EXAMPLE 13.11 shows the MainActivity class, Version 3. We include a ListView instance variable, listView, at line 13.

Inside the displayList method (lines 23–36), we populate listView with all the titles from the ArrayList items. We generate titles, an ArrayList of Strings containing the titles in items at lines 25–28. At lines 30–31, we create an ArrayAdapter containing titles. We use the constructor listed in TABLE 13.7, passing three arguments. The first argument is this, a reference to this activity (Activity inherits from Context). The second argument is

```
1    package com.jblearning.webcontentv3;
2
3    import android.os.AsyncTask;
4    import android.widget.Toast;
5    import java.util.ArrayList;
6    import javax.xml.parsers.SAXParser;
7    import javax.xml.parsers.SAXParserFactory;
8
9    public class ParseTask extends AsyncTask<String, Void, ArrayList<Item>> {
10     private MainActivity activity;
11
12     public ParseTask( MainActivity fromActivity ) {
13       activity = fromActivity;
14     }
15
16     protected ArrayList<Item> doInBackground( String... urls ) {
17       try {
18         SAXParserFactory factory = SAXParserFactory.newInstance( );
19         SAXParser saxParser = factory.newSAXParser( );
20         SAXHandler handler = new SAXHandler( );
21         saxParser.parse( urls[0], handler );
22         return handler.getItems( );
23       } catch( Exception e )  {
24         Toast.makeText( activity, "Sorry - There was a problem parsing",
25                 Toast.LENGTH_LONG ).show( );
26         return null;
27       }
28     }
29
30     protected void onPostExecute ( ArrayList<Item> returnedItems ) {
31       activity.displayList( returnedItems );
32     }
33   }
```

EXAMPLE 13.10 The ParseTask class, Web Content app, Version 3

```
1    package com.jblearning.webcontentv3;
2
3    import android.os.Bundle;
4    import android.support.v7.app.AppCompatActivity;
5    import android.widget.ArrayAdapter;
6    import android.widget.ListView;
7    import android.widget.Toast;
8    import java.util.ArrayList;
9
```

EXAMPLE 13.11 The MainActivity class, Web Content app, Version 3 (*Continued*)

```
10    public class MainActivity extends AppCompatActivity {
11      private final String URL
12               = "http://blogs.jblearning.com/computer-science/feed/";
13      private ListView listView;
14
15      protected void onCreate( Bundle savedInstanceState ) {
16        super.onCreate( savedInstanceState );
17        setContentView( R.layout.activity_main );
18        listView = ( ListView ) findViewById( R.id.list_view );
19        ParseTask task = new ParseTask( this );
20        task.execute( URL );
21      }
22
23      public void displayList( ArrayList<Item> items ) {
24        if( items != null ) {
25          // Build ArrayList of titles to display
26          ArrayList<String> titles = new ArrayList<String>( );
27          for( Item item : items )
28            titles.add( item.getTitle( ) );
29
30          ArrayAdapter<String> adapter = new ArrayAdapter<String>( this,
31                  android.R.layout.simple_list_item_1, titles );
32          listView.setAdapter( adapter );
33        } else
34          Toast.makeText( this, "Sorry - No data found",
35                  Toast.LENGTH_LONG ).show( );
36      }
37    }
```

EXAMPLE 13.11 The `MainActivity` class, Web Content app, Version 3

TABLE 13.7 Selected constructor of the `ArrayAdapter` class

Constructor	Description
ArrayAdapter(Context context, int textViewResourceId, List<T> objects)	Context is the current context; textViewResourceId is the id of a layout resource containing a TextView; objects is a list of objects of type T.

`android.R.layout.simple_list_item_1`, a constant of the `R.layout` class. It is a simple layout that we can use to display some text. The third argument is `titles`, an `ArrayList` and therefore a `List`.

We retrieve the `ListView` defined in activity_main.xml using its id at line 18 and assign it to `listView`. At line 32, we assign the list of titles as the list to display inside `listView`, calling the `setAdapter` method of the `ListView` class, shown in **TABLE 13.8**. The `adapter` reference is

TABLE 13.8 The `setAdapter` method of the `ListView` class	
Method	**Description**
void setAdapter(ListAdapter adapter)	Sets the ListAdapter of this ListView to adapter; adapter stores the list of data backing this ListView and produces a View for each item in the list of data.

actually an `ArrayAdapter` and therefore a `ListAdapter` because `ArrayAdapter` inherits from the `ListAdapter` interface. `ListAdapter` is a bridge between a `ListView` and its list of data.

At this point, we do not set up any list event handling; we do that in Version 4. If `items` is `null`, we show a `Toast` at lines 34–35.

FIGURE 13.6 shows the app, Version 3, running inside the emulator.

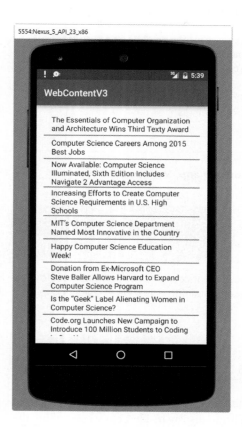

FIGURE 13.6 The Web Content app, Version 3, running inside the emulator

13.5 Opening a Web Browser Inside the App, Web Content App, Version 4

In Version 4, we open the browser at the URL chosen by the user from the list. In order to do that, we do the following:

▶ Implement event handling when the user selects an item from the list.
▶ Retrieve the link associated with that item.
▶ Open the browser at the URL contained in the link.

In Version 3, our list shows the titles of the `ArrayList` of `Item` objects that we generated parsing the XML document. In Version 4, we actually need to access the link values. In order to retrieve the link for a given `Item` object, we add an instance variable to the `MainActivity` class that represents the list of `Item` objects. When the user selects an item from the list, we retrieve its index, retrieve the `Item` object from the `ArrayList` at that index, and retrieve the value of the `link` instance variable of that `Item`.

EXAMPLE 13.12 shows the `MainActivity` class, Version 4. At line 18, we declare the `listItems` instance variable, an `ArrayList` of `Item` objects. Inside `displayList`, at line 29, we assign its `items` parameter to `listItems`.

```
1    package com.jblearning.webcontentv4;
2
3    import android.content.Intent;
4    import android.net.Uri;
5    import android.os.Bundle;
6    import android.support.v7.app.AppCompatActivity;
7    import android.view.View;
8    import android.widget.AdapterView;
9    import android.widget.ArrayAdapter;
10   import android.widget.ListView;
11   import android.widget.Toast;
12   import java.util.ArrayList;
13
14   public class MainActivity extends AppCompatActivity {
15     private final String URL
16         = "http://blogs.jblearning.com/computer-science/feed/";
17     private ListView listView;
18     private ArrayList<Item> listItems;
19
20     protected void onCreate( Bundle savedInstanceState ) {
21       super.onCreate( savedInstanceState );
22       setContentView( R.layout.activity_main );
```

EXAMPLE 13.12 The `MainActivity` class, Web Content app, Version 4 (*Continued*)

```
23      listView = ( ListView ) findViewById( R.id.list_view );
24      ParseTask task = new ParseTask( this );
25      task.execute( URL );
26    }
27
28    public void displayList( ArrayList<Item> items ) {
29      listItems = items;
30      if( items != null ) {
31        // Build ArrayList of titles to display
32        ArrayList<String> titles = new ArrayList<String>( );
33        for( Item item : items )
34          titles.add( item.getTitle( ) );
35
36        ArrayAdapter<String> adapter = new ArrayAdapter<String>( this,
37                android.R.layout.simple_list_item_1, titles );
38        listView.setAdapter( adapter );
39
40        ListItemHandler lih = new ListItemHandler( );
41        listView.setOnItemClickListener( lih );
42      } else
43        Toast.makeText( this, "Sorry - No data found",
44                Toast.LENGTH_LONG ).show( );
45    }
46
47    private class ListItemHandler
48            implements AdapterView.OnItemClickListener {
49      public void onItemClick( AdapterView<?> parent, View view,
50                              int position, long id ) {
51        Item selectedItem = listItems.get( position );
52        Uri uri = Uri.parse( selectedItem.getLink( ) );
53        Intent browserIntent = new Intent( Intent.ACTION_VIEW, uri );
54        startActivity( browserIntent );
55      }
56    }
57  }
```

EXAMPLE 13.12 The `MainActivity` class, Web Content app, Version 4

OnItemClickListener is a public inner interface of the AdapterView class. It includes one abstract callback method, onItemClick. That method is automatically called when the user selects an item from a list associated with an AdapterView, provided that an OnItemClick-Listener object is listening for events on that list. **TABLE 13.9** shows the onItemClick method. In order to implement list event handling, we do the following:

▸   We code a private handler class that extends OnItemClickListener at lines 47–56, and override its only abstract method, onItemClick, at lines 49–55.

TABLE 13.9 The `OnItemClickListener` interface	
Method	**Description**
void onItemClick(AdapterView<?> parent, View view, int position, int id)	This method is called when an item is selected in a list: parent is the AdapterView; view is the view within the AdapterView that was selected; position is the position of view within the AdapterView; id is the row index of the item selected.

TABLE 13.10 The `parse` method of the `Uri` class	
Method	**Description**
static Uri parse(String uriString)	Creates a Uri that parses uriString and returns a reference to it.

▶ We declare and instantiate an object of that class at line 40.
▶ We register that handler on the `List-View` at line 41 so that it listens to list events.

The parameter `position` of the `onItemClick` method stores the index of the item in the list that the user selected. We use it to retrieve the `Item` object in `listItems` at that index at line 51. At line 52, we use the `static parse` method of the `Uri` class, shown in **TABLE 13.10**, to create a `Uri` object with the `String` stored in the `link` instance variable of that `Item` object. At line 53, we create an `Intent` to open the web browser at that `Uri`. We pass the `ACTION_VIEW` constant of the `Intent` class and the `Uri` object to the `Intent` constructor. At line 54, we start a new activity with that `Intent`. Since the activity is to open the browser, there is no layout file and class associated with that activity.

FIGURE 13.7 shows the app, Version 4, running inside the emulator, after the user selects an item from the list. If we click on the back button of the emulator, we go back to the list of links, which then becomes the activity at the top of the activity stack.

FIGURE 13.7 The Web Content app, Version 4, running inside the emulator, after the user selects an item from the list

Chapter Summary

- There are two types of XML parsers: DOM and SAX.
- A DOM parser converts an XML document into a tree. A SAX parser reads the XML document sequentially and reports what it finds. We can use it to convert the XML document to a list of objects.
- We can use the SAXParserFactory class to get a SAXParser reference.
- The SAXParser class contains several methods to parse an XML document.
- We can extend the DefaultHandler class to parse an XML document using a SAX parser.
- The DefaultHandler class includes callback methods that are automatically called when parsing an XML document. For example, the startElement method is called when the parser encounters a start tag.
- The latest versions of Android do not allow us to open a URL on the app's main thread. We need to do that on a separate thread.
- We can extend the AsyncTask class to provide threading functionality.
- A call to the execute method of the AsyncTask class triggers execution of its preExecute, doInBackground, and postExecute methods, in that order.
- The argument passed to execute is in turn passed to doInBackground, and the return value of doInBackground is then passed as the argument of postExecute.
- In order to access the Internet from an app, we need to include a uses-permission element for it in the AndroidManifest.xml file.
- We can use a ListView to display a list of items.
- To perform event handling on a ListView, we can implement the OnItemClickListener inner interface of the AdapterView class and override its onItemClick method.
- The Uri class encapsulates a Uniform Resource Identifier.
- We can create an intent to open the browser using the ACTION_VIEW constant of the Intent class and an Uri object.

Exercises, Problems, and Projects

Multiple-Choice Exercises

1. What does DOM stand for?
    - Direct Object Model
    - Document Object Model
    - Document Oriented Model
    - Direct Oriented Model

2. What does SAX stand for?
    - Super Adapter XML
    - Simple API eXtension
    - Simple API for XML
    - Simple Android for XML

3. What method of the DefaultHandler class is called when the parser encounters a start tag?
    - startElement
    - startTag
    - start
    - tag

4. What method of the DefaultHandler class is called when the parser encounters an end tag?
    - endElement
    - endTag
    - end
    - tag

5. What method of the DefaultHandler class is called when the parser encounters character data?
    - data
    - characterData
    - foundCharacters
    - characters

6. What method of the AsyncTask class do we call to start the task?
    - start
    - run
    - execute
    - startTask

7. The argument of the method in question 7 becomes the argument of which method?
   - preExecute
   - doInBackground
   - postExecute
   - publishProgress

8. The return value of the doInBackground method becomes the argument of which method?
   - preExecute
   - doInBackground
   - postExecute
   - publishProgress

9. What constant of the Intent class can we use to create an intent to open the browser?
   - ACTION_BROWSER
   - ACTION_VIEW
   - WEB_VIEW
   - WEB_BROWSER

Fill in the Code

10. This code starts parsing a file named myFile.xml located in the raw directory of the res directory, using the DefaultHandler myHandler (assume that SAXHandler extends DefaultHandler).

```
SAXParserFactory factory = SAXParserFactory.newInstance( );
SAXParser saxParser = factory.newSAXParser( );
SAXHandler myHandler = new SAXHandler( );
// Your code goes here
```

11. Inside the characters method of the DefaultHandler class, assign to a String named myString the characters read by the parser.

```
public void characters( char ch [ ], int start, int length )
     throws SAXException {
  String myString;
  // Your code goes here
}
```

12. We are coding a class named MyTask, extending AsyncTask. We expect to pass an array of Integers to the execute method, and we expect the doInBackground method to return an ArrayList of Doubles. We do not care about reporting progress. Write the class header of MyTask.

13. We are coding a class named MyTask2, extending AsyncTask. We expect to pass a Double to the execute method, and we expect the doInBackground method to return a String. We want to report progress as an Integer. Write the class header of MyTask2.

14. We have already coded a class named MyTask, extending AsyncTask. The doInBackground accepts a variable number of Integers as parameters. Start executing the task, passing one or more values.

    ```
    // We are inside an activity class
    MyTask myTask = new MyTask( this );
    // Your code goes here ( one statement only )
    ```

15. Write a private class that implements the OnItemClickListener interface and override its method(s) as do-nothing method(s).

16. Inside an activity, write the code to open the browser at http://www.google.com.

Write an App

17. Write an app similar to the app in the chapter: use a different URL and display the published date along with the title.

18. Write an app similar to the app in the chapter: use a different URL and display only the titles that have been published within the last 30 days.

19. Write an app similar to the app in the chapter: use a different URL and add a text field to let users specify how recent they want the data to be. For example, if a user enters 45, then only display results with a published date that is within the last 45 days.

20. Write an app similar to the app in the chapter: use a different URL and add a front end activity with a text field to let the user specify a search term so that the titles displayed include that search term.

21. Write an app that presents the user with a list of websites of your choice in a ListView. When the user clicks on one, the browser opens that website.

CHAPTER FOURTEEN

Making an Android Widget

CHAPTER CONTENTS

Introduction

App widgets, also known as **widgets**, are small apps that are embedded in other apps, called **app widget hosts**. The Home screen and the Lock screen are examples of app widget hosts. We can also implement our own app widget host, but that is beyond the scope of this chapter. Widgets can receive periodic updates and update their view accordingly. The minimum frequency of automatic periodic updates is 30 minutes. Many Android devices come with native widgets already installed. A well-known and common widget is a weather app widget from www.accuweather.com. In this chapter, we create a widget that displays the current temperature at a location specified by the user during the installation of the widget.

14.1 Steps in Making a Widget, Temperature Widget, Version 0

In order to create a widget, we first start by creating a standard Android application project using the Empty Activity template. Although we could reuse (and modify) the activity_main.xml file, we choose to create a new layout file in the layout directory for the widget. We name it widget_layout.xml.

The `android.appwidget` package contains classes that enable us to create and manage widgets. TABLE 14.1 lists some of these classes.

In order to create a widget, we do the following:

▸ Add a `receiver` element inside the `application` element in the AndroidManifest.xml file.
▸ Define an `AppWidgetProviderInfo` object in an eXtensible Markup Language (XML) resource located in the res/xml directory.
▸ Define an app widget layout in an XML file in the res/layout directory.
▸ Extend the `AppWidgetProvider` class or the `BroadcastReceiver` class.

In Version 0, we create a very simple widget that displays a hard coded `String`.

TABLE 14.1 Selected classes of the `android.appwidget` package

Class	Description
AppWidgerProvider	A convenience class we can extend to implement a widget provider. This class contains life-cycle methods for a widget that we can override.
AppWidgetProviderInfo	Describes the metadata in a widget provider, such as icon, minimum width and height, update frequency, etc.
AppWidgetManager	Manages the widget provider and the widgets.

First, we update the AndroidManifest.xml file. We include a `receiver` element inside the `application` element in the AndroidManifest.xml file using the following pattern:

```
<receiver android:name="AppWidgetProviderClassName" >
  <intent-filter>
    <action android:name="android.appwidget.action.APPWIDGET_UPDATE" />
  </intent-filter>
  <meta-data android:name="android.appwidget.provider"
             android:resource="@xml/name_of_widget_info_file" />
  </meta-data>
</receiver>
```

In this example, `TemperatureProvider` is the name of our class that extends `AppWidget-Provider`, and widget_info.xml is the name of the file inside the xml directory of the res directory that contains the widget information such as size and update frequency.

EXAMPLE 14.1 shows the AndroidManifest.xml file. At lines 12–22, the `receiver` element replaces the default `activity` element. The `android:name` attribute inside the `receiver` element at line 12 is mandatory. Its value is the name of the class that extends `AppWidgetProvider`. The `action` element (lines 14–15) inside the `intent-filter` element is mandatory and must have

```
1    <?xml version="1.0" encoding="utf-8"?>
2    <manifest package="com.jblearning.temperaturewidgetv0"
3              xmlns:android="http://schemas.android.com/apk/res/android">
4
5      <application
6          android:allowBackup="true"
7          android:icon="@mipmap/ic_launcher"
8          android:label="@string/app_name"
9          android:supportsRtl="true"
10         android:theme="@style/AppTheme">
11
12        <receiver android:name="TemperatureProvider">
13          <intent-filter>
14            <action android:name=
15              "android.appwidget.action.APPWIDGET_UPDATE" />
16          </intent-filter>
17
18          <meta-data
19              android:name="android.appwidget.provider"
20              android:resource="@xml/widget_info" />
21
22        </receiver>
23      </application>
24
25    </manifest>
```

EXAMPLE 14.1 The AndroidManifest.xml file

an `android:name` attribute whose value is the equivalent of the `ACTION_APPWIDGET_UPDATE` constant of the `AppWidgetManager` class. That means that this widget receives an update broadcast at the frequency specified in the widget info xml file. The `meta-data` element, at lines 18–20, specifies the `AppWidgetProviderInfo` information via its `android:name` and `android:resource` attributes, both mandatory:

▶ The `android:name` attribute specifies the metadata name: the value `android.appwidget.provider` is used to identify the metadata as the `AppWidgetProviderInfo` type (line 19).

▶ The `android:resource` attribute specifies the resource location and name of the xml file that contains the `AppWidgetProviderInfo` information (line 20).

EXAMPLE 14.2 shows the widget_info.xml file. It defines an `AppWidgetProviderInfo` object in an XML resource. **TABLE 14.2** shows some `public` instance variables and corresponding XML attributes of the `AppWidgetProviderInfo` class.

```
1   <?xml version="1.0" encoding="utf-8"?>
2   <appwidget-provider
3       xmlns:android="http://schemas.android.com/apk/res/android"
4       android:initialLayout="@layout/widget_layout"
5       android:minHeight="50dp"
6       android:minWidth="200dp"
7       android:updatePeriodMillis="1800000">
8   </appwidget-provider>
```

EXAMPLE 14.2 The widget_info.xml file

The res directory does not contain an xml directory by default, so we need to create it. Since we specify widget_info as the name of the xml file defining the `AppWidgetProviderInfo` object in the AndroidManifest.xml file in Example 14.1, we add an xml file in the xml directory named widget_info.xml. That file must contain a single `appwidget-provider` element. It is defined at lines 2–8 of Example 14.2. At line 4, we specify widget_layout.xml, located in the res/layout directory, as the layout resource of the widget. At lines 5–6, we set its minimum height and width to 50 and 200 pixels. These will be the width and height of the widget when it is created and added to the host. An Android home screen is organized as a grid of cells in which widgets (and icons) can be placed. The grid can vary by device.

It could be 4×4 for a phone or 8×7 for a tablet, for example. The number of horizontal or vertical cells that the widget requires is the minimum number of cells required to accommodate `minWidth` or `minHeight` pixels, respectively. **TABLE 14.3** shows Google's recommendations. For example, if we have a widget whose `minWidth` value is 200 and whose `minHeight` value is 70, its graphical representation is allocated a 2×4 rectangle of cells: the 200 density pixels require 4 vertical cells and the 70 density pixels require 2 horizontal cells.

TABLE 14.2 Selected `public` instance variables and XML attributes of the `AppWidgetProviderInfo` class

Public Instance Variable	XML Attribute	Description
int minWidth	android:minWidth	The width of the widget when added to the host, in dp.
int minHeight	android:minHeight	The height of the widget when added to the host, in dp.
int minResizeWidth	android:minResizeWidth	The minimum width the widget can be resized to, in dp.
int minResizeHeight	android:minResizeHeight	The minimum height the widget can be resized to, in dp.
int updatePeriodMillis	android:updatePeriodMillis	The frequency of updates for the widget, in ms. Minimum frequency is 30 minutes.
int widgetCategory	android:widgetCategory	Specifies whether this widget can be displayed on the Home screen, Lock screen (Keyguard), or both.

TABLE 14.3 Number of cells versus widget size per dimension

# of Cells per Dimension	Widget Maximum Dimension in Density Pixels (dp)
n	$70 * n - 30$
1	40
2	110
3	180
4	250

At line 7, we set the update frequency to be `1800000` milliseconds, which is equal to 30 minutes. This is the minimum frequency at which a widget can be automatically updated. However, we can trigger a widget update by code by setting up some event handling on the widget, for example, if the user touches the widget. We do that in Version 2.

Example 14.2 specifies at line 4 that the layout of the widget is defined in the widget_layout.xml file. Although a widget is typically small with a simple GUI, a widget can have a complex GUI, but with some restrictions. TABLE 14.4 lists the Views and layout managers that a widget can use.

TABLE 14.4	Views and layout managers that we can use in a widget
Views	AnalogClock, Button, Chronometer, ImageButton, ImageView, ProgressBar, TextView, ViewFlipper, ListView, GridView, StackView, AdapterViewFlipper
Layout Managers	FrameLayout, LinearLayout, RelativeLayout, GridLayout

EXAMPLE 14.3 shows the widget_layout.xml file. It is organized in a `LinearLayout` (line 2) and contains only a `TextView` (lines 7–12), which in this version shows some hard coded text using the string resource `city_and_temp` (line 11); `city_and_temp` is defined in strings.xml as follows:

```
<string name="city_and_temp">New York, NY\n75\u00B0F</string>
```

It uses the Unicode character `\u00B0` to encode the degree sign (°). Inside strings.xml, we change the value of the `app_name` `String` from `TemperatureWidgetV0` to `TemperatureV0`.

```
1   <?xml version="1.0" encoding="utf-8"?>
2   <LinearLayout xmlns:android="http://schemas.android.com/apk/res/android"
3                 android:orientation="vertical"
4                 android:layout_width="match_parent"
5                 android:layout_height="match_parent">
6
7     <TextView
8         android:layout_width="match_parent"
9         android:layout_height="match_parent"
10        style="@android:style/TextAppearance.Large"
11        android:text="@string/city_and_temp" >
12    </TextView>
13
14  </LinearLayout>
```

EXAMPLE 14.3 The widget_layout.xml file

We now create a class that extends `AppWidgetProvider`. As specified in the AndroidManifest.xml file in Example 14.1, we name it `TemperatureProvider`. **TABLE 14.5** shows some life-cycle methods of the `AppWidgetProvider` class. The constants in column 2 are from the `AppWidgetManager` class. At the minimum, we need to override the `onUpdate` method so that we display the widget. The `onUpdate` method provides three parameters:

▶ A `Context` reference to the context in which this `AppWidgetProvider` is running.
▶ An `AppWidgetManager`: it enables us to update one or more widgets of the current type.
▶ An array of widget ids: the ids of the widgets of that provider for which an update is needed.

TABLE 14.5 Selected methods of the `AppWidgetProvider` class

Method	Type of BROADCAST (or Action Value of Intent)	Description
void onUpdate(Context context, AppWidgetManager manager, int [ ] appWidgetIds)	ACTION_APPWIDGET_ UPDATE	Called when this widget first runs and when it is updated (at the frequency defined in updatePeriodMillis).
void onAppWidgetOptionsChanged(Context context, AppWidgetManager manager, int appWidgetId, Bundle newOptions)	ACTION_APPWIDGET_ OPTIONS_CHANGED	Called when this widget has been resized.
void onEnabled( )	ACTION_APPWIDGET_ ENABLED	Called when the first widget of that type is added to the host screen.
void onDeleted( )	ACTION_APPWIDGET_ DELETED	Called when a widget of that type is deleted from the host screen.
void onDisabled( )	ACTION_APPWIDGET_ DISABLED	Called when the last widget of that type is deleted from the host screen.
void onReceive(Context context, Intent intent)	Automatically called before the onUpdate method before a widget is configured and after the widget's configuration activity has finished.	Overrides this method to dispatch calls to the other methods of this class.

It is possible that several widgets of that class are installed. This is why we refer to an array of widget ids rather than a single widget id. For example, if this widget is customizable based on some location, we could have a widget of that class displaying the temperature in New York, NY, and another one displaying the temperature in Palo Alto, CA.

Inside the onUpdate method, we loop through all the widget ids of type `TemperatureProvider` and update them using the `AppWidgetManager` parameter.

Note that we could choose to only update the widgets that need an update by using the appWidgetIds parameter of the onUpdate method.

TABLE 14.6 shows some methods of the `AppWidgetManager` class.

The `RemoteViews` class, from the `android.widget` package, describes a hierarchy of Views that can be displayed. It can be inflated from an XML resource. It also includes methods

TABLE 14.6 Selected methods of the `AppWidgetManager` class

Method	Description
int [ ] getAppWidgetIds(ComponentName provider)	Returns the list of widget ids for the widgets of the type of this AppWidgetProvider provider
void updateAppWidget(int appWidgetId, RemoteViews views)	Sets views as the RemoteViews for the widget whose id is appWidgetId.

TABLE 14.7 Selected Methods of the `RemoteViews` class

Constructor	Description
RemoteViews(String packageName, int layoutResourceId)	Creates and returns a RemoteViews from the resource identified by layoutResourceId in the package named packageName.

that can manage the contents of the hierarchy of Views. **TABLE 14.7** shows a constructor of the `RemoteViews` class.

EXAMPLE 14.4 shows the `TemperatureProvider` class. The `onUpdate` method is at lines 9–17. At lines 13–14, we instantiate a `RemoteViews` object for the layout defined in the

```
1   package com.jblearning.temperaturewidgetv0;
2
3   import android.appwidget.AppWidgetManager;
4   import android.appwidget.AppWidgetProvider;
5   import android.content.Context;
6   import android.widget.RemoteViews;
7
8   public class TemperatureProvider extends AppWidgetProvider {
9     @Override
10    public void onUpdate ( Context context,
11      AppWidgetManager appWidgetManager, int [ ] appWidgetIds ) {
12      super.onUpdate( context, appWidgetManager, appWidgetIds );
13      RemoteViews remoteViews = new RemoteViews(
14          context.getPackageName( ), R.layout.widget_layout );
15      for ( int widgetId : appWidgetIds )
16        appWidgetManager.updateAppWidget( widgetId, remoteViews );
17    }
18  }
```

EXAMPLE 14.4 The `TemperatureProvider` class

FIGURE 14.1 The app icons, including the Widget Preview icon, inside the emulator

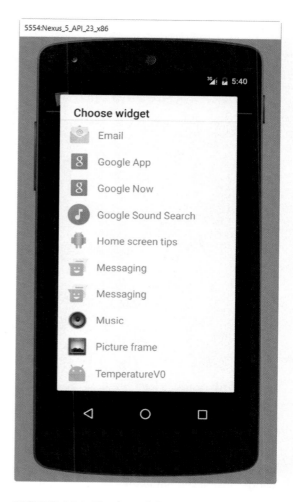

FIGURE 14.2 The list of the widgets in the emulator

widget_layout.xml file. The `appWidgetIds` parameter stores the widget ids of the widgets that need to be updated. At lines 15–16, we loop through all of them with the `appWidgetManager` parameter.

If there are several widgets of the same provider class installed on a device, they have most likely been installed at different times. In Example 14.4, we only update those that need to be updated. We can also update all of them regardless of which ones need to be updated, so that they are synchronized. We do that later in the chapter.

We can test a widget inside the emulator. If we click on the apps icon, then click on the Widget Preview icon (see **FIGURE 14.1**), and then click on the widget (see **FIGURE 14.2**), we can see a preview of the widget (see **FIGURE 14.3**).

FIGURE 14.3 A preview of the TemperatureWidgetV0 widget inside the emulator

FIGURE 14.4 The tablet after a long press showing a menu

After we run Example 14.4 on a device like a tablet, we need to install the widget on the tablet. In order to do that, we do the following:

▶ Long press on the screen in order to bring the menu shown in **FIGURE 14.4** (we can also click on the Apps icon),

▶ Choose Apps and widgets and click on the Widgets tab at the top of the screen. Depending on how many widgets are already installed on the device, we may have to swipe the screen in order to get to the screen that shows the widget, which is shown in **FIGURE 14.5**.

▶ In order to install it, we press on it and move it to the location we want. When we release it, the widget is running.

FIGURE 14.6 shows the widget running on the Home screen. Note that we can repeat that operation and install a second widget of the same provider class on the Home screen.

FIGURE 14.5 The tablet showing the TemperatureWidget, Version 0, widget

FIGURE 14.6 The TemperatureWidgetV0 widget running inside the home screen of the tablet

14.2 Styling the Widget, Temperature Widget, Version 1

In Version 1, we style the widget so that it looks more like the widgets we are accustomed to, but we do not improve its functionality yet. We style it in two ways:

▶   We give it a background.
▶   We style the TextView that displays the text.

To define a background, we create an XML file in the drawable directory and define a rectangular shape (line 3) as shown in **EXAMPLE 14.5**. At line 5, we specify that the corners of the rectangle be rounded with a radius of 10 for each corner. At lines 7–9, we specify the stroke of the rectangle:

```
1    <?xml version="1.0" encoding="utf-8"?>
2    <shape xmlns:android="http://schemas.android.com/apk/res/android"
3           android:shape="rectangle" >
4
5      <corners android:radius="10dp" />
6
7      <stroke
8        android:width="2dp"
9        android:color="#FFA6FF9B" />
10
11     <gradient
12       android:startColor="#FFFFFFF0"
13       android:endColor="#AA008080"
14       android:angle="45" />
15
16   </shape>
```

EXAMPLE 14.5 The `widget_shape.xml` file

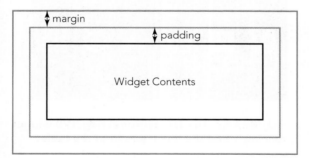

FIGURE 14.7 Margin and padding of a widget

its width is 2 pixels (line 8) and its color is sea foam green (line 9). At lines 11–14, we specify a gradient to fill the rectangle with. Its starting color is ivory (line 12) and its ending color is teal (line 13) with two different opacity levels. It is a linear gradient going from left to right at a 45 degree angle (line 14).

Google recommends to leave a margin between the edges of the widget's bounding rectangle and the widget's frame, and some padding inside the widget's frame, as shown in **FIGURE 14.7**. The red outside rectangle is the bounding rectangle, or bounding box, of the widget. The blue rectangle is the frame of the widget. The widget contents, in particular `Views`, are inside the black rectangle.

EXAMPLE 14.6 shows the updated widget_layout.xml file. The widget_layout.xml file defines the layout for the widget using a `LinearLayout` element. At line 7, we assign the value `@drawable/widget_shape` to the `android:background` XML attribute to specify that the background of the `LinearLayout` element is defined by the widget_shape.xml file. We set the margin to 5 pixels at line 6. At line 14, we center the text inside the `TextView` element both horizontally and vertically. We set the padding to 5 pixels at line 15. Since we need to access the `TextView` by code in Versions 2 and after, we give an id at line 10.

FIGURE 14.8 shows our widget, Version 1, running inside the tablet alongside a widget from Version 0.

```
1    <?xml version="1.0" encoding="utf-8"?>
2    <LinearLayout xmlns:android="http://schemas.android.com/apk/res/android"
3                  android:orientation="vertical"
4                  android:layout_width="match_parent"
5                  android:layout_height="match_parent"
6                  android:layout_margin="5dp"
7                  android:background="@drawable/widget_shape">
8
9       <TextView
10          android:id="@+id/display"
11          android:layout_width="match_parent"
12          android:layout_height="match_parent"
13          style="@android:style/TextAppearance.Large"
14          android:gravity="center_horizontal|center_vertical"
15          android:padding="5dp"
16          android:text="@string/city_and_temp" >
17      </TextView>
18
19   </LinearLayout>
```

EXAMPLE 14.6 **The** `widget_layout.xml` **file**

FIGURE 14.8 **The Version 0 and Version 1 widgets inside the Home screen of the tablet**

14.3 Updating the Data in the Widget, Temperature Widget, Version 2

In Version 2, we make the widget dynamic: we retrieve the date and time dynamically from the device, and display it inside the widget. In order to implement this feature, we do the following:

- Retrieve the date and time by code and build a `String` that includes it.
- Use that `String` to update the `TextView` inside the widget.

The `Date` class of the `java.util` package enables us to retrieve the data and time dynamically. The `DateFormat` class of the `java.text` package enables us to format that date and time into a `String`.

The `RemoteViews` class contains methods that enable us to manage Views inside the widget like we manage Views inside an app. **TABLE 14.8** shows some methods of the `RemoteViews` class as well as their equivalent methods and classes for a regular app. The methods of `RemoteViews` include an additional parameter to identify the `View` that is the subject of the method call. That parameter is typically the id of the `View`.

For example, if the layout XML file for our widget is widget_layout.xml and it contains a `TextView` whose id is `display`, we could set the text of that `TextView` to `Hello Widget`, its color to `green`, and its size to `32` as follows:

```
RemoteViews remoteViews = new RemoteViews( context.getPackageName( ),
                                           R.layout.widget_layout );
remoteViews.setTextViewText( R.id.display, "Hello Widget");
remoteViews.setTextColor( R.id.display, Color.parseColor("#00FF00"));
remoteViews.setTextViewTextSize( R.id.display, TypedValue.COMPLEX_
UNIT_SP, 32.0f );
```

TABLE 14.8 Selected methods of the `RemoteViews` class and their equivalent methods (and their classes)

Method of RemoteViews	Equivalent Method	From Class
void addView(int viewId, RemoteViews nestedView)	void addView(View child)	ViewGroup
void setTextViewText(int viewId, CharSequence text)	void setText (CharSequence text)	TextView
void setTextViewTextSize(int viewId, int units, float size)	void setTextSize(int units, float size)	TextView
void setTextColor(int viewId, int color)	void setTextColor(int color)	TextView

```
1    package com.jblearning.temperaturewidgetv2;
2
3    import android.appwidget.AppWidgetManager;
4    import android.appwidget.AppWidgetProvider;
5    import android.content.Context;
6    import android.content.res.Resources;
7    import android.widget.RemoteViews;
8
9    import java.text.DateFormat;
10   import java.util.Date;
11
12   public class TemperatureProvider extends AppWidgetProvider {
13     @Override
14     public void onUpdate ( Context context,
15       AppWidgetManager appWidgetManager, int [ ] appWidgetIds ) {
16       super.onUpdate( context, appWidgetManager, appWidgetIds );
17       Date dateToday = new Date( );
18       String today = DateFormat.getDateTimeInstance( ).format( dateToday );
19       Resources resources = context.getResources( );
20       String displayString
21          = today + "\n" + resources.getString( R.string.city_and_temp );
22
23       RemoteViews remoteViews = new RemoteViews(
24          context.getPackageName( ), R.layout.widget_layout );
25       remoteViews.setTextViewText( R.id.display, displayString );
26       for ( int widgetId : appWidgetIds )
27         appWidgetManager.updateAppWidget( widgetId, remoteViews );
28     }
29   }
```

EXAMPLE 14.7 **The `TemperatureProvider` class, app Version 2**

EXAMPLE 14.7 shows the updated `TemperatureProvider` class. At lines 9–10, we import the `DateFormat` and `Date` classes. At line 17, we get a reference to today's date, `dateToday`. We format it to a simpler `String`, `today`, at line 18, eliminating the day of the week and the time zone. At line 19, we get a `Resources` reference so we can convert the `city_and_temp` `String` resource into a `String` (line 21). `Resources` is imported at line 6. At lines 20–21, we concatenate `today` and our default city, state, and temperature into the `String displayString`. At line 25, we set the text inside the `TextView` whose id is `display` to `displayString`.

FIGURE 14.9 shows our widget, Version 2, running inside the tablet alongside widgets from Versions 0 and 1.

FIGURE 14.9 The Versions 0, 1, and 2 widgets running inside the Home screen of the tablet

14.4 Updating the Data in the Widget by Clicking on It, Temperature Widget, Version 3

A widget can update itself automatically at a specified frequency. The minimum frequency is 30 minutes. Often, the user does not want to wait 30 minutes but wants to force an immediate update. In Version 3, we implement that functionality. We set up event handling so that, by clicking on the widget, the widget calls the onUpdate method and updates itself.

The setOnClickPendingIntent method of RemoteViews, shown in TABLE 14.9, enables us to specify an intent that has been created as a pending intent that will be launched when the user clicks on a View within the RemoteViews hierarchy identified by its id.

The PendingIntent class encapsulates the concept of a **pending intent**. A pending intent comprises an intent and an action to perform when the intent is launched. A PendingIntent

TABLE 14.9 The `setOnClickPendingIntent` method of the `RemoteViews` class

Method	Description
void setOnClickPendingIntent(int viewId, PendingIntent pendingIntent)	When the user clicks on the View whose id is viewId, pendingIntent is launched.

TABLE 14.10 The `getBroadcast` Method of the `PendingIntent` class

Method	Description
static PendingIntent getBroadcast(Context context, int requestCode, Intent intent, int flags)	Creates and returns a PendingIntent in the Context context; requestCode is currently not used (use 0 as default value); intent is the Intent to be broadcast; flags may be one of the FLAG_. . . constants.

TABLE 14.11 Selected constants of the `PendingIntent` class

Constant	Description and Use
FLAG_UPDATE_CURRENT	Pending intent, if it exists, is reused but its extras are replaced with the extras of the new intent.
FLAG_ONE_SHOT	Pending intent can only be used once.
FLAG_CANCEL_CURRENT	Pending intent, if it exists, is cancelled before a new one is generated.

can be created using the `getBroadcast static` method of the `PendingIntent` class, shown in TABLE 14.10, in conjunction with some of its constants, shown in TABLE 14.11.

EXAMPLE 14.8 shows the updated `TemperatureProvider` class. At lines 29–33, we create the `Intent intent` of the type `TemperatureProvider` (line 30), set its action so that it updates the widget defined by the `TemperatureProvider` class (line 31), and put the array of widget ids as extras in it (line 32–33). When the intent is launched, that triggers a call to the `onUpdate` method of `TemperatureProvider`.

At lines 35–36, we create a `PendingIntent` (the `PendingIntent` class is imported at line 3) using `intent` and we specify to reuse the current intent and only update the extras. The extras contain the array of widget ids, and it is possible that we delete existing widgets or install more widgets of the `TemperatureProvider` type on our device. Thus, the list of widget ids can vary. At line 37, we specify that clicking on the `View` whose id is `display` will trigger the pending intent to be launched.

```
1    package com.jblearning.temperaturewidgetv3;
2
3    import android.app.PendingIntent;
4    import android.appwidget.AppWidgetManager;
5    import android.appwidget.AppWidgetProvider;
6    import android.content.Context;
7    import android.content.Intent;
8    import android.content.res.Resources;
9    import android.widget.RemoteViews;
10
11   import java.text.DateFormat;
12   import java.util.Date;
13
14   public class TemperatureProvider extends AppWidgetProvider {
15     @Override
16     public void onUpdate ( Context context,
17       AppWidgetManager appWidgetManager, int [ ] appWidgetIds ) {
18       super.onUpdate( context, appWidgetManager, appWidgetIds );
19       Date dateToday = new Date( );
20       String today = DateFormat.getDateTimeInstance( ).format( dateToday );
21       Resources resources = context.getResources( );
22       String displayString
23           = today + "\n" + resources.getString( R.string.city_and_temp );
24
25       RemoteViews remoteViews = new RemoteViews(
26           context.getPackageName( ), R.layout.widget_layout );
27       remoteViews.setTextViewText( R.id.display, displayString );
28       for ( int widgetId : appWidgetIds ) {
29         // Set up event handling when the user clicks on the widget
30         Intent intent = new Intent( context, TemperatureProvider.class );
31         intent.setAction( AppWidgetManager.ACTION_APPWIDGET_UPDATE );
32         intent.putExtra( AppWidgetManager.EXTRA_APPWIDGET_IDS,
33                         appWidgetIds );
34
35         PendingIntent pendingIntent = PendingIntent.getBroadcast( context,
36             0, intent, PendingIntent.FLAG_UPDATE_CURRENT );
37         remoteViews.setOnClickPendingIntent( R.id.display, pendingIntent );
38
39         appWidgetManager.updateAppWidget( widgetId, remoteViews );
40       }
41     }
42   }
```

EXAMPLE 14.8 The `TemperatureProvider` class, app Version 3

FIGURE 14.10 shows our widget, Version 3, running inside the tablet (second from the top on the left) alongside widgets from Versions 0, 1, and 2. If we touch the Version 3 widget, the data and time are updated, as opposed to Versions 0, 1, and 2 for which the data is static.

FIGURE 14.10 The Versions 0, 1, 2, and 3 widgets running inside the Home screen of the tablet

14.5 Retrieving the Temperature Data from a Remote Source, Temperature Widget, Version 4

In Version 4, we display live temperature data that we retrieve from a remote source. In order to do that, we need to do the following:

▶ Identify a remote source that supplies the data we are looking for.
▶ Identify what data to pass and how to pass it to the remote source.
▶ Understand the data returned by the remote source and how it is formatted.
▶ Retrieve data from the remote source:
  ■ Connect to the remote source.
  ■ Read data from the remote source into an appropriate data structure.
▶ Parse that data structure so that we retrieve the data we want.
▶ Display the desired data inside the widget (or the app).

Weather data is collected at weather stations. In the United States, there are around 2,000 weather stations, and each weather station has an id and geographical data associated with it, such as address, latitude, longitude, etc. The **National Weather Service** (**NWS**) provides an abundance of free weather data. In order to get weather data for a particular location, we first retrieve a list of weather stations close to that location from NWS, calculate the distances from the location to each weather station, choose the weather station that is the closest, and read data from that weather station.

In addition to NWS, there are many available sources of weather data: some are free, some are not, some require a key to get access, some do not. They may accept one or several types of input, such as zip code, city, or latitude and longitude coordinates, and they use different ways to format data, such as XML or **JavaScript Object Notation** (JSON), which is a lightweight way of formatting data. JSON is often used to format data transmitted over the Internet between a server and client and vice versa, because it is not as cumbersome as XML and is easy to parse.

A JSON string can include two data structures:

▶   An object representing a hashtable.
▶   An array.

An object is enclosed in curly braces ({}) and consists of a list of name/value pairs separated by a comma (,). A colon (:) separates the name and the value. Values can be strings enclosed in double quotes, numbers, true, false, null, an object, or an array (i.e., those two data structures can be nested). An array is a list of comma-separated values enclosed in square brackets ([]).

Here are some examples of valid JSON strings:

```
{ "name": "mike", "age": 22 }
{ "states": { "MD": "Maryland", "CA": "California", "TX": "Texas" } }
[ "Chicago", "New York", "Palo Alto" ]
{ "countries": [ "USA", "Mexico", "China" ] }
```

In this app, we use openweathermap.org as our source of weather data. It is very easy to obtain a key and it is free for limited use. The URL accepts a simple input such as a city, country string, and its output is a JSON string. One of the possible URL formats to query that site is:

```
http://api.openweathermap.org/data/2.5/weather?q=city,country&appid=your_key
```

The key is a long `String` made up of hexadecimal digits, for example:

```
8f4fc1b7ccx025gga22ac2db344a3hj8z
```

The URL also accepts a US state instead of a country. The `String` after the question mark character (?) (i.e., `q=city,country&appid=key` in this case) is called the **Query String**.

For example, we could use:

```
http://api.openweathermap.org/data/2.5/weather?q=London,UK&appid=YOUR_KEY
http://api.openweathermap.org/data/2.5/weather?q=New York,NY&appid=YOUR_KEY
http://api.openweathermap.org/data/2.5/weather?q=Baltimore,MD&appid=YOUR_KEY
```

If we open a browser and paste the first of these three examples (using an actual key) into the URL field, the browser displays the JSON string shown in **FIGURE 14.11**.

```
{"coord":{"lon":-0.13,"lat":51.51},"weather":[{"id":520,"main":"Rain",
"description":"light intensity shower rain","icon":"09d"},{"id":311,"main":
"Drizzle","description":"rain and drizzle","icon":"09d"}],"base":"cmc stations",
"main":{"temp":283.09,"pressure":994,"humidity":93,"temp_min":282.15,"temp_max":
284.15},"wind":{"speed":7.2,"deg":140},"rain":{"1h":2.29},"clouds":{"all":90},
"dt":1451744717,"sys":{"type":1,"id":5168,"message":0.005,"country":"GB",
"sunrise":1451721962,"sunset":1451750600},"id":2643743,"name":"London","cod":200}
```

FIGURE 14.11 JSON String from openweathermap.org for London, UK

TABLE 14.12 Temperature conversions between Kelvin, Celsius, and Fahrenheit degrees

Kelvin	Celsius	Fahrenheit
K	C = K – 273.15	F = (C * 9/5) + 32
273.15	0	32
298.15	25	77

There is more information returned than we actually want for this widget. We keep the widget simple and only show the current temperature. Figure 14.11 indicates a temperature of 283.09, the value for the field temp. The temperature is given in degrees Kelvin. **TABLE 14.12** shows the conversion formulas between the various temperature scales.

As we build a Model to parse such a JSON string, we note that our Model depends on the formatting of the data that we receive. Although it is not expected that the data source will change its data format frequently, it is a good idea to subscribe to notifications from the data source in order to be able to edit our code as quickly as possible to adapt to any change in the data and its formatting. The JSONObject class, part of the org.json package, includes methods to parse a JSON string. **TABLE 14.13** shows some of them.

In Figure 14.11, the value mapped to coord is a JSONObject. The value mapped to weather is a JSONArray. The value mapped to name is a String, London. The constructor and the methods in Table 14.13 throw a JSONException. It is a checked exception so we must use try and catch blocks when calling these methods. Assuming that we have created a JSONObject named jsonObject with the JSON string shown in Figure 14.11, we can retrieve these values as follows:

```
// jsonObject is a JSONObject created from the String in Figure 14.11
try {
    JSONObject coordJSONObject = jsonObject.getJSONObject( "coord" );
    JSONArray weatherJSONArray = jsonObject.getJSONArray( "weather" );
    String city = jsonObject.getString( "name" );
} catch( JSONException jsonE ) {
    // handle the exception here
}
```

TABLE 14.13 Selected methods of the `JSONObject` class

Constructor and Methods	Description
JSONObject(String json)	Creates a JSONObject object for json.
JSONObject getJSONObject(String name)	Returns the JSONObject mapped by name if there is one and it is a JSONObject.
JSONArray getJSONArray(String name)	Returns the JSONArray mapped by name if there is one and it is a JSONArray.
int getInt(String name)	Returns the int value mapped by name if there is one and it can be cast to an int.
double getDouble (String name)	Returns the double value mapped by name if there is one and it can be cast to a double.
String getString(String name)	Returns the String value mapped by name if there is one.

In order to retrieve the current temperature within the JSON string of Figure 14.11, we can use the following code sequence:

```
// jsonObject is a JSONObject created from the String in Figure 14.11
try {
  JSONObject mainJSONObject = jsonObject.getJSONObject( "main" );
  double temperature = mainJSONObject.getDouble( "temp" );
  // process temperature here
} catch ( JSONException jsonE ) {
  // handle the exception here
}
```

EXAMPLE 14.9 shows the `TemperatureParser` class, part of our Model for this app. Its main functionality is to extract the temperature data from the JSON String. The constructor, at lines 13–18, instantiates `jsonObject`, the only instance variable, calling the `JSONObject` constructor and passing its `String` parameter. The `getTemperatureK` method, at lines 20–27, returns the value associated with the key `temp` inside the json object associated with the key `main`. Note that we catch a generic `Exception` at line 24 rather than a `JSONException`, because `jsonObject` could be `null`. When a `TemperatureParsing` object is instantiated, if the argument passed to the constructor cannot be converted to a `JSONObject`, then `jsonObject` is `null`. Calling the `getJSONObject` method with a `null` reference would cause a `NullPointerException`. By catching a generic `Exception`, we catch either a `NullPointerException` or a `JSONException`. If an exception occurs at that time, we use the default value of 25 degrees Celsius at line 25. The `getTemperatureC` (lines 29–31) and `getTemperatureF` (33–35) methods, return the Celsius and Fahrenheit temperatures, respectively, as rounded integers.

```
1     package com.jblearning.temperaturewidgetv4;
2
3     import org.json.JSONObject;
4     import org.json.JSONException;
5
6     public class TemperatureParser {
7       public static final double ZERO_K = -273.15;
8       private final String MAIN_KEY = "main";
9       private final String TEMPERATURE_KEY = "temp";
10
11      private JSONObject jsonObject;
12
13      public TemperatureParser( String json ) {
14        try {
15          jsonObject = new JSONObject( json );
16        } catch( JSONException jsonException ) {
17        }
18      }
19
20      public double getTemperatureK( ) {
21        try {
22          JSONObject jsonMain = jsonObject.getJSONObject( MAIN_KEY );
23          return jsonMain.getDouble( TEMPERATURE_KEY );
24        } catch( Exception jsonException ) {
25          return 25 - ZERO_K;
26        }
27      }
28
29      public int getTemperatureC( ) {
30        return ( int ) ( getTemperatureK( ) + ZERO_K + 0.5 );
31      }
32
33      public int getTemperatureF( ) {
34        return ( int ) ( ( getTemperatureK( ) + ZERO_K ) * 9 / 5 + 32 + 0.5 );
35      }
36    }
```

EXAMPLE 14.9 The `TemperatureParser` class, app Version 4

In addition to the `TemperatureParser` class, we include in our Model a class to read data from a remote location, `RemoteDataReader`. That class is a utility class that reads data from a remote location defined by two `String`s: a base URL and a query string.

In order to read data from a remote location, we do the following:

▸   Connect to the remote location.
▸   Get an input stream from that remote location.
▸   Read that input stream into a `String`.

TABLE 14.14 Selected classes and methods to read data from a remote location

Class	Constructor or Method	Description
URL	URL(String url)	Creates a URL for url.
URL	URLConnection openConnection( )	Creates and returns a URLConnection with this URL.
URLConnection	InputStream getInputStream( )	Returns an InputStream that reads from this URLConnection.
URLConnection	void setDoInput(boolean doInputFlag)	We call this method with the argument true if we want to read, or false if we do not want to read (the default is true).
URLConnection	void setDoOutput(boolean doOutputFlag)	We call this method with the argument true if we want to write, or false if we do not want to write (the default is false).
HttpURLConnection (inherits from URLConnection)	void setRequestMethod(String method)	Sets the method for this request to method—typically GET or POST. The default is GET.
HttpURLConnection (inherits from URLConnection)	void disconnect( )	Disconnects from the server located at the URL of this HttpURLConnection.
InputStream	void close( )	Closes this InputStream and releases the memory resources associated with it.
InputStreamReader (inherits from Reader)	InputStreamReader(InputStream is)	Constructs an InputStreamReader to read from the input stream is.
BufferedReader	BufferedReader(Reader r)	Constructs a BufferedReader, and uses buffering for more efficient reading.
BufferedReader	String readLine( )	Reads and returns a line of text.
BufferedReader	void close( )	Closes the input stream and releases the memory resources associated with it.

TABLE 14.14 shows various classes and methods that we use to perform those steps. HttpURL-Connection is a subclass of URLConnection with added support for the HTTP protocol. Input-StreamReader is a subclass of Reader, thus, an InputStreamReader reference that can be used as the argument of the BufferedReader constructor.

EXAMPLE 14.10 shows the RemoteDataReader class. The instance variable urlString, declared at line 12, represents a full url. The constructor, at lines 14–25, constructs urlString,

```
1     package com.jblearning.temperaturewidgetv4;
2
3     import java.io.BufferedReader;
4     import java.io.InputStream;
5     import java.io.InputStreamReader;
6     import java.io.UnsupportedEncodingException;
7     import java.net.HttpURLConnection;
8     import java.net.URL;
9     import java.net.URLEncoder;
10
11    public class RemoteDataReader {
12      private String urlString;
13
14      public RemoteDataReader( String baseUrl, String cityString,
15                               String keyName, String key ) {
16        try {
17          urlString = baseUrl
18                    + URLEncoder.encode( cityString, "UTF-8" );
19          if( keyName != null && key != null )
20            urlString += URLEncoder.encode( "&", "UTF-8" )
21                       + keyName + "=" + key;
22        } catch( UnsupportedEncodingException uee ) {
23          urlString = "";
24        }
25      }
26
27      public String getData( ) {
28        try {
29          // Establish the connection
30          URL url = new URL( urlString );
31          HttpURLConnection con = ( HttpURLConnection ) url.openConnection( );
32          con.connect( );
33
34          // Get the input stream and prepare to read
35          InputStream is = con.getInputStream( );
36          BufferedReader br =
37              new BufferedReader( new InputStreamReader( is ) );
38
39          // Read the data
40          String dataRead = new String( );
41          String line = br.readLine( );
42          while ( line != null ) {
43            dataRead += line;
44            line = br.readLine( );
45          }
46
```

EXAMPLE 14.10 **The** `RemoteDataReader` **class, app Version 4 (*Continued*)**

```
47        is.close( );
48        con.disconnect( );
49        return dataRead;
50     } catch( Exception e ) {
51        return "";
52     }
53   }
54 }
```

EXAMPLE 14.10 **The `RemoteDataReader` class, app Version 4**

concatenating its four `String` parameters: the second one is a query string and may contain characters, such as the space or comma characters, that are considered unsafe and need to be encoded. The third and fourth parameters may be `null`, in case there is no key needed to read data from that URL. We encode the second parameter to URL standards at line 18 before concatenating it to `baseUrl`. If the third and fourth parameters are not `null` (line 19), we add the `&` character, encode it, and concatenate them to form the full URL. We expect that second `String` parameter to represent user input in Version 5 of the widget, so we want to make sure that special characters, in particular the space character, which we are almost certain to get from user input, are encoded.

The `getData` method, at lines 27–53, reads data from the URL location represented by `urlString` and returns it. We open a connection at lines 29–32 and create a `BufferedReader` object at lines 34–37 that we use to read the data at that URL location. We initialize `dataRead`, a `String` that accumulates the data read, at line 40 and prime the read at line 41. We use a `while` loop at lines 42–45 to read the data into `dataRead`, which we return at line 49. We catch any exception that may happen during the whole process at line 50 and return the empty `String` at line 51 if an exception occurs.

We have completed the Model for this version. Now we need to edit the Controller for the widget, which is the `TemperatureProvider` class. For this version of our widget, we go on the Internet and retrieve some data from a remote server. Thus, we include two `uses-permission` elements in the AndroidManifest.xml file inside the `manifest` element as follows:

```
<uses-permission android:name="android.permission.INTERNET"/>
<uses-permission android:name="android.permission.ACCESS_NETWORK_STATE"/>
```

Because we are accessing the Internet, we need to do this on a separate thread. We create the `TemperatureTask` class, a subclass of the `AsyncTask` class, in order to read temperatures from a remote server. Appendix D explains the `AsyncTask` in great detail. The `AsyncTask` class uses three generic types that we must specify when extending it. The class header of a subclass is as follows:

```
AccessModifier ClassName extends AsyncTask<Params, Progress, Result>
```

TABLE 14.15 Selected methods of the `AsyncTask` class	
Method	**Description**
AsyncTask execute(Params. . . params)	params represent an array of values of type Params, a generic type.
Result doInBackground(Params. . . params)	params is the argument passed to execute when we call it.
void onPostExecute(Result result)	is automatically called after doInBackground finishes; result is the value returned by doInBackground.

where `Params`, `Progress`, and `Result` are placeholders for actual class names and have the following meanings:

▶ `Params` is the data type of the array that is passed to the `execute` method of `AsyncTask` when we call it.

▶ `Progress` is the data type used for progress units as the task executes in the background. If we choose to report progress, that data type is often `Integer` or `Long`.

▶ `Result` is the data type of the value returned upon execution of the task.

We expect the retrieval of the data to be fast and, therefore, we do not intend to give the user any feedback about its progress. The input to our task is a URL string, and the output of our task is a `String` that we retrieve from the remote server. Thus, the class header of `TemperatureTask` is:

```
public class TemperatureTask extends AsyncTask<String, Void, String>
```

After we call the `execute` method with a `TemperatureTask` reference, the `doInBackground` method executes and its argument is the same as the one we passed to `execute`. Its return value becomes the argument of `onPostExecute`, which is called automatically after `doInBackground` finishes. **TABLE 14.15** shows these three methods. The `execute` and `doInBackground` method headers show that they both accept a variable number of arguments.

We expect to instantiate a `TemperatureTask` object and call its `execute` method from the `onCreate` method of the `TemperatureProvider` class. The `doInBackground` method executes and its return value becomes the argument of the `postExecute` method. Thus, we need to update the widget from inside the `postExecute` method. However, in order to update the widget, we need to use the parameters of the `onCreate` method. In order to have access to these parameters inside the `onPostExecute`, we pass them to the `TemperatureTask` constructor and assign them to instance variables of the `TemperatureTask` class. From the `postExecute` method, we can then call a method of the `TemperatureProvider` class and pass these references to that method so it can update the widget. Note that in order to call a method of the `TemperatureProvider` class, we need a reference to a `TemperatureProvider` object, which we can also pass to the `TemperatureTask` constructor and assign it to an instance variable.

EXAMPLE 14.11 shows the `TemperatureTask` class. We declare three instance variables to match the three parameters of the `onCreate` method of `TemperatureProvider` at lines

```
1    package com.jblearning.temperaturewidgetv4;
2
3    import android.appwidget.AppWidgetManager;
4    import android.content.Context;
5    import android.os.AsyncTask;
6
7    public class TemperatureTask extends AsyncTask<String, Void, String> {
8      private TemperatureProvider provider;
9      private Context context;
10     private AppWidgetManager appWidgetManager;
11     private int [ ] appWidgetIds;
12
13     public TemperatureTask( TemperatureProvider fromTemperatureProvider,
14                            Context fromContext,
15                            AppWidgetManager fromAppWidgetManager,
16                            int [ ] fromAppWidgetIds ) {
17       provider = fromTemperatureProvider;
18       context = fromContext;
19       appWidgetManager = fromAppWidgetManager;
20       appWidgetIds = fromAppWidgetIds;
21     }
22
23     protected String doInBackground( String... urlParts ) {
24       String baseUrl = "", cityString = "", keyName = "", key = "";
25       if( urlParts != null ) {
26         baseUrl = urlParts[0];
27         cityString = urlParts[1];
28         keyName = urlParts[2];
29         key = urlParts[3];
30       }
31
32       RemoteDataReader rdr =
33         new RemoteDataReader( baseUrl, cityString, keyName, key );
34       String json = rdr.getData( );
35       return json;
36     }
37
38     protected void onPostExecute ( String returnedJSON ) {
39       TemperatureParser parser = new TemperatureParser( returnedJSON );
40       provider.updateWidget( parser.getTemperatureF( ), context,
41                              appWidgetManager, appWidgetIds );
42     }
43   }
```

EXAMPLE 14.11 The `TemperatureTask` class, app Version 4

9–11. We also declare a `TemperatureProvider` instance variable at line 8, so that we can call a method of the `TemperatureProvider` class with it. The constructor, at lines 13–21, assigns four parameter references to these four instance variables. We will call it from the `onCreate` method of the `TemperatureProvider` class using `this` as the first argument, and the three parameters of the `onCreate` method as the other three arguments.

The `doInBackground` method, which is automatically called after the `execute` method is called and given the same arguments as the ones passed to `execute`, is coded at lines 23–30. It instantiates a `RemoteDataReader` object at lines 32–33, and reads the data at that URL location into a `String` named `json` (line 34), and returns it.

The `postExecute` method, at lines 38–42, instantiates a `TemperatureParser` object with its `String` parameter (the `String` returned by the `doInBackground` method) at line 39. It retrieves the temperature value in Fahrenheit and calls the `updateWidget` method of the `Temperature-Provider` class at lines 40–41, passing the temperature and the three instance variables that are references to the three parameters of the `onCreate` method.

EXAMPLE **14.12** shows the `TemperatureProvider` class. We include the constants `DEGREE` and `STARTING_URL` at lines 14–16. Instead of using a resource for the city value, we declare an instance variable named `city` at line 19. We will need it in Version 5, when we allow the user to modify it. We declare a constant and an instance variable for the key name and the key value at lines 17 and 20. Note that for privacy and security reasons, we have substituted the key value for YOUR KEY HERE.

```
1    package com.jblearning.temperaturewidgetv4;
2
3    import android.app.PendingIntent;
4    import android.appwidget.AppWidgetManager;
5    import android.appwidget.AppWidgetProvider;
6    import android.content.Context;
7    import android.content.Intent;
8    import android.widget.RemoteViews;
9
10   import java.text.DateFormat;
11   import java.util.Date;
12
13   public class TemperatureProvider extends AppWidgetProvider {
14     public static final char DEGREE = '\u00B0';
15     public static final String STARTING_URL
16         = "http://api.openweathermap.org/data/2.5/weather?q=";
17     public static final String KEY_NAME = "appid";
18
19     private String city = "New York, NY";
20     private String key = "YOUR KEY HERE";
```

EXAMPLE 14.12 **The** `TemperatureProvider` **class, app Version 4 (*Continued*)**

```
21
22      @Override
23      public void onUpdate ( Context context,
24             AppWidgetManager appWidgetManager, int [ ] appWidgetIds ) {
25        super.onUpdate( context, appWidgetManager, appWidgetIds );
26        // execute task to retrieve current temperature for city
27        TemperatureTask task = new TemperatureTask( this, context,
28            appWidgetManager, appWidgetIds );
29        task.execute( STARTING_URL, city, KEY_NAME, key );
30      }
31
32      public void updateWidget( int temp, Context context,
33             AppWidgetManager appWidgetManager, int [ ] appWidgetIds ) {
34        Date dateToday = new Date( );
35        String today = DateFormat.getDateTimeInstance( ).format( dateToday );
36        String displayString = today + "\n" + city + "\n";
37        displayString += new String( temp + "" + DEGREE + "F" );
38
39        RemoteViews remoteViews = new RemoteViews( context.getPackageName( ),
40            R.layout.widget_layout );
41
42        remoteViews.setTextViewText( R.id.display, displayString );
43        for( int widgetId : appWidgetIds ) {
44          // Set up event handling when the user clicks on the widget
45          Intent intent = new Intent( context, TemperatureProvider.class );
46          intent.setAction( AppWidgetManager.ACTION_APPWIDGET_UPDATE );
47          intent.putExtra( AppWidgetManager.EXTRA_APPWIDGET_IDS,
48                        appWidgetIds );
49
50          PendingIntent pendingIntent = PendingIntent.getBroadcast( context,
51              0, intent, PendingIntent.FLAG_UPDATE_CURRENT );
52          remoteViews.setOnClickPendingIntent( R.id.display, pendingIntent );
53
54          appWidgetManager.updateAppWidget( widgetId, remoteViews );
55        }
56      }
57    }
```

EXAMPLE 14.12 **The** `TemperatureProvider` **class, app Version 4**

The `onUpdate` method (lines 22–30) instantiates a `TemperatureTask` object at lines 27–28 and calls its `execute` method at line 29. The four arguments of `execute` are automatically passed to the `doInBackground` method of the `TemperatureTask` class.

The `updateWidget` method is at lines 32–56. It is called by the `postExecute` of the `TemperatureTask` class with the retrieved temperature as the first argument and the parameters of `onUpdate` as the other three arguments. It builds the `String` to display, including the temperature, at lines 34–37. The rest of the code is the same as the code in the `onUpdate` method of Version 3.

TABLE 14.16 Model-View-Controller classes and files, Version 4	
Model	RemoteDataReader.java, TemperatureParser.java
View	widget_layout.xml
Controller	TemperatureProvider.java, TemperatureTask.java

FIGURE 14.12 The Versions 0, 1, 2, 3, and 4 widgets running inside the Home screen of the tablet

TABLE 14.16 shows the various components of our widget, Version 4: the Model is comprised of the `RemoteDataReader` and `TemperatureParser` classes, and they are both reusable in other projects. The widget_layout.xml file is the View. The `TemperatureProvider` and `TemperatureTask` classes make up the Controller.

FIGURE 14.12 shows our widget, Version 4, running inside the tablet (third from the top on the left) alongside widgets from Versions 0, 1, 2, and 3. Notice that the temperature shows live data (77°F), not a hard coded value as with the previous versions.

14.6 Using an Activity to Customize the Widget, Temperature Widget, Version 5

In Version 4, the location is hard coded to be New York, NY. In Version 5, we allow the user to specify the location for which we show the current temperature. When the user installs the widget, he or she can set the city and state or the city and country. In this way, we allow the user to **configure** the widget. We can do this by adding an activity to the project. This activity runs first and collects user input. We use the user input, in this case the city and state (or city and country) to set the appropriate parameters of the widget provider. In this case, we set the value of the `city` variable inside the **TemperatureProvider** class.

In order to configure the widget, we modify our project as follows:

▶ We add an `activity` element in the AndroidManifest.xml file.
▶ We create a layout XML file for the activity that collects user input.
▶ We add an `android:configure` attribute to the `AppWidgetProviderInfo` XML file.
▶ We create a class for the activity.
▶ We provide a mechanism to pass data from the activity to the `TemperatureProvider` class.
▶ We update the `TemperatureProvider` class as necessary.

EXAMPLE 14.13 shows the updated AndroidManifest.xml file. At lines 16–21, we add an `activity` element inside the `application` element and before the `receiver` element for the widget. At line 16, we specify `.TemperatureWidgetConfigure` as the value for the `android:name` attribute of the `activity` element. That means that the name of our class that extends the `Activity` class is `TemperatureWidgetConfigure`. The dot (.) in front of it means that it is located in the current package. At lines 18–19, we specify that the action for the intent of the activity is to configure a widget by assigning the value of the `ACTION_APPWIDGET_CONFIGURE` constant of the `AppWidgetManager` class (see **TABLE 14.17**) to the `android:name` attribute of the `action` element of the `intent-filter` element of the `activity` element. The widget host, in this case the Home screen, launches the activity with an `ACTION_APPWIDGET_CONFIGURE` action, so we need to specify this in the manifest.

```
1   <?xml version="1.0" encoding="utf-8"?>
2   <manifest package="com.jblearning.temperaturewidgetv5"
3           xmlns:android="http://schemas.android.com/apk/res/android">
4
5     <uses-permission android:name="android.permission.INTERNET"/>
6     <uses-permission
7         android:name="android.permission.ACCESS_NETWORK_STATE"/>
8
```

EXAMPLE 14.13 The AndroidManifest.xml file, app Version 5 (*Continued*)

```
 9     <application
10         android:allowBackup="true"
11         android:icon="@mipmap/ic_launcher"
12         android:label="@string/app_name"
13         android:supportsRtl="true"
14         android:theme="@style/AppTheme">
15
16        <activity android:name=".TemperatureWidgetConfigure">
17          <intent-filter>
18            <action
19              android:name="android.appwidget.action.APPWIDGET_CONFIGURE"/>
20          </intent-filter>
21        </activity>
22
23        <receiver android:name="TemperatureProvider">
24          <intent-filter>
25            <action
26              android:name="android.appwidget.action.APPWIDGET_UPDATE" />
27          </intent-filter>
28
29          <meta-data
30            android:name="android.appwidget.provider"
31            android:resource="@xml/widget_info" />
32
33        </receiver>
34      </application>
35    </manifest>
```

EXAMPLE 14.13 **The AndroidManifest.xml file, app Version 5**

TABLE 14.17 Selected constants of the `AppWidgetManager` class

Constant	Description
ACTION_APPWIDGET_ CONFIGURE	Action sent to start the activity specified in the AppWidgetProviderInfo metadata.
EXTRA_APPWIDGET_ID	Use this constant to retrieve the widget id from the extras of an intent.
INVALID_APPWIDGET_ID	Has value 0, a value that an AppWidgetManager never returns as a valid widget id.

The widget_config.xml file, which we create in the layout directory, defines the layout for the activity that configures the widget. The user interface includes a text field to enter data and a button to process the data entered. **EXAMPLE 14.14** shows the widget_config.xml file. At lines 6–10, we code a `TextView` element telling the user what to do. The `EditText` element is defined at lines 11–15 and is given the id `city_input` at line 12 so that we can retrieve it by code using the

```
1    <?xml version="1.0" encoding="utf-8"?>
2    <LinearLayout xmlns:android="http://schemas.android.com/apk/res/android"
3        android:orientation="vertical"
4        android:layout_width="match_parent"
5        android:layout_height="match_parent" >
6        <TextView
7            android:layout_width="match_parent"
8            android:layout_height="wrap_content"
9            style="@android:style/TextAppearance.Large"
10           android:text="Enter city,country or city,state" />
11       <EditText
12           android:id="@+id/city_input"
13           android:layout_width="match_parent"
14           android:layout_height="wrap_content"
15           style="@android:style/TextAppearance.Large" />
16       <Button
17           android:layout_width="wrap_content"
18           android:layout_height="wrap_content"
19           android:layout_gravity="center"
20           android:onClick="configure"
21           android:text="CONFIGURE WIDGET" />
22   </LinearLayout>
```

EXAMPLE 14.14 **The widget_config.xml file, app Version 5**

findViewById method. The button is defined at lines 16–21. At line 20, we specify configure as the method to execute when the user clicks on the button.

It is mandatory to declare the activity in the AppWidgetProviderInfo XML file using the android:configure attribute. Thus, we update the widget_info.xml file, shown in **EXAMPLE 14.15**. At lines 8–9, we specify the TemperatureWidgetConfigure class of the com.jblearning.temperaturewidgetv5 package as the value for the android:configure attribute of the appwidget-provider element.

```
1    <?xml version="1.0" encoding="utf-8"?>
2    <appwidget-provider
3        xmlns:android="http://schemas.android.com/apk/res/android"
4        android:initialLayout="@layout/widget_layout"
5        android:minHeight="50dp"
6        android:minWidth="200dp"
7        android:updatePeriodMillis="1800000"
8        android:configure=
9            "com.jblearning.temperaturewidgetv5.TemperatureWidgetConfigure" >
10   </appwidget-provider>
```

EXAMPLE 14.15 **The widget_info.xml file, app Version 5**

Next, we create `TemperatureWidgetConfigure`, the activity class that configures the widget. In order to configure a widget inside an activity, we do the following:

▶ Get user input as needed.
▶ Get the widget id.
▶ Update the widget.
▶ Create the return intent.
▶ Pass the user input data to the `AppWidgetProvider` class.
▶ Exit the activity.

When we use a configuration activity to customize a widget, it is the responsibility of the activity to first update the widget. Also, the configuration activity should return a result that should include the widget id that was passed by the intent that launched the activity.

EXAMPLE 14.16 shows the `TemperatureWidgetConfigure` class. At line 15, we set the result to the value of the `RESULT_CANCELED` constant of the `Activity` class, shown in TABLE 14.18. When the result is set to `RESULT_CANCELED`, the widget is not installed if the user does not complete the configuration activity.

```
1    package com.jblearning.temperaturewidgetv5;
2
3    import android.app.Activity;
4    import android.appwidget.AppWidgetManager;
5    import android.widget.EditText;
6    import android.widget.RemoteViews;
7    import android.content.Intent;
8    import android.content.Context;
9    import android.os.Bundle;
10   import android.view.View;
11
12   public class TemperatureWidgetConfigure extends Activity {
13     protected void onCreate( Bundle savedInstanceState ) {
14       super.onCreate( savedInstanceState );
15       setResult( RESULT_CANCELED );
16       setContentView( R.layout.widget_config );
17     }
18
19     public void configure( View view ) {
20       // Get user input
21       EditText cityText = ( EditText ) findViewById( R.id.city_input );
22       String cityInput = cityText.getText( ).toString( );
23
24       // Update city variable of TemperatureProvider
25       TemperatureProvider.city = cityInput;
26
```

EXAMPLE 14.16 The `TemperatureWidgetConfigure` class, app Version 5 (*Continued*)

```
27      // Get widget id
28      Intent intent = getIntent( );
29      Bundle extras = intent.getExtras( );
30      int appWidgetId = AppWidgetManager.INVALID_APPWIDGET_ID;
31      if ( extras != null )
32        appWidgetId =
33            extras.getInt( AppWidgetManager.EXTRA_APPWIDGET_ID,
34                         AppWidgetManager.INVALID_APPWIDGET_ID );
35
36      if( appWidgetId != AppWidgetManager.INVALID_APPWIDGET_ID ) {
37        // Update the widget
38        Context context = TemperatureWidgetConfigure.this;
39        AppWidgetManager appWidgetManager =
40            AppWidgetManager.getInstance( context );
41        RemoteViews views = new RemoteViews( context.getPackageName( ),
42                                          R.layout.widget_layout );
43        appWidgetManager.updateAppWidget( appWidgetId, views );
44
45        // Create the return intent
46        Intent resultIntent = new Intent( );
47
48        resultIntent.putExtra( AppWidgetManager.EXTRA_APPWIDGET_ID,
49                             appWidgetId );
50        setResult( RESULT_OK, resultIntent );
51      }
52
53      // exit this activity
54      finish( );
55    }
56  }
```

EXAMPLE 14.16 The `TemperatureWidgetConfigure` class, app Version 5

TABLE 14.18 Constants of the `Activity` class

Constant	Description
RESULT_CANCELED	0: means that the activity was cancelled.
RESULT_OK	−1: means that the activity ended successfully.

At lines 20–22, we retrieve user input. To pass simple data from an activity to another, we typically use the `putExtra` and `getExtra` methods of the `Intent` class. However, there is no intent associated with the `AppWidgetProvider` class, so we cannot use that strategy here. Furthermore, the default constructor of an `AppWidgetProvider` class is called automatically and re-initializes the instance variables to their default values. Thus, it is not practical to store widget data in an instance variable whose value can change over time. In Version 4, we used the instance variable `city` of the `TemperatureProvider` class, declared at line 19 of Example 14.12, to store the city and state (or country), even though it is hard coded to the value `New York, NY` for that version. In Version 5, we make that variable global by specifying it as `public` and `static` so that we can access it and modify it from the `TemperatureWidgetConfigure` class. That is a very simple and convenient way of passing data from an activity class to a widget provider class. At lines 24–25, we access the `public static` variable `city` of the `TemperatureProvider` class and update it with the value input by the user.

At lines 27–34, we retrieve the widget id from the incoming intent. We set its default value to `0` (the value of the `INVALID_APPWIDGET_ID` constant, shown in Table 14.17) at line 30. At line 31, we test if there is some data stored in the `Bundle` of the incoming intent. If there is, we attempt to retrieve the widget id at lines 32–34. If the `Bundle extras` has a key entry equal to the value of the `EXTRA_APPWIDGET_ID` constant of the `AppWidgetManager` class (see Table 14.17), then that key maps to the widget id value and that widget id value is returned by calling `getInt`. If not, the call to `getInt` returns the second argument, the value of `INVALID_APPWIDGET_ID` (i.e., `0`).

We test if the widget id value is valid at line 36. If it is, we update the widget at lines 37–43, create a return intent at lines 45–46, place the widget id in it at lines 48–49, and set the result to the value of `RESULT_OK` at line 50. After that, or if the widget id value is invalid, we terminate the activity at lines 53–54.

EXAMPLE 14.17 shows the `TemperatureProvider` class. At line 19, we change the access modifier to the `city` variable from `private` to `public` and `static` so we can modify its value in the `TemperatureWidgetConfigure` class (see line 25 of Example 14.16).

```
1    package com.jblearning.temperaturewidgetv5;
2
3    import android.app.PendingIntent;
4    import android.appwidget.AppWidgetManager;
5    import android.appwidget.AppWidgetProvider;
6    import android.content.Context;
7    import android.content.Intent;
8    import android.widget.RemoteViews;
9
10   import java.text.DateFormat;
11   import java.util.Date;
12
13   public class TemperatureProvider extends AppWidgetProvider {
14     public static final char DEGREE = '\u00B0';
15     public static final String STARTING_URL
16         = "http://api.openweathermap.org/data/2.5/weather?q=";
17     public static final String KEY_NAME = "appid";
```

EXAMPLE 14.17 The `TemperatureProvider` class, app Version 5 (*Continued*)

```
18
19      public static String city = "New York, NY";
20      private String key = "YOUR KEY HERE";
21
22      @Override
23      public void onUpdate ( Context context,
24           AppWidgetManager appWidgetManager, int [ ] appWidgetIds ) {
25        super.onUpdate( context, appWidgetManager, appWidgetIds );
26        // execute task to retrieve current temperature for city
27        TemperatureTask task = new TemperatureTask( this, context,
28           appWidgetManager, appWidgetIds );
29        task.execute( STARTING_URL, city, KEY_NAME, key );
30      }
31
32      public void updateWidget( int temp, Context context,
33           AppWidgetManager appWidgetManager, int [ ] appWidgetIds ) {
34        Date dateToday = new Date( );
35        String today = DateFormat.getDateTimeInstance( ).format( dateToday );
36        String displayString = today + "\n" + city + "\n";
37        displayString += new String( temp + "" + DEGREE + "F" );
38
39        RemoteViews remoteViews = new RemoteViews( context.getPackageName( ),
40           R.layout.widget_layout );
41
42        remoteViews.setTextViewText( R.id.display, displayString );
43        for( int widgetId : appWidgetIds ) {
44          // Set up event handling when the user clicks on the widget
45          Intent intent = new Intent( context, TemperatureProvider.class );
46          intent.setAction( AppWidgetManager.ACTION_APPWIDGET_UPDATE );
47          intent.putExtra( AppWidgetManager.EXTRA_APPWIDGET_IDS,
48                     appWidgetIds );
49
50          PendingIntent pendingIntent = PendingIntent.getBroadcast( context,
51             0, intent, PendingIntent.FLAG_UPDATE_CURRENT );
52          remoteViews.setOnClickPendingIntent( R.id.display, pendingIntent );
53
54          appWidgetManager.updateAppWidget( widgetId, remoteViews );
55        }
56      }
57
58      public void onReceive( Context context, Intent intent ) {
59        super.onReceive( context, intent );
60        AppWidgetManager appWidgetManager =
61           AppWidgetManager.getInstance( context );
62        int appWidgetId =
63           intent.getIntExtra( AppWidgetManager.EXTRA_APPWIDGET_ID,
```

EXAMPLE 14.17 The `TemperatureProvider` class, app Version 5 (*Continued*)

```
64                     AppWidgetManager.INVALID_APPWIDGET_ID );
65
66         if( appWidgetId != AppWidgetManager.INVALID_APPWIDGET_ID ) {
67           int [ ] appWidgetIds = { appWidgetId };
68           onUpdate( context, appWidgetManager,  appWidgetIds );
69         }
70       }
71     }
```

EXAMPLE 14.17 The `TemperatureProvider` class, app Version 5

TABLE 14.19 The sequence of method calls when installing the widget, Version 5		
Event and Method Call Sequence	**Widget id**	**Method Call**
Install the widget		
TemperatureProvider:onReceive	Invalid	Automatic
TemperatureProvider:onUpdate		Automatic
TemperatureWidgetConfigure:onCreate		Automatic
Enter the city and state, click on CONFIGURE WIDGET		
TemperatureWidgetConfigure:configure	Valid	Event handling
TemperatureProvider:onReceive	Valid	Automatic
TemperatureProvider:onUpdate		Called by onReceive

The onReceive method of the AppWidgetProvider class is automatically called after the TemperatureWidgetConfigure activity finishes. It is coded at lines 58–70. At lines 62–64, we use its Intent parameter in order to retrieve the app widget id. If it is a valid widget id (line 66), we update the widget by calling the onUpdate method at line 68. TABLE 14.19 shows the sequence of method calls and the nature of the method calls.

TABLE 14.20 shows the state of the Model, View, and Controller for our widget Version 5. As compared to Version 4, the Model is unchanged. We added the widget_config.xml file to the View to define the layout of the activity that configures the widget, and we added the TemperatureWidgetConfigure class and modified the TemperatureProvider class in the Controller.

FIGURE 14.13 shows the user configuring the city and state during the configuration of the widget, Version 5. FIGURE 14.14 shows our widget, Version 5, running inside the tablet alongside widgets from Versions 0, 1, 2, 3, and 4. The city and state of the widget, Version 5 (San Francisco, CA), are different from the others, and it shows live data like Version 4.

TABLE 14.20 Model-View-Controller classes and files, Version 5	
Model	RemoteDataReader.java, TemperatureParser.java
View	widget_layout.xml, **widget_config.xml**
Controller	TemperatureProvider.java, TemperatureTask.java, **TemperatureWidgetConfigure.java**

FIGURE 14.13 The configure screen when installing the widget, Version 5

FIGURE 14.14 The Versions 0, 1, 2, 3, 4, and 5 widgets running inside the Home screen of the tablet

14.7 Hosting the Widget in the Lock Screen, Temperature Widget, Version 6

Since Android Version 4.2, it is also possible to host a widget on the Lock screen, also called the **Keyguard**. We enable hosting of a widget on the Lock screen by assigning the value keyguard to

TABLE 14.21 Selected constants of the `AppWidgetProviderInfo` class

Constant	Description
WIDGET_CATEGORY_HOME_SCREEN	Has value 1. Widget can be displayed on the Home screen.
WIDGET_CATEGORY_KEYGUARD	Has value 2. Widget can be displayed on the Keyguard (Lock screen).

the `android:widgetCategory` attribute of the `appwidget-provider` element in the widget info file as follows:

```
android:widgetCategory="keyguard"
```

We assign the values `keyguard`, `home_screen`, or `keyguard | home_screen` values to the `android:widgetCategory` attribute, depending on whether we want to allow the Lock screen, the Home screen, or both to be possible Host screens for the widget. If none is specified, the default host for the widget is the Home screen. These values correspond to the `WIDGET_CAT-EGORY_KEYGUARD` and `WIDGET_CATEGORY_HOME_SCREEN` constants of the `AppWidgetProviderInfo` class, shown in **TABLE 14.21**.

EXAMPLE 14.18 shows the updated widget_info.xml file. At line 8, we specify that the widget can be hosted on either the Home screen or the Lock screen.

```
 1    <?xml version="1.0" encoding="utf-8"?>
 2    <appwidget-provider
 3        xmlns:android="http://schemas.android.com/apk/res/android"
 4        android:initialLayout="@layout/widget_layout"
 5        android:minHeight="50dp"
 6        android:minWidth="200dp"
 7        android:updatePeriodMillis="1800000"
 8        android:widgetCategory="keyguard|home_screen"
 9        android:configure=
10            "com.jblearning.temperaturewidgetv6.TemperatureWidgetConfigure" >
11    </appwidget-provider>
```

EXAMPLE 14.18 The `widget_info.xml` file, app Version 6

It is possible to design a widget that has a different appearance on the Lock screen from its appearance on the Home screen. For this, we create a different XML layout file for the widget when it is hosted on the Lock screen. We also need to specify the name of that file in the `AppWidgetProviderInfo` XML file. If the name of the XML layout file for the Lock screen

TABLE 14.22 The `OPTION_APPWIDGET_HOST_CATEGORY` constant and the `getAppWidgetOptions` method of the `AppWidgetManager` class

Constant and Method	Description
OPTION_APPWIDGET_HOST_CATEGORY	A String constant used as a key to retrieve the value of the widget host category stored as an extra.
Bundle getAppWidgetOptions(int widgetId)	Returns the Bundle storing the extras for the widget whose id is widgetId.

TABLE 14.23 The `getInt` method of the `BaseBundle` class, inherited by `Bundle`

Method	Description
int getInt(String key)	Returns the integer value associated with key, 0 if there is none.

is widget_layout_keyguard.xml, then we add the following attribute/value pair in the `appwidget-provider` element of the `AppWidgetProviderInfo` XML file.

```
android:initialKeyguardLayout="@layout/widget_layout_keyguard"
```

Inside the `AppWidgetProvider` class, we can test if the widget host is the Home screen or the Lock screen. The host information is stored in the `Bundle` associated with the widget. Inside the `onUpdate` method of the `AppWidgetProvider` class, we have an `AppWidgetManager` reference as a parameter of that method. We can retrieve that `Bundle` by calling the `getAppWidgetOptions` method of the `AppWidgetManager` class (see **TABLE 14.22**), passing the widget id as its only argument. With the `Bundle` reference, we can call the `getInt` method, shown in **TABLE 14.23**, passing the `OPTION_APPWIDGET_HOST_CATEGORY` constant of the `AppWidgetManager` class (see Table 14.22), and retrieve the widget host category as an `int`. We can then compare that integer value to the `WIDGET_CATEGORY_HOME_SCREEN` and `WIDGET_CATEGORY_KEYGUARD` constants of the `AppWidgetProviderInfo` class (see Table 14.21), whose values are 1 and 2 respectively, in order to test what host the widget is on.

We can use the following sequence to test if the host is the Home screen or the Lock screen.

```
Bundle bundle = appWidgetManager.getAppWidgetOptions( widgetId );
int host =
  bundle.getInt( AppWidgetManager.OPTION_APPWIDGET_HOST_CATEGORY, -1 );
if( host == AppWidgetProviderInfo.WIDGET_CATEGORY_KEYGUARD ) {
  // code for Lock screen host
} else if( host == AppWidgetProviderInfo.WIDGET_CATEGORY_HOME_SCREEN ) {
  // code for Home screen host
}
```

Designing a widget that looks and behaves differently on the Lock screen is left as an exercise.

Chapter Summary

- App widgets, also known as widgets, are small apps that are embedded in other apps, called app widget hosts.
- The Home screen and the Lock screen are examples of app widget hosts.
- To create a widget, we can extend the `AppWidgetProvider` class and override its `onUpdate` method.
- The widget info file, located in the xml directory of the res directory, defines an `appwidget-provider` element that specifies the characteristics of a widget such as size and frequency of updates.
- Not all `View` and layout manager classes can be used inside a widget.
- A widget can use a drawable resource for its background.
- A widget can update its display automatically at a certain frequency. The minimum frequency is 30 minutes.
- We can update the widget via user interaction with the widget, such as a click.
- It is possible to update the data displayed by the widget dynamically. That data can be retrieved locally or from a remote source.
- A widget can be customizable by the user at installation by adding an activity that captures user input.
- Not only can we install a widget on the Home screen, we can also install a widget on the Lock screen.

Exercises, Problems, and Projects

Multiple-Choice Exercises

1. What method of AppWidgetProvider do we override to update a widget?
   - update
   - onUpdate
   - widgetUpdate
   - broadcast

2. The third parameter of the method in question 1 is
   - A Context reference
   - An AppWidgetManager reference
   - A widget id
   - An array of widget ids

3. What class do we use to manage the View hierarchy inside a widget?
    - Views
    - View
    - RemoteViews
    - Remotes

4. What element do we define in the widget info XML file?
    - appwidget
    - appwidget-provider
    - provider
    - widget-info

5. The data type of a widget id is
    - A char
    - A String
    - An int
    - An AppWidgetInfo

6. The minimum frequency of automatic update for a widget is
    - 1 second
    - 30 seconds
    - 60 seconds
    - 30 minutes

7. We can allow a widget to be updated via user interaction
    - No, that is not possible
    - Yes, by clicking on it for example
    - Yes, but only every 60 seconds
    - Yes, but only every 30 minutes

8. The data displayed by a widget
    - cannot be changed
    - can be changed, but only using data stored inside the device
    - can be changed, by retrieving data from an external source
    - can only be changed every 30 minutes

9. How can we customize a widget at installation time?
    - It is not possible
    - We can run an activity at that time and capture and use user input to customize the widget
    - We use the CustomizeWidget class of the android.widget package
    - We use the SpecializeWidget class of the android.widget package

10. What are examples of a Host screen for a widget?
    - There is no such thing as a Host screen for a widget
    - The Home screen and only the Home screen
    - The Lock screen and only the Lock screen
    - The Home screen and the Lock screen

Fill in the Code

11. Write the code so that the widget's update frequency is 1 hour

```xml
<?xml version="1.0" encoding="utf-8"?>
<appwidget-provider
    xmlns:android="http://schemas.android.com/apk/res/android"
    android:initialLayout="@layout/widget_layout"
    android:minHeight="40dp"
    android:minWidth="180dp"
    <!-- your code goes here -->


</appwidget-provider>
```

12. Inside the onUpdate method of an AppWidgetProvider class, update all the widgets of the type of that AppWidgetProvider class.

```java
public void onUpdate ( Context context,
        AppWidgetManager appWidgetManager, int[ ] appWidgetIds ){
    super.onUpdate( context, appWidgetManager, appWidgetIds );
    RemoteViews views = new RemoteViews( context.getPackageName( ),
                                        R.layout.widget_layout );
    // Your code goes here

}
```

13. Write the code to set the text inside a TextView whose id is my_view to HELLO WIDGET.

```java
RemoteViews remoteViews = new RemoteViews( context.getPackageName( ),
                                        R.layout.widget_layout );
// Your code goes here
```

14. Inside the onUpdate method of the MyProvider class, write the code to update the widget every time the user clicks on a View whose id is my_view inside the widget.

```
RemoteViews remoteViews = new RemoteViews( context.getPackageName( ),
                                           R.layout.widget_layout );
// widgetId is the id of the current widget
Intent intent = new Intent( context, MyProvider.class );
intent.setAction( AppWidgetManager.ACTION_APPWIDGET_UPDATE );
intent.putExtra( AppWidgetManager.EXTRA_APPWIDGET_IDS, appWidgetIds );
// Your code goes here

appWidgetManager.updateAppWidget( widgetId, remoteViews );
```

15. Consider the following JSON string named json. Write the code to retrieve the value of a country (i.e., Italy).

```
{"coord":{"lon":12.495800018311,"lat":41.903049468994},"sys":{"country":
"Italy","sunrise":1374033016,"sunset":1374086531 } };

// Your code goes here
```

16. Write the code so that the widget is configured by an activity named MyActivity and located in the com.xyz.q16 package.

```
<?xml version="1.0" encoding="utf-8"?>
<appwidget-provider
    xmlns:android="http://schemas.android.com/apk/res/android"
    android:initialLayout="@layout/widget_layout"
    android:minHeight="40dp"
    android:minWidth="180dp"
    <!-- your code goes here -->


</appwidget-provider>
```

17. Inside a configuration activity, write the code to put current_widget_id, a widget id, as an extra stored in the Intent resultIntent.

```
// the app widget id is widget_id
Intent resultIntent = new Intent( );
// Your code goes here
```

18. Write the code so that the widget can be installed on the Home screen or the Lock screen.

```
<?xml version="1.0" encoding="utf-8"?>
<appwidget-provider
    xmlns:android="http://schemas.android.com/apk/res/android"
    android:initialLayout="@layout/widget_layout"
    android:minHeight="40dp"
    android:minWidth="180dp"
    <!-- your code goes here -->


</appwidget-provider>
```

Write a Widget

19. Modify Version 4 of the example in the chapter so that it displays something different from the temperature, for example, the humidity level.

20. Modify Version 4 of the example in the chapter so that it displays two pieces of data, not one, and different from the temperature, for example, the pressure and the humidity level.

21. Modify Version 5 of the example in the chapter so that it displays the temperature for two cities, not one.

22. Modify Version 5 of the example in the chapter so that it displays data for two cities, not one, and that data should be different from the temperature, for example, the humidity level.

23. Modify Version 5 of the example in the chapter so that the user can customize how the temperature is displayed, not the location. The user can choose between degrees Celsius and degrees Fahrenheit.

24. Modify Version 5 of the example in the chapter so that the user can customize the background color of the widget, not the location.

25. Create a widget of your choice that pulls data from a remote source of your choice.

26. Create a widget of your choice that pulls data from a remote source of your choice and is customizable by the user.

27. Modify Version 5 of the example in the chapter so that the data is pulled from the NWS. Use the strategy described at the beginning of paragraph 14.5 of the chapter.

CHAPTER FIFTEEN

In App Advertising

CHAPTER CONTENTS

Introduction

An important issue when building an app is how to monetize it. With so many apps out there, most people will first try a free app whenever possible. The Android SDK provides developers with the ability to include advertising inside their apps and leverage Google's advertising resources to upload ads at runtime.

15.1 The View, Stopwatch App, Version 0

We want to build a stopwatch app that enables users to start the clock, stop it, reset it, restart it, etc. In Version 0, we only build the GUI, reserving a space for an ad banner at the bottom. **FIGURE 15.1** shows the version 3 of the app running inside the emulator. The screen is divided into three parts:

▶ At the top, we have the clock.
▶ In the middle, we have a start/stop toggle button and a reset button.
▶ At the bottom, we have the ad banner.

FIGURE 15.1 The Stopwatch app, Version 3

For the two round buttons, we use three drawables, shown in **EXAMPLES 15.1, 15.2,** and **15.3.** We place them in the drawable directory. For the start/stop button, we will toggle the background of the button between start_button.xml and stop_button.xml. The start button has a green circle outline and the stop button has a red circle outline (line 6 of Examples 15.1 and 15.2). The reset button has a gray circle outline (line 6 of Example 15.3).

```xml
1   <?xml version="1.0" encoding="utf-8"?>
2   <shape
3       xmlns:android="http://schemas.android.com/apk/res/android"
4       android:shape="oval">
5       <solid android:color="#FFFF" />
6       <stroke android:width="2dp" android:color="#F0F0" />
7   </shape>
```

EXAMPLE 15.1 **The start_button.xml file, Stopwatch app, Version 0**

```xml
1   <?xml version="1.0" encoding="utf-8"?>
2   <shape
3       xmlns:android="http://schemas.android.com/apk/res/android"
4       android:shape="oval">
5       <solid android:color="#FFFF" />
6       <stroke android:width="2dp" android:color="#FF00" />
7   </shape>
```

EXAMPLE 15.2 **The stop_button.xml file, Stopwatch app, Version 0**

```xml
1   <?xml version="1.0" encoding="utf-8"?>
2   <shape
3       xmlns:android="http://schemas.android.com/apk/res/android"
4       android:shape="oval" >
5       <solid android:color="#FFFF" />
6       <stroke android:width="2dp" android:color="#F444" />
7   </shape>
```

EXAMPLE 15.3 **The reset_button.xml file, Stopwatch app, Version 0**

To display the stopwatch, we use a `Chronometer`. The `Chronometer` class inherits from `TextView` and encapsulates the functionality of a running clock. We want to style the `Chronometer` so we code the `textViewStyle` style at lines 11–15 in the styles.xml file, shown in **EXAMPLE 15.4.**

```
 1    <resources>
 2
 3        <!-- Base application theme. -->
 4        <style name="AppTheme" parent="Theme.AppCompat.Light.DarkActionBar">
 5            <!-- Customize your theme here. -->
 6            <item name="colorPrimary">@color/colorPrimary</item>
 7            <item name="colorPrimaryDark">@color/colorPrimaryDark</item>
 8            <item name="colorAccent">@color/colorAccent</item>
 9        </style>
10
11        <style name="textViewStyle" parent = "@android:style/TextAppearance">
12            <item name = "android:gravity">center</item>
13            <item name = "android:textStyle">bold</item>
14            <item name = "android:textSize">96sp</item>
15        </style>
16
17    </resources>
```

EXAMPLE 15.4 **The styles.xml file, Stopwatch app, Version 0**

EXAMPLE 15.5 shows the activity_main.xml file, organizing the GUI. A vertical (line 10) LinearLayout (line 2) organizes the screen into three parts:

▶ A Chronometer (lines 13–18).
▶ A horizontal (line 21) LinearLayout (lines 20–59) contains the start/stop and reset buttons.

```
 1    <?xml version="1.0" encoding="utf-8"?>
 2    <LinearLayout xmlns:android="http://schemas.android.com/apk/res/android"
 3        xmlns:tools="http://schemas.android.com/tools"
 4        android:layout_width="match_parent"
 5        android:layout_height="match_parent"
 6        android:paddingBottom="@dimen/activity_vertical_margin"
 7        android:paddingLeft="@dimen/activity_horizontal_margin"
 8        android:paddingRight="@dimen/activity_horizontal_margin"
 9        android:paddingTop="@dimen/activity_vertical_margin"
10        android:orientation="vertical"
11        tools:context="com.jblearning.stopwatchv0.MainActivity">
12
13        <Chronometer
14            android:layout_weight="4"
15            android:layout_width="match_parent"
16            android:layout_height="0dp"
17            android:id="@+id/stop_watch"
18            style="@style/textViewStyle" />
19
```

EXAMPLE 15.5 **The activity_main.xml file, Stopwatch app, Version 0 (*Continued*)**

```
20        <LinearLayout
21            android:orientation="horizontal"
22            android:layout_weight="4"
23            android:layout_width="match_parent"
24            android:layout_height="0dp"
25            android:gravity="center" >
26
27            <LinearLayout
28                android:orientation="vertical"
29                android:layout_width="0dp"
30                android:layout_weight="1"
31                android:layout_height="match_parent"
32                android:gravity="center" >
33                <Button
34                    android:id="@+id/start_stop"
35                    android:layout_width="150dp"
36                    android:layout_height="150dp"
37                    android:text="START"
38                    android:textSize="36sp"
39                    android:background="@drawable/start_button"
40                    android:onClick="startStop" />
41            </LinearLayout>
42
43            <LinearLayout
44                android:orientation="vertical"
45                android:layout_width="0dp"
46                android:layout_weight="1"
47                android:layout_height="match_parent"
48                android:gravity="center" >
49                <Button
50                    android:id="@+id/reset"
51                    android:layout_height="150dp"
52                    android:layout_width="150dp"
53                    android:text="RESET"
54                    android:textSize="36sp"
55                    android:background="@drawable/reset_button"
56                    android:onClick="reset" />
57            </LinearLayout>
58
59        </LinearLayout>
60
61        <LinearLayout
62            android:orientation="horizontal"
63            android:layout_weight="1"
64            android:layout_width="match_parent"
65            android:layout_height="0dp"
66            android:background="#FDDD" >
67        </LinearLayout>
68
69    </LinearLayout>
```

EXAMPLE 15.5 The activity_main.xml file, Stopwatch app, Version 0

▶ Another `LinearLayout` (lines 61–67), a placeholder for the ad banner (we later change this `LinearLayout` to a fragment as recommended by Google).

We assign 4/9 (weight 4 – line 14) of the screen to the `Chronometer` element, 4/9 to the buttons (weight 4 – line 22), and 1/9 (weight 1 – line 63) to the `LinearLayout` at the bottom. We give an id to the `Chronometer` at line 17 because we need to access it from the `MainActivity` class. We style it at line 18.

The horizontal `LinearLayout` in the middle of the screen contains two `LinearLayout`s (lines 27–41 and 43–57), each containing a button (lines 33–40 and 49–56). Each button has a diameter of size 150 pixels (lines 35–36 and 51–52) and a text size of 36. Although it is generally not good practice to hard code dimension values, we do so here to keep the example simple. Furthermore, these dimensions are reasonably small and are expected to work on any device. At lines 39 and 55, we set the background of each button to its corresponding drawable resource. Clicking on the Start/Stop button will trigger a call to the `startStop` method (line 40) and clicking on the Reset button will trigger a call to the `reset` method (line 56).

In this version, we color the bottom `LinearLayout` in light gray (line 66) so that we can visualize where the ad banner will go.

We add do-nothing `startStop` and `reset` methods to the `MainActivity` class (**EXAMPLE 15.6**) so that the app does not crash when the user clicks on either button.

FIGURE 15.2 shows a preview of the Stopwatch, Version 0, in the environment.

```
1    package com.jblearning.stopwatchv0;
2
3    import android.support.v7.app.ActionBarActivity;
4    import android.os.Bundle;
5    import android.view.View;
6
7    public class MainActivity extends ActionBarActivity {
8
9      @Override
10     protected void onCreate( Bundle savedInstanceState ) {
11       super.onCreate( savedInstanceState );
12       setContentView( R.layout.activity_main );
13     }
14
15     public void startStop( View view ) {
16     }
17
18     public void reset( View view ) {
19     }
20   }
```

EXAMPLE 15.6 The `MainActivity` class, Stopwatch app, Version 0

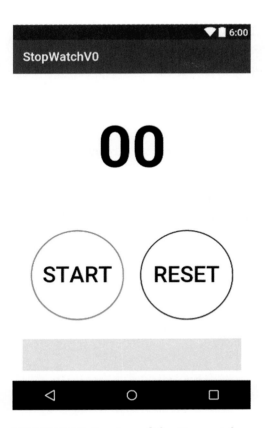

FIGURE 15.2 Preview of the Stopwatch app, Version 0

15.2 The Controller: Running the Stopwatch App, Version 1

In Version 1, we will code the `startStop` and `reset` methods to give the app its functionality. In order to do this, we use the functionality of the `Chronometer` class, which represents the Model for this app: the `start`, `stop`, and `setBase` methods of the `Chronometer` class, shown in TABLE 15.1, enable us to start, stop, and reset the `Chronometer`.

The parameter of `setBase`, `base`, is typically set using the `elapsedRealtime` method of the `SystemClock` class. Its API is:

```
public static long elapsedRealtime( )
```

The `elapsedRealTime` method returns, in milliseconds, the amount of time since the last boot, including sleep time.

TABLE 15.1 Selected methods from the Chronometer class	
Method	**Description**
void start( )	Start counting (or restart counting).
void stop( )	Stop counting.
void setBase(long base)	Set the time of reference for the count.

EXAMPLE 15.7 shows the updated MainActivity class. Since the Start/Stop button toggles between two states, we keep track of that state with a boolean instance variable, started (line 12). Since we need access to the Chronometer in both methods, we add an instance variable for it, chrono (line 11). Inside the onCreate method, we instantiate it at line 18 using the findViewbyId method.

```
1   package com.jblearning.stopwatchv1;
2
3   import android.os.Bundle;
4   import android.os.SystemClock;
5   import android.support.v7.app.ActionBarActivity;
6   import android.view.View;
7   import android.widget.Button;
8   import android.widget.Chronometer;
9
10  public class MainActivity extends ActionBarActivity {
11    private Chronometer chrono;
12    private boolean started = false;
13
14    @Override
15    protected void onCreate( Bundle savedInstanceState ) {
16      super.onCreate( savedInstanceState );
17      setContentView( R.layout.activity_main );
18      chrono = ( Chronometer ) findViewById( R.id.stop_watch );
19    }
20
21    public void startStop( View view ) {
22      Button startStopButton = ( Button ) findViewById( R.id.start_stop );
23      if( started ) {
24        chrono.stop( );
25        started = false;
26        startStopButton.setText( "START" );
27        startStopButton.setBackgroundResource( R.drawable.start_button );
28      } else {
```

EXAMPLE 15.7 The MainActivity class, Stopwatch app, Version 1 (*Continued*)

```
29            chrono.start( );
30            started = true;
31            startStopButton.setText( "STOP" );
32            startStopButton.setBackgroundResource( R.drawable.stop_button );
33          }
34        }
35
36      public void reset( View view ) {
37        if( !started )
38          chrono.setBase( SystemClock.elapsedRealtime( ) );
39      }
40    }
```

EXAMPLE 15.7 The `MainActivity` class, Stopwatch app, Version 1

The `startStop` method is coded at lines 21–34. If the `Chronometer` has already started (line 23), then the Start/Stop button is in its "started" state and we do the following:

▶ Stop the `Chronometer`: we do this by calling `stop` with `chrono` at line 24.

▶ Turn `started` to `false` (line 25) to specify that the button is now in a "stopped" state.

▶ Change the text of the button to START (line 26).

▶ Switch the background of the button to the drawable defined in start_button.xml (line 27).

Otherwise (line 28), the `Chronometer` has not started yet or was stopped, the button is in its "start" state and we do the following:

▶ Start the `Chronometer`: we do this by calling `start` with `chrono` at line 29.

▶ Turn `started` to `true` (line 30) to specify that the button is now in a "started" state.

▶ Change the text of the button to STOP (line 31).

▶ Switch the background of the button to the drawable defined in stop_button.xml (line 32).

The `reset` method (lines 36–39) resets `chrono` to `00:00` by calling the `setBase` method, passing the current time in milliseconds. Thus, when we call reset at time `t`, `00:00` is considered to be time `t`.

FIGURE 15.3 shows the Stopwatch, Version 1, running inside the emulator. The clock is running and the Start/Stop button has a red circle outline and says STOP.

FIGURE 15.3 The Stopwatch app, Version 1

15.3 Improving the Stopwatch App, Version 2

There is one issue with Version 1: if we stop the clock and restart it later, it does not restart where we stopped it. In fact, when we stop the Chronometer, it keeps running in the background. In Version 2, we fix that problem so that when we stop the Chronometer at time t, it restarts at time t.

To implement this, when we start or restart the Chronometer, we need to subtract the time elapsed since we stopped the Chronometer from the value returned by the elapsedRealtime method. Rather than doing this inside the MainActivity class, the Controller, we create a utility class, ClockUtility, shown in **EXAMPLE 15.8**. The Model for this app is now comprised of the Chronometer and ClockUtility classes. Furthermore, the functionality of the ClockUtility class is reusable in other apps.

The ClockUtility contains one static method, milliseconds: it converts a String that is formatted like a String displayed inside a Chronometer to its equivalent number of milliseconds. The format of the String clock (line 10) is expected to be hh:mm:ss or mm:ss where hh

```
1   package com.jblearning.stopwatchv2;
2
3   public class ClockUtility {
4     /*
5      * This method computes and returns the equivalent number of milliseconds
6      *   for its parameter, a String that represents a clock
7      * @param  clock, a String, expected to look like mm:ss or hh:mm:ss
8      * @return a long, the equivalent number of milliseconds to clock
9      */
10    public static long milliseconds( String clock  ) {
11      long ms = 0;
12      String [ ] clockArray = clock.split( ":" );
13
14      // compute milliseconds
15      try {
16        if( clockArray.length == 3 ) {
17          ms = Integer.parseInt( clockArray[0] ) * 60 * 60 * 1000
18              + Integer.parseInt( clockArray[1] ) * 60 * 1000
19              + Integer.parseInt( clockArray[2] ) * 1000;
20        } else if ( clockArray.length == 2 ) {
21          ms = Integer.parseInt( clockArray[0] ) * 60 * 1000
22              + Integer.parseInt( clockArray[1] ) * 1000;
23        }
24      } catch( NumberFormatException nfe ) {
25        // should never get here if clock has proper format
26      }
27      return ms;
28    }
29  }
```

EXAMPLE 15.8 The ClockUtility class, Stopwatch app, Version 2

represents the number of hours (between 00 and 23), mm the number of minutes (between 00 and 59), and ss the number of seconds (between 00 and 59). In order to convert the `String clock` to a number of milliseconds, we use the `parseInt` method of the `Integer` class, which throws a `NumberFormatException`. Although it is not mandatory because `NumberFormatException` is unchecked, we prefer to use `try` and `catch` blocks (lines 15–26).

We convert `clock` to an array at line 12. If there are three elements in that array (line 16), the number of milliseconds is equal to `hh * 60 * 60 * 1000 + mm * 60 * 1000 + ss * 1000` (lines 17–19). If there are two elements in that array (line 20), the number of milliseconds is equal to `mm * 60 * 1000 + ss * 1000` (lines 21–22). If `clock` does not have the proper formatting, the method returns 0.

EXAMPLE 15.9 shows the updated `MainActivity` class. Inside the `startStop` method, if we restart the `Chronometer` (lines 29–33), we first reset it to where it had previously stopped at line 29 by calling the `resetChrono` method. Inside `resetChrono` (lines 42–46), we convert the current value of `chrono` to a number of milliseconds at lines 43–44. At line 45, we reset its base (i.e., its starting value) to its value when it stopped. **TABLE 15.2** shows possible values returned by the `elapsedRealtime` and `milliseconds` methods when the user clicks on START, then STOP when `chrono` shows `10:00`, then START again.

```
1    package com.jblearning.stopwatchv2;
2
3    import android.os.SystemClock;
4    import android.support.v7.app.ActionBarActivity;
5    import android.os.Bundle;
6    import android.view.View;
7    import android.widget.Button;
8    import android.widget.Chronometer;
9
10   public class MainActivity extends ActionBarActivity {
11     private Chronometer chrono;
12     private boolean started = false;
13
14     @Override
15     protected void onCreate( Bundle savedInstanceState ) {
16       super.onCreate( savedInstanceState );
17       setContentView( R.layout.activity_main );
18       chrono = ( Chronometer ) findViewById( R.id.stop_watch );
19     }
20
21     public void startStop( View view ) {
22       Button startStopButton = ( Button ) findViewById( R.id.start_stop );
23       if( started ) {
24         chrono.stop( );
25         started = false;
26         startStopButton.setText( "START" );
```

EXAMPLE 15.9 The `MainActivity` class, Stopwatch app, Version 2 (*Continued*)

```
27            startStopButton.setBackgroundResource( R.drawable.start_button );
28         } else {
29            resetChrono( );
30            chrono.start( );
31            started = true;
32            startStopButton.setText( "STOP" );
33            startStopButton.setBackgroundResource( R.drawable.stop_button );
34         }
35      }
36
37      public void reset( View view ) {
38         if( !started )
39            chrono.setBase( SystemClock.elapsedRealtime( ) );
40      }
41
42      public void resetChrono( ) {
43         String chronoText = chrono.getText( ).toString( );
44         long idleMilliseconds = ClockUtility.milliseconds( chronoText );
45         chrono.setBase( SystemClock.elapsedRealtime( ) - idleMilliseconds );
46      }
47   }
```

EXAMPLE 15.9 The `MainActivity` class, Stopwatch app, Version 2

TABLE 15.2 Values returned by `elapsedRealtime` and `milliseconds` assuming a START, STOP, START sequence

Action	Chrono	Time	Value Returned by `elapsedRealtime`	Value Returned by `milliseconds`
Start	00:00	t1	695064	0
Stop	00:10	t2	705777	10000
Start	00:10	t3	859134	10000

Now, when we run the app, we can stop the Chronometer and it will restart where it was stopped. For example, if the Chronometer says 00:15 when we stop it and we wait 10 seconds before clicking on the Start/Stop button, the Chronometer will restart at 00:15, not 00:25.

15.4 Placing the Ad, Stopwatch App, Version 3

In Version 3, we place an ad at the bottom of the screen. The com.google.android.gms.ads package provides a set of classes to display an ad and manage the ad. **TABLE 15.3** shows some of these classes.

TABLE 15.3 Selected classes from the `com.google.android.gms.ads` package	
Class	**Description**
AdView	A subclass of View to display an ad banner.
AdSize	Encapsulates the size of a banner ad.
AdRequest	Encapsulates a set of marketing characteristics such as location, birthday, keywords, etc., so that the ad can target demographics related to the app.

However, the `com.google.android.gms.ads` package is not part of the standard Android SDK, but it is part of Google Play services. Thus, in order to use it, we edit the build.gradle file as shown in **EXAMPLE 15.10**. Since we edited the build.gradle file, we need to sync the project.

```
1    apply plugin: 'com.android.application'
2
3    android {
4        compileSdkVersion 23
5        buildToolsVersion "23.0.2"
6
7        defaultConfig {
8            applicationId "com.jblearning.stopwatchv3"
9            minSdkVersion 15
10           targetSdkVersion 23
11           versionCode 1
12           versionName "1.0"
13       }
14       buildTypes {
15           release {
16               minifyEnabled false
17               proguardFiles getDefaultProguardFile('proguard-android.txt'),
18                       'proguard-rules.pro'
19           }
20       }
21   }
22
23   dependencies {
24       compile fileTree( dir: 'libs', include: ['*.jar'])
25       testCompile 'junit:junit:4.12'
26       compile 'com.android.support:appcompat-v7:23.4.0'
27       compile 'com.google.android.gms:play-services:9.4.0'
28   }
```

EXAMPLE 15.10 The edited build.gradle file

We edit the activity_main.xml file and give an id to the last `LinearLayout`, where we place the ad, as shown at line 60 in **EXAMPLE 15.11**. Since we do not fully control the size of the ad that will be served, we want the width of the screen to be maximal. Thus, we delete lines 7 and 8 of Example 15.5 so that we do not have any left and right padding for the overall `LinearLayout`.

```
58
59        <LinearLayout
60            android:id="@+id/ad_view"
61            android:orientation="horizontal"
62            android:layout_weight="1"
63            android:layout_width="match_parent"
64            android:layout_height="0dp"
65            android:background="#FDDD"  >
66        </LinearLayout>
67    </LinearLayout>
```

EXAMPLE 15.11 The end of the activity_main.xml file

The `AdSize` class encapsulates the size of a banner ad. It provides constants to match various industry standard sizes, as well as constants to cause the width and height to be relative to the device's width and height. **TABLE 15.4** shows some of these constants. We can use the `FULL_WIDTH` and `AUTO_HEIGHT` constants to create an `AdSize` object using an `AdSize` constructor, whereas we can use the other constants, such as `SMART_BANNER`, to specify a premade `AdSize` object.

The `AdView` class includes methods to create and manage a banner ad. Its direct superclass is `ViewGroup`, itself a subclass of `View`. Thus, `AdView` inherits from `View`. **TABLE 15.5** shows some methods of the `AdView` class.

We must set the size and ad unit id of an `AdView` before we can load an ad into the `AdView`. Otherwise, an (unchecked) `IllegalStateException` will be thrown when we try to load the ad. In order to obtain an ad unit id from Google, we must be a registered Android developer. Among

TABLE 15.4 Selected constants of the `AdSize` class

Constant	Data Type	Description
AUTO_HEIGHT	int	Causes the height of the ad to scale based on the height of the device.
FULL_WIDTH	int	Causes the width of the ad to match the width of the device.
BANNER	AdSize	Mobile Marketing Association ad size of 320 × 50 dip.
SMART_BANNER	AdSize	Dynamically sized to full width and auto height.

TABLE 15.5 Selected methods of the `AdView` class

Method	Description
public AdView(Context context)	Constructs an AdView.
public void setAdSize(AdSize adSize)	Sets the size of the banner ad. The argument can be one of the constants of the AdSize class.
public void setAdUnitId(String adUnitId)	Sets the ad unit id.
public void loadAd(AdRequest request)	Loads the ad on a background thread.

other things, the developer uses the ad unit id to generate ad revenues. The ad unit id is a `String` that we can obtain from **AdMob**, the platform that Google uses for managing ads, at the following URL:

`https://support.google.com/admob/v2/answer/3052638`

AdMob ad unit ids have the following format:

`ca-app-pub-XXXXXXXXXXXXXXXX/NNNNNNNNNN`.

For developers who are not registered and want to test an app containing an `AdView`, Google provides a test ad unit id. We include it in the strings.xml file, shown in **EXAMPLE 15.12** (lines 3–4). We actually do not use that `String` in Version 3, but we do use it in Versions 4 and 5.

```
1    <resources>
2        <string name="app_name">StopWatchV3
3        <string name="banner_ad_unit_id">
4            ca-app-pub-3940256099942544/6300978111
5    </resources>
```

EXAMPLE 15.12 **The strings.xml file, Stopwatch app, Version 3**

The following shows a code sequence creating an `AdView`, setting its size and setting its ad unit id, assuming we are inside an `Activity` class:

```
// Create a banner ad; assume this is an Activity reference
AdView adView = new AdView( this );
// Set ad size
adView.setAdSize( AdSize.SMART_BANNER );
// Set the ad unit id; use the default String from Google
String adUnitId = "ca-app-pub-3940256099942544/6300978111";
adView.setAdUnitId( adUnitId );
```

TABLE 15.6 Selected methods of the `AdRequest.Builder` class	
Method	**Description**
public AdRequest.Builder( )	Default constructor.
public AdRequest.Builder addKeyword(String keyword)	Adds a keyword for targeting purposes and can be called several times to add several keywords.
public AdRequest.Builder setGender(int gender)	Sets the user's gender for targeting purposes.
public AdRequest.Builder setBirthday(Date birthday)	Sets the user's birthday for targeting purposes.
public AdRequest.Builder setLocation(Location location)	Sets the user's location for targeting purposes.
public AdRequest.Builder addTestDevice(String deviceId)	Sets up a device to receive test ads rather than live ads. Use the constant DEVICE_ID_EMULATOR from the AdRequest class to use the emulator.
public AdRequest build( )	Constructs and returns an AdRequest with the attributes specified by this AdRequest.Builder.

Once we have created an `AdView`, set its size and ad unit id, we need to create an ad request and load it into the `AdView`. The `AdRequest` class encapsulates the concept of an ad request. It includes a `static` inner class, `Builder`, that we can use to set the characteristics of an `AdRequest`. **TABLE 15.6** shows some methods of the `AdRequest.Builder` class. The `addKeyword` allows us to add keywords, one per method call, that relate to the app, so that the ad can be better targeted at the typical app user. The `setGender` method allows us to target the ad at women, men, or both. The `AdRequest` class provides three `int` constants, `GENDER_FEMALE`, `GENDER_MALE`, and `GENDER_UNKNOWN`, which we can use as arguments of that method. We can use the `setLocation` method to target the ad based on a location. The app can access the GPS, retrieve the location of the user dynamically, and include it in the ad request so that Google services can use the location to better choose and target the ad. All these methods return the `AdRequest.Builder` reference that called them so that method calls can be chained. Once all the characteristics of the ad request are set, we can use the `build` method to create an `AdRequest` object.

The following shows a code sequence creating an `AdRequest`, and loading it onto an `AdView`:

```
// Create the ad request using an AdRequest.Builder object
AdRequest.Builder adRequestBuilder = new AdRequest.Builder( );
// Define target data for adRequest ( this is optional )
adRequestBuilder.setGender( AdRequest.GENDER_UNKNOWN );
adRequestBuilder.addKeyword( "fitness" );
adRequestBuilder.addKeyword ( "workout" );
```

FIGURE 15.4 Logcat output showing the device id

```
// Create the AdRequest
AdRequest adRequest = adRequestBuilder.build( );
// load the ad
adView.loadAd( adRequest );
```

If we want to use the emulator to test our app, we add this line before calling `build` to create the `AdRequest`:

```
adRequestBuilder.addTestDevice( AdRequest.DEVICE_ID_EMULATOR );
```

If we are a registered developer and we have obtained a valid ad unit id from Google, we can add this line before calling `build` to create the `AdRequest` for testing purposes. In the final version of the app, before submitting our app to Google Play, we should either delete that line or comment it out.

We can obtain the device id, a 32-digit hexadecimal string, for a device we use to test our app. We can obtain it by looking at the Logcat output when running the app on a connected device. For the author's device, here is the Logcat output, also shown in **FIGURE 15.4** (if you cannot find it in Logcat, screen the messages using the Ads tag as shown):

```
Use AdRequest.Builder.addTestDevice( "DE4??????????????7A" ) to
get test ads on this device.
```

Thus, for the author's device, we can include the following code to test the app on the tablet (for security and privacy reasons, the device id is partially hidden on Figure 15.4 and has been filled with ? characters below).

```
String deviceId = "DE4??????????????7A";
adRequestBuilder.addTestDevice( deviceId );
```

EXAMPLE 15.13 shows the updated `MainActivity` class, which includes creating an `AdView`, then an `AdRequest`, and loading the ad. The only edits are at lines 25–48 of the `onCreate` method. At lines 25–30, we create an `AdView` and set its size using `SMART_BANNER` and unit ad id using the default Google supplied ad unit id. At lines 32–41, we create and define an `AdRequest`. The ads served will target users interested in `fitness` and `workout` (lines 36—37). If we run the ad on the emulator, we ask for test ads, not live ads, to be sent (lines 38–39). We call `build` with the `AdRequest.Builder` reference `adRequestBuilder` at line 41 to create an `AdRequest`. At lines 43–45, we retrieve the `LinearLayout` whose id is `ad_view` and place the `AdView` in it. At lines 47–48, we load an ad conforming to `adRequest` inside the `AdView`.

```
1    package com.jblearning.stopwatchv3;
2
3    import android.os.Bundle;
4    import android.os.SystemClock;
5    import android.support.v7.app.ActionBarActivity;
6    import android.view.View;
7    import android.widget.Button;
8    import android.widget.Chronometer;
9    import android.widget.LinearLayout;
10
11   import com.google.android.gms.ads.AdRequest;
12   import com.google.android.gms.ads.AdSize;
13   import com.google.android.gms.ads.AdView;
14
15   public class MainActivity extends ActionBarActivity {
16     private Chronometer chrono;
17     private boolean started = false;
18
19     @Override
20     protected void onCreate( Bundle savedInstanceState ) {
21       super.onCreate( savedInstanceState );
22       setContentView( R.layout.activity_main );
23       chrono = ( Chronometer ) findViewById( R.id.stop_watch );
24
25       // create a banner ad
26       AdView adView = new AdView( this );
27       // Set ad size and ad unit ID
28       adView.setAdSize( AdSize.SMART_BANNER );
29       String adUnitId = "ca-app-pub-3940256099942544/6300978111";
30       adView.setAdUnitId( adUnitId );
31
32       // define an ad request
33       AdRequest.Builder adRequestBuilder = new AdRequest.Builder( );
34       // Define target data for the ad request ( optional )
35       adRequestBuilder.setGender( AdRequest.GENDER_UNKNOWN );
36       adRequestBuilder.addKeyword( "fitness" );
37       adRequestBuilder.addKeyword ( "workout" );
38       // request test ( not live ) ads for emulator
39       adRequestBuilder.addTestDevice( AdRequest.DEVICE_ID_EMULATOR );
40       // build the AdRequest
41       AdRequest adRequest = adRequestBuilder.build( );
42
43       // add the AdView to the LinearLayout
44       LinearLayout adLayout = ( LinearLayout ) findViewById( R.id.ad_view );
45       adLayout.addView( adView );
46
```

EXAMPLE 15.13 The `MainActivity` class, Stopwatch app, Version 3 (*Continued*)

```
47        // load the ad into the AdView
48        adView.loadAd( adRequest );
49      }
50
51    public void startStop( View view ) {
52        Button startStopButton = ( Button ) findViewById( R.id.start_stop );
53        if( started ) {
54          chrono.stop( );
55          started = false;
56          startStopButton.setText( "START" );
57          startStopButton.setBackgroundResource( R.drawable.start_button );
58        } else {
59          resetChrono( );
60          chrono.start( );
61          started = true;
62          startStopButton.setText( "STOP" );
63          startStopButton.setBackgroundResource( R.drawable.stop_button );
64        }
65      }
66
67    public void reset( View view ) {
68        if( !started )
69          chrono.setBase( SystemClock.elapsedRealtime( ) );
70      }
71
72    public void resetChrono( ) {
73        String chronoText = chrono.getText( ).toString( );
74        long idleMilliseconds = ClockUtility.milliseconds( chronoText );
75        chrono.setBase( SystemClock.elapsedRealtime( ) - idleMilliseconds );
76      }
77    }
```

EXAMPLE 15.13 The `MainActivity` class, Stopwatch app, Version 3

There are three things to add to the AndroidManifest.xml file, shown in **EXAMPLE 15.14**. A uses-permission element to access the Internet (lines 5–6), a required meta-data element in order to use Google services (lines 15–17), and another activity element as shown at lines 29–32. Note that lines 30 and 31 should be in a single line in the AndroidManifest.xml file.

Figure 15.1, at the beginning of this chapter, shows the Stopwatch app, Version 3, running, including the banner ad at the bottom of the screen. If we are a registered developer and are using our own app unit id, we should not click on the live ad for testing purposes: it is against Google policy to do so. If we want to test the functionality of the banner ad, then we should use test ads, which we can get as follows:

▶ Use the Google provided test ad unit id, or
▶ Request test ads by using AdRequest.Builder.addTestDevice.

```
1   <?xml version="1.0" encoding="utf-8"?>
2   <manifest xmlns:android="http://schemas.android.com/apk/res/android"
3     package="com.jblearning.stopwatchv3" >
4
5     <!-- required permissions for Google Mobile Ads -->
6     <uses-permission android:name="android.permission.INTERNET"/>
7
8     <application
9       android:allowBackup="true"
10      android:icon="@mipmap/ic_launcher"
11      android:label="@string/app_name"
12      android:supportsRtl="true"
13      android:theme="@style/AppTheme" >
14
15      <!--required meta-data tag to use Google Play Services.-->
16      <meta-data android:name="com.google.android.gms.version"
17          android:value="@integer/google_play_services_version" />
18
19      <activity
20        android:name=".MainActivity"
21        android:screenOrientation="portrait" >
22        <intent-filter>
23
24          <action android:name="android.intent.action.MAIN" />
25          <category android:name="android.intent.category.LAUNCHER" />
26        </intent-filter>
27      </activity>
28
29      <activity android:name="com.google.android.gms.ads.AdActivity"
30        android:configChanges="keyboard|keyboardHidden|orientation|
31                  screenLayout|uiMode|screenSize|smallestScreenSize"
32        android:theme="@android:style/Theme.Translucent" />
33
34    </application>
35
36  </manifest>
```

EXAMPLE 15.14 The AndroidManifest.xml file, Stopwatch app, Version 3

In both cases, we can run on the emulator or a device.

> **COMMON ERROR:** Be sure that the View showing the ad is big enough. Either specify the full width of the device and WRAP_CONTENT for its height, or test that ads have enough space and load correctly by testing your app on many devices or emulators.

15.5 Placing the Ad in a Fragment, Stopwatch App, Version 4

Google recommends using a fragment in which to place the AdView. A benefit is that a fragment's XML layout file is reusable in other apps. In Version 4, we place the AdView inside a fragment instead of a LinearLayout. Going from Version 3 to 4 involves the following steps:

▶ Create an XML layout file for the fragment.
▶ Change the last LinearLayout in the activity_main.xml file to a fragment.
▶ Code the fragment class.
▶ Update the MainActivity class.

EXAMPLE 15.15 shows the XML layout file for our fragment. We place the AdView element (lines 7–15) inside a RelativeLayout element (line 2). We give the AdView an id at line 8 so we can retrieve it inside the fragment class using the findViewById method. We specify the size and the ad unit id of the AdView at lines 13–14. At lines 11–12, we center the AdView horizontally and vertically within the RelativeLayout.

```
1   <?xml version="1.0" encoding="utf-8"?>
2   <RelativeLayout xmlns:android="http://schemas.android.com/apk/res/android"
3       xmlns:ads="http://schemas.android.com/apk/res-auto"
4       android:layout_width="match_parent"
5       android:layout_height="match_parent" >
6
7   <com.google.android.gms.ads.AdView
8       android:id="@+id/ad_view"
9       android:layout_width="match_parent"
10      android:layout_height="wrap_content"
11      android:layout_centerHorizontal="true"
12      android:layout_centerVertical="true"
13      ads:adSize="SMART_BANNER"
14      ads:adUnitId="@string/banner_ad_unit_id">
15  </com.google.android.gms.ads.AdView>
16
17  </RelativeLayout>
```

EXAMPLE 15.15 **The fragment_ad.xml file, Stopwatch app, Version 4**

EXAMPLE 15.16 shows the updated activity_main.xml file: we have replaced the last LinearLayout element with a fragment element (lines 59–64). We give it an id at line 60 and specify that it is an instance of the AdFragment class at line 61. Although we are not using its id in this app, the app will crash at runtime if we do not give a fragment either an id or a tag.

```
1    <?xml version="1.0" encoding="utf-8"?>
2    <LinearLayout xmlns:android="http://schemas.android.com/apk/res/android"
3        xmlns:tools="http://schemas.android.com/tools"
4        android:layout_width="match_parent"
5        android:layout_height="match_parent"
6        android:paddingBottom="@dimen/activity_vertical_margin"
7        android:paddingTop="@dimen/activity_vertical_margin"
8        android:orientation="vertical"
9        tools:context="com.jblearning.stopwatchv4.MainActivity">
10
11       <Chronometer
12           android:layout_weight="4"
13           android:layout_width="match_parent"
14           android:layout_height="0dp"
15           android:id="@+id/stop_watch"
16           style="@style/textViewStyle" />
17
18       <LinearLayout
19           android:orientation="horizontal"
20           android:layout_weight="4"
21           android:layout_width="match_parent"
22           android:layout_height="0dp"
23           android:gravity="center" >
24
25           <LinearLayout
26               android:orientation="vertical"
27               android:layout_width="0dp"
28               android:layout_weight="1"
29               android:layout_height="match_parent"
30               android:gravity="center" >
31               <Button
32                   android:id="@+id/start_stop"
33                   android:layout_width="150dp"
34                   android:layout_height="150dp"
35                   android:text="START"
36                   android:textSize="36sp"
37                   android:background="@drawable/start_button"
38                   android:onClick="startStop" />
39           </LinearLayout>
40
41           <LinearLayout
42               android:orientation="vertical"
43               android:layout_width="0dp"
44               android:layout_weight="1"
45               android:layout_height="match_parent"
46               android:gravity="center" >
47               <Button
```

EXAMPLE 15.16 The activity_main.xml file, Stopwatch app, Version 4 (*Continued*)

```
48                          android:id="@+id/reset"
49                          android:layout_height="150dp"
50                          android:layout_width="150dp"
51                          android:text="RESET"
52                          android:textSize="36sp"
53                          android:background="@drawable/reset_button"
54                          android:onClick="reset" />
55                  </LinearLayout>
56
57          </LinearLayout>
58
59          <fragment
60              android:id="@+id/fragment_ad"
61              android:name="com.jblearning.stopwatchv4.AdFragment"
62              android:layout_width="match_parent"
63              android:layout_height="wrap_content"
64              android:layout_weight="1" />
65
66      </LinearLayout>
```

EXAMPLE 15.16 The activity_main.xml file, Stopwatch app, Version 4

EXAMPLE 15.17 shows our fragment class, which we name AdFragment. Inside the onCreateView method, we inflate the fragment_ad.xml file at line 15. Inside the onActivityCreated method, we retrieve the AdView specified in the fragment using its id (lines 21–22), we build an AdRequest (lines 23–31), and load it into the AdView (line 32–33).

```
1    package com.jblearning.stopwatchv4;
2
3    import com.google.android.gms.ads.AdRequest;
4    import com.google.android.gms.ads.AdView;
5    import android.app.Fragment;
6    import android.os.Bundle;
7    import android.view.LayoutInflater;
8    import android.view.View;
9    import android.view.ViewGroup;
10
11   public class AdFragment extends Fragment {
12     @Override
13     public View onCreateView( LayoutInflater inflater, ViewGroup container,
14                               Bundle savedInstanceState ) {
15       return inflater.inflate( R.layout.fragment_ad, container, false );
16     }
17
```

EXAMPLE 15.17 The AdFragment class, Stopwatch app, Version 4 (*Continued*)

```
18        @Override
19        public void onActivityCreated( Bundle bundle ) {
20          super.onActivityCreated( bundle  );
21          // retrieve the AdView
22          AdView adView = ( AdView ) getView( ).findViewById( R.id.ad_view );
23          // build the ad request
24          AdRequest.Builder adRequestBuilder = new AdRequest.Builder( );
25          // Define target data for the ad request ( optional )
26          adRequestBuilder.setGender( AdRequest.GENDER_UNKNOWN );
27          adRequestBuilder.addKeyword( "fitness" );
28          adRequestBuilder.addKeyword ( "workout" );
29          // request test ( not live ) ads for emulator
30          adRequestBuilder.addTestDevice( AdRequest.DEVICE_ID_EMULATOR );
31          AdRequest adRequest = adRequestBuilder.build( );
32          // load the ad
33          adView.loadAd( adRequest );
34        }
35      }
```

EXAMPLE 15.17 The `AdFragment` class, Stopwatch app, Version 4

Since all banner ad–related code is in the `AdFragment` class, the `MainActivity` class is the same as the one in Version 2.

> **COMMON ERROR:** Be careful to use test ads and not live ads when testing your app. Clicking on a live ad while testing an app on a device is against Google's policy. When we are ready to publish our app, we should comment out the code that specifies the emulator or a specific device id to test the app.

15.6 Managing the Life Cycle of the AdView, Stopwatch App, Version 5

The `AdView` class includes life-cycle methods, shown in **TABLE 15.7**, so that we can avoid unnecessary processing when the app goes to the background or is exited. Inside the fragment class, the `onPause`, `onResume`, and `onDestroy` life-cycle methods are automatically called as the parent's activity goes into the background, the foreground, or is exited. Thus, we can call the `AdView` life-cycle methods from the fragment's life-cycle methods.

EXAMPLE 15.18 shows the updated `AdFragment` class of our app, Version 5. All the other classes and files remain identical. Because we need to access the `AdView` from onPause (lines 38–42), onResume (lines 44–48), and onDestroy (lines 50–54), we make the `AdView` an instance variable

TABLE 15.7 The life-cycle methods of the `AdView` class	
Method	**Description**
public void pause( )	Pauses any extra processing associated with this AdView.
public void resume( )	Resumes processing associated with this AdView following a call to pause.
public void destroy( )	Destroys this AdView.

```
1   package com.jblearning.stopwatchv5;
2
3   import android.app.Fragment;
4   import android.os.Bundle;
5   import android.view.LayoutInflater;
6   import android.view.View;
7   import android.view.ViewGroup;
8   import com.google.android.gms.ads.AdRequest;
9   import com.google.android.gms.ads.AdView;
10
11  public class AdFragment extends Fragment {
12    private AdView adView;
13
14    @Override
15    public View onCreateView( LayoutInflater inflater, ViewGroup container,
16                              Bundle savedInstanceState ) {
17      return inflater.inflate( R.layout.fragment_ad, container, false );
18    }
19
20    @Override
21    public void onActivityCreated( Bundle bundle ) {
22      super.onActivityCreated( bundle  );
23      // retrieve the AdView
24      adView = ( AdView ) getView( ).findViewById( R.id.ad_view );
25      // build the ad request
26      AdRequest.Builder adRequestBuilder = new AdRequest.Builder( );
27      // Define target data for the ad request ( optional )
28      adRequestBuilder.setGender( AdRequest.GENDER_UNKNOWN );
29      adRequestBuilder.addKeyword( "fitness" );
30      adRequestBuilder.addKeyword ( "workout" );
31      // request test ( not live ) ads for emulator
32      adRequestBuilder.addTestDevice( AdRequest.DEVICE_ID_EMULATOR );
33      AdRequest adRequest = adRequestBuilder.build( );
```

EXAMPLE 15.18 The `AdFragment` class, Stopwatch app, Version 5 (*Continued*)

```
34      // load the ad
35      adView.loadAd( adRequest );
36    }
37
38    public void onPause( ) {
39      if( adView != null )
40        adView.pause( );
41      super.onPause( );
42    }
43
44    public void onResume( ) {
45      super.onResume( );
46      if( adView != null )
47        adView.resume( );
48    }
49
50    public void onDestroy( ) {
51      if( adView != null )
52        adView.destroy( );
53      super.onDestroy( );
54    }
55  }
```

EXAMPLE 15.18 **The `AdFragment` class, Stopwatch app, Version 5**

(line 12) so that we can have a direct reference to it. Inside the three methods, we pause, resume, or destroy the `AdView` and call the `super` method. Note that inside `onPause` and `onDestroy`, we first `pause` or `destroy` the `AdView` before calling the `super` method: we want to pause the processing of the `AdView` or destroy the `AdView` inside the fragment before pausing or destroying the fragment itself. Inside `onResume`, we call the `super` method before calling `resume` with the instance variable `adView`: we want to resume the processing of the fragment before resuming the processing of the `AdView`, which is inside the fragment.

Note that the `AdFragment` is not reusable as is because the gender and the keywords of this ad request are specific to this app. We could make the ad request builder an instance variable and provide methods inside `AdFragment` to set these parameters. This is left as an exercise.

Chapter Summary

- The `Chronometer` class encapsulates a stopwatch.
- `elapsedRealtime`, a `static` method of the `SystemClock` class, returns, in milliseconds, the amount of time since the last boot, including sleep time.
- The `com.google.android.gms.ads` package provides a set of classes to display an ad and manage the ad.

- The `com.google.android.gms.ads` package is part of Google Play services. In order to use it, we need to edit the build.gradle file accordingly.
- The `AdView` class, which inherits from `View`, encapsulates a `View` that can display an ad banner.
- The `AdSize` class encapsulates the size of a banner ad. It includes constants for various industry standard banner sizes.
- The `AdRequest.Builder` class provides methods to define data, such as gender, location, and keywords, that enable an ad to target a certain type of demographic.
- The `build` method of the `AdRequest.Builder` class returns an `AdRequest` reference.
- We can use the following ad unit id for testing purposes:
  `ca-app-pub-3940256099942544/6300978111`
- We must set the size and ad unit id of an `AdView` before the `AdView` calls the `loadAd` method to load an ad.
- We can use a fragment for the banner ad, per Google's recommendations.
- Including a Google ad requires three additions to the AndroidManifest.xml file:
  - The `INTERNET` permission is required since the Internet is used in any app that displays a Google ad.
  - A `meta-data` element showing use of Google play services is also required.
  - An additional `activity` element for `AdActivity` is required.

Exercises, Problems, and Projects

Multiple-Choice Exercises

1. The com.google.android.gms.ads package is part of Google Play services
   - True
   - False

2. What class is not in the com.google.android.gms.ads package?
   - AdView
   - AdBuilder
   - AdSize
   - AdRequest

3. The Builder class is an inner static class of which class?
   - AdView
   - AdRequest
   - AdSize
   - AdListener

4. What method can we use to be sure that we only receive test ads and not live ads during testing?
   - addTest
   - addDevice
   - addTestDevice
   - addEmulator

5. If we are not an Android developer and therefore cannot obtain an ad unit id from Google, we cannot test an app that includes banner ads.
   - True
   - False: we could use a default ad unit id provided by Google

6. What method is not one of the methods that can specify the target demographics of an ad request?
   - setLocation
   - setBirthday
   - setGender
   - setKeyword

7. What Exception is thrown by the loadAd method when the size or the ad unit id of the AdView has not been set?
   - IOException
   - IllegalStateException
   - LoadException
   - AdViewException

8. What element is not one that we need to include in the AndroidManifest.xml file for an app that uses banner ads?
   - activity
   - uses-permission
   - meta-data
   - uses-storage

Fill in the Code

9. Inside an Activity class, create an AdView and set its size so that it meets the IAB leaderboard ad size (you need to look at the AdSize class for that).

10. Inside an Activity class, create an AdView and set its ad unit id to the default String provided by Google for testing purposes.

11. Create a simple AdRequest so that we use test ads and not live ads.

12. Create an AdRequest for men, using the two keywords `game` and `video`.

13. Create an AdRequest for women, using a birthday of 1/1/2000.

14. Create an AdRequest, considering that we will test the app in the emulator, and we only want test ads, not live ads.

15. Assuming the AdView myAdView has been created, its size and ad unit id have been set, and the AdRequest myRequest has been built, load the ad into myAdView.

16. Inside the AndroidManifest.xml, code the permission-related element for an app that includes banner ads.

17. Inside the AndroidManifest.xml, code the extra activity element for an app that includes banner ads.

18. Inside the AndroidManifest.xml, code the metadata-related element for an app that includes banner ads.

Write an App

19. Make a simple flashlight app with a banner ad at the bottom. The flashlight is a yellow View taking the whole screen except the banner ad.

20. Make a flashlight app with a banner ad at the top. The flashlight is a yellow View taking the whole screen except the banner ad and a SeekBar. The yellow View is dimmable, which you should implement with the SeekBar. Include a Model.

21. Make an app of your choice (it should have some functionality) with a banner ad whose display is triggered by an event, for example the user clicking on a button.

22. Make an app of your choice (it should have some functionality) with a banner ad that shows 50% of the time the user runs the app.

23. Make an app of your choice (it should have some functionality) with a banner ad. The app should include some form of user input (either an EditText, or some list to pick from). You need to use the user input as a keyword for the ad request.

24. Modify the Stopwatch app, Version 5, making the AdFragment class fully reusable (i.e., it should not set specific gender and keywords). Limit the customization of the ad to gender and keywords.

CHAPTER **SIXTEEN**

Security and Encryption

CHAPTER CONTENTS

Introduction

Security is a very important concern for every user of a computer in general, and a mobile device in particular. Valuable data, such as credit card numbers, can be stolen if not properly protected. One way to protect data is to encrypt it. As technology evolves and computers get more and more powerful, encryption algorithms that were once thought to be robust and safe may become weaker. When choosing an encryption algorithm, it is wise to check that it is still safe at the time we use it. In this chapter, we learn about various encryption algorithms and how we can use them to encrypt data.

16.1 Symmetric and Asymmetric Encryption

Encryption typically involves using a particular algorithm and a key in order to encrypt a message. A key is usually a string of characters. In cryptography, in order to test the strength of an encryption algorithm, we typically assume that the algorithm is known and assess the difficulty of finding its associated key. Thus, in addition to understanding how an encryption algorithm works, it is also important to understand how to generate a key for that algorithm.

An encryption system can be one way or two ways. One way means that once we have encrypted something, it is not possible to decrypt it. A one-way encryption system can be used to encrypt passwords. Usernames and encrypted passwords are typically stored in a database located on a server. Users connect to that server from a remote location and log in. The plaintext passwords are only known by the individual users and never stored on the server. Because the encryption process takes place on the server side and not on the client side, we do not cover one-way encryption in this chapter.

A two-way encryption system can be either symmetric or asymmetric. **Symmetric encryption** means that the key used to encrypt the plain message is the same as the key used to decrypt the encrypted message: there is only one key. That means that both the sender and the recipient of the message need to have that key. That, in turn, means that at least one person must have given the key to the other person. Since that key is secret, a challenge is to distribute that key in a secure manner, so that nobody else has access to it. If more than two people are involved, the challenge is even greater. People can decide to use a different key every time they send a message, in order to decrease the risk of having the key stolen by a third party. As always, there is a trade-off between practicality and security.

Asymmetric encryption means that the key used to encrypt the plain message is different from the key used to decrypt the encrypted message: there are two keys. One such system is **RSA**, which stands for **Rivest, Shamir, and Adleman**, its three inventors. In the RSA system, every person has a set of two keys, a public one (published) and a private one (secret). For example, if Alice and Bob are two users of the system, Alice can send a message to Bob, encrypting the message using the public key of Bob as follows:

```
encryptedMessage1 = rsa( publicKeyBob, message1 )
```

Alice knows Bob's public key because it is public and published. Because that message has been encrypted using Bob's public key, it can only be decrypted using Bob's private key. Since Bob's private key is private and secret, only Bob knows it. Thus, only Bob can decrypt that message. Bob decrypts the message as follows:

```
decryptedMessage1 = rsa( privateKeyBob, encryptedMessage1 )
```

Bob can reply to Alice, encrypting a message using Alice's public key as follows:

```
encryptedMessage2 = rsa( publicKeyAlice, message2 )
```

Bob knows Alice's public key because it is public and published. Because that message has been encrypted using Alice's public key, it can only be decrypted using Alice's private key. Since Alice's private key is private and secret, only Alice knows it. Thus, only Alice can decrypt that message. Alice decrypts the message as follows:

```
decryptedMessage2 = rsa( privateKeyAlice, encryptedMessage2 )
```

RSA relies on the fact that finding the factors of a very large composite number is very hard. A composite number is the product of two prime numbers. For example, 143, which is equal to 13 times 11, is a composite number. The underlying mathematical foundations of RSA include group theory and modular algebra.

16.2 Symmetric Encryption: The Model (AES), Encryption App, Version 0

In Version 0, we explore symmetric encryption via a simple app. We also look into the issue of key distribution. We build a Model for encrypting and decrypting text using symmetric encryption and test it. There are many symmetric encryption algorithms available in the Android library. We use **Advanced Encryption Standard** (**AES**). We can access the list of encryption algorithms available on a device via the `Security` class by calling its `getProviders` method, and then iterating through all the providers. This is beyond the scope of this chapter.

The `javax.crypto` package contains classes and interfaces that encapsulate cryptology concepts, such as `Cipher`, `KeyGenerator`, and `SecretKey`. The `Cipher` class provides access to implementations of encryption and decryption algorithms. All of its methods are `final` (i.e., we cannot override them). TABLE 16.1 shows some selected methods of the `Cipher` class. `Cipher` does not have a `public` constructor. We use its `getInstance` static method to get a reference to a `Cipher` object. The parameter of the `getInstance` method is a `String` representing the name of the encryption algorithm, for example, `AES`. The `doFinal` method encrypts or decrypts an array of bytes into another array of bytes. Before calling `doFinal`, we should call the `init` method in order to specify three things:

▶ Whether `doFinal` is going to encrypt or decrypt (the operation mode).
▶ The encryption/decryption key.
▶ An element of randomness.

TABLE 16.1 Selected methods of the `Cipher` class

Method	Description
public static Cipher getInstance(String transformation)	Returns a Cipher for transformation, the name of an encryption algorithm. Throws a NoSuchAlgorithmException and a NoSuchPaddingException.
public byte [ ] doFinal(byte [ ] input)	Encrypts input and other previously buffered bytes, and returns the resulting encrypted bytes. Throws an IllegalBlockSizeException, a BadPaddingException, and an IllegalStateException.
public void init(int opMode, Key key, SecureRandom random)	Initializes this Cipher with the operation opMode, key and with random as a randomness source. Throws an InvalidKeyException and an IllegalParameterException.

TABLE 16.2 Selected constructor of the `SecureRandom` class

Method	Description
public SecureRandom( )	Constructs a SecureRandom object using the default algorithm. We can use it to generate pseudo-random numbers.

TABLE 16.3 Selected methods of the `KeyGenerator` class

Method	Description
public static KeyGenerator getInstance(String algorithm)	Returns a KeyGenerator that can generate a key for an encryption algorithm named algorithm. Throws a NoSuchAlgorithmException and a NullPointerException.
public void init(int keySize)	Initializes this KeyGenerator for a key whose size is keySize bits.
public SecretKey generateKey( )	Returns a SecretKey reference for this KeyGenerator.

We can use the ENCRYPT_MODE and DECRYPT_MODE constants of the Cipher class to specify the mode, encryption or decryption. Key is an interface so it cannot be instantiated. The Secret-Key class implements the Key interface and encapsulates a secret key for a symmetric encryption algorithm. Thus, we can use it for the second parameter of init.

The third parameter's type is SecureRandom. The SecureRandom class encapsulates the ability to generate cryptographically secure pseudo-random numbers. We can instantiate a SecureRandom object using the default constructor of the SecureRandom class, a subclass of Random, shown in TABLE 16.2. We can use the KeyGenerator class, shown in TABLE 16.3, to create a SecretKey.

KeyGenerator does not have a `public` constructor. We use the `getInstance static` method to get a reference to a KeyGenerator object. The parameter of the `getInstance` method is a `String` representing the name of the encryption algorithm, for example, AES. The `generateKey` method returns a secret key of type `SecretKey`. Before calling `generateKey`, we should call the `init` method in order to specify the size of the key in bits.

We first write a class, part of our Model, to encapsulate the ability to encrypt and decrypt a `String` using the AES algorithm. **EXAMPLE 16.1** shows the `AESEncryption` class. We can use it to generate a secret key and also to perform encryption and decryption using any key. It has a default constructor, two accessors for the `secretKey` instance variable, and the `crypt` method, which we can use to encrypt or decrypt a `String`. We need a `SecretKey`, a `Cipher`, and a `SecureRandom` reference in order to encrypt or decrypt a `String`. Thus, we declare three instance variables (`secretKey`, `cipher`, and `rand`) of these types (lines 11–13) so we can access them in the `crypt` method. Inside the constructor (lines 15–24), we instantiate `cipher` at line 17 and `rand` at line 18. We instantiate a `KeyGenerator` object for the AES algorithm at line 19, initialize it with a key size of 256 bits at line 20, and instantiate `secretKey` with it at line 21. We catch either a `NoSuchAlgorithmException` or a `NoSuchPaddingException` at line 22.

```
 1    package com.jblearning.encryptionv0;
 2
 3    import java.security.GeneralSecurityException;
 4    import java.security.SecureRandom;
 5    import javax.crypto.Cipher;
 6    import javax.crypto.KeyGenerator;
 7    import javax.crypto.SecretKey;
 8
 9    public class AESEncryption {
10      public static String ALGORITHM = "AES";
11      private SecretKey secretKey;
12      private Cipher cipher;
13      private SecureRandom rand;
14
15      public AESEncryption( ) {
16        try {
17          cipher = Cipher.getInstance( ALGORITHM );
18          rand = new SecureRandom( );
19          KeyGenerator keyGen = KeyGenerator.getInstance( ALGORITHM );
20          keyGen.init( 256 );
21          secretKey = keyGen.generateKey( );
22        } catch ( GeneralSecurityException gse ) {
23        }
24      }
25
```

EXAMPLE 16.1 The `AESEncryption` **class of the Encryption app, Version 0 (*Continued*)**

```
26      public String crypt( int opMode, String message, SecretKey key ) {
27        try {
28          cipher.init( opMode, key, rand );
29          byte [ ] messageBytes = message.getBytes( "ISO-8859-1" );
30          byte [ ] encodedBytes = cipher.doFinal( messageBytes );
31          String encoded = new String( encodedBytes, "ISO-8859-1" );
32          return encoded;
33        } catch( Exception e ) {
34          return null;
35        }
36      }
37
38      public SecretKey getKey( ) {
39        return secretKey;
40      }
41
42      public byte [ ] getKeyBytes( ) {
43        return secretKey.getEncoded( );
44      }
45    }
```

EXAMPLE 16.1 The `AESEncryption` class of the Encryption app, Version 0

We provide two accessors for the key of the algorithm, secretKey. The first one, getSecret-Key, (lines 38–40), returns secretKey. The second one, getKeyBytes (lines 42–44), returns a representation of secretKey as an array of bytes. Generally, we need to distribute a key to remote users. If we want to distribute a key electronically, we can send an array of bytes to a user via a secure connection, using the getKeyBytes method to get a byte array representation of the key. We can also encrypt a key when we send it. Inside getKeyBytes, we call the getEncoded method of SecretKey, inherited from the Key interface, and shown in **TABLE 16.4**.

We can use the crypt method (lines 26–36) to either encrypt or decrypt a String using a given key. Its first parameter specifies whether we encrypt or decrypt. If we want to encrypt, we pass Cipher.ENCRYPT_MODE as the first argument. If we want to decrypt, we pass Cipher.DECRYPT_MODE. The third parameter represents an encryption key. In this example, we pass the key of this AESEncryption object. We initialize cipher using the mode specified by opMode with the key parameter key and rand (line 28). The doFinal method accepts an array

TABLE 16.4 The `getEncoded` method of the `Key` interface

Method	Description
byte [ ] getEncoded( )	Returns the encoded form of this Key as an array of bytes.

of bytes parameter, so we convert the `String` parameter into an array of bytes at line 29. We use the `ISO-8859-1` encoding standard to convert the array of bytes to a `String`: `ISO-8859-1` is the default encoding standard for transmitting documents via the HTTP protocol with the MIME type; it provides a one-to-one mapping between a `String` and an array of bytes. At line 30, we call `doFinal` to crypt that array of bytes into another array of bytes, and convert that array of bytes to a `String` at line 31. We return that `String` at line 32. We catch all possible `Exceptions` at line 33 and return `null` at line 34 if an `Exception` occurs.

In the `MainActivity` class, shown in **EXAMPLE 16.2**, we use the `AESEncryption` class to encrypt a `String` and decrypt its encrypted version into the original `String`. We also test that we can convert a key to an array of bytes, reconstruct a key from that array of bytes, and that the reconstructed key matches the original key. That is the type of operation that happens when we

```
1   package com.jblearning.encryptionv0;
2
3   import android.os.Bundle;
4   import android.support.v7.app.AppCompatActivity;
5   import android.util.Log;
6   import java.util.Arrays;
7   import javax.crypto.Cipher;
8   import javax.crypto.SecretKey;
9   import javax.crypto.spec.SecretKeySpec;
10
11  public class MainActivity extends AppCompatActivity {
12    public static final String MA = "MainActivity";
13    private AESEncryption aes;
14
15    @Override
16    protected void onCreate( Bundle savedInstanceState ) {
17      super.onCreate( savedInstanceState );
18      setContentView( R.layout.activity_main );
19
20      aes = new AESEncryption( );
21
22      // testing encryption and decryption
23      String original = "Encryption is fun";
24      Log.w( MA, "original: " + original );
25      String encrypted =
26        aes.crypt( Cipher.ENCRYPT_MODE, original, aes.getKey( ) );
27      Log.w( MA, "encrypted: " + encrypted );
28      String decrypted =
29        aes.crypt( Cipher.DECRYPT_MODE, encrypted, aes.getKey( ) );
30      Log.w( MA, "decrypted: " + decrypted );
```

EXAMPLE 16.2 The `MainActivity` class of the Encryption app, Version 0 (*Continued*)

```
31
32        // testing key distribution
33        byte [ ] keyBytes = aes.getKeyBytes( );
34        // distribute keyBytes to a user
35        String keyString = Arrays.toString( keyBytes );
36        Log.w( MA, "original key: " + keyBytes + ": " + keyString );
37
38        // having received keyBytes, reconstruct the key
39        SecretKey reconstructedKey = new SecretKeySpec( keyBytes, "AES" );
40        // check that the reconstructed key is the same as the original key
41        byte [ ] bytesFromReconstructedKey = reconstructedKey.getEncoded( );
42        String stringFromReconstructedKey =
43          Arrays.toString( bytesFromReconstructedKey );
44        Log.w( MA, "reconstructed key: "
45             + bytesFromReconstructedKey + ": " + stringFromReconstructedKey );
46    }
47 }
```

EXAMPLE 16.2 The `MainActivity` class of the Encryption app, Version 0

distribute a key electronically. At line 20, we instantiate aes, an AESEncryption instance variable. We encrypt the String original at lines 25–26 and output the encrypted String to Logcat the result at line 27. We decrypt the encrypted String at lines 28–29 and output the result to Logcat at line 30, which, as **FIGURE 16.1** shows, is identical to the String we started with.

At lines 32–45, we simulate distributing a key and check that the key received matches the key sent. We start with the key of aes and convert it to an array of bytes at lines 32–33. At lines 34–36, we output the array of bytes as an object and a String equivalent of that array of bytes. We then assume that that array of bytes is sent to a user and reconstruct a key with it at lines 38–39. We retrieve the equivalent array of bytes for that reconstructed key at lines 40–41. Finally, at lines 42–45, we output the array of bytes as an object and a String equivalent of that array of bytes.

```
original: Encryption is fun
encrypted: ±ÈÃ1Pb}°mn×°_Ô7zý;Gµ9,-åZ
decrypted: Encryption is fun
original key: [B@1edb46d: [-21, -86, -2, 7, -121, 112, 118, 76, 42, -66, -31,
15, -95, 99, 72, -33, -60, -13, 101, 87, -31, -79, 41, 3, -89, -71, 75, -79,
16, 88, 66, 88]
reconstructed key: [B@87d38a2: [-21, -86, -2, 7, -121, 112, 118, 76, 42, -66,
-31, 15, -95, 99, 72, -33, -60, -13, 101, 87, -31, -79, 41, 3, -89, -71, 75,
-79, 16, 88, 66, 88]
```

FIGURE 16.1 Logcat output from the Encryption app, Version 0

Figure 16.1 shows the output in Logcat. We can see two things: the memory addresses for both arrays of bytes are different, and their values are identical. Thus, this example shows that we can transfer a key from one user to another by transferring bytes.

16.3 Symmetric Encryption: Adding a View, Encryption App, Version 1

In Version 1, we add a user interface to enable the user to enter a `String`. We provide a button to encrypt that `String` and decrypt the encrypted String, thus, retrieving the original `String`.

EXAMPLE 16.3 shows the activity_main.xml file. We use a `RelativeLayout` to organize the various elements. We also make references to styles and strings defined in the styles.xml and

```
1   <?xml version="1.0" encoding="utf-8"?>
2   <RelativeLayout
3       xmlns:android="http://schemas.android.com/apk/res/android"
4       xmlns:tools="http://schemas.android.com/tools"
5       android:layout_width="match_parent"
6       android:layout_height="match_parent"
7       android:paddingBottom="@dimen/activity_vertical_margin"
8       android:paddingLeft="@dimen/activity_horizontal_margin"
9       android:paddingRight="@dimen/activity_horizontal_margin"
10      android:paddingTop="@dimen/activity_vertical_margin"
11      tools:context="com.jblearning.encryptionv1.MainActivity">
12
13      <TextView
14          android:id="@+id/label_original"
15          style="@style/LabelStyle"
16          android:layout_marginTop="50dp"
17          android:minWidth="120dp"
18          android:text="@string/label_original" />
19
20      <EditText
21          android:id="@+id/string_original"
22          style="@style/InputStyle"
23          android:layout_toRightOf="@+id/label_original"
24          android:layout_alignBottom="@+id/label_original"
25          android:layout_alignParentRight="true"
26          android:hint="@string/hint_original" />
27
28      <TextView
29          android:id="@+id/label_encrypted"
30          style="@style/LabelStyle"
31          android:layout_marginTop="30dp"
```

EXAMPLE 16.3 The activity_main.xml file of the Encryption app, Version 1 (*Continued*)

```
32          android:layout_below="@+id/label_original"
33          android:layout_alignLeft="@+id/label_original"
34          android:layout_alignRight="@+id/label_original"
35          android:text="@string/label_encrypted" />
36
37      <TextView
38          android:id="@+id/string_encrypted"
39          style="@style/CenteredTextStyle"
40          android:layout_toRightOf="@+id/label_encrypted"
41          android:layout_alignBottom="@+id/label_encrypted"
42          android:layout_alignRight="@id/string_original" />
43
44      <TextView
45          android:id="@+id/label_decrypted"
46          style="@style/LabelStyle"
47          android:layout_marginTop="30dp"
48          android:layout_below="@id/label_encrypted"
49          android:layout_alignLeft="@+id/label_original"
50          android:layout_alignRight="@+id/label_original"
51          android:text="@string/label_decrypted" />
52
53      <TextView
54          android:id="@+id/string_decrypted"
55          style="@style/CenteredTextStyle"
56          android:layout_toRightOf="@+id/label_decrypted"
57          android:layout_alignBottom="@+id/label_decrypted"
58          android:layout_alignRight="@id/string_original" />
59
60      <Button
61          style="@style/ButtonStyle"
62          android:layout_marginTop="30dp"
63          android:layout_centerHorizontal="true"
64          android:layout_below="@+id/string_decrypted"
65          android:text="@string/button_aes"
66          android:onClick="encryptAndDecryptAES" />
67
68  </RelativeLayout>
```

EXAMPLE 16.3 The activity_main.xml file of the Encryption app, Version 1

strings.xml files. The styles.xml file uses colors that we have defined in the colors.xml file. **EXAMPLES 16.4**, **16.5**, and **16.6** show those three files. The activity_main.xml file includes three TextViews on the left that we use as labels for the EditText (lines 20–26) and the two TextViews on the right (lines 37–42 and 53–58). We give ids to these three elements (lines 21, 38, 54) so we can retrieve them using the findViewById method in the MainActivity class. When the user enters something in the EditText and clicks on the button (lines 60–66), the encryptAndDecryptAES method executes (line 66). We update the two TextViews on the right accordingly, showing the encrypted String and the result of decrypting the encrypted String.

```
1   <resources>
2     <string name="app_name">EncryptionV1</string>
3     <string name="label_original">Original</string>
4     <string name="hint_original">Type a String to encode</string>
5     <string name="label_encrypted">Encrypted</string>
6     <string name="label_decrypted">Decrypted</string>
7     <string name="button_aes">AES</string>
8   </resources>
```

EXAMPLE 16.4 The strings.xml file of the Encryption app, Version 1

```
1    <?xml version="1.0" encoding="utf-8"?>
2    <resources>
3      <color name="colorPrimary">#3F51B5</color>
4      <color name="colorPrimaryDark">#303F9F</color>
5      <color name="colorAccent">#FF4081</color>
6
7      <color name="lightGray">#DDDDDDDD</color>
8      <color name="lightGreen">#40F0</color>
9      <color name="darkBlue">#F00F</color>
10   </resources>
```

EXAMPLE 16.5 The colors.xml file of the Encryption app, Version 1

```
1    <resources>
2
3      <!-- Base application theme. -->
4      <style name="AppTheme" parent="Theme.AppCompat.Light.DarkActionBar">
5        <!-- Customize your theme here. -->
6        <item name="colorPrimary">@color/colorPrimary</item>
7        <item name="colorPrimaryDark">@color/colorPrimaryDark</item>
8        <item name="colorAccent">@color/colorAccent</item>
9      </style>
10
11     <style name="TextStyle" parent="@android:style/TextAppearance">
12       <item name="android:layout_width">wrap_content</item>
13       <item name="android:layout_height">wrap_content</item>
14       <item name="android:textSize">22sp</item>
15       <item name="android:padding">5dp</item>
16     </style>
17
18     <style name="LabelStyle" parent="TextStyle">
19       <item name="android:background">@color/lightGray</item>
20     </style>
```

EXAMPLE 16.6 The styles.xml file of the Encryption app, Version 1 (*Continued*)

```
21
22      <style name="CenteredTextStyle" parent="TextStyle">
23        <item name="android:gravity">center</item>
24      </style>
25
26      <style name="InputStyle" parent="CenteredTextStyle">
27        <item name="android:textColor">@color/darkBlue</item>
28      </style>
29
30      <style name="ButtonStyle" parent="TextStyle">
31        <item name="android:background">@color/lightGreen</item>
32      </style>
33
34    </resources>
```

EXAMPLE 16.6 **The styles.xml file of the Encryption app, Version 1**

EXAMPLE 16.7 shows the MainActivity class. Inside the encryptAndDecryptAES method (lines 21–34), we retrieve user input and update the two TextViews on the right side of the screen. We get references to the EditText and the two TextViews at lines 22, 26–27, and 29–30. At line 23, we retrieve the user input. At lines 24–25, we encrypt it. We place the result in the TextView in the middle right of the screen at line 28. We decrypt the encrypted String at lines 31–32 and place the result in the other TextView at line 33.

```
1     package com.jblearning.encryptionv1;
2
3     import android.os.Bundle;
4     import android.support.v7.app.AppCompatActivity;
5     import android.view.View;
6     import android.widget.EditText;
7     import android.widget.TextView;
8
9     import javax.crypto.Cipher;
10
11    public class MainActivity extends AppCompatActivity {
12      private AESEncryption aes;
13
14      @Override
15      protected void onCreate( Bundle savedInstanceState ) {
16        super.onCreate( savedInstanceState );
17        aes = new AESEncryption( );
18        setContentView( R.layout.activity_main );
19      }
20
```

EXAMPLE 16.7 **The MainActivity class of the Encryption app, Version 1 (*Continued*)**

```
21      public void encryptAndDecryptAES( View v ) {
22        EditText et = ( EditText ) findViewById( R.id.string_original );
23        String original = et.getText( ).toString( );
24        String encrypted =
25            aes.crypt( Cipher.ENCRYPT_MODE, original, aes.getKey( ) );
26        TextView tvEncrypted =
27            ( TextView ) findViewById( R.id.string_encrypted );
28        tvEncrypted.setText( encrypted );
29        TextView tvDecrypted =
30            ( TextView ) findViewById( R.id.string_decrypted );
31        String decrypted =
32            aes.crypt( Cipher.DECRYPT_MODE, encrypted, aes.getKey( ) );
33        tvDecrypted.setText( decrypted );
34      }
35    }
```

EXAMPLE 16.7 **The** `MainActivity` **class of the Encryption app, Version 1**

FIGURE 16.2 shows the app running inside the emulator after the user typed in `Android is fun` and clicked on the button.

FIGURE 16.2 **The Encryption app, Version 1, running inside the emulator**

16.4 Asymmetric Encryption: Adding RSA to the Model, Encryption App, Version 2

In Version 2, we add RSA encryption to our Model and test it in the `MainActivity` class. We can use the `RSAEncryption` class, shown in **EXAMPLE 16.8**, to generate a set of private and public keys, and also to perform encryption and decryption using any key. This design is similar to the `AESEncryption` class. We declare three instance variables at lines 11–13: `cipher`, a `Cipher` reference, and the two keys—`privateKey` and `publicKey`. The constructor, at lines 15–25, instantiates `cipher` at lines 17 and generates the two keys at lines 18–22.

```
1   package com.jblearning.encryptionv2;
2
3   import java.security.GeneralSecurityException;
4   import java.security.Key;
5   import java.security.KeyPair;
6   import java.security.KeyPairGenerator;
7   import javax.crypto.Cipher;
8
9   public class RSAEncryption {
10     public static String ALGORITHM = "RSA";
11     private Cipher cipher;
12     private Key privateKey;
13     private Key publicKey;
14
15     public RSAEncryption( ) {
16       try {
17         cipher = Cipher.getInstance( ALGORITHM );
18         KeyPairGenerator generator = KeyPairGenerator.getInstance( ALGORITHM );
19         generator.initialize( 1024 );
20         KeyPair keyPair = generator.genKeyPair( );
21         privateKey = keyPair.getPrivate( );
22         publicKey = keyPair.getPublic( );
23       } catch( GeneralSecurityException gse ) {
24       }
25     }
26
27     public Key getPrivateKey( ) {
28       return privateKey;
29     }
30
31     public Key getPublicKey( ) {
32       return publicKey;
33     }
```

EXAMPLE 16.8 The `RSAEncryption` class of the Encryption app, Version 2 (*Continued*)

```
34
35      public byte [ ] getPrivateKeyBytes( ) {
36        return privateKey.getEncoded( );
37      }
38
39      public byte [ ] getPublicKeyBytes( ) {
40        return publicKey.getEncoded( );
41      }
42
43      public String crypt( int opMode, String message, Key key ) {
44        try {
45          cipher.init( opMode, key );
46          byte [ ] messageBytes = message.getBytes( "ISO-8859-1" );
47          byte [ ] encryptedBytes = cipher.doFinal( messageBytes );
48          String encrypted = new String( encryptedBytes, "ISO-8859-1" );
49          return encrypted;
50        } catch( Exception e ) {
51          return null;
52        }
53      }
54    }
```

EXAMPLE 16.8 The `RSAEncryption` class of the Encryption app, Version 2

The `KeyPairGenerator` class has methods to generate a `KeyPair`, which encapsulates a pair of keys, one private and one public. **TABLE 16.5** shows methods of these two classes. The `KeyPairGenerator` class is `abstract` and cannot be instantiated. However, we can use its `getInstance` static method to get a reference to a `KeyPairGenerator` (line 18). The `getInstance`

TABLE 16.5 Selected methods of the `KeyPair` and `KeyPairGenerator` classes

Class	Method	Description
KeyPairGenerator	public static KeyPairGenerator getInstance(String algorithm)	Returns a KeyPairGenerator that uses the specified algorithm.
KeyPairGenerator	initialize(int keySize)	Initializes this KeyPairGenerator with keySize (in bits).
KeyPairGenerator	KeyPair genKeyPair( )	Generates and returns a new KeyPair.
KeyPair	PrivateKey getPrivate( )	Returns the private key of this KeyPair.
KeyPair	PublicKey getPublic( )	Returns the public key of this KeyPair.

method accepts a `String` parameter that represents the algorithm that the `KeyPairGenerator` will use to generate a `KeyPair`. The `genKeyPair` method (called at line 20) returns a `KeyPair`: we can retrieve the two keys using the `getPrivate` and `getPublic` methods of the `KeyPair` class (lines 21 and 22). The `getPrivate` and `getPublic` methods return a `PrivateKey` and `PublicKey`, respectively. Both are interfaces that inherit from the `Key` interface. Thus, we can assign their return values to the `privateKey` and `publicKey` instance variables (lines 21 and 22). We provide accessors for the two keys at lines 27–29 and 31–33. We also provide accessors for the byte array representation of the two keys, so that they can be transferred electronically. We can transfer the public key to a central location, probably on a server, so that other users can retrieve it. If we provide client software that generates the keys, there is no need to transfer the private key to each user and therefore the risk of compromising one or more private keys is much lower. If we have to transfer the private key to a particular user in a secure manner, we can encrypt it using an algorithm like `AES`.

The `crypt` method (lines 43–53) is identical to the `crypt` method of the `AESEncryption` class, except that it uses a `Cipher` reference for `RSA` instead of `AES`.

The `MainActivity` class, shown in **EXAMPLE 16.9**, demonstrates how we can use the `RSAEncryption` class. Because the `RSA` encryption algorithm is asymmetric, we perform two

```
1    package com.jblearning.encryptionv2;
2
3    import android.os.Bundle;
4    import android.support.v7.app.AppCompatActivity;
5    import android.util.Log;
6    import android.view.View;
7    import android.widget.EditText;
8    import android.widget.TextView;
9
10   import javax.crypto.Cipher;
11
12   public class MainActivity extends AppCompatActivity {
13     public static final String MA = "MainActivity";
14     private AESEncryption aes;
15     private RSAEncryption rsa;
16
17     @Override
18     protected void onCreate( Bundle savedInstanceState ) {
19       super.onCreate( savedInstanceState );
20       aes = new AESEncryption( );
21       rsa = new RSAEncryption( );
22       setContentView( R.layout.activity_main );
23
```

EXAMPLE 16.9 The `MainActivity` class of the Encryption app, Version 2 (*Continued*)

```
24        // encrypt with public key, decrypt with private key
25        String original1 = "Hello";
26        Log.w( MA, "original1: " + original1 );
27        String encrypted1 =
28          rsa.crypt( Cipher.ENCRYPT_MODE, original1, rsa.getPublicKey( ) );
29        Log.w( MA, "encrypted1: " + encrypted1 );
30        String decrypted1 =
31          rsa.crypt( Cipher.DECRYPT_MODE, encrypted1, rsa.getPrivateKey( ) );
32        Log.w( MA, "decrypted1: " + decrypted1 );
33
34        // encrypt with private key, decrypt with public key
35        String original2 = "Hello";
36        Log.w( MA, "original2: " + original2 );
37        String encrypted2 =
38          rsa.crypt( Cipher.ENCRYPT_MODE, original2, rsa.getPrivateKey( ) );
39        Log.w( MA, "encrypted2: " + encrypted2 );
40        String decrypted2 =
41          rsa.crypt( Cipher.DECRYPT_MODE, encrypted2, rsa.getPublicKey( ) );
42        Log.w( MA, "decrypted2: " + decrypted2 );
43      }
44
45    public void encryptAndDecryptAES( View v ) {
46      EditText et = ( EditText ) findViewById( R.id.string_original );
47      String original = et.getText( ).toString( );
48      String encrypted =
49        aes.crypt( Cipher.ENCRYPT_MODE, original, aes.getKey( ) );
50      TextView tvEncrypted =
51        ( TextView ) findViewById( R.id.string_encrypted );
52      tvEncrypted.setText( encrypted );
53      TextView tvDecrypted =
54        ( TextView ) findViewById( R.id.string_decrypted );
55      String decrypted =
56        aes.crypt( Cipher.DECRYPT_MODE, encrypted, aes.getKey( ) );
57      tvDecrypted.setText( decrypted );
58      }
59  }
```

EXAMPLE 16.9 The `MainActivity` class of the Encryption app, Version 2

tests. We declare an `RSAEncryption` instance variable at line 15 and instantiate it at line 21. We first encrypt with the public key and decrypt with the private key (lines 24–32), then we encrypt with the private key and decrypt with the public key (lines 34–42). **FIGURE 16.3** shows that in both scenarios, we end up with the original `String` after successively encrypting and decrypting. We two encrypted `String`s illustrate that the encryption is not symmetric. As indicated on the figure, the encrypted `String`s are much longer than shown.

```
original1: Hello
encrypted1: µD2 â,%.z¹{Ã;ûßÿösÎ... ( partial output )
decrypted1: Hello
original2: Hello
encrypted2: 9D*f•Ð/³ö^™ddvÀ′tTg+*Ù%3À... ( partial output )
decrypted2: Hello
```

FIGURE 16.3 Logcat output of the Encryption app, Version 2

16.5 Symmetric and Asymmetric Encryption: Modifying the View, Encryption App, Version 3

In Version 3, we present the user with three buttons: the first one triggers AES encryption and decryption, as before, and the other two trigger RSA encryption and decryption, using the two scenarios available to us:

▶ One encrypting with the private key and decrypting with the public key.
▶ The other one encrypting with the public key and decrypting with the private key.

We modify the activity_main.xml file, the View, and add two buttons. The two buttons are coded at lines 67–74 and 76–83 of **EXAMPLE 16.10**. We give the AES button an id (line 60) so we can position the two new buttons relative to it. Also, since we now have three buttons, the AES button is no longer centered. Because RSA encrypting results in a String much larger than AES encrypting, we specify a bigger margin than before between the first row and second row of components (line 30).

We also define the button_rsa1 and button_rsa2 Strings in strings.xml.

```
1    <?xml version="1.0" encoding="utf-8"?>
2    <RelativeLayout
3        xmlns:android="http://schemas.android.com/apk/res/android"
4        xmlns:tools="http://schemas.android.com/tools"
5        android:layout_width="match_parent"
6        android:layout_height="match_parent"
7        android:paddingBottom="@dimen/activity_vertical_margin"
8        android:paddingLeft="@dimen/activity_horizontal_margin"
9        android:paddingRight="@dimen/activity_horizontal_margin"
10       android:paddingTop="@dimen/activity_vertical_margin"
11       tools:context="com.jblearning.encryptionv3.MainActivity">
12
13    <TextView
14        android:id="@+id/label_original"
15        style="@style/LabelStyle"
16        android:minWidth="120dp"
17        android:text="@string/label_original"/>
18
```

EXAMPLE 16.10 The activity_main.xml file of the Encryption app, Version 3 (*Continued*)

```
19      <EditText
20          android:id="@+id/string_original"
21          style="@style/InputStyle"
22          android:layout_toRightOf="@+id/label_original"
23          android:layout_alignBottom="@+id/label_original"
24          android:layout_alignParentRight="true"
25          android:hint="@string/hint_original" />
26
27      <TextView
28          android:id="@+id/label_encrypted"
29          style="@style/LabelStyle"
30          android:layout_marginTop="200dp"
31          android:layout_below="@+id/label_original"
32          android:layout_alignLeft="@+id/label_original"
33          android:layout_alignRight="@+id/label_original"
34          android:text="@string/label_encrypted"/>
35
36      <TextView
37          android:id="@+id/string_encrypted"
38          style="@style/CenteredTextStyle"
39          android:layout_toRightOf="@+id/label_encrypted"
40          android:layout_alignBottom="@+id/label_encrypted"
41          android:layout_alignRight="@id/string_original" />
42
43      <TextView
44          android:id="@+id/label_decrypted"
45          style="@style/LabelStyle"
46          android:layout_marginTop="30dp"
47          android:layout_below="@id/label_encrypted"
48          android:layout_alignLeft="@+id/label_original"
49          android:layout_alignRight="@+id/label_original"
50          android:text="@string/label_decrypted" />
51
52      <TextView
53          android:id="@+id/string_decrypted"
54          style="@style/CenteredTextStyle"
55          android:layout_toRightOf="@+id/label_decrypted"
56          android:layout_alignBottom="@+id/label_decrypted"
57          android:layout_alignRight="@id/string_original" />
58
59      <Button
60          android:id="@+id/button_aes"
61          style="@style/ButtonStyle"
62          android:layout_marginTop="30dp"
63          android:layout_below="@+id/string_decrypted"
64          android:text="@string/button_aes"
65          android:onClick="encryptAndDecryptAES" />
66
```

EXAMPLE 16.10 The activity_main.xml file of the Encryption app, Version 3 (*Continued*)

```
67      <Button
68          android:id="@+id/button_rsa1"
69          style="@style/ButtonStyle"
70          android:layout_marginTop="30dp"
71          android:layout_below="@+id/string_decrypted"
72          android:layout_centerInParent="true"
73          android:text="@string/button_rsa1"
74          android:onClick="encryptAndDecryptRSA1" />
75
76      <Button
77          android:id="@+id/button_rsa2"
78          style="@style/ButtonStyle"
79          android:layout_marginTop="30dp"
80          android:layout_below="@+id/string_decrypted"
81          android:layout_alignParentRight="true"
82          android:text="@string/button_rsa2"
83          android:onClick="encryptAndDecryptRSA2" />
84
85  </RelativeLayout>
```

EXAMPLE 16.10 **The activity_main.xml file of the Encryption app, Version 3**

EXAMPLE 16.11 shows the updated MainActivity class. Because we need to access the GUI components in three different methods, we add three instance variables for them at lines 14–16. We instantiate them using the findViewById method at lines 24–26. Note that it is important to set the content View (line 23) before we retrieve them. Otherwise, they will be null and the app

```
1   package com.jblearning.encryptionv3;
2
3   import android.os.Bundle;
4   import android.support.v7.app.AppCompatActivity;
5   import android.view.View;
6   import android.widget.EditText;
7   import android.widget.TextView;
8
9   import javax.crypto.Cipher;
10
11  public class MainActivity extends AppCompatActivity {
12    private AESEncryption aes;
13    private RSAEncryption rsa;
14    private EditText etOriginal;
15    private TextView tvEncrypted;
16    private TextView tvDecrypted;
17
```

EXAMPLE 16.11 **The MainActivity class of the Encryption app, Version 3 (Continued)**

```
18        @Override
19        protected void onCreate( Bundle savedInstanceState ) {
20          super.onCreate( savedInstanceState );
21          aes = new AESEncryption( );
22          rsa = new RSAEncryption( );
23          setContentView( R.layout.activity_main );
24          etOriginal = ( EditText ) findViewById( R.id.string_original );
25          tvEncrypted = ( TextView ) findViewById( R.id.string_encrypted );
26          tvDecrypted = ( TextView ) findViewById( R.id.string_decrypted );
27        }
28
29        public void encryptAndDecryptAES( View v ) {
30          EditText et = ( EditText ) findViewById( R.id.string_original );
31          String original = et.getText( ).toString( );
32          String encrypted =
33              aes.crypt( Cipher.ENCRYPT_MODE, original, aes.getKey( ) );
34          TextView tvEncrypted =
35              ( TextView ) findViewById( R.id.string_encrypted );
36          tvEncrypted.setText( encrypted );
37          TextView tvDecrypted =
38              ( TextView ) findViewById( R.id.string_decrypted );
39          String decrypted =
40            aes.crypt( Cipher.DECRYPT_MODE, encrypted, aes.getKey( ) );
41          tvDecrypted.setText( decrypted );
42        }
43
44        public void encryptAndDecryptRSA1( View v ) {
45          String original = etOriginal.getText( ).toString( );
46          String encrypted =
47              rsa.crypt( Cipher.ENCRYPT_MODE, original, rsa.getPrivateKey( ) );
48          tvEncrypted.setText( encrypted );
49          String decrypted =
50              rsa.crypt( Cipher.DECRYPT_MODE, encrypted, rsa.getPublicKey( ) );
51          tvDecrypted.setText( decrypted );
52        }
53
54        public void encryptAndDecryptRSA2( View v ) {
55          String original = etOriginal.getText( ).toString( );
56          String encrypted =
57              rsa.crypt( Cipher.ENCRYPT_MODE, original, rsa.getPublicKey( ) );
58          tvEncrypted.setText( encrypted );
59          String decrypted =
60              rsa.crypt( Cipher.DECRYPT_MODE, encrypted, rsa.getPrivateKey( ) );
61          tvDecrypted.setText( decrypted );
62        }
63    }
```

EXAMPLE 16.11 The `MainActivity` class of the Encryption app, Version 3

FIGURE 16.4 The Encryption app, Version 3, after the user clicks on RSA 1

FIGURE 16.5 The Encryption app, Version 3, after the user clicks on RSA 2

will eventually crash at runtime. The `encryptAndDecryptRSA1` and `encryptAndDecryptRSA2` methods are very similar to the `encryptAndDecryptAES` method. The `encryptAndDecryptRSA1` method encrypts with the private key (lines 46–47) and decrypts with the public key (lines 49–50). The `encryptAndDecryptRSA1` method encrypts with the public key (lines 56–57) and decrypts with the private key (lines 59–60).

FIGURES 16.4 and **16.5** show the app after the user enters `Android is fun` and clicks on the RSA 1 button and RSA 2 button, respectively.

Chapter Summary

- Encryption algorithms can be one way (something encrypted cannot be decrypted), symmetric (the same key is used for encryption and decryption), or asymmetric (a different key is used for encryption and decryption).
- The `javax.crypto` package provides interfaces and classes that encapsulate various cryptology concepts and functionalities.
- We can use the `KeyGenerator` class to generate a key for a symmetric encryption algorithm.
- We can use the `KeyPairGenerator` class to generate a pair of keys for an asymmetric encryption algorithm.
- Classes that encapsulate a key provide methods to convert a key object to an array of bytes and to reconstruct a key from an array of bytes. In this way, we can transfer a key electronically. Key distribution is an important issue.
- We can use the `SecureRandom` class to generate a cryptographically secure pseudo-random number.
- The `Cipher` class provides access to implementations of encryption and decryption algorithms.
- The `doFinal` method of the `Cipher` class encrypts or decrypts an array of bytes into another array of bytes.
- We can use the `ISO-8859-1` encoding standard to convert an array of bytes to a `String` and vice versa. It provides a one-to-one mapping between a `String` and an array of bytes.
- Before calling the `doFinal` method to encrypt or decrypt, we call `init` to specify the mode (encryption or decryption), the key, and set an element of randomness.

Exercises, Problems, and Projects

Multiple-Choice Exercises

1. An asymmetric encryption algorithm uses the same key for encryption and decryption
   - True
   - False

2. In what package do we find interfaces and classes that encapsulate cryptology concepts and functions?
   - java.crypto
   - javax.crypto
   - android.crypto
   - android.algorithm

3. What class can we use to generate a private key and its corresponding public key for the RSA algorithm?
   - Key
   - KeyGenerator
   - KeyPairGenerator
   - SecretKey

4. What is the name of the class that provides implementations of various encryption and encryption algorithms?
   - Crypt
   - Encrypt
   - RSA
   - Cipher

5. The doFinal method of the class in question 4 converts
   - An array of bytes to a String
   - A String to an array of bytes
   - A String to a String
   - An array of bytes to an array of bytes

6. The first parameter of the init method of the class in question 4 is an int. If we want to encrypt, what value can we use?
   - Cipher.ENCRYPT_MODE
   - Cipher.ENCRYPT
   - Cipher.DECRYPT
   - Cipher.DECRYPT_MODE

7. The first parameter of the init method of the class in question 4 is an int. If we want to decrypt, what value can we use?
   - Cipher.ENCRYPT_MODE
   - Cipher.ENCRYPT
   - Cipher.DECRYPT
   - Cipher.DECRYPT_MODE

Fill in the Code

8. Write the code to declare and instantiate a Cipher object for the AES algorithm.

9. Write the code to declare and instantiate a Cipher object for the RSA algorithm.

10. Write the code to declare and instantiate a KeyGenerator object for the AES algorithm.

11. Write the code to declare and instantiate a KeyPairGenerator object for the RSA algorithm.

12. The variable keyPair is a KeyPairGenerator reference and has already been instantiated for the RSA algorithm. Write the code to retrieve the array of bytes for its private key.

13. The variable keyPair is a KeyPairGenerator reference and has already been instantiated for the RSA algorithm. Write the code to retrieve the array of bytes for its public key.

14. A String named s has been initialized. Write the code to convert it to an array of bytes using the ISO-8859-1 encoding standard.

15. An array of bytes has been initialized with some values. Write the code to convert it into a String using the ISO-8859-1 encoding standard.

16. A Cipher reference named myCipher has been declared and instantiated. The key myKey has also been declared and instantiated. Write the code to initialize myCipher so that it is ready to encrypt something with myKey.

17. A Cipher reference named myCipher has been declared, instantiated, and initialized for encryption with some key. Write the code to encrypt the array of bytes myBytes. Assign the result to a variable of your choice.

Write an App

18. Code an app similar to Version 1 in this chapter. Choose an encryption algorithm different from AES.

19. Code an app similar to Version 1 in this chapter. Use the init method whose second parameter is a Certificate instead.

20. Code an app that sends an email. Encrypt the body of the email with AES.

21. Code an app, using RSA, asking the user to enter a sentence. One button encrypts the sentence with the private key of user 1 and the public key of user 2 and displays the result in a TextView (user 2 can decrypt the sentence knowing that it comes from user 1). Another button decrypts the result back to the original sentence and displays it in another TextView.

22. Make an app that encrypts some user input using a Caesar cipher (every letter on the alphabet is shifted by a fixed number: for example, if the shift is 3, a becomes d, b becomes e, etc.).

23. Look at the Security class from the java.security package. Make an app that uses that class in order to retrieve all the encryption algorithms that are supported by your Android devices.

APPENDIX A

Retrieving the Height of the Status Bar and the Action Bar Dynamically

If we define a View programmatically, we often need to retrieve the height of the content view, which is the total height of the screen minus the heights of the status bar and the action bar.

FIGURE A.1 shows the various parts of a device's screen. The device's status bar is shown in yellow: it typically includes some icons for system and application notifications, including the clock. In red is the app's action bar, which typically includes the app name on the top left and a menu on the right, although it can be different depending on the app. The app content View is shown in blue. This is where the contents of our app go. The visible display frame is made up of the app's action bar (in red) and the app content View (in blue).

At the time of this writing, and according to Google's design guidelines, the height of the status bar is 24 dp and the height of the action bar is 56 dp. These numbers are given in density independent pixels, so in order to compute the actual number of pixels, we need to multiply them by the logical pixel density of the device. There is no guarantee that the height of the status and action bars will not change in the future. Thus, it is better to retrieve them programmatically.

The following code sequence shows how to retrieve the logical pixel density of a device.

```
Resources res = getResources( );
DisplayMetrics metrics = res.getDisplayMetrics( );
float pixelDensity = metrics.density;
```

We first obtain a Resources reference by calling the getResources method inherited from the ContextWrapper class by the Activity class. We can use the Resources class to access the app's resources. Using the

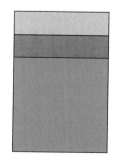

FIGURE A.1 **View components of the screen**

643

TABLE A.1 The `getResources`, `getDisplayMetrics` methods, and the ensity field of `DisplayMetrics`

Class	Method or field	Description
ContextWrapper	Resources getResources( )	Returns a Resources reference for this app's package.
Resources	Display getDisplayMetrics( )	Returns the display metrics for this Resources object.
DisplayMetrics	density	The scaling factor for the density independent pixel unit.

`Resources` reference `res`, we call the `getDisplayMetrics` method to obtain a `Display-Metrics` reference for the device. The `DisplayMetrics` class contains information about the display, including its size, its density, and font scaling. The `density` field of the `DisplayMetrics` class stores the logical pixel density of the device. **TABLE A.1** shows the `getResources` method from the `ContextWrapper` class, the `getDisplayMetrics` from the `Resources` class, and the `density` field from the `DisplayMetrics` class.

Once we have the density of the device, we can assign a default value to the action bar height and the status bar height as follows:

```
int actionBarHeight = ( int ) ( pixelDensity * 56 );
int statusBarHeight = ( int ) ( pixelDensity * 24 );
```

Now that we have a default value for the action bar height, we can attempt to retrieve its value dynamically using the following sequence. If we are not successful, we use the action bar default value.

```
// set default value for action bar height
int actionBarHeight = ( int ) ( pixelDensity * 56 );
TypedValue tv = new TypedValue( );
if( getTheme( ).resolveAttribute( android.R.attr.actionBarSize, tv, true ) )
    actionBarHeight = TypedValue.complexToDimensionPixelSize( tv.data,
                         getResources( ).getDisplayMetrics( ) );
```

The height of the action bar is part of the theme of the app. The `getTheme` method, shown in **TABLE A.2**, inherited from `ContextThemeWrapper` by `Activity`, returns the `Theme` associated with the current `Context`. `Theme` is an inner class of the `Resources` class: it stores the attribute values for a particular theme. The `resolveAttribute` method of the `Theme` class, shown in **TABLE A.3**, checks if an attribute is present in a theme. If it is, it returns `true` and assigns the attribute value to its `TypedValue` parameter, the second one. The resource id for the action bar height is `android.R.attr.actionBarSize`. We declare and instantiate a `TypedValue` reference, `tv`, for the purpose of passing it as the second argument to the `resolveAttribute` method. If the method returns `true`, we assign its value to `actionBarHeight`.

TABLE A.2 The `getTheme` method of the `ContextThemeWrapper` class	
Resources.Theme getTheme( )	Returns the Theme associated with the current Context.

TABLE A.3 The `resolveAttribute` method of the `Resources.Theme` class	
boolean resolveAttribute(int resourceId, TypedValue outValue, boolean resolveRefs)	Returns true if the attribute resourceId is present in this Theme. If it is, it assigns its value to outValue; resolveRefs is used to determine the type of resource of the attribute.

TABLE A.4 Resources of the `TypedValue` class	
public int data	The data in this TypedValue.
public int type	The type of data in this TypedValue.
static int complexToDimensionPixelSize(int data, DisplayMetrics metrics)	Returns the number of pixels corresponding to data using metrics as the display metrics. The type of data must be TYPE_DIMENSION (value 5)

We use the `complexToDimensionPixelSize` static method of the `TypedValue` class, shown in TABLE A.4, to convert the data inside `tv`, `tv.data`, to an integer representing its number of pixels. If we output the type of `tv`, `tv.type`, we can see that its value is 5, the value of the `TYPE_DIMENSION` constant of the `TypedValue` class.

To retrieve the value of the status bar height dynamically, we use the following sequence. If we are not successful, we use the status bar default value.

```
// set default value for status bar height
int statusBarHeight = ( int ) ( pixelDensity * 24);
// res is a Resources reference
int resourceId =
    res.getIdentifier( "status_bar_height", "dimen", "android" );
    // res.getIdentifier( "android:dimen/status_bar_height", "", "" );
if( resourceId != 0 ) // found resource for status bar height
  statusBarHeight = res.getDimensionPixelSize( resourceId );
```

We can get the id of a resource given its name and the type of resource it is by calling the `getIdentifier` method of the `Resources` class shown in TABLE A.5. If the value returned

TABLE A.5 The `getIdentifier` and `getDimensionPixelSize` methods of the `Resources` class	
int getIdentifier(String name, String type, String package)	Returns the resource id for the resource named name; type specifies the type of the resource (color, dimen, etc.), and package is the package that the resource is in. Both type and package are optional if name includes them (i.e., is a String like "package:type/resourceName"). Returns 0 if not found.
int getDimensionPixelSize(int id)	Returns the number of pixels of a resource whose id is id.

is not 0, we have successfully retrieved it. We can then obtain its dimension by calling the `getDimensionPixelSize` method of `Resources`, passing the id value. Table A.5 also shows that method.

EXAMPLE A.1 shows the `MainActivity` class for a simple app that retrieves the status bar and action bar heights.

```
1   package com.jblearning.statusandactionbars;
2
3   import android.content.res.Resources;
4   import android.os.Bundle;
5   import android.support.v7.app.AppCompatActivity;
6   import android.util.DisplayMetrics;
7   import android.util.Log;
8   import android.util.TypedValue;
9
10  public class MainActivity extends AppCompatActivity {
11    public static int STATUS_BAR_HEIGHT = 24; // in dp
12    public static int ACTION_BAR_HEIGHT = 56; // in dp
13
14    @Override
15    protected void onCreate( Bundle savedInstanceState ) {
16      super.onCreate( savedInstanceState );
17      setContentView( R.layout.activity_main );
18
```

EXAMPLE A.1 The `MainActivity` class, showing how to retrieve the status bar and action bar heights of the current device (*Continued*)

```
19      Resources res = getResources( );
20      DisplayMetrics metrics = res.getDisplayMetrics( );
21      float pixelDensity = metrics.density;
22      Log.w( "MainActivity", "pixel density = " + pixelDensity );
23
24      TypedValue tv = new TypedValue( );
25      int actionBarHeight = ( int ) ( pixelDensity * ACTION_BAR_HEIGHT );
26      if( getTheme( ).resolveAttribute( android.R.attr.actionBarSize,
27          tv, true ) ) {
28        actionBarHeight = TypedValue.complexToDimensionPixelSize( tv.data,
29            res.getDisplayMetrics( ) );
30        Log.w( "MainActivity", "retrieved action bar height = "
31            + actionBarHeight );
32      }
33
34      int statusBarHeight = ( int ) ( pixelDensity * STATUS_BAR_HEIGHT );
35      int resourceId =
36          res.getIdentifier( "status_bar_height", "dimen", "android" );
37      Log.w( "MainActivity", "resource id for action bar height = "
38          + resourceId );
39      if( resourceId != 0 ) { // found resource for status bar height
40        statusBarHeight = res.getDimensionPixelSize( resourceId );
41        Log.w( "MainActivity", "retrieved status bar height = "
42            + statusBarHeight );
43      }
44    }
45
46  }
```

EXAMPLE A.1 **The `MainActivity` class, showing how to retrieve the status bar and action bar heights of the current device**

FIGURE A.2 shows the output of Example A.1 when running in the Nexus 5 emulator. The retrieved action bar height, 168, is equal to 3 (the pixel density) times 56 (the height given by Google for the action bar in dp units). The retrieved status bar height, 72, is equal to 3 (the pixel density) times 24 (the height given by Google for the status bar in dp units).

```
pixel density = 3.0
retrieved action bar height = 168
resource id for action bar height = 17104919
retrieved status bar height = 72
```

FIGURE A.2 **The output of Example A.1 for the Nexus 5 emulator**

```
pixel density = 2.0
retrieved action bar height = 112
resource id for action bar height = 17104919
retrieved status bar height = 48
```

FIGURE A.3 The output of Example A.1 for the Nexus 4 emulator

FIGURE A.3 shows the output of Example A.1 when running in the Nexus 4 emulator. The retrieved action bar height, 112, is equal to 2 (the pixel density) times 56 (the height given by Google for the action bar in dp units). The retrieved status bar height, 48, is equal to 2 (the pixel density) times 24 (the height given by Google for the status bar in dp units). We can verify that the resource id is the same as for the Nexus 5 emulator.

APPENDIX B

Setting the Font Size of a TextView Dynamically

Sizing the font inside a TextView is one issue that arises often when building an app. Since the app will run on many devices with various screen sizes, it could look awkward on some devices if we use the same font size for all the devices. There are many ways to set the size of the font inside a TextView so that the text fits well. We explore how to set it so that the text fits in one line and the font size is maximal. We assume that there is no padding inside the TextView.

We build a utility class, DynamicSizing, that includes a static method that works as follows:

▶ It sets the size of the font in the TextView so that the text fits on one line and that the font size is maximal.

Another possible implementation of this functionality is to subclass TextView and define the method mentioned previously as a non static method.

One strategy to compute the optimal font is to start with a very large font, for example of size 200, and decrease the font size by 1 as long as it takes two lines or more to fit the text inside the TextView, as in the following pseudo-code:

```
font size = 200
while( text needs 2 or more lines to fit inside TextView ) {
  decrease font size by 1
}
```

We can use the getLineCount method, shown in **TABLE B.1**, of the TextView class to access the number of lines that the text occupies within the TextView. One issue that arises when resizing a View or a property of a View dynamically is to have access to the View's properties, such as width, height, or the number of lines that the text occupies. If the View has not been displayed yet, the methods getWidth, getHeight, and getLineCount all return 0. We can call the measure method of the View class (see Table B.1) in order to access the width, height, and number of lines

TABLE B.1 Selected methods of the `View` and `TextView` classes

Class	Method	Description
View	int getWidth( )	Returns the width of the View in pixels, 0 if it has not been displayed yet.
View	int getHeight( )	Returns the height of the View in pixels, 0 if it has not been displayed yet.
View	void measure(int widthMeasureSpec, int heightMeasureSpec)	Called if we want to find out the size of the View; widthMeasureSpec and heightMeasureSpec represent the horizontal and vertical requirement imposed by the parent View.
View	int getMeasuredWidth( )	Returns the width of the View in pixels as measured by the call to measure.
View	int getMeasuredHeight( )	Returns the height of the View in pixels as measured by the call to measure.
View	ViewParent getParent( )	Returns the parent view of this View.
TextView	int getLineCount( )	Returns the number of lines of text inside the TextView, 0 if the TextView has not been displayed yet.
TextView	void setTextSize(int unit, float size)	Sets the size of the text inside the TextView to size units.
TextView	void setWidth(int w)	Sets the width of TextView to w pixels.
TextView	void setHeight(int h)	Sets the height of TextView to h pixels.

of text inside a `TextView`. If we call `measure` first, then the call to `getLineCount` returns the actual number of lines that the text takes inside the `TextView`. To obtain width and height information after calling `measure`, we should call the `getMeasuredWidth` and `getMeasuredHeight` methods. The `measure` method takes two `int` parameters, specifying the type of size constraint that the parent of the `View` has imposed or not imposed on it. **TABLE B.2** shows three constants of the `MeasureSpec` class that we can use to specify values for these two parameters.

EXAMPLE B.1 shows our `DynamicSizing` utility class. We declare the `MAX_FONT_SIZE` constant, equal to `200`, at line 8. We use it as the starting size for the font before we decrease it by `1` to find the correct value so that the text fits on one line. We also declare another constant, `MIN_FONT_SIZE`, whose value is set to `1` (line 9), and we use this value as the minimum font size for the `TextView`.

The `setFontSizeToFitInView` method, at lines 11–32, accepts a `TextView` parameter, `tv`, and modifies its font size. It returns its modified font size. We assign the value of `MAX_FONT_SIZE`

TABLE B.2 Constants of the MeasureSpec class

Constant	Description
UNSPECIFIED	Parent has not imposed any constraint on the child View.
EXACTLY	Parent has determined the exact size of the child View.
AT_MOST	Parent has determined the maximum size of the child View.

```
1    package com.jblearning.dynamicfontsizing;
2
3    import android.util.TypedValue;
4    import android.view.View.MeasureSpec;
5    import android.widget.TextView;
6
7    public class DynamicSizing {
8      public static final int MAX_FONT_SIZE = 200;
9      public static final int MIN_FONT_SIZE = 1;
10
11     /*
12      * Sets the maximum font size of tv so that the text inside tv
13      *      fits on one line
14      * @param  tv    the TextView whose font size is to be changed
15      * @return the resulting font size
16      */
17     public static int setFontSizeToFitInView( TextView tv ) {
18       int fontSize = MAX_FONT_SIZE;
19       tv.setTextSize( TypedValue.COMPLEX_UNIT_SP, fontSize );
20       tv.measure( MeasureSpec.UNSPECIFIED, MeasureSpec.UNSPECIFIED );
21       int lines = tv.getLineCount( );
22       if( lines > 0 ) {
23         while( lines != 1 && fontSize >= MIN_FONT_SIZE + 2 ) {
24           fontSize--;
25           tv.setTextSize( TypedValue.COMPLEX_UNIT_SP, fontSize );
26           tv.measure( MeasureSpec.UNSPECIFIED, MeasureSpec.UNSPECIFIED );
27           lines = tv.getLineCount( );
28         }
29         tv.setTextSize( TypedValue.COMPLEX_UNIT_SP, --fontSize );
30       }
31       return fontSize;
32     }
33   }
```

EXAMPLE B.1 The DynamicSizing utility class

TABLE B.3 Constants of the `TypedValue` class

Constant	Description
COMPLEX_UNIT_IN	Value in inches.
COMPLEX_UNIT_PX	Value in raw pixels.
COMPLEX_UNIT_SP	Value in scaled pixels.

to the variable `fontSize` at line 18 and set the font size of `tv` to `fontSize` at line 19. We use the integer constant `COMPLEX_UNIT_SP` from the `TypedValue` class as the first argument of the `setTextSize` method of the `TextView` class to specify the units. It means that the unit is a scaled pixel. **TABLE B.3** shows several constants of the `TypedValue` class.

Before we get the number of lines in the text by calling `getLineCount` at line 21, we call `measure` at line 20, so that `getLineCount` does not return 0. If it does not, we loop at lines 23–28 until the number of lines, stored in the variable `lines`, is equal to 1 or the font size goes down to 2. If for some reason, for example, if the text is very long, the font size reaches size 2, we exit the loop. This is unlikely to happen, but it is good defensive programming practice to guard against the unexpected. If we get inside the loop and the font size is greater than 2, it means that the number of lines is greater than 1, and therefore the font size needs to be reduced. We decrease `fontSize` by 1 at line 24, reset the font size of `tv` to reflect that at line 25, call `measure` at line 26 to reset the measured values, and update `lines` at line 27. Since the font size decreases inside the loop, either the value of `lines` will reach 1 or the value of `fontSize` will reach 2.

After exiting the loop, we reset the font size of `tv` to `fontSize - 1` at line 29, to be sure that the text fits on one line within `tv`. We return `fontSize` at line 31. Note that we do not account for any padding inside the `TextView`.

COMMON ERROR: If a `TextView` has not been displayed yet, `getWidth`, `getHeight`, and `getLineCount` will all return 0. If we are interested in getting width, height, or line count information, we should call `measure` first, before calling `getMeasuredWidth`, `getMeasuredHeight`, and `getLineCount`.

We now build a simple app and edit the activity_main.xml file and the `MainActivity` class to test the `setFontSizeToFitInView` method of the `DynamicSizing` class. **EXAMPLE B.2** shows the activity_main.xml file. We give an id to the `TextView` at line 15 so we can get a reference to it in the `MainActivity` class in order to modify its width text, and the font size of its text. We set the background of the `TextView` to yellow at line 16 so we can visualize its bounds.

EXAMPLE B.3 shows the `MainActivity` class. At lines 13–14, we retrieve the `TextView`. At lines 15–17, we set its width and text. At lines 18–19, we set its font size so that the text inside

```
1   <RelativeLayout xmlns:android="http://schemas.android.com/apk/res/android"
2     xmlns:tools="http://schemas.android.com/tools"
3     android:layout_width="match_parent"
4     android:layout_height="match_parent"
5     android:paddingLeft="@dimen/activity_horizontal_margin"
6     android:paddingRight="@dimen/activity_horizontal_margin"
7     android:paddingTop="@dimen/activity_vertical_margin"
8     android:paddingBottom="@dimen/activity_vertical_margin"
9     tools:context=".MainActivity">
10
11    <TextView
12      android:text="Hello World!"
13      android:layout_width="wrap_content"
14      android:layout_height="wrap_content"
15      android:id="@+id/tv"
16      android:background="#FFF0" />
17
18  </RelativeLayout>
```

EXAMPLE B.2 The activity_main.xml file

```
1   package com.jblearning.dynamicfontsizing;
2
3   import android.os.Bundle;
4   import android.support.v7.app.AppCompatActivity;
5   import android.widget.TextView;
6
7   public class MainActivity extends AppCompatActivity {
8     @Override
9     protected void onCreate( Bundle savedInstanceState ) {
10      super.onCreate( savedInstanceState );
11      setContentView( R.layout.activity_main );
12
13      // retrieve TextView
14      TextView tv = ( TextView ) findViewById( R.id.tv );
15      // set width and text of TextView
16      tv.setWidth( 600 );
17      tv.setText( "PROGRAMMING" );
18      // set optimal font size
19      DynamicSizing.setFontSizeToFitInView( tv );
20    }
21  }
```

EXAMPLE B.3 The MainActivity class

FIGURE B.1 The Test app running inside the emulator

it fits on one line. We do not need the returned value of `setFontSizeToFitInView` so we make the call to `setFontSizeToFitInView` as a stand-alone statement.

FIGURE B.1 shows the app running inside the emulator. Try changing the text (to PRO or PROGRAM, for example) and/or the width (to 300, for example) of the `TextView` and test the app again. The font size adjusts accordingly.

APPENDIX C

How to Download and Install Google Play Services, Use Maps

The Android Standard Development Kit (Android SDK) does not include all the packages and classes we need for development. For example, maps and advertising-related classes may not be included. However, we can download and install them with the Android SDK Manager. TABLE C.1 shows the possible extra steps needed.

Steps 1 and 2 relate to the development environment, and we only need to perform them once. Steps 3, 4, and 5 are project related, and we need to perform them for each project.

TABLE C.1 Steps to use Google Play services

Step	Description
1	Download and install Google Play Services (if not already done).
2	Download and install Google APIs (if not already done).
3	Update the build.gradle (Module: app) file (if not already done— that depends on the Android template we use).
4	For an app using Google Maps, obtain a key from Google (if not already done).
5	Add the appropriate elements to the AndroidManifest.xml file (if not already done— that depends on the Android template we use).

Step 1 (to do once, and periodically if needed): Install Google Play services

Select Tools, select Android, select SDK Manager (or click on the SDK Manager icon), select the SDK Tools tab. Look for Google Play services. If it indicates `Not installed`, check its checkbox and click on Install x Packages (x is likely to be more than 1 and can vary depending on our current version of the development environment). Accept the license terms and click on Install. Depending on how many files are downloaded and installed, this may take between a few seconds or several minutes. In **FIGURE C.1**, we can see that Google Play services are installed.

Step 2 (to do once, and periodically if needed): Install the Google APIs if necessary

The library we need may or may not have been installed as part of Step 1. For example, the Google Maps Android API Version 2 is part of the Google Play Services SDK. It may have been installed as part of Step 1 (it may have been checked by default and was installed along with Google Play services). If not, we must install it in order for us to use maps. Reopen the SDK Manager (Select Tools, select Android, select SDK Manager). Select Android SDK, then select the SDK Platforms tab. Select the most recent Android directory (for the author, at the time of this writing, it is Android 6.0 API 23), and click on the Show Package Details button at the bottom right of the panel. In **FIGURE C.2**, we can see that the Google APIs are already installed but there is an update available. If Google APIs indicates `Not installed`, we need to select it and then click on Install

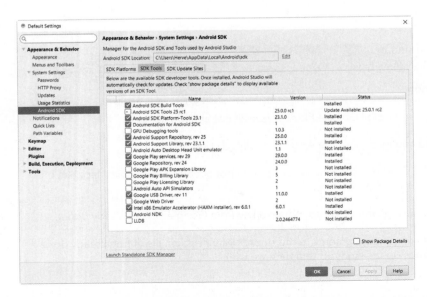

FIGURE C.1 The Android SDK manager before Google Play services are installed

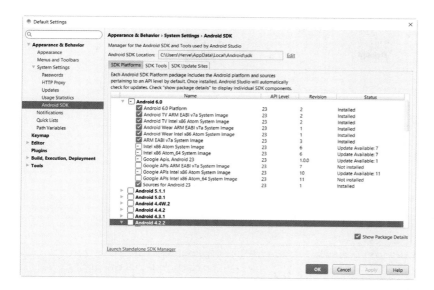

FIGURE C.2 The Android SDK manager: Google APIs are installed and there is an update available

packages. If there is an update available, we should update. We can also update by selecting Check for Update. . . from the Help menu and following the directions. This may take several minutes.

Step 3 (to do for each project): Make Google Play services libraries available to an app

In order to do this, we need to modify the build.gradle file (there are two such files. We need to edit the one for the module). **EXAMPLE C.1** shows the edited file. The only addition is at line 27: we need to include the appropriate version of the Google Play services libraries. This example shows edition 9.4.0. Any time we modify a gradle file, we should sync the project. We can do that by clicking on the sync icon. **FIGURE C.3** shows the sync icon. After this step, the project should compile properly.

Note that if we use an existing Android template such as the Google Maps Activity template when creating a new project, the build.gradle file already contains line 27.

Step 4 (to do only once): In order to use Google maps, obtain a key from Google

To obtain a key from Google that we can use for development, we need to do the following:

1. Obtain a debug certificate fingerprint.
2. Register a project in the Google APIs Console and add the Maps API as a service for the project.
3. Request and obtain a key.

```
1    apply plugin: 'com.android.application'
2
3    android {
4        compileSdkVersion 23
5        buildToolsVersion "23.0.2"
6
7        defaultConfig {
8            applicationId "com.jblearning.maptest"
9            minSdkVersion 15
10           targetSdkVersion 23
11           versionCode 1
12           versionName "1.0"
13       }
14       buildTypes {
15           release {
16               minifyEnabled false
17               proguardFiles getDefaultProguardFile('proguard-android.txt'),
18                                               'proguard-rules.pro'
19           }
20       }
21   }
22
23   dependencies {
24       compile fileTree( dir: 'libs', include: ['*.jar'])
25       testCompile 'junit:junit:4.12'
26       compile 'com.android.support:appcompat-v7:23.4.0'
27       compile 'com.google.android.gms:play-services:9.4.0'
28   }
```

EXAMPLE C.1 The edited build.gradle (Module: app) file

FIGURE C.3 The sync icon

When it is time to release our app to Google Play, we need to obtain a release certificate fingerprint instead of a debug certificate fingerprint, and the process is similar. However, in order to do that, we need to be a registered developer with Google Play.

In order to obtain a debug certificate fingerprint, do the following at the command line:
For Linux or Unix systems:

```
keytool -list -v -keystore ~/.android/debug.keystore -alias
androiddebugkey -storepass android -keypass android
```

For Windows systems:

```
keytool -list -v -keystore "C:\Users\your_user_name\.android\debug.
keystore" -alias androiddebugkey -storepass android -keypass android
```

For the author's computer, it is:

```
keytool -list -v -keystore "C:\Users\Herve\.android\debug.keystore"
-alias androiddebugkey -storepass android -keypass android
```

If the keytool command is not recognized by the system, we can either add the directory where it is located to the path, or run the keytool command from inside its directory. The executable file for keytool, keytool.exe, should be located inside the bin directory of the Java jdk directory. On the author's computer, keytool.exe is located in the C:\Program Files\Java\jdk1.8.0_60\bin directory.

In Windows, we should see an output similar to the one shown in **FIGURE C.4** (note that the author has replaced the certificate fingerprints and key identifier with random values). The

```
C:\Users\Herve>keytool -list -v -keystore "C:\Users\Herve\.android\debug.
keystore" -alias androiddebugkey -storepass android -keypass android
Alias name: androiddebugkey
Creation date: Sep 15, 2015
Entry type: PrivateKeyEntry
Certificate chain length: 1
Certificate[1]:
Owner: CN=Android Debug, O=Android, C=US
Issuer: CN=Android Debug, O=Android, C=US
Serial number: 64c2e50f
Valid from: Tue Sep 15 19:16:08 EDT 2015 until: Thu Sep 07 19:16:08 EDT 2045
Certificate fingerprints:
        MD5: 40:A1:7F:2C:18:2C:DD:45:67:A4:4D:C3:C6:F3:12:34
        SHA1: A4:C4:23:B6:C5:D4:25:67:89:CC:3C:84:8A:21:89:34:36:E5:2E:F5
        SHA256: 56:56:89:01:0F:DE:E4:E5:C4:A3:34:45:56:78:4D:E3:23:34:7E:D3:B3:
C6:F7:A4:B6:C5:23:56:67:72:88:D4
        Signature algorithm name: SHA256withRSA
        Version: 3

Extensions:

#1: ObjectId: 2.5.29.14 Criticality=false
SubjectKeyIdentifier [
KeyIdentifier [
0000: 76 C4 D4 B4 66 D4 A7 F4 44 23 78 82 DC 90 A3 66  P^.=.:...l.c..e^.
0010: AA 23 56 B4                                       .As.
]
]
```

FIGURE C.4 Possible output when running keytool

fingerprint is the sequence of 20 two-digit hexadecimal numbers separated by colons that appear after SHA1.

Fingerprint certificates are unique and provide a way to identify an app. That enables Google to track the app in Google Play as well as track the use of map resources by our app.

Now, we need to go the Google APIs Console to register a project. At the time of this writing, the URL is:

```
https://console.developers.google.com/
```

If we have already registered a project, the project shows on the web page. Otherwise, click on Create project. Enter a name for our project and click on Create. Then, select Use Google APIs.

Among the list of available services, locate Google Maps Android API, as shown in **FIGURE C.5**, and click on it. Next, click on Enable API, as shown in **FIGURE C.6**. At that time, unless we have done it before, we will be asked to enter our credentials.

Google Maps APIs

Google Maps Android API

Google Maps SDK for iOS

Google Maps JavaScript API

Google Places API for Android

Google Places API for iOS

Google Maps Roads API

⌄ More

FIGURE C.5 **Finding Google Maps Android API in Google Play services**

FIGURE C.6 **Enabling the Google Maps Android API**

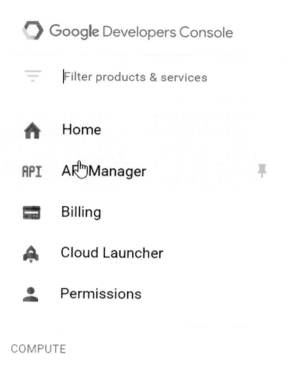

FIGURE C.7 **Selecting the API Manager**

Next, we need to obtain a key. On the top left, click on the three small horizontal lines next to Google Developers Console. From the menu, choose API Manager (see **FIGURE C.7**). Then select Credentials. From the New Credentials menu, select API key (see **FIGURE C.8**), then choose Android key. At that point, we should enter the package name of our app and the SHA-1 fingerprint from Figure C.4, as shown in **FIGURE C.9**. Note that we have hidden the author's fingerprint in the figure. We then click on Create and the key shows.

A key depends on the fingerprint certificate and the application package, so we recommend that you get a different key for each app, but it is not required.

Step 5 (to do for each project): Add the appropriate permissions to the AndroidManifest.xml file

Depending on the app, we need to edit the AndroidManifest.xml file as follows:

- ▶ List permissions using the `permission` element.
- ▶ List use permissions using the `uses-permission` element.

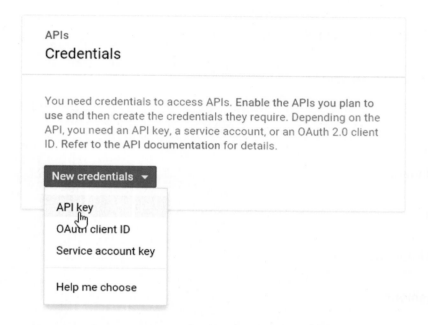

FIGURE C.8 **Selecting API key from the New credentials menu**

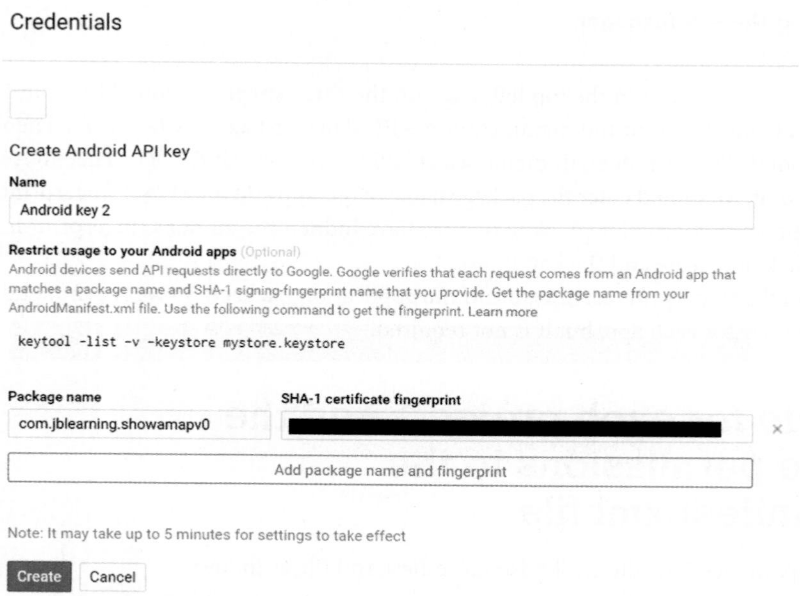

Credentials

Create Android API key

Name

Android key 2

Restrict usage to your Android apps (Optional)

Android devices send API requests directly to Google. Google verifies that each request comes from an Android app that matches a package name and SHA-1 signing-fingerprint name that you provide. Get the package name from your AndroidManifest.xml file. Use the following command to get the fingerprint. Learn more

```
keytool -list -v -keystore mystore.keystore
```

Package name   **SHA-1 certificate fingerprint**

com.jblearning.showamapv0   ▓▓▓▓▓▓▓▓▓▓▓▓▓▓▓▓▓▓▓▓▓▓   ✕

Add package name and fingerprint

Note: It may take up to 5 minutes for settings to take effect

Create   Cancel

FIGURE C.9 **Entering package name and SHA-1 fingerprint**

- ▶ List use features using a `uses-feature` element.
- ▶ If the app is using Google Maps, specify the name and value of the key to access map data using a `meta-data` element.
- ▶ If the app is using Google Maps, list the Google Maps library using a `uses-library` element.

If we use the Google Maps Activity template, some of these may have been included in the AndroidManifest.xml automatically.

APPENDIX D

The AsyncTask Class

A **Thread** is a sequence of code that executes inside an existing process. The existing process is often called the **Main Thread**. For an Android app, it is also called the **User Interface Thread**. There can be several threads executing inside the same process, and threads can share resources, such as memory.

When we start the app, our code executes in the main thread. Sometimes, we need to start another thread. For example, we may need to retrieve data from a remote location. Furthermore, we may need that other thread to finish before we use and place its data inside a GUI component. The AsyncTask class, from the android.os package, allows us to perform a background operation and then access the main thread to communicate its results. It is designed to execute short tasks, lasting a few seconds or less, and should not be used to start a thread that runs for a long time. AsyncTask is abstract so we must subclass it and instantiate an object of the subclass in order to use it.

The AsyncTask class uses three generic types that we must specify when extending it. The syntax for the header of a subclass is as follows:

```
AccessModifier ClassName extends AsyncTask<Params, Progress, Result>
```

where Params, Progress, and Result are placeholders for actual class names and have the following meanings:

▶ Params is the data type of the array that is passed to the execute method of AsyncTask when we call it.
▶ Progress is the data type used for progress units as the task executes in the background. If we choose to report progress, that data type is often Integer or Long.
▶ Result is the data type of the value returned upon execution of the task.

We may not be interested in using some of these types. If we are not interested in using one, we use `Void`. For example, let's assume that the name of our class is `TestTask` and that we pass an array of `Integers` as the argument of the `execute` method. Let's further assume that we do not care about reporting progress, and the task returns a `String`. Then, we use the following class header:

```
public TestTask extends AsyncTask<Integer, Void, String>
```

In order to launch a task using the `AsyncTask` class, we do the following:

▶ Create a subclass of `AsyncTask`.
▶ Declare and instantiate an object of that subclass.
▶ With that object, call the `execute` method to start the task.

The `execute` method is `public` and `final`. `AsyncTask` includes some `protected` methods that can be overridden by a subclass. **TABLE D.1** lists some of the methods of the `AsyncTask` class. As discussed previously, `Params`, `Progress`, and `Result` are placeholders for actual class names.

The three dots syntax after the data type in the parameter list indicates that a method accepts a variable number of arguments, also known as **varargs**. Varargs must be at the final parameter position in the parameter list. The syntax for a method header using a variable number of arguments is as follows:

```
AccessModifier returnType methodName( someParameterList, DataType...
variableNames )
```

TABLE D.1 Selected methods of the `AsyncTask` class

Method	Description
AsyncTask execute(Params. . . params)	Public and final; params represent an array of values of type Params, a generic type; returns this instance of AsyncTask.
void onPreExecute( )	Protected. Automatically called after we call execute and before doInBackground starts.
Result doInBackground(Params. . . params)	Protected. Abstract method that we need to override to perform the task; params is the argument passed to execute when we call it.
void publishProgress(Progress. . . values)	Protected and final. Calling that method triggers a call to onProgressUpdate.
void onProgressUpdate(Progress. . . values)	Protected. Automatically called if we call publishProgress.
void onPostExecute(Result result)	Protected. Automatically called after doInBackground finishes; result is the value returned by doInBackground.

Note that there is no space between the data type and the three dots. The `execute`, `doIn-Background`, `publishProgress`, and `onProgressUpdate` methods accept a variable number of arguments.

For example, and assuming we have defined a class named `Item`, we could override the `doIn-Background` method using the following method header:

```
protected ArrayList<Item> doInBackground( Integer... numbers )
```

When calling a method that accepts a variable number of arguments, we can pass no argument, a single argument, several arguments, or an array of arguments. For example, to call a `doInBack-ground` method that has the method header defined above with an `AsyncTask` reference named `task`, we could do it four different ways:

```
// #1: pass no argument
task.execute( );
// #2: pass only 1 argument
task.execute( 7 );
// #3: pass several arguments
task.execute( 6, 8, 15 );
// #4: pass an array of arguments
int [ ] values = { 10, 20, 30, 40, 50 };
task.execute( values );
```

When we call the `execute` method, the following methods of the `AsyncTask` class execute in this order: `onPreExecute`, `doInBackground`, and `onPostExecute`.

Before the task executes, if we want to perform some initialization, we can place that code inside the `onPreExecute` method. We place the code for the task we want to execute in the `doIn-Background` method. That method is `abstract` and must be overridden. The argument that is automatically passed to the `doInBackground` method is the same argument that we passed to the `execute` method when we call it. Inside `doInBackground`, as the task is executing, if we want to report progress to the main thread, we can call the `publishProgress` method. That in turns triggers a call to the `onProgressUpdate` method, which we can override: for example, we can update a progress bar in the user interface thread. When the `doInBackground` method finishes executing, the `onPostExecute` method is automatically called. We can override it to update the user interface with the results of the task that just completed. The argument that is automatically passed to the `onPostExecute` method is the value that is returned by the `doInBackground` method.

To summarize the flow of data, the argument that we pass to `execute` is automatically passed to `doInBackground`, and the returned value of `doInBackground` is automatically passed as the argument of `onPostExecute`.

Inside the `onPostExecute` method, it is very likely that we want to update the activity of the user interface thread. There are essentially two ways to do this:

▸ We can code the subclass of `AsyncTask` as a `private` inner class of the activity class that executes the task. In this case, we can call methods of the activity class from inside the `onPostExecute` method,

▸ We can code the subclass of AsyncTask as a separate public class. In this case, we need a reference to the activity class that executes the task so that we can call methods from that activity class from inside the onPostExecute method.

We show an example of the second solution (i.e., we code a separate public subclass of AsyncTask). It illustrates how to pass an Activity reference from one class to another. We perform the following steps:

▸ We create TestTask, a subclass of AsyncTask.
▸ We override the doInBackground method so that it performs the task we are interested in.
▸ Inside TestTask, we include an instance variable that is a reference to the Activity that starts the task. This enables us to call methods of the Activity class from TestTask.
▸ We override the onPostExecute method and call one or more methods of the Activity class to update the activity with the results of the task that just completed.
▸ Inside the Activity class, we create and instantiate an object of TestTask.
▸ We pass a reference to this Activity to the TestTask object.
▸ We call the execute method of AsyncTask, passing whatever input data is appropriate (for example a URL if we need to retrieve data from a remote website), to start executing the task.

We now build a very simple app in order to illustrate how to use the AsyncTask class. We use the Empty Activity template. **EXAMPLE D.1** shows the TestTask class. In the class header

```
1   package com.jblearning.asynctasktest;
2
3   import android.os.AsyncTask;
4   import android.util.Log;
5
6   public class TestTask extends AsyncTask<Integer, Void, String> {
7     private MainActivity activity;
8
9     public TestTask( MainActivity fromActivity ) {
10      Log.w( "MainActivity", "Inside TestTask constructor" );
11      activity = fromActivity;
12    }
13
14    protected String doInBackground( Integer... numbers ) {
15      Log.w( "MainActivity", "Inside doInBackground" );
16      return "Changed using AsyncTask";
17    }
18
19    protected void onPostExecute( String message ) {
20     Log.w( "MainActivity", "Inside onPostExecute" );
21     activity.updateView( message );
22    }
23  }
```

EXAMPLE D.1 The TestTask class

(line 6), we specify `Integer` as the `Params` data type, `Void` as the `Progress` data type (we are not interested in reporting progress here), and `String` as the `Result` data type.

At line 7, we declare the `activity` instance variable, a reference to `MainActivity`. The constructor (lines 9–12) accepts a `MainActivity` parameter and assigns it to `activity`. When we call the `TestTask` constructor from the `MainActivity` class, we pass `this` as the argument.

We override the `doInBackground` method at lines 14–17. The method header specifies that it returns a `String` (the `Result` data type) and that it accepts `Integers` as parameters (the `Params` data type). The parameters are never used in this simple example and therefore insignificant.

We override the `onPostExecute` method at lines 19–22. When it is called automatically after the `doInBackground` method finishes execution, the value of its parameter `message` is the `String` returned by `doInBackground`. We call the `updateView` method of the `MainActivity` class with the `activity` instance variable, passing `message` at line 21. The `updateView` method, which we need to add to the `MainActivity` class, is expected to update the View based on the value of its argument.

Inside all the methods, we add an output statement (lines 10, 15, 20) so that we can trace the order in which all the methods are called.

EXAMPLE D.2 shows the `MainActivity` class. At line 16, we declare and instantiate a `TestTask` object and call the `execute` method at line 18, passing 1. In this simple example,

```
1    package com.jblearning.asynctasktest;
2
3    import android.os.Bundle;
4    import android.support.v7.app.AppCompatActivity;
5    import android.util.Log;
6    import android.widget.TextView;
7
8    public class MainActivity extends AppCompatActivity {
9
10       @Override
11       protected void onCreate( Bundle savedInstanceState ) {
12         super.onCreate( savedInstanceState );
13         setContentView( R.layout.activity_main );
14
15         Log.w( "MainActivity", "Instantiating TestTask object" );
16         TestTask task = new TestTask( this );
17         Log.w( "MainActivity", "Starting TestTask" );
18         task.execute( 1 );
19         Log.w( "MainActivity", "Started TestTask" );
20       }
21
22       public void updateView( String s ) {
23         Log.w( "MainActivity", "Inside updateView" );
24         TextView tv = ( TextView ) findViewById( R.id.tv );
25         tv.setText( s );
26       }
27    }
```

EXAMPLE D.2 The `MainActivity` class

the argument we pass is never used and therefore irrelevant. However, its data type must match the data type of the parameters of the `doInBackground` method of the `TestTask` class. Since the `execute` method accepts a variable number of arguments, we can pass 0, 1, or more arguments. We could have passed an array of `Integers` containing only one element, 1, as follows:

```
task.execute( new Integer[ ] { 1 } );
```

At lines 22–26, we code the `updateView` method. At this point, it outputs some feedback to Logcat and updates the text in the `TextView` at line 25.

Note that the sequencing of our code is important when we use an `AsyncTask`. After the call to `execute` at line 18, execution would continue inside the `onCreate` method if there were statements after line 18. In that case, there would be interleaved execution between those statements and the statements executing inside the `TestTask` class. If we attempted to retrieve the value or values generated by a task right after calling `execute` (even though the value[s] generated by the task is inside the `TestTask` class, it would be easy to write them as `public static` data of another class and read that `public static` data from the `MainActivity` class), in this example inside the `onCreate` method, that value or those values would very likely be `null`. The correct way to process the value generated by a task is to do it inside the `onPostExecute` method.

EXAMPLE D.3 shows the activity_main.xml file. We add an id for the `TextView` at line 16 and set the font size to 32 at line 17 so we can see it better on the screen.

```
1   <?xml version="1.0" encoding="utf-8"?>
2   <RelativeLayout xmlns:android="http://schemas.android.com/apk/res/android"
3     xmlns:tools="http://schemas.android.com/tools"
4     android:layout_width="match_parent"
5     android:layout_height="match_parent"
6     android:paddingLeft="@dimen/activity_horizontal_margin"
7     android:paddingRight="@dimen/activity_horizontal_margin"
8     android:paddingTop="@dimen/activity_vertical_margin"
9     android:paddingBottom="@dimen/activity_vertical_margin"
10    tools:context=".MainActivity">
11
12    <TextView
13      android:text="Hello World!"
14      android:layout_width="wrap_content"
15      android:layout_height="wrap_content"
16      android:id="@+id/tv"
17      android:textSize="32sp" />
18
19  </RelativeLayout>
```

EXAMPLE D.3 The activity_main.xml file

COMMON ERROR: Do not attempt to process the results of an `AsyncTask` immediately after calling the `execute` method. It is likely that the task has not finished executing and the results are not ready. Instead, process the results inside the `onPostExecute` method.

FIGURE D.1 shows the Logcat output when we run, in particular the order of execution. It shows that the Logcat output statement at line 19 of the `MainActivity` class executes before the `doInBackground` method of the `TestTask` class executes. This very simple simulation confirms that the correct way to process the value generated by a task is to do it inside the `onPostExecute` method. **FIGURE D.2** shows the text inside the `TextView` has changed from `Hello World!` to `Changed using AsyncTask`.

FIGURE D.2 **The app running inside the emulator**

```
Instantiating TestTask object
Inside TestTask constructor
Starting TestTask
Started TestTask
Inside doInBackground
Inside onPostExecute
Inside updateView
```

FIGURE D.1 **Logcat output of Example D.2**

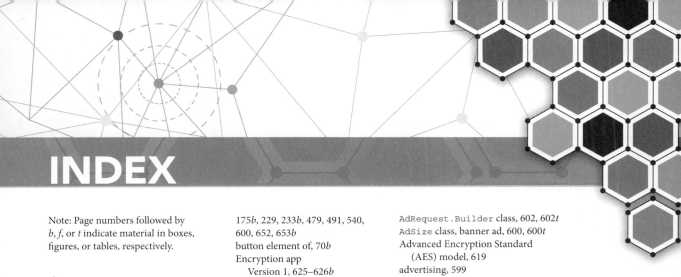

INDEX

Note: Page numbers followed by *b*, *f*, or *t* indicate material in boxes, figures, or tables, respectively.

673